Romania

Romania

The Industrialization of an Agrarian Economy under Socialist Planning

Report of a mission sent to Romania by the World Bank

Andreas C. Tsantis and Roy Pepper
Coordinating Authors

The World Bank : Washington, D.C.

 THE WORLD BANK
1818 H Street, N.W., Washington, D.C. 20433 U.S.A.

Manufactured in the United States of America

This report is a working document and is, as such, part of an informal series based wholly on materials originally prepared for restricted use within the Bank. The text is not meant to be definitive, but is offered so as to make some results of internal research widely available to scholars and practitioners throughout the world. Titles of all Bank publications may be found in the *Catalog of Publications*, which is available free of charge from World Bank, Publications Unit, at the address shown above or 66, avenue d'Iena, 75116 Paris, France.
The views and interpretations in this book are the authors' and should not be attributed to the World Bank, to its affiliated organizations, or to any individual acting in their behalf. The five maps in this book have been prepared by the staff of the World Bank exclusively for the convenience of readers of this book. The denominations used and the boundaries shown do not imply, on the part of the World Bank and its affiliates, any judgment on the legal status of any territory or any endorsement or acceptance of such boundaries.

Library of Congress Cataloging in Publication Data
Tsantis, Andreas C. 1942–
Romania, the industrialization of an agrarian economy under Socialist planning.
Bibliography: p. 703
1. Romania—Economic conditions—1945–
2. Romania—Economic policy. I. Pepper, Roy, 1949– joint author. II. International Bank for Reconstruction and Development. III. Title.
HC405.T812 330.9′498′03 79–84315
ISBN 0–8018–2269–6
ISBN 0–8018–2262–9 pbk.

Contents

TABLES

FIGURES

MAPS

Glossary

Terms

Accumulation fund: The part of national income used in the form of investment and change in stocks in both the productive and nonproductive sectors.

Benefit: The difference between the value of output measured in delivery prices and total cost of production plus turnover tax; equal to gross profit.

Central: An economic unit subordinate to, but separate from, a ministry, with responsibilities for planning, supervising, and coordinating the operations of enterprises under its jurisdiction. It is also responsible, through subordinate enterprises, for research, design, and foreign trade.

Combinat: A large enterprise that is usually vertically or horizontally integrated.

Comparable price: A form of constant price used to value many statistical series, particularly social product, national income, and aggregated production data. Romanian statistics for 1950–76 and expressed in comparable prices present data in 1963 prices. Such series are not equivalent, however, to a pure constant price measure, since the aggregations are made in terms of different price weights; for 1950–59, the aggregations are based on weights derived from 1950 prices; for 1959–65, on 1955 prices; and for 1965–76, on 1963 prices.

Consumption fund: The part of national income allocated for the consumption of material products and services. Consumption of nonproductive services is included only insofar as they constitute part of material expenditures.

Cooperative: A form of economic organization in both productive and nonproductive sectors in which assets are collectively owned by its members. There are four types of cooperatives: agricultural, craft, consumer, and credit. Their activities cover arable agriculture and livestock, small-scale industry, nonproductive services, credit, and retail sales in rural areas.

Delivery price: Producer price plus turnover tax: that is, a wholesale price at which goods are delivered to retail outlets.

Employed population: The total number of wage earners in the socialist sector; it includes workers, technical and economic personnel, engineers, managers, and administrators.

Enterprise: The basic unit of economic and social activity. Published statistics include only those enterprises with legal status (Chapter 10, Table 10.5). For details of industrial enterprises, see Appendix C; for agricultural enterprises, see Chapter 11.

Fiscal year: January 1 to December 31.

Global or gross product: A gross output concept, measured in delivery prices, that measures and aggregates the production of enterprises; it includes (and thus double-counts) the value of intermediate goods used as inputs except those produced in the same enterprise. The sum of global products of all productive sectors equals social product. (See **Gross production** and **Social product.**)

Gross production: A gross output concept, valued in producer prices, that measures and aggregates the production of enterprises; it includes the value of intermediate goods used as inputs, whether produced in the same enterprise or purchased from other enterprises. (See **Global product** and **Social product.**)

Group A industry: Producer goods industry.

Group B industry: Consumer goods industry.

Judet: Territorial and administrative unit (Appendix B).

Labor productivity: Measured as social product for each employee, it is a gross output concept of the value of production for each employed person in the socialist sector.

Leu valuta: The "foreign exchange leu;" a unit of currency expressing the formal gold price of the leu, which is termed the official rate. At present, the official rate is 4.47 lei valuta : US$1. The leu valuta is used only to express the value of foreign trade in government statistics.

Local budget: The budget of judets (districts), under the management of the People's Councils.

Local sector: State enterprises and institutions which are responsible to the People's Councils.

Material balance: A physical measure, used in the planning process, of the sources and uses of a product or resource (Chapter 3).

Material expenditure: The cost of all material inputs (including depreciation) used in production.

National income: A value-added concept measured in delivery prices and the sum of net products in the productive sector, where net product equals global product less material expenditures. It does not include the net products of the nonproductive sector or depreciation expenditures; these items constitute the main difference between national income in the Romanian definition (system of material production) and the United Nations definition (system of national accounts) (Appendix D).

Nonproductive sector: Includes those activities not directly related to production: municipal services (not including distribution of water, gas, electricity, and urban transport); housing; education; health services; scientific services (not including scientific research related to production); finance; administration; and political and social organizations (Appendix D).

Norm: Quantitative expression of existing rules and standards; for example, time for each operation and material expenditures for each unit of output.

Occupied population: The total number of persons working in all sectors of the economy.

People's Council: Local body of state power in judets, towns, or villages responsible for planning and management of economic and social activities under its jurisdiction.

Producer price: The ex-factory price, defined as the branch-average cost of production (including a profit margin) and the price at which state enterprises conduct transactions for inputs and outputs in the process of production (Chapter 4).

Productive sector: Includes industry, agriculture, forestry, construction, transport, trade, telecommunications, and other productive branches. Since 1970 it has specifically included services rendered to agriculture by agricultural mechanization stations, veterinary dispensaries, passenger transport, telecommunications servicing the population, and administrative and sociocultural units, services rendered by hotels, catering units in hospitals and health resorts, scientific research for production, laundries, cleaning, dyeing, and photographic shops (Appendix D).

Real income: Personal income of the population in money and kind (goods and services) coming from labor and social funds.

Real remuneration: Real wages: that is, money wages deflated by the retail price index.

Regularization tax: A tax on excess profits that was established in 1970 and was abolished in 1977 (Appendix G).

Republican sector: All state enterprises of national importance responsible to ministries and other central state bodies.

Socialist retail trade: Distribution and sale of goods through socialist sector outlets.

Socialist sector: The state sector plus the cooperative sector.

Social product: The sum of global products of the productive sector.

Sociocultural expenditure: The cost of education, health, arts and culture, physical education and sport, social assistance, and so forth.

State budget: The state financial plan, including centralized incomes of the state and their distribution.

Synthetic indicator: A measure that summarizes and aggregates values of other variables; for example, national income.

Titular: An administrative body responsible for implementing specific tasks of the plan.

Tonne: A metric ton or 1.1 tons.

Turnover tax: A tax levied on a good between production and wholesale (see **Producer price** and **Delivery price,** and Chapter 4).

Wage fund: The total value of wage payments to employees.

Acronyms

ARCOM — The foreign trade enterprise in the Ministry of Industrial Construction

BAFI — Bank for Agriculture and Food Industries

CAP — Agricultural producer cooperatives

CFR — Romanian railways

CMEA — Council for Mutual Economic Assistance; also referred to as COMECON

CNST — National Council for Science and Technology

CPPC	Committee for the Problems of the People's Councils
GIGCDC	General Inspectorate for Guidelines, Control, and Directions in Construction
IAS	State agricultural units
ICA	Inter Cooperative Association
ICOR	Incremental capital output ratio
IOVR	Military pension scheme
ITA	State Warehousing and Distribution Company
ORDGC	Organization for Research Design and Guidelines in Construction
RCP	Romanian Communist Party
SAM	Stations for agricultural mechanization
SCESD	Supreme Council of Economic and Social Development
SGIIC	State General Inspectorate for Investments and Construction
SMP	System of Material Production (Romanian accounting methodology)
SNA	System of National Accounts (United Nations accounting methodology)
SPC	State Planning Committee

Currency Equivalents

Conversions from lei and lei valuta into dollars using the official and conversion rates are made according to the exchange rates in force at the time. Exchange rates and the periods in which they were in force are given in footnotes 7 and 8 to Chapter 4.

Official Rate

4.47 lei = US$1.00
1.00 leu = US$0.22

Tourist Rate

12.00 lei = US$1.00
1.00 leu = US$0.08

Conversion Rate for Traded Goods

18.00 lei = US$1.00
1.00 leu = US$0.06

Social Indicators Data Sheet

	Romania[a]			Reference countries (1970)		
	1960	*1970*	*Most recent estimate*	*Yugo-slavia*	*Italy*	*Germany, Federal Republic of*[b]
Gross national product per capita (U.S. dollars)	—	550.0[c]	1,450.0[c]	830.0[d]	1,910.0[d]	4,420.0[d]
			Population and vital statistics			
Population (mid-year, million)	18.4	20.3	21.4[e]	20.4	53.7	61.6
Population density						
(per square kilometer)	77.0[f]	85.0[f]	90.0[e,f]	80.0	178.0	240.0
(per square kilometer of agricultural land)	126.0[f]	136.0[f]	144.0[e,f]	139.0	266.0	439.0
Vital statistics						
Crude birth rate (per thousand, average)	23.9	19.0	19.7	21.0	18.6	17.3
Crude death rate (per thousand, average)	10.9	8.9	9.3	9.1	9.7	11.6
Infant mortality rate (per thousand)	75.7	49.4	34.7	55.5	29.6	23.6
Life expectancy at birth (years)	65.9	67.7	69.1	67.7	71.9	70.3
Gross reproduction rate (percent)	1.2	1.3	1.3	1.3	1.3	1.2
Population growth rate (percent)						
Total	1.2	1.0	1.0	1.0	0.8	1.0
Urban	3.8	3.4	2.1	4.6	0.8	4.1
Urban population (percent of total)	32.0	40.8	43.0	38.7	51.5	82.4
Age structure (percent)						
0 to 14 years	27.9[g]	25.9	25.4[e]	28.3	24.4	23.2
15 to 64 years	64.9[g]	65.5	64.8[e]	64.3	65.2	63.6
65 years and over	7.2[g]	8.6	9.8[e]	7.4	10.4	13.2

			Population and vital statistics			
Age dependency ratio	0.5	0.5	0.5	0.6	0.5	0.6
Economic dependency ratio	0.7[h]	0.7[h]	0.7[e,h]	—	0.9[h]	0.9
Family planning						
Acceptors (cumulative, thousands)	—	—	—	—	—	—
Users (percent of married women)	—	—	—	—	—	—
			Employment			
Total labor force (thousands)	9,600.0	9,900.0	10,200.0[e]	—	19,600.0	26,500.0
Labor force in agriculture (percent)	66.0	49.0	36.0[e]	—	19.0	8.9
Unemployed (percent of labor force)	—	—	—	—	3.1	0.7
			Income distribution			
Percent of private income received by						
Highest 5 percent of households	—	—	—	15.1	—	—
Highest 20 percent of households	—	—	—	41.4	—	—
Lowest 20 percent of households	—	—	—	6.6	—	—
Lowest 40 percent of households	—	—	—	18.4	—	—
			Distribution of land ownership			
Percent owned by top 10 percent of owners	—	—	—	15.1[i]	—	—
Percent owned by smallest 10 percent of owners	—	—	—	84.9[j]	—	—
			Health and nutrition			
Population per physician	740.0	680.0	620.0	1,010.0	550.0	580.0
Population per nursing person	300.0	200.0	180.0	410.0[l]	470.0[m]	350.0
Population per hospital bed	180.0[k]	140.0[k]	120.0[k]	170.0	90.0	90.0

(Table continues on the following pages)

Social Indicators Data Sheet—Continued

	Romania[a]			Reference countries (1970)		
	1960	1970	Most recent estimate	Yugo-slavia	Italy	Germany, Federal Republic of[b]
			Health and nutrition			
Per capita supply of						
Calories (percent of requirements)	105.0	118.0	118.0[n]	124.0	126.0	121.0
Protein (grams per day)	81.0	92.0	90.0[n]	92.0	100.0	88.0
Animal and pulse	24.0	28.0	—	29.0	42.0	56.0
Death rate for ages 1 to 4 (per thousand)	4.9[g]	2.4	2.1	2.6	1.0	0.9
			Education			
Adjusted enrollment ratio						
Primary school	98.0	113.0	108.0	94.0	110.0	129.0
Secondary school	24.0	44.0	49.0	45.0	60.0	66.0
Years of schooling provided (first and second levels)	12.0	14.0	14.0	12.0	13.0	15.0
Vocational enrollment (percent of secondary)	54.0	58.0	67.0	72.0	26.0	48.0
Adult literacy rate (percent)	—	—	98.0[o]	85.0	97.0	99.0
			Housing			
Persons per room—urban	—	1.3[p]	—	—	—	0.7[q]
Occupied dwellings without piped water (percent)	—	88.0[p,r]	—	—	—	0.3[r]
Access to electricity (percent of all dwellings)	—	49.0[p]	—	—	—	100.0
Rural dwellings connected to electricity (percent)	—	27.0[p]	—	—	—	—

			Consumption			
Radio receivers (per thousand population)	109.0	152.0	146.0	165.0	218.0	318.0
Passenger cars (per thousand population)	—	—	—	35.0	190.0	220.0
Electricity (kilowatt-hours per year per capita)	414.0	1,615.0	2,411.0	1,288.0	2,262.0	4,128.0
Newsprint (kilograms per year per capita)	2.1	2.6	2.1	4.3	5.3	17.7

a. Unless otherwise noted, data for 1960 refer to any year between 1959 and 1961; for 1970, between 1968 and 1970; and for most recent estimate, between 1973 and 1975.

b. The Federal Republic of Germany has been selected as an objective country because it is an industrialized European country with major trade ties with Romania.

c. These figures should not be compared with those for other centrally planned economies. They are derived by using the *World Bank Atlas* methodology, by adjusting official Romanian national accounts data and converting them into U.S. dollars at the effective exchange rate for foreign trade transactions, which approximates 20 lei per U.S. dollar.

d. GNP per capita data are based on the *World Bank Atlas* methodology (1974–76 basis).

e. 1976.

f. The total surface area comprising land area and inland waters is 237,500 square kilometers; the most recent estimate of agricultural area used temporarily or permanently for crops, pastures, market and kitchen gardens, or to lie fallow is 149,000 square kilometers.

g. 1962.

h. Ratio of population under 15 and over 65 to total labor force.

i. Agricultural land held by social sector "Kambinate."

j. Agricultural land held by private small-holders; "10 hectares maximum."

k. Hospitals only; excludes sanitaria and maternity homes.

l. Including midwives, assistant midwives, assistant nurses, and nursing auxiliaries.

m. Hospital personnel.

n. 1969–71 average.

o. 1974 official estimate is 100 percent.

p. 1966.

q. Total, urban, and rural.

r. Inside only.

Definitions of Social Indicators:

GNP per capita (US$): GNP per capita estimates at current market prices. It is calculated by same conversion method as the *World Bank Atlas* (1973–75 basis) and contains 1960, 1970, and 1975 data.

Population (mid-year, million): As of July 1: If not available, the average of two end-year estimates was used: 1960, 1970, and 1975 data.

Population density per square kilometer: Mid-year population per square kilometer (100 hectares) of total area.

Population density per square kilometer of agricultural land: Computed as above, but for agricultural land only.

Crude birth rate per thousand, average: Annual live births per thousand of mid-year population; ten-year arithmetic averages ending in 1960 and 1970, and five-year average ending in 1975 for most recent estimate.

Crude death rate per thousand, average: Annual deaths per thousand of mid-year population; ten-year arithmetic averages ending in 1960

(Definitions continue on the following pages)

and 1970, and five-year average ending in 1975 for most recent estimate.

Infant mortality rate (per thousand): Annual deaths of infants under one year old per thousand live births.

Life expectancy at birth (years): Average number of years of life remaining at birth; usually five-year averages ending in 1960, 1970, and 1975 for developing countries.

Gross reproduction rate (percent): Average number of live daughters a woman will bear in her normal reproductive period if she experiences present age-specific fertility rates; usually five-year averages ending in 1960, 1970, and 1975 for developing countries.

Population growth rate (percent)—total: Compound annual growth rates of mid-year population for 1950–60, 1960–70, and 1970–75.

Population growth rate (percent)—urban: Computed as above. Different definitions of urban areas may affect comparability of data among countries.

Urban population (percent of total): Ratio of urban to total population. Different definitions of urban areas may affect comparability of data among countries.

Age structure (percent): Children (0–14 years), working-age (15–64 years), and retired (65 years and over) as percentages of mid-year population.

Age dependency ratio: Ratio of population under 15 and over 65 to those between 15 and 64 years old.

Economic dependency ratio: Ratio of population under 15 and over 65 to the labor force, between 15 and 64 years old.

Family planning—acceptors (cumulative, thousands): Cumulative number of those accepting birth-control devices under the auspices of the national family planning program since its inception.

Family planning—users (percent of married women): Percentages of married women of child-bearing age (15 to 44 years) who use birth-control devices to all married women in same age group.

Total labor force (thousands): Economically active persons, including armed forces and unemployed, but excluding housewives, students, and so forth. Definitions in various countries are not comparable.

Labor force in agriculture (percent): Agricultural labor force (in farming, forestry, hunting, and fishing) as a percentage of the total labor force.

Unemployed (percent of labor force): Unemployed are usually defined as persons who are able and willing to take a job, are out of a job on a given day, remain out of a job, and are seeking work for a specified minimum period not exceeding one week. Data may not be comparable between countries because of different definitions of unemployed and source of data, for example, employment office statistics, sample surveys, compulsory unemployment insurance.

Income distribution: Percentage of private income (both in cash and kind) received by richest 5 percent, richest 20 percent, poorest 20 percent, and poorest 40 percent of households.

Distribution of land ownership: Percentages of land owned by wealthiest 10 percent and poorest 10 percent of land owners.

Population per physician: Population divided by the number of practicing physicians qualified from a medical school at the university level.

Population per nursing person: Population divided by the number of practicing male and female graduate nurses, "trained" or "certified" nurses, and auxiliary personnel with training or experience.

Population per hospital bed: Population divided by the number of hospital beds available in public and private general and specialized hospitals and rehabilitation centers. This excludes nursing homes and establishments for custodial and preventive care.

Per capita supply of calories (percent of requirements): Computed from energy equivalent of net food supplies available in country per capita per day. Available supplies comprise domestic production, imports less exports, and changes in stock; net supplies exclude animal feed, seeds, quantities used in food processing, and losses in distribution. Requirements were estimated by FAO based on physiological needs for normal activity and health, considering environmental temperature, body weights, age and sex distributions of population, and allowing 10 percent for waste at household level.

Per capita supply of protein (grams per day): Protein content of per capita net supply of food per day. Net supply of food is defined as above. Requirements for all countries were established by the USDA Economic Research Services and provide for a minimum allowance of 60 grams of total protein per day and 20 grams of animal and pulse protein, of which 10 grams should be annual protein. These standards are lower than those of 75 grams of total protein and 23 grams of animal protein as an average for the world, proposed by FAO in the Third World Food Survey.

Per capita protein supply from animal and pulse (grams per day): Protein supply of food derived from animals and pulses.

Death rate (per thousand) ages 1 to 4: Annual deaths per thousand for ages 1 to 4 years. It is suggested as an indicator of malnutrition.

Adjusted enrollment ratio—primary school: Enrollment of all ages as percentage of primary school-age population. It includes children 6 to 11 years old, but is adjusted for different lengths of primary education. For countries with universal education, enrollment may exceed 100 percent since some pupils are below or above the official school age.

Adjusted enrollment ratio—secondary school: Computed as above. Secondary education requires at least four years of approved primary instruction and provides general, vocational, or teacher training instructions for pupils 12 to 17 years old. Correspondence courses are generally excluded.

Years of schooling provided (first and second levels): Total years of schooling. At the secondary level, vocational instruction may be partially or completely excluded.

Vocational enrollment (percent of secondary): Vocational institutions include technical, industrial, or other programs, which operate independently or as departments of secondary institutions.

Adult literacy rate (percent): Literate adults (able to read and write) as a percentage of total adult population aged 15 years and over.

Persons per room—urban: Average number of persons per room in occupied conventional dwellings in urban areas. Dwellings exclude nonpermanent structures and unoccupied parts.

Occupied dwellings without piped water (percent): Occupied conventional dwellings in urban and rural areas without inside or outside piped water facilities, as a percentage of all occupied dwellings.

Access to electricity (percent of all dwellings): Conventional dwellings with electricity in living quarters as a percentage of total dwellings in urban and rural areas.

Rural dwellings connected to electricity (percent): Computed as above, but for rural dwellings only.

Radio receivers (per thousand population): All types of receivers for radio broadcasts to the general public, per thousand of population. This excludes unlicensed receivers in countries and in years when registration of radio sets was in effect. Data for recent years may not be comparable, since most countries abolished licensing.

Passenger cars (per thousand population): Passenger cars comprise motor cars seating less than eight persons and excludes ambulances, hearses, and military vehicles.

Electricity (kilowatt-hours per year per capita): Annual consumption of industrial, commercial, public, and private electricity. It is generally based on production data, without allowance for losses in grids, but allowing for imports and exports of electricity.

Newsprint (kilograms per year per capita): Annual consumption estimated from domestic production plus net imports of newsprint.

22°
24°
48°
46°
44°
U. S.
HUNGARY
YUGOSLAVIA
SATU-MARE
Satu-Mare
MARAMUREȘ
Baia-Mare
SĂLAJ
Zalău
BIHOR
Oradea
CLUJ
Cluj
Tîrgu Mureș
ARAD
Arad
ALBA
Alba Iulia
SIBIU
Sibiu
TIMIȘ
Timisoara
HUNEDOARA
Deva
CARAȘ-SEVERIN
Resita
GORJ
Tîrgu-Jiu
VÎLCEA
Rîmnicu-Vîlcea
MEHEDINȚI
Turnu-Severin
DOLJ
Craiova
POLAND
U.S.S.R.
CZECH.
HUNGARY
ROMANIA
Bucharest
YUGOSLAVIA
BULGARIA
Black Sea
ALBANIA
GREECE
TURKEY

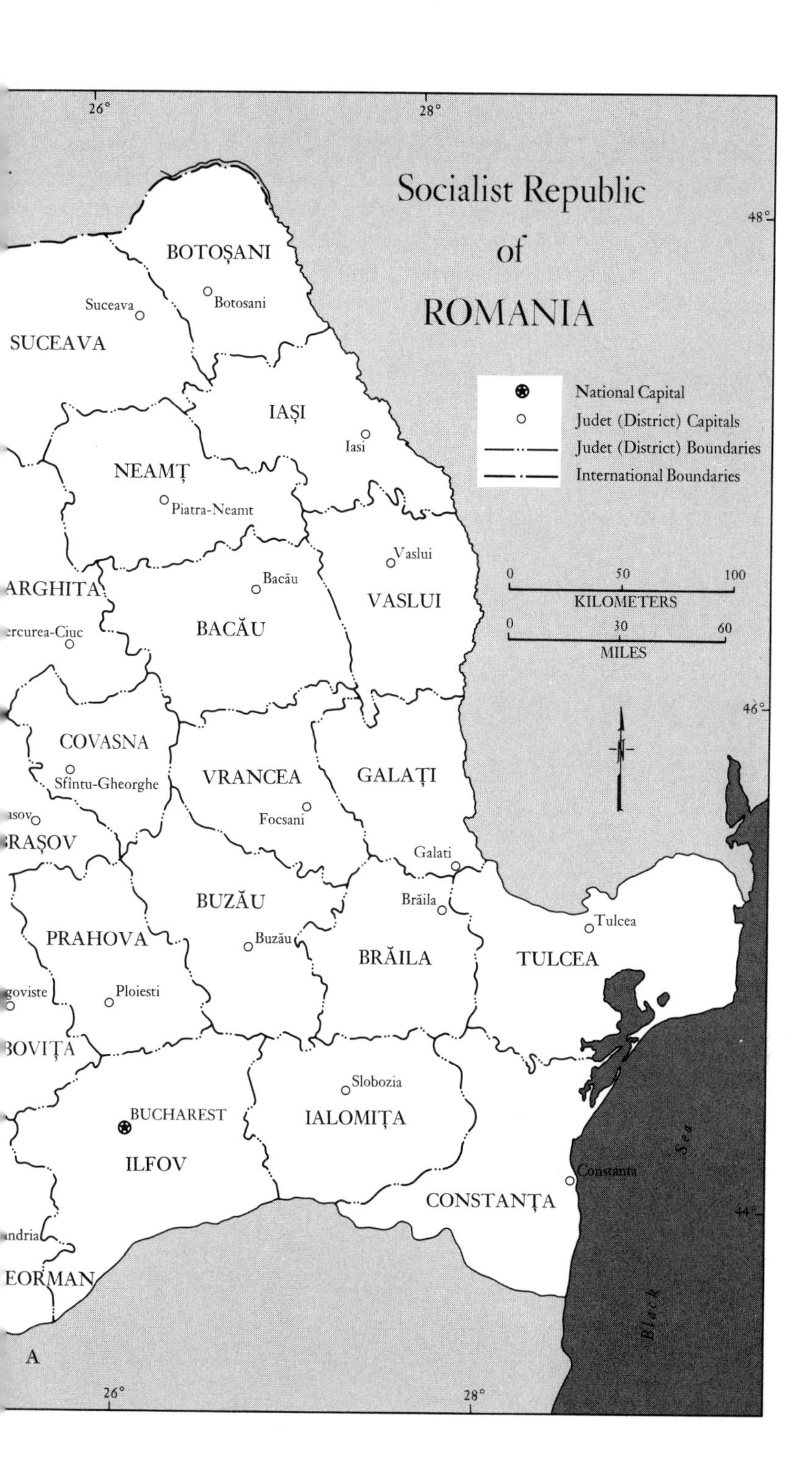
Socialist Republic
of
ROMANIA
National Capital
Judet (District) Capitals
Judet (District) Boundaries
International Boundaries
0 50 100
KILOMETERS
0 30 60
MILES
26°
28°
48°
46°
44°
BOTOŞANI
Botosani
Suceava
SUCEAVA
IAŞI
Iasi
NEAMŢ
Piatra-Neamt
Vaslui
VASLUI
Bacău
BACĂU
COVASNA
Sfîntu-Gheorghe
VRANCEA
Focsani
GALAŢI
Galati
Brăila
BRĂILA
Tulcea
TULCEA
BUZĂU
Buzău
PRAHOVA
Ploiesti
Slobozia
IALOMIŢA
BUCHAREST
ILFOV
Constanta
CONSTANŢA
Black Sea

Preface

THIS IS THE WORLD BANK'S FIRST BASIC ECONOMIC REPORT on the Romanian economy. Romania joined the Bank in December 1972, and since that time the Bank's economic work has been oriented toward obtaining a gradual understanding of the economy, chiefly to support its lending operations. Two economic reports have been issued: "The Economy of Romania" (no. 181b-RO, November 1973) and "Current Economic Position and Prospects of Romania" (no. 492a-RO, October 1974). An Economic Memorandum (no. 818a-RO, December 1975) has also been issued. Sector work in this country has been undertaken in connection with the Bank's lending operations, but the only sector report published to date has been "Romania: Agricultural Sector Survey" (no. 953a-RO, October 1976). The circulation of all these studies, however, is restricted to World Bank staff.

It is against this background that the present study was prepared. It provides the first comprehensive review of the development of the Romanian economy and its prospects and also establishes a data base for future economic and sector work. The report is both descriptive and analytical, but it makes no attempt to be exhaustive. Only the most important economic sectors are examined. In several areas, it is not over-analytical, since the data available are sufficient for a general economic review, but not for an in-depth analysis of certain important sectors. In addition, because this is the first basic report on Romania, the procedures and institutions involved in the planning and management of the economy are described in some detail.

This study is also limited chronologically: it examines the economy to the end of July 1977. Since that time the Romanian government has announced several important changes in plans and policies. In December 1977 the National Conference of the Romanian Communist Party (RCP) adopted a supplementary program containing higher targets for the 1976–80 Plan period, including the increases in targets for living standards and pensions originally announced in July. In March 1978 the Plenum of the Central Committee of the RCP announced measures to enable workers to participate in the profits of enterprises and to improve the functioning of the economic system through greater use of self-management techniques and financial instruments. As a result, it is planned that workers' bonuses will be based in part upon profits and foreign exchange earnings, that wages will be linked to net production instead of to global output, and that enterprises will be able to retain part of the profits for the construction of workers' houses and for other sociocultural activities. The announced measures will also increase the role of profit in the planning and implementation of enterprise activity. The major indicator against which performance is to be measured will be net, rather than gross, production, and each economic unit will be given greater responsibility for carrying out its economic and financial plan within both the domestic and export markets. As a part of these self-management measures, it is intended that financial institutions will have a strengthened role. These measures, which are now being debated in detail within the country, are not discussed in the report, since they have not yet been analyzed by the World Bank and discussed with the Romanian authorities. They will be reviewed during the Bank's forthcoming economic work on Romania.

The study is divided into three sections. The first section is divided into four parts and describes the organization and operation of this centrally planned economy and its major sectors; reviews and assesses the economic achievements of the past twenty-five years (1950–75), both at the macro level and in selected sectors; and discusses the prospects for development during the next decade. Particular attention is given to the management tools, especially the plans used to plan and administer the economy; the 1971–75 Plan and the prospects for the 1976–80 Plan are treated in detail. The second section, Appendixes A to K, provides additional information on issues and subsectors that is not discussed in the main report, but that is important in conveying a comprehensive view of the economy. The last section, the Statistical Appendix, along with the text tables, provides a detailed data base, chiefly using published information, but containing some previously unpublished data and discussing data interpretation.

The findings of two missions have been particularly important for the completion of this study. A basic economic mission visited Romania in October and November 1976. It consisted of Andreas Tsantis (mission leader), Roy Pepper (general economist), Peter Davies (general economist), Darrel G. Fallen-Bailey (energy sector specialist), Wolfgang Wipplinger (industrial economist), and Hendrik Van Helden (consultant, transport sector specialist). The basic mission had been preceded by a preparatory special economic mission in March 1976 consisting of Otto Maiss (mission leader), Andreas Tsantis (general economist), Roy Pepper (general economist), Pierre Biraben (general economist), Tito Lejano (national accounts specialist), Jayanta Roy (quantitative planner), Richard Sabot (manpower economist), James L. Theodores (education sector specialist), and Shahid Yusuf (fiscal economist). The chapter on agriculture is based on the World Bank's agricultural sector report and that on tourism on the findings of Bernard Snoy, who visited Romania in April and May 1975.

Peter Davies assisted the authors in the earlier stages of writing the study. Virginia deHaven Orr edited the final text, Goddard W. Winterbottom edited the tables, and Brian J. Svikhart directed the design and production of the book.

Andreas C. Tsantis
Roy Pepper

Washington, D.C.
March 1979

Introduction and Summary

ROMANIA'S PROGRESS OVER THE PAST TWENTY-FIVE YEARS shows that the economy has experienced a major transformation. Before World War II, Romania was one of the least developed countries of eastern Europe. Its economic structure was predominantly agrarian, with approximately three-quarters of the population living in the rural areas and a similar proportion of the labor force working in agriculture. Organized mainly in large estates, despite spasmodic and limited attempts at land reform, agriculture was poorly developed, providing the subsistence requirements of the population and oriented toward producing export crops for sale in western Europe. For most of the population, economic and social conditions were poor. Standards of living, dependent largely on low-productivity agriculture, were low, and the limited access to education and medical services resulted in high rates of illiteracy and infant mortality and low life expectancy. Despite the efforts of successive governments to stimulate industrial development, industrial production and employment had grown only slowly, the latter constituting only 8 percent of the labor force in 1938. Industrial development was limited sectorally and regionally and was mainly in consumer goods and associated with the production of raw materials for export; little heavy industry existed, and the only large-scale modern industry was oil production. Furthermore, industry and commerce were concentrated in only a few urban areas, evidence of the limited progress made in transforming the economy from its backward state.

By 1975 the economy had made considerable progress toward the Romanian Communist Party's (RCP's) long-term development goal of a highly industrialized economy providing a high standard of living for the population. The more important progress had been made in expanding the productive base of the economy. The level of industrial production had increased rapidly, and, with the creation of a broad industrial base (especially heavy industry), the composition of output had been diversified. This provided the means to modernize other economic sectors and a general increase in labor productivity and national income. Standards of living, although they remained below levels in most other European countries, had improved substantially, not only because of the growth of personal incomes resulting from both general wage increases and the transfer of labor from low-productivity agriculture to higher-productivity industry, but also because of greater expenditures on medical services, housing, and other social sectors provided through the state budget. Per capita gross national product in 1975 was approximately US$1,170.[1]

Development Strategy

The changes in the level and structure of economic activities between 1950 and 1975 are the result of a development strategy that has aimed to accelerate the growth rate and to catch up as soon as possible to the level and structure of economic activities in the developed socialist and capitalist countries. The essential features of this strategy can be summarized as follows:

(a) High and increasing rates of saving and investment. This has been a key element in the strategy. An acceleration in the growth rate of the economy has required the diversion of a high proportion of incremental income to investment and its allocation to generate the maximum increase in production. This is seen as necessary to provide a steady and sustained growth of living standards.

(b) Creation of a broad industrial base able to provide both capital and consumer goods. Industry has been viewed as the key to economic progress, to the provision of high living standards, and to economic and political independence. Industrialization policy has stressed the creation of a capital goods industry that can provide the means to modernize and to increase the productive potential of other sectors. Domestic production of a wide range of industrial goods and the incorporation of scientific and technological gains through the use of the most modern production techniques are also stressed. Over the past decade, the industrialization strategy has shifted in emphasis from the creation of a wide foundation of basic industries toward the development of technologically advanced secondary industries, chief of which are in the engineering, metallurgical, and chemical subsectors.

1. This figure was calculated using the United Nations methodology and official statistics on national income. Under the *World Bank Atlas* methodology, per capita gross national product in 1975 is estimated at US$1,300.

(c) Development of local natural resources. The strategy has given importance to the exploitation of all local resources of fuels (oil, gas, coal, and hydroelectric power), metals, and minerals to ensure as much self-sufficiency in these areas as possible and to meet the needs of industry and its related sectors.

(d) Reorganization and modernization of agriculture. Agriculture plays an important role in Romania's development strategy because of its importance as a sector and as an employer. Its role has been to supply food and inputs for industry and the newly urbanized industrial work force, to provide a livelihood for a large percentage of the population, and to produce a surplus over domestic requirements for export, thus permitting the import of goods needed for industrial development. In view of the fragmented and underdeveloped nature of the sector, the RCP's strategy has had two major components: reorganization and the expansion of production. Reorganization into large-scale units, that is, state farms and cooperatives, has been necessary to plan effectively the growth of the sector and to make use of modern management techniques and mechanization. The policy to stimulate production has centered on developing arable production through irrigation, improved inputs, and better management. The aim has been to increase the share of land used to produce industrial crops as well as fodder for the livestock industry, whose share in total agricultural production has increased substantially and is planned to increase further in the future.

(e) Balanced regional distribution of production and incomes. Increasing attention has been paid during the past three plan periods (1960–75) to the distribution of investment and economic activities to reduce inequalities in levels and structures of production and incomes in each judet (district). In view of the unified national wage structure, the allocation of investment is seen as a way to improve the regional distribution of personal incomes.

(f) Expansion of foreign trade and international economic relations. Although the development strategy has emphasized self-sufficiency as much as possible, Romania is too small and not endowed with enough natural resources to be totally self-sufficient. Certain raw materials must be imported because they are not available locally, and others must be purchased abroad because the growth of the economy has outrun domestic raw material resources. Furthermore, the change of emphasis in the industrialization strategy over the past decade toward developing sophisticated manufacturing using technology not yet available within Romania has generated the need for capital goods imports. Thus, it has been an important element of Romania's development strategy to develop foreign trade at a sufficiently rapid rate to ensure that the economy is supplied with enough raw materials and capital goods. To this end, it has been government policy to expand exports to pay for imports. Important elements of this policy have been the expansion of trade with all countries, attempts to improve the efficiency of trading activities by increasing the share in exports of highly processed goods, particularly products of the engineering, metallurgical, and chemical industries, and, furthermore, signing cooperation agreements with trading partners to tie trade more closely to joint production, technological and scientific research, and technical assistance. Over the past decade, the government's view of the role of foreign trade has been modified by Romania's success in industrializing. In the past, participation in foreign trade was viewed largely as a way to secure resources not available domestically. Exports now have a more positive role, however, since Romania's economic structure produces a comparative advantage, which permits it to compete on a more equal basis with other developed countries. Exports are promoted as a way to improve efficiency and quality of production, as well as to obtain faster growth and economies of scale not available through the domestic market.

(g) Development of human resources. To improve the standards of living of the population as the beneficiary of the development process, the government has pursued policies to make better use of the population as a factor of production. The most important policies in this respect have been a commitment to full employment, introduction of an education and training system geared to the needs of economic growth, transfer of the labor force from rural areas and agriculture to urban areas and industry, and transformation of some rural towns into urban centers. An essential feature of the overall manpower policy has been to raise participation rates and to stimulate an increase in birth rates.

The main instrument for carrying out this strategy has been the system of comprehensive central planning and management. Upon taking power in 1947, the RCP began to bring all activities under social control, in keeping with its belief that the economy could not be transformed under a decentralized market system. Since then, the RCP has emphasized the need to create and continuously improve the planning and management system and to involve the population in formulating and implementing plans.

Economic Development, 1950–75

Between 1950 and 1975 the economy grew rapidly within the framework of comprehensive economic planning, which was made possible by the state's control of the major productive resources and its monopoly over foreign trade. Through this control, the state was able to mobilize the resources required for the economy's rapid growth rate and to finance the development programs laid out in the five-year plans. Development planning has been evolving continuously, with periodic changes introduced to deal with weaknesses in previous practices and to respond to changes in the level and structure of activity. Until the mid-1960s planning and implementation by central directive was reasonably effective in a simple economy, but thereafter it became necessary to adapt it to a more complex economy. As a result, new measures have been introduced in the past decade to improve the planning process and to secure better results in plan implementation.

According to official statistics, between 1950 and 1975 the Romanian economy sustained the highest growth rate in eastern Europe and one of the highest in the world. Social product and national income grew at 9.8 percent and 9.7 percent a year, respectively.[2] Since population growth was of the order of only 1.1 percent a year, per capita growth of social product and national income was also high by international standards, 8.7 percent and 8.6 percent a year, respectively. The driving force behind these growth rates was the high and increasing volume of investment. Between 1950 and 1975 investment grew at an annual average rate of 13.1 percent. As a result of this high marginal propensity to invest (approximately 0.4 throughout the period and approaching 0.5 in some years), which documents clearly the government's ability to mobilize resources for growth and to maintain the growth of consumption below that of national income, the economy raised the proportion of national income used as the accumulation fund from 17.6 percent in 1951–55 to 34.1 percent in 1971–75.[3] The allocation of investment to the sectors throughout the period reflected the priority

2. These figures should be interpreted with care, because of the statistical methodologies used to calculate them (Chapter 5).

3. Gross investment amounted to 36.6 percent of national income in 1971–75, which corresponded to approximately 29 percent of GNP.

given to industrialization; approximately 50 percent was allocated to industry, and, of this, by far the largest part was directed to the producer goods subsector.

Industry

As a result, the leading sector in the economy was industry, which grew at an average annual rate of 13 percent between 1950 and 1975; the output of producer goods increased at 14.5 percent a year, faster than that of consumer goods (10.5 percent). During the first three plan periods, 1951–65, the difference between growth rates of producer and consumer goods widened because of the strong emphasis given to engineering goods and to basic chemicals industries. It was only during the past decade that this trend was reversed, since consumer goods industries have been given more emphasis without, however, affecting the leading role of producer goods industries. As a result, the share of producer goods in total industrial production rose from approximately 50 percent in 1950 to 72 percent in 1975. Throughout the period, the leading sectors of industry were chemicals and engineering goods, and, propelled by high and increasing volumes of investment, their joint share of total industrial production rose from 16.4 percent in 1950 to 43.7 percent in 1975. Another important feature of structural change and growth within industry was the lagging growth of some subsectors that supply raw materials and of the consumer goods industry. With the output of domestic raw materials, particularly oil, gas, coal, and iron ore, growing less quickly than the user industries because of limited domestic reserves, the dependence on imports has increased substantially.

This study provides a largely statistical picture of the impressive rate of industrial growth, but it is unable to provide a full assessment of the sector's past developments. It does, however, draw attention to a number of the sector's characteristics that reflect the efficiency of the industrialization process and industrial production. Industrialization has produced generally large-scale enterprises in many subsectors. Large size (by international standards Romania has a high number of employees for each enterprise) was seen as necessary for applying advanced technology and for securing economies of scale. Between 1960 and 1975 average employment for each enterprise doubled, reaching 1,554 persons in 1975, when 82 percent of gross industrial production and the industrial labor force was concentrated in enterprises employing more than 1,000 persons. The growth in the average size of an enterprise reflected normal expansion of existing production lines and the addition of new lines and administrative reorganization in existing enterprises. In recent years, enterprises employing more than

2,000 persons have been the major generators of new employment. This may explain why, as yet, labor productivity increases in this group have been below average and why economies of scale have not been fully utilized. Some inefficiencies in the utilization of capital are also identified. In some subsectors, such as machine-building, wood processing, and some light industry enterprises, capacities have exceeded domestic market requirements. This was caused by investment decisions determined by technological scale rather than by the size of the market, and led to underutilization of capital stock or the production of surplus goods for export in which Romania has had no particular advantage. In addition, in the past, there has been a certain lack of coordination between policies to modernize production and to reduce the wasteful use of capital; this has led to obsolete machinery being retained or to new equipment being used alongside older and less productive equipment. Such difficulties have stood in the way of more efficient use of the capital stock.

Energy

One industrial sector (as categorized in the Romanian classification) which receives special attention in this study is energy. Rapid industrialization has increased energy consumption about 8.6 percent a year, eventually outpacing domestic production. In 1950, Romania was a net exporter of energy, through its crude oil exports. Over the next two decades, despite large investments in oil, gas, and coal that resulted in significant production increases, domestic consumption expanded more quickly. In 1972, according to World Bank estimates, Romania became a net importer of energy, largely in the form of crude oil imports, which had begun in 1968. In anticipation of this, as well as because of the increases in 1973 in the price of crude oil, plans were made to increase domestic supplies of coal and to economize on the consumption of all energy supplies.

Construction

The large volumes of investment directed toward new production facilities necessitated the rapid expansion of the construction sector. In 1975 construction was the third-largest sector in the economy, providing 7.6 percent of national income and having grown annually an average of 11.3 percent between 1950 and 1975. Construction's share in total investment, however, has been diminishing, particularly during the past decade. This appears to reflect two aspects of the sector: first, the diminishing share of construction investment, since there has been a gradual but continuous shift from investment in new facilities to the modernization and expansion of existing enterprises; and, second, the reduction in the relative price of construction resulting from substantial improvements in efficiency.

In 1950 the sector was labor intensive, unmechanized, and unsophisticated; by 1975 construction was mechanized and efficiency conscious. For much of this period, the growth of the sector was propelled by increases in labor and capital, but in the past plan period, difficulties in recruiting labor led to accelerated capitalization of the sector, at an increasing cost. The result of these efforts to prevent construction from becoming a constraint was an attempt to increase efficiency by increasing mechanization, economizing on materials, improving design work (especially eliminating overdesign), and improving training. Successful implementation of these measures has become more urgent following the 1977 earthquake. The reconstruction program imposes additional tasks on the construction sector beyond those already set out in the 1976–80 Plan, especially in the field of housing.

Transport

The other major sector that has grown rapidly in response to the demands of industry is transport. In 1950, Romania had a fairly well-developed and evenly distributed rail system. Over the past twenty-five years, government policy has concentrated chiefly on improving all transport and on minimizing the cost of transporting goods. Between 1950 and 1975 the growth of goods transport grew annually an average of 11.7 percent, somewhat faster than national income and social product, but the growth of passenger traffic was substantially smaller. As a result of government's policy to improve the existing system and to concentrate traffic on the railways, the capital productivity of the sector has risen. There have been indications in recent years, however, that the capacity of the rail system is being reached and that further increases in traffic will necessitate costly upgrading and construction programs. Road transport has expanded rapidly over the past decade, carrying as much tonnage in 1975 as did rail, but much less in ton-kilometers, because of the limitations imposed on length of haul. The development of road transport has also been inhibited by the condition of the road system. An expanded use of road transport is becoming more urgent with the development of trading and tourist links with western Europe, where speed of transport and delivery service for goods are regarded as more important than in Romania.

Agriculture

As a basic sector of the economy, agriculture has contributed to the economy's development over the past twenty-five years. Between 1950 and

1975 social product and national income in agriculture increased at average annual rates of 5 and 3 percent, respectively. Production grew even though the sector's manpower diminished, and this led to a tripling of labor productivity between 1955 and 1975. The growth of production was greater in livestock than in crop production, 4.3 percent a year compared with 2.1 percent between 1955 and 1975. As a result, the share of livestock production, as a proportion of total agricultural production, increased from 35 percent in 1955 to 43 percent in 1975. The major features of agricultural development over the period were reorganization into state farms and cooperatives between 1949 and 1962 and irregular improvements in production. These improvements included increased cereal production generated by large increases in yields (as a result of improved farming practices), improved inputs, and irrigation. This permitted the acreage devoted to cereals to be reduced. On the land thus released, other food crops (such as potatoes, vegetables, and fruit), fodder crops (green feed and silage in particular), and industrial crops (flour, sugar, beet, sunflower, tobacco, and so forth) were expanded to provide inputs for industry and feed for the livestock industry, the chief components of which are cattle, pork, and poultry.

In spite of these improvements, agricultural performance throughout the period seldom approached the potential of the sector. During the 1950s the sector received relatively few investment funds despite its underdeveloped state, and most of the gains from production in this period reflected recovery from the war, reorganization of land into larger units, and price incentives given for private farmers. Since 1960 investments have increased more rapidly, and the growth rate of gross agricultural production accelerated, as irrigation, improved inputs, and mechanization were provided. Steady gains have not been made in production, however, because of annual fluctuations in rainfall. In spite of such difficulties, the sector has played an important role in the economy. It has provided enough food to increase the nutritional standards of the population and to supply a surplus for export. It has also supplied the nonagricultural sectors with labor while maintaining and increasing production, and, in addition, it has supplied inputs for industrial expansion.

Structure of the Economy

As a result of these developments in the sectors, the structure of the economy changed considerably between 1950 and 1975, with industry becoming the dominant sector. Between 1950 and 1975 the proportion of national income originating in industry rose from 44 percent to 56.2 percent in current prices, whereas that originating in agriculture declined from 27.8 to 16 percent. Because of the large relative price changes over the period, the extent of the structural change is somewhat veiled. Expressed in constant prices, the decline in agriculture and increase in industry would be more prominent. The employment figures express the change more clearly. Whereas in 1950, 74.1 percent of the labor force was employed in agriculture, the proportion was only 37.8 percent in 1975. This reallocation of employment involved an increase in urban population, although at a slower rate than that at which nonagricultural jobs were created. This is an uncommon feature in developing countries, but it has been achieved in Romania by the coordinated control of employment and labor movement and by official policies to distribute new capacities evenly and to control urban growth. Between 1950 and 1975 the proportion of the population living in urban areas increased from 23 to 43 percent. In spite of these policies, the demand for housing has been such that 10 to 15 percent of all investment over the period has been allocated to housing; this investment has grown some 12 percent a year. The sectoral reallocation of employment also generated the need for education and training. Comprehensive efforts have been made to provide proper training for all the population. One of the first programs introduced was literacy training, and since 1948, when the basis for the present system was established, the education and training system has been developed, along with the manpower planning system, to meet the needs of the economy. The system has improved the educational qualifications of the labor force and has adapted continually to the needs of the economy for trained manpower.

The pattern of development in Romania has had implications for the level and structure of foreign trade and for its economic cooperation with all trading partners. Between 1950 and 1975 the volume of foreign trade increased almost 13 percent a year. Throughout the period, foreign trade played an important role in the growth of the economy and also served as an index of the success of the development policy. The total level of imports rose because of the need for raw materials and capital goods. The policy of diversifying sources of supply of raw materials and the industrialization strategy stressing the development of technologically advanced industries both led to a more rapid increase in trade with developing countries and developed market economies, particularly after 1965. The structure of exports in turn mirrored the transformation of the economy. Between 1950 and 1975 the structure of exports moved away from being predominantly raw materials toward industrial products. Whereas in 1950, 75 percent of all exports were raw materials, in 1975 industrial goods constituted 55 percent of all exports. The extent of Romania's industrialization has been shown, however, by the structure of trade with developed market economies; in contrast to its trade with developing and socialist countries, raw materials and relatively unsophisticated products continue to constitute a sizable share of the exports, although industrial exports are increasing rapidly. In its trade with developed market economies, Romania has typically been in deficit and has financed imports by recourse to suppliers and financial credits. As a result, Romania has increased its external debt in the past decade, but a conservative debt policy has been followed so that financing the debt imposes no undue burdens on the economy.

The changes in the level and structure of economic activity have been accompanied by changes in the standard of living, although in view of the increasing savings and investment rate, it was less substantial than the increase in national income. In the early 1950s the authorities took on the commitment to provide all the population with a basic needs package, partly through providing a job and a wage for all people of working age and partly through providing social consumption, such as education, health, and housing. From this subsistence level, the government planned annual increases in living standards. Between 1950 and 1975 the real incomes of the population rose at an annual average of 6.2 percent, with the growth rate gradually increasing. The main component of real incomes—wages and salaries—increased at 4.8 percent a year, whereas sociocultural expenditures, measured in current prices, increased annually at 11.6 percent.

The major conclusion to be derived from a review of the past is that Romania, although still a developing country, has been successful so far in its development efforts and that the problems identified so far have not prevented targets from being met, although they may have increased the cost of meeting them. The Romanian economy, however, has reached an important phase in its development. Maintaining the high growth rates of the past decade might become increasingly difficult and require new measures to deal with some problems that in the past have not been serious constraints, but that might become so at the new stage of Romania's development.

Future Plans and Prospects

The assessment of Romania's development prospects is based upon the government's proposals for the next fifteen years laid out in the perspectives for 1976–90, and more specifically in the five-year plan for 1976–80. The perspectives provide a general impression of where the economy will stand in 1990. In short, it will have caught up with the more developed socialist countries in living standards and level and structure of production, having a national income of some US$3,000 per capita (Romanian methodology) in 1963 prices. It is planned that national income will be 3.5 to 3.8 times the 1975 level. Growth will continue to be fueled by increases in investment, which in 1976–80 will be 1.8 times more than in 1971–75 and in 1981–90 two times larger than in 1971–80, and by increases in efficiency. The allocation of investment will continue to favor industry, whose growth will lead to a gross industrial production in 1990 of 3.5 to 4.0 times the 1975 level. As a result, industry will produce about 70 to 75 percent of national income in 1990. Within industry, the major subsectors, constituting 55 to 60 percent of industrial output by 1990, will continue to be chemicals and engineering. Complementary investments will be made in energy resources, and these will be coupled with a program to conserve energy which, it is planned, will contain the rate of growth of energy consumption to approximately two-thirds that of national income.

In agriculture, the emphasis will be placed on livestock development, which will amount to 50 percent of gross agricultural production in 1990; on the irrigation of all irrigable land of about 5 million hectares by 1990 (amounting to half of the arable land); and on increased fertilizer use, reaching around 300 kilograms per hectare by 1990. Furthermore, the perspectives envisage a reduction in the agricultural labor force to 12 to 15 percent of the total and thus a corresponding increase in mechanization. In foreign trade, a more than threefold increase is anticipated, in constant prices, thereby maintaining the relative importance of trade by 1990.

The perspectives for 1976–90 also provide targets for consumption and living standards. They provide for doubled real wages (a 5.6 percent increase a year), increased social consumption to the level where it accounts for 30 to 32 percent of total incomes, and a work week reduced to 40 to 42 hours by 1990.

A comparison of the 1976–80 Five-Year Plan with the perspectives to 1990 indicates clearly that the fifteen-year period breaks down into two distinct parts. Between 1976–80 the high growth rates of 1971–75 are to be continued, after which the momentum is expected to slacken. The high growth rates of 1976–80 support the contention that the 1970s have been viewed as a decisive period in achieving the long-term development objectives. During the decade the economy is to make the transition from a developing country to an industrially based and technologically advanced economy.

Between 1976 and 1980 national income is planned to grow at 10 to 11 percent a year, only a little lower than the rate achieved between 1971 and 1975. Gross industrial production will increase at 10.2 to 11.2 percent a year, a little lower than before, but gross agricultural production is expected to overcome its previous poor results by increasing at 5 to 7.6 percent. In addition, investment is to increase considerably more quickly than before, at 12.7 percent a year. The volume of foreign trade is planned to double in real terms, which is a much faster growth rate than in 1971–75 when trade merely doubled in current prices. Furthermore, the growth of exports is intended to exceed that of imports, to allow the liquidation of most external debt and the accumulation of international reserves. The targets for consumption growth are below those of production, but with a target of 6.2 to 7.0 percent growth in real incomes, the increase is similar to that attained in 1971–75. Real wages for all workers are to grow at 5.4 percent a year.

The picture for 1981–90 is considerably different. Although the perspectives indicate a constant growth in standards of living, the production targets imply a relative deceleration in the growth rate. National income would grow at 8 to 8.4 percent a year, which remains high by international standards, and gross industrial production would increase at 8 to 8.9 percent. Investment growth would decelerate, and growth of foreign trade would also be slower.

Both the perspectives and the Sixth Five-Year Plan specify a number of additional objectives. These are to improve regional distribution of production and incomes, to encourage internal scientific and technological development, to reduce consumption of energy and raw materials, and to improve the efficiency of production and the quality of goods. Regional development is to be improved through distributing industrial and agricultural investment. Scientific and technological development is to be secured through organizational improvements gearing scientific work more closely to industrial needs and through simply allocating more funds to it. Consumption of raw materials is to be controlled through planning and design and the institution of norms and indicators. Improvements in efficiency and marketability are sought from improvements in the use of capital and labor and more rigorous use of available economic tools: for example, prices, product planning, and export incentive.

The targets must be assessed by considering these aspects of the Romanian plans. The ambitious levels at which targets are set are not sufficient grounds for doubting that they can be achieved, because the government has succeeded in implementing ambitious plans before. In assessing Romania's plans, two major issues must be considered: first, the gradual shift of emphasis from an extensive to an intensive development strategy, with its implications for increased complexity and interdependence of the economy and its effect on the planning system and efficiency of production, and, second, the deterioration in Romania's energy and raw material balance with its implications for foreign trade and the marketability of Romanian exports. The connection of these two issues in the foreign trade sector provides the basis for the conclusion that implementation of Romania's present five-year plan will be more difficult than those of the past. This conclusion is drawn without considering the effect of the earthquake; it is, of course, clear that the damage caused by the earthquake will make implementation more difficult.

During the 1976–80 plan period, the high target for foreign trade is generated by the projected increase in imports of raw materials and capital goods. It is planned that total imports will grow at more than 10 percent a year. Having become a net energy importer in the early 1970s, Romania will be importing some US$1.2 billion of crude oil in 1980 to meet forecast demand. It will also have increased imports of raw materials to keep industry running at full capacity. In addition, imports will increase because of the need for capital goods to develop advanced secondary industries in chemicals, engineering, and metallurgy and thereby to push these leading subsectors toward the technological frontier. Thus not only the continued operation of the economy, but also future investment will depend more heavily on foreign trade and therefore on the ability of Romania to increase its exports. Exports are required to increase at 11.2 percent a year in real terms.

The ability to fulfill this trade plan will be constrained in some degree by the condition of the world economy, over which Romania has little control, but it will be affected also by internal developments. First, it will depend upon whether imports can be limited to the target level that were set on the basis of the norms laid down to reduce consumption of raw materials. In view of previous performance, it would seem ambitious to try to trim material expenditures by 8.5 to 9.5 percent per 1,000 lei of marketable production. Second, holding imports to planned levels will depend on domestic sources of raw materials being developed on schedule. The 1976–80 Plan contains an ambitious lignite mining program, which is already behind schedule and which threatens to increase crude oil and coal imports more than planned. Third, fulfillment of the trade plan will depend upon the ability of the economy to generate marketable exports, particularly in the subsectors of chemicals, machinery and equipment, and industrial consumer goods. It is planned that most export growth should originate in these industrial subsectors; achievement of total exports will require a substantially higher growth rate of exports from these sectors than has been achieved in the past. These are product areas requiring high quality and responsiveness to customer demand. In addition, the intended destination of these products, the developed market economies, are highly competitive markets protected frequently by tariffs and quotas. Through vigorous bilateral and multilateral negotiations, Romania is trying to break down such barriers to market entry, but merely gaining the opportunity to compete does not guarantee export sales in these areas.

The achievement of export targets will require improvements in the quality of products and responsiveness to customer demands, areas in which the economy appears to have lagged behind targets in past years. In spite of measures taken to improve performance—for example, giving enterprises more direct contact with foreign customers and repricing products to give a premium for quality and export suitability—progress has been limited in making the trade sector responsive to world markets. This, again, requires further improvements in planning to incorporate into economic management more effective tools to meet the diverse and multitudinous objectives of an increasingly sophisticated economy. Important problems exist, such as the stimulus for standardization, the emphasis on volumetric indexes, and the need for improving investment criteria to establish optimum resources allocation.

There are alternative possibilities should foreign trade be constrained (for external or internal reasons), but the most likely possibility will be to expand external borrowing within prudent limits and, beyond that, to maintain tight control over imports.

In focusing on the internal and external problems facing Romania in the future, this study does not attempt to belittle the achievements of the economy or to suggest that it faces insurmountable problems. Although the issues discussed above are not easily resolved, it remains probable that Romania will continue to enjoy one of the highest growth rates among developing countries over the next decade and that it will largely succeed in implementing its development targets. As a result of the comprehensive control of economic activities and the cautious policy of the government toward the use of foreign borrowing, external constraints will not reduce the country's creditworthiness.

PART ONE

Development Objectives and Planning

I

Geographic and Historical Perspective

THE SOCIALIST REPUBLIC OF ROMANIA covers an area of 237,500 square kilometers (91,300 square miles) and shares common borders with four countries: to the south Bulgaria, to the west Hungary and Yugoslavia, and to the north and east the U.S.S.R. Romania is not a landlocked country, however; it has a 245-kilometer (152-mile) coastline on the Black Sea, and along much of its southern border with Bulgaria flows the Danube, the largest navigable river in southeastern Europe.

Topography

Romania has a varied topography with three principal relief zones of approximately equal size. In the middle of the country lie the Carpathian Mountains, part of the Alpine chain, which rise to more than 2,500 meters (8,200 feet). Around this mountain core there are hills and tablelands ranging in height from 200 to 500 meters. Finally, there are the lowlands, the largest of which are the Tisa Plain (Cimpia Tisei) in the west and the Romanian Plain (Cimpia Romana) in the south. Reflecting the relief features, drainage is basically radial, although in the north of the country it is largely westwards into the Tisa by the Muresul and the Somesul Rivers. Parts of the tablelands of the northwest, particularly where glacial soils are found, have poor drainage. In the south the major rivers—the Oltul, Siretul, and Argesul—flow toward the Danube. All these tributaries have large seasonal and annual variations in flow, and, in years of heavy rainfall, flooding occurs. The last major flood was in 1975, when all the rivers overflowed, damaging crops and physical structures.

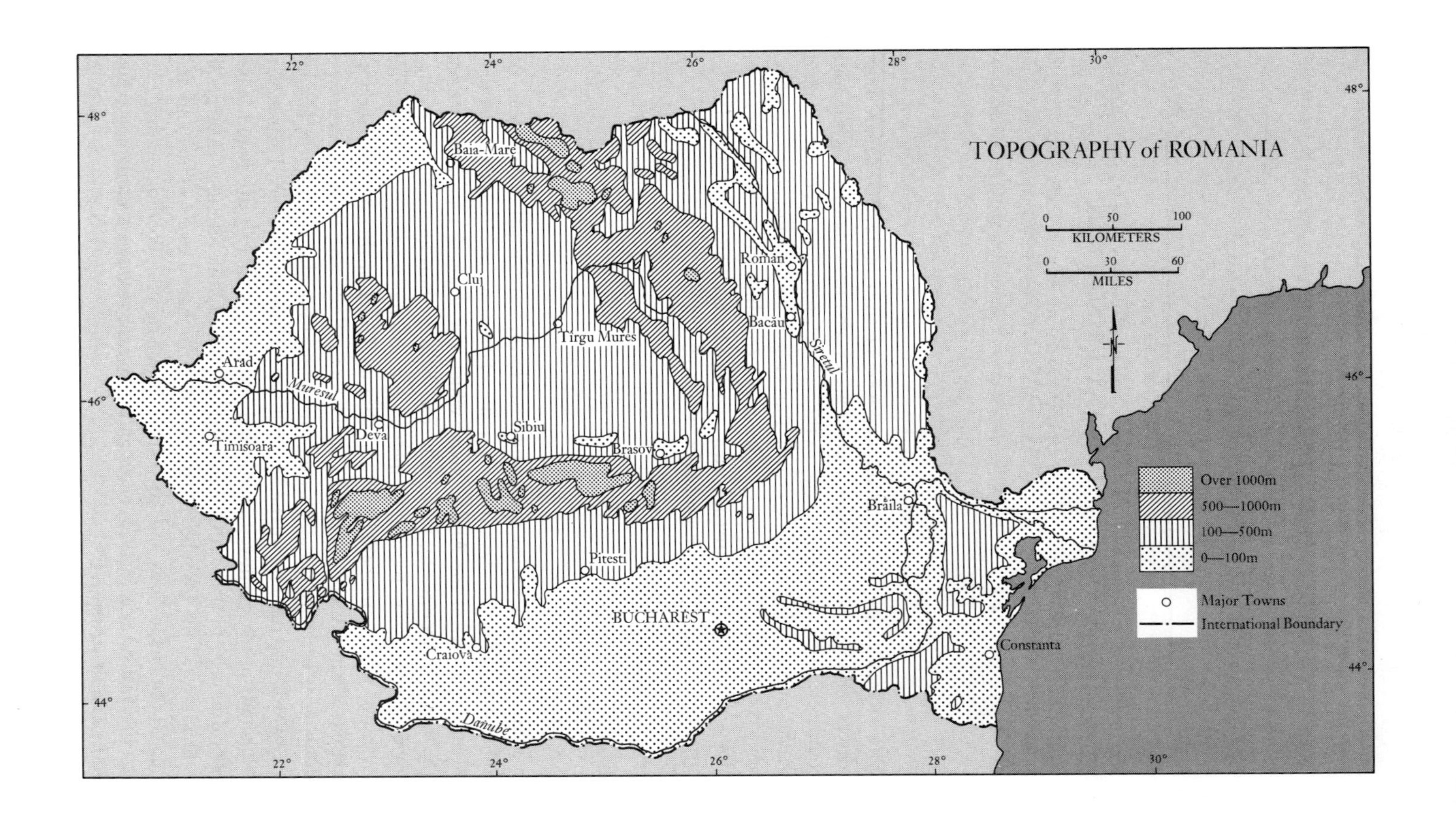
TOPOGRAPHY of ROMANIA
0
50
100
KILOMETERS
0
30
60
MILES
N
Over 1000m
500—1000m
100—500m
0—100m
Major Towns
International Boundary
Baia-Mare
Cluj
Roman
Bacau
Siretul
Tirgu Mures
Arad
Muresul
Timisoara
Deva
Sibiu
Brasov
Braila
Pitesti
BUCHAREST
Craiova
Danube
Constanta
22°
24°
26°
28°
30°
48°
46°
44°

Climate

Romania's climate can be described generally as continental, but there is considerable local variation because of relief features and the influence at different times of the year of the Atlantic Ocean, the Mediterranean, and the Eurasian landmass. In the north and northeast, Eurasian continental influences are strong, bringing heavy snowfalls and strong winds (the crivat) in winter. The Danubian plains are influenced in summer by tropical air masses that produce temperatures of up to 44°C. In general, rainfall declines from northwest to southeast, with annual precipitation of up to 1,500 millimeters (60 inches) in the mountains and as little as 400 millimeters (16 inches) in the southeast, where the substantial variation in rainfall has made agriculture an uncertain undertaking in unirrigated areas. At the same time, the low rainfall on the Black Sea coast, coupled with mild winters and moderately hot summers, has encouraged tourism.

Natural Resources

Romania has a wide range of natural resources of varying size and quality. More than 60 percent of its area is suitable for agriculture, with climatic and relief characteristics favoring both arable and pastoral farming. The plains consist largely of fertile soils that permit the cultivation of a wide range of cereals, foods, and industrial crops. Arable agriculture, especially in vineyards and orchards, can also be carried out in much of the upland areas, whereas in the mountains, pastoral farming is found wherever grazing is available. Some 27 percent of the country, chiefly upland and mountain areas, is forested; the lowlands have been largely deforested for farming. Forestry has been an important industry for many years, with replanting and forest management programs renewing and conserving the lumber reserves. The delta, the rivers, and the Black Sea also contain large fish resources.

Romania has significant resources of fossil fuels, comprising oil, natural gas, coal, and lignite, but because of their quantity and quality, the capacity of reserves and production to meet the country's needs varies considerably. The high-grade fuels, oil and gas, are in increasingly short supply, whereas the largest deposits of solid fuels are predominantly low-grade lignite. Oil and gas are found in an extensive belt around the east and southern flanks of the Carpathian Mountains and in the Danube Plain bordering it; the area has a history of commercial exploitation going back to 1860, but the largest deposits, in the Ploiesti region, are almost depleted, and the present annual oil production level of around 14 million tons is obtained from many wells having low individual productivity. Exploration continues for deeper-producing horizons and for new production on the continental shelf of the Black Sea, but this is not expected to increase production significantly in the short term.

Nonassociated natural gas, found in the Transylvanian Basin, has been extensively exploited since World War II, supplanting oil as the largest single source of energy in the Romanian economy. Oil and natural gas now supply the greater part of the fuel needs of the Romanian economy and also form the basis of an extensive refining and petrochemical industry.

Romania also has substantial reserves of solid fuels, the greater part of which are lignites of relatively low calorific value. These are, nevertheless, being rapidly developed as a fuel for industry and for thermal power generation, and it is intended that they will replace oil and gas as the main source of energy in Romania. The principal mining district is Gorj in the southwest, where lignite is mined by both opencast and underground methods. Bituminous coal also is mined in relatively small quantities in the southwest, near Petrosani, but geologic conditions in the deposits are very difficult, and no significant production increases are foreseen. Some of the coals have weak coking properties and are used in the metallurgical industry. Small deposits of brown coal and of anthracite are mined also, but they are not of major economic significance. Romania has an appreciable hydroelectric potential, most of it concentrated on the Danube. In the Iron Gates region it is being developed jointly with Yugoslavia. Elsewhere, most of the hydroelectric schemes are multipurpose, serving for flood control and irrigation as well as for power generation, and are relatively small.

Romania possesses a wide range of ferrous and nonferrous minerals but few large deposits, and it relies increasingly upon imports, especially of iron ore, for its rapidly expanding industrial needs. Iron ore is mined in the southwest, whereas nonferrous metals—particularly copper but also gold, silver, lead, zinc, and bauxite—are found in the north and west. Romania also has deposits of nonmetallic minerals, most notably salt in the foothills of the Carpathians in the oil field belt; many of the oil-bearing structures are associated with salt plugs and extrusions. In some areas, the salt plugs include potassium salts in addition to common salt. Also found are deposits of refractory sands, the basis of a long-established glass industry, materials for the brick and cement industries, and, in smaller quantities, sulfur, mica, talc, asbestos, and gypsum.

Population and Education

The population of Romania at the time of the January 1977 census was 21.6 million, and it is increasing at approximately 1 percent a year. The present crude birth and death rates—19.5 and 9.6 per 1,000, respectively, in 1976—are low by international standards and have fallen steadily from levels that produced annual population growth rates of approximately 1.2 percent during the 1950s. The decrease in the birth rate, which continued steadily until 1967 when the government introduced measures to reverse the decline, reflects, in large part, changes in social habits associated with industrialization and urbanization. The measures succeeded in almost doubling the birth rate in the late 1960s, after which a new decline occurred. The decrease in the death rate, and, more spectacularly, the decline in infant mortality, from 142.7 per thousand in 1948 to 31.4 per thousand in 1976, attests to improvements in standards of living and increased access to medical services.

By 1977 the urban population had risen to 47.5 percent, the steady (but, compared with many other countries, relatively slow) increase since 1947 resulting from the coordination of economic development and settlement patterns. Considerable internal migration has taken place in the last three decades in response to urbanization, industrialization, and the government's attempts to distribute economic activities equitably throughout the country. The transformation of the economy has also been associated with widespread improvements in education. Illiteracy, about 40 percent in the 1930s, has been virtually eliminated, and a comprehensive system of education has been developed to improve the skills and cultural level of the population.

The Economy before 1950

Before the outbreak of World War II, Romania was one of the least developed countries in Europe. Formed from the two principalities of Wallachia and Moldavia, which united in 1859, Romania became an independent state in 1877. Over the following four decades, economic growth was slow, reflecting the unstable political and economic conditions in the country and within southeastern Europe in general. Transylvania joined Romania in 1918, forming a unified Romanian state, and the potential for development improved. But because of war damage and in spite of government actions to stimulate industrial development through protective tariffs, state investment in infrastructure, and direct assistance to private enterprise, the Romanian economy remained a peripheral appendage of industrial western Europe, supplying agricultural products and mineral and energy resources. Industrial production and employment grew slowly, the latter constituting only 8 percent of the labor force in 1938. Such industrial development as occurred was limited sectorally and regionally and was mainly in consumer goods and associated with the production of raw materials for export: little heavy industry existed, and the only large-scale modern industry was oil production, much of which was controlled by foreign firms. Industry and commerce, furthermore, was concentrated in a few urban areas, evidence of the limited progress in diffusing industry throughout the economy. The great majority of the population lived in the rural areas working in a low-productivity agricultural sector. Organized largely in large feudal estates (despite spasmodic attempts at land reform), agriculture was poorly developed, providing the subsistence requirements of the population and increasingly oriented toward the production of export crops. For most of the population, economic and social conditions were poor; illiteracy rates were high, infant mortality rates were the highest in eastern Europe, and life expectancy was low.

Just as World War I damage to the economy posed massive reconstruction problems that further impeded the largely ineffectual efforts of the government to develop a comprehensive industrial base, so World War II severely affected the country, weakening the economic base and destroying much of the industrial capacity. A popular uprising removed from power the representatives of the prewar regime; a broadly based progressive government was formed in 1944 and prepared the way for the People's Republic, which was established in 1947. Under the guidance of the Romanian Communist Party (RCP), reconstruction of the economy began, and coordinated programs of development in all sectors were initiated, with the intention of converting the backward agricultural economy into a modern industrialized and independent state. In the early years, however, the extent of the war damage and scarcity of investment resources constrained economic growth. It was not until 1950 that national income reached 1938 levels and not until 1953 that the prewar level of agricultural production was attained. From then on, development proceeded at a rapid pace.

2

Development Objectives and Strategy

THE LONG-TERM ECONOMIC OBJECTIVES of the Romanian Communist Party (RCP), established by the Eleventh Congress in 1974, can be summarized as:

(a) The transformation of the economy, through rapid and sustained growth in the production of goods and services and by the application of science and technology, into a technologically advanced and multilaterally developed state;
(b) The predominant position, and thus rapid growth, of industry and agriculture as the material basis of the economy;
(c) The balanced and equal development of the whole country and the elimination of regional disparities in production and income;
(d) The elimination of rural-urban inequalities and the diminution of differences between manual and intellectual work, through education, mechanization, and automation;
(e) The restructuring of the labor force to increase the weight of nonagricultural employment;
(f) Participation in the world economy "on an equal basis" with developed economies: that is, as an exporter of highly processed industrial and agricultural products;
(g) The provision of an improved standard of living for the whole population at a level comparable with that in developed countries.

These goals represent one major element of the overall development goal of the RCP: that is, the construction of socialism and the eventual transition to a communist society. Interpreted in terms of the materialist framework of modes of production, the economic goals are concerned with developing the forces of production and are regarded by the RCP as necessary for the creation of socialism.[1] The second major element of the RCP's overall goal has been the evolution of the social relations of production: that is, the economic, political, and social relations between classes and individuals within society. Although Romanian government statements on development stress both elements, this study concentrates on the country's economic objectives and discusses the social relations of production only indirectly, insofar as the effect on economic growth of the planning, organization, and implementation of production is concerned.

Any description of a development strategy must be anchored to a particular period since, as the economy progresses along a development path, the details, emphases, and, in some cases, foundations of the strategy change. In the case of Romania, the fundamental features of the development strategy have remained unchanged throughout the period covered by this study; the strategy can be summarized as the rapid and diversified industrialization of an initially agrarian economy through high rates of investment and under comprehensive central planning of economic activities. The changes in the strategy largely result from attempts of the RCP to move the economy from an "extensive" to an "intensive" development path after the mid-1960s. Strategy between 1950 and 1965 emphasized unbalanced growth that was centered on the creation of new industry, in particular, the producer goods sector, with the intention of eliminating what was seen by the RCP as the uneven development of the economy inherited after World War II and of establishing a broad base for a "sustained drive towards socialism." After 1965, although the emphasis remained on industrial growth, greater attention was given to a more intensive strategy—capital deepening as well as broadening, developing specialized secondary industries, and obtaining greater efficiency from existing inputs as well as additional endowments of capital and labor. Furthermore, greater emphasis has been given to the development of agriculture, with increased investment funds being applied to mechanization and the development of the productive base. This chapter discusses the present development strategy as it is laid out in the 1976–80 Plan and the 1981–90 Perspective Program.

The major components of the strategy are high increasing rates of saving and investment; rapid and comprehensive industrialization based upon modern scientific and technological methods; development of local natural resources, including the modernization and reorganization of agriculture; balanced regional distribution of production and income; expansion of

1. "We set out from the fact that the development of the productive forces propels social development, the general progress of mankind." Nicolae Ceaucescu (speech to the Plenary meeting of the Central Committee of the Romanian Communist Party, November 23, 1976).

foreign trade to supply raw materials and capital goods for industry; and, finally, efficient use of human resources. The main instrument for achieving the development strategy is comprehensive and compulsory planning.

Consumption and Investment

A key feature of Romania's development strategy, and a necessary condition for implementing the other components of the strategy, has been the allocation of a high and increasing proportion of national income to investment. In the absence of capital flows of any size, it has been necessary to achieve this by increasing the rate of domestic savings. During the first plan period, the government divided national income between consumption and investment to provide for the basic needs of the population. Since then, it has been government policy to plan for a steady growth of consumption while channeling a large proportion of incremental income toward investment. The allocation of national income between consumption and investment has been based on the fact that although investment and consumption constitute competitive claims on resources in any single period, a high rate of growth of accumulation and thus of national income is, in the long run, the only viable basis for a high and increasing level of consumption. Thus, high rates of investment generate high levels of income, which permit higher absolute levels of consumption and investment than would have been the case with a lower rate of accumulation.

The planning of consumption in aggregate terms, therefore, has been generally subordinated to the growth of accumulation and of national income. The development strategy has provided for the steady growth of both private and social consumption from the level of basic needs established by the government during the first plan period and for the development of a countrywide network of socialist retail outlets. The growth and increasing diversity of private consumption has been correlated with the increased remuneration of the labor force to avoid excess demand and forced savings; it has also been government policy to expand the level of social consumption through state expenditures.

Industrialization

Industrialization has been the core of Romania's development strategy. Comprehensive industrialization is seen as necessary to create a modern and developed socialist society, to raise the standard of living, and to ensure the country's economic and political independence. Furthermore, the importance of industrialization, particularly heavy industry, in developing the technical basis of other sectors, especially agriculture, in raising the productivity of labor in all sectors, and in stimulating the more efficient exploitation of raw materials has been emphasized in the development plans. The program of industrial development has stressed the creation of heavy industry and the construction of new plants.

The industrialization strategy emphasizes the use of the most modern technologies and the incorporation of scientific and technological advances. Although great efforts have been made to develop the required technology, it has been necessary to import many investment goods. The interdependence of different components of the development strategy appears most clearly here. An increased ability to import capital goods (and the raw materials needed for industry) has depended upon the growth of exports that, especially in the 1950s and 1960s, were chiefly agricultural raw materials and food products; in turn, the growth of exports has depended upon increases in agricultural production, which are largely a function of investments in mechanization, fertilizers, and so forth: that is, industrial goods. During the past decade, a more balanced export structure has been developed as a result of large increases in industrial exports. Romania's development strategy for industry has thus required complementary investment in all other sectors of the economy and the development of foreign trade.

Development of Natural Resources

The development of industry generates both the potential for using natural resources more effectively and an increased demand for such resources. To supply the rapidly expanding needs of the Romanian economy, the state has instituted comprehensive planning of the exploration for and exploitation of raw materials, combining these efforts with policies to economize on their use wherever possible. Investment funds have been allocated throughout 1950–75 to produce ferrous and nonferrous metals (notably iron ore, manganese, copper, and bauxite) and nonmetallic minerals (such as sulfur, mica, gypsum, and limestone). Local resources, however, have increasingly been insufficient to meet demand, and imports have been necessary. Particularly in the past decade, the government has secured such raw materials under long-term supply agreements and, furthermore, has shown interest in investing in joint production facilities abroad.

Economic growth has also generated increasing demand for energy resources. The development of the four major energy sources—oil, gas, coal, and hydroelectric power—has been worked out explicitly within the framework of a national energy plan, the chief goals of which are to maximize the use of domestic energy resources and to minimize waste of energy resources. As a result, the government has invested heavily in energy production and has built into its planning targets explicit indicators requiring enterprises to reduce energy consumption. In addition, new factories are designed for the most appropriate energy source—frequently lignite—and considerable research has been conducted to devise less energy-intensive methods. It has, furthermore, been an important parameter of government's policy to minimize the use of oil and gas as fuels and to use them in higher value-added activities. They form the basis of a rapidly expanding chemical industry. Oil production has been stabilized during the past decade, an expanding excess demand being met by imports of crude oil, and refineries and chemical works have been established to provide for both domestic needs and the export market.

The present energy strategy foresees the major sources of power for the future as being lignite, hydroelectric power (HEP), and, somewhat farther into the future, nuclear power. Production of lignite has grown rapidly since 1947, particularly in the past decade, reflecting the world energy situation and mechanization of mining operations. The first national plan for HEP as a source of power and irrigation was drawn up in 1950. A national grid system for electricity distribution has been established to supply electricity to all parts of the country and, thus, to permit an equitable distribution of industry and rural electrification, two important features of development policy.

Modernization of Agriculture

The relation between industrial and agricultural development in terms of foreign trade and imports of investment goods and industrial raw materials has been pointed out already. There are other aspects of this relation that demonstrate not only the role of industry in modernizing agriculture, but also the role of agriculture in stimulating industrial expansion and the overall development of the economy. In addition to providing, through exports of agricultural goods, the means of importing investment goods (especially in the 1950s before the industrial sector was large enough to generate a significant export potential), agricultural development has been required to provide food for the industrial work force and raw materials for processing in the industrial sector. In addition, it has provided a source of labor for industrial expansion and a source of surplus for investment before the industrial sector became large enough to generate its own reinvestable resources. To fulfill these functions, investment in agriculture has been required to raise the productivity of a declining labor force.

Government strategy in agriculture has had two major components: reorganization and the growth and diversification of production and its reorientation to high value-added goods. Reorganization was accomplished primarily through creating state farms and collectives during the 1950s and subsequently through refinements in their basic organization. It was meant to create large farming units capable of using modern agricultural techniques efficiently. The strategy for the growth of production has been to reduce the land area used for grain production (production levels being increased through investments to produce higher yields) and to use the released land for industrial crops and for fodder crops for livestock. The main source of production increases has been investment in mechanization; improved inputs, such as seeds, feed concentrates, and fertilizers; and irrigation to increase both land and labor productivity and to reduce the impact of the climate. The restructuring of production toward products for industrial processing and livestock reflects the government's policy to produce higher value-added goods in agriculture, as does the decision to divert grain output from direct export to livestock production, where part of the output is exported as processed products.

Development of International Economic Relations

Rapid income growth based on the creation of a modern industrial sector generates a greatly increased demand for investment goods and raw materials. As the demand of industry for raw materials has outgrown domestic production, regular importation has become necessary. Furthermore, the development of advanced secondary industries has generated a demand for imports of sophisticated capital goods that, despite the increased capacity of the domestic capital goods sector, cannot be produced yet in Romania. Consequently, the continued growth of the Romanian economy has depended a great deal upon the steady expansion of foreign trade. Throughout 1950–75 foreign trade policy was geared primarily to expanding exports to pay for necessary imports. In recent years, however, exports have been stimulated not only to finance imports, but also to continue high growth rates in sectors where the size of the domestic market constrains continued growth or the achievement of economies of scale. It also appears that, especially in the leading sectors of industry—chemicals, metallurgy, and engineering—foreign trade is viewed as a way to improve efficiency and product quality by exposing these sectors more to international markets.

For diverse reasons, Romania has, particularly since 1960, followed a policy of diversifying the source of its imports and, thus in turn, the destination of its exports. Although the volume of trade with socialist countries has increased through bilateral agreements, trade has been expanded more rapidly with nonsocialist countries in the past decade to obtain the capital goods and raw materials required for the development program. In particular, it has been government policy to develop trade with the developing countries to secure directly materials previously obtained through intermediaries in the developed market economies. At the same time, Romania has attempted to change the structure of its exports to sell goods embodying a higher domestic value-added than agricultural products and raw materials. Successive five-year plans have included ambitious targets to expand the sale of manufactures, both investment goods and consumer products, to all trading partners.

Romania's attempts to increase and to diversify its foreign trade have been carried out within the wider context of a very active policy of international cooperation. It has been government policy to establish agreements with trading partners covering not only trade, but also joint production facilities, scientific and technological exchange, and a wide range of economic cooperation activities. Furthermore, the government has joined several multilateral organizations, particularly the World Bank, the United Nations Committee on Trade and Development (UNCTAD), the International Monetary Fund (IMF), and the General Agreement on Tariff and Trade (GATT).

Regional Development Policy

Within the past decade, more attention has been paid to the equitable distribution of production throughout the economy, and the government has introduced an active regionalization policy to distribute industrial investment and production more equitably and thereby, through the growth of industrial employment in each judet, to equalize income inequalities in the country. The regional policy has been three-pronged. First, the basis for effective implementation of regional policies has been laid by creating machinery for regional planning and management. Second, measures are taken to limit the further concentration of the population and to correlate the movement of the population with the labor requirements of the economy. The most important features have been balancing urban growth, restraining the growth of Bucharest, expanding small and medium-sized urban centers, and upgrading villages into small towns. In addition, many public services have been extended to villages. Third, industrial investment has been allocated, where feasible, to judets that have little industry (and consequently, because of the national incomes policy, lower personal incomes).

Development of Human Resources

Romania's development strategy has also emphasized, as a means to and an end of development, improvements in the level of human resources through the relocation of the labor force, education and training, and improvements in living standards. Government policy has been, particularly since the mid-1960s, to stimulate population growth, both by encouraging the birth rate and by improving medical services and nutrition. The annual population growth, however, remains about 1 percent, and the accomplishment of the development program has necessitated major changes in the location and structure of the labor force. The government has implemented an urbanization program and, through investment and training programs, has enabled population to be transferred productively from agriculture to industry and other nonagricultural sectors.

The education and training system plays a major role in preparing the population for employment, and it is an integral part of government strategy to tie education and training closely to the needs of the economy. To ensure that education programs are an efficient and effective investment for economic development, the government periodically reviews the sector and restructures enrollments and program content in keeping with projections of manpower and skill requirements.

Importance of Centralized Economic Control

The comprehensive and coordinated planning and management of economic activities is viewed by the RCP as a necessary condition for implementing its development strategy. "To accept the idea that the economy should be left to develop by itself, through the spontaneous mechanism of the law of value, means to give up one of the most important advantages of the new system: the conscious direction of the economy with a view to rationally utilizing all the country's resources to the satisfaction of the general interests of the people."[2] Accordingly, under the overall guidance of the RCP, the economic resources of the country were brought under the control of the state, and comprehensive economic and social planning was introduced. The basis for managing the economy was laid during 1948 and 1949, with the nationalization of large-scale industry and banks, the establishment of a State Planning Committee (SPC), and legislation providing for the collectivization of agriculture. The centralized control of the economy's resources provided the necessary condition for an integrated program for economic growth, and the establishment of a SPC and planning bodies in all sectors and at all levels of activity provided the means to plan and to administer development (Chapters 3 and 4).

Centralized economic control has remained strong in Romania. In the 1950s and 1960s, when the industrialization strategy focused on a limited number of strategic choices, centralized planning and control by directives provided an effective way to meet targets. Increasing sophistication of the economy produced strains upon this system, however, and toward the end of the 1960s a more detailed planning structure embodying some elements of decentralized management and planning evolved. In general, however, central control has remained strong, and the reforms introduced in the name of decentralization and efficiency have been concerned largely with improving the implementation of plans, the outlines of which remain fixed by the center, and with improving the flow of information on which decisions are based.

2. Nicolae Ceaucescu, "Report Concerning Measures for Perfecting the Management and Planning of the National Economy and for Improving the Administrative and Territorial Organization of Romania" (report delivered to the National Conference of the Romanian Communist Party, December 6, 1967) (Bucharest: Meridiane Publishing House, 1967).

3

Nature and Techniques of Romanian Planning

DEVELOPMENT OBJECTIVES, as outlined in Chapter 2, are being pursued within the framework of comprehensive economic planning. The major instrument of economic management is the national plan for economic and social development, which sets out specific tasks and activities for economic and social entities for the economy as a whole, by sector and branch, and on a regional (judet) basis. Financial resources to implement this plan are ensured through a financial plan prepared concurrently. In addition, other supplementary instruments are being used (for example, prices, taxes, and credits) to help achieve the socioeconomic objectives set by the Romanian Communist Party (RCP) and the government. Comprehensive planning is facilitated by the social ownership of the major productive resources of the country and by the state's monopoly on foreign trade.

Evolution of Development Planning

Development planning in Romania, as an instrument of the state's economic management and control, has been evolving continually. It began with the development of two one-year plans in 1949 and 1950. The basic planning period of five years was introduced in 1951–55. As economic needs

Note: This chapter presents Romania's planning process as World Bank staff have come to understand it in their discussions with central authorities. The object of this chapter is primarily to convey an understanding of how planning is reported to be organized and undertaken. The principles of sector planning are discussed in subsequent sector chapters. This chapter does not provide a World Bank assessment of the actual operation of Romania's planning system and techniques.

and priorities have been changing through the different stages of the country's development, so has the system of planning been adapting to new goals. At times this has required major organizational and procedural changes involving the creation of new institutions or the modification and abandonment of existing ones. With the 1966–70 Plan, the principle of continuous planning was introduced, and for the first time the plan contained sections for each year, sector, ministry, region, and enterprise. The number of targets was increased in the Fifth Plan (1971–75), and this and the Sixth Plan (1976–80) are the most detailed ones yet developed by the authorities.

In addition to the scope of the plan itself, the process of plan elaboration has also changed substantially. Three periods can be distinguished in this respect:

(a) Up to 1959 plan elaboration was centralized, and targets were handed down to lower-level units. The State Planning Committee (SPC) drafted the plan's targets based on the directives of the RCP. Upon government approval, these were given to ministries, which allocated control figures to their general departments; these, in turn, applied the targets to their enterprises;

(b) During 1960–66 the essentials of a dialogue in plan elaboration were established. The ministries drew up proposals for the plan after discussion with their subordinate units; these were submitted to the SPC. The SPC then drafted a plan based on the RCP's directives and the proposals. The plan, after approval by the government, was divided by ministries and subsequently by the subordinate units of each ministry.

(c) Since 1967 the present, more elaborate system has been used, in which plan preparation starts both at the enterprise level and at the SPC and other agencies for economic analysis, with an extensive reconciliation process at national, ministry, and district levels when differences exist. This process is explained further below.

Since the National Conference of the RCP in 1967 called for the "raising of economic activity onto a higher qualitative level"[1] and for the "strengthening of the role of the plan in guiding socioeconomic processes,"[2] the Romanian authorities have undertaken a wide range of institutional, economic, and procedural changes designed to improve the planning system

1. Report of the National Party Conference, December 1967, p. 6.
2. Ibid., p. 54.

and to increase the efficiency of economic management. The changes have not been confined to the institutional organizations alone, but have included changes in the policy and practice of pricing in financing and investment procedures and in the conduct of foreign trade among others.[3] Many of the new procedures have been introduced recently, and most of these are discussed separately in this study.

Principles of Planning

Planned economic management is viewed as an essential attribute of Romanian sovereignty and national independence. It is an attribute that follows logically from the social ownership of the means of production and the state's control of distribution and exchange. Apart from this, four major principles can be distinguished in the Romanian planning system: comprehensiveness of the plan; continuity of planning; complementarity of economic activity; and democratic centralism.

In Romania, the plan is a comprehensive instrument that covers the bulk of economic activity in all sectors and administrative jurisdictions. Even the limited resource requirements of sectors outside the direct purview of the plan (for example, private farming and housing) are included when establishing material balances in the economy for any period of time. The plan is the sole basis for executing economic activity at any one time.

The process of planning is continuous. During each of the planning periods, all economic units seek to reconcile present achievements and medium-term plans, adjusting these to coincide with longer-term perspectives. Monthly, quarterly, and annual plans are constantly adjusted. Five-year plans are made compatible with the perspective program reflecting longer-term trends. It is difficult for an outside observer to understand how this continuous reconciliation process works with the many intricate adjustments required in diverse economic activities. It appears likely that the microeconomic implications of new directives or national campaigns are left to the enterprise to reconcile in the course of plan implementation.

3. The range of changes is illustrated by new laws that were passed: Law (no. 71) on Economic Contracts of 1969; Law (no. 72) on the Organization, Planning, and Execution of Investment Projects of 1969; Law (no. 2) on Assurance and Control of Product Quality of 1970; Law (no. 1) on Foreign Trade of 1971, Law (no. 9) on the Transfer of Fixed Assets and Supply of Materials of 1971; Law (no. 11) on the Organization and Management of State Socialist Units of 1971; Law (no. 8) on the Planned Social and Economic Development of Romania of 1972; and Law (no. 9) on Finance of 1972.

Economic activities are viewed as complementary, not competitive; they are oriented toward achieving a common end: the objectives set out by the RCP (Chapter 2). Competing demands are reconciled in formulating the plan so that it can be derived either from an aggregation of sector/subsector plans (vertical aggregation) or of judet plans (horizontal aggregation). Participation in the production process is undertaken through contractual obligations resulting from the plan and is encouraged by material, financial, pricing, and other incentives. Despite a recent emphasis on improving product quality, performance is still largely judged on the basis of achieving volumetric targets. Increasing importance is, however, being given to improving efficiency.

Democratic centralism entails popular participation in formulating the plan at the enterprise level. This deliberation, however, can only be undertaken in tandem with central decisions concerning the growth rates and resource mobilization, since resource allocation in the economy at large is a political option. The draft plan is elaborated through a combination of central directives and individual aggregation: that is, draft planning is both downward and upward, and any differences are reconciled through a continuous dialogue between the ministries, the judets, and the central planning authorities. Although this dialogue provides a degree of participation for the entities in the planning process, some proposals of these entities cannot always be included in the final plan.

Institutions Involved in the Planning Process

All state and socialist institutions are involved in the process of planning and plan execution. The following paragraphs give a brief description of the division of responsibilities between the major institutions involved (see also Figure 3.1):

(a) The Romanian Communist Party (RCP). The Congress of the RCP, which is usually held every five years, is the supreme forum for determining the direction of Romania's development, and it issues the directives that become the preliminary basis for formulating each five year plan. The last congress, the Eleventh, was held in November 1974. Between congresses, the Central Committee of the RCP deals with most of the important issues. When necessary, National Party conferences can be convened to discuss important problems arising between congresses.

(b) The Grand National Assembly. The assembly is the Romanian parliament. It is the supreme legislative organ and adopts the laws concern-

Figure 3.1. *Structure of the Government*

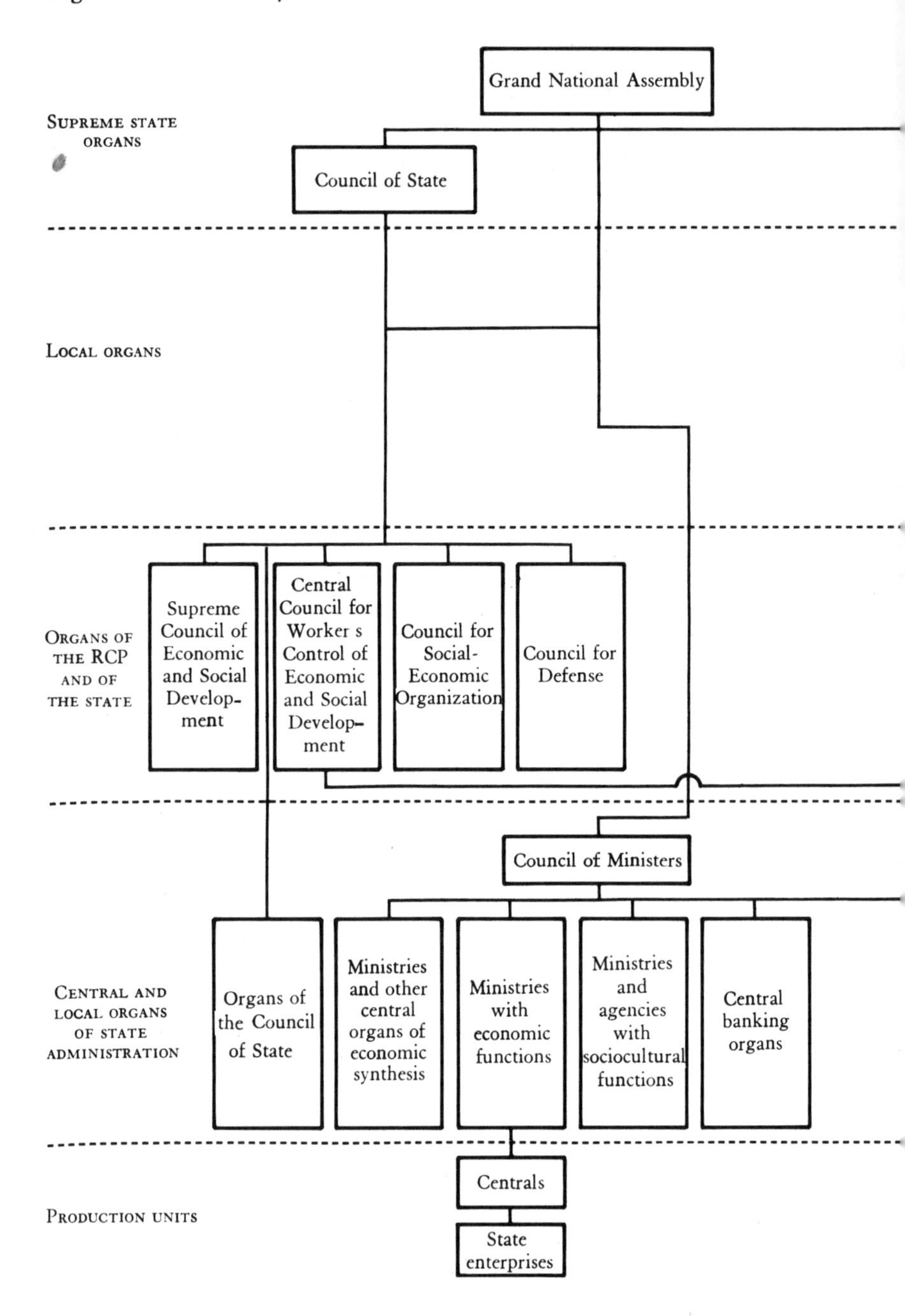

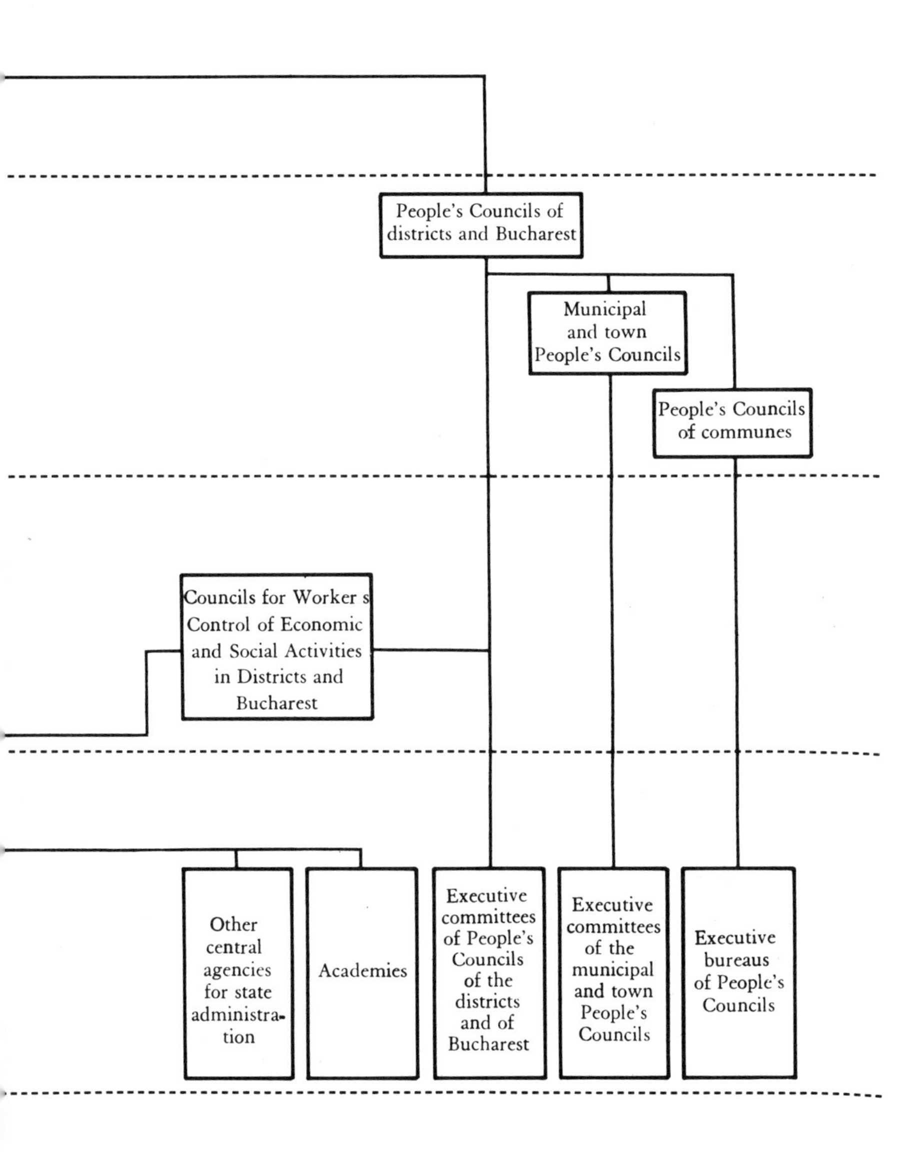
People's Councils of districts and Bucharest
Municipal and town People's Councils
People's Councils of communes
Councils for Worker s Control of Economic and Social Activities in Districts and Bucharest
Other central agencies for state administra-tion
Academies
Executive committees of People's Councils of the districts and of Bucharest
Executive committees of the municipal and town People's Councils
Executive bureaus of People's Councils

ing the annual and five-year plans. It has permanent commissions in some branches and fields of the economy that advise the Assembly on the passage of legislation. The Assembly elects the State Council, which acts for it between sessions and controls the application of laws and the activities of all organs of state administration. After adoption of five-year and annual plans, the Council of State divides the plan targets among the ministries, other central bodies, and People's Councils.

(c) The Supreme Council of Economic and Social Development (SCESD). Established in 1973, this council is the chief advisory and deliberative agency in the planning field. It is composed of 150 to 260 members who represent all areas of Romanian economic and social life. As a joint state-party organ, the SCESD presents studies and conclusions on the long-term prognoses to the State Council and Central Committee of the RCP. It also reports to the Grand National Assembly on the efficiency and consistency of the five-year and annual plans.

(d) The Legislative House of People's Councils. The House consists of deputies, who are members of the executive committees of the People's Councils of each judet. Its responsibility is to ensure the correlation of centrally planned and local activities and to discuss, approve, and submit to the National Assembly those measures affecting local activities, including the regional plans.

(e) The Council of Ministers. This is the highest body of state administration. It is responsible for managing all economic and social activities.[4] In the area of planning, it is responsible for elaborating plans and submits these to the National Assembly and to the State Council. After their adoption, it supervises their fulfillment.

(f) The State Planning Committee (SPC). The SPC, which is represented by its president in the Council of Ministers, is responsible for the actual elaboration of the draft plan and for technical tasks involved in planning. The SPC designs several plan variants based on its own studies and on the proposals from the technical ministries, other central agencies, and the People's Councils. It proposes which indicators and which norms will be used for such matters as raw material use, inventory levels, employment, and remuneration. It draws up synthetic balances of the national economy, as well as material balances for strategic products decided upon by the Council of Ministers. In terms of plan implementation, the SPC, along with

4. The composition of the Council of Ministers is given in Appendix A.

other agencies, oversees plan fulfillment, proposes corrections of imbalances, and reallocates resources. Together with the Ministry of Foreign Trade, the SPC works on five-year plans with other members of the Council for Mutual Economic Assistance (CMEA).

(g) The People's Councils. The local elected governing body in each of the thirty-nine judets and Bucharest is called the People's Council. The Executive Committee of the Council, consisting of a chairman, two or more deputy chairmen, and several other members chosen for the life of the Council, is the chief administrative organ of each district Council and directs the planning activity in each district for areas in which it has direct responsibility (housing, maintenance of local public facilities, certain education levels, and so forth.) The Council also plays a major role in coordinating all economic activities in the region.[5] Meeting every five years, the Congress of the District People's Councils and of the presidents of the People's Councils has been established to discuss common problems and to serve as a forum for working out programs under their jurisdiction and the means of implementing them within the framework of the national development plan.

(h) Technical Ministries, Centrals, and Enterprises. Each major sector of the economy has a technical ministry responsible for its planning. The centrals are independent units of the ministries and were set up in 1968 to assist them in economic administration. The centrals, each of which directs the operations of a group of enterprises (horizontally or vertically integrated), perform important tasks in the planning process.[6] They elaborate their own plans based on the proposals of their constituent enterprises, then pass them upward as proposals to the ministries. They also disaggregate final plan targets of the ministries to their enterprises. The centrals have become "titulars" to the plans of their respective ministries, responsible for fulfilling plan targets. The enterprise is the unit that executes the plan and has to achieve its targets. Enterprises exist not only for production, but also for distribution of goods, trade, and services.

(i) The Agencies for Economic Synthesis. These agencies, many of which are ministries, deal with aspects of the economy that are not specific to particular sectors. The agencies represented in the Council of Ministers that are involved in the planning process are the Ministry

5. The system of regional government and its financing are discussed in Appendix B.
6. Industrial organization is discussed in Appendix C.

of Finance (assisted by the banking system), the Ministry of Labor, the Ministry of Technical Material Supply and Fixed Assets Administration, the Ministry of Foreign Trade and International Cooperation, the National Council for Science and Technology, the General State Inspectorate for Investment and Construction, the State Committee for Prices, the General Directorate of Statistics, the General State Inspectorate for Production Quality Control, and the Ministry of Domestic Trade. These agencies collaborate with the SPC and with the technical ministries to coordinate plan aggregates within their respective fields.

Planning Techniques

Although econometric models are used as a general reference and comparative framework, their use is rather recent and not extensive or sophisticated. Traditional eastern European planning techniques still predominate. These consist of synthetic and material balances drawn up for the major products by the Council of Ministers, ministries, and centrals and the elaboration of special programs for various branches and subbranches of economic activities and for groups of products. For the current five-year plan, about 160 such programs were developed.

Balances and the system of advance contracting

During plan elaboration, macroeconomic equilibrium is achieved through a number of synthetic balances. The process of preparing synthetic balances is essential in the planning system. Synthetic balances are compiled for such measures as national income, social product, labor force, production capacity, foreign payments, incomes, and expenses of population. But the most numerous balances, which are also discussed more extensively below, are material balances. Balances are compiled at all levels to ascertain the feasibility of plan proposals. In the case of an imbalance, one organization negotiates with another to reduce demand or to increase supply. A change in one quantity may necessitate changes in other variables, which may generate more imbalance and a new series of negotiations.

In determining material balances, each balance has two sections: one lists the source of a particular resource and the other enumerates its uses. Before the balance can be finalized (which is done by successive approximations) and its components can be incorporated in the plan, sources must be made equal to uses. The Council of Ministers determines the products for which material balances should be compiled (these are the products of major importance) and designates the coordinator of the balance (usually the unit that directs the largest share of the production or consumption of the product). With the help of the SPC, the Council of Ministers is responsible for compiling about 200 material balances for products of national importance. Balances for other products are struck by the ministries and centrals. The basic form followed in determining the balances is presented below:

Sources	*Uses*
Beginning stock	Consumption
Production	Production
Imports	Investment
Releases from state reserve	Export
Other sources	Other uses
	Increased state reserve
	Plan reserves
	Ending stock

The coordination of material balances by the central authorities is a difficult process. It has encountered numerous problems in the past. An inefficient geographic distribution of local and central agencies and their warehouses as well as growing shortages of some materials at a time of accumulation of unwanted inventories led to two reforms in 1968 and 1971. These reforms included changes in the norms of inventories to be held and the establishment of a new institution in planning and management, the Ministry of Technical Material Supply and Fixed Assets Administration. This ministry, in consultation with the SPC and other state agencies, is responsible for drawing up the plan for material supplies and for determining the allocation of stocks, supply contracts, and the like.

The equilibrium in material balances is crucial to plan implementation. As a rule, for the enterprise plan to become effective, enterprises must complete contracts for the purchase of inputs and sale of output consistent with the plan. In this way the planning authority attempts to ensure that the actual demand for inputs and supply of output (including changes in stocks) are balanced and consistent with the plan. The enterprises are legally bound to their procurement contracts. If changes in an enterprise's plan targets require modifications to these contracts, these changes cannot be effected without renegotiating the contract with the consent of the supplier. This encourages strict adherence to initially established plan targets. In such cases as the recent campaign to reduce consumption of raw materials, however, a process of accommodation is implicitly required between the contractor and the supplier so that national goals can be achieved. Except for items covered by material balances at the level of the central and above, the enterprises generally are free to choose suppliers or buyers, and such factors as quality, size, and delivery date are negotiated. This must be of little significance to most enterprises, however, because of the limited number of suppliers, particularly for industrial and intermediate goods. Disputes among the contracting parties are submitted for settlement to the ministries concerned or to the Ministry of Technical Material Supply and Fixed Assets Administration.

Econometric models

The quantitative technical basis for Romanian planning is provided primarily by two research institutes under the SPC. The first of these, the Institute of Planning and Prognosis, is concerned with overall planning methodology and long-term forecasting techniques. The other, the Computer and Cybernetics Center for Planning, does all the computations connected with the plans and develops the sectoral models that form the basis of the sectoral plans. The models can be divided into three categories:

(a) Models for long-term projections, covering 1976–90, with extensions up to 2000;
(b) Medium-term models, focusing on the five-year plan;
(c) Sector models for important sectors of the economy.

These are discussed in more detail in Appendix E.

Although the use of input-output tables has had limited significance so far in Romanian planning, their obvious relevance to planning problems has resulted in extensive research efforts. An input-output table for twenty-seven sectors was completed around 1974, with the sectors roughly corresponding to the structure of the ministries, and was used to establish macroeconomic balance for the 1976–80 Plan. This table was actually reduced from an earlier (and the first) input-output table prepared in 1972 that contained seventy-four industrial sectors. Its application to the Romanian planning, however, was found to be extremely difficult.

Despite the problems in developing and applying the new technique, experimentation with the models is continuing, and some useful applications have been observed. They have helped to identify those branches and sectors which contribute most to national income in relation to the energy, materials, national resources, and, especially, to imports required. In addition, they have indicated some discrepancies in the balance between sectors.

Use of Plan Indicators and Norms

Indicators

The responsibilities of the various economic units are established and monitored through the use of indicators, which are in essence obligatory targets through which the economic activities of enterprises, centrals, and ministries are controlled. Generally, such indicators are established at three levels: for the macroeconomic parameters of the economy; for the various branches of economic activities (that is, for ministries and centrals); and for enterprises. The indicators of the national plan—which include, for example, gross value of output, wage bill, outlays for each 1,000 lei of marketable output, labor productivity, investment levels, supplies for domestic markets, and exports—are established by law when the plan is approved. The rest of the targets are established by the ministries, centrals, and People's Councils and are enacted into law by a Council of Ministers decree.

At each level of economic activity, responsibility for performance rests at the next higher level. Thus, the ministries establish the targets for the activities of the centrals, and the centrals for the enterprises. This decentralization in target-setting has introduced a certain flexibility in meeting overall plan targets. A central, for example, can accept reductions in the targets of some of its constitutent enterprises if these reductions have no effect on the central's performance as a whole: that is, if there are indications that they would be offset by above-target performance of other units. Similarly, changes in targets of a central of a certain ministry are considered in the context of the ministry's overall performance. Reductions or substantial modifications of targets approved for a ministry are subject to approval by the State Council.

The nature and particular use of indicators in Romania's planning have encouraged a growth-oriented economic performance. One of the most important indicators, for example, is that of gross value of output. Because a bonus system is partially tied to this indicator (Chapter 4), all units strive to maximize output to meet established targets. A corrective measure was introduced experimentally in 1973, incorporating net output into a target indicator, but its use is still limited.[7] The emphasis on improv-

7. The use of net output as a target indicator differs from that of gross production (which includes both material inputs, goods in process, services, and depreciation), because it emphasizes the production of a finished product, net of inputs. This indicator discourages gross output maximization, and, since it makes no allowance for raw material input, it also discourages enterprises from adopting a product mix favoring heavy or high-value products.

ing product quality and efficiency in the production process has, however, been gradually increasing, and currently several indicators address such factors as improvements in labor productivity and reduction in the consumption of raw materials. The fulfillment or underfulfillment of such indicators has also been incorporated in the bonus/penalties system. The general fulfillment of such indicators has, however, proven to be difficult.

Norms

In Romanian planning, norms, which are quantitative expressions of existing rules, are prepared for virtually all activities in both productive and nonproductive sectors. Among the most important norms are work time necessary to complete an operation, fixed assets required for each unit of output, working capital consumed for each unit of output, and material input for each thousand lei of output. A system of progressive norms is applied in the elaboration of all plans. This means that future input requirements are not determined by reference to an average result of the past but are based on a combination of the best and average results.

Norms are established in many different ways. Where information is abundant, norms are fixed on the basis of time, production, and staffing studies of specific industries or even plants. When data are limited or a technology is imported, norms are purportedly based on cadre-personnel-production structures in similar sectors in other countries. It is apparent from plant visits, however, that this is not always the case, as overmanning of enterprises, including those with imported modern technology, has been observed. Norms are also calculated by extrapolating from enterprises of the same size and with the same production profile. If a norm is inaccurate, it would affect target fulfillment.

The Planning Process and Kinds of Plans

Plan preparation is a lengthy and time-consuming process in which all entities are involved. The major undertaking is the formulation of the five-year plan. Preparations for the elaboration of the five-year plan begin when the RCP congress issues the plan directives. The preparation of these begins two to three years before the end of the current five-year plan. Available studies or prognoses are used, and new ones are commissioned at selected levels of organization and economic activity to provide the foundation for drafting the plan directives. These studies, which usually cover each branch and subbranch of national and regional economic activity, pinpoint products of special importance to the development effort and of strategic value to the country. A subsequent effort is undertaken to establish macroeconomic balance by aggregating the results of these studies in the draft outline of the plan.

The draft outline of the plan, together with the long-term macroeconomic prognosis drawn up by economic branch and by district, is analyzed and approved by the Council of Ministers and then is submitted to the Political Executive Committee of the RCP. Shortly after the Committee approves the outline and prognosis, the draft directives to be issued by the RCP Congress are elaborated. A version of the emerging concensus is then received by the SCESD and is submitted for adoption first to the Executive Committee and then to a plenary session of the Central Committee of the RCP. The current five-year plan outline and the prognosis up to 1990, as well as the draft directives, were approved by the Political Executive Committee in June 1974. The draft directives for the plan period 1976–80 and the principal guidelines for development for the subsequent ten-year period (1981–1990) were adopted by the plenary session of the Central Committee of the RCP in November 1974.

Five-year development plan

Within the bounds of the general directives issued, the five-year development plan is elaborated by the ministries and judets. This process involves the participation of all economic and administrative units in the state hierarchy, which then engage in a process of successive submission and consolidation of information upward from the enterprise and downward from the plan directives as follows:

(a) On the basis of their current operations and their expected expansion of output and capacity, enterprises submit to the centrals estimates of their production, together with their needs for current inputs and for investment and working capital. At the same time, these estimates are submitted to the local authority in whose area the enterprise is located. This enables the regional plans to be elaborated simultaneously with the branch ministerial plans.

(b) The central elaborates a plan for its particular branch of industry. In this way, enterprise plans are consolidated in a first degree of aggregation, considering both the suggested plans of other enterprises and the overall plan directives. After discussion with their constituent enterprises, the centrals arrive at agreed first drafts of their plans, which are then submitted to their respective ministries.

(c) The ministries prepare the plan for their fields of activity. They try to achieve sector consistency between requirements and availabilities in the light of national priorities. The ministries bear primary responsibility for proposing the creation of new enterprises or the expansion of existing ones, and, together with the local authorities, for the location of new plants.

(d) At the same time, regional and local authorities are required to prepare regional development plans for the rational use of resources within their respective areas. In continuous consultation with the respective ministries (which have their own representative in a coordinating function attached to the People's Councils), the local administrative bodies play an important role in proposing the nature and location of new investment projects in this area, so regional plans do not conflict with the plans of each ministry.

(e) Together with other "organs of economic synthesis,"[8] the SPC is responsible for correlating the projects proposed by ministries and local authorities and for ensuring macroeconomic consistency of both the material and synthetic balances. The SPC together with other organs of economic synthesis, elaborates the draft of the plan and prepares it for the Council of Ministers.

Once the plan reaches the final draft, it must be approved successively by the various government and party organs in hierarchical order. First, review and approval is obtained from the Council of Ministers. The endorsed plan is examined by the Supreme Council of Socioeconomic Development and subsequently is submitted with recommendations to the Central Committee of the RCP. The latter, in its plenary session, authorizes the plan objectives as contained in the draft. The plan is finally discussed, approved, and ratified by the Grand National Assembly, which passes the enabling legislation.

This Law of the Plan provides the only available published information on the five-year plan.[9] Because the information presented in the Law of the

8. "Organs for economic synthesis" are bodies such as the Ministries of Finance and Foreign Trade, the Central Statistical Office, and others engaged in the economy in a general capacity, as described in the text.

9. In its final unpublished form, the plan is comprehensive and extremely detailed with some twenty-one chapters. Each chapter, a self-contained plan for each respective field, forms an integral part of the plan as a whole. The principal chapters of the plan are: (1) Industrial Production; (2) Agriculture; (3) Water Administration; (4) Forestry; (5) Transportation and Telecommunications; (6) Technological Research and Development; (7) Improvement of Product and Production Quality; (8) Investment in Construction; (9) Geological Exploration; (10) Technical Material Supply; (11) Foreign Trade; (12)

Plan is in an aggregative form, it is possible to know the plan's policy objectives and action themes but not to evaluate the efficiency of inter- and intrasectoral resources allocation, except in very general terms.

The Law of the Plan provides the macroeconomic policy objectives of the RCP by setting targets for the economy against which performance will be evaluated and by establishing the basic themes for the plan's implementation (for example, improvement in efficiency, technology, product quality, or energy conservation). Included in the document are such macroeconomic targets as national income growth, investment level, gross production for the industrial and agricultural sectors and for their major products, employment and productivity, standards of living, and increases in the volume of international trade.

The investment requirements are determined in aggregate terms. Apparently only a few major projects are identified at that stage; most projects are analyzed after their inclusion in the plan. This leads to a double bind situation at the time of project analysis, since subsequent disapproval of a project would jeopardize the fulfillment of an entity's investment target.

Although sector targets may be summarily presented in the most aggregate form in the Law of the Plan, each sector ministry is fully aware of its being a titular of the plan. And, to ensure plan fulfillment, performance indicators are developed for each ministry, to be achieved at each level of responsibility by the centrals. The centrals, in turn, set the targets for the enterprises. This disaggregation of indicators, eventually to the enterprise level, is exercised within a range of discretion, accommodating as much as possible the economic conditions prevailing in different centrals and enterprises as long as the aggregate targets are met.

Annual plan

Following practically the same procedures as those for the elaboration of the five-year plan, the draft of the annual plan is prepared in detail about six months before it is scheduled to be executed: that is, by the middle of the preceding year. It contains the same chapters as the five-year plan, and in its published form it is almost a replica of the five-year one in structure,

International Economic Cooperation; (13) Training and Improvement of the Labor Force; (14) Labor Force, Population Wages, and Incomes; (15) Production Costs; (16) Prices; (17) The Supply of Goods and Services for the Population; (18) Development of the Material Basis of Education, Health Care, Culture, Housing, Local Public Facilities, and Environment Protection; (19) Social Product and National Income; (20) Centralized Financial Plan, Balance of the Incomes, and Money Expenses of Population; and (21) Regional Development.

content, and style. As an illustration, an informal translation of the 1976 Annual Plan is given in Appendix E. The targets of the annual plan are based on:

(a) The provisions within the five-year plan for the year in question;
(b) The availability of new resources or reserves and the possibility of using more fully existing production capacities as well as of increasing labor productivity;
(c) Achievements in the previous year, the rate of growth of domestic and external markets, and other factors warranting an adaptation of the original five-year plan targets.

Because of some flexibility in the planning process, which is finally made concrete in the annual plan, a summation of the annual plans for five years may not yield the targets of the five-year plan. It also follows that enterprises may not meet annual plan targets but still may meet and surpass the five-year plan, depending on the level at which the former are set.

In the process of annual plan elaboration, many new projects are introduced. As a rule, these have to be fully prepared about six months before the year of execution, including relevant technoeconomic studies and information on the financing and procurement of supplies. In earlier years the proportion of prepared projects was much smaller, and this may explain occasional lags in fulfilling investment targets. The project selection criteria combine technical/economic and social considerations.[10] As many as seventeen technical and economic indicators are legally specified for consideration for each project, but in reality a smaller number is used in approving the projects. Decisions to invest are a matter of policy priorities, and a project must integrate first into the plan priorities. Once it is approved, resources will be allocated for it. So, implicitly, a decision to incorporate a project in the plan implies that there is no alternative use of funds that can provide a higher rate of return. Also, since the merit of each investment is judged individually and since there is not a single criterion upon which all costs and benefits can be measured, tradeoffs between the individual criteria used must be established at some stage of the appraisal process. This calls for a decision on the weights given in each project to each criterion. In many cases the weights can be derived by the priorities in the government's strategy. Finally, to the extent that prices used in evaluating costs and benefits differ from border prices, the real net benefits cannot be easily determined.

10. For a detailed review of project selection and investment criteria, see Appendix E.

After the plan is drafted, the SPC, the ministries, centrals, and enterprises begin to arrange for supply and marketing contracts (above) to make the plan concrete. In the fall, the final amendments to the draft plan are incorporated to include the most updated information on economic performance under the current plan: that is, harvest results and preliminary estimates of performance for the other major sectors. This draft plan is then presented to the Supreme Council of Economic and Social Development, subsequently to the House of People's Councils, the plenum of RCP, and finally to the Grand National Assembly.

When the plan is approved, the process of its disaggregation begins. This involves, among other things, what is called the "nominalization" of production targets: that is, the setting of fixed and obligatory objectives in stated production lines. The Grand National Assembly, through the State Council, and the Council of Ministers nominalize targets only for a range of major products (in 1977 the Assembly nominalized about 60 products, the State Council about 1,300). The ministries and centrals allocate responsibilities for these centrally nominalized products and specify the different types and qualities of the products to be produced; they also nominalize an additional range of products for the enterprises. Thus, the enterprises receive some targets that are nominalized by the State Council, some by the ministries, and others by the centrals. Any capacities that the enterprises still have available can be used to produce products of their own choice, provided supply and purchase contracts can be found.[11] Once the enterprise, in consultation with the central, has decided upon its additional targets, these become obligatory and are entered in the plan of the enterprises and centrals. In the end, therefore, nominalization is always 100 percent. In the process of elaboration, however, there is a range of discretion in setting targets at each level, from ministry and central to the enterprise.

Financial Planning

As already mentioned, parallel with the major national effort to formulate the five-year and annual development plans, the various units prepare financial plans that identify the resources they will require to implement their physical plans. Financial planning plays a significant role in helping

11. An enterprise cannot begin production of any product before contracts have been completed.

the government attain its development objectives. It has these main objectives:

(a) Ensuring the availability of financial resources required by the economic development plan of the country and establishing the necessary correlations between these financial resources and the various programs of development;
(b) Ensuring a financial balance within the economy—a financial equilibrium between resources and expenditures, a monetary equilibrium between the money supply and the availability of goods and services, and a currency equilibrium between resources and expenditures in foreign currency;
(c) Enhancing economic efficiency in all sectors of activity, both productive and nonproductive.

The Ministry of Finance is responsible for financial planning at the national level and collaborates with the banking system and other agencies of economic synthesis. The banking system consists of the National Bank of the Socialist Republic of Romania and four specialized banks: the Investment Bank, the Bank for Agriculture and Food Industry, the Romanian Bank for Foreign Trade, the Savings Bank (Appendix H).

Centralized five-year financial plan

The centralized financial plan for the five-year period provides a synthetic balance sheet for the entire economy. The financial plan is prepared with reference to the targets set in the development plan, and its main purpose is to consolidate the relevant financial information and to determine the consistency of the planning effort. Included in the centralized financial plan are all financial resources and their respective uses; equilibrium between resources and expenditures thus is supposed to become a test of the financial consistency of the comprehensive plan. The centralized financial plan is elaborated on the basis of established value relations especially concerning the domestic and foreign price levels. When preparing the centralized financial plan annually, the impact of changing domestic and foreign prices is considered, and, accordingly, the five-year centralized financial plan is corrected. For example, the centralized financial plan for 1976–80 was originally finalized in the prices prevailing at that date (the domestic prices were expressed in 1963 prices). Several modifications have been introduced, however, with the 1974–76 resetting of production and delivery prices. First, the state budget for 1977 was expressed in 1977 prices, which were known when the draft budget was being prepared, and, second, the 1977–80 centralized financial plan was also corrected to reflect the different price base.

Annual financial plan

While the annual plan of the economy is being drawn up, the annual centralized financial plan is also being prepared. Initially, the data contained in the five-year financial plan are disaggregated and placed at the disposal of the ministries to provide guideposts for the preparation of the annual plan. Preparation of the annual financial plan also leads to the preparation of the first draft of the state budget by the Ministry of Finance. The annual financial plan is an operational document that presents the targets and financial indexes for the coming year and assists in checking the feasibility of government directives and the intersectorial consistency of the economic plan.

Plan Fulfillment and Control

Once the plan has been approved, the various levels of the economy are responsible for its implementation. Monitoring and modification procedures allow the plan to be a flexible working document.

Plan implementation

The Council of Ministers oversees the execution of the plan, but the centrals also play a key supervisory role, since the enterprises are directly responsible to their centrals for the plan's implementation. Plan execution is monitored continuously by the centrals, the ministries, local administrative bodies, financial and banking institutions, the SPC, and the Central Council for Workers' Control of Socioeconomic Activity, all of which report systematically on progress in target fulfillment. Thus, at any given time, the central authorities have an updated and accurate knowledge of the state of national economic performance. An incentive/penalty mechanism is also built into the monitoring system, designed to promote fulfillment—even overfulfillment—of the plan's targets and a more efficient use of resources.

Financial control

Financial control is exercised in two ways: preventive and auditing (ex-post control). The main role of preventive financial control is to identify and eliminate illegal spending and, thus, to ensure that business is being conducted efficiently and according to the plan. It is exercised continuously at various levels. At the enterprise level, the chief accountant reviews and approves all financial transactions. The Ministry of Finance and the Investment or Agriculture Bank ensure that no transfer of funds is permitted except within plan guidelines and according to the approved techno-economic documentation for specific investments. Finally, the Superior Court of Financial Control, as a body of the State Council, exercises control functions for the ministries and other centralized state agencies. Ex-post control is undertaken to check whether the financial transactions have been performed according to the plan. First, there is internal financial (budgetary) control organized at the enterprise, central, and ministries level. This is undertaken at least once a year. Second, the Ministry of Finance has its own control organizations, the State General Financial Inspectorate and, at the district level, the Territorial Financial Inspectorate, that check on economic, financial, and exchange transactions to ensure that they conform to existing laws. Third, the National Bank and the other specialized banks use their inspectors in connection with their credit operations, investment financing, and so forth. Fourth, the Superior Court of Financial Control undertakes similar control for the ministries and other state agencies and checks up on the Ministry of Finance.

Plan modification

The plan can be modified during its operation by the authority that approved it at each level of responsibility, provided that no contract is underfulfilled. Without outside permission, an enterprise can change an output target nominalized at the level of the enterprise, provided no contracts are broken or new legally acceptable contracts are concluded. For an enterprise to change an output target assigned by the central, it must demonstrate justifiable cause, and the central can authorize the modification only as long as the central can continue to meet output targets assigned by the ministry. Likewise, the ministry can approve, again given sufficient reason, only those plan changes by the centrals that do not adversely affect the output targets set by the State Council.

A Further Assessment

In the late 1960s and early 1970s, Romania undertook measures in planning and management that were intended to increase the responsibility of the enterprises in elaborating and implementing the plan and to orient the economy to a more efficient use of its resources. Although these changes were not broad in nature and scope, they were significant in the context of the centrally planned and managed Romanian economy. Success in their implementation, however, has varied. In the course of the discussion above, some of the implications and difficulties arising have been highlighted. Additional selected topics are reviewed briefly in this section and in the following chapter.

One of the more important new measures was the introduction in 1969 of a newly found entity: the central or industrial association. It was established as an organ of management between the enterprises and the ministries. The centrals were supposed to assist the ministries in a more efficient management of their constituent enterprises by taking over some of the functions of the enterprises, such as marketing and budgeting, but not production. The potential gains from that reorganization, however, cannot be realized in all cases. Although not involved directly in production, the centrals have been responsible for overseeing the productive activities of the enterprises. Some of the centrals maintain a role that is similar to previous functions of the ministerial directorates that they replaced. In spite of these decentralization measures, therefore, decisionmaking has remained centralized. Decentralization of authority would allow the centrals to seek economies of scale in production operations and to internalize externalities.

Certain conflicts have developed from the role of prices in the resource allocation process. Managers may be directed to use certain materials when they can meet cost-reducing targets by selecting alternate inputs. For example, in the 1960s government attempts to convert energy use from gas to coal, which were included in the targets of various enterprises, were frustrated largely because of unchanged lower gas prices.

4

Other Management Instruments

THE GOVERNMENT USES A WIDE RANGE OF INSTRUMENTS to assure the implementation of the plan and the mobilization of resources required for its success. These include the system of prices; the institution of a uniform exchange rate to serve not only as a means of linking Romanian prices to world prices, but also as an efficiency indicator of which goods should be traded; financial incentives to stimulate workers and management to meet or surpass production targets; and, finally, financial instruments that include the state budget (Appendix G), the banking system, and the use of credit, interest rates, and money supply (Appendix H).

Prices and Pricing Policy

The present system of prices in Romania dates from 1950 when Decree 142 removed responsibility for setting prices from individual producers to responsible government bodies—the Council of Ministers, relevant ministries, and People's Councils. The decree also established three basic pricing principles that have governed all subsequent price regulations: uniformity of prices of similar commodities throughout the country; stability of prices through permanent control; and monitoring of prices with respect to costs, quality of products, and general economic conditions.

Note: This chapter presents the operation of management instruments in Romania as World Bank staff have come to understand it in discussions with central authorities. The objective of this chapter is primarily to convey how the instruments are reported to be used, not to provide an assessment of how they operate.

Role of prices

The principal functions of prices at the present time are formally laid out in the Law (no. 19) on Prices and Tariffs of 1971, which was updated and republished on January 1, 1977. These functions carry out the role of "attaining the economic policy objectives for socialist industrialization and intensive development of agriculture, for enlarging domestic and foreign trade, ensuring monetary stability and elevating the people's standard of living"[1] and are:

(a) To serve as a means of aggregation and an indicator of value for measuring inputs and outputs and the contribution of each enterprise and economic unit to social product and national incomes;
(b) To reflect the social cost of production and thereby to help to allocate resources to different sectors of the economy;
(c) To stimulate economic efficiency and qualitative improvement of production and to encourage reduction of production costs and increases in labor productivity;
(d) To distribute national income and goods.

In this formal sense, therefore, the role of the pricing system in Romania is essentially similar to that of all other economies: that is, it provides data for the valuation of goods and economic calculations. Since prices, however, are only one of several measures and instruments used for and subordinated to the coordinated planning and implementation of development objectives and are established by the state at fixed levels or within narrow boundaries, a more detailed examination of prices at wholesale and retail levels and their relation to other instruments available to the government is required to explain the specific functions of prices in Romania. The operation of the pricing system is discussed later.

Categories and components of price

There are two principal categories of prices in the Romanian economy: in industry, there are wholesale (producer and delivery) and retail prices, and in agriculture, there are producer, contract, acquisition, delivery, and retail prices.

Wholesale prices have been defined as "the economic means whereby

1. Law (no. 19) on Prices and Tariffs of 1971. Preamble. *Official Bulletin of the Socialist Republic of Romania*, no. 154 (December 16, 1971).

economic enterprises and organizations in the socialist sector conclude the process of buying and selling in the delivery of goods among themselves."[2] Producer prices are ex-factory prices usually paid by enterprises in their sales to each other, whereas delivery prices (producer prices plus turnover tax) are the prices obtained by enterprises when selling to internal trading enterprises.[3] Retail prices are the prices at which goods are sold to the population by the trading enterprises.

Producer prices consist of the planned branch average unit cost of production (that is, branch average production cost) covering all direct and indirect outlays, plus a predefined profit (benefit) that ensures a reasonable profitability for all branches, for most of the enterprises in each branch and for most products within each enterprise. The production expenditures included in the calculation of the producer price were established under the Law (no. 19) on Prices and Tariffs of 1971 as follows:

(a) Raw materials
(b) Fuel, energy, and water
(c) Wages and social security contributions
(d) Depreciation of fixed assets
(e) Tax on production funds (capital)
(f) Land tax
(g) Research and development expenses
(h) Interest on short-term credits and other financial expenses
(i) Profit

The law also allowed for a regularization tax to be levied on the profits of enterprises in cases where excess profits were made as a result of decreases in production expenses over time. In January 1977 the Law on Prices and Tariffs was republished to incorporate some changes in the system of price formulation. First, the tax on land was no longer counted as a production expenditure but became a tax to be paid from profits. Second, the tax on productive assets was abolished, and a separate tax on profits was introduced through the Law of Taxes on Profits (Decree 391). Finally, the regularization tax was removed.

For the state agricultural units (IAS's), the pricing structure is similar to that in industry; there is a single wholesale price, known as the delivery price, at which all state farm produce is sold to state trading enterprises. For

2. G. H. Sica, *Projection and Planning of Wholesale Prices* (Bucharest: Editura Academii, 1973).

3. Goods delivered for export are sold to foreign trade enterprises at producer prices.

the agricultural producer cooperatives (CAP's) and private farms, there are three prices at which producers can dispose of produce. Most produce is sold to the trading enterprises at contract prices (contracts being drawn up at the beginning of the crop year); produce in excess of contracted amounts is also usually disposed of at these prices, contracted amounts simply being increased to cover the surplus. Produce can also be sold to trading enterprises at acquisition prices. Since they are generally lower than contract prices, they usually apply to unforeseen sales made when a CAP member or private farmer needs to dispose quickly of a few animals or small amount of produce. Produce from the private plots of CAP members and from private farmers is also marketed directly to the population in peasant markets at flexible prices, within bounds established by People's Councils. For produce sold by the state, fixed retail prices, uniform across the country but incorporating seasonal variations, are established.

Price reassessments and operation of the pricing system

The functions of the pricing system presented above represent the legislative culmination of a debate on the role of prices, profit, and the socialist market, which took place in Romania during the 1960s. The debate arose from the increasing complexity and interdependence of the economy and from the recognition that the planning and implementation of economic activities required more indirect and decentralized instruments to complement or to replace the system of directive planning. In 1967 the Central Committee of the Romanian Communist Party (RCP) issued directives[4] proposing several changes in the planning and administration of economic activities, in which the active role of prices in implementing and planning development objectives was considered.

Until this time, prices for many products had largely had an accounting function only; their role in allocating resources in the socialist sector and in providing appropriate signals concerning economic efficiency was small. This was, perhaps, for the best, since, as the Directives put it, "one of the main drawbacks of the price system in our country lies in the fact that a series of prices are established without the social expenditures incorporated in the given products being taken into account and that the criteria of the law of value which still governs in one form or another any economy based

4. *Directives of the Central Committee of the Romanian Communist Party On the Perfecting of Management and Planning of the National Economy in Keeping with the Conditions of the New Stage of Romania's Socialist Development.* (Bucharest: Agerpres, October 1967.)

on commodity production are being ignored."[5] If prices gave the wrong signals to economic units, the effect was negligible as long as the allocation of resources and the implementation of production plans were governed by other instruments and management tools, which took little account of prices.

The increased sophistication of the economy and the increasing impossibility of covering all economic activities with physical indicators raised the possibility that economic units would pursue their financial interests as indicated by the structure of prices and thereby make the fulfillment of development objectives more difficult. As the 1967 Directives stated, the use of inappropriate prices, in particular, made it difficult to raise the efficiency of production, to lower the consumption of inputs, and to improve the quality of goods. Thus, the major concerns of price assessments have been wholesale prices.

In 1956 a State Committee for Prices (SCP) was established to administer the pricing system, and, following discussions of the Central Committee's directives by the National Conference of the RCP and its Tenth Congress, an Interministerial Commission, under the supervision of the SCP, was appointed to make proposals for improving wholesale prices. Out of these proposals came the 1971 Law on Prices and Tariffs, which established the legal and analytical framework for the new pricing policies. In 1974 the application of new producer and delivery prices began.[6] This was formally completed at the end of 1976, although some corrective changes have been made since then. As the Commission on Prices indicated in its report, in view of the past decisions that have shaped Romania's economic progress, it can only be a gradual process by which prices can be brought closer to social valuations, whether measured in terms of internal values or international prices.

The price reassessment can be discussed most usefully from two angles; first, the extent to which the price changes reflect more accurately and fully the social costs of production, and, second, the extent to which the price system working with other managerial tools has been able to carry out the functions delineated in the 1971 Law.

In one sense, the price reassessment unequivocably led to improved calculations of the social cost of production, since between 1963 (the date of the previous price resetting) and 1974, producer prices and actual produc-

5. Ibid.

6. For the stages of implementation, see World Bank, "Current Economic Position and Prospects of Romania," report no. 492a-RO (a restricted circulation document) (Washington, D.C., October 1974; processed), Annex B.

tion costs had diverged as a result of technological change and changes in factor productivities. The major discussion on prices as a measure of the social cost of production centered, however, on what should be included within the producer price as an appropriate charge for the use of capital. Before 1974 improvements in producer prices (which took place in 1955 and 1963) had not dealt effectively with the question of the calculation and distribution of net profit. Producer prices before 1974 had included charges for capital only insofar as depreciation expenditures were concerned. Thus, no charges for the use of capital stock were incorporated, because funds for these purposes were generally provided through the state budget. Once the overall amount of profit and, thus, the average rate of profit had been determined for each industrial branch, the rate of profit for each enterprise and each product was determined based on production expenditures.

The 1974–76 producer and delivery price reassessment introduced, for the first time, explicit charges on total assets and working capital as a component of production expenditures to stimulate more efficient use of fixed assets and to prevent overcapitalization of production. The rate of profit for each product was recalculated based on all production expenses and the average branch rate of profit to take into account fixed assets and working capital. Beginning in January 1977 the tax on productive assets was abolished. At the same time, a tax on profits was introduced as a way to transfer to the state budget the difference between producer price and production expenditures in excess of planned profit (Appendix G). This was done because the authorities wished to increase the role of profit, along with other indicators, as an instrument for stimulating greater efficiency at the enterprise level.

Insofar as the functions of prices in planning and implementing economic activity of enterprises are concerned, producer prices are more important in implementing plans than in determining the allocation of resources. Resources are allocated chiefly through the planning process, and the fact that the allocation is made increasingly by indicators of value reflects the fact that the overall structure of producer prices has been made consistent with the development objectives of the country. This is of practical importance in the planning process, because reconciliation of enterprise plans aggregated upward and the macroeconomic plan parameters of the SPC can only be achieved speedily and efficiently if the combination of physical, financial, and pricing instruments applied at the enterprise level orients units in the same direction as do the central plans.

In the areas where physical indicators do not constrain the allocation of resources, producer prices clearly do have an effect on production planning. This is most obvious in agriculture, where the structure of input and output prices clearly affects the production of goods by private farmers and members of CAP's on their private plots, but it also occurs to some degree in industry, particularly where enterprises have some say over product mix and factor use.

Producer prices are also used to encourage enterprises toward fulfilling their plans and to evaluate performance in executing plan objectives, such as cost reduction and improved quality of goods, insofar as the structure of prices provides appropriate signals. The fact that specific plan targets for cost reduction and new improved products have been necessary suggests that the structure of prices, although improved by the recent exercise, is not yet sufficiently finely tuned to act in every case in favor of these objectives. The Law on Prices and Tariffs provides for the continuous review and improvement of prices, and the government has indicated that, in the future, more frequent reviews of price levels will occur, although the government still maintains a constant structure of prices within each plan period. The need for continued improvement is shown by the adjustments that have been made, particularly in construction, since the producer price exercise was completed.

Although the policies of the government toward producer and delivery prices have led to considerable changes in their levels and structure, the relative lack of change demonstrates government policy toward retail prices: the government maintains as stable a level of retail prices as possible. To this end, each five-year plan contains a target for the maximum permissible increase in retail prices, the fulfillment of which is the primary responsibility of the Council of Ministers, the State Committee of Prices, and the People's Councils.

Foreign Trade Pricing and the Exchange Rate

Just as the planning and organizational changes stemming from the Directives of the 1967 National Conference of the RCP concerned both the internal organization of the economy and external economic relations (Chapters 3 and 7), so the reorganization of the pricing system affected both internal and external transactions. The major effect of the pricing reforms on external transactions has been to expand the influence of international prices on Romania's domestic price levels and to make limited use of the relation between domestic and international prices to help determine the goods suitable for export and import. This has been achieved through the institution of an exchange rate in 1973 and of a more appropriate domestic pricing system, which together permit a more instructive comparison of Romanian and international prices.

Before 1973 there was no link between internal and external prices in the form of a generalized exchange rate, which could be used to assess the profitability of Romanian foreign trade or to signal enterprises that goods could be profitably exported or imported. In view of this and the fact that domestic prices themselves had several deficiencies, as well as being dissimilar to the international price structure, the profitability of foreign trade could only be calculated through shadow pricing exercises. These were carried out largely within the planning process. The decision to import was taken mainly on the basis of the comparison between the needs of the domestic economy and the resources available to fulfill the plan, and export targets were established chiefly to finance the imports. Moreover, the financial results of foreign transactions were not reflected in the books of producing enterprises; they paid for imports and received for exports the domestic price of the good, irrespective of its foreign price. Thus, the gains from trade flowed directly to the state.

For these reasons and because the leu was not freely convertible, the exchange rates quoted by the government under this foreign trade regime had limited application. Two rates were quoted. The official rate, which was and remains the official gold price of the leu,[7] is used only to express the value of foreign trade in official statistics. The unit of currency is the leu valuta or foreign exchange leu. The official rate with premium,[8] which was and remains in use for noncommercial transactions (among others, for tourist transactions) was the only operational rate, in the sense that it was the only rate at which non-Romanians could obtain lei.

In 1973 the government established an exchange rate (also known as the trading rate or internal conversion coefficient), of 20 lei : US$1, which was intended for use in comparing foreign and domestic prices of goods. The rate was fixed at 20:1, because it approximated the weighted average of all actual exchange rates for export and import transactions over the previous three years; it therefore represented the average rather than marginal cost of foreign exchange. Its introduction as an efficiency indicator, which would show more clearly the comparative advantage of Romanian producers in international markets, followed from the recommendations of the 1967 National Conference Directives and subsequent studies that economic calculations in the allocation and use of resources should be influenced

7. Defined equal to 0.148112 grams of fine gold, yielding an exchange rate against the U.S. dollar of 6 : 1 before December 1971; 5.53 : 1 until February 1973; 4.97 : 1 until March 1978; and 4.47 : 1 from then.

8. Before December 1971, 18 lei : US$1; 16 lei : US$1 until February 1973; 14.38 lei : US$1 until October 1974; since then, the rate has been 12 lei : US$1.

more directly than previously by the level and structure of international prices. In March 1978 the trading rate was revalued to 18 lei: US$1.

The trading rate has two major roles: to determine whether, in principle, a particular good should be traded or not and as a starting point for determining the division of foreign exchange gains between the state and the producing enterprise. The ground rule for determining whether a product should be exported is that the foreign exchange earned must, when converted into lei at the trading rate, be equal to or greater than the domestic price of the good; in other words, the export of a good must cover the full cost of production, including the profit margin. In principle, the basic decision to import is determined in a similar fashion. The foreign price of an imported good is compared with the domestic price at the trading rate. Because the structure of Romanian relative prices does not correspond to the international price structure and because enterprises may not see reflected in their domestic cost the full foreign exchange cost of imported inputs or in their receipts the full foreign price of an export, (below) the basic comparison of foreign and domestic prices using the trading rate is complemented by what amounts to a comprehensive shadow pricing operation. For each tradable good, the profitability of trade is also calculated by costing all inputs (traded and nontraded) and outputs in international prices. These calculations are made first in the technoeconomic study that is made when production within Romania or the expansion of production is being considered. They are also made annually by the foreign trade enterprises and more frequently for commodities whose international price fluctuates a great deal. These calculations also provide the basis on which the Council of Ministers determines whether products with an effective exchange rate less favorable than 18 lei : US$1 can be authorized for export.

Because the structure of Romanian prices does not fully correspond with international price structures, the shadow pricing calculations produce situations in which the export of goods may be economically profitable, even when the basic ground rule cannot be met. (Conversely, there may be cases where the ground rule is met, but export is not profitable.) Such cases may also reflect situations where enterprises have not yet attained planned productivity levels. In these cases, exports may be authorized for a year by the Council of Ministers, after individual review when the annual plan is prepared. Enterprises exporting under this approval have to improve their productivity and export performance so that they can export profitably at the trading rate in the future. In the meantime, the enterprises that exchange the foreign exchange earned from export into lei at the trading rate receive payment from a trade equalization fund to help to recover the full producer price.

The exchange rate also enters into the distribution of foreign exchange gains between producing enterprises and the state. For exports, standard foreign prices are established annually, calculated on the basis of external prices obtained by enterprises in the previous period, and updated to account for the expected world market situation. These prices are used to express, in value terms, the volume of exports included in the annual plan and to prepare balance of payments projections. Their major operational role is to serve as a benchmark for determining the division of foreign exchange receipts between the enterprise and the state: that is, the price equalization fund. In the case of goods that are exported profitably—when the price obtained is higher than the domestic price converted at the trading rate—the producing enterprises receive the domestic price in lei, and the difference between the standard foreign price and the domestic price is paid into the equalization fund: that is, the profit from trade accrues to the state. Where the enterprise secures an actual price above the standard price, it receives all of the difference as a bonus. Conversely, if it can secure only a price lower than the standard price, the enterprise must pay the difference into the equalization fund, so that in effect the fund receives the full difference between standard and domestic price. (The situation in which exports occur when the actual foreign price is below the domestic price was discussed above.) Thus, the standard foreign price serves as an incentive for firms to seek the most profitable market.[9] Enterprises also receive bonuses in lei for distribution to employees if they overfulfill their foreign exchange targets.[10]

For some "conjunctural" goods,[11] those goods with large and unpredictable short-term fluctuations in their foreign prices, the system of distribution between producing or importing enterprises and the equalization fund has been modified to protect exporters and importers from exchange losses and gains. For these goods, the equalization fund absorbed all but 5 percent of any difference between the actual price and standard foreign price.

The arrangements for imports have also changed considerably over the past few years. When the trading rate was introduced, the cost of all imports were to be translated into domestic prices at the trading rate, thereby eliminating the need for a price equalization fund, and differences between

9. Foreign trade enterprises are encouraged to seek high prices for the producing enterprises, because their commission is a percentage of the price.

10. Before 1974 bonuses were in foreign exchange and could be used for additional imports.

11. Conjunctural commodities are wheat, maize, sunflower oil, sugar, sheep, cattle, live pigs, meat, softwood and beechwood lumber, cement, gas, diesel oil, black oil, nitrogenous fertilizer, caustic soda, sheet iron, concrete iron, profiles, rolled metal, and aluminum in lumps.

international and domestic prices were to be dealt with through a system of tariffs. In 1974 import tariffs were established, and, for a few months, the equalization fund was abolished. The international inflation of 1974 and 1975, however, necessitated the reintroduction of the equalization for raw material imports to prevent the profitability of import-using enterprises from being impaired and financial flows through the economy from being disturbed. Since enterprises received fixed prices for outputs, increasing outlays for raw material inputs would have reduced their profits. At present, enterprises pay the established domestic price for imports, any differences between domestic price and foreign price converted at the trading rate being settled with the equalization fund. As for exports, a standard price system induces enterprises to seek the most economic source of supply. For the import of machinery and equipment, the domestic price paid by the final user is established by the conversion of the foreign price at the trading rate plus the appropriate tariff. For consumer goods, the foreign price is converted at the trading rate and the appropriate tariff added to determine the domestic cost of the import. Any difference between the cost and the domestic price is reflected in the financial accounts of the importing enterprise. Thus, the import of investment goods and consumer goods is regulated through the tariff and, in the last resort, through the issue of trade licenses. In 1977 new custom tariffs were established to take into account the changes since 1974 in domestic-international price relations.

Incentives and Penalties

The present system of wage and salary bonuses has evolved since 1970 when substantial changes were made in the prevailing system, which lacked a sufficient incentive effect. In the earlier system, the bonuses had amounted to a substantial 20 to 25 percent of the wage fund, and they were paid out of the wage fund. Because they were linked only to the fulfillment of plan indicators, there was almost no additional bonus when targets were overfulfilled. In the case of plan underfulfillment, penalties were not imposed on salaries. Thus, in practice, the system did not provide an incentive effect.

The 1970 measures raised basic wages and salaries to incorporate previous bonuses. Basic wages and salaries now average about 95 percent of total earnings. Integrated into the wage system is a new incentive scheme that rewards performance above plan targets and penalizes shortcomings. The maximum effect on wages under this scheme is ± 20 percent. Additional end-of-year bonuses are also available to workers, and these are discussed further below. Wage or salary increases or decreases are usually determined mainly on the basis of the fulfillment or underfulfillment of four indicators. These are divided into quantitative indicators (planned output targets and exports, where applicable) and efficiency indicators (labor productivity and material costs for each 1,000 lei of marketable output). Some ministries and centrals may establish other indicators as well, depending on the production patterns of their constituent units. As a rule, the above four indicators have the same weight, but ministries can also set different weights.

Salaries of employees, technical, and administrative personnel are increased or decreased by 1 percent for each percent of over- or underfulfillment of the indicators, up to a maximum of 20 percent. For management staff, a 1 percent over- or underfulfillment of the indicators leads to a 4 percent salary increase or decrease up to a maximum of 20 percent. The salary adjustments are applied monthly, but an enterprise can partly or fully make up its shortfalls in these indicators in subsequent months, and salaries will reflect that. Increases or decreases of salaries in centrals and ministries for over- or underfulfillment of indicators are subject to the same rules.

End-of-year bonuses can also be paid to the staff of an enterprise (as well as a central and a ministry). The bonus fund amounts to 2 percent of the wage fund. If excess profits are realized, the bonus fund can be augmented up to 8 percent of the wage fund of an enterprise.[12] There is a formula determining what proportion of excess profits from different activities would be allocated to the bonus fund.[13] Although the maximum bonus fund corresponds to a month's wages and salaries for an entity, bonuses can reach up to three monthly salaries for individuals. The existing bonus fund is distributed according to salaries, but half of the fund developed from excess profits is distributed by the management according to salaries and the rest selectively. In addition, the management of a unit has at its disposal another bonus fund amounting to 1 percent of the wage fund, which it can distribute during the year to reward exceptional performance. Similarly, the management can penalize an individual up to 10 percent of his monthly salary if he has underfulfilled personal tasks, even if the unit at large may have overfulfilled its targets.

Although the new scheme provides substantially more incentives than that before 1970, its effects have not yet been fully assessed. To an outside

12. Before July 1, 1977 these percentages applied to the gross wage fund. Since then, they are applied to the net wage fund, since the enterprises (centrals and ministries) now pay a tax calculated on their wage fund.

13. The following formula was used before July 1, 1977, and it has been slightly modified since then: 20 percent of excess profits arising from increases in productivity and from decreases in material costs, 16 percent from increases in output, and 10 percent from other activities.

observer, it is not clear what tradeoffs the enterprise establishes between consistent and significant target overfulfillment that leads to increased salaries as well as bonuses and the risk that its targets or norms may be reassessed if it continues to perform successfully.

Financial Instruments

The objective of the public finance and banking measures in the early 1970s was to introduce additional elements of profit orientation in the economy and to assist in decentralizing decisionmaking by devolving more resources to local governments and enterprises. The measures have been implemented with some success, but, for various reasons, some of their initial impact had dissipated by 1975 (Appendixes B, G, and H). Thus, the dependence on fiscal flows through the state budget has continued to increase. In the rest of this chapter, only the role and functions of the principal financial instrument, the state budget, and of the major monetary aggregates are discussed.

State budget

The principal financial instrument for plan implementation is the state budget, which includes the republican and the local budgets. Under the law, it is drawn up balanced, but when executed, it is regularly in surplus, and the government has never had to borrow from the National Bank to cover expenditures. These persistent surpluses are not necessarily deflationary in a planned economy such as that of Romania, and they may be explained by various factors, such as, for example, increased incomes or unspent investment funds from shortages of materials and machinery. The budgetary balance is monitored closely through detailed biweekly and quarterly reports of the financial and banking system.

The resources of the republican budget are collected mainly from state enterprises and institutions operating on a republican scale and from taxes paid by the population. The republican budget finances national economic and social objectives, such as fixed investments and other important economic projects, sociocultural activities, national defense, and so forth. The local budgets of districts, municipalities, towns, and villages are financed by transfers of profits from local enterprises and institutions and from taxes paid by individuals, cooperatives, and economic units of other public agencies. The local budgets finance the economic and social activities carried out by the People's Councils and local administration.

Both the republican and local budgets include reserve funds for contingencies. The use of the reserve funds and any additional financing requirements that develop unexpectedly during the year have to be thoroughly justified and ultimately may have to be approved by the State Council.

Taxes, quotas, and other payments

The high growth rates of the Romanian economy attest to the ability of the government to mobilize domestic resources (Chapter 5). The chief instrument for resource mobilization is the system of profit transfers, taxes, and other quotas, and the government appears to have used it with considerable effect to meet its needs for investment capital. Most of the resources are collected at the enterprise level, since the strict control exercised by the state over individual incomes makes it unnecessary to tax the population heavily.[14] Most of the taxes are state taxes, but, as mentioned earlier, there are some local taxes. A synopsis and definition of the taxes, quotas, and other payments to the state and local governments, including the new 1977 measures, are given in Appendixes B and G.

Monetary Instruments

The role and function of the three major monetary instruments—bank credit, interest rates, and the money supply—are discussed briefly below. Recent changes and their current levels are given in Appendix H.

Bank credit

An important financial instrument developed in recent years has been bank credit. This instrument was improved in 1970, and the current lending conditions are set out in the Financial Law of November 1972, implemented on January 1, 1973. The law states that credits can be extended only for specific purposes, such as production (including working capital), marketing, and investments or minor improvements in an enterprise's plant and are to be secured by the unit's assets. Credits can be extended only by the banking system and never by enterprises. The decision of the government to substitute certain financial for fiscal flows is an important recognition of the

14. As of July 1977, the personal salary tax was removed, and, in its place, a tax on the wage fund paid by the enterprise was introduced.

competing demands for capital and its cost. Further, the measures adopted on credit terms recognize the need for a more efficient capital use by the enterprises. The average interest rate for such credits increased, and the terms were established to reward efficient performers and to penalize less efficient enterprises. The total planned increase in funds under the credit plan indicates how many new credits can be issued, whereas the increases in the individual categories for which credit funds are used are, in effect, limits beyond which banks cannot extend credit.

The level of short-term credit in the economy is provided in the quarterly credit plan, drawn up by the National Bank in collaboration with the Ministry of Finance, the other banks, and other agencies of economic synthesis. It is based on an analysis, undertaken with the sector ministries, of the activities determined by the development plan and the state budget. The Investment Bank and the Bank for Agriculture and Food Industry (BAFI) draw up, for investment purposes, the plan for medium- and long-term credit, in addition to the short-term credit plan. Bank credit can be divided into three categories: long- and medium-term credit, primarily to finance investment needs of enterprises; short-term credit to finance working capital needs; and consumer credit extended to the public for durable goods purchases and housing. Long- and medium-term credits can be granted for two purposes:

(a) To finance centrally planned investments. The extension of long-term credit for this purpose is a recent phenomenon and of small scale. About 88 percent of long-term investment by enterprises is financed through the state budget and depreciation funds.

(b) To supplement internal resources of the cooperatives and economic units of other public organizations. This might involve a new investment such as the modernization of facilities, or, in the agricultural sector, it might be used to purchase animals for breeding.

The maturity for long-term credit is up to ten years (for agricultural cooperatives some credits are extended for up to twelve to twenty-five years), and for medium-term credit is up to five years. Two fundamental provisions for extending any bank credit are that the items financed must have been included in the annual plan, and their production must be profitable enough to cover the repayment of the loan within ten years. Investment credit is also available, with one-year maturity, to offset frictional disturbances in the investment program of the firm, when rescheduling a project causes a higher level of disbursement.

The largest percent of bank credit operations in Romania is composed of short-term credit, chiefly to meet the working capital needs of enterprises; of these, trade, construction, and agricultural organizations are the biggest users. The annual growth in this credit depends, of course, on the production increases. On the average, 45 percent of the working capital requirements of the enterprises is financed by bank credit, whereas the working capital needs of new enterprises are met by the state budget. Bank credits are repaid from the profits of the enterprises or from other specific funds. The repayment period is typically twelve months, but it can vary for some branches of the economy. For example, in agriculture the repayment terms are longer, and in industry they are shorter. The National Bank extends credits to industry, trade, and transport. BAFI extends credit to agriculture, forestry, and the food industry. Agricultural cooperatives and private farmers can borrow 45 to 60 percent of the value of their contracts with state organizations to finance working capital needs. Finally, the Investment Bank extends credits to the construction sector. The funds of the last two banks can be supplemented by the National Bank. Foreign trade enterprises engaged in exporting borrow from the Bank of Foreign Trade (Chapter 3), repaying their debts once they receive payment from their foreign trading partners.

Consumer credit is extended through two banks, and its availability and terms, as well as the items for which it can be used, vary, depending on the consumer credit policy of the government at any time. Installment credits are extended by the National Bank through the state trade units. Consumer demand to purchase particular goods can be manipulated by changing the credit terms for these goods, as illustrated by the 1974 case in which the government eased credit terms for passenger cars to eliminate an accumulation of unwanted inventories. In general, changes in credit conditions are used for inventory control. Credits for housing are extended through the National Savings Bank, and these usually cover 70 to 80 percent of the total housing costs with a maturity of fifteen to twenty-five years. Low-income earners obtain the most favorable terms.

The banking system fulfills a complementary auditing function in supervising the financial and economic operations of enterprises, specifically their use of credits and of state budget funds. In fact, the banks supervise the operations of the enterprises in many diverse ways. Because of the limitations placed on cash transactions, the enterprises depend on banks to settle their accounts. Banks may extend credits to economic units for up to ninety days if they are in temporary financial difficulties. In more severe cases, when an enterprise, for example, encounters certain operational difficulties, it may request the bank to extend special credit, which would be extended on the condition that remedial economic measures be undertaken by the enterprise. Such credits are extended for a maximum of six months, and the interest rate is set two percentage points higher than current applicable rates. For all outstanding credits and for credits without guarantees, a penalty interest of a maximum of 12 percent is applied by the bank. In 1974 only 5 percent of all the bank loans were at the penalty rate, reflecting the financial discipline of most economic units. In effect, through their tight control over credit, the banks can force the enterprises to comply with the plan.

Interest rates

Interest rates are paid on all credits. These rates are set by the central authority and are not influenced by the demand for and supply of capital, nor do they reflect risk, since there is no money market in Romania. Conceptually they are more a tax on the use of capital than the price of capital. By the same token, they do not necessarily reflect the social opportunity cost of capital, because the return on capital investment is derived not only from interest payments, but also from taxes and from the net surplus after operations returned by the state enterprises to the state budget. Interest rates, therefore, are relatively low. Since there is little price increase in the economy, however, the relatively low rates result in quite high real rates compared with those in many other countries today.

The government looks upon interest payments as a device to increase the efficiency of resource use. Enterprises can borrow only for projects that have an adequate rate of return, and all interest obligations are serviced out of the profits of the firm. Although it is difficult to know the sensitivity of enterprises and consumers to interest rate levels, undoubtedly it exists. It induces enterprises to follow their stock position more closely, and the penalty interest of 12 percent induces them to use resources more efficiently. The increased propensity of the consumer to save and his response to credit charges for some categories of consumer goods also suggest responsiveness to the level of interest rates.

Interest rates are pegged at a level somewhat below the average profitability of enterprises, and the rate structure favors sectors with a particularly heavy demand for working capital. Trading enterprises pay the low rate of 3 percent on their borrowings, agriculture is charged 4 percent, and industry pays the top 5 percent. A State Council decree in December 1974 simplified the regulations on interest rates, but it left the rate structure largely unchanged except for some special credits, which were lowered from the 6 to 12 percent range to 4 to 7 percent. The present rate structure is given in Appendix H.

The money supply

Money supply is defined as the sum of the balances in the bank accounts of enterprises, organizations, and institutions and the state budget; the savings deposits of the population; and the currency in circulation. Cash in circulation is limited mainly to individuals and arises from their transactions with enterprises and among themselves. All other transactions do not use cash. Settlement occurs through transfer of funds from one bank account to another.

Since consumers are free to use their cash income for current consumption, acquisition of dwellings, durable goods, and savings deposits, the government pays particular attention to the planning and control of the money in circulation. For this purpose, the balance of consumer cash income and expenditure and of cash plans is drawn on a quarterly basis. The purpose is to match the portion of the income of the population devoted to consumption with the output of goods and services available to consumers. The cash plan is, thus, a component of the annual plan, and it attempts to project the future behavior of households, in terms of expenses and savings, to attain an equilibrium in the cash circuit of the economy.

Every effort is made to keep the increase of cash in circulation in line with the output of consumer goods, taking into account the requirements of stable retail prices and the increasing monetization of the economy. Since the money supply is basically determined by the level of production and by current credit and cash plans, however, its effectiveness as an instrument of economic management is actually rather limited.

PART TWO

Development Trends and Structural Changes

5

Long-Term Trends, 1950 to 1975

THIS CHAPTER EXAMINES THE CHANGES in the Romanian economy over the past twenty-five years; it traces the performance of the economy through its major macro-elements and examines the most important issues arising during the period. Further details on the stages of economic growth between 1950 and 1975 are given in Appendix F. In addition, the chapter provides the general background for the detailed examination of performance between 1971 and 1975 (Chapters 6 and 7) and the more specific discussions of plans and performance in various economic sectors in subsequent chapters.

Economic Growth, Structural Change, and Resource Allocation

Between 1950 and 1975 the Romanian economy underwent a radical transformation (Figures 5.1, 5.2, and 5.3). The level and diversification of industrial production increased rapidly, providing the basis for the modernization and expansion of other economic sectors and a general increase in labor productivity and national income. With the transfer of labor from agriculture to industry, the population became increasingly urbanized. Standards of living improved substantially, not only because of the growth of personal incomes, but also because of the provision, through the state budget, of expanded and improved education, medical services (both of which are free), housing, and social expenditures of all kinds. Finally, reflecting the changes in economic structure, Romanian participation in the world economy changed significantly as the level of trade rose and its composition altered. This section provides a largely quantitative picture of the transformation. Although the data clearly indicate the extent of rapid economic progress,

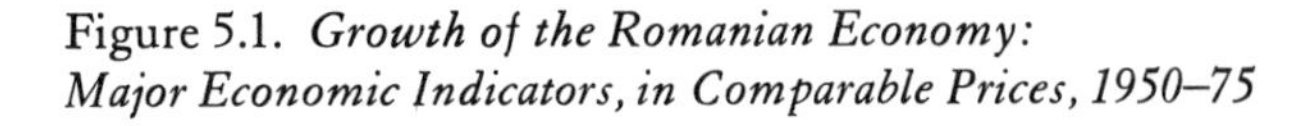

Figure 5.1. *Growth of the Romanian Economy: Major Economic Indicators, in Comparable Prices, 1950–75*

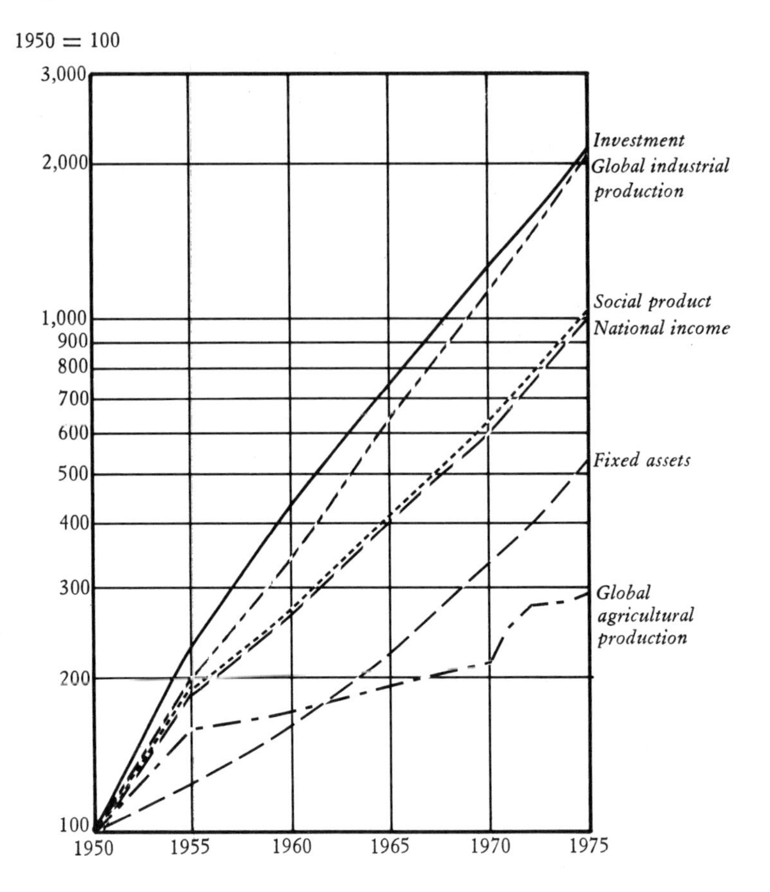

some care is required in interpreting them, because of the methodologies used in their computation by the Romanian Statistics Office.[1]

According to official statistics, the Romanian economy sustained the highest growth rate in eastern Europe between 1950 and 1975 and one of the highest in the world. During this period, social product and national income increased approximately ten times. Measured in comparable prices, social

1. See the Glossary for a definition of national accounting terms used in Romania and Appendix D on social product and national income.

Figure 5.2. *Growth of the Romanian Economy: Income Indexes, in Comparable Prices, 1950–75*

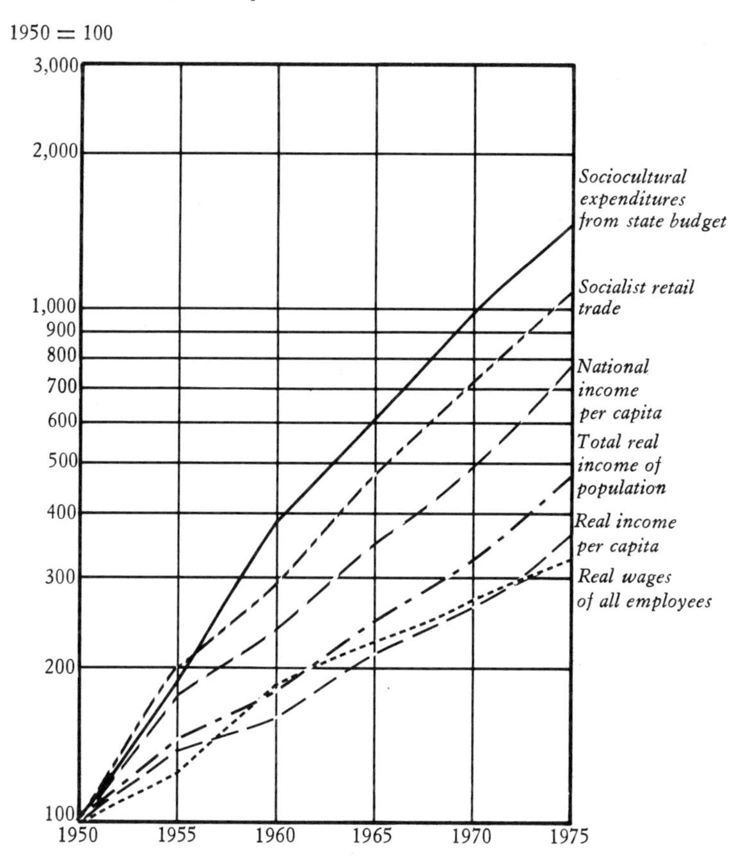

product rose from 83 billion lei in 1950 to 864 billion in 1975, and national income grew from 35.4 to 362 billion lei.[2] The average annual growth rates of social product and national income over the twenty-five years have therefore been 9.8 percent and 9.7 percent, respectively. Since the annual population growth rate for the same period was only 1.1 percent, per capita social product and national income have also risen at very high rates compared with other developing countries; the average annual growth rates have been 8.7 and 8.6 percent, respectively. These aggregate figures should, however,

2. See the Glossary for an explanation of comparable prices.

Figure 5.3. *Structure of Output and of Employment, 1950–75*

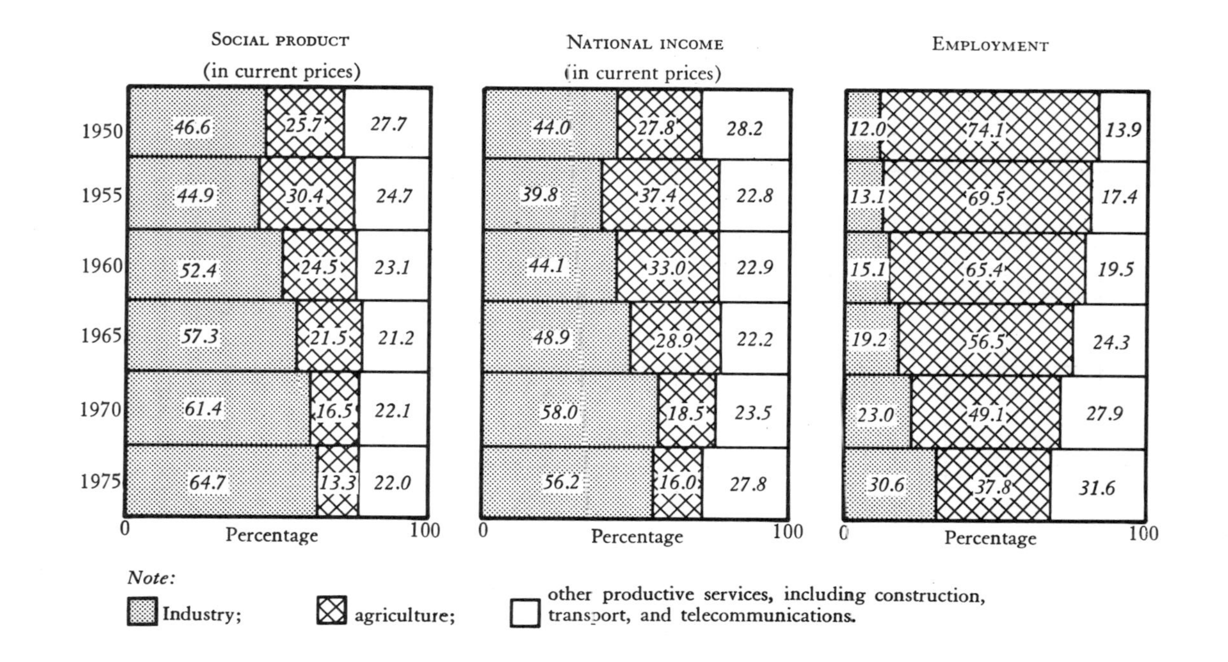

Note: Industry; agriculture; other productive services, including construction, transport, and telecommunications.

be regarded as approximations of the real economic growth, rather than precise measures of it for several reasons. In all economies, it is difficult to value outputs for periods of significant structural change and large relative price changes. In Romania, these problems have been compounded by the facts that comparable price series are not exactly constant price series and that gross output has been used as the primary plan target at all levels of the economy during 1950–75. Nevertheless, it is clear that Romania has enjoyed an internationally high economic growth rate over the past twenty-five years.

The driving force behind the high rates of economic growth has been the high and rapidly expanding volume of investment resulting from the ability of the government to maintain consumption growth below the annual increases in overall productivity and so to raise the saving rate. Between 1950 and 1975 gross investment increased 22 times, from 6.3 billion lei (measured in 1959 prices) to 137.7 billion lei (in 1963 prices) (Table SA3.3); this represented an average annual increase of 13.1 percent, considerably more than the growth of national income. This growth can be represented more dramatically by the fact that in each plan period, the volume of investment has exceeded the volume in the previous ten years. As a result of the high marginal propensity to invest, which in some years has approached 0.5, the proportion of national income allocated to the accumulation fund rose from 17.6 percent in 1951–55 to 34.1 percent during 1971–75 (Table 5.1).

The mobilization and allocation of savings and investment in all sectors has been under full central control. By far the largest proportion of domestic savings has been appropriated and deployed by the state budget, which in turn has operated as a component of the central planning mechanism. All other resources that fall outside the budget (for example, depreciation funds and savings by agricultural cooperatives and individuals) have been closely regulated and monitored to ensure that their use complements the budgetary resources in implementing the development plan.

Romania's fiscal system has been shaped to provide consistently the bulk of the resources required for the planned development effort of the country. Over the past twenty-five years, the growth of budget revenues has exceeded that of national income, and their structure has changed markedly, indicating the expansion and deepening of economic activities, as well as the effects of the government fiscal measures to enhance the financial viability of the state enterprises. The aim has been to make the economic activities of these enterprises more profitable in the context of the Romanian pricing system, and this is clearly reflected in the sharply increased share of the profit remissions of the enterprises in total budgetary revenues.

In 1950–75, revenues of the state budget increased at an average annual

Table 5.1. *Use of National Income (in Comparable Prices) for Consumption and Accumulation, 1951–55 to 1971–75*
(percentage)

Five-year period	*Consumption fund*[a]	*Accumulation fund*[b]
1951–55	82.4	17.6
1956–60	84.0	16.0
1961–65	75.7	24.3
1966–70	71.2	28.8
1971–75	65.9	34.1

Source: Anuarul Statistic al Republicii Socialiste Romania (Bucharest: Directia Centrala de Statistica, published yearly).
Note: National income data exclude nonproductive services.
a. Consumption of material products and services by individuals, the state, and other institutions.
b. Includes net investment plus change in stocks.

rate of 10.5 percent, from 20 to 239 billion lei, versus a corresponding national income growth rate of 9.7 percent.[3] As a proportion of national income, budget revenues have remained consistently in the high range of 60 to 65 percent. They have been at about 50 percent of gross national product (GNP) during 1965–75.

The effect of the high investment rates on the growth of social product and national income has been magnified by the large share given to the productive sector. Approximately 80 percent of total investment over the period was allocated to the productive sector, and most of that allocated to the nonproductive sector was used to support the expansion of productive activities; for example, investments in education and housing for the newly urbanized labor force. The high growth rate of net investment, embodied largely in the form of new plants and the diversification of the production base, led to a constant increase in the volume of fixed assets. Between 1950 and 1975, the average annual growth rate of fixed assets was 6.9 percent.

The patterns of investment financing reflect the nature of the centralized economic system. As noted above and in Table 5.1, the dramatic growth of investment is highlighted by the fact that in each plan period, the volume of investment has exceeded the volume in the previous ten years. The volume of investment in 1971–75 was about nine times that of 1951–55. State funds

3. National income data are available in comparable prices, whereas budget data are in current prices. Accurate direct comparison of the data is, therefore, not possible. Also, if allowance was made for the expansion in 1955 of the activities included in the socialist sector and if the respective growth rates were calculated for 1955–75, the respective annual growth rates would be 8.7 percent for national income and 8.8 percent for revenues.

account for the financing of most gross investment in the economy. Of these, the centralized funds and particularly the budget play the major role, as illustrated in Table 5.2. Investment financed by foreign borrowing is included in the amount reported for state budget financing and is not available separately.

Just as the overall level of investment and its distribution between productive and nonproductive sectors illustrates the priority given by the Romanian Communist Party (RCP) to rapid growth of production and national income, so the sectoral distribution of investment reflects the priority given to industrialization. Throughout the period, approximately 50 percent of the total investment was directed toward industry, and, of this, by far the largest amount was allocated to the producer goods industry (Table 5.3). The importance of industry and related sectors in the allocation of investment is reflected in sectoral growth rates and in the changing structure of social product and national income since 1950. Compared with the 9.7 percent average annual growth rate of national income, national income from industry increased 13.5 percent, construction by 11.5 percent, and transport by 11.5 percent, whereas agriculture grew only 3.1 percent. Relative growth rates were similar in terms of social product. Consequently, the structure of social product and national income changed significantly, with industry becoming the leading branch of the economy. Figure 5.3 illustrates to some degree the change in structure, but it essentially underestimates the extent of the changes, since relative prices over the period moved heavily in favor of agricultural goods.[4]

Demographic and Employment Changes

The changes in economic structure between 1950 and 1975 were accompanied by changes in the growth and distribution of population, the structure of the labor force, and the level and diversification of its skills. The growth of population and of the labor force was quite low over the period; population grew at a little over 1 percent a year whereas the labor force increased still less quickly, at 0.8 percent a year (Chapter 8). The most notable changes in employment were in its regional and sectoral distribution. Between 1950 and 1975 the rapid growth of industry and its related sectors resulted in a transfer of labor from agriculture and an associated increase in urbanization. During this period, the agricultural labor force fell from 6.2 to 3.8 million, whereas nonagricultural employment almost tripled, rising from 2.2 to 6.3 million: that is, from 26 to 62 percent of the

4. Between 1950 and 1959 the price of agricultural goods tripled in relation to industrial goods. Thus, the change in structure during the 1950s is greatly underestimated in Figure 5.1.

Table 5.2. *Fixed Investment, by Financing Source, 1951–75*
(billions of lei)

Source	*1951–55*[a]		*1956–60*[a]		*1961–65*[a]		*1966–70*[b]		*1971–75*[b]	
	Amount	*Percentage*	*Amount*	*Percentage*	*Amount*	*Percentage*	*Amount*	*Percentage*	*Amount*	*Percentage*
Total fixed investment	*61.9*	*100*	*100.2*	*100*	*199.7*	*100*	*330.8*	*100*	*549.0*	*100*
					Socialist sector investment					
Total	*57.7*	*93.2*	*88.2*	*88.0*	*187.7*	*94.0*	*314.5*	*95.1*	*516.7*	*94.1*
State sector contribution	56.7	91.6	84.5	84.3	173.7	87.0	297.3	89.9	495.6	90.3
Centralized state funds	55.0	88.9	79.7	79.5	168.9	84.6	286.5	86.6	478.0	87.1
Enterprises' own funds	1.7	2.7	4.8	4.8	4.8	2.4	10.8	3.3	17.6	3.2
Cooperative sector contribution	0.9	1.5	3.0	3.0	12.6	6.3	15.5	4.7	18.9	3.5
Cooperative and mass organizations funds	0.5	0.8	0.9	0.9	1.6	0.8	4.2	1.3	6.4	1.2
Agricultural cooperatives	0.4	0.7	2.1	2.1	11.0	5.5	11.3	3.4	12.5	2.3
Contribution of population[c]	0.2	0.3	0.7	0.7	1.4	0.7	1.7	0.5	2.1	0.4
					Private sector investment					
Total	*4.2*	*6.8*	*12.0*	*12.0*	*12.0*	*6.0*	*16.3*	*4.9*	*32.3*	*5.9*

a. Data for 1951–65 in 1959 prices.
b. Data for 1966–75 in 1963 prices.
c. Services contributed for community works.
Source: Anuarul Statistic, various issues.

Table 5.3. *Distribution of Investment, by Sector, 1950–75*
(percentage)

Sector	*1951–55*[a]	*1956–60*[a]	*1961–65*[a]	*1966–70*[b]	*1971–75*[b]
Industry	53.8	44.9	46.5	50.0	50.5
Group A	46.8	39.2	41.5	42.4	42.1
Group B	7.0	5.7	5.0	7.6	8.4
Construction	3.7	2.5	3.4	3.9	4.7
Agriculture and silviculture	11.3	17.3	19.4	16.0	14.4
Transport	9.4	7.5	8.1	9.6	9.1
Telecommunication	0.9	0.6	0.7	0.7	1.1
Trade	2.4	2.1	2.5	2.9	3.5
Nonproductive services	18.5	25.1	19.5	17.0	16.7
Housing	10.1	15.6	11.6	9.5	9.3
Education	1.5	1.3	1.7	1.5	1.6
Health	1.8	1.7	1.2	1.2	0.9

a. In 1959 prices.
b. In 1963 prices.
Source: Anuarul Statistic, various issues.

labor force (Figure 5.3). Urbanization progressed with industrialization, but at a slower rate; Romania has been one of the few developing countries in which growth of nonagricultural employment increased more quickly than the growth of urban areas. In 1950, 75 percent of the population lived in rural areas, and 72 percent of the labor force worked in agriculture. In 1975 the proportions had changed to 57 and 38 percent, respectively. These trends reflected the efforts of the government to locate industrial employment in both rural and urban areas and to control the influx into cities, thereby economizing on housing expenditures (Chapter 8).

The increases in national income and the transfer of labor from low-income agriculture to higher-income industry have generated substantial improvements in the standard of living since 1950, although the increases were below the growth of national income per capita. Whereas the latter rose at 8.6 percent a year between 1950 and 1975, the total real income of the population rose at an annual rate of 6.4 percent. As Figure 5.2 shows, a major reason for this increase has been the rapid increase in sociocultural expenditures, which grew at an annual rate of 11.4 percent. Wages grew at a more modest rate, 6.6 percent a year (Chapter 9).

Growth of Foreign Trade

The growth of the economy has had implications for the level and structure of foreign trade. Between 1950 and 1975 the volume of foreign trade, measured in current prices, rose from 2.7 to 53.1 billion lei valuta, an average annual growth rate of almost 13 percent. Throughout the period, foreign trade both played an important role in the growth of economy and also mirrored the success of development policies through changing levels and structure of exports. The level of imports rose throughout the period, more or less at the same rate as national income (Table SA4.1), whereas the structure of the import bill was dominated by capital goods and raw materials. Despite the technological improvements and productive capacity of its capital goods industry, Romania's industrialization strategy has required a continued increase in capital goods imports, and they have constituted some 35 percent of total imports during the period. As Romania's requirements for capital imports became more sophisticated during the 1960s, Romania had to develop its trade with the developed market economies, largely because such goods were not available within the Council for Mutual Economic Assistance (CMEA). Imports of raw materials also maintained their high share of the total, reflecting the rapidly expanding needs of industry for materials either not available in the country or for which domestic reserves and production were inadequate. The other category of imports that indicates Romania's growth trends is industrial consumer goods. Its declining share throughout the period demonstrated, in part, the success at the final stage of Romania's import-substitution strategy and also the limitations maintained during the period on the imports of such goods.

The transformation of the Romanian economy between 1950 and 1975 was most clearly mirrored, however, in the structure of exports. Although exports increased between 1950 and 1975 at virtually the same rate as imports, their composition changed significantly. In 1950, 75 percent of all exports were raw materials, chiefly agricultural products and oil, whereas industrial goods constituted only 11 percent of the total. In 1975 industrial exports had risen to 55 percent, and raw material exports, although growing at an annual average of approximately 10 percent, had diminished to 34 percent of the total. Although of lesser relative importance in recent years, exports of industrial raw materials and agricultural products have played an important role in financing imports from developed market economies. Unlike other European countries, which generally ran a deficit in agricultural trade, Romania's surplus enabled the country to expand trade with the West before developing competitive industrial exports. One other particular feature of Romania's exports has been the rapid growth of capital goods exports, from 4.2 percent of the total in 1950 to 25.3 percent in 1975—an increase of some 120 times (Chapters 7 and 10).

6

The Fifth Plan, 1971 to 1975

THIS CHAPTER COMPLETES THE ASSESSMENT, started in Chapter 5, of Romania's economic performance since 1950, by examining development policies, plans, and achievements during the Fifth Five-Year Plan, 1971–75. In looking at the policies, the indicators, and targets of the Directives and the final Plan, the process of implementation, and the overall achievements of the economy during the five years, the 1971–75 Plan period illustrates the operation of the planning and management system outlined in Chapters 3 and 4. The performance of each economic sector is not discussed in detail; such discussions are found in the relevant sectoral chapters. Overall developments in the economy are assessed and the most important macroeconomic issues are discussed, in particular regional development, qualitative improvement, and production efficiency. Because of the importance given to foreign trade by the Romanian government and by the study in its discussion of Romania's prospects, foreign trade between 1971 and 1975 is discussed in a separate chapter, Chapter 7.

Major Features of the Plan

The preparation of the Fifth Plan began formally in 1969 at the Tenth Congress of the Romanian Communist Party (RCP) with the publication of general guidelines for the development of the economy between 1971 and 1980 and specific directives for the preparation of the 1971–75 Five-Year Plan. In view of the progress made between 1966 and 1968 in fulfilling the targets of the 1966–70 Plan, the guidelines for the decade emphasized the continuation of a high rate, and even an acceleration, of economic growth. They also indicated a continuation of the strategy adopted in previous plan periods—high investment rates, the primary importance of industry, in-

Table 6.1. *Economic Indicators for 1971–75 Plan*

Indicator	*1975 level (1970 = 100) (in comparable 1963 prices)*		
	Directives of the Tenth Congress of the RCP	*Law of the Five-Year Plan*	*Achievement*
Social product	n.a.	n.a.	165
National income	145–150	169–176	170.6
Gross industrial production	150–157	169–176	184.7
Gross agricultural production[a]	128–131	136–149	125.4
Volume of freight transport	130–142	n.a.	154.8
Volume of foreign trade[b]	140–145[b]	161–172[b]	206.1[c]
Volume of investment from state funds[a]	148–153	165	168.3
Value of fixed capital activated from state funds[a]	n.a.	n.a.	167.8
Increase in the number of personnel in the national economy	107.8–109.8	119.6	123.3
Labor productivity for each worker			
In republican industry	137–140	142	137
In construction and assembly	127–131	135	146.1
In railroad transport	133–135	133	127.2
Reduction of expenses per 1,000 lei in commodity output in national industry (percentage)	6–7	11–12	9.2
Socialist retail trade sales	130–135	140–147	148.3
Volume of services for the population	140–145	155–161	168.6
Number of houses constructed[d]	500,000	522,000	511,700
Wage fund	130–135	153	n.a.
Real wages of personnel	116–120	120	120
Real incomes of peasants	115–120	122–130	n.a.
Total real income of the population	n.a.	140–146	146
National income per capita	137–142	n.a.	162.6

n.a. Not available.

a. 1971–75 annual average compared with 1966–70 annual average.

b. 1971–75 volume in 1970 prices compared with 1966–70 volume in current prices.

c. 1971–75 volume in current prices compared with 1966–70 volume in current prices.

d. From state funds and with assistance of state funds.

Sources: Directives of Tenth Congress of the Romanian Communist Party Concerning the 1971–75 Plan and the Guidelines for the Development of the National Economy in the 1976–80 Period; draft (Bucharest: Meridiane Publishing House, 1969).

creases in labor productivity and economic efficiency, and the introduction throughout the economy of improved technologies—while introducing new emphases that mirrored the progress made by the economy in the previous decade. The guidelines stressed improvements in the structure of industry (reflecting concern about the appropriate division of national income between investment and consumption) and the increased importance of electrotechnical, chemical, metallurgical, and engineering industries; promotion of technical progress in all branches of the economy; development of indigenous technological and scientific research; improved regional distribution of production; and changes in the level and structure of foreign trade.

The Directives for 1971–75 were prepared within this framework. Measured against the 1966–70 Directives, they represented the commitment of the RCP at least to maintaining the rate of economic growth (see Table 6.1). A comparison of the two directives produces several noteworthy points. First, despite a slowdown in the growth rate of gross industrial production and the same growth rate of investment as between 1966 and 1970, national income was projected to grow more rapidly than in the previous plan. It is assumed that this resulted from both a planning assumption of lower incremental capital output ratios (ICOR's) and lower unit expenditures on raw materials and labor and also from anticipated improvements in the performance of nonindustrial sectors, especially agriculture. Second, the 1971–75 Directives envisaged a significant deceleration in the expansion of wage earners, thereby predicting the success of steps to economize on labor (as well as other inputs), to obtain most of the planned production increases from more efficient use of existing inputs, and to strike a more desirable balance of labor between production and administration. In both cases, the targets reflected the anticipated effect on the economy of the reforms in planning and management approved by the National Conference of the RCP in 1967 (Chapter 3). Third, the Directives indicated the continuing increase in the proportion of national income allocated to investment. The increase in the consumption fund (which was to constitute 68 to 70 percent of national income between 1971 and 1975), measured indirectly by the growth rates of wages, retail sales, services, and sociocultural expenditures, was to be below that of national income. Indeed, the Directives for 1971–75

Law (no. 10) of October 21, 1971 on the Adoption of the Five-Year Plan for 1971–75 for the Economic and Social Development of the Socialist Republic of Romania, *Official Bulletin of the Socialist Republic of Romania*, no. 129 (October 21, 1971).

Communiqué Regarding the Fulfillment of the Unified National Plan for Social and Economic Development of the Socialist Republic of Romania during the 1971–75 Period. (Bucharest: Publishing Office for Political Literature, 1976.)

indicated that the growth rates of wages and retail sales were to be a little below the rates in the 1966–70 Directives.

Between the Tenth Congress and the publication of the Law of the Plan in November 1971, the indicators were revised upward several times in response to progress during the past two years of the 1966–70 Plan and the gradual refinement of the draft Plan. In May 1971 targets were raised following a more optimistic assessment of the effect of the 1970 floods; further increases were built into the plan in October of the same year, resulting from expectations that Romania could anticipate further improvements in her foreign trade performance. As Table 6.1 shows, the final draft published as the Law of the Plan envisaged that the economy would grow at a substantially faster rate than originally intended[1] and that the additional resources and growth possibilities identified during the preparation of the plan were to be directed largely toward investment rather than consumption, so that the accumulation fund between 1971 and 1975 would amount to 30 to 32 percent of national income. National income was planned to grow at 11.1 to 12.0 percent a year, compared with 7.7 to 8.5 percent in the Directives; gross industrial production was planned to grow at 11.1 to 12.0 percent a year compared with the earlier target of 8.5 to 9.5 percent; and gross agricultural production at 6.4 to 8.3 percent compared with 5.1 to 5.6 percent in the Directives. The targets in the Law of the Plan indicated that the increased growth would be assured both by increases in, and more efficient use of, resources. On the one hand, a larger volume of investment, (some 470 billion lei instead of the 420 to 435 billion lei of the Directives) and a larger increase in personnel (one million instead of 400,000 to 500,000) were planned. On the other hand, targets for increased labor productivity and reductions in the costs of production were increased, in keeping with the attention given to more efficient use of productive resources and the embodiment of technical progress in new investment. The increased targets for production and investment generated greater import require-

1. Since the projected 1975 levels are based on different 1970 levels in the Directives and in the Plan Law (in the former, it is an estimate of 1970; in the latter, the preliminary results), the increased targets in the Law of the Plan may indicate not only a real increase, but also a change in the base-year figures. A similar word of caution is required concerning evaluation of plan achievements. Straightforward comparisons of targets and actuals given in percentage terms do not necessarily show whether targets have been met or not, because targets are based on preliminary results of the previous planning period and achievements on actual results of the previous period. For example, in year t, the preliminary production estimate is 100 units. The plan target for the following year, $t + 1$, requires growth of 10 percent, meaning 110 units. Suppose actual production in year t is 105 units and production in year $t + 1$ is 110 units. Target output in year $t + 1$ is attained, but not the target growth rate.

ments of raw materials and investment goods, as well as greater export potential. The Law of the Plan projected a substantial increase in Romania's foreign trade, a 1971–75 volume of 61 to 72 percent above that of 1966–70, compared with a 40–45 percent increase in the Directives.

Although the Law of the Plan projected larger increases in targets for the productive sector, targets for consumption were changed less, the latter maintaining the rates of per capita growth planned for the previous plan period. The increase in the growth rate of the wage fund (53 percent over the five years compared with 30 to 35 percent in the Directives) represented a revised target for the number of wage earners and a 20 percent increase in real wages for each employee. The upgrading of targets for socialist retail trade and services to the population also mirrored the accelerated transfer of labor, whereas the requirements laid out in the Plan for diversification of consumer goods production, qualitative improvements, and improved territorial distribution of production were an aggregate of measures to meet the needs of the population more effectively. The Plan also projected increases in other components of sociocultural expenditures, notably pensions (planned to increase by 18 percent between 1970 and 1975), children's allowances (planned to increase by 27 percent), and housing, in which 522,000 units were to be constructed from state funds. Finally, one area in which the Plan did envisage a larger increase than the Directives was the real incomes of peasants. This reflected the wish of the RCP to reduce the gap between wages of cooperative members and of state employees and to stimulate agricultural production through price and wage incentives as well as through greater volumes of investment. Taking these elements of private and public consumption together, the Plan projected that the real incomes of the population should increase 40 to 46 percent over the five-year period.

The Plan was revised further following its publication as law. In 1972 the National Conference of the RCP adopted a resolution calling for fulfillment of the Plan in four-and-a-half instead of in five years. This acceleration was planned on the basis of the successful fulfillment of targets for industrial production and investment during 1966–70 and the achievements of the 1971 Annual Plan; during 1971 the growth of industrial output exceeded the target, and agricultural production grew rapidly following the poor 1970 harvest. As a result, the Conference stipulated that 1975 levels of industrial output should be 40 to 60 billion lei higher than initial targets, thereby permitting national income to be 200 billion lei above the level in the Law of the Plan. To obtain this improved performance, emphasis was to be placed not upon increasing the volume of investment, but upon improving the efficiency of production through fuller use of capacity, technical progress, reduction in the use of fuels and raw materials, improved organization, and reallocation of personnel.

Table 6.2. *Economic Indicators for the Annual Plans, 1970–75*

Indicator	1970 Achievement	1971 Plan	1971 Achievement
Social product (b. lei[a])	523.4	—[b]	584
National income (b. lei[a])	212.1	—[b]	240
Gross industrial production (b. lei[a])	319.5	326.8	357
Gross agricultural production (b. lei[a])	68.6	91.4	81
Volume of freight transport (b. tonnes per kilometer)	93.9	102.4	102
Volume of foreign trade (b. lei valuta[c])	22.9	27.0	25
Volume of investments from state funds (b. lei[a])	68.2	75.8	75
Increase in the number of personnel in the national economy	5.1[e]	—[b]	250,000
Labor productivity[f]			
In republican industry (lei[a])	159,300	168,935	168,441
In construction and assembly (lei[a])	64,100	68,555	69,092
In railroad transport (tonnes per kilometer)	343,500	357,420	359,295
Maximum expenses per 1,000 lei of commodity output in republican industry (lei[g])	872.9	874.1	879
Socialist retail trade sales (b. lei[g])	93.7	100.4	102
Volume of services for the population (b. lei[h])	—[b]	—[b]	—
Number of houses constructed[i]			
Wage fund (b. lei[g])		103.0	103
Real wages of personnel (lei per month)	1,302		
Real incomes of the peasantry[j] (lei per month)		—[b]	—
Total real income of the population (b. lei)	160	—[b]	181

a. In comparable 1963 prices.
b. Not available from Plan Law or Communiqué on Achievements.
c. Plan figures are in projected current prices, whereas achievements are in actual current pri
d. Total investment in the national economy.
e. Total number of personnel, in millions.
f. Social product for each employee.

Plan Implementation and Achievements

The achievements of the fifth plan period are shown in Tables 6.1, 6.2, and 6.3; they demonstrate that the Romanian economy enjoyed considerable success in meeting the targets laid out in the Law of the Plan and thus in overfulfilling the Directives of the 1969 Congress. Indeed, industrial production and investment overfulfilled their respective plan targets. The

1972		1973		1974		1975	
Plan	*Achievement*	*Plan*	*Achievement*	*Plan*	*Achievement*	*Plan*	*Achievement*
—[b]	641.0	—[b]	708.0	—[b]	788.0	—[b]	863.7
—[b]	264.7	—[b]	293.0	—[b]	329.5	—[b]	361.9
368.6	399.4	414.2–428.7	457.0	501.0	524.0	582–591	586.9
97.8	89.2	106.8	89.9	113.0	91.2	—[b]	93.8
110.6	100.3	107.6	107.4	120.0	119.1	129.9	145.4
30.3	28.8	35.0	36.0	50.9	49.8	60.7	53.1
87.2	83.4	93.8	91.0	118.0[d]	119.7[d]	142.7[d]	137.7[d]
5,000	255,000	235,000	185,000	250,000	195,000	6.4[e]	6.3[e]
1,921	180,931	198,650	197,466	216,600	210,794	239,000	225,760
3,300	73,881	78,230	80,622	85,370	87,240	95,500	94,220
8,400	374,572	452,430	454,185	475,000	479,940	498,500	495,780
852.7	863.7	837.4	853.7	879.7	897.8	875.0	873.6
108.8	108.8	120.9	117.2	128.7	129.5	140.8	140.8
20.1	20.5	22.8	22.8	25.6	25.9	28.4	27.8
109.4	109.3	120.9	117.7	134.0	129.6	154.5	137.1
				1,456	1,442	1,602	1,542
—[b]	—[b]	—[b]	—[b]	950	980	980	
—[b]	194	—[b]	203	—[b]	219	—[b]	234

g. In current prices.
h. In prices in effect on January 1, 1971.
.. From state funds.
. Including proceeds of private plots.
Sources: Anuarul Statistic al Republicii Socialiste Romania (Bucharest: Directia Centrala de Sta-ica, published yearly); Law (no. 10) on the Five-Year Plan for 1971–75; and Annual Plans aw (no. 64) of 1974, Law (no. 105) of 1973; Law (no. 11) of 1972, and Law (no. 16) of 71].

economy fell a little short of the accelerated targets adopted at the 1972 National Conference, however.

During the five years, social product and national income, measured in comparable 1963 prices, increased from 523 to 864 billion lei and from 212 to 362 billion lei, respectively. These increases represented average annual growth rates of 10.5 and 11.3 percent, respectively, the latter just exceeding the lower bound of the Plan target. In keeping with the priorities and tar-

Table 6.3. *Annual Growth Rates of Major Economic Indicators (in Comparable Prices), 1971–75*
(percentage)

Indicator	*1971*	*1972*	*1973*	*1974*	*1975*	*1971–75 average*
Social product	11.7	9.8	10.4	11.3	9.6	10.5
National income	13.5	10.0	10.7	12.5	9.8	11.3
Gross industrial production	12.0	11.7	14.6	14.7	11.8	12.9
Group A	12.0	11.7	14.8	15.5	14.4	13.7
Group B	10.7	11.9	14.7	11.9	6.3	11.1
Gross agricultural production	18.9	9.5	0.8	1.1	2.8	6.5
Volume of freight transport	9.0	−2.0	7.0	11.0	21.9	9.1
Construction output	7.7	7.2	7.2	3.8	7.9	6.9
Volume of foreign trade[a]	10.3	14.3	24.8	38.3	6.6	18.4
Volume of investment	10.5	10.4	8.3	13.3	15.1	11.5
Fixed assets	9.2	8.2	8.8	10.4	11.7	9.6
Number of personnel	5.2	4.7	3.8	3.3	4.6	4.3
Labor productivity						
In republican industry	4.5	5.7	7.8	6.0	7.2	6.4
In construction and assembly	5.9	7.5	9.0	9.0	7.6	7.9
In rail transport	4.7	4.9	6.5	5.7	3.2	4.9
Socialist retail trade sales[b]	9.1	6.3	7.5	10.2	7.7	8.2
Sociocultural expenditures	7.6	9.7	10.6	7.4	6.8	8.4
Real wages of personnel	2.2	1.8	3.2	4.5	6.9	3.7
Total real income of the population	13.2	6.8	5.6	7.2	7.0	7.9
National income per capita	12.4	8.9	9.8	11.3	8.7	10.2

a. In current prices.
b. In prices in force on January 1, 1971.
Source: Anuarul Statistic, various issues.

gets established in the Plan, the sector with the highest rate of growth was industry, which overfulfilled its aggregate plan target, whereas agricultural growth was considerably below target. Gross industrial production,[2] measured in comparable 1963 prices, rose from 319.5 billion lei in 1970 to 586.9 billion lei in 1975, the average annual growth rate of 13 percent exceeding the Plan target's upper bound of 12 percent. As a result, the Plan target was fulfilled two months before the end of 1975, and some additional 30 billion lei of production was obtained. Achievements, therefore, fell only a little short of the revised target adopted by the 1972 National Conference. Both group A and B industries exceeded the upper limits of their respective plan targets, with group A industry, as in previous plans, exceeding the target by a wider margin. The average annual growth rate of group A was 13.7 percent compared with the Plan target of 11.7 to 13 percent and of group B was 11.1 percent compared with a target of 9.5 to 11.0 percent (Chapter 10).

Gross agricultural production, measured in comparable 1963 prices, rose from 68.6 billion lei in 1970 to 93.8 billion lei in 1975, a 37 percent increase and an average annual growth of 6.5 percent. Measured in terms of a plan target, however, which required the average annual production during 1971–75 to be 36 to 49 percent higher than the annual average for 1966–70, the increase was only 25.4 percent. As Table 6.2 shows, the major gains in agricultural production during the period were made in 1971, when production rose 19 percent after a poor harvest in 1970, and again in 1972. As a result, further increases above the plan targets were anticipated at the RCP Conference of 1972, but agricultural production stagnated in the face of poor climatic conditions between 1973 and 1975 (Chapter 11).

The sectoral growth rates led to further structural change within the productive sector, with industry strengthening its position as the leading branch of the economy. The extent of the change is shown, in differing ways, by Tables 6.4 and 6.5. The former provides indexes of the growth of each sector's contribution to social product and national income measured in comparable prices and shows the relatively high growth of industry. Table 6.5 shows the changing structure of social product and national income in current prices. Between 1970 and 1975 industry's share of social product increased from 61.4 to 64.7 percent, whereas agriculture's fell from 16.5 to 13.3 percent, and construction's declined from 10.6 to 8.6 percent. For national income, Table 6.5 does not show the increasing weight of industry because of relative price changes during 1973–75.

2. See the Glossary for the distinction between gross industrial (agricultural) production and social product in industry (agriculture).

Table 6.4. *Index of Growth of Social Product and National Income, by Branch of the Economy (in Comparable 1963 Prices), 1970–75*
(1970 = 100)

Year	*Total*	*Industry*	*Construction*	*Agriculture*	*Transport and telecommunications*
			Social product		
1970	100	100	100	100	100
1971	112	111	109	121	108
1972	123	123	117	130	116
1973	135	141	123	132	126
1974	151	159	129	134	135
1975	165	176	140	139	156
			National income		
1970	100	100	100	100	100
1971	113	111	110	131	109
1972	125	126	119	140	119
1973	138	147	124	133	132
1974	155	167	131	130	144
1975	171	186	144	130	169

Source: Anuarul Statistic, various issues.

The growth in production and the changes in economic structure between 1971 and 1975 were accompanied, and to a large extent generated, by a large investment program designed to ensure "the steady growth of the entire production potential of the country, improvement in the territorial distribution of the forces of production, amelioration in the structure of the national economy, improvement in the population's housing conditions and development of the material resources of sociocultural activities."[3]

The Plan target for investments from centralized state funds (which constituted 87 percent of total investments in the national economy between 1971 and 1975) was slightly overfulfilled, achievements being 8 billion lei above the target of 470 billion lei, and, according to the Plan communiqué, the actual sectoral distribution of investment approximated the planned amounts, with industry receiving 57.2 percent of total centralized state funds,

3. *Communiqué Regarding the Fulfillment of the Plan during the 1971–75 Period.*

Table 6.5. *Structure of Social Product and National Income (in Current Prices), 1970–75*
(percentage)

Year	*Industry*	*Construction*	*Agriculture*	*Transport and telecommunications*	*Other productive services including trade*
			Social product		
1970	61.4	10.6	16.5	4.7	6.8
1971	60.4	10.3	18.1	4.5	6.7
1972	61.1	10.1	17.1	4.5	7.2
1973	62.2	9.6	16.1	4.4	7.7
1974	63.6	8.9	14.1	4.1	9.3
1975	64.7	8.6	13.3	4.2	9.2
			National income		
1970	58.0	10.4	18.5	6.0	7.1
1971	56.0	9.6	22.2	5.5	6.7
1972	56.5	9.5	21.2	5.5	7.3
1973	58.1	9.1	18.5	5.6	8.7
1974	56.6	8.3	15.9	5.4	13.8
1975	56.2	7.6	16.0	5.8	14.4

Source: Anuarul Statistic, various issues.

agriculture 16.1 percent, transport and telecommunications 11.4 percent, and construction 5 percent (Table 6.6).

The total volume of investment in the national economy during the Fifth Plan was 549 billion lei, a larger amount than was invested during the Third and Fourth Plans together (Table SA3.3). As a result, the proportion of national income directed toward the accumulation fund between 1971 and 1975 was 34.1 percent (Table 5.1), which surpassed the Plan target of 30 to 32 percent. This is a strong indication of the efforts made during 1971–75 to accelerate the growth rate of the economy, as well as being evidence of the difficulties facing the economy in implementing the targets of the 1972 National Conference. As the later discussion on efficiency indicates, the accelerated growth called for by the Conference could not be provided by improvements in resource use and efficiency but had to be secured through additional inputs of capital and labor (below).

The distribution of the total investment volume followed closely the priorities laid out in the Plan: 83.3 percent of the total was allocated to the productive sector, and the sectoral distribution continued the previous

Table 6.6. *Planned and Actual Investments from Centralized State Funds (in Comparable 1963 Prices), 1971–75*

Sector	*Planned, 1971–75*		*Achievement, 1971–75*	
	Billions of lei	*Percentage*	*Billions of lei*	*Percentage*
Total	*470.0*[a]	*100*	*478.0*	*100*
Industry	281.2	58.1	273.3	57.2
Construction	18.5	3.8	23.9	5.0
Agriculture	81.4	16.8	76.8	16.1
Transport and telecommunications	53.6	11.1	54.4	11.4
Trade	13.2	2.7	—[b]	—
Municipal services	8.1	1.7	—[b]	—
Housing	14.3	3.0	—[b]	—
Education and health	9.6	2.0	—[b]	—
Scientific research	4.5	0.9	3.8	0.8

a. Components do not add to total but equal 484.4 billion lei. Percentages for sectors are based on this higher figure.

b. Not reported in Plan communiqué.

Sources: Law (no. 10) of the Five-Year Plan for 1971–75; *Communiqué Regarding the Fulfillment of the Plan during the 1971–75 Period.*

plan period's emphasis upon industry (Table SA3.4). Some 277 billion lei (50.5 percent of the total) was directed toward industry, of which 231 billion lei (42.1 percent) went to group A industries, in particular to metallurgy, machine building, chemicals, fuels, and energy. As a result of these allocations, Romania was able to supply a higher proportion of its own capital goods; in 1975 almost 75 percent of all equipment investments were produced domestically. Group B industries were allocated 45.9 billion lei (8.4 percent), and, as a result of this increased allocation and the higher investment during the 1966–70 plan period, light industry enjoyed one of the highest annual growth rates of the industrial subsectors—13 percent. The next largest investments were in agriculture with 79.2 billion lei (14.4 percent of the total) and in transport and telecommunications with 55.7 billion lei (10.2 percent), followed by construction with 25.9 billion lei (4.7 percent). During the 1971–75 plan period, greater attention was given to regional distribution of investment (below).

The overfulfillment of the plan target for investment was matched by overfulfillment of the target for the number of wage earners. Although the occupied population increased from 9.9 to 10.2 million, the number of personnel rose from 5.1 to 6.3 million, an increase of 1.2 million (23.3 percent above the 1970 level) compared with a Plan target of 1 million (19.6 percent). The increase in the number of personnel involved essentially a transfer of labor from agriculture. The occupied population in agriculture declined from 4.85 to 3.84 million (49.1 to 37.8 percent), whereas the number working in industry rose from 2.28 to 3.11 million (23 to 30.6 percent). Further details of employment and, in particular, of participation rates and urbanization, are discussed in Chapter 8.

In terms of the percentage of national income allocated to the consumption fund, the economy between 1971 and 1975 failed to fulfill the target of 68 to 70 percent, since only 65.9 percent of national income was reported as going to the consumption fund. The growth of national income, however, was such that the growth of the consumption fund, 7.5 percent a year over the Plan period, was higher than in previous plans and made possible large enough increases in personal incomes and sociocultural expenditures of the government to fulfill Plan targets. Total purchasing power of the population, expressed in terms of real income, increased by 46 percent between 1970 and 1975, thereby meeting the upper bound of the Plan target. According to the Communiqué, the wage fund rose by 51 billion lei (53 percent) during the plan period, indicating a slight overfulfillment of the plan target, which was caused by the higher-than-targeted increase in personnel. Nominal and real wages more or less increased according to the targets. Through increases in the minimum wage and general wage increases, the nominal monthly wage rose to an average of 1,813 lei in 1975, just over the target set in the Plan, and to 1,975 lei in December 1975, thereby attaining the goal set out in the National Conference of the RCP in 1972. The increase in real wages was 18.4 percent over the five years, just short of the 20 percent target of the Plan. Increases in the incomes of peasants also occurred through the introduction of minimum wage and increases in procurement prices. It is not clear whether the Plan target of a 22 to 30 percent increase in real incomes was attained, but monetary incomes are reported in the Plan Communiqué to have increased by 28.7 percent.

Funds allocated from the state budget for sociocultural needs also increased by 50 percent over 1970. Expenditures totalled 50.9 billion lei in 1975, an average of 7,420 lei for each family, and financed improvements in education, health, and pensions (Chapters 8 and 9 and Appendix J). State funds were also used to construct 511,700 housing units, virtually meeting the Plan target of 522,000 (Chapter 12).

In the absence of plan targets, the growth of consumption must be estimated through the surrogate measures of socialist retail trade sales and through the volume of services carried out for the population. In both cases, the upper bounds of the targets established in the Plan were exceeded.

Socialist retail trade sales increased by 48.3 percent over the five-year period compared with a plan target of 40 to 47 percent. In 1975 sales totaled 140.8 billion lei, measured in current prices. The volume of services for the population totaled 27.8 billion lei, measured in 1971 prices in 1975, an increase of 68.6 percent over 1970. This exceeded the planned growth of 55 to 61 percent (Chapter 9). Savings by the population, mainly for the purchase of houses and durable consumer goods, which were in increased supply during the Fifth Plan, also grew. Savings deposits of the population reached 44.9 billion lei in 1975, an average annual growth of 16 percent over the plan period.

In summary, Romania's economic performance during the Fifth Plan indicates that the country succeeded to a large extent in formulating and carrying out consistent plans. Except for agriculture, production targets were largely met, and although they were assured by additional injections of investment and labor to offset the less-than-planned improvements in efficiency, the transfer from consumption to investment was not sufficient to prevent targets for consumption from being met.

Economic and Technical Efficiency

Although the main engine for economic growth has been the expanding level of investment in all sectors and the transfer of labor from agriculture to industry, as shown in earlier chapters and in the next section of this chapter, increasing attention has been paid to improvements in the efficiency of economic operations since the beginning of the 1966–70 plan period. This has included measures to improve the allocation of resources (through improvements in planning and management of the economy), as well as their use (through the introduction of specific plan targets for cost reduction, qualitative improvements, and reduction in resource consumption). Guidelines for specific programs and legislation were mapped out by the National Conference of the RCP in 1967.[4] They stipulated better organization and management of the branches of material production by allotting more responsibility to enterprises and by creating large-scale units; improved planning at central and enterprise levels; improved organization of the supply of materials for production; better use of financial tools and indicators and, in consequence, a more effective financial plan; reforms in

4. Nicolae Ceausescu, "Report Concerning Measures for Perfecting the Management and Planning of the National Economy and for Improving the Administrative and Territorial Organization of Romania" (report presented to the National Conference of the Romanian Communist Party, December 6, 1967) (Bucharest: Meridiane Publishing House, 1967).

the price system to provide correct signals to enterprises in their implementation of the plan; and finally, as a major task, the overall improvement of efficiency. This last task was to be achieved by shortening the commissioning period for new assets, increasing the degree of capacity use, ensuring a high degree of raw material processing, improving the quality of products for both internal and external markets, incorporating scientific and technological research in production, and minimizing consumption of inputs.

After 1967 and particularly during the Fifth Plan period, steps were taken to implement these measures through both legislation and new procedures. The details of the planning and organizational changes are given in Chapters 3 and 4; this section looks at the effect of these measures, insofar as an assessment can be made, and compares them with the targets published in the Plan.

Two efficiency targets were published in the Plan: labor productivity for each worker in industry, construction, and rail transport and the reduction of expenses for each 1,000 lei of marketed industrial output. Both are synthetic indicators, combining in a single index changes in more than one economic variable. Thus, an improvement in labor productivity (which is defined as gross product for each worker) may measure capital deepening, improved labor skills, improved management, higher-value product mix, and so forth. Nevertheless, in the absence of more direct measures of efficiency, they serve as a useful starting point.

Labor productivity in republican industry increased by 37 percent over the plan period, an average annual increase of 6.5 percent, reflecting the infusion of investment and new technology and managerial improvements (Chapter 10). The increase, however, fell short of the targeted increase of 42 percent, according to the Plan Communiqué, because of deficiencies in production organization and in capacity use; it may also have resulted from overmanning (see above and Chapter 10). Labor productivity in construction, growing 46 percent, exceeded its plan target of 35 percent, a performance attributable to the accelerated capitalization and mechanization of the sector (Chapter 12). Labor productivity in rail transport increased 27 percent compared with a target of 33 percent. The shortfall appears to have resulted from a lower-than-planned increase in goods traffic.

The Plan Communiqué also reported improved efficiency of fixed capital; the volume of gross production for each 1,000 lei of fixed capital increased 8 percent during the plan period. As in the case of the labor productivity figures, this measure is a synthetic indicator, summarizing the impact of changes in various variables. In the absence of a plan target or more detailed information, it is not possible to evaluate the result.

Since both the published plan targets are defined in gross output terms, they contain the influence of many factors. For example, an increase in

Table 6.7. *Sectoral Capital/Output Ratios, 1970–75*
(1970 = 100)

	Capital/output ratio[a]			
Year	*Industry*	*Construction*	*Agriculture*	*Transport and telecommunications*
1970	100	100	100	100
1971	101.8	105.5	84.0	100
1972	99.2	112.6	85.7	98.3
1973	95.2	119.4	98.5	96.2
1974	95.8	128.2	110.0	97.2
1975	99.5	139.6	121.5	92.9

a. Ratio of fixed assets to national income (in comparable prices).
Source: Anuarul Statistic, various issues.

labor productivity, measured as gross product for each worker, could as well denote increased material expenditures or an increase in the complexity and stages of production as increased net output for each worker. In principle, more appropriate measures of efficiency would be the proportion of national income in social product and capital-output ratios, but some care is required in interpreting them, since the aggregate ratios also measure several factors.[5] According to published data,[6] the capital-output ratio[7] for the productive sector as a whole did not change between 1970 and 1975; in both years, its value was 2.55, and the incremental capital-output ratio (ICOR)[8] for 1971–75 was 2.56. Changes in the sectoral ratios, absolute values of which are not available from published data, are shown in Table 6.7. In spite of the constant increase in the ratio for construction and for agriculture after 1973, the stability of the overall rate was maintained by the increasing weight of declining ratios for industry and transport.

The decline in industry's capital-output ratio reversed itself in 1975; it is unclear whether this resulted from inefficient use of new capital assets or from the fact that, with the large effort in 1975 to commission new capital before the end of the Plan, gains in output were delayed to the following plan period. The overall ICOR of 2.56 for 1971–75 was quite low by inter-

5. Such as natural resource endowment, present economic structure, present level of infrastructure, structure of investment, and short-run factors such as capacity use, as well as pricing of capital.
6. *Anuarul Statistic*, various issues.
7. The ratio of fixed assets to national income.
8. The ratio of change in fixed assets to change in national income.

national standards.[9] Although international comparison of ICOR's can be spurious for many reasons, it remains the only measure of the efficiency of capital available, in the absence of detailed data on capital good costs and information on enterprise activities. In view of the fact that the ICOR during the 1971–75 Plan was similar to the overall capital-output ratio and that the Romanian ICOR was not substantially different from those of other countries at a similar level of development, it may be concluded that there was no great change during the plan period in the overall efficiency of capital.

In principle, an increasing ratio of national income to social product also indicates improved economic efficiency: that is, increased value-added for given material expenditures. During the Fifth Plan, national income grew more quickly than social product. As a result, the ratio of national income to social product rose from 40.5 percent in 1970 to 41.9 percent in 1975. A similar trend was shown for each sector for agriculture, where increased inputs did not achieve large production gains, largely because of climatic difficulties. Again, these aggregate measures suggest a trend but can not be cited as certain evidence of increased efficiency, because in some cases changes in the ratio reflect changes in sectoral and intrasectoral composition of output quite unrelated to efficiency.

Nevertheless, the above figures and statements from the Plan Communiqué do suggest that the efficiency of economic operations increased between 1971 and 1975, especially by moving toward a product mix with a higher value-added and by producing economies in the use of fuels and raw materials. The Communiqué reported that the value of products obtained for each unit of processed raw materials increased substantially in several branches, especially in mechanical engineering and metallurgy, where it rose by 43 percent over the five years. Particular attention was paid to increasing value-added and the quality of processing in exported goods to improve the efficiency of foreign trade. The Plan also established targets to reduce material expenditures. In industry, material expenditures were to be reduced by 11 to 12 percent, but a reduction of only 9.2 percent was achieved, the shortfall being attributed to managerial deficiencies and failure to commission on time and to use new technologies fully.

Special efforts were made to economize on raw materials and fuels, particularly following the rise in the price of oil in 1973 (Chapter 14). Scientific research was directed toward improving industrial techniques to minimize use of fuels. For example, it was announced in 1975 that improvements in iron smelting technology would reduce the use of coal.

9. Comparable figures (1968–73) were 3.4 for Spain, 3.3 for Greece, 2.2 for South Korea, 2.9 for Turkey, and 1.4 for Brazil.

Studies were commissioned within government branches to identify economies, for example, in transport (Chapter 13), and sector and subsector-specific targets were established (for example, in 1974 it was announced that 25 percent of future paper needs were to be met through recyling used paper). Finally, producer prices of basic materials were reset during 1974–76, during the repricing exercise, to reflect more accurately their real cost and to encourage more efficient use of resources.

Regional Development

Regional development policy, first given special prominence in the 1966–70 Directives, was emphasized more strongly during the 1971–75 plan period. To distribute production, employment, income, education, and medical services more equitably through the country and to reduce substantially the imbalances in economic and social conditions, the Plan stipulated that increased investment in productive facilities and nonproductive services should be allocated to less industrialized and poorer judets. The Plan proposed that, as a result, industrial production in the poorer judets would increase annually by 20 to 27 percent compared with the national increase of 11 to 12 percent. No further specific targets were published in the Law of the Plan.

The implications for location of investment and employment and for regional distribution of production were reported in more detail in the Plan Communiqué. It indicated that for the less-developed judets, the growth of investment between 1970 and 1975 exceeded the national average. Compared with a 70 percent increase in total investment, investment rose by 220 percent in Dimbovita, 190 percent in Gorj and Tulcea, and above 100 percent in Dolj, Bistrita-Nasaud, Botosani, Alba, Satu Mare, and Vaslui. As a result, these areas experienced a higher-than-average growth of fixed assets. The poorer judets also enjoyed higher rates of growth of gross output than the economy as a whole. Information provided by the government indicates that all but three of the nineteen judets that had gross industrial production of less than five billion lei in 1970 fulfilled or overfulfilled their plan target[10] (Table 6.8). As a result, the number of districts with a low volume of industrial production decreased, as shown in Table 6.9.

The growing importance of an industrial work force in the poorer dis-

10. The rapid pace of growth in the less-developed judets, however, was not sufficient, except for Harghita, to meet the ambitious provisions established at the National Conference of the RCP in 1972. In the Directives, annual growth rates for the following judets were given: Bistrita-Nasaud 20.3 percent, Teleorman 21.6 percent, Harghita 15.8 percent, Dimbovita 22.6 percent, Salaj 25.4 percent, and Tulcea 28.1 percent.

tricts also reflects the increasing industrialization of the less-developed regions. In 1975 thirty-two districts had more than one-fifth of their inhabitants categorized as personnel, compared with twenty-seven in 1970, and only eighteen in 1965. Similarly, the population employed in nonagricultural activities was more than 50 percent of the occupied population in twenty-seven districts in 1975 compared with only thirteen in 1970. A trend toward greater urbanization accompanied these increases. This permitted efficient provision of social and cultural services, including improved medical services (for example, between 1970 and 1975, infant mortality rates in the poorer districts radically improved), centralized water and sewerage systems, better education, and so forth (Chapter 8).

The above statistics provide some evidence of the positive achievements of regional development policy. They demonstrate changing levels of production and employment in each judet, however, rather than changes in their distribution or in per capita terms. Therefore, the changes in regional distribution of per capita output were analyzed. Since figures on output from each judet are not published, an approximate figure was calculated using published data on social product in industry, agriculture, and construction and was converted into per capita terms. Such series were obtained for 1967 and 1974, and a coefficient of variation[11] of this output variable was calculated in both absolute and per capita terms, including and excluding Bucharest (Table 6.10).

These calculations show that industrial production has become more equally distributed; in other words, they demonstrate that the government policy for regional development, which is phrased in terms of industrial distribution, has been implemented successfully. The conclusion is supported further by calculating the coefficient of variation for the distribution of the population engaged in industrial production. Figures on the number of employees in industry by judet were converted into a proportion of population, and a coefficient of variation was calculated, as given below.

	1967	*1974*
(i)	58.66	46.45
(ii)	60.92	48.16

The figures show that, in addition to a general increase in the proportion of the occupied population in each judet working in industry, the disparity between judets in the distribution of the industrial work force has declined.

11. The coefficient of variation is a normalized variance defined as:

$$cv\ (x) = (\mathrm{Var}\ (x)/x) \times 100$$

Table 6.8. *Gross Industrial Production, by Judet (in Comparable 1963 Prices), 1970–75*

Judet	*Gross industrial production*			
	1970 (*thousands of lei*)	*1975* (*thousands of lei*)	*Plan target, 1975 ÷ 1970*	*Achievements 1975 ÷ 1970*
Alba	4,409	8,106	124	184
Arad	6,951	11,585		167
Arges	10,441	21,937		210
Bacau	10,659	16,336		153
Bihor	7,738	14,036		181
Bistrita-Nasaud	898	1,808	201	201
Botosani	1,811	3,388	147	187
Brasov	21,838	38,295		175
Braila	6,751	11,198		166
Buzau	3,602	9,058	231	251
Caras-Severin	8,643	11,478		133
Cluj	11,446	20,334		178
Constanta	6,619	12,842		194
Covasna	1,658	3,494		211
Dimbovita	4,864	11,372	217	234
Dolj	10,166	18,073		178
Galati	10,497	25,425		242
Gorj	3,374	5,802	173	172
Harghita	3,154	6,579	184	209
Hunedoara	16,747	21,503		128
Ialomita	2,872	5,272	161	184
Iasi	8,731	19,113		219
Ilfov	4,312	7,433	170	172
Maramures	5,068	7,952		157
Mehedinti	2,451	6,447	233	263
Mures	10,827	17,171		159
Neamt	8,175	15,933		195
Olt	3,858	13,456	341	349
Prahova	20,142	32,247		160
Satu-mare	3,610	7,688	160	213
Salaj	782	2,082	260	266
Sibiu	11,414	21,287		186
Suceava	5,906	9,928		168
Teleorman	3,040	6,970	255	229
Timis	11,544	20,659		179
Tulcea	1,453	2,675	250	184

Table 6.8. *Continued*

Vaslui	2,243	4,907	209	219
Vilcea	2,777	5,638	200	203
Vrancea	2,058	4,223	145	205
Bucharest municipality	55,947	103,147		184
Total or average	*319,476*	*586,878*		*183.7*

Source: Anuarul Statistic, various issues.

The calculations also show that, between 1967 and 1974, the distribution of agricultural production became less equal, so much so that the overall distribution of output between judets became no more equal. The increasing inequality in the distribution of agricultural production results from the constraints imposed by natural conditions on the regional allocation of investment in the sector. The government has announced that attempts will be made to distribute agricultural production more equitably, insofar as

Table 6.9. *Levels of Gross Industrial Production, by Judet (in Comparable 1963 Prices), 1965, 1970, and 1975*

Value of production (billions of lei)	*Number of judets*		
	1965	*1970*	*1975*
Less than 5	30	19	8
5–10	6	12	11
10–15	3	5	7
15–25		3	11
More than 25			2

Source: Communiqué Regarding on the Fulfillment of the Plan during the 1971–75 Period.

Table 6.10. *Coefficient of Variation of Per Capita Output, by Judet, 1967 and 1974*

	1967	*1974*
Absolute (i)	54.09	55.27
(ii)	83.36	90.90
Per capita (i)	42.34	42.84
(ii)	43.26	44.30

Note: (i) excludes Bucharest; (ii) includes Bucharest.

there are plans to make each judet as self-sufficient as possible in food production and to distribute large-scale livestock operations equitably. Such measures, however, are unlikely to have more than a marginal effect upon the inequality of the distribution of agricultural production.

So far, this discussion of regional distribution has been phrased in terms of output and employment. Lack of data on wages by judet prevents any conclusion that the regional distribution of incomes has also improved. Since the wage levels in industry are higher than those in agriculture, however, it is likely that the reduced disparity in levels of industrialization has also led to a reduced income disparities between judets. Partial data was supplied by Romanian authorities and is given below.

	Average income (lei per month)		
	Lowest judet	*Highest judet*	*Highest ÷ lowest*
1970	1,260	1,613	1.29
1975	1,631	2,035	1.26

According to these figures the gap between the average incomes of the richest and poorest judets diminished a little between 1970 and 1975. It is probable that the gap is reduced further, in terms of total real income of the population, by the allocation of sociocultural expenditures on the basis of national norms.

As a result of the government's figures and additional calculations, it can be concluded that Romanian regional policy has been successful in directing both industrial investment and production toward the less-developed judets. Furthermore, the data indicate that the pace of these changes has been, in general, as fast as or faster than planned.

Table 6.11. *Coefficient of Variations of per Capita Output, in Industry and Agriculture, 1967 and 1974*

	Industry		*Agriculture*	
	1967	*1974*	*1967*	*1974*
Absolute (i)	75.45	67.88	46.65	53.06
(ii)	132	111	49.00	54.19
Per capita (i)	66.83	56.37	40.03	41.08
(ii)	68.48	58.47	43.19	43.87

7

Foreign Trade and International Economic Relations

THE DEVELOPMENT OF THE ROMANIAN ECONOMY over the past twenty-five years has been accompanied by the rapid growth of foreign trade and the expansion of international economic relations with socialist, developed market, and developing countries. Between 1950 and 1975 the volume of foreign trade measured in current prices rose from 2.7 to 53.1 billion lei valuta,[1] an average annual growth rate of approximately 12.6 percent. Over the past decade, there has been a distinct acceleration in the rate of growth, the average annual expansion for 1965–75 equaling 15 percent and for 1970–75 18.4 percent. To some extent, this is explained by international inflation, but more importantly, underlying the current price data, there has been a steady acceleration in the real growth of foreign trade. This can be measured not only in terms of the ratio of trade to gross national product (GNP)—approximate calculations by the World Bank suggest the ratio in 1975 to have been somewhat above 20 percent compared with 12 to 14 percent in the early 1960s[2]—but also by the fact that the sectors upon which the economy depends for much of its growth, for example, chemicals, metallurgy, and engineering, have been those in which the importance of foreign trade has increased most. The impetus for the expansion has come largely from the

1. See the Glossary and Chapter 4 for the definition of this currency unit.
2. The figures for the early 1960s are quoted from J. M. Montias, *Economic Development in Communist Romania* (Cambridge, Mass.: MIT Press, 1967), p. 147.

side of imports to meet the needs of Romania's industrialization. On the one hand, the pace of industrial development has outpaced the domestic resource base, initially iron ore and coal in particular and since 1968 crude oil also. On the other hand, the change of emphasis in the industrialization strategy toward the development of advanced secondary industries has generated a demand for imported capital goods.

It has been the needs of the leading sectors of industry for raw materials and investment goods that have led to larger growth rates of trade with nonsocialist countries. Between 1960 and 1975 the average annual growth rate of imports from developed market economies was approximately 18 percent and from developing countries substantially more, albeit from a low base. To pay for these imports, Romania has made great attempts to expand exports, particularly industrial products, to all three trading areas. Romania has adopted a very comprehensive approach toward international economic relations. It has formalized trade relations through agreements that have also established the basis for technological and scientific exchange and for cooperation in production; it has tried to reduce trade barriers; and it has joined and participated actively in several international organizations such as the World Bank, the International Monetary Fund (IMF), the General Agreement on Tariff and Trade (GATT), and the United Nations Committee on Trade and Development (UNCTAD). These outward-looking actions have increased exports and economic cooperation of various kinds, most especially with the developing countries. A surplus in its trade with the developing countries has enabled Romania to finance some of its deficit with the developed market economies, whose markets have been harder to penetrate. The overall deficit that Romania has typically run with the convertible currency area has been financed by external borrowing.

This chapter explains the importance and operation of foreign trade in the Romanian economy by describing the role of foreign trade in the Romanian economy and the changes in that role as the country's economic profile has changed; by outlining the foreign trade planning system; and by examining in some detail foreign trade and international economic relations during the 1971–75 Plan period. The chapter should be read in conjunction with several other sections in the report: the section on foreign trade pricing in Chapter 4, the discussion of foreign trade in Chapter 5, and Appendix E, which all examine the development of trade and international economic relations during 1950–75, as well as the paragraphs on trade in the sectoral chapters. Wherever possible, the discussions are supported by official data and information from unofficial sources, but since information on balance of payments and external debt is given to the World

Bank by the government on a confidential basis, the discussion of these elements is necessarily nonquantitative.

Role of Foreign Trade

The major role played by foreign trade over the past two-and-a-half decades has mainly been to obtain resources that have been unavailable domestically and that are required to meet production plans. In pursuing a development strategy emphasizing the broadening of its economic base and rapid and comprehensive industrialization, Romania explicitly rejected the notion that its development should be governed by its comparative advantage as it appeared immediately after the war. During the 1950s and for much of the following decade, Romania's participation in world trade was determined largely by the size and structure of an import bill generated through planning domestic supply and demand; exports were regarded, in principle, as desirable only to finance imports as efficiently as possible.

During the past decade, trade has gradually become a less passive element of the economy, mainly as a result of changes on the sides of exports. Whereas the size and structure of trade continues to be derived largely from domestic supply and demand conditions that are determined within the planning process, the government has become more willing to exploit, within limits, a newly established comparative advantage, especially in industry. As the next section and the section on foreign trade pricing in Chapter 4 show, planning and pricing reforms have been adopted to reduce the insulation of the economy from international influences and to help to determine the export activities in which Romania can most profitably specialize. As a result, export activities are exposing enterprises to increasing international competition and are stimulating improvements in efficiency and product quality and the assimilation of new production processes, and thereby improving the marketability of Romanian exports. In addition to providing a more appropriate basis for establishing Romania's comparative advantage, such measures have secured imports with the minimum expenditure of domestic resources.

Export activities have also helped to maintain the growth rate, particularly in sectors where the size or growth of the domestic market has been a limiting factor. In such cases, exports have enabled growth rates to continue beyond the capacity of the domestic market or have allowed production at a level sufficient to secure economies of scale.

Foreign Trade Planning

Foreign trade is a state monopoly in Romania.[3] This monopoly encompasses not only all import and export operations, but also all international accounts, thus also thus creating a monopoly of foreign exchange. It exists to ensure that foreign trade activities are fully subordinated to the development strategy of the country and are implemented through the planning system. Since every branch of the economy is connected directly or indirectly with foreign trade, questions of control and administration of trade are inseparable from those concerning domestic economic activities. Therefore, this section should be read in conjunction with Chapter 3. The nature of foreign trade planning and the changes it has undergone in the past decade parallel, to a great extent, the arrangements in the internal economy. This section looks at the institutions and planning process governing the foreign trade sector as World Bank staff have come to understand them in discussions with government officials.

Foreign trade institutions

The institutions that plan and implement foreign trade operations are set out, and have their responsibilities outlined, in the Law (no. 1) on Foreign Trade, 1971. Prior to this law, responsibilities for carrying out foreign trade were vested in a single ministry, the Ministry of Foreign Trade, which had under its general direction several foreign trade enterprises responsible for securing imports and selling exports. By the mid-1960s the insulation of domestic enterprises from international markets was hindering the development of foreign trade, especially exports. Along with proposals for improving the organization for domestic economic activities, the Directives of the Central Committee of the Romanian Communist Party (RCP),[4] issued

3. The scope of foreign trade is defined in Article 3, Law (no. 1) on Foreign Trade of 1971 as "commercial and economic and technicoscientific cooperation transactions with foreign countries with regard to: sales, purchases, and exchanges of commodities, services, international transportation and forwarding, designing and commissioning of projects, technical assistance and cooperation, sale consignment and warehousing of goods, agencies and commissions, financial and foreign currency operations, insurance, tourism, and, in general, any act or facts of trade, as well as market research, tenders, proceedings, negotiations and agreements to such operations." (*Official Bulletin of the Socialist Republic of Romania*, no. 33 (March 17, 1971).

4. *Directives of the Central Committee of the Romanian Communist Party on the Perfecting of Management and Planning of the National Economy in Keeping with the Conditions of the New Stage of Romania's Socialist Development.* (Bucharest: Agerpres, October 1967.)

in 1967 as a blueprint for a more sophisticated management system, recommended that foreign trade be reorganized to carry out its functions more effectively and, in particular, that the sole responsibility over the sector of the Ministry of Foreign Trade be ended by decentralizing some foreign trade responsibilities to the sectoral ministries, centrals, and producing enterprises. Over the past decade, the government has adopted a series of laws and measures establishing new institutions and delineating the responsibilities of all bodies involved in trade. The most important and comprehensive of the measures was the Law (no. 1) on Foreign Trade of 1971. The present division of responsibilities between the major institutions involved is summarized below.

(a) Council of Ministers. The highest body of state administration, it has general responsibility for administering and controlling international economic relations.

(b) Ministry of Foreign Trade. This Ministry has overall responsibility for planning and implementing foreign trade activities. The major elements include the preparation, in coordination with the SPC, and implementation of the foreign trade plan, which comprises a separate chapter of the five-year plan; the authorization of imports and exports through the issue of licenses; joint responsibility with the State Planning Committee (SPC), Ministry of Finance, National Bank, and Bank of Foreign Trade for working out and securing the balance of payments; negotiation, in collaboration with the Ministry of Foreign Affairs and other interested bodies, of agreements with trading partners; investigation of foreign markets; organization of economic representation through diplomatic missions or trade offices in foreign countries; and general coordination of external economic relations.

(c) Ministry of Finance. This Ministry is responsible for foreign currency and, with the Ministry of Foreign Trade, controls international transactions in which foreign currency is involved.

(d) Bank for Foreign Trade. Established in 1968 as a specialized unit of the External Operations Department of the National Bank, the Bank primarily facilitates trade by organizing trade payments, obtaining domestic and foreign credits, and concluding banking arrangements required domestically and internationally. It administers Romania's foreign exchange reserves and payments agreements (Appendix H).

(e) Ministries. Each sectoral ministry is responsible for coordinating the planning and implementation of external economic relations specific to its sector and for ensuring the fulfillment of its part of the foreign trade plan. The Ministry of Transport has the specific responsibility for overseeing the implementation of the external transport plan.

(f) Centrals, foreign trade enterprises, and productive enterprises. The Law on Foreign Trade widened the category of economic units able to carry out foreign trade, stipulating that trade could be carried out directly by centrals, production enterprises, specialized foreign trade enterprises, units supplying services or goods in foreign countries or to foreign interests in Romania (for example, ARCOM), and any other such economic units that are authorized to trade. In 1969 most specialized foreign trade enterprises previously under the Ministry of Foreign Trade were made the responsibility of their respective sectoral ministries, and since 1971 there have been several reorganizations that have affected both the number of units operating directly in the foreign trade sector and their responsibilities. Since December 1974 foreign trade has been carried out by forty-one specialized foreign trade enterprises (thirty-four under sectoral ministries and seven under industrial centrals) and by export and import bureaus of the ministries and centrals. The foreign trade enterprises, which are jointly responsible to their sectoral ministry and the Ministry of Foreign Trade, are established as separate legal entities with their own management and employees and specific commercial responsibilities established by law. They are required to support all their activities from their revenues and to operate at a profit. At the same time, production enterprises were made directly responsible for their own trade activities, even when they were carried out through the centrals or foreign trade enterprises. Centrals and production enterprises now have responsibilities for preparing a trade plan and for implementing the final trade targets built into the annual plan and handed down from the ministry.

(g) Other bodies. Several other institutions play an important role in Romania's foreign trade. The Chamber of Commerce is responsible for developing relations with foreign firms, economic organizations, and professional associations and for staging trade fairs at home and abroad. It has affiliated with it an Arbitration Commission to settle foreign trade disputes. Also affiliated with the Chamber is Argus, an agency established in 1971, whose original function was to represent foreign firms in Romania, but which has recently moved into assisting firms to set up their own offices and acting as the channel for recruiting Romanian personnel. The State General Inspectorate for Product Quality Control has responsibilities, in cooperation with the ministries, for controlling the quality of goods and services supplied and purchased by Romania in the foreign trade sector. In 1967 the Institute for the Study of International Economic Conjuncture[5] was formed to study the appropriate development of Romania's foreign

5. Renamed in 1977, The Institute of World Economy.

trade, and in 1971 the Romanian Association for Marketing (AROMAR) was established to improve the quality of market research and services for Romanian exports.

Planning process

Foreign trade is planned within the same overall framework as the planning of domestic activities. The five-year plan for the economy contains a separate chapter on foreign trade and payments, which sets out the overall targets for exports and imports and specifies responsibilities and targets for each level of organization. In essence, the central foreign trade plan is a volumetric and financial projection of exports and imports for the five-year period in the field of trade, which constitutes the main part of the overall balance of payments. The five-year plan does not project the balance of payments, but this can be put together from the provisions of the tourist and transport plans and the guidelines for actual capital flows. During the implementation of the five-year plan, balance of payments projections are drawn up for use as management instruments for the overall development of international economic relations.

The planning process for foreign trade occurs simultaneously with that of domestic activities and is essentially similar to the planning for other sectors with a derived demand for goods and services. Each economic unit prepares, as part of its draft plan, projections of export and import needs based on surveys of foreign markets and data on domestic production and demand forecasts. Aggregation of enterprise plans through centrals and ministries to the level of the SPC produces projections of import requirements for the economy as a whole and permits their comparison with the results of the SPC's summary schemes and econometric models. The process of iteration and negotiation at each level of the organizational pyramid produces a final plan, which, after approval, is disaggregated and presented to each level in the form of export targets and import allocations expressed in value and volume terms. Because of the inherent uncertainty of foreign trade, targets in the five-year plan are expressed in general terms. More detailed targets are given in the annual plans.

The overall foreign trade plan is divided into two chapters, covering plans for convertible and nonconvertible currencies separately. Before the 1976–80 Plan, the plan was also divided into separate chapters for socialist, developed market, and developing countries, but no such division is included now. This development—and the fact that it is the total plan, rather than the two chapters, that is divided into import and export plans—illustrates the increasing commercial orientation of foreign trade activities. The import plan is specified by various categories. The most important commodities are designated in volume terms, others are in value terms, and there is also a residual category, not specified by commodity but allocated by value and ministry. The plan also is divided into three categories on the basis of use.

(a) Imports for production include raw materials, designated primarily in volume terms and calculated according to production norms and technical coefficients, and parts and other production inputs, designated in volume or value terms.
(b) Imports for investment include capital goods for specific projects, broken down by project, and capital goods not specified by project, for which a total value is given for each ministry and technical specifications defined.
(c) Imports for final consumption include important goods, for which volumes are specified, and all other goods, for which value terms are used.

The export plan is also broken down into value or volume terms for major commodities. In general, the predominant target for each administrative level is given in value terms, but in certain cases volumetric targets are also given.

In addition to planning foreign trade internally, the Romanian government organizes its economic relations with its trading partners to reduce as much as possible the uncertainty in the sector and to avoid jeopardizing internal development programs that depend on foreign inputs. Romania has conducted most of its trade and payments through specific intercountry agreements. In the past, these agreements were generally bilateral for both trade and payments, but in recent years the payments have tended to become multilateral, payments with nonsocialist countries being made increasingly in convertible currencies. At the end of 1975, Romania had signed 112 general cooperation agreements, 185 sectoral agreements, and 235 joint venture agreements and had many still under negotiation.

The most institutionalized trade agreements signed by Romania are those with socialist countries. They are negotiated bilaterally, for a five-year period, during the preparation of the five-year plan and consist of a general framework agreement supplemented by annual protocols that settle details of purchases and deliveries. The agreements generally contain binding quotas: that is, quotas up to which import and export licenses must be issued. Prices for transactions are set at "negotiated world prices," which are now based on moving averages of international prices adjusted for speculation, fluctuations, and so forth. Settlements for trade under these agreements are carried out in transferable rubles through the International Bank for Economic Cooperation in Moscow. The institution of a multilateral settlement system within the Council for Mutual Economic Assistance (CMEA) means that Romania no longer has to balance trade with each country.

Agreements with nonsocialist countries have involved similar attempts to guide the development of trade along predictable lines, but in general, the stipulations in the agreements have been more indicative than binding. The agreement usually runs for up to five years and provides a framework for trade and, in many cases, for scientific and technological cooperation, joint production and commercial ventures, exploration for raw materials, and technical assistance agreements. Further details are given in the following section.

Foreign Trade and International Economic Relations in the Fifth Plan (1971–75)

The goals set for the development of the Romanian economy between 1971 and 1975 necessitated a further considerable increase in the volume of foreign trade. Continued growth of material production, particularly in industry, generated additional imports of raw materials and capital goods which, in view of Romania's cautious approach toward expanding its external debt, had to be financed largely by increased exports of industrial and agricultural goods. Thus, Romania's participation in world trade during the Fifth Plan, as before, was largely subordinated to the requirements of the domestic economy and was dictated by the insufficiency of domestic resources and raw materials and the inability to supply internally all the sophisticated capital goods and installations required for complex industrialization. As a result, much of foreign trade policy in this period was concerned with developing marketable export goods and with obtaining stable long-term supplies of raw materials and access to industrial technology.

The Law of the Plan projected an increase of 61 to 72 percent in the volume of trade, measured in 1970 prices, during the Fifth Plan compared with the volume achieved during 1966–70. Translated into absolute terms, the target equalled 151 to 160 billion lei valuta. The Plan forecast that imports during the 1971–75 plan period would total approximately 75 billion lei valuta in 1970 prices, an increase of 54 percent compared with the 1966–70 volume measured in current prices. In keeping with the internal development of the economy, it was envisaged that the major elements of import growth would be raw materials and machinery and equipment. The Plan envisaged that raw material imports would increase at approximately the same rate as total imports, whereas purchases of machinery and equipment would more than double.

The Plan established both quantitative and qualitative goals for exports between 1971 and 1975. The target for the growth of exports, 14.3 percent a year, was considerably higher than that of imports and reflected the government's plan to secure a positive trade balance by 1975 in both total and convertible currency trade and to minimize the growth of external debt. In absolute terms, the target implied a volume of exports totalling 85 billion lei valuta during the plan period. The Plan also indicated that there would be changes in the geographic distribution of trade. Although the CMEA countries would remain Romania's largest export market,[6] trade with developed market economies and developing countries was to increase rapidly to finance the increased imports of raw materials and technology. In addition, the Law of the Plan required that the efficiency of exports be increased; all bodies involved in foreign trade were to ensure "the increase in export efficiency, the diversification of the forms of foreign trade, the exploration of the foreign market and the study of conjunctural trends in perspective."[7] The increased efficiency of exports, that is, the improvement of Romania's resource terms of trade, was to be brought about largely by the general increase in productivity of the Romanian economy, reductions in production cost, improved quality, and the availability of more highly processed and technologically advanced goods for export. In particular, it was planned that exports of machinery and equipment, and chemicals (projected to constitute 41 percent of total export value in 1975 compared with 30 percent in 1970) and the products of light industry—notably clothing, footwear, and wood products, all embodying a high degree of added value—would be increased rapidly. Although general improvements in productivity and in quality and sophistication of products provided an important basis for increased efficiency, it is clear, from the measures proposed at the National Conference of the RCP in 1967, that further improvements in efficiency were anticipated from the more efficient organization of foreign trade under the Ministry of Foreign Trade and International Economic Cooperation and also from the more direct exposure of enterprises to the international market (Chapters 3 and 4).

In addition to these policies, development of economic cooperation with

6. Trade with CMEA was planned to increase by 50 percent during the plan period.

7. Law (no. 10) of October 21, 1971 on the Adoption of the Five-Year Plan for 1971–75 for the Economic and Social Development of the Socialist Republic of Romania. Article 24. *Official Bulletin of the Socialist Republic of Romania*, no. 129 (October 21, 1971).

all trading partners was emphasized. The primary purpose of agreements for cooperation was similar to the bilateral trade agreements they in some cases replaced: that is, to introduce a measure of stability and certainty into foreign trade. A further purpose was to provide a framework for joint ventures, cooperation in production, the transfer of technology, and similar forms of interstate cooperation. For imports, emphasis was placed on negotiating long-term contracts for raw materials and for joint exploration and exploitation enterprises, especially in developing countries, to ensure a continuous supply at advantageous terms. Such agreements were also intended to permit the establishment of joint ventures within Romania, to develop economic cooperation, and to introduce advanced technology, modern management techniques, and scientific research into the Romanian economy. For exports, the foreign trade plan envisaged the establishment of joint production and commercial ventures in other countries, as a way to export Romanian-made machinery and equipment and technology. Although the major emphasis during the fifth plan period was clearly the development of widespread cooperation with the developed market economies and developing countries, Romania also was to continue to expand its economic relations with all socialist countries, including CMEA members.

Trade performance

The total volume of foreign trade between 1970 and 1975 increased from 22.9 to 53.1 billion lei valuta in current prices, an average annual growth rate of 18.4 percent. Imports increased 2.26 times from 11.8 to 26.5 billion lei valuta and exports 2.39 times from 11.1 to 26.5 billion lei valuta over the plan period, average annual growth rates of 17.7 and 19.0 percent, respectively (Table SA4.1). As a result of the faster growth of exports, Romania succeeded in balancing its overall trade in 1975 (Table 7.1). Measured in the same terms as the Five-Year Plan target, the volume of trade during 1971–75 was 106 percent higher than in 1966–70. An immediate comparison between achievements and the targeted increase of 61 to 72 percent over the 1966–70 volume is not possible, since the former is expressed in current prices and the latter in 1970 prices. In the absence of price indexes relating specifically to Romanian trade, it is difficult to separate volume and price effects, especially for trade with non-CMEA countries, and to assess Romanian trade performance during the period accurately by using these aggregate data.

There are two further reasons why an assessment at the aggregate level is not useful. First, Romania participates in two discrete trade areas, the nonconvertible currency area of socialist countries and some trade with develop-

Table 7.1. *Volume of Trade, by Convertible and Nonconvertible Areas, 1970–75*
(millions of lei valuta)

Item	*1970*	*1971*	*1972*	*1973*	*1974*	*1975*
			Total trade			
Exports	11,105	12,606	14,373	18,576	24,226	26,547
Imports	11,761	12,616	14,465	17,418	25,563	26,548
Balance	−656	−10	−92	+1,158	−1,337	−1
			Convertible currency trade			
Exports		4,980	5,950	8,181	13,016	14,110
Imports		5,285	6,348	8,509	14,637	14,661
Balance		−305	−398	−328	−1,621	−551
			Nonconvertible currency trade			
Exports		7,626	8,423	10,395	11,209	12,438
Imports		7,330	8,117	8,909	10,927	11,888
Balance		+296	+306	+1,486	+282	+550

Source: Ministry of Finance; data supplied during discussions with the authors.

ing countries and the convertible currency area encompassing most trade with developed market economies and the developing countries. As the tables on trade balances and commodity structure of trade show,[8] Romania's trading position in the two areas (and within the convertible currency area, its position in relation to the developing countries and the developed market economies) differed considerably. Second, the state's monopoly in foreign trade means that the trade figures reflect changes in trade policy in response to both internal and international circumstances. Thus, the rest of this section attempts to assess performance of foreign trade during the Fifth Plan by examining more disaggregated figures.

The major features of Romania's trade are shown in Tables 7.1, 7.2, and SA4.1 to SA4.8. Between 1970 and 1973, the growth of trade proceeded at a fairly rapid rate, although, as Table 7.2 shows, somewhat less rapidly than projected in the annual plans.[9] Average annual growth rates for exports and imports were 10.8 and 8.2 percent, respectively. This permitted a reduction in the overall deficit from its 1970 level of 656 million

8. Tables 7.1, 7.2, SA4.6, SA4.7, and SA4.8.

9. Since the targets for foreign trade in the annual plan are cast in estimated current prices, whereas achievements are in actual prices, a shortfall in performance may, in principle, result from either inaccurate price predictions or from lower volumes of trade.

Table 7.2. *Volume of Trade with Developing Countries and with Developed Market Economies, 1970–75*
(millions of lei valuta)

Item	*1970*	*1971*	*1972*	*1973*	*1974*	*1975*
			Total trade with developing countries and developed market economies			
Exports	4,652.3	5,448.8	6,351.6	8,966.8	13,726.0	14,333.6
Imports	5,417.8	5,825.3	6,995.7	9,173.9	15,561.7	14,990.0
Balance	−765.5	−376.5	−644.1	−207.1	−1,835.7	−656.4
			Trade with developed market economies			
Exports	3,284.5	3,992.6	4,549.0	5,980.2	9,455.4	8,225.0
Imports	4,534.0	4,880.6	5,767.7	7,212.1	12,108.5	10,762.3
Balance	−1,249.5	−888.0	−1,218.7	−1,231.9	−2,653.1	−2,537.3
			Trade with developing countries			
Exports	1,367.8	1,456.2	1,802.6	2,986.6	4,270.6	6,108.6
Imports	883.8	944.7	1,228.0	1,961.8	3,453.2	4,227.7
Balance	+484.0	+511.5	+574.6	+1,024.8	+817.4	+1,880.9

Sources: Ministry of Finance and *Anuarul Statistic*, various issues.

lei valuta, and in 1973 the economy actually had a surplus of 1,158 million lei valuta. Furthermore, Romania's trading position with each trading area improved.[10] Trade with socialist countries increased by almost 40 percent between 1970 and 1973, compared with a target growth of 50 percent between 1970 and 1975. The greater growth of exports (49 percent against only 30 percent for imports) increased Romania's surplus in nonconvertible currency trade. The surplus with developing countries also increased, the growth rate of imports (mainly crude oil, minerals and metals, and raw materials) exceeding marginally that of exports (122 percent compared with 118 percent). In its trade with developed market economies, however, Romania reduced its deficit only a little from 1,250 million lei valuta in 1970 to 1,230 million lei valuta in 1973; in that period exports rose by 82 percent, whereas imports increased by only 60 percent.

Trends in trade were much less favorable, however, in the remaining two years of the plan period. In 1974 the surplus on total trade was replaced

10. Care is required in interpreting the figures for trade with developing and developed market economies, since exports and imports are categorized in Romania by country of payment rather than by country of origin or destination. Thus, trade figures quoted by Romania for countries with important commodity exchanges may not equal those countries' own figures.

by a deficit of 1.3 billion lei valuta, since exports grew less rapidly than planned and imports increased considerably faster than anticipated. The causes were both internal and external. The growth of exports, 30.6 percent compared with an annual plan target of 43.5 percent, was constrained by the harvest failure, which reduced agriculture's exportable surplus, and by the world recession, which severely affected the growth of exports of machinery and equipment, textiles, and garments. In addition, trade restrictions were imposed on important Romanian exports such as beef, textiles, shoes, and fertilizer. Large increases in the price of oil and other raw materials and of machinery and equipment raised the cost of imports substantially, and the total import bill increased by 46.8 percent compared with the plan target of 38.8 percent. Consequently, the favorable developments of the previous three years were reversed. The trade deficit with the developed market economies grew to 2.65 billion lei valuta, as imports rose by 68 percent, whereas exports increased by only 58 percent; the surplus with the socialist countries decreased to less than half a billion lei valuta, in part because export goods were shifted to convertible currency markets. In trade with the developing countries as a group, Romania's trade balance deteriorated only slightly, partly because the prices of exports rose to compensate for the increased cost of oil and other raw material imports and partly because of the trading and cooperative agreements established with many developing countries during the fourth and fifth plan periods.

In 1975 the foreign trade sector experienced further problems. The world recession continued to limit demand for Romanian goods, especially textiles, machinery, and wood products, and less foreign exchange than anticipated was earned, because international market prices (particularly of chemicals, cement, and timber) stopped rising. Internally, severe floods reduced the planned supply of export goods, mainly from agriculture, but also from some industrial sectors, by 1.1 to 1.2 billion lei valuta. Although in 1974 the large deficit had been financed through capital inflows without imposing restraints on imports in 1975, the government dealt with the unfavorable developments by accepting the need to reduce or to delay some planned imports, particularly from the convertible currency area, and by running down stocks. As a result, imports grew by only 3.9 percent, and, with an export growth of 9.6 percent, the overall trade account was practically in balance. The deficit with the developed market economies was reduced by a small amount to 2.54 billion lei valuta, with both exports and imports falling by 13 and 11 percent, respectively. In trade with developing countries, Romania's surplus increased rapidly, reflecting further success in expanding exports of machinery and equipment and industrial consumer goods to the oil-producing countries. Exports to developing countries increased 41 percent in 1975, whereas imports increased by 22 percent. Trade with socialist countries continued to grow steadily, exports and imports increasing by 16.4 and 15.5 percent, respectively.

Thus, in the last year of the plan period, the foreign trade sector registered a lower growth rate than planned, because internal and external factors inhibited the growth of exports. In some cases, this led to a decrease in imports of machinery and equipment; in others, to the substitution of imports from CMEA for goods from developed market economies; and, in yet other cases, to the substitution of local investment goods.

During the fifth plan period, substantial changes occurred in the geographic distribution and commodity structure of trade. In current price terms, the weight of socialist countries in Romania's foreign trade diminished. In 1970, 58.1 percent of exports were sold to, and 53.9 percent of imports were obtained from, this source. In 1974 the percentages had fallen to 43.3 and 39.1 percent, respectively, before rising again in 1975 to 46.0 and 43.6 percent, respectively. In the meantime, both developed market economies and developing countries had assumed more important positions, with the growth of the latter the most striking. Although the proportion of exports to and imports from developed countries had risen from 29.6 to 31.0 percent and from 38.6 to 40.5 percent of the total, respectively, trade with developing countries increased over four times in current price terms. A radical change in the level and relative importance of trade with the developing countries occurred with the oil price increase. In 1974, Romania's trade with them rose by 56 percent (exports increasing 43 percent and imports by 76 percent). A further increase in total trade of 34 percent in 1975 (43 percent for exports and 22 percent for imports) meant that, in that year, total trade with developing countries was 19.5 percent of overall trade, more than double the 1970 proportion.

The changes in geographic distribution of Romania's trade, however, were less striking once the effect of different price changes within convertible and nonconvertible trade is accounted for. Approximate calculations using world price indexes suggest that, measured in constant prices, the socialist countries maintained their share of trade with Romania and that the major change in distribution was the declining share of trade with the developed market economies and, correspondingly, the rapid growth of trade with the developing countries. Examination of the foreign trade data indicates that, although the oil price increase caused the terms of trade to move heavily against Romania[11] (notwithstanding the benefits Romania derived from

11. An analysis of Romania's trade with developing countries carried out by the World Bank suggests that a bundle of exports capable of purchasing 100 lei worth of imports from developing countries in 1970 would obtain only 60 lei worth in 1975.

price increases for its chemical fertilizer, petroleum products, and energy exports), Romania took full advantage of its economic and political relations with developing countries in general, and the oil-producing countries in particular, by exchanging large amounts of machinery and equipment, food and raw materials for food production, and industrial consumer goods for the oil it required.

The commodity structure of trade also continued to change between 1971 and 1975, especially in exports where the changes implied some success in implementing plan targets for improving the efficiency of exports (Table SA4.4). The structural changes reflected both the relative price changes and the changing needs and productive resources of the economy. In aggregate, the structure of imports changed little during the period, comprising almost exclusively imports of capital goods and raw materials. The proportion of capital goods in total imports declined from 40.3 percent in 1970 to 34.7 percent in 1975. The decrease occurred in 1974 and 1975, reflecting the foreign exchange constraints in those years and the increased ability of the Romanian economy to provide its own capital goods. The proportion of fuels, minerals, and metals rose from 30.4 to 38.2 percent during the same period, not only because of the increased price of crude oil (and increased volume of its import), but also because of increased requirements of metals and minerals. If imports of other raw materials are included, the proportion of raw material imports rose from 42.8 percent in 1970 to 52.0 percent in 1975 (Table SA4.5).

The changes in the structure of exports mirrored to a great extent the progress of industrialization in Romania and also the limitations of the process. Industrial goods (machinery and equipment, chemicals, and industrial consumer goods) continued to increase their proportion of exports, increasing from 47.9 to 52.2 percent. Although the growth of industrial consumer good exports was no greater than the growth of exports as a whole, machinery and equipment and chemicals enjoyed the highest growth rates, their combined share of exports rising from 29.8 percent in 1970 to 36.1 percent in 1975 (but falling short of the plan target of a 41 percent share in 1975). Correspondingly, the share of raw materials in exports declined. The decline in the share of exports of foodstuffs and agricultural raw materials reflected the growth of domestic processing industries and the relatively low growth rate in agriculture, whereas the slight decline in the share of fuels, metals, and minerals masked the offsetting effects of price increases and volume decreases as domestic needs took a higher proportion of supply.

The structure of exports and imports also varied by trading area, demonstrating Romania's position in the world economy (Tables SA4.7

and SA4.8) In its trade with developing countries, Romania sold machinery and equipment and other industrial products in return for raw materials. In its trade with socialist countries, Romania supplied capital goods and consumer products in return for capital goods and raw materials. In its trade with the developed market economies, Romania stood as a developing country, exporting raw materials and simple industrial manufactures in return for sophisticated capital equipment and raw materials.

Cooperation agreements and joint ventures

In recent years Romania has become a strong advocate of international and technical cooperation; this represents an important change from previous periods when cooperation focused mainly on CMEA. The diversity of these relations is exemplified by Romania's participation since 1971 in GATT and since 1972 in the IMF and the World Bank and by the signature of some 250 agreements covering various forms of cooperation to develop raw material and energy supplies, for access to advanced technology, and to stimulate Romania's exports of goods and technology.

Romanian cooperation with foreign countries and companies was intensified during the Fifth Plan, both within Romania and in developing and developed countries. It was abroad, however, where most headway was made through partnerships in the construction of industrial units, provision of Romanian equipment and know-how mostly in geologic exploration, provision of turnkey projects, establishment of joint production and commercial ventures, and, last but not least, in the field of technical assistance.

The erection of industrial plants abroad has been an important instrument of export promotion for machinery and equipment, and the composition of such projects gives some idea of the relative strengths of Romanian equipment manufactures. In the past ten years, Romania has taken part in the construction of over fifty industrial units, of which about ten were in the chemical industry, seven in petroleum and mining, seven in wood processing and building materials, and six in the field of mechanical and electrical engineering. From the available limited project list, it appears that Romanian efforts were concentrated on countries in the Middle East and Asia. In the field of chemicals and petroleum, plants were set up or are being set up for the production of sulfuric acid and fertilizers (Turkey, Egypt), sodium products (Iran, Egypt), and for oil refining (Syria, India, Pakistan). Other projects included wood processing plants (Iran, Sri Lanka, People's Republic of the Congo), cement works (Syria), cotton mills

(Sudan, People's Republic of the Congo), power plants (Egypt, Philippines), and several production and assembly plants for transport equipment, notably tractors (Iran, Egypt, but also Canada, the United States). More recently, Romania has participated in geologic exploration, concentrated mainly in the Middle East, Africa, and Latin America and in covering exploration for phosphates, a wide range of ferrous and nonferrous ores, and oil. Many projects are at present being constructed or are under negotiation.

Romania's capital participation in joint ventures abroad rose substantially between 1970 and 1975. Romania is currently[12] a shareholder in twenty-eight production enterprises abroad[13] and in thirty-five commercial joint ventures. Joint ventures abroad have various purposes. Probably most of them are geared toward increasing and broadening raw material supplies of Romanian industry and include both production and shipping companies. Others have been established to promote Romanian exports and to gain a foothold in new markets. This type of joint company focuses on production and export of Romanian products and is found both in developing countries and in some industrial countries. Others have the more general objective of trade promotion, such as the joint banking companies set up in Egypt, the United Kingdom, France, and the Federal Republic of Germany.

Of the twenty-eight production-oriented joint ventures, eleven are in mining; seven in agro-industries, including cotton; four in the exploitation of tropical hardwood; two in light industry; and one each in machine building, construction materials, rubber, and transport. The remaining three companies are servicing and assembling enterprises. Within the total number, Romania also is participating in international consortia to exploit iron ore in Gabon and Guinea and natural rubber in Liberia. Commercial joint ventures serve mainly marketing objectives. They usually provide Romania with access to distribution and servicing facilities for its exports and are important in establishing a more permanent presence in foreign markets. Participation in commercial firms abroad enables Romanian products to be sold through already existing distribution networks (normally those of the partner firm), to keep adequate stocks of spare parts, and to perform essential servicing jobs. Romania has established such commercial partnerships in western Europe, North America, and in some developing countries. Romania has also increased its exports of technical and consultancy services, particularly in chemicals, power, and petroleum refining through the agencies RomConsult and ROMENERGY.

12. Since October 1977.

13. Romania is also participating in three ventures in cooperation with socialist countries.

International economic and technical cooperation within Romania has also developed quickly, especially within the past two years. No joint ventures with CMEA members have yet been established, although at least one is under negotiation, but considerably more progress has been made in joint ventures with nonsocialist countries. Following the formulation of a legal framework for establishing joint companies in Romania (Decree no. 424 of November 2, 1972), Romania has established up to the end of 1977, eight production joint ventures in industry and transport, of which three have begun production. The formation of two more such ventures has been announced, but they have not been formally established yet. The eight ventures established so far operate, or will be operating, in the production and marketing of chemical fibers, reducing gears, EDP equipment, electronic-medical equipment, precision chains, feedstuff, and passenger cars and in the operation of marine transportation. The latest two ventures will produce aircraft and petrochemicals. The foreign capital participation, limited to a maximum of 49 percent, has come from Italy, the Federal Republic of Germany, the United States, France, Austria, Japan, and Libya. Operating in areas of advanced technological requirements, the companies are expected to contribute to increasing Romania's export potential by providing new production lines and by upgrading existing ones. Moreover, training programs in these plants are to contribute to the dissemination of technical and organizational know-how. (Details of capital plans associated with these ventures are given below.)

Another form of foreign cooperation with Romanian firms within Romania, more important so far than joint ventures, takes place through licensing and technical assistance agreements. Some cases of major effect are generally known, such as the licensing and assistance agreements between Renault and the Dacia Automobile Works and between the Swedish ASEA and the Electro-puters Works (diesel-electric locomotives). On the whole, however, little information is available on this subject.

Invisibles

Romania recorded a deficit on invisible transactions as a whole throughout the fifth plan period, as a result of developments in both trade and capital accounts. An increasing surplus in tourism (Chapter 15) was more than offset by net payments for transport, telecommunications, and other services, particularly interest on external debt. The expansion of Romania's trade was accompanied by a rapid expansion in payments to other countries for transport services, whereas the growth of receipts was constrained by the limited growth of Romania's merchant fleet (Chapter 13). Similarly, net payments for other services grew over the period as interest payments on foreign borrowings were made.

Romania ran a small surplus on invisibles with the nonconvertible currency area that was insufficient to offset the deficit with the convertible currency area. The surplus, however, diminished during the plan period from 200 million lei valuta in 1971 to 75 million in 1975. This reflected both growth in Romanian tourist expenditures in eastern Europe and the gradual transition from surplus to deficit in transport services. The deficit with the convertible currency area doubled between 1971 and 1975, from 345 to 750 million lei valuta. Deficits in transport and other services increased steadily throughout the period, offsetting the surplus on tourism. A major feature of the latter was the very slow growth of tourist payments to convertible currency countries.

Capital flows and external debt

In overall terms, Romania was a net importer of capital during the fifth plan period, thereby financing a large part of its deficit on trade and services and increasing the size of its external debt. An overall assessment of capital flows and external debt, however, is not very useful, since Romania's position with convertible and nonconvertible currency areas differed greatly. With the convertible currency area, Romania was a capital importer, whereas with the nonconvertible currency area, it had a net capital outflow, which, in fact, consisted of goods.

Between 1971 and 1973 the inflow of medium- and long-term capital from the convertible currency area was sufficient to cover the deficit on current account, to repay credits made available to Romania between 1966 and 1970, and to permit a restructuring of foreign debt. It was government policy during this period to liquidate the outstanding short-term debt. The capital flow and external debt figures show that the policy was successfully carried out to the extent that less than 700 million lei valuta of short-term debt remained at the end of 1975. In 1974 medium- and long-term capital inflows increased greatly. The inflow was required to finance the large current account deficit and to reduce further short-term debt. In 1975 the inflow declined to 4.1 billion lei valuta, as attempts were made to reduce imports of goods. The net inflow also decreased substantially, since the size of annual capital repayments continued to increase. A further feature of the capital account between 1971 and 1975 was the increasing importance of medium- and long-term credits extended by Romania to finance its exports of machinery and equipment. The growth of such credits was limited to some extent, however, by Romania's ability to exchange its exports directly for crude oil and raw materials, particularly in its trade with developing countries.

In all years of the plan period, the trade surplus with the nonconvertible currency area was offset by a net capital outflow, which constituted chiefly repayments of principal on medium- and long-term loans (given during previous plan periods to finance investment projects) and credits extended by Romania on short-, medium-, and long-term to finance exports to developing country trading partners. Capital inflows were relatively small, comprising mainly loans from the International Investment Bank (IIB) and repayments of export credits advanced by Romania in previous years.

The implications of the capital movements for Romania's external debt were that, between 1972 and 1975, total external debt almost doubled. Most of the debt was held in convertible currencies. Repayments by Romania in the early years of the plan period reduced nonconvertible currency debt, and, by the end of 1975, it was a small amount only, the largest part being short-term. Romania now appears to be a creditor country in the nonconvertible currency areas.

Between 1972 and 1975, Romania's convertible currency debt also almost doubled. At the end of 1975 all but 4 percent was medium- and long-term debt, reflecting the successful attempts to reduce the level of short-term debt. Almost all of the external debt (about 80 percent) was suppliers' and financial credits from major trading partners, particularly Germany, Italy, the United Kingdom, and France. Of this, a large portion, about 40 percent, was guaranteed suppliers' credits. Almost alone of CMEA countries, Romania has not greatly expanded borrowing from U.S. and European banks. In 1975 total net borrowing from such sources totaled US$670 million,[14] approximately US$80 million less than in 1974. The term structure of suppliers' credits, many of which are government guaranteed, is five to eight years at 7 to 8 percent, whereas financial credits have maturities of five to six years at 8 to 9 percent. At the end of 1975 approximately half of the debt was due for repayment within three years, and all but 15 percent within five years. In 1975 the debt service ratio was 17 percent, approximately the same as it had been throughout the plan period, since trade receipts and debt repayments both grew rapidly.

In the past, the Romanian government has displayed a cautious approach to external debt, as demonstrated by the debt service ratio and attempts both to improve the structure of debt and to expand exports as rapidly as possible.

14. The sources of these data were *East-West Markets* (April 5, 1976) and *East-West*, no. 150 (March 25, 1976). *East-West Markets* (October 4, 1976) suggested that total indebtedness to western banks at the end of 1975 was approximately U.S.$1 billion.

It has also tried to diversify sources of borrowing and to negotiate long-term loans. The operations of the Franco-Romanian and Anglo-Romanian Banks were expanded during the fifth plan period, and in early 1977, the creation of a German-Romanian Bank was announced. As discussed above, long-term equity capital has been secured in this form of joint ventures; so far, the six ventures that have progressed beyond the signing stage have led to an inflow of only US$10 to 15 million. The ventures announced during 1977 will have a far more substantial capital inflow; OLT-CIT, the venture with Citroen to produce passenger cars, will involve a total transfer of some US$250 million. Even larger flows are expected as a result of an agreement with Kuwait, still to be signed, to construct a petrochemical complex costing US$1.25 million.

Furthermore, the government attempted to secure capital from three new sources: the multilateral agencies (IMF and the World Bank), bilateral sources including the Organization of Petroleum Exporting Countries (OPEC), and the Eurocurrency market. Romania joined the IMF and the World Bank in 1972. By October 1977, Romania's gross borrowings from the IMF stood at US$363.5 million (not including the gold tranche), with a further US$45.7 million of the latest standby arrangement undrawn. Romania became an active borrower from the World Bank in 1974, and, between then and 1977, secured loans totaling US$697 million. So far, the World Bank remains the most important source of long-term funds available to Romania, and only limited progress has been made in tapping other sources. In 1975 a US$100 million loan was negotiated from Kuwait as part of a general cooperation agreement; the loan carries a 9.4 percent interest rate with a maturity of eight years and a grace period of three years. In the same year, the U.S. Eximbank, having suspended lending in 1974 following loans of US$40 million, approved a US$22 million loan to finance machinery imports. The eight-year loan carries an interest rate of 8.25 percent. Romania has also borrowed on the Eurocurrency market. A small initial borrowing of some US$6 million was made in 1974 to finance the first joint venture, Resita-Renk. In 1976 arrangements were made to borrow US$50 million, but the loan was canceled because the terms were not acceptable to the government. Subsequently, in early 1977 a US$50 million loan was successfully floated, at a rate of 1.25 percent above LIBOR, and an additional US$75 million loan was negotiated in April.

In conclusion, Romania has been largely successful in financing its current account deficit with the convertible currency area through capital inflows, and it has improved the structure of outstanding debt. It has been less successful, however, in diversifying the sources of its debt, especially at the long-term end of the market where the World Bank remains the main lender. As a result, most of Romania's outstanding debt remains in the form of medium-term suppliers and financial credits.

Balance of payments and international reserves

As a result of the trade and capital movements described above, Romania ran a deficit on its overall balance of payments in three of the five plan years, but in no year was the deficit significant in relation to the size of transactions. It is more instructive, however, to consider separately the balance of payments results for convertible and nonconvertible currency areas. The convertible balance was in deficit for three of the five years—1971, 1973, and 1975. In 1971, 1972, and 1974, capital inflows more or less offset the deficit in current account, whereas the large deficits of 1973, in particular, and of 1975 were offset by monetary movements, chiefly by borrowings from the IMF. As a result, Romania's convertible currency reserves remained fairly constant over the period, although measured in terms of the import bill, they declined markedly. Although this decline is not as significant as in market economies in view of the Romanian state's monopoly over trade, it does indicate the scarcity of convertible foreign exchange.

The nonconvertible currency balance was in deficit for four of the five years, capital outflows exceeding the current account deficit in all but 1973. Monetary movement adjustments were made through payment agreements with each trading partner.

8

Human Resources—Population, Manpower Planning, Education, and Training

According to the census of January 1977, Romania's population totaled 21.6 million. The population pyramid is well structured, with about 25 percent of the people fourteen years or younger and about 10 percent sixty-four years or older. (The 1975 population pyramid is given in Figure 8.1.) Life expectancy is seventy years.

Population

For more than a decade, the government has been strongly in favor of a high birthrate; its policy has been to improve the age structure of the population and to meet the expected needs of the economy for labor in the late 1980s. At that time, the demand for manpower in a rapidly expanding industrial sector will no longer be able to be met by transfers from the agricultural sector.

In the early postwar period, and especially between 1949 and the mid-1950s, the birth and death rates had declined moderately; population growth then was approximately 1.3 percent a year. Birth rates, after peaking at 27 a thousand in 1949, also began to decline gradually. A decline in birth rates continued for the next ten years, encouraged by government legislation that made abortion readily available. By 1966 it had reached the low point of 14.3 a thousand, with population growth down to 0.7 percent. At this point the government reversed its demographic policy.

The new pronatalist program was wide-ranging. Abortions were severely

Figure 8.1. *Population Pyramid, 1966, 1975*

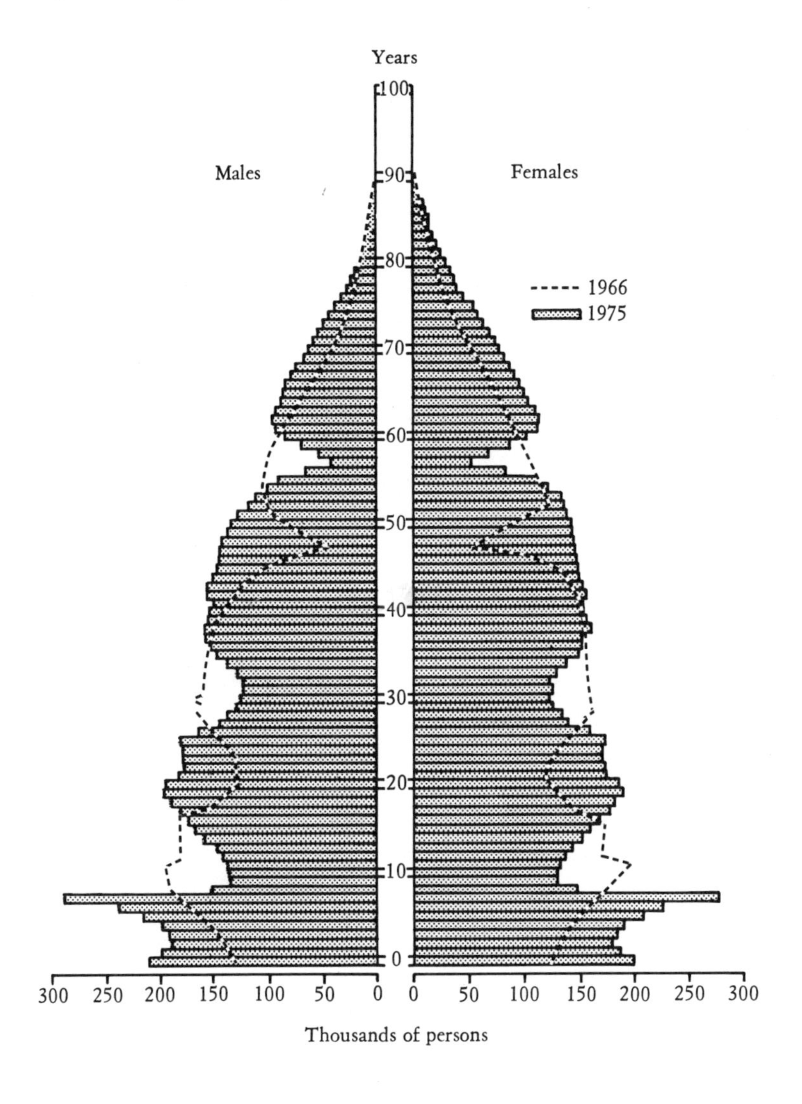

restricted, child payments were increased, and extra allowances were given to families with more than five children. There were also special tax concessions to parents. A liberal maternity leave policy during pregnancy and for child raising guaranteed 80 percent of wages and full credit for seniority.

The policy had an immediate impact. In one year, 1966–67, the birth rate nearly doubled from 14.3 to more than 27.4 a thousand; it eventually stabilized at 20 a thousand. The growth of the population rose to slightly more than 1 percent a year, the approximate rate currently prevailing.

A new population census, the first since 1966, was taken in January 1977. Significant new detailed demographic data are expected to be available in 1979. In the meantime, it is useful to look at the United Nations population estimate issued in May 1975. Using their high variant population projection (with an annual population growth of 1.1 percent), total population is estimated at 28 million in the year 2000. (Even this high variant projection of 28 million is 2 million under present Romanian estimates for that year.) Table 8.1 compares composition by urban-rural residence, as well as by sex and age, for the years 1975 and 2000.

Table 8.1. *Population and Demographic Characteristics, 1975 and 2000*

	1975 Actual	*2000 United Nations estimate*
Total (millions)	21.25	28.0
Urban (percent)	43	63
Rural (percent)	57	37
Sex (percent)		
Male	49	50
Female	51	50
Age (percent)		
0–14	25	27.6
15–64	65	60.8
65 and over	10	11.5

Sources: Data for 1975 from *Anuarul Statistic al Republicii Socialiste Romania* (Bucharest: Directia Centrala de Statistica, published yearly); data for 2000 from United Nations Secretariat, Department of Economic and Social Affairs, Population Division, *Selected World Demographic Indicators by Countries, 1950–2000* (New York: United Nations, May 1975).

The most substantive trend projected here is that of an increasing urban population (over half of it will be urban by 1982) and the increasing proportion of the population fourteen years and younger and sixty-five and over. The dependency ratio is expected to increase to about 644 a thousand, and life expectancy should reach seventy-two years.

Urbanization

The changing pattern of urbanization after 1950 is best illustrated by comparing it with the population movement in earlier years.[1] During 1930–48, total urban population increased by 22 percent, at an annual growth rate roughly equal to the national population growth rate (Table SA1.4). Of this 662,000 increase, 60 percent was concentrated in the capital city, Bucharest. During the later period of more rapid urbanization, 1948–75, when urban population increased by 147 percent, Bucharest's population increase was substantial, but its share of the total urban growth declined dramatically to 12 percent. No other city approached its scale, however. In 1975 the size of Bucharest was 7.1 times that of the next largest city, Cluj-Napoca.

In the late 1940s the government instituted a policy to curb migration to the bigger cities (although these later were referred to as "closed cities," they were not really closed, but entry into them was restricted). The policy is considered to have been successful. It continues to the present day, but in more recent years, it has become more closely linked to the dispersion of employment opportunities outside the metropolitan areas. One measure of its success is the higher proportion of rural migrants in small towns in 1973 than twenty-five years earlier. Although the proportion of population living in urban areas increased from 23 to 43 percent, the number of districts that were more than 25 percent urbanized nearly tripled. The largest segment of the population, 54 percent, lived in judets that were 25–50 percent urbanized (Table SA1.7).

Migration, rather than differences in birthrates, accounts for the character and extent of urbanization within Romania. Actually, it was not until 1974 that the urban birthrate caught up with and passed the rural. A study of the seven largest urban areas (Table SA1.8) provides a detailed analysis

1. In Romania, urban, semiurban, and rural areas are defined by law and not by a common statistical denominator. This makes comparisons of migrant flows with those of other countries very difficult.

Figure 8.2. *Internal Migration Flows, 1968–73*
(percentage)

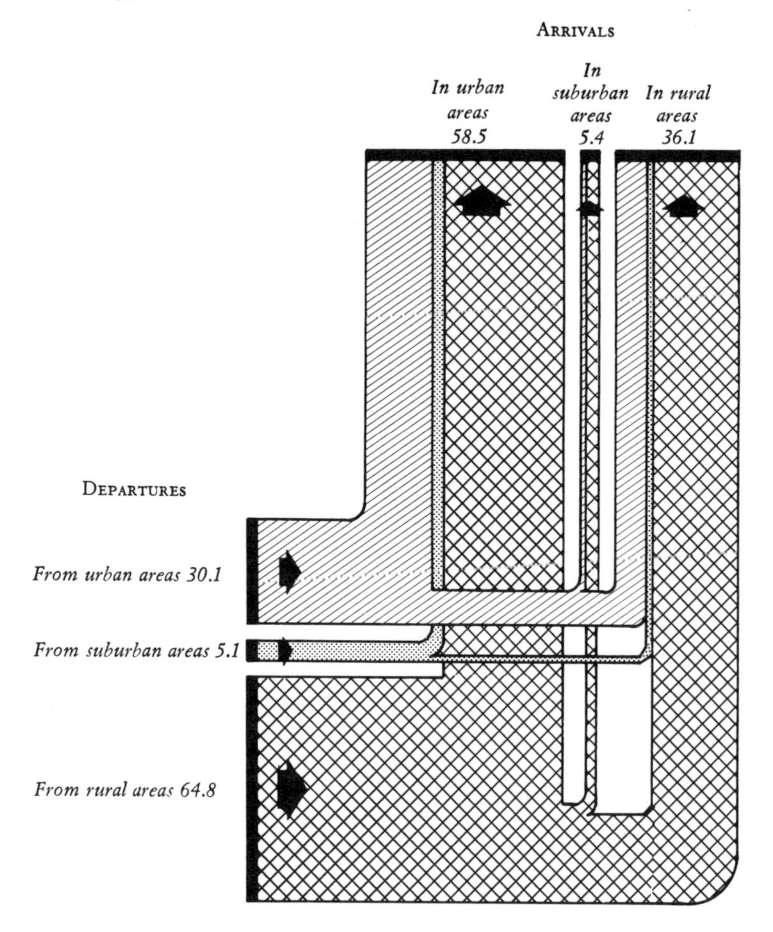

Note: The percentage relate to the total migration flow of 1,885,597 persons between 1968 and 1973

of the population influx during the entire period, 1930–73. One of the more interesting findings is that in 1966 almost 60 percent of the population in these seven centers was born elsewhere. Detailed evidence of the size and direction of migratory flows during 1968–73 is shown in Figure 8.2 and in Table SA1.9.

Of the 1,885,597 migrants from one locality to another, the rural-urban stream was dominant. About two-thirds of the migrants were from rural areas, and, of these, 60 percent headed for urban centers. The urbanization of the country, however, has lagged behind the growth in industrial employment. Consequently, although less than 40 percent of its labor force is presently employed in agriculture, about 57 percent of the people continue to live in rural areas.

The pattern of age distribution among migrants remained much the same during this period. The migration rates from rural areas to urban centers were highest among those between twenty and twenty-four years old (Table SA1.10). Roughly 60 percent of those arriving in urban areas were between fifteen and twenty-nine years old. Urban net immigration—the balance between departures and arrivals—rose steadily from 9.9 a thousand urban residents in 1968 to 15.3 a thousand in 1973. Correspondingly, rural areas have had a greater net population loss: from 6.3 to 9.8 a thousand. Variance in the rate of arrivals from other urban areas did not influence the total urban migration balance, and the rate of immigration from suburban areas has remained constant. This suggests that virtually all of the increase in the urban migratory balance has resulted from an increase in the rate of rural-urban migration.

The migratory pattern is unlike that of many other countries in which older people leave the cities for rural areas. On the contrary, the net rate of migration into the urban areas has increased for those between fifty-five and fifty-seven years old and again for those sixty years and older. It is in the middle years—from twenty-five to fifty-four—that there is a steady decline in urban influx. This may possibly be attributed to the effect of the government's regional industrialization policy.

Table 8.2 shows the net immigration by sex within the five districts with the largest gain in population. Apparently, women have been much more on the move than men, especially to the capital city, Bucharest. A partial explanation for this is the rapid rise in the education of rural women—from 25 percent of total enrollments in 1950 to 50 percent in 1973. Finding themselves better equipped educationally, women may have more persistently sought employment in the fast-growing urban centers. Undoubtedly, many nonworking women have also followed male heads of households who had migrated and settled in new urban jobs.

Table 8.2. *Immigration by Sex in the Five Districts with Highest Population Gain, 1968–73*
(per 1,000 residents)

Sex	*Arad*	*Brasov*	*Bucharest*	*Constanta*	*Timis*
Male	2.6	2.6	11.5	3.2	3.2
Female	2.7	3.4	15.1	4.4	4.5

Source: Anuarul Demografic al Republicii Socialiste Romania (Bucharest: Central Statistics Office and National Demographic Commission, 1974).

Labor Force

Total employment increased from 8.4 million in 1950 to 10.2 million in 1975 (Table SA1.11), at an average annual rate of 0.8 percent. This is lower than the population growth rate, which is explained below. As a result of the government's rapid growth and full employment strategies, employment in the state sector has expanded rapidly. In state-salaried agricultural and nonagricultural activities, employment tripled between 1950 and 1975, from 2.1 to 6.3 million.

Growth and structure of employment

Table 8.3 shows the growth of the labor force and the dynamic changes that have taken place in its structure, paralleling the transformation of the economy from a predominantly agrarian to an industrialized one.

During the past twenty-five years, industry has generated about 2 million jobs and has become the most important source of employment in Romania. Growing at an average annual rate of 5.1 percent during 1951–75, industrial employment rose from 0.8 million in 1950 to 2.8 million in 1975. The emerging job opportunities were filled largely by recruiting agricultural and nonagricultural labor, predominantly people under twenty-five years old with no prior job experience in industry. Although, since the 1948 education reform, the educational system has been increasingly oriented toward meeting the training requirements of the growing economy, particularly during 1950–60 and in some industrial subsectors, the demand for trained manpower was not satisfied by the available supply, and extensive on-the-job training and in-plant short training courses had to be organized to compensate for the excess demand of skilled labor.

Government policies have deliberately sought to mobilize female labor for industrial work, particularly during the past decade. As a result, female

Table 8.3. *Growth and Structure of Employment, 1950–75*

Sector	*1950*	*1960*	*1970*	*1975*	*Growth index, 1975 (1950 = 100)*
Total employment (thousands of persons)	8,377.2	9,537.7	9,875.0	10,150.8	121
Agricultural employment (percent)[a]	74	66	49	34	62
Industrial employment (percent)[b]	19	26	39	49	316
Services employment (percent)[c]	7	8	12	13	227

a. Includes agriculture and forestry.
b. Includes industry, building, transport, telecommunications, and trade.
c. Includes municipal services, education, art and culture, public health, social assistance, physical culture, and science and scientific research administrations.
Source: Anuarul Statistic, various issues.

employment in industry increased from 375,200 in 1961 to 534,100 in 1967. Its expansion during the past decade brought it to over 1 million in 1975. In 1975 about 36 percent of the total industrial labor force was women. Industry now employs more women than does any other branch of the state sector of the economy.

The intensity of employment generation in industry had resulted in a rapidly growing demand for physical and social infrastructure and for additional social services. This demand has often been greater than the supply, causing a considerable strain on existing facilities. Despite the large housing program in urban areas, housing demands are still unsatisfied, especially in Bucharest. Elsewhere, too, there have been problems in housing and other social infrastructure, but the industrial firms themselves have helped to alleviate the situation by providing dwellings and other facilities. In addition, transport facilities have been in increasing demand throughout the country, since many industrial laborers have to commute, sometimes over fairly long distances. Another consequence of the rapid expansion of industrial employment has been the need for extensive training and retraining facilities, both within industrial plants and outside, because of the background and age composition of the new labor force (discussed above).

With a substantial portion of the labor force still employed in agriculture, where the potential for productivity increases from advanced technology is quite high, Romania's unabated industrialization drive is not yet constrained by any anticipated serious labor shortages. Some shortages of specific labor, however, exist in the growth industries. The government has emphasized the potential contribution of the economy's "labor reserves" to the future industrial development of the country. Official reference is made primarily to the "reserves" of the rural sector, and the government has sought either to attract them to urban centers or to locate industrial production activities in rural areas, a policy that would probably reduce the social cost of migration. Although not yet a problem, the changing age structure of the rural labor force, because of the migration of the younger element, may soon require more careful selection of the type of industry that should be located in these rural areas. Already special attention is being given to the reserve of rural women able to undertake industrial jobs, and this consideration has entered into project selection criteria. In this context, the Ministry of Labor has developed a nomenclature of jobs in handicrafts and other specialties more suitable for women, which established the guidelines for the participation of rural women in industrial activities.

Analysis of labor participation rates and employment practices in the various sectors, which is discussed in more detail later in the study, clearly suggests two additional sources of labor reserves in the economy: urban women and labor reserves in industrial enterprises.

Labor mobility

In Romania everyone of working age who wants a job is entitled to one by law, and the state ensures the placement of all individuals. Therefore, open unemployment does not exist. At any given time, however, there are a certain number of labor force members who are not employed. These, in Romania, are not classified as unemployed but as "in the process of changing work."[2] (In many respects this parallels the frictional or search component of unemployment found in labor markets of industrialized economies.) There is no way to estimate the size of this phenomenon or the characteristics of those without work and the duration of the waiting period of unemployment, all of which are relevant to assessing resource costs. With-

2. The "occupied population" working in organizations is counted annually but does not include job seekers. The "active population," which is larger than the "occupied" population because it includes job seekers and military trainees, is estimated by the census, but there is no distinction between the employed and job seekers. The latter are classified as employed in the occupation to which they will eventually be allocated; so, in effect, this component of unemployment is statistically defined away.

drawals and reentries into the labor force are frequent, and rates of turnover and interenterprise transfers are quite high. Because of the emphasis on the use of all available manpower (below), such shifts are subject to regulation. Withholding productive labor from the economy is considered antisocial (except, for example, where medically justified or when child-caring responsibilities of women are greatest) and is basically not tolerated. At the extreme, the people are directed by the government to work in their area of qualification.

Although there are few formal limitations to labor mobility, such mobility is rather restricted. If a worker is not to lose accumulated seniority rights, his transfer to a new job must be agreed upon by his current employer. Where such a job change leads to a promotion or to better use of skills, the current employer cannot block it in principle. Seeking employment in enterprises in "closed cities" (above) is difficult but can be done through "temporary" residence that is obtained with the assistance of these enterprises. In some sectors it is possible to obtain seasonal labor services. For example, an agricultural cooperative worker can enter into a contract with a construction enterprise for a specified number of days' work that also allows him to meet his full working obligations to the cooperative.

Qualified workers (graduates of vocational and industrial schools) are free to apply for transfer to another enterprise after fulfilling their contractual obligations to their first employer (generally three years). Nonskilled workers can ask to transfer at any time. Evidence on turnover rates indicates that such shifts are not uncommon among lower-paid and young workers who are seeking higher pay or among professionals seeking greater job satisfaction. Fulfilling the "employment guarantee" is made still more difficult by the fact that, in Romania, the aim is not just to provide any job to a seeker but one within the worker's field of specialization.

Participation rates

Questions regarding the nature of imbalances in the supply and demand for labor are also raised by some labor force trends, in particular those of participation rates. Between 1956 and 1972 the ratio of the total labor force to the population of working age declined steadily (Table 8.4).

In a period when the total working-age population rose 19 percent, the participation rate of workers fell 7 percent. This is not explained alone by the expanding student population and the increased average duration of schooling, since students sixteen years and older are included in the active population. The authorities have advanced two additional explanations: an increasing number of pensioners between fifty-five and sixty years old and the withdrawal of women for several years (up to seven) to raise children.

Table 8.4. *Employment of Working-Age Population, 1955–75*

Year	*Percentage employed*	*Year*	*Percentage employed*
1955	85.0	1966	83.1
1956	86.8	1967	82.5
1957	85.0	1968	81.8
1958	84.8	1969	81.2
1959	84.5	1970	80.1
1960	84.8	1971	79.8
1961	84.4	1972	79.3
1962	84.3	1973	79.1
1963	84.0	1974	78.9
1964	83.4	1975	79.0
1965	82.8		

The fall in participation rates may also reflect the lower rates in urban compared with rural areas during a period of relatively rapid urbanization. The participation rate for males, however, is virtually the same in rural and urban areas, whereas that for females is nearly 50 percent higher in rural areas. This probably reflects three factors. First, family incomes are higher in urban areas, thus encouraging women to substitute leisure for work. Second, there may be relatively fewer unskilled jobs suitable for women in urban as compared with rural areas. Third, in the past women have received less education than men. In 1966 the proportion of men with education beyond the primary level was roughly double that of women. Women, who in the past had received less education, would be at a disadvantage when competing for jobs in urban areas, although there is legislation that stipulates complete income equality between sexes.

The imbalances that have accompanied urbanization—a scarcity of unskilled urban jobs and current or projected scarcity of skilled urban labor—are not easily susceptible to short-run solutions. As previously noted, the government's pronatalist policy is designed to meet the needs of a rapidly growing industrial sector that is expected to be skill and capital intensive by the late 1980s. The rapid increase in educational opportunities for women above the primary level should also be beneficial.

Skill and educational attainments

The substantial national educational efforts of the past twenty-five years are documented in Table SA2.1. From 1950 to 1975, when total population increased by about 20 percent, the size of the total student population more than doubled. In 1956 only 13.2 percent of all men and 9.6 percent of all women had attended school for more than four years; by 1966, these proportions had risen to 22.8 and 16.6 percent, respectively (Table SA2.2). The more substantial increases were in the rural population, particularly among women. The limited published data on the educational and occupational matrix of the labor force show dynamic improvements in its educational and skill composition and particularly in the increases of technical and administrative personnel (Table 8.5).

Role and Functions of Trade Unions

Most of Romania's workers are organized into trade unions, which are established in all enterprises, institutions, and communes. These unions have a multifaceted role in the political, economic, and social spheres. On the one hand, they are the main vehicles for the Romanian Communist Party (RCP) to communicate with the workers, to organize mass education campaigns, to provide feedback on draft laws, and also to act in an indirect role monitoring worker performance and behavior. On the other hand, the unions exercise the rights and duties of workers as both producers and owners of the means of production. In this role, they may propose legislation affecting the working people or may ensure equity in the distribution of

Table 8.5. *Composition of the Labor Force, by Education and Skill, 1961–68*
(thousands of persons)

Kind of employment	*June 1961*	*June 1964*	*September 1968*
Total employment	*3,377.4*	*3,924.8*	*4,550.1*
Workers	2,456.3	2,888.7	3,403.0
Qualified	1,939.6	2,225.1	2,777.0
Not qualified	516.7	663.6	626.0
Technical or administrative	670.2	803.6	967.1
With higher education	235.5	284.6	337.6
With secondary education	434.7	519.0	585.8
Unclassified positions requiring primary or less than primary education	250.9	232.5	180.0

Source: Revista de Statistica, Bucharest (November 21, 1970).

benefits and pay system as guaranteed by law. Because of the many functions and mass representation of the trade unions, they, by law, participate in all executive bodies, for example, in the Council of Ministers, People's Councils, and the enterprises' or institutions' management committees. Consistency of union activities with national sociopolitical and economic objectives is achieved through the Socialist Unity Front, which is a standing union political body under RCP leadership and also through the participation of the union chairmen in the executive bodies mentioned above. The horizontal and vertical coordination of these activities is provided by the General Union of the Trade Unions of Romania, under which the individual unions are grouped in thirteen branches of economic activity.

Manpower Planning

In Romania, in contrast to other countries where it is practiced, manpower planning is not concerned solely with forecasting the demand of the labor market for new entrants from the educational system. Rather, the allocation of the labor force among sectors, occupations, and geographic areas, as well as its training, is subject to comprehensive planning. Though subordinated to the planning of capital investment, it is subject to the legal requirements both of full employment of the labor force and of a minimum ten years of education. Although responsibility for all decisions rests wholly with the central authorities, enterprises and other institutions help to formulate and implement the plan, particularly in determining specific labor requirements and equilibrating supply and demand. Manpower planning directs the options available to job seekers, but individuals still have a say in selecting a field of study, career, place of residence, and employer.

Manpower planning seeks to attain its objectives through the educational system (and its planning). To the extent feasible, the policy aims to redistribute the labor force to meet the needs of a rapidly growing economy. Occupational rigidity, for example, father-to-son skills, is much reduced, because of the changing skill requirements and greater educational opportunities. Emphasis is on orienting new entrants toward workpaths different from their parents rather than on shifting workers from activities in which they are already well established. The crux of the problem is to orient those who are younger and with little or no experience to work in the newer and more sophisticated industries.

Planning is coordinated by the State Planning Committee (SPC) in conjunction with the Ministries of Education, Labor, and Finance. The Ministry of Education and other interested agencies are responsible for education planning, which ensures that the physical school capacity and teaching staff provide the necessary training at each level of education; this is based primarily upon national and regional demographic projections and on estimated manpower requirements.

Planning by the Ministry of Labor is concerned with achieving future balances between the demand and supply of labor within skill categories. Within this category, demand projections are based on anticipated growth of production, as well as on changes within its structure. Other factors are the degree of technological development, the labor intensity of work, the use rate of capital, and the optimality of the base year employment level.

Supply projections are derived from calculations of the number of entrants from the educational system and of losses from deaths and migration or from occupational change. Also considered are changes in participation rates, hours, and intensity of work. As a general rule, adjustments in the system are made on the supply side through control of entry and orientation of enrollments in the educational and training system.

The Romanian projections of labor demand and supply are more comprehensive and more frequently revised than in the manpower plans of other developing countries. They cover all categories of labor and are updated annually. Projections are not only made for the four broad occupational categories (workers, foremen, technicians, and professionals), corresponding roughly to the three educational attainments (respectively, basic education of ten years, lycee, and higher education), but also for over 100 occupational specializations within these categories.

Demand projections

Because the increase in output and changes in labor productivity over the planning period are given parameters, demand projections are restricted to estimates of output elasticity for labor demand. In effect, the manpower required to fulfill a production target is estimated. This does not mean that output targets are determined without regard to conditions of labor supply. If there is not enough labor to achieve the output target in some enterprises, their plan will be adapted, and necessary labor will be trained. If there is surplus labor, either the output target, the technological configuration of production, or a combination of the two are adjusted or the surplus labor will be transferred to other enterprises in need of it.

To account for the likelihood of technological change, the estimates of the output elasticity of the demand for labor are based on microstudies of the relation of output to employment in both foreign and domestic enterprises of varying sizes and technological sophistication. From the perspective of educational planning, the influence of technical change on the occupational composition of demand is of equal, if not greater, importance than its influence on the aggregate output elasticity of demand. Disaggregation, therefore, of the projected demand for labor is essential. There are two procedures for estimating the output elasticity of demand within specializations, and the selection of either depends on the information available on the organization of production within sectors.

Where information is relatively scarce, the "coefficients method" is used. First, the number of workers required to fulfill the target output is estimated. Then the requirements for the other occupational categories are estimated on the basis of the existing ratios among workers and other personnel. These are disaggregated to the level of the subsector and to enterprise level, because of variance at that level in technology and organization of work and, hence, in the shape of the occupational pyramid. The estimated occupational structure of demand is then modified to allow for expected changes during the following five to ten years resulting from technical progress.

Where there is more detailed knowledge of the equipment to be adopted and the future occupational structure of production, the "job list method" is used. This involves determining the number and categories of work stations manned by specified numbers of workers at various skill levels that are required to accomplish the enterprise production target, on the basis of studies estimating the physical output of each station. The approach requires established "work norms" for each category of workers and tasks. These are determined by time studies of production activities, but more frequently by less rigorous methods, which may explain some of the overmanning in the enterprises.

Errors in demand projections can arise either from difficulties in estimating accurately the effect of technical change or from different timing of the education and production plans. The latter is likely to be of greater significance, since the detailed production plans are drawn up only for five-year periods, and there are no detailed estimates of output on which to base longer-run estimates of labor demand and, hence, the education plan. For example, to plan in 1970 the number of first-year entrants into a five-year training program for each of the years 1971–75 requires production targets for 1976–80. But in 1970 the production targets for 1976–80 are only indicative. The long gestation periods associated with investments in many types of formal training and the inability of forecasting techniques to eliminate uncertainty regarding labor requirements five to ten years ahead, both suggest that short-run imbalances of supply and demand are inevitable. This, in turn, implies that, when forecasting demand, any disequilibrium at the base year must be taken into account.

A notable feature of the demand projection procedures for labor is the apparent disregard of changes, over the planning period, in the level and structure of wages. This is not because no changes are anticipated; on the contrary, wages are expected to continue their steady rise. Not to include wage changes in assessing labor requirements is equivalent to assuming that the wage elasticity of labor demand is zero. Since economic criteria, as well as engineering criteria, are applied in choosing production techniques, however, a zero wage elasticity of the demand for labor would be justified only where, both before and after, the elasticity of substitution between capital and labor is zero. There is a growing body of evidence that this elasticity of substitution is positive. Thus, it appears that, where they have competence to decide, managers apply economic rules of thumb to determine capital/labor ratios, and the implicit shadow wage varies positively with expectations regarding the actual level of wages. Although information is available on wage trends for the five years following the year in which the manpower plan is formulated, there is no firm information for the subsequent five years, the period directly relevant to the demand projections intended to guide education planning. The lack of explicit guidelines on procedures to account for wage changes may result in misestimates by managers of the economic tradeoffs involved in substituting between capital and labor. This situation may contribute to errors in the demand projections.

Supply projections

Base-year supply for a specialized category of labor is simply the number of employed workers with the requisite training. For subsequent years, estimating gross supply is equivalent to determining two figures: (a) the output from the relevant program within the school system, which is estimated quite systematically and which accounts fully for the internal efficiency of the education system (for example, dropouts, repeaters, and so forth); and (b) the training of active workers in short-term courses, undertaken to meet constraints in the rate of expansion of the school system and unpredicted scarcities in some specializations. Adjustments for natural losses include variance of losses within specializations among industries and sexes. For the economy as a whole, the annual reduction of labor force resulting from retirement or disability is approximately 2.5 percent for men and 2.55 percent for women; the loss from death is approximately 0.49 percent for men and 0.23 percent for women.

Equilibrating supply and demand

The projections of demand for specialized workers by occupation requires the future educational composition of the labor force to be specified. For supply, the educational composition of the labor force is projected initially on the assumption that the distribution of students among specializations will remain constant. The burden of synchronizing the two pictures to equilibrate the markets for specific occupations five to ten years ahead is borne almost entirely by the institutions on the supply side; the structure of educational opportunities adjusts to the desired future occupational structure. Students in some specialized programs will be increased as a proportion of the total and decreased in others. Since altering the size of an entering class will not affect the supply of labor until two to five years later, however, there are few adjustments of the formal educational system that can rectify differences between the supply and demand in the short term. The approach of the authorities in correcting such imbalances is quite systematic.

First, since scarcity or surplus of a particular specialization at the enterprise level does not imply that the occupational category is out of balance in aggregate, an enterprise with an unexpected labor deficit first determines if there is another enterprise with a surplus of that type of labor. There are two institutions that reallocate labor. The headquarters of centrals register deficits and surpluses of member enterprises, and, if equilibrium cannot be achieved within a central, it will contact other central headquarters regarding labor availability and requirements. When a new enterprise begins operations, the central will form a nucleus of experienced personnel from existing enterprises, designated by these enterprises, to guide and train the workers at the beginning of the new operations. Most of these workers are recruited from among school graduates who, following their studies, have worked for two to three years in enterprises in the same line of production as the new one. The additional new workers are recruited through the mass media or word of mouth.

Second, if the imbalance cannot be eliminated by interenterprise mobility, the labor office, a municipal specialized organization for registering jobs and job seekers, places the job seekers in the municipality. The labor office does not duplicate the role of the central, because employed workers who desire a change of employer, whether or not they are in surplus, will register there and, more important from the perspective of trying to eliminate imbalances, so will workers reentering the labor force after a period of absence.

If a net scarcity within a specialization still remains, the enterprises' remedial policies to minimize output losses resulting from the short-term labor constraints include (a) restructuring the workers' work program in that specialty, to concentrate workers' time on those tasks for which their training is most essential; and (b) providing short-term training courses. Rarely, if ever, do enterprises resort to increasing the working hours to meet labor scarcities. Since the short-term courses are intended to meet immediate staff needs, they are included and budgeted for in the annual plan, not in the five-year plan.

It is conceivable that within a given occupation there could be scarcity at the enterprise level, even though the aggregate output of the school system matches employers' requirements for additional labor, and no enterprises have surpluses. Such a situation could arise if workers trained in a specialty enter jobs in another field. In Romania, this is unlikely, because the distribution of graduates is directly regulated. The procedures for assigning students to vacant positions are based on the premise that all graduates are expected to work within the broad occupational category for which they have been trained. The adaptability of graduates to different technologies has been enhanced by reducing the number of technical specialties at the lycée level from over 150 to less than 100 and through the organization of in-plant and on-the-job training.

The distribution plan for graduates of institutions of higher education is the responsibility of both the schools and organizations in which they will be employed. Students are given the opportunity to express preferences for particular vacancies, and those who have excelled in their studies are the most likely to have their choices fulfilled. Priority is usually given to graduates who want to be assigned to their own communities or to the community in which their spouse is working. Special consideration is also given to those who require access to a particular area for medical treatment. Once they are assigned, the students sign a contract obliging them to remain in their jobs for three years before seeking transfer. Students from vocational and foreman's schools also sign three-year contracts, but their distribution among employers is determined before their training. This is true as well of students of postsecondary schools who receive scholarships from employers. The rest are allocated to jobs upon the completion of their training.

Manpower distribution is monitored through a balance sheet of labor force utilization, which is drawn up twice a year. It is used for both short-term and medium-term manpower planning and is a basic reference for training plans.

Students are admitted to the specialized lycees on the basis of their academic performance and other aptitude and psychological tests. Entrance to universities is achieved wholly through examinations, which in effect are also used to regulate the number attending the various higher educational institutions. Students are induced to attend the rapidly expanding technical facilities or other educational areas marked for expansion by more fellowships and higher salaries of graduates. In recent years, for example, engineers and economists have been the highest paid professionals.

Efficiency of the Manpower Planning System

Two criteria can be used to assess the performance of the manpower planning system in training citizens and directing them to the appropriate tasks in the community. One is the efficiency of the allocation system; the other is whether the targets specified in the plan for training and for the supply and demand of various specialized categories of labor have been fulfilled.

The distribution of the labor force among sectors, occupations, and geographic areas has altered dramatically in recent decades, with the increased mobility of workers who have been well established in their vocation and residence and, to an even greater extent, with the orientation of new labor force members to training and workpaths different from those of the preceding generations. Although the system has been able to shift labor in response to changes in production patterns and techniques, and hence in labor requirements, there is still room for improvement. Manpower planning has been centralized, but certain improvements have been undertaken, as explained below. Its main instrument is the elaboration of manpower balances derived through successive reconciliation between enterprises, ministries, and the SPC. This procedure has some important disadvantages. First, it is a rather static approach in which the emphasis is on striking balances between the manpower needs and existing and apparent labor reserves. Within the reconciliation process mentioned above, this method facilitates the allocation of labor only in aggregate terms, with greater weight given to industry. Despite attempts, it is also obvious that it has not always been successful in achieving a balance in labor demand and supply in some sectors. This is evident, for example, in the existing excess demand in the construction sector (Chapter 12).

The second disadvantage is that although the method provides a comprehensive picture of the distribution of labor, it leaves little scope for review of the effective use of labor among different sectors and subsectors and at the enterprise level. This review has become increasingly important, partly because of emerging labor shortages in several more industrialized regions (for example, Brasov and Bucharest). The government has apparently recognized the need for a more dynamic and decentralized approach in manpower planning and allocation, and it has recently begun to prepare additional labor force balances for judets and several urban areas. Although this may not be sufficient, it indicates government awareness that future productivity increases in industry and its competitive position on world markets will depend more and more on labor efficiency. Reallocation of labor among industries and the promotion of labor mobility in general should offer considerable opportunities for improvement.

The fulfillment of plan targets for recruitment and distribution of the labor force—which presumably has been accomplished to a great degree but cannot be confirmed because of lack of data—is another indication of the ability of the system to mobilize labor resources. Plan fulfillment by itself, however, does not imply a high level of allocative efficiency, unless the plan targets for labor use were precisely those that would equalize the social marginal productivity of labor in all uses. Since, in formulating the plan, no explicit attempt is made to estimate shadow prices of labor, fulfillment would not preclude variances in the marginal social productivity of labor between sectors or occupations or even between enterprises within the same sector.

A close examination of the system of labor allocation in Romania reveals three situations in which people may either not be employed or may be underemployed. The first is the inevitable temporary unemployment of workers who are moving from one job to another or are reentering the labor force. Both groups need jobs in their specialization. The second situation is indicated by the evidence of an excess supply of labor that is concentrated in urban areas and consists mainly of women. Some of the possible reasons for a lower participation rate for women in urban areas were discussed above. Third, there is underemployment that may occur in the agricultural sector or where workers trained in one specialization or in particular skills end up in jobs requiring a different specialization or skills. For vocational school graduates, however, this problem has been minimized in recent years. Schools are located adjacent to the factories, the school curricula are determined on the advice of the factory managers, the equipment used for training is the same the students will use on the job, and, in some programs, practical training is taking place in the factory rather than in a school workshop. Since, on entering the school, most of the students commit themselves to employment in the factory for several years, the likelihood of a graduate taking a job outside of his specialization is remote.

Development of the Education System

The education system has been recognized and used effectively as a vital tool for Romania's political, social, cultural, and economic development. Changes in its structure and reorientation correspond closely to the transformation of Romania's economic policies and have been undertaken to increase the sensitivity of the sector to the economy's technological advances and to the changing structure and needs of its labor force.

The program is justified as a national investment in human resource development, and it is intended to realize the potential of each individual within the productive process. Any bias in favor of academic work on the part of parent or student is systematically undermined, and the young are prepared to enter the productive process as soon as they are trained. The concept of lifelong education for all members of society is encouraged, and this applies to the nonformal technically oriented fields that prepare the labor force to assimilate technological change as well as to art and science areas that broaden the sociocultural background of individuals.

The present modernized system has evolved from a major reform in 1948 and subsequent corrective actions in 1956, 1968, 1973, and 1977 to increase the system's efficiency. The 1948 reform nationalized all educational institutions; its main goals were to prepare the younger entrants to the labor force for a more effective participation in the country's development effort and to eradicate illiteracy. Compulsory education was increased from four to seven years, at that time the duration of elementary schooling. The next adjustment in the educational system was undertaken in 1955 in conjunction with the second five-year plan in Romania's industrialization program. The major modification at this time was the restructuring of secondary schools along polytechnical lines to better synchronize academic studies with industrial and agricultural production. (The diversification of secondary education was not legislated until ten years later, however.) Under this reform, primary and secondary schools were unified into a system of general education consisting of eight grades with compulsory attendance. In addition, institutions of higher learning were organized to correlate with the requirements of the economy and to diversify the social composition of university students.

Significant shortcomings in the 1956 measures began to emerge in the early 1960s. The system had become overcentralized, and it was not keeping pace with technological developments in the society. Their key needs were for new programs and materials in the rapidly advancing sciences; for less fragmentation in academic and scientific specializations, particularly at the higher level; and for expanded studies in such areas as cybernetics, automation, genetics, and sociology. A major investigation of all levels of education led to the corrective measures introduced in 1968.

These measures were designed to correct skill shortages and to improve labor productivity, consistent with the country's efforts to improve production quality and to compete successfully in the international markets. In addition to strengthening a more diversified secondary education, new intermediate schools for subprofessional training were established, and a national system of refresher and upgrading courses was organized. Compulsory education was raised to ten years.

With the 1973 measures adopted in the plenary session of the RCP, efforts were made to integrate training and development and to strengthen the socioideological base of the system. Guidelines were established for a comprehensive long-term manpower and education plan in which education was integrated with practical production training at all levels and with research at higher education levels. New programs were developed to train and integrate women in production activity, particularly in newly developed industries. Directives were issued to establish a unified education system, beginning with preprimary and ending with higher education. Permanent education was strengthened by expanding courses that improved skills, and the social status distinctions between manual and intellectual work were eradicated.

Finally, in 1977 new efforts were undertaken to strengthen the link of practical training with the requirements of the economy so that secondary graduates can be directly and immediately incorporated in the economy's production activities. The 1977 measures also eliminated the one-to-two years postlycée specialization and reduced secondary education from five to four years.

As previously noted, these measures have been generally effective. The education system has been linked to the transformation of the economy in a dynamic way and has provided, both in quality and quantity, the manpower required by the national development efforts. The main structural pattern of the system, also depicted in Figure 8.3 is as follows:

(a) One to four years of preprimary education for three-to-six year olds;
(b) Eight years of compulsory education (grades 1–8) for six-to-thirteen year olds;
(c) Four years of secondary education for fourteen-to-seventeen year olds, encompassing a compulsory level (grades 9–10) and an optional one (grades 11–12);
(d) Three to six years of higher education.

Access to secondary and higher levels of education is by examination, with enrollments determined on the basis of manpower demand prognosis (above). Specialized education begins effectively at grade 9, either in specialized lycées or in vocational training schools. There are nine types of lycées (industrial, agro-industrial and forestry, economic and administrative law, medical, pedagogical, mathematics and physics, philosophy, history, and science and arts), in which eighty-two specialties are offered (forty-seven

Figure 8.3. *Organization of the Education System, 1975*

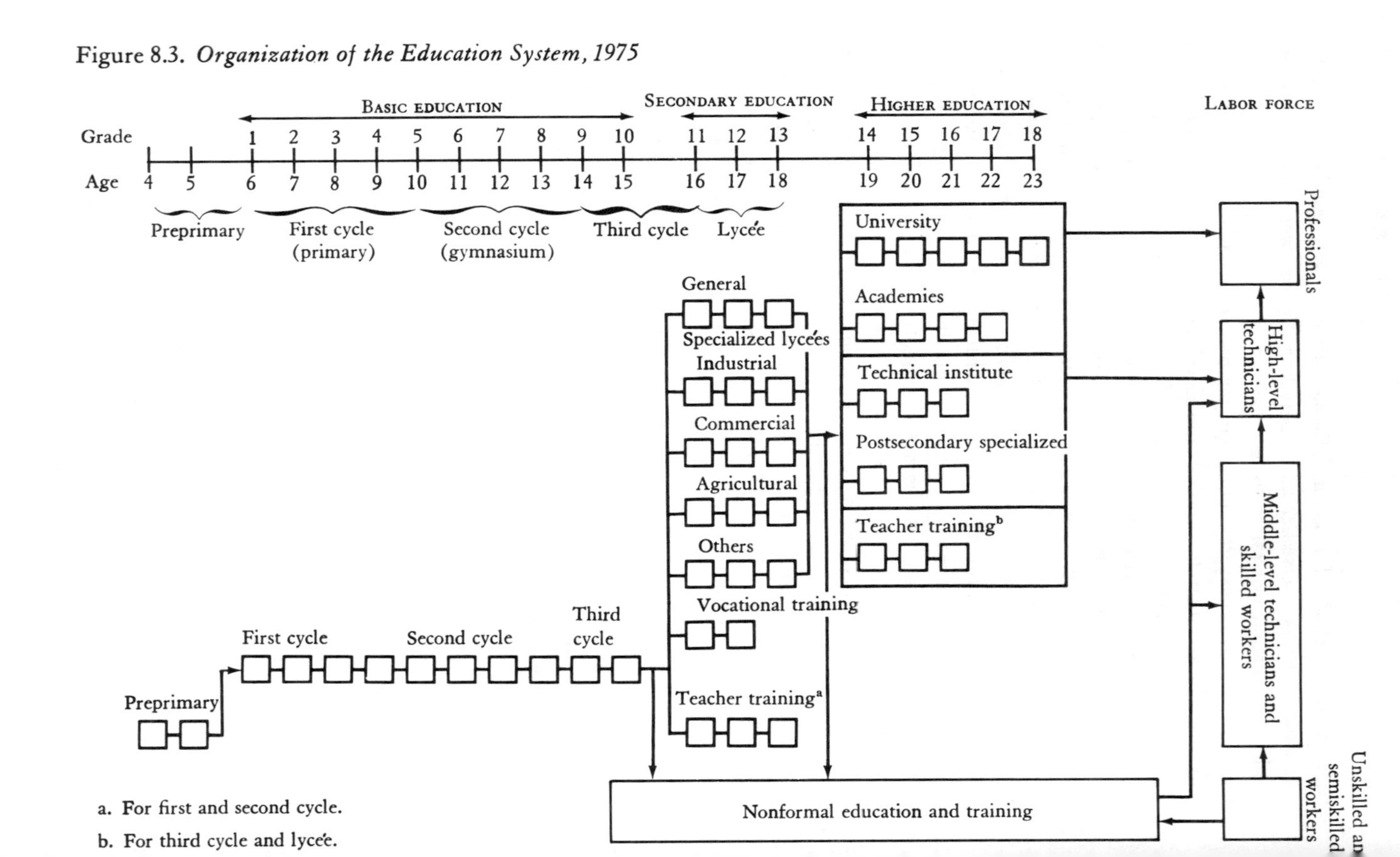

a. For first and second cycle.

b. For third cycle and lycée.

of these are industrial in nature). Vocational education is offered, either in vocational schools or in on-the-job apprenticeship programs, with about 40 percent of the students trained in metallurgy and mechanical engineering. An additional type of vocational training is provided for master craftsmen or foremen. Until 1976–77 young people had been trained in postsecondary schools, with one-to-three-year courses for certain technical specialties.

Management and Administration of the Education System

The Ministry of Education and Training (referred to thereafter as the Ministry of Education) manages and supervises all education activities throughout Romania. Only higher institutions are administered directly by the Ministry; the rest are subordinate to a "dual jurisdiction" system. Although the Ministry of Education directs and supervises the educational activities (teaching and curricula), the schools are under the administrative control of district governments, specialized ministries, and other central agencies[3] (Figure 8.4).

District administrative control extends to all schools offering eight years of education and to about half of preprimary and lycée education. Only a handful of vocational schools are under local government control. Each district has a school inspectorate, with its education activities supervised by the Ministry of Education and with its physical operating requirements supervised by the Executive Committee of the District's People's Council. The other institutions are administered by republican agencies. These agencies provide the schools with the resources they require for normal operation and also supervise their administration. At the same time, all the ministries and central agencies collaborate closely with the SPC and the Ministry of Education to determine their personnel needs at all levels, including management.

Educational Planning

The links between education and manpower planning have been discussed above. As previously noted, education planning consists of two

3. These include the District People's Councils, the Ministries of Metallurgy, Industry of Machine Construction, Mining, Oil and Geology, Electric Power, Chemical Industry, Industrial Construction, Forestry Economics and Construction Materials, Transport and Telecommunications, Light Industry, Agriculture and Food Industry, Domestic Trade, and Health, the Council of Culture and Socialist Education, and the Ministry of Finance.

Figure 8.4. *Organization of the Education System (Dual Jurisdiction System)*

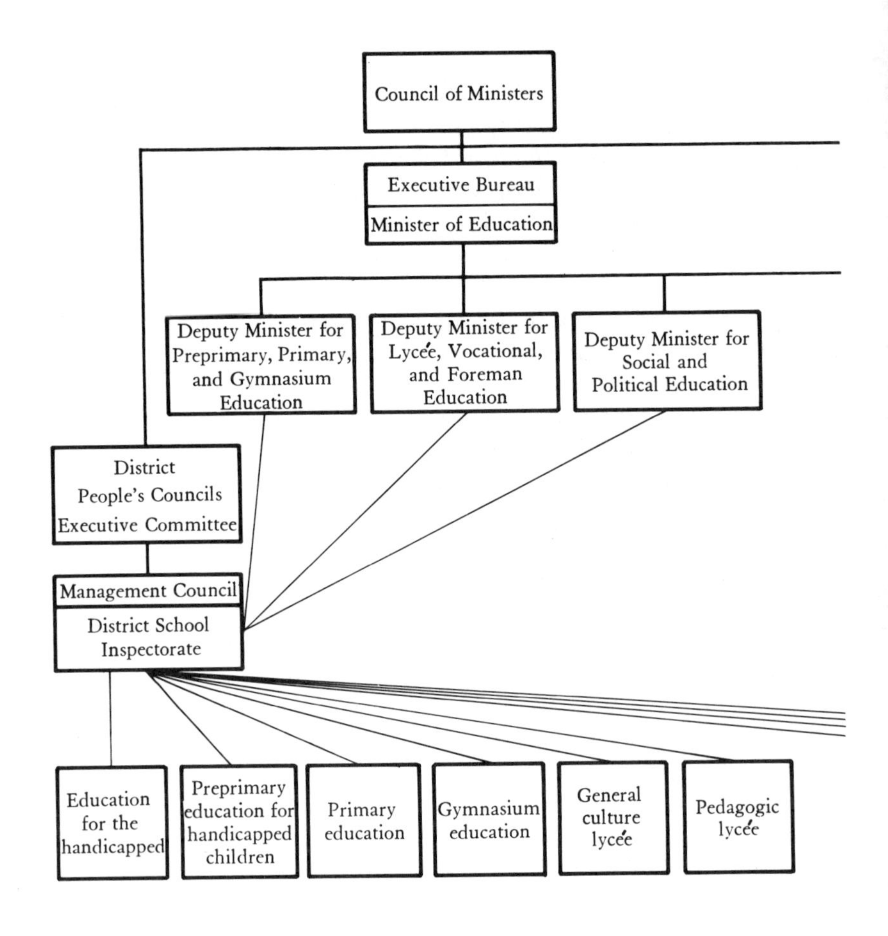

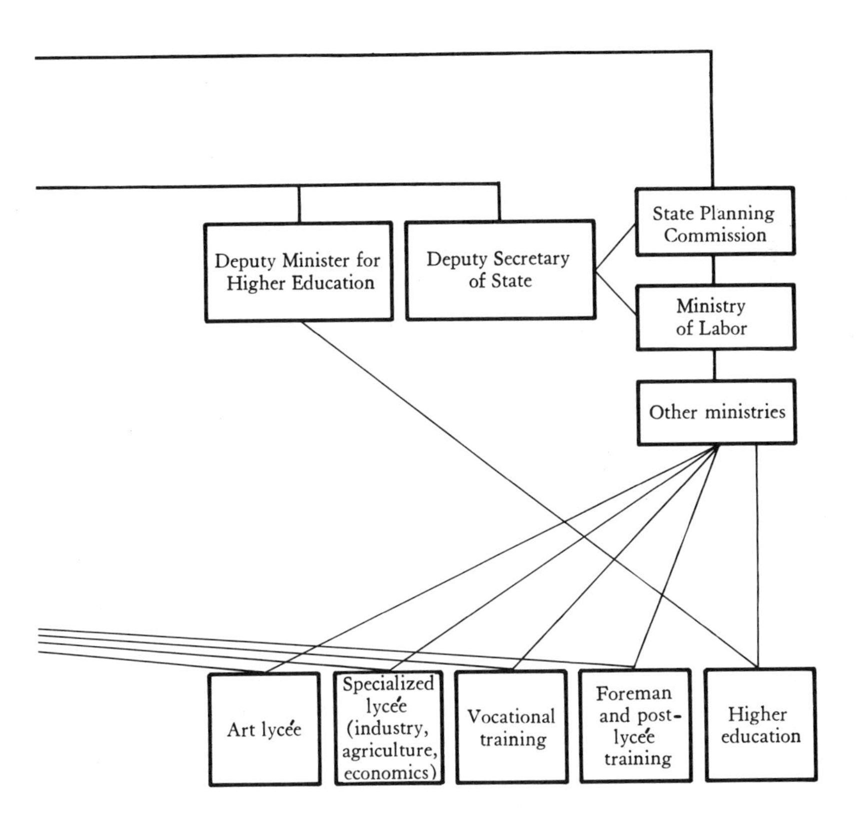
State Planning Commission
Deputy Minister for Higher Education
Deputy Secretary of State
Ministry of Labor
Other ministries
Art lycée
Specialized lycée (industry, agriculture, economics)
Vocational training
Foreman and post-lycée training
Higher education

parallel exercises—enrollment and physical facilities planning. The former consists of formulating plans for the compulsory education, for lycée-level education, and for specialized technical and professional education or training.

The school enrollment plan for basic education is very straightforward. All but the disabled students have to attend school; the latter attend special schools. The plan is thus prepared on the basis of population data, a yearly census of school-age children, and statistical data on student flows in the system of the previous years. The People's Council of each district prepares the district plan. It is reviewed by the Ministry of Education, which subsequently develops a national plan from an aggregate of all district plans.

The enrollment plan for lycée-level education requires a more detailed analysis, and it also involves determination of the distribution of enrollments by types of lycées and prospects of enrollments in higher education. Built-in assumptions in this exercise include estimates regarding enrollments by occupations and take into account dropouts and repeaters.

The plan for specialized training, known as the training plan, is linked to the estimates of the future manpower needs of the economy. Some of the possible errors that may develop in formulating the quantitative targets of this plan, in view of the fact that training for most specializations extends beyond the five-year plan's estimated manpower requirements, were discussed above. The training plan, however, reflects the needs of a more distant future by orienting the training toward the future qualitative needs of the labor force: that is, for a continuously increasing level of general education, closer linkages of academic education and of practical work, and a broader curriculum that includes the more recent developments in science and technology. The training plan is based on the data of the balance sheet of use of the labor force (above).

The physical facilities planning in the sector is undertaken along with the other planning exercises and is usually based on a two-year lead assessment of the adequacy of existing facilities to accommodate future required increases. The evaluation of space use is systematic, since it is governed by Ministry of Education norms. Investment proposals are prepared by the agency that has administrative jurisdiction over the school facilities in question and are all aggregated and reviewed, initially by the Department of Planning of the Ministry of Education and subsequently by the SPC and the Ministry of Finance, in the context of the major indicators of the five-year plan and budget. Except for universities, all other education or training institutions are based on standard design, which reduces cost and minimizes the period of implementation.

Contribution of the Education System to Romania's Growth

One of the cornerstones in Romania's development effort has been its education and skill development program. As noted above, there has been a certain lag in responding to the manpower needs of the economy, especially for the more sophisticated skills required by technological advances. But on the whole, considering the extent of the undertaking, the program has been remarkably successful.

External efficiency

IMPROVING THE LABOR FORCE'S EDUCATIONAL QUALIFICATIONS. Expansion of the education system and its access for the whole population have brought dramatic changes. Illiteracy, estimated at 27 percent of the population in the 1945 census, was eliminated by 1956, and universal ten-year basic education was attained in 1975. The 1974–75 enrollments estimated as a proportion of the respective age groups stood at 101 percent for basic, 49 percent for secondary, and 10 percent for higher education, which compare favorably with similar participation rates in most other countries.[4] The disparities in enrollment ratios by region and sex have also been eliminated. The growth and changing structure of enrollments is summarized in Table 8.6 (also in Table SA2.1).

The striking effect of the 1966 measures, designed to orient secondary education to the economy's more specialized needs, is clearly demonstrated. With the attainment of universal basic schooling, primary and general secondary enrollments have stabilized. In fact, since 1966 the full expansion of the system has been exclusively in the nonacademic areas—an impressive record (Table SA2.3). The changes in the structure of enrollments illustrate further the growth of middle-level manpower training, an area where shortages developed in the 1960s. This orientation of enrollments to satisfy the demand of the rapidly growing sectors of the economy can also be seen in the growth of the related secondary and vocational schools and university facilities. For example, 61 industrial lycées enrolled 5,300 students in 1966; in the 1974–75 school year, their number had grown

4. Estimated respectively as percentage of the following age groups: 6–14, 15–19, and 20–24 of mid-1974 populations. The excess in basic education may be attributed to repeaters.

Table 8.6. *Growth and Structure of Educational Enrollment, 1950–75*

Level of education	Enrollment (thousands)[a]			Index of growth (1950/51 = 100)		Structure (percentage)		
	1950–51	1965–66	1974–75	1965–66	1974–75	1950–51	1965–66	1974–75
Primary[b]	1,779	2,993	2,890	168	162	84	80	73
Secondary	93	372	708	400	761	4	10	17
General	(60)	(360)	(344)	(600)	(573)	(3)	(10)	(9)
Specialized	(33)	(12)	(363)	(36)	(1,100)	(1)	(—)	(9)
Vocational	99	182	192	183	194	5	4.5	5
Technical postsecondary	95	68	35	72	39	4	2	1
Higher	53	131	153	247	289	3	3.5	4
Total	*2,119*	*3,746*	*3,978*	*177*	*188*	*100*	*100*	*100*

a. Excludes preprimary.
b. Includes eight years of education.
Source: Anuarul Statistic, various issues.

to 382 and enrollments to 252,000. Agricultural secondary schools almost doubled during the same period, and enrollments more than quadrupled. In vocational training, the growth (1950–51 to 1974–75) in enrollments has been particularly high in such areas as mining (200 percent), metallurgy and engineering (67 percent), industrial chemistry (389 percent), infrastructure (construction, transport, and telecommunications), and light industries (Table SA2.4). The effect of the formal education system's growth on the diversified secondary level has not yet been fully felt because of the training period required and the rapid enrollment acceleration in the most recent years. For example, only 27,000 graduated from specialized lycées in 1974. This is still a remarkable performance, however, as in 1967 there were no graduates at all with such training. The growth and distribution of graduates by level of education is given in Table SA2.5.

RELEVANCE OF TRAINING. The content and quality of education and training programs has been quite efficiently related to the real needs of the economy. The adaptation of graduates to the world of work has been productive and immediate. This is a product both of building early receptive attitudes toward production training and of implementing a curriculum that starkly reflects the nation's priorities: that is, one that has increased emphasis on exact sciences and production training. To illustrate this point, Table 8.7 gives the basic distribution of subjects in 1973–74 for three types of schools. The percentages have been drawn on groupings of subjects during each cycle. Those for practical work and exact sciences are quite high.

The outstanding aspect of these programs concerns production training. All schools at all levels are "sponsored" by neighboring production enterprises, and they are linked in a unique and relatively low-cost training and production program. In essence, there is a business arrangement in which enterprises subcontract the manufacture of product components to school workshops rather than to other enterprises.

For grades 5–8, a sequential series of training modules and related lesson plans, increasing gradually in complexity, are prepared by Ministry of Education specialists for woodworking, electrical, and metalworking. From among the products manufactured by the "sponsoring" enterprise, the production components that best relate to the training programs and modules are selected for school workshop production and assembly (in consultation with management from the enterprises and also a sponsoring secondary education institution). Production targets and schedules are established along with the equipment, tools, and materials required for production. Pupils in the school workshop receive related instruction on the tools, materials, design, and function of the respective components.

Table 8.7. *Distribution of General Curricula, by Kind of School, 1973–74*
(percentage)

	Basic education (grades 1–8)	*General secondary lycée (grades 9–12)*	*Industrial secondary lycée (grades 9–12)*
Humanities	43	36	19
Exact sciences	32	39	27
Arts and physical education	18	8	5
Production training	7	17	49

Source: Ministry of Education; data supplied during discussions with the authors.

In actual practice, a production line approach is generally followed, with the higher grades producing the more difficult components. All students are rotated through the various operations, including quality controls, to facilitate their skill training and their understanding of the interdependency and need for accuracy in each operation. Finally, each completed training-production lot is also checked for quality control by a representative of the enterprise and, upon acceptance, the school receives full compensation for the work produced.

For specialized lycées and vocational schools, production training is even more integrated with the enterprises. Partly, this has been designed to increase student exposure to actual working conditions. It is also probable, however, that with the rapid expansion of specialized education, qualitative training could not have been implemented without using actual enterprise workshops. Whatever the cause, the combination of training in the academic environment and the world of work has been made effectively. In vocational training, for example, students are trained in the enterprises' workshops during their last year of training; during the second year of training, the use of these facilities depends on the availability of facilities on school premises. In the case of specialized lycées, because of comparatively less intensive practical training, the use of enterprises' facilities is more common in the advanced grades.

Efforts are made to relate academic work to real life situations. Thus formal education system. In 1971 the concept of lifelong education was lems facing the economy or work on actual draft plans of the country. Technical faculty students participate in research that is incorporated in production projects.

The state's efforts to increase labor productivity are not limited to the formal education system. In 1971 the concept of lifelong education was introduced, providing for the periodic updating of the labor force's skills. Annually about two million workers in almost all fields attend this form of in-service training course. During the 1971–75 five-year plan period, most of the active work force completed at least one organized form of in-service training, in courses ranging from one week to a few months.

Finally, adult education courses have been organized in workers' and peoples' "universities" under the sponsorship of municipalities and large enterprises. These offer a variety of courses at various levels. In 1971, 171 such universities offered 1,231 courses attended by about 100,000 people. Courses were about evenly split among social sciences, natural sciences, and foreign languages. (The number of trainees attending vocational courses was relatively limited.) More than half of those attending were over thirty years old. Students represented all occupational and social groups.

Internal efficiency

Another contribution of the education system to the country's development efforts has been its improved internal efficiency. Currently, a greater proportion of students complete their studies and join the labor force with better qualifications than previously. The increase in compulsory education to ten years is one of the measures contributing to that development. Others have reduced the number of dropouts and repeaters by providing systematic remedial help for students, particularly in the primary grades, parental guidance, and special program offerings.

One of the greatest accomplishments of the system has been the improvement in the quality of the teaching and administrative staff. Only about 4 percent of the teaching force for the first eight grades is unqualified by current standards, and most of these are now enrolled in university correspondence training programs. Romania's success in overcoming what in other countries is a severe constraint to fast expansion of the education system results mainly from the facts that (a) teaching has long enjoyed an important and prestigious role in the country; (b) salary scales are considered within the context of a national income policy, eliminating differences in compensation that have discouraged entry to the teaching force in the past; and (c) educational research and educational management are recognized as integral and vital to the development of education at all levels.

Apart from the relatively high level in the qualifications required of the teaching force, several other factors contribute to maintaining quality standards and efficiency. Some of these are:

(a) Establishment of pupil/teacher ratios and of contact hours at various levels on the basis of on-going research;
(b) The requirement that administrators must spend a specified amount of their time (5 to 50 percent) in teaching or other direct pupil contact;
(c) Restandardization of specialty posts within school inspectorates (on the average, one such post for every 250 teachers);
(d) The requirement that general inspectors of the Ministry spend at least 50 percent of their time in field visits at the district level.

To accommodate the changing requirements of the economy and to achieve a high degree of teacher use, most teachers are required to be qualified in two specialties, so that later on they won't have to be retrained in a completely new field. Finally, in teacher training programs, emphasis is placed on guidance and counseling work, to prepare each teacher to address the needs of those students for which he will be responsible during their primary or gymnasium schooling.

One conspicuous shortage in the specialized lycées has been in teachers of technical subjects. As an interim move, the teaching staff has been augmented by engineers and specialists from enterprises who now make up an estimated 50 percent of the lycées' technical teachers.

The internal efficiency of the present system, as measured by the extremely high rates of student promotion, is shown in Table 8.8. This probably results from the rigorous screening of students through placement exams as well as from the improvements in teaching and administrative staff mentioned earlier.

Expected contribution of preprimary education

One of the fastest growing segments of the education system in recent years has been preprimary education. Enrollments have grown from 199,000 in 1950–51 to 770,000 in 1974–75, representing about 68 percent of the relevant age group. The fastest enrollment growth has been registered since 1966 (9 percent a year) and results from the government's social and economic objectives. The first objective is to affect the development of the childrens' social and personality traits during the formative years and to prepare them for the tasks required by the elementary schools. The economic objective is to assist gainfully employed mothers with childcare and to release women to the labor force. The lower participation rates of urban

Table 8.8. *Rate of Student Promotions*
(percentage)

Level of education	*1970–71*	*1971–72*	*1972–73*	*1973–74*	*1974–75*
General	92.9	93.7	94.2	97.6	97.9
Lycée					
Humanities	92.6	94.4	95.1	96.3	95.6
Specialized	93.9	95.1	96.2	97.3	96.4
Vocational					
Vocational school	98.3	98.3	98.7	99.0	99.2
Apprentice	96.9	97.5	98.3	98.4	98.8
Foremen schools	99.1	99.4	99.4	99.4	99.5
Postlycée technical	95.4	97.9	98.8	99.1	99.0
Higher					
Day students	90.0	92.0	94.2	94.4	93.0
Evening students	97.6	83.9	90.3	92.6	90.4
Correspondence students	67.9	66.5	66.5	65.7	62.3

Source: Ministry of Education.

women, however, suggests that this objective is not being met and that other factors may have a more serious impact (above).

Educational Finance

Educational finance is complex, and not all expenditures are included in the national budget, which accounts for about 85 percent of total expenditures on education and training.

Educational expenditures

Romania's budget expenditures on education and training understate the country's commitment to the sector and the real amount of national resources allocated to it. The factors leading to the large understatement have been identified to be:

(a) The shifting of the burden of financing of materials and teaching staff and facilities and workshop equipment use to enterprises where a substantial proportion of practical training has been increasingly undertaken;

(b) Materials for workshop training in the formal system, including

vocational training, are given to the schools by the enterprises subcontracting the production of goods;
(c) Payments to schools by the enterprises for the finished products are not reflected in the schools' budgets;
(d) Payment toward vocational student labor in enterprises is reflected only in the production cost;
(e) Scholarships paid by enterprises for students they sponsor, mainly in vocational training, are absorbed in the enterprises' other costs;
(f) Financing of upgrading courses from production funds is not included in the training budget (there were reported to be approximately 1.2 billion lei in 1975); and
(g) In-service training expenditures for all agencies are not reported separately.

Thus, in 1975 apparent education and training expenditures amounted to 15.1 billion lei or about 6.4 percent of total government expenditures (5.5 percent of recurrent and about 2.8 percent of capital expenditures). They represented 3.1 percent of estimated gross national product (GNP), a comparatively low allocation considering the educational effort of the country and the fact that it is offered free. A more representative estimate of the allocation of national resources to the sector would be close to 4 percent of GNP, which is within 10 percent of the ratio for a "representative" OECD country.[5]

There is a noteworthy constancy in the historical allocation of capital resources to the education sector. The latter's share in total investment expenditures has remained mostly within the range of 1.6 to 2.0 percent (1950, 1.6 percent; 1960, 1.8 percent; 1970, 1.6 percent; and 1975, 1.7 percent), which implies a very high annual growth rate and also demonstrates the commitment of the government to providing training facilities and equipment to implement its educational objectives. An evaluation of the historical allocation of recurrent expenditures is not possible because of lack of data series. As Table 8.9 illustrates, these expenditures have declined as a percentage of total recurrent expenditures in 1975, as compared with 1970. Also, their share of total sociocultural recurrent expenditures has declined (Chapter 9). The commitment of resources to meet the rapid expansion of enrollments in technical and vocational training, discussed earlier, is illustrated in Table 8.10 for 1960–75. During the past ten years especially, although overall recurrent expenditures for education about

5. Manuel Zymelman, "Patterns of Educational Expenditure," World Bank Staff Working Paper, no. 246 (Washington, D.C.: World Bank, November 1976).

Table 8.9. *Allocation of State Recurrent Expenditures to Education, 1970 and 1975*

Item	*1970*	*1975*
(1) Total recurrent expenditure (billions of lei)	130.9	236.2
(2) Total sociocultural recurrent expenditure (billions of lei)	34.0	50.9
(3) Recurrent expenditure on education (billions of lei)	9.2	12.9
3 as percent of 1	7.0	5.5
3 as percent of 2	27.2	25.3
2 as percent of 1	26.0	21.6

Source: Anuarul Statistic, various issues.

doubled, those for technical and vocational education and training almost tripled.

A substantial portion (64 percent) of recurrent education expenditures is financed by local government. In 1975 local government financed 85 percent of preprimary education, all of primary, about half of lycée, and only 4 percent of vocational training expenditures. Table 8.11 illustrates the division of responsibility in the financing of the main levels of education for that year.

The expenditures for materials are clearly limited because, as mentioned earlier, production-related materials are given by enterprises to be used in the production of goods. This, along with factors (a), (c), (d), and (e) mentioned above, lead to a considerable distortion of unit cost, especially for

ıble 8.10. *Distribution of Recurrent Expenditures, Kind of Education, 1960–75*

	Total expenditures on education		*Level and distribution of expenditure*					
			General[a]		*Technical or vocational*		*Higher*	
ear	*Millions of lei*	*Growth index (1960 = 100)*	*Millions of lei*	*Growth index (1960 = 100)*	*Millions of lei*	*Growth index (1960 = 100)*	*Millions of lei*	*Growth index (1960 = 100)*
'60	3,496	100	1,968	100	561	100	526	100
'65	6,533	187	3,474	177	1,318	235	1,027	195
'70	9,235	264	4,657	237	1,944	346	1,385	263
'75	12,893	369	6,121	311	3,717	662	1,713	326

a. Includes primary or basic and general secondary education.
Source: Anuarul Statistic, various issues.

Table 8.11. *Financing of Expenditure on Principal Levels of Education, 1975*

		Republican		*Local*	
Level of education	*Total (thousands of lei)*	*Amount (thousands of lei)*	*Percentage*	*Amount (thousands of lei)*	*Percentage*
Preprimary	1,397,853	203,925	4.9	1,193,928	16.2
Basic	4,723,550	—		4,723,550	64.1
Lycée	2,508,193	1,146,309	27.4	1,361,884	18.5
Vocational	1,209,055	1,118,261	26.7	90,794	1.2
Higher	1,712,522	1,712,522	41.0	—	—
Total	*11,551,173*	*4,181,017*	*100*	*7,370,156*	*100*

Source: Ministry of Finance; data supplied during discussions with the authors.

basic, lycée, and professional schools. For example, based upon field data from a few sporadic school visits, the distortion from factor (d) would average about 10 percent of unit cost, whereas that from factor (e) for vocational schools could amount to as high as one-third of unit cost.

Irrespective of levels of unit cost, it is striking that the ratios of the unit costs among different levels of education are exceptionally low, about 1:2 for basic-to-lycée and for lycée-to-university. Even allowing for corrections in the substantial understatement of the levels of unit costs, the ratios would not be much affected. This unusual relation, which in other developing countries is close to the order of 1:5, is explained by the very limited difference in teacher salaries, as well as by the understated expenditures for instruction materials. For example, the salary of a university professor is only about two-and-a-half times that of a primary school teacher.

Unit cost

An analysis of detailed education cost data for 1975 by level of education and by type of recurrent expenditure confirms the understatement of education expenditures and the factors that explain it. An analysis of key data is presented in Table 8.12.

The 1976–80 Plan to Develop Education

The Plan is designed to continue the momentum of the sector's growth and its contribution to the development of the economy. The achievement of four key targets is central to the Plan's success.

Table 8.12. *Distribution of Recurrent Educational Expenditure and Unit Costs, by Level, 1975*

Level of education	*Total (millions of lei)*	*Distribution (percentage)*			*Total expenditure per pupil (lei)*[b]
		Salaries	*Student aid*[a]	*Instructional materials*	
Preprimary	1,397	77	19	4	1,793
Basic	4,724	93	5	2	1,668
Lycée	2,508	78	19	3	3,479
Vocational	1,209	48	49	3	6,494
Higher	1,713	69	26	4	13,402
Other[c]	1,341	69	26	4	—
Total	*12,893*				

a. Includes scholarships, students' food, and expenditure for materials used in social events.
b. Expenditure per pupil has been calculated by averaging 1974/75 and 1975/76 enrollments.
c. Special education, sports schools, foremen training, and upgrading courses.
Source: Ministry of Finance.

(a) At preprimary level, an enrollment ratio of 89 percent by 1980 to provide these children with early sociopolitical and educational orientation, as well as to tap the urban women labor reserves.
(b) A generalized ten-year compulsory basic education plan by 1977, with continuing emphasis in the later years on practical courses. The already successful implementation of this target sets the ground for the gradual introduction of a twelve-year universal and compulsory education plan by 1990.
(c) Acceleration of the graduation of students from the engineering facilities (83,000 over the five-year period), as well as of higher-level institutes at large (190,000 to 200,000 graduates compared with 155,000 in 1971–75).
(d) Provision to about one-fifth of the labor force (1.9 million workers) of retraining and refresher courses in the context of the national campaign of lifelong education.

An adequate amount of financial resources appears to have been allotted to implement the 1976–80 targets, although the total and specific breakdowns have not been published. The investment allocation to education over the five-year period is estimated to be about 16.5 billion lei, about double the expenditures of the previous five-year period. The sector is thus expected to retain its share of about 1.5 percent of the rapidly growing total investment expenditure. The allocations should support a doubling of student places in preprimary education over the 1971–75 Plan (159,000 versus 72,000); an over 50 percent increase in boarding spaces (139,000 versus 88,000); a substantial increase in new classrooms (14,400 versus 10,900), and a physical expansion in institutions of higher learning of 186,700 square meters (versus the previous plan's 221,000 square meters).

Performance of the Education Sector

There are two further areas that can be assessed with regard to the performance of Romania's education system: whether the sector has been successful in its contribution to the country's development efforts and whether the earlier plans (their targets for enrollments, internal efficiency, cost reduction, and so forth) have been efficiently fulfilled. Unfortunately, information on past five-year plans is not publicly available, so the second judgment cannot be made. This assessment will be restricted to the first area.

The earlier discussion has demonstrated the significant inroads made by Romania's education system. Planning has been largely successful and, contrary to the experience in most developing countries, human resource development has not lagged significantly behind the rapid economic development of the country.

The capacity of the system to respond in a timely and efficient way to the economy's labor needs results largely from the administration of education. The ministries are basically the trainers and the users of manpower. They are keenly aware of their specific production targets and technologies and can develop reliable estimates of their own manpower requirements, as well as of their facility to meet them.

In response to the demand posed by the rapid rate of industrialization and by specialized manpower needs sometimes exceeding the training capacity of the educational system, the joining of schools and enterprises has emerged as a viable mechanism for manpower training. This wide-scale practice was developed by design, and the results appear to be cost effective. It has enhanced the external efficiency of the education system and has reduced, sometimes even eliminated, costs associated with the on-the-job training of newly graduated students. The placement of students is also more efficient, since most of the graduates of any given training institution are absorbed by one of the associated enterprises.

A major correction in the system has been the reduction in the number of specialties offered in lycées and vocational training schools. Earlier, the training program had been designed to meet the enterprises' own specialized manpower needs. Romania's broadening industrial base and the improving production technology require skilled labor able to adapt quickly to new technologies with limited on-the-job training. Trainees are now being given a much broader theoretical and practical preparation. Until the recent changes in the training programs are fully implemented, however, some inefficiencies are bound to occur, and additional in-service training may have to be undertaken.

Conclusion

The educational system has been linked to the transformation of the economy in a dynamic way and, by and large, has been successful in providing both the quality and quantity of manpower required by the national development efforts. Its growth and diversification has evolved in the context of a continuous self-evaluation. Reforms have brought about a more equitable educational system with access for all and have provided lifelong learning opportunities through various adult education programs. In addition, cultural standards have been raised, and the mix of academic and manual work has lessened the distinctions between white- and blue-collar workers. Although it is not possible to assess the cost effectiveness of this impressive record, it is reasonable to conclude that the sector has basically met its challenge, as well as the planners' expectations, and has been a highly effective component of Romania's development effort.

Romania's decision to introduce universal and compulsory education of twelve years, a goal stated in the country's perspective prognosis for 1976–90, is based on similar action by developed countries at an earlier stage of their development. The implementation of such a program will be very costly in terms of space, equipment, and technical teaching requirements. Also, the economic justification for universal middle-level technical training has not been established concretely at this time. The implementation period of such a program is sufficiently long, however, to enable the government to proceed at a pace that is justified by the economy's training requirements and is documented by relevant studies.

9

Consumption and the Standard of Living

Romania's development strategy, as discussed in Chapter 2, has consistently emphasized rapid economic growth through the expansion of a modern capital-intensive industrial sector. Thus, in the allocation of resources, priority has been given to investment over consumption, although consumption has been increased with increases in income. The government policy has been to ensure that, initially, the basic needs of the population were met and, in the long run, that a high and increasing consumption level is attained.

Consumption: Its Composition and Growth

As Tables 9.1 and 9.2 show, this policy has been quite effective over the past two decades. The rising proportion of national income accumulated and national product invested has helped build a strong economic base, which will yield increasing material returns to the population in the future.

Between 1960 and 1975 national income[1] grew at an average rate of 9.3 percent. Although the consumption fund was allocated a smaller share of national income, it increased in absolute size, and, as Table 9.3 indicates, its rate of growth also went up during the period. In per capita terms, the increase has been substantial, since population growth during the period averaged less than 1 percent a year.

1. Measured in 1963 comparable prices.

Table 9.1. *Use of National Income (in Comparable Prices) for Consumption and Accumulation, 1956–60 to 1971–75*

(percentage)

Five-year period	*Consumption fund*[a]	*Accumulation fund*[b]
1956–60	84.0	16.0
1961–65	75.7	24.3
1966–70	71.2	28.8
1971–75	65.9	34.1

Note: National income data exclude nonproductive services.

a. Consumption of material products and services by individuals, the state, and other institutions.

b. Includes net investment plus change in stocks.

Source: Anuarul Statistic al Republicii Socialiste Romania (Bucharest: Directia Centrala de Statistica, published yearly).

Table 9.2. *Investment as a Percentage of Gross National Product (in Comparable 1963 Prices), 1961–65 to 1971–75*

Five-year period	*Investment*
1961–65	24.5
1966–70	26.7
1971–75	27.1

Source: World Bank estimates from official statistics.

The three chief elements of the consumption fund are private consumption of goods, direct government consumption, and consumption by bodies providing social services to the population (for example, health, education, and sports). The largest element, constituting approximately two-thirds of the consumption fund, is private consumption, and this is closely reflected in the volume of socialist retail trade.[2] Between 1960 and 1975 it increased

2. This excludes the retail trade in peasant markets and consumption of self-produced products, which in 1975 were about 35 billion lei (showing an increase of about 32 percent over 1970). This also excludes nonsocialist retail trade, which has been negligible since 1960.

Table 9.3. *Average Annual Growth of the Consumption Fund, 1956–60 to 1971–75*
(percentage)

Five-year period	*Average annual growth*
1956–60	4.8
1961–65	5.3
1966–70	6.2
1971–75	7.5

Source: World Bank calculations.

from 41.5 to 145.6 billion lei,[3] an average annual rate of 8.7 percent, with retail price inflation under 1 percent a year. Significantly, retail sales of food were a high proportion of the total, increasing faster than sales of nonfood commodities (Table 9.4). This is a different pattern than that observed in countries at similar levels of development. The authorities have advanced several factors to explain this, such as the urbanization process, the increased demand for food products produced by the government, and changes in the relative prices of food and nonfood products. Another explanation is that nonfood commodities have not been always readily available in the required quantities and of sufficient quality, and there may also have been insufficiencies in the marketing of goods.

In addition to trade, total private consumption includes services for the population that are mainly carried out by the state and cooperatives. Those provided by the state include, among others, services in transport and telecommunications whereas those of the cooperatives include most forms of personal services, such as hairdressing, shoe repairs, laundries, and maintenance of housing. The volume increased by 68.6 percent between 1971 and 1975 (11 percent a year). This increase, however, has not kept pace with demand, particularly in the case of repairs and maintenance of housing, repairs of consumer durable goods (such as televisions), and some domestic and laundry services.

The other major element of the consumption fund is the consumption of material products in the sociocultural sector. The more relevant concept

3. In current prices.

Table 9.4. *Average Annual Increases in Socialist Retail Trade (in Current and Comparable Prices), 1961–65 to 1971–75*
(percentage)

	1961–65		*1966–70*		*1971–75*	
	Current prices	*Comparable prices*	*Current prices*	*Comparable prices*	*Current prices*	*Comparable prices*
Total	10.3	9.8	7.4	8.3	8.5	8.2
Foodstuffs and public catering	12.3	10.5	7.7	7.4	8.6	7.8
Nonfood commodities	8.7	9.2	7.1	9.1	8.4	8.4

Sources: Anuarul Statistic, various issues, and data provided by Romanian authorities during discussions with the authors.

for real consumption, however, is the total value of sociocultural expenditures, since this includes the value added in the services provided.[4] The data in Table SA8.2 show the expenditures by the government on sociocultural activities since 1960. These do not represent the consumption element alone, since pensions and other transfer payments are included in the total. Taking sociocultural expenditures as an aggregate, the increase between 1971 and 1975 was 8.4 percent a year, a figure comparable with the increase in retail trade. State budget allocations alone represented 7,240 lei for each family in 1975 as against 5,200 lei in 1970. These are significant amounts considering the average wages of 1,813 and 1,434 lei a month, respectively, that prevailed in these years. Basic education is provided completely free, and health services are provided substantially free to the population.

State social assistance also provides consumer goods and services directly and free to the population. Goods, in the form of "material helps," are provided to people in temporary difficulty because of some mishap. The state also provides free centers or homes for those unable to work and look after themselves. These include homes for the old and the handicapped, as well as for "special children," the blind, and the deaf.

4. For example, for education, the consumption fund as part of national income will include only goods consumed in education (such as books, pens, electricity), whereas total consumption, as part of gross national product, will include the total "cost" of education, which includes the valuation of the services performed by the teaching staff.

Table 9.5 *Estimate of Housing Services Consumed (in Comparable 1963 Prices), 1965 and 1970–75*

Year	*Amount (billion of lei)*
1965	7.0
1970	8.8
1971	9.2
1972	9.6
1973	10.0
1974	10.4
1975	10.7

Source: This volume, Table SA3.2.

The final element in the consumption fund is government consumption, which consists of material goods consumed by the state in carrying out its functions. It is a minor part of total consumption, however. In 1975, for example, the state budget allocation for administrative, judicial, and other government organs amounted to 2.7 billion lei.

As consumption includes both goods and services, the services rendered by the housing stock must be considered. In Romania, rents are not based solely on the value of the property, but take into account the size of the property and the income of the tenant. The maximum rent is 20 percent of the highest individual income in the household, but the average is between 7 and 12 percent of that income. Consequently, the value of housing services must be calculated in a different way to reflect the true return to society. An estimate of these services is given in Table 9.5.

The data show an annual average increase between 1971 and 1975 of about 11.8 percent, as against 8.8 percent between 1965 and 1970 and 10.4 percent between 1961 and 1965. The 1971–75 increase is marginally greater than the increase in gross national product (GNP) and national income, but a significant housing shortage still exists. The quality of housing is low, particularly with respect to size (the average size of dwellings constructed in 1975 was only 33.7 square meters).[5] The state envisages that the housing shortage will have disappeared by 1990, and beginning in 1977 larger minimum sizes for new dwellings have been introduced (Chapter 12).

5. Floor area of bedrooms plus living rooms, excluding kitchen and bathroom.

Income

So far only consumption has been considered. But if the standard of living is to be assessed accurately, savings, as well as consumption, should be taken into account. The Romanians do not prepare data on GNP as such, because they use a system of material product balances rather than the standard United Nations system of national accounts, which values services as well as material production. The World Bank, however, has itself estimated the GNP per capita (Table 9.6).[6] The real growth rates represent a signifi-

Table 9.6. *Gross National Product per Capita (in 1963 Comparable Lei), 1965 and 1970–75, and Its Average Annual Growth Rate*

Year	GNP *per capita*	*Five-year period*	*Average annual growth of* GNP *(percentage)*
1965	9,592	1961–65	8.7
1970	13,278	1966–70	6.7
1971	14,895	1971–75	10.0
1972	16,208		
1973	17,793		
1974	19,863		
1975	21,662		

Sources: World Bank estimates based on *Anuarul Statistic*, various issues, and data provided by Romanian authorities during discussions with the authors.

cant and continuous increase in the economic strength of the country and form one of the best growth records for any economy during this period.

In absolute terms, however, the annual GNP per capita of 21,662 lei is still low. Using the World Bank Atlas methodology, this represents a figure of $1,300 a year. Romania remains one of the least affluent countries in Europe.

Even GNP does not reflect fully the standard of living of the Romanian people as individuals. Because it includes investment from state funds, it represents some elements of national wealth, but does not give a feeling of the real income that an individual perceives as his own rather than

6. For full methodology and the concept of material product balances, see Appendix D.

Table 9.7. *Real per Capita Income of the Population (in Comparable Prices): Index and Its Average Annual Growth Rate*

Year	*Index (1950 = 100)*	*Five-year period*	*Average annual growth (percentage)*
1950	100	1951–55	6.5
1955	137	1956–60	3.3
1960	161	1961–65	5.8
1965	214	1966–70	4.2
1970	263	1971–75	6.8
1971	294		
1972	311		
1973	326		
1974	346		
1975	366		

Source: Anuarul Statistic, various issues.

society's in general. A series is published in index form only, entitled "Real Income of the Population" (Table 9.7), which incorporates both personal incomes and imputed incomes in the form of government goods and services provided. In other words, it represents consumption (including that self-produced, but not housing services), plus personal savings. The rates of growth are substantial, but less than GNP per capita, because of the increasing growth rate of investment from national income.

There are two components of personal incomes: the money income of the population and income in the form of goods produced and consumed. As stated earlier, little is known about the latter element, except that it is an important factor in the agricultural sector. Money incomes consist of wages, bonuses, transfer payments from the state, and "other payments."

Wages are determined by law in Romania, and, as Table 9.8 shows, in

Table 9.8. *Average Rates of Growth of Wages, 1961–65 to 1971–75*

Five-year period	*All employees*	*Workers*
1961–65	5.5	5.5
1966–70	5.2	4.9
1971–75	4.8	5.3

Source: Anuarul Statistic, various issues.

the state sector they have been growing constantly in nominal terms, but at a slower rate than real incomes. This suggests that nonearned incomes (in the form of sociocultural services) have been growing faster than earned incomes. Cooperative wages are based on identical scales, and so similar trends should be expected in that sector.

For workers at all levels, basic wages average about 95 percent of total remuneration (but for any individual, the proportion may be considerably less). These are supplemented by various forms of bonus payments and increments for uninterrupted employment or for work performed under extraordinary conditions (Chapter 4 and Appendix I).

Transfer payments represent the second branch of the social welfare system. The largest part of this is state social insurance (Table SA5.3), which provides pensions, sickness insurance, and recuperation plans for state employees. Expenditures in this category increased by 14 percent a year between 1971 and 1975 against 8.6 percent a year between 1966 and 1970. The plan is noncontributory: that is, it is financed by state enterprises, which make payments totaling 15 percent of the wage fund. Cooperative workers are not covered by the state plan, but the law requires that they establish one of their own under similar rules. These state and cooperative plans form the backbone of the social welfare system for those who are able-bodied and who work in the socialist sector. Those working outside the socialist sector were not covered until 1977, when a new pension plan was introduced (below).

Various other transfer payments are also made. These include state assistance for children, maternity benefits, educational scholarships, and what are termed "money helps." These "money helps" contribute to the comprehensiveness of the social welfare system, since they help to provide, for example, money to those earning less than 3,400 lei a year.

The final element is "other payments," the miscellaneous category that includes such things as interest on savings deposits and income received from the sale of an individual's own produce on the open market. It is not thought to be a large component of total income.

To obtain a more complete picture of the standard of living in Romania, it is necessary to go beyond the various components of income and to examine their distribution. Once again, the unavailability of a more comprehensive data base precludes a thorough examination of this problem, but there are sufficient published statistics to indicate the degree of income equality in Romania.

Taking wages in the state sector first, the minimum wage for unskilled workers was set in 1975 at 1,200 lei a month and for skilled workers at 1,406 lei. The average monthly nominal wage in 1975 amounted to 1,813

Table 9.9. *Distribution of Wages, by Groups of Employees in the State Sector, 1960, 1965, 1970, and 1975*
(percentage)

Wages of group (lei)	*1960*	*1965*	*1970*	*1975*
Less than 900	65.4	39.6	7.0	...
901–1,100	16.0	23.1	20.3	...
1,101–1,300	8.9	14.2	22.2	3.5
1,301–1,500	4.7	9.2	15.7	16.8
1,501–2,000	3.9	10.1	20.8	44.6
2,001–2,500	0.8	2.6	8.2	25.8
More than 2,500	0.3	1.2	6.0	9.3

... Zero or negligible.
Sources: Anuarul Statistic, various issues, and data provided by Romanian authorities during discussions with the authors.

lei (Table SA1.14), indicating a narrow dispersion at the lower end. Furthermore, the Law on Remuneration[7] requires that the maximum wage or salary be five-and-a-half times the minimum. Table 9.9 shows the distribution of wage earners between income groups within the state sector. These data imply that the distribution of wages within the state sector has become more equal over the past ten years. So in the state sector, not only have wages been growing, but the benefits have accrued more to those at the lower end than at the higher.

Figure 9.1 plots the cumulative frequency of each wage group expressed in terms of the average wage of that year. The nearer to vertical the graph, the more equal the distribution. The results show that in 1975 only 50 percent of the state employees received less than the average wage, whereas in 1970 the figure was 60 percent and in 1965 was 65 percent.

Guaranteed incomes also exist in the cooperative sector.[8] In livestock breeding, the figure is 1,500 lei a month; in vegetable, vine, and fruit tree growing, it is 1,200 lei; and for other crops and agricultural works, daily remuneration is fixed at 40 lei.

Guaranteed minimum wages do not cover those on piece work. If piece workers fulfill their norms, they receive their contracted wage. Over- or underfulfillment of production targets is proportionately linked with in-

7. Law (no. 57) on Remuneration According to the Quantity and Quality of Labor, *Official Bulletin of the Socialist Republic of Romania*, no. 133–134 (November 1, 1974).
8. Introduced in 1971.

Figure 9.1. *Distribution of Wages in the State Sector, 1965, 1970, and 1975*

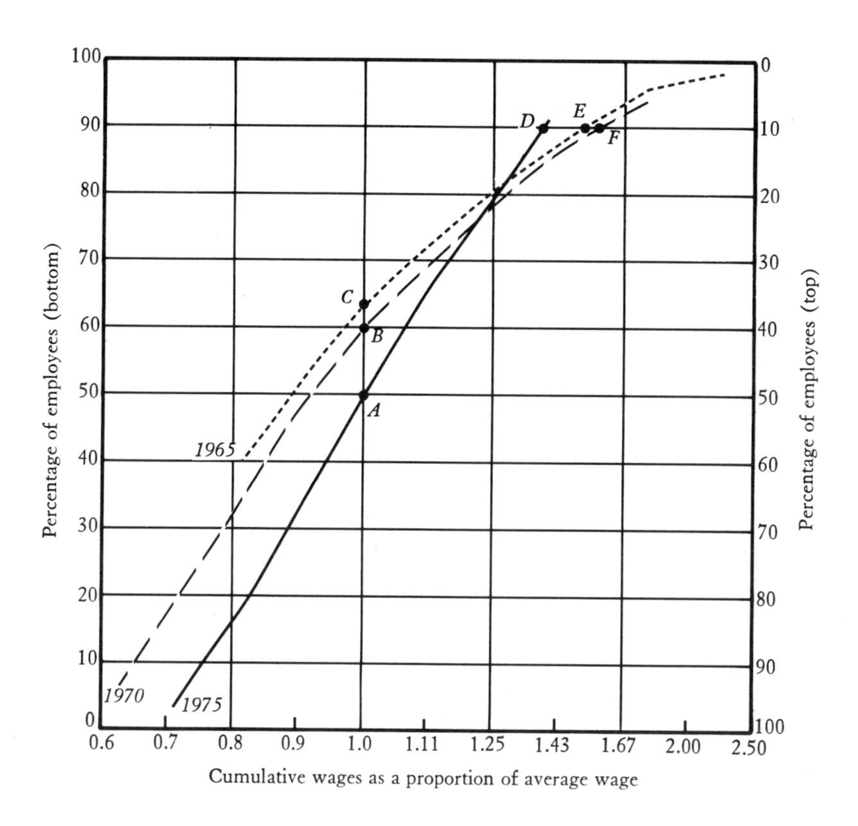

Note: A implies that in 1975 the bottom 50 percent of the population received less than average wage. *B* implies that in 1970 the bottom 60 percent received less than the average wage. *C* implies that in 1965 the bottom 65 percent received less than the average wage. *D* implies that in 1975 the top 10 percent received at least 40 percent more than the average wage. *E* implies that in 1965 the top 10 percent received at least 50 percent more than the average wage. *F* implies that in 1970 the top 10 percent received at least 55 percent more than the average wage.

creases or decreases in wages, respectively. Most cooperative workers and many state workers are on piece work.

To put this into perspective, however, it must be realized that in Romania everyone has sufficient food, clothing, housing, education, and health care. The basic needs of all people are met. Wages received are only part of real income. The comprehensive social welfare system and state provision of services exist for the benefit of all according to their needs (Appendix J). In addition, the price system attempts to provide goods at prices reflecting their social cost, with the result that the basic necessities of life are relatively low in price, whereas the rest are relatively high.[9]

Planning Consumption and Personal Incomes

A basic tool in determining the split between consumption and investment is the unisectoral macroeconomic model of the State Planning Committee (SPC), which maximizes consumption over a fifteen-year period. This provides the given consumption/investment split and implicitly determines the low rate of time preference by using the fifteen-year horizon. The extent of the problem can be seen by referring to Figure 9.2, which gives a simplified picture of the circular flow of income in Romania.

For a given output, the problem is to determine the level of household income that is consistent with the given consumption/investment split. In this calculation, various other constraints have to be adhered to. First, the level of sociocultural expenditure is predetermined. Such services are considered to be first priority and are taken as a given. Second, the taxation system is also a given. Income taxes have been progressive to create an equitable distribution of income. Turnover taxes are used mainly to set social prices. They represent the difference between financial cost and the derived selling price, which is set low. Third, there is the constraint of the wage structure, which is also determined by law.

Thus, the problem becomes twofold: what level of household income will lead to the desired levels of private consumption, private investment (mainly in housing), and private savings and what split between wages and profit will lead to that level of household income. The first problem is dealt with by selective consumer budget surveys covering a representative cross section of the population (11,000 families). Each respondent provides

9. For example, the cost of a new Dacia car is 70,000 lei, which represents thirty-six months' earnings for the individual earning the average income in 1976; rents average 7 to 12 percent of income.

Figure 9.2. *Income Flow*

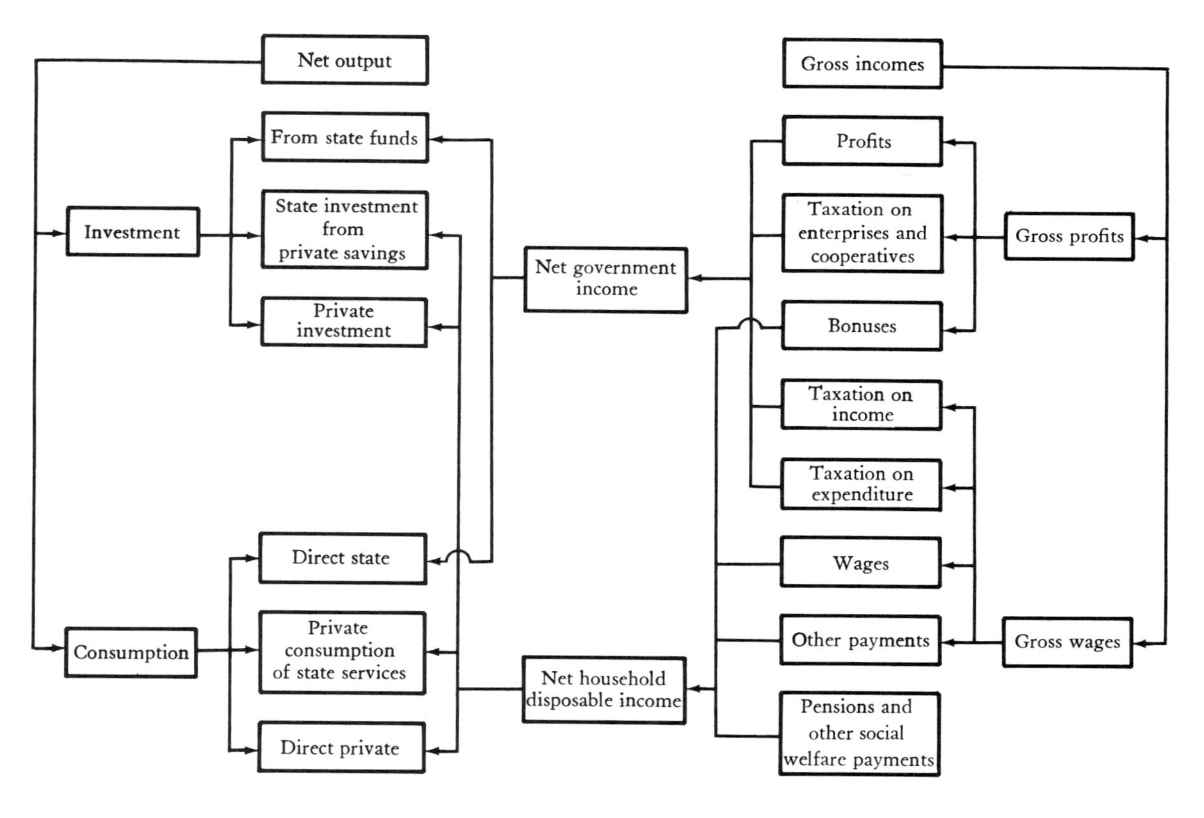

information on income, family size, and other socioeconomic indicators, as well as a daily questionnaire showing his expenditure on various items. In addition, systematic and periodic surveys of the population are organized regarding the demand, preferences, and opinions in connection with existing and new products. Annual consumer goods fairs are also organized in different parts of the country where the appeal of various new products is tested. This information, together with records of actual retail sales and prognosis studies, can then be analyzed and used to project the future pattern of demand and to determine the expected propensity to consume and the material balances in consumer supplies. Other conventional and more indirect methods of influencing consumer demand, such as changes in the tax structure or credit conditions, are not often used.[10] Tax levels and credit conditions are already set at the socially optimal levels.

The estimation of the wage/profit split, or the absolute level of wages, then becomes an arithmetic calculation, given the parameters that are already fixed. Total incomes are already determined by the level of output, as is the government/household disposable income ratio. Thus, given the level of disposable income and its structure, which are based on such parameters as the Law on Remuneration and the level of transfer payments in sociocultural expenditures, the size of the wage fund can be calculated and the system made closed and consistent.

1976–80 Plan Targets

Substantial progress has been made in recent years in increasing the level of consumption and standard of living in Romania.

Initial targets

The main targets for the 1976–80 Five-Year Plan are given in Table 9.10. National income (measured in comparable prices) is expected to continue to grow at 10 to 11 percent, with the consumption fund (measured in comparable prices) expected to increase at 8 percent and remaining at 66 to 67 percent of it. As the rate of increase of both real incomes and retail trade (in volume terms) is planned to be slightly lower, the indication is that the relative price of consumer goods and services will increase and that the real share of the consumption fund in national income will fall.

10. Consumer credit is available for most durable goods.

Table 9.10. *Plan Targets and Achievements*

		1976–80 Plan	
	Achieved, 1971–75	*Initial plan*	*Revised estimates*
	(percentage increase during period)		
National income	71	61–68.5	
Real incomes of population	46	35–40	
Real wages	20	18–22	30.2
Real incomes of peasantry	31.6	20–29	30.0
Services	68.6	61–68.6	75.0
Retail trade	48	45.0–47.5	52.0
Real pensions	19	15–16	16.0
State allowance for children	36	25–30	30.0
	(number of units constructed)		
Housing	750,000	815,000	1,000,000
	(percentage of national income)		
Consumption fund as percent of national income	66	66–67	

Sources: Law (no. 4) on Adoption of the Unified National Plan of Economic and Social Development for 1976–80, *Official Bulletin of the Socialist Republic of Romania,* no. 65 (July 7, 1976), and data provided by the Romanian authorities during discussions with the authors.

Nevertheless, although the momentum may be slightly reduced, living standards should continue to rise rapidly. Real incomes are expected to increase annually at 7 percent, retail trade at 8.7 percent, and services at 11 percent. These are bold targets, but if Romanian past experience is a guide, they will at least be fulfilled on average.

Since the increase in real income is generally greater than that of real wages (above) and because of the increases in salaried personnel, the greatest increases in consumption can be expected in the sociocultural sectors. Education, public health services, and cultural activities will receive particular attention. The building of over one million new housing units[11] is intended to help solve the chronic housing shortage. Early reports of achievements in 1976 and new targets for 1977 indicated that at least the initial targets for the five-year period should be achieved.

Retail supplies will (as noted above) increase by approximately 8.7 percent a year. The increases for some of the major commodities are shown in Table 9.11. During this five-year plan, particular emphasis seems to be

11. This is a revised five-year plan target (Chapter 12).

Table 9.11. *Retail Trade*
(percentage)

	Increase in 1975 over 1970	*Increase in 1980 over 1975*
Meat and meat products	52.5	55–63
Milk for consumption	50.2	65–78
Butter	41.5	75–108
Cheese	36.1	60–84
Edible oil	11.7	35–47
Sugar	29.7	30–39
Eggs	115.5	50–60
Vegetables	5.1	65–76
Fruits (including grapes)	63.3	100–154
Knitwear	64.0	60–68
Footwear	38.7	50–55
Radios	41.9	55–63
Televisions	62.9	45–50
Refrigerators	80.7	50–54
Furniture	52.4	45–50
Passenger automobiles	78.4	45–50

Source: Law (no. 4) on Adoption of the Plan for 1976–80.

going to foodstuffs, as before, with the biggest increases planned for fruit, vegetables, and dairy products, as against staple goods. The increase in consumer durables, however, seems to be getting less priority than in the last five-year plan.

The plan law states that the supply of goods to the public will be improved "through . . . rigorous application of the provisions of the programs relating to production and marketing of consumer goods, achievement of regularity of supply of commodities as market allocations in a diversified assortment structure and of a suitable quality."[12] In other words, consumer preferences should be satisfied more fully.

Further improvements are also envisaged that will not be mirrored in the standard indexes. For instance, the working week was planned to be reduced to forty-four to forty-six hours by 1980 from the present forty-eight, but because of the earthquake, this began in 1978 instead of 1977 and

12. Law (no. 4) on the Adoption of the Plan for 1976–80.

will be implemented by 1982 instead of 1980. Also, the minimum sizes of state apartments will be increased, and they will tend to be of a higher standard. Finally, along with these definitive increases in the standard of living projected for the five-year period, 33 to 34 percent of national income is to be invested in returns for the future.

Revised (1977) targets

In mid-1977, a new program was adopted with higher targets for wages and pensions during the 1976–80 Five-Year Plan. Some of the revised targets are given in Table 9.10.

INCREASES IN WAGES IN NONAGRICULTURAL ACTIVITIES. An additional 35 billion lei have been added to the wage fund over and above the increases specified in the 1976–80 Five-Year Plan. This would entail an increase in real wages over the period of about 30 percent compared with the 18 to 22 percent envisaged earlier. The authorities attribute this additional increase in the wage fund to "savings realized through lowering of the cost of investments and sounder management of social consumption funds."

The additional increase in the wage fund is substantial and should lead to corresponding increases in the volume of sales of certain consumer goods. The net benefit that will accrue to the workers, however, needs to be reviewed within a broader context and is not quite clear at this time. For example, total sociocultural expenditures which make up a substantial portion of family income are not increasing as much over the previous five-year plan period as they did in the past. The increase in the 1976–80 period was 42.7 percent over the corresponding expenditures in 1971–75, whereas in 1971–75 the increase over 1966–70 was 53.6 percent. To the extent that this relatively smaller increase results from "sounder management of social consumption funds," there is a real gain for the consumer, but commensurate with that has been a recent government announcement to reduce further sociocultural expenditures.

For the savings realized by lowering the costs of investment, there is no published data available to analyze what proportion of these savings has been passed on to the workers. Concurrent with the revision of the wage targets, the initial targets for productivity changes over the plan period have also been substantially increased (in industry, for example, by 10 percent). The wage increases are contingent on attaining the revised targets for productivity increases. The last phase of the wage increases is scheduled for 1979–80, which are the last years of the plan. Finally, the real wage increase will depend upon the level of the retail price index.

CHANGES AFFECTING INCOMES AND PENSIONS OF AGRICULTURAL WORKERS. The new program increases the incomes of the workers of state agricultural enterprises, cooperative farmers, and individual farmers over the 1976–80 period. The increases in the incomes of workers in state enterprises will amount to 30 percent, as against 18 to 22 percent initially planned. The real incomes of cooperative farmers will increase by about 30 percent, which is close to the upper range of the previously expected increase (20 to 29 percent). The real incomes of independent farmers would increase by 16 percent, but no previous comparative target is available for reference.

A more important series of measures has been that increasing the pensions of farmers in cooperatives and the institution of a pension system for independent farmers. The pensions would be funded by cooperative or individual monthly contributions and a contribution by the state of 2 percent of the value of products delivered to the state fund either by the cooperatives or by the independent farmers. Without further details on the funding of these schemes, it is not possible to assess the net benefits that will accrue to the farmers.

PART THREE

Growth and Prospects of Major Sectors

10

The Industrial Sector

ROMANIA'S PERCEPTION OF INDUSTRY[1] as the key to economic progress has, as noted earlier, determined its overall development strategy.

Pattern of Industrial Development

The concentrated effort to expand industry has had impressive results. According to the Romanian statistics, gross industrial production grew at an average rate of 13 percent a year between 1951 and 1975, a pace that was one of the highest among developing countries and that can be compared with the rates of Japan, Spain, and Greece. Worldwide, only Korea, Singapore, and Iran appear to have shown significantly higher rates of industrial production growth.[2]

1. Industry is defined in Romania to include the following economic activities: (a) extraction of fuels and mineral resources; (b) production, transmission, and distribution of thermo- and hydroelectric energy, excluding distribution of such energy by general public utilities enterprises; (c) processing of materials, except in cottage industries (defined as the processing of raw materials in the same peasant family household that produces them); (d) repairs of machinery and equipment and of consumer goods; and (e) cold storage plants. Based on this broad definition, the Romanian classification of economic activities divides industry into eighteen branches, with the individual activities in these branches being further classified according to the predominant destination of their output. Group A comprises the production of producer goods and group B that of consumer goods. The industrial classification is uniform in all published basic Romanian statistics, except foreign trade statistics, and provides the main yardstick for the planning process. Cottage industries are listed in the Romanian classification of economic activities under "Other branches of the economy."

2. Any growth comparisons with market economies are subject to considerable margins of errors because of the different conceptual and pricing procedures applied to calculate relevant aggregate data.

Relative importance of industry in the economy

As a result of this strong performance, industry's share in social product, expressed in current prices, rose from about 47 percent in 1950 to 65 percent in 1975, about five times the contribution of agriculture. In national income, also expressed in current prices, the share of industry increased more slowly, from 44 percent in 1950 to 56 percent in 1975. This may be explained by a higher rise in the material costs of production, which are not a component of national income (Appendix D). Because material costs and depreciation are excluded, the national income concept reflects the relative weight of industry in the economy better than any other global concept used in Romania.

In this context, it should be recalled that industry, as defined in Romania, comprises mining and the extraction of hydrocarbons. Thus, it includes activities that had been well established before manufacturing was given the impetus to develop on a broad basis. This and the fact that industrialization in Romania actually began sometime before World War II—even though on a relatively small scale—may explain why in 1950 industry already had made a rather significant contribution to the economy. Recognition of this belittles by no means the achievements of the past twenty-five years.

Added to these achievements are the two million industrial jobs created since 1950 (Chapter 8). Total industrial employment rose to 3.1 million in 1975 compared with about one million in 1950; industrial labor's share in total labor force grew from 12 percent in 1950 to 31 percent in 1975. Absorption of the labor force in Romanian industry has been greater than in countries with similar records of industrial growth.

Growth and structural change in industry

Romania's gross industrial production, calculated in comparable prices, rose at an average annual rate of 13 percent a year during 1951–75, with the output of producer goods growing at an average annual rate of 14.5 percent, faster than that of consumer goods (10.5 percent).

The gross industrial production indicator is the aggregated value of the productive industrial activities. It is calculated from the enterprise level up and comprises mainly the value of finished and semifinished products manufactured for delivery, the value of industrial services rendered to other enterprises, repairs, and changes in stocks of semimanufactured and unfinished products. It may have an element of overestimation mainly because of the effect of double-counting in the process of adding the productions of the individual industrial units.

Table 10.1 compares the index numbers of gross industrial production with those of gross industrial product and net output for the past twenty-five years. It shows that net production—the value of gross production minus material inputs—has grown more rapidly than gross production and gross product. This reflects increased production efficiencies, including the effects of vertical integration. It may be more appropriate, however, to compare net production and gross product, since both are expressed in delivery prices, whereas gross production is expressed in producer prices.

The published indexes of gross industrial production suggest that the rate of industrial growth has been consistently greater than 10 percent in each of the five planning periods since 1950, with producer goods industries (group A) maintaining higher rates of growth than the consumer goods branches (group B). Because of the strong emphasis given in industrial policies to basic chemical and engineering goods industries, the difference between the growth rates of group A and group B industries actually widened during the first three five-year plan periods (1951–65). It was only during the last two plan periods (1966–75) that the difference between the growth rates of groups A and B industries diminished as consumer goods industries were given greater emphasis, although the group A industries continued to lead (Table SA6.1).

ble 10.1. *Indexes of Industrial Growth (in Comparable 1963 Prices)*
d Average Annual Growth Rates, 1950–75

Item	*1950*	*1955*	*1960*	*1965*	*1970*	*1975*
lexes (1950 = 100)						
oss production (in comparable prices)	100	202	340	649	11 times	21 times
oss product (in comparable lelivery prices)	100	201	338	606	10 times	18 times
t production (in omparable lelivery prices)	100	218	372	710	13 times	24 times
erage annual rowth rates (percent)	*1951–55*	*1956–60*	*1961–65*	*1966–70*	*1971–75*	*1951–75*
oss production	15.2	11.0	13.8	11.9	12.9	13
oss product	15.0	10.9	12.4	11.5	12	12
t production	16.9	11.3	13.8	12.8	13	13–14

ource: Anuarul Statistic al Republicii Socialiste Romania (Bucharest: Directia Centrala de Statis-, published yearly).

Table 10.2 indicates the growth performance of major industrial branches for the five five-year periods since 1950. It shows that the leading growth sectors of industry were chemicals and engineering goods, whose output grew consistently faster than the output of industry as a whole. The chemical industry exceeded other branches of industry for nearly twenty years until about 1970, when it lost its leading position to the engineering goods sector because of lower growth rates of chemical production. Other producer goods industries also showed periods of overproportionate growth. In iron and steel, for example, output grew faster than gross industrial production during the five-year periods of 1956–60 and 1966–70. In other pe-

Table 10.2. *Average Annual Growth Rates of Gross Industrial Production, 1950–75*
(percentage)

Industry	*1951–55*	*1956–60*	*1961–65*	*1966–70*	*1971–75*
Total industry	*15.2*	*11.0*	*13.8*	*11.9*	*12.9*
Electric power	18.4	12.7	20.6	16.6	9.8
Fuels	13.3	7.6	8.1	6.0	5.3
Ferrous metallurgy[a]	8.8	19.8	11.4	12.3	11.3
Ferrous metallurgy only	(8.5)	(20.2)	(11.7)	(12.3)	(11.5)
Nonferrous metallurgy[b]	16.4	12.7	13.4	12.4	10.0
Engineering and metal-working	22.7	16.1	16.9	15.8	18.1
Chemicals	24.0	17.5	25.5	21.4	15.8
Construction materials	20.3	10.2	16.0	13.0	10.0
Lumber and wood processing	12.7	8.0	13.1	6.5	6.4
Wood processing only	(12.7)	(11.7)	(15.1)	(9.0)	(7.9)
Pulp and paper	6.5	10.9	19.1	14.3	9.1
Textiles	11.7	6.2	10.5	11.1	12.1
Clothing	8.4	10.0	11.2	12.4	17.1
Leather, furs, and footwear	11.3	7.6	10.2	9.5	9.1
Food processing	11.1	7.1	8.5	6.5	7.4
Soap and cosmetics	17.6	4.3	8.5	9.3	10.7
Printing	16.0	10.8	14.8	7.1	1.7
Group A	16.8	12.8	15.7	12.9	13.7
Group B	13.1	8.4	10.5	9.8	11.1

a. Includes mining and dressing of ferrous ores.
b. Includes mining and dressing of nonferrous ores.
Source: Anuarul Statistic, various issues.

riods under review, including 1971–75, ferrous metallurgy production grew at lower rates than industry as a whole. This growth pattern is quite usual for such industries as iron and steel, since it reflects the various stages in capacity buildup. A similar feature, that is, the erection of comparatively large production units, exists in the particular growth pattern of the construction materials industry. Except for the 1956–60 and 1971–75 periods, the output of construction materials expanded faster than the output of industry as a whole. Throughout the twenty-five years under review, it also exceeded the growth of the construction sector, thus permitting the export of a significant proportion of production (for example, of cement).

Another important feature of past industrial development is reflected in Table 10.2: the lagging growth of some industrial branches that supply basic inputs for expanding industries. In domestic fuels (petroleum, gas, coal), but also in iron ore and timber, the domestic resource base became a major constraint, because available raw materials could not fully support the rapid industrial expansion. Particularly for oil and iron ore, where output has grown more slowly than the main user industries, this has increased substantially the dependence of user industries on imports over the years, thereby affecting their cost structure. To cope with this situation, the government, at the beginning of the current plan period, introduced measures to reduce the specific consumption of basic industrial materials in the manufacturing process. Similar measures were taken in late 1973 to reduce the consumption of electric energy. They were successful in reducing considerably the growth of energy consumption and in explaining in part the slower growth of power output during 1971–75.

As stated earlier, the growth of consumer goods industries has, on the whole, lagged behind that of total industrial output. This has been largely the result of the relatively slow expansion of food processing activities, which weigh heavily on the group's performance and is closely related with the development of agriculture. Clothing and, since 1966, textiles have been important exceptions. Expansion of output in these two branches was above the average of the group; in clothing it has even exceeded the average of all industries since 1966. Since both branches were particularly suited to provide employment for the female labor reserve in Romania—including areas in which industrialization had lopsidedly promoted the employment of male labor—and to achieve a better balance in regional development, these industries enjoyed greater government attention than did other consumer goods industries. In addition, both branches have become important convertible foreign exchange earners, owing to considerable labor cost advantages. The export potential in clothing and textiles was only recently fully realized.

Table 10.3. *Per Capita Production of Selected Industrial Commodities Compared with Other Countries, 1975*

Commodity	*Romania*	*Poland*	*Germany, F.R. of*	*Spain*	*Unit Stat*
Crude steel (kilograms)	449	440	653	313	54
Sulfuric acid, 100 percent H_2SO_4 (kilograms)	68	100	66	66	12
Caustic soda (kilograms)	27	12	40	10	4
Plastics and synthetic resins, 100 percent (kilograms)	16	16	82	16	3
Synthetic rubber (kilograms)	5	3	5	5[b]	
Nitrogenous fertilizers (kilograms of nitrogen)	61	43[b]	25[c]	23[b]	4
Phosphate fertilizers (kilograms of P_2O_5)	19	24[b]	15[c]	19[b]	2
Cement (kilograms)	542	544	542	675	27
Paper and paper board[e] (kilograms)	28[b]	33[b]	97[b]	55[b]	23
Cotton fabrics (square meters)	28[f]	—	—	—	–
Woolen fabrics (square meters)	5[g]	—	—	—	–
Shoes (pairs)	4	—	2	4	–
Sugar (kilograms)	24	47[b]	40[b]	19[b]	2

a. Dry basis only.
b. 1974.
c. July 1, 1974 to June 30, 1975.
d. Shipments only.
e. Except newsprint.
f. Compares with 7 square meters in the Republic of Korea, 19 square meters in Japan, an square meters in the U.S.S.R.
g. Compares with 0.5 square meters in the Republic of Korea, 3.2 square meters in Japan, 2.9 square meters in the U.S.S.R.

Sources: Anuarul Statistic, various issues; United Nations Statistical Office, *Statistical Year* (New York: United Nations, 1975); United Nations Statistical Office, *Monthly Bulletin of Stat* (October 1976); *Eurostat* No. 2-1976 (1976); and *Anuario Estadístico de España* (Madrid: Inst Nacional de Estadística, 1976).

Table 10.3 shows the production levels reached in some principal industrial commodities in 1975, expressed on a per capita basis (Table SA6.2). In this context, the favorable picture in basic industrial product is only one aspect of the situation. In many consumer goods, particularly in durable items, the gap between levels reached in other countries and levels in Romania is still relatively wide and results from the comparatively low priority that has been given in Romania to nonessential consumer items.

As a result of the strong growth in the output of producer goods, their share in Romania's gross industrial production, expressed in comparable prices, rose from approximately 50 percent in 1950 to 72 percent in 1975. Chemicals and engineering goods, representing the main components of the producers' goods output, reached a combined share of 44 percent in total industrial output in 1975. Table 10.4 shows structural changes in gross industrial production in greater detail, and the data reflect the relative decline in the share of the production of fuels, iron ore, and timber (above). The petroleum sector, in particular, the largest branch of group A industries in prewar Romania (13 percent of total industrial output in 1938), had its share in gross industrial production dwindle to 2 percent by 1975, following the rapid increase of the processing industries. The food industry, with 24 percent in 1950, had the largest share of total industry, which is typical of an agrarian economy with a weak industrial sector. As a result of the rapid growth of the other industrial branches and the level of development

Table 10.4. *Gross Industrial Production, 1950–75*
(percentage)

Industry	*1950*	*1960*	*1965*	*1965*	*1970*	*1975*
	in 1955 prices (lei)			*in 1963 prices (lei)*		
Electric power	1.9	2.5	3.2	2.6	3.2	2.7
Fuels	11.3	9.1	7.0	7.0	5.3	3.6
Petroleum and methane gas	(8.0)	(6.6)	(5.1)	(5.1)	(3.7)	(2.4)
Ferrous metallurgy[a]	5.4	6.3	5.6	8.3	8.5	7.9
Ferrous metallurgy only	(5.1)	(6.1)	(5.5)	(8.1)	(8.2)	(7.8)
Nonferrous metallurgy[b]	2.1	2.1	2.1	3.2	3.3	2.8
Engineering and metalworking	13.3	24.0	28.3	21.2	25.0	32.4
Chemicals	3.1	6.1	10.0	6.7	10.1	11.3
Construction materials	2.4	3.2	3.6	3.3	3.4	3.1
Lumber and wood processing	9.9	7.5	7.1	8.2	6.4	4.7
Wood processing only	(5.5)	(5.1)	(5.3)	(5.9)	(5.2)	(4.1)
Pulp and paper	1.3	1.0	1.2	1.2	1.4	1.2
Textiles	11.1	7.9	6.8	7.4	7.2	6.8
Clothing	7.5	5.6	5.0	4.2	4.3	5.1
Leather, furs, and footwear	4.0	2.8	2.4	2.4	2.1	1.9
Food processing	24.2	18.9	14.8	22.0	17.3	13.1
Others	2.5	3.0	2.9	2.3	2.5	3.4
Group A	53.0	62.9	70.0	65.2	70.5	72.3
Group B	47.0	37.1	30.0	34.8	29.5	27.7

a. Includes mining and dressing of ferrous ores.
b. Includes mining and dressing of nonferrous ores.
Source: Table SA6.3.

in agriculture, its share in gross industrial production had declined to 13 percent by 1975. The food industry was then about two-fifths the size of the engineering and metalworking industries and was only marginally larger than the chemical industry.

Size of enterprises

The industrialization process in Romania has produced generally large-scale industrial enterprises, and this trend has not been limited to heavy industries only, but is also evident in consumer goods and other more specialized branches of industry. Size considerations have usually tipped the scale in investment decisions, since large enterprises were considered essential for applying advanced technologies and for achieving economies of scale. Also, large industrial enterprises are more suitable for industrial planning and plan control than many smaller production units. It was generally considered that any disadvantages, such as domestic market constraints and some management difficulties, were temporary and that later benefits from economies of scale would justify the investment.

The following data reflect the changes in the size structure of industrial enterprises since 1960 (Table 10.5). Although no information on this subject is available for 1950–1960, the general process of size concentration appears clear. As the table shows, there was only a small increase in the number of industrial enterprises between 1960 and 1975, despite the intensive diversification of the industrial structure. The average employment for each enterprise doubled, however, from 748 in 1960 to 1,554 in 1975. The trend toward larger enterprises appears evident in both state enterprises and handicraft cooperatives. But it has been particularly strong at the level of the handicraft cooperatives, in which the average employment for each unit rose to almost 670 persons. An interesting development has been the consolidation of local state enterprises in recent years. A sweeping reorganization of local industries in 1973 cut their number in half. At the same time, average employment in local enterprises has quadrupled to over 2,600, well above the average of other state enterprises. In 1977 the main part of the local industrial units was transferred to the state enterprise sectors.

In republican industry, which comprises about 80 percent of total industrial employment and 88 percent of gross industrial production, average employment for each enterprise is largest in ferrous metallurgy, including mining and dressing of ferrous ores. In this branch of industry, it reached over 4,700 persons in 1974, up from about 3,700 in 1960. In nonferrous metallurgy (including mining and dressing of nonferrous ores), as well as in engineering and chemical industries, enterprises employed an average

Table 10.5. *Number of Industrial Enterprises and Size of Employment, 1960–75*

		State enterprises		
Year	*Total industry*	*Republican industry*	*Local industry*	*Handicraft cooperatives*
		Number of enterprises[a]		
1960	1,658	1,001	318	339
1965	1,572	1,065	207	300
1970	1,731	1,126	246	359
1974	1,699	1,251	102	346
1975	1,731	1,276	99	356
		Employment (thousands)[b]		
1960	1,241	1,003	149	89
1965	1,648	1,409	137	102
1970	1,997	1,629	207	161
1974	2,565	2,072	258	235
1975	2,691	2,191	262	238
		Average employment per enterprise		
1960	748	1,002	469	263
1965	1,048	1,323	662	340
1970	1,154	1,447	841	448
1974	1,510	1,656	2,529	679
1975	1,554	1,717	2,646	669

a. At end of year. Excluded from the number of enterprises are the units without a legal status, which are considered economically independent (see the Glossary).

b. In determining the number of employees used by industrial enterprises, the number of employees used in all shifts has been considered (including the number of employees in training for new enterprises).

Source: Anuarul Statistic, various issues.

of 2,000 to 3,000 persons in 1974. Compared with 1960, average employment for each enterprise more than doubled in both the engineering and the chemical branches. In lumber and wood processing, pulp and paper, glass and ceramics, textiles, and leather goods and shoes, the average employment for each enterprise reached a relatively uniform high of 1,600 to 1,700 persons. Only construction materials, food processing, and printing have remained substantially below the average size of an industrial enterprise in Romania (Table SA6.4). This may be explained by the fact that these branches of industry normally have a more limited scope of operations, both because of the materials they process and because of the markets they serve. This makes them clearly less suitable for consolidation.

Table 10.6. *Number of Employed Persons for Each Industrial Enterprise, in Selected Countries, 1973*

Socialist countries		*Industrial market economies*		*Developing countries*	
Romania	1,480	Federal Republic of Germany[a]	149	Colombia[a]	71
Hungary	1,070	Austria[a]	96	Brazil[a,b]	54
U.S.S.R.	712	United Kingdom (1972)[a]	87	Korea[a]	49
Yugoslavia	531	Sweden	68	Greece[b]	41
Bulgaria	520	Canada	58	Israel	35
German Democratic Republic	297	Belgium	35		
Poland	114				

a. Manufacturing only.
b. Figure for 1972.
Sources: United Nations Statistical Office, *Yearbook of Industrial Statistics* (New York: United Nations, 1974), except for Romania, which is based on data from *Anuarul Statistic*, 1974.

By international standards, Romania has probably the highest number of employed persons for each industrial enterprise. This is illustrated in Table 10.6.

The development in Romania of concentrated industrial production in large enterprises has several important aspects:

(a) In 1975 about 82 percent of gross industrial output and 82 percent of the industrial labor force was concentrated in enterprises employing more than 1,000 persons. These enterprises represented 45 percent of all industrial establishments. In 1960 the group of enterprises with employment of 1,000 and over represented only 15 percent of all industrial establishments, but this group accounted for 53 percent of total industrial labor and 52 percent of gross industrial output (Table SA6.6).

(b) Large enterprises employing more than 2,000 workers became the main generators of new employment. This development is somewhat unexpected after years of concentrated efforts in building up heavy industries and other capital-intensive and technologically advanced production processes. The use of large plants to generate substantial employment has meant that industries have remained unusually labor-intensive, despite the modernization and automation that has taken place.

(c) The concentration of new employment in large industrial plants has also had a significant effect on changes in labor productivity. If the size distribution of Romanian industry is disaggregated (Table SA6.6), enterprises in the range of 500 to 3,000 employees, and those in the 3,000-to-5,000 bracket until about 1970, showed inverse labor productivity ratios. This implies that labor productivity changes have been below the industrial average. Only in very large enterprises (over 5,000 workers) and in smaller establishments (up to 500 workers) have labor productivity changes been above the industrial average. Labor productivity in Romanian industry is discussed later in this chapter.

(d) The dominance of the large production unit has contributed to broad product mixes and to limited specialization. Particularly in the more labor-intensive engineering goods plants and in light industries, the great number of simultaneous production lines has frequently overtaxed the capabilities of production management and has made it difficult to increase productivity. As part of current rationalization efforts in industry, there has been a greater emphasis on specialization.

Industrial Investment and Employment

Capital investments have been the main engine of Romania's industrial expansion since 1950. Fixed assets in industry increased by approximately 10.5 percent a year during 1951–75, and industry's share in the total fixed assets of the economy (expressed in inventory values)[3] rose from 20 percent in 1950 to 4.2 percent in 1975. At this rate of growth, which was surpassed only by the construction sector, industrial investment grew about twice as fast as industrial employment.

Investment patterns

Investment in industry has been concentrated in iron and steel, chemicals, and the engineering sectors. Although these three branches combined had absorbed only 17 percent of total industrial investment in 1950, their share in industrial investment has grown rapidly, from about 28 percent in 1960 and 40 percent in 1970 to about 46 percent in 1975. The investment share of petroleum exploration and development, however, declined as a result of industrial diversification. In 1950 it represented the largest capital outlay of Romanian industry, accounting for almost 40 percent of total industrial investment. By 1975 its share in total industrial investment was well below

3. The published industrial investment data include outlays for the replacement of fixed assets. This should be kept in mind in comparing investment data among industrial subsectors and by type of investment. Net investment figures are not published in Romania.

10 percent. As a result of these major trends of industrial investment, there has been little change in the distribution of investments between producer goods and consumer goods industries. In 1975 the former accounted for about 85 percent of total industrial investment and the latter for about 15 percent (Table SA6.5).

Within the broad types of investment, machinery and other equipment have substantially increased their weight in total industrial investment outlays, from 36 percent in 1965 to 51 percent in 1975 (Table SA6.7). This results partly from the increasing diversification of industry, which has produced new activities with high technological requirements, involving new and costlier types of equipment that had to be supplied largely from specialized firms abroad. Replacement investment has contributed to the larger share of machinery and equipment, but statistical evidence of their proportion is not available. On the whole, the growth in industrial investment has been the main factor behind the exceedingly rapid expansion and diversification of equipment manufacturing in Romania, although exports also contributed (below).

The share of civil works in industrial investment has declined from 47 percent in 1965 to 38 percent in 1975, reflecting the government's policies to reduce construction cost to the necessary minimum and to emphasize the expansion and modernization of existing facilities. In absolute terms, outlays for civil works in industry have grown little in recent years, and there has even been an absolute decline of such outlays in the consumer goods industries. The increasing application of simpler construction methods, in part by using prefabricated elements, and, more generally, the recent drive to reduce the specific consumption of materials in construction works might explain this trend (Chapter 12).

Government policies affecting investment and the choice of technology

To achieve maximum use of its natural resources, as well as efficient use of its labor potential, Romania from the beginning has placed great emphasis on creating basic industries that would use domestic raw materials and also would provide a base for more specialized secondary industries with good potential for employment and improved labor productivity. A first priority was to develop chemical industries to use Romania's resources of hydrocarbons and other chemical raw materials, as well as metallurgical industries to use available minerals and energy sources. The pattern of investments in industry clearly shows this sequence, with priorities shifting gradually from basic industries to processing industries, notably engineering.

In the past twenty-five years, an increasing proportion of national income has been made available for investment by keeping consumption growth below that of national income. Emphasis was put on the creation of producer goods industries and the rapid growth of capital-intensive production. Since employment generation remained the other irrevocable objective of industrial policies, however, there have been situations in several industries where capital-intensive productions did not ensure in all cases the best use of labor, as discussed further below.

In the allocation of investments, priority has been given to those industries oriented mainly to the domestic market, since the achievement of certain levels of industrial self-sufficiency has long been an important objective. Until a few years ago, it would have been difficult to identify industrial projects that were developed primarily for the export market. Because of the rapidly growing need for imported equipment, technologies, and material supplies, however, there has been a greater urgency to develop industrial exports in recent years.

In investment decisions, regional policy objectives are now being considered to a significant extent (Chapter 2). In its regional industrialization efforts, Romania has increasingly preferred to establish enterprises within designated industrial areas to facilitate the common use of utilities and other services, to ensure cooperation among enterprises, and to restrict the industrial land use to what is strictly necessary. With this orientation, several specific problems have been addressed recently concerning cooperation between industries; use of land better suited for agriculture, public utilities, and other services; use of industrial waste materials; and, finally, effective treatment of industrial effluents.

Criteria for investment selection

All major investment decisions in Romania are made autonomously by the highest authorities of party and government[4] and are the basis for implementing projects drawn up at the ministry level (ministries, central research, and design institutes) with participation of centrals and enterprises. Decisions to invest in particular activities are essentially a matter of policy priorities, as spelled out in the development plan (the Five-Year Plan) and in the RCP guidelines of long-term economic and social development. Once priority has been given in the plan or guidelines to developing a certain industry, based on comparative studies on the development of indus-

4. See Appendix E for the distribution of competencies in the approval of industrial projects and on investment selection criteria.

trial branches, this industry will be given preference in the allocation of investment resources.[5]

Assessment

Investment decisions are made within the framework of the plan. Projects must contribute to meeting plan priorities and targets. The decision to incorporate a project within the plan implies that there is no alternative use of funds that can provide a higher rate of return. Once a project is approved, resources are released for implementation. Project appraisals are based upon a set of criteria that are assigned weights, which may be changed from project to project according to government priorities. To the extent the prices used to evaluate costs and benefits differ from border prices, the real net benefits cannot be easily determined.

If the criteria are used to compare different alternative solutions that satisfy most individual policy objectives, however, this method can be used with considerable benefit. Besides, many of the economic criteria used to assess project choices become important parameters of the physical and financial planning and execution work that follow after approval. And in aggregated form, they become part of the material balances that have to be established for products of national importance, of manpower balances, and of the national development and financial plans.

Choice of technology

Investment policies have generally given preference to advanced technological equipment and to installations with large processing capacity. This had an important effect on the growth of labor productivity in industry and the use of the capital stock. In some branches of industry, such as tires, light industry, machinery, and parts of the wood processing industry, the selected capacities were of a minimum technical size that not only met domestic market requirements, but also provided production for export. Some of the export products were not always in commodity groups in which Romania had a particular comparative advantage, and, in several cases, the country had to compete with established name brands in world markets, as well as with exports of developing countries. Romania succeeded in selling these products abroad, thereby maintaining a relatively high level of

5. Notwithstanding the establishment of overall sectoral priorities, Romanian planners adhere quite closely to some basic principles of resource allocation in selecting projects. These tenets include the principle of complementarity and diversification; the principle of cost-effectiveness (that is, the project's objective has to be achieved at minimum cost); and the principle of minimum rate of return.

capacity use. Several exports were sold at prices below average foreign market prices. If Romania could not sell products for export as planned, stocks accumulated, and output was cut. For these reasons, Romania has tried to negotiate foreign long-term contracts to secure firm outlets and to increase the productivity of capital.

Although considerable progress has been made in replacing obsolete equipment—over two-thirds of total fixed assets in industry are officially claimed to be less than ten years old—there is still deadwood in the existing capital stock. Pre-World War II machinery is still operating in some plants of engineering and light industries.

In the past, policies of industrial modernization and renovation and policies to reduce the wasteful use of capital have not always been well coordinated. In the latter case, enterprises have been encouraged in the past to keep and maintain equipment long after its economic life has expired.[6] Thus, despite the global reevaluations of fixed assets in 1950 and 1964 and the introduction of higher rates of depreciation in 1968, old machinery was used side-by-side with modern automated equipment in some enterprises, in some cases adversely affecting the overall efficiency of the enterprise. Although this machinery required higher maintenance outlays, it had been kept in operation to produce larger outputs and to save investment funds.

Some industrial centrals and enterprises with regionally dispersed production units have transferred older and mechanically simpler equipment to other locations. Since this kind of equipment has often been better suited to the skills available in the new locations, training costs have been saved, and the risk of stoppages resulting from inappropriate handling of equipment have been reduced considerably.

The problem of replacing obsolescent machinery with technologically advanced fixed capital is a permanent concern to ensure an increase in industrial capital productivity. Although the promotion of smaller production units (in part through breaking up existing large enterprises and specialization) would ease this problem in many cases, other more comprehensive measures may be needed, including measures to improve the depreciation system.

In several industrial branches it has been difficult to reconcile the need for technological advance with the need to create more jobs in industry. One example is provided by engineering, where priority was given both to

6. Two factors have contributed to this in the past: (a) equipment that in a formal sense had been written off could continue to be depreciated at the same linear rate, and depreciation allowances could be retained by the enterprise for reinvestment (this regulation was abolished in December 1976); and (b) to a much lesser extent, the 6 percent production fund tax, abolished in January 1977, encouraged the continued use of older equipment. Depreciation amounts imposed on equipment during its established economic life had to be transferred to the industrial central.

modernization—reflected in its rapidly increasing share in total industrial investment—and to creating as many jobs as possible in the industry. This eventually led to overstaffing. In addition, expensive automated equipment was frequently used to compensate for lower levels of skill. As a result, overall factor productivity was low.

Trends in capital productivity

Although high growth rates of capital investment have helped sustain the growth of labor productivity, official statistics suggest that capital productivity slackened until the 1971–75 period. This is a phenomenon that also can be observed in other industrializing countries, implying that marginal returns on new investments tend to decline with increasing modernization and sophistication of industrial production. The prevailing practice of overdesigning productive installations also contributed.

Analysis of capital productivities in Romanian industry is constrained by an index series based on different prices. Investment data are expressed only in initial values (full initial cost) and are based on different sets of prices. Questions of comparability also arise with respect to the various published output index series, which are expressed in comparable prices derived from different price series. Because of this, published output and capital series cannot strictly be matched, and any findings on capital productivity may have a considerable margin of error.[7] Published Romanian data do not permit any analysis of absolute capital-output ratios other than at the aggregate level. The published index series can be used, however, to trace relative changes of capital productivity over a period of time, also expressed in an index number.

Another difficulty in measuring trends in capital productivity with a reasonable degree of accuracy arises from the fact that industrial output indexes by branches of industry all refer to gross output. Keeping in mind the caveats referred to above, the general findings on capital productivity stated below should only be taken as rough indicators. This applies in particular to the apparent productivity trends at the disaggregated branch level. Nevertheless, it appears sufficiently clear that capital productivity in industry remained stagnant in the 1966–70 period but increased in the 1971–75 period. Yet the Romanian leadership has been increasingly concerned about the recent levels of industrial capital productivity, which are reflected in the actions taken to improve the situation in this field.

Estimated by branches of industry, capital productivity appears to be

7. Since 1965, Romania has published data for investment and output in comparable prices of 1963.

increasing in virtually all basic industries, notably in chemicals, nonferrous metallurgy, nonmetallic minerals, and, to a much lesser extent, ferrous metallurgy. In construction materials, temporary gains in the 1950s have been followed by a relative decline in capital productivity, reflecting the rising capital intensity of production. The engineering subsector appears to be a somewhat peculiar case in which the increases in capital productivity in the 1950s have been gradually lost as a result of high investments and some changes in the production structure. In pulp and paper, textiles, clothing, and food processing, capital efficiencies declined, mainly because of the move toward capital-intensive production.

Employment and labor productivity

Industrial employment expanded most strongly in engineering and metalworks, which accounted for 37 percent of the absolute increase in industrial employment during 1951–75. Employment generation in engineering actually accelerated, and during 1971–75 every second industrial job in Romania was created in this branch of industry. This strong growth of employment has meant an increased need for job preparation and on-the-job training. Other important employment generators were textiles and clothing, which together accounted for about 18 percent of the 1951–75 employment increase in industry. As in engineering, employment growth in textiles and clothing has accelerated in recent years, in this case reflecting increased employment of women. Table SA6.9 shows details of labor force absorption in industry during the past twenty-five years.

As a leading generator of new industrial employment, the engineering branch expanded its share in Romania's industrial labor force from 21 percent in 1950 (when it was already the most important industrial employer) to 33 percent in 1975. Textiles, lumber, and wood processing each accounted for about 11 percent of total industrial employment in 1975, followed by food processing, chemicals, and clothing (Table 10.7).

Despite the rapid growth of industrial employment, labor productivity in Romanian industry improved substantially because of the use of more sophisticated equipment and improvements in production management. Official Romanian statistics indicate increases in labor productivity just under an average 8 percent a year during 1951–75, with iron and steel, engineering, chemicals, and construction materials, as expected, recording the largest gains. The Romanian practice of expressing labor productivity in gross terms (that is, social product for each employed person) is only a rough indicator of actual productivity increases in industry. In particular, it may tend to inflate such gains in branches which, in the course of industrial diversification and specialization, depend on semifabricated inputs from

Table 10.7. *Distribution and Growth of Employment among Specific Industries, 1950–75*

Industry	*Absolute increase in employment 1950–75*		*Total industrial employment in 1975*	
	Thousands of persons	*Percent*	*Thousands of persons*	*Percent*
Electric power	31.6	1.6	41.9	1.5
Fuels	40.3	2.0	101.5	3.6
Ferrous metallurgy[a]	62.1	3.1	96.6	3.5
Nonferrous metallurgy[b]	57.4	2.9	73.7	2.6
Engineering and metal-working	739.3	37.2	912.2	32.6
Chemicals	170.6	8.6	191.8	6.9
Construction materials	74.1	3.7	121.5	4.3
Lumber and wood processing	173.4	8.7	313.5	11.2
Pulp and paper	26.1	1.3	35.1	1.3
Textiles	213.9	10.8	317.1	11.3
Clothing	145.2	7.3	179.6	6.4
Leather, furs, and footwear	58.9	3.0	102.7	3.7
Food processing	125.5	6.3	215.0	7.7
Others	70.2	3.5	99.9	3.4
Total industry	*1,988.6*	*100.0*	*2,802.1*	*100.0*

a. Includes mining and dressing of ferrous ores.
b. Includes mining and dressing of nonferrous ores.
Source: Anuarul Statistic, various issues.

other industrial branches. Because of some double-counting, which is inherent in all gross industrial production data, productivity increases shown for some branches (probably including engineering) may be partly attributable to increases achieved in their supplier industries (for example, iron and steel). The use of social product as a labor efficiency indicator can be misleading in another respect. For example, if an industrial operation saves material inputs to produce the same volume of output as previously, this would involve a relative decline in productivity as such. The official productivity data, presented in Table SA6.10, should consequently be used with discretion.

Aside from these statistical problems, the published data appear to reflect trends correctly. As the data in Table SA6.10 indicate, productivity increases in industry have slowed considerably, especially in recent years. Engineering industries, in particular, appear affected by this relative decline, as do chemicals and construction materials.

In industrial planning, both job creation and intensive equipment use were emphasized. As a result, many enterprises have combined labor-intensive operations in the production process with the use of sophisticated machinery. This has not always led to the best use of labor, and, in some enterprises, particularly within the machine-building industry, there are still productivity reserves that can be mobilized through better organization of the production process.

The past tendency of overdesigning industrial projects, which the government is correcting (Chapter 12), explains in large part why there is as yet little evidence of a serious strain on existing capacities. In fact, productivity reserves are apparent almost everywhere and could be mobilized by rationalization measures, including a more efficient allocation of labor. Staff can be shifted within the group of enterprises of an industrial central, a rather common practice during the buildup and expansion of such enterprises. With the average labor productivity increase experienced in Romania during 1971–75 (6.4 percent annually), the country compares quite favorably with most of the other countries for which comparative data are available, as shown in Table 10.8.

Coordination and Specialization

From what is known about selected product lines in new and expanded industrial plants, it would appear that Romania has rightly given preference to production with limited variation of specification, reduced number of types, and large serial volumes.

Product mix and specialization

Product lines with relatively short average runs, requiring frequent adjustments of equipment and tools and a rearrangement of process flows have generally been avoided. By keeping the product mix narrow, it has not only ensured higher equipment use, but also has employed to a certain extent labor with lower skill levels. In addition, testing requirements could usually be held to a minimum, since the relative product uniformity and quality involved only limited variations. Since the same production lines have frequently been maintained for several years without any major changes in engineering and design, it can be assumed that past production choices have generally helped to improve the cost effectiveness of production. This favorable effect has

Table 10.8. *Average Growth in Industrial Productivity in Selected Countries, 1971–75*

Country	*Percentage growth*
Poland	7.6
Bulgaria	7.1
Romania	6.4
Hungary	6.3
German Democratic Republic	6.1
U.S.S.R.	5.9
Greece	4.8[a]
Japan	4.6[a]
Spain	4.6[a]
Ireland	4.1[a]
Israel	3.8
Yugoslavia	3.4
Germany, Federal Republic of	2.6[a]

Note: The average annual growth for the countries of the Council for Mutual Economic Assistance (CMEA) is based on gross production values and for the rest of the countries on gross value added.

a. Manufacturing only.

Source: United Nations Economic Commission for Europe, *Economic Survey of Europe* (Geneva, 1975), and United Nations Statistical Office, *Monthly Bulletin of Statistics* (October 1976).

been further enhanced by the prevalence of large production units in almost all branches of industry.

In some industrial subsectors, however, the prevailing product mix has created some less-efficient productions and lower levels of capacity use. In these cases, the existence of large-sized production facilities has become a burden, raising difficult problems of production management. This was the case in some enterprises in the engineering subsector, notably mechanical engineering. These enterprises had relatively short production runs, and, because of certain adjustments and rearrangements of process flows, there were lower levels of equipment use, all of which tended to result in higher production costs. For these reasons the engineering subsector had shown a lower degree of capacity use than other industrial branches of Romania.

In the engineering industry, as in all other branches of industry, serial changes, the introduction of new products, and the technologies to be applied are established plan targets that take into account the specific suggestions made by the enterprises, centrals, ministries, and the economic synthesis organs. In determining the specific plan targets, centrals and enterprises may generally give a preference to a more limited number of new products and processes, which they see as being more compatible with the plan targets. Any possible differences in the approach to new products and process are, however, finally decided upon by the central authorities.

Throughout industry in Romania, the emphasis on size has led to long production runs and infrequent model changes. In addition, the planning system gives very limited incentives for continuous industrial innovation beyond the planned technological efforts. As in other centrally planned economies, an institutionalized sellers' market tends to be created, where the industrial consumer must buy what is offered to him. All these factors explain why there is considerable scope for further industrial specialization and for more cooperation between enterprises belonging to different centrals and ministries.

To a large extent, past specialization has occurred within existing large industrial complexes, leading to a rapid multiplication of different production lines and involving only limited cooperation and integration with other plants. Under these conditions, an enterprise producing transport equipment might also manufacture a range of materials and components aside from machine tools and other instruments. Tehnofrig, a food equipment manufacturer at Cluj, has a product mix ranging from refrigeration and milling equipment to equipment for the beverage, dairy, brewing, canning, edible oil, and baking industries. And a manufacturer of equipment for producing construction and refractory materials at Bistrita also produces equipment for ordinary bricks, firebricks, glass, and ceramic materials and other items such as dust-retaining filters. Specialization is also quite limited in the chemical subsector, but it has advanced in recent years more rapidly in machine building. Although the enterprises themselves have a highly diversified product list and are oriented toward long production runs, integration with secondary processing plants and specialization in output of final products is still rather limited.

In general, enterprises supplying general purpose materials and components are still unable to cover the entire range of types and dimensions that are in demand, despite the fact that their product list is very extensive. The insufficient capacity and small number of medium-sized and small suppliers able to economically manufacture small batches of materials and components, which are not established by the plan, still create problems for industrial plants. This forces them to postpone the manufacture of some products requested by the customer.[8]

Enterprise diversification and cooperation has been slow in the past and

8. Serban Orascu, *Specializarea si Cooperarea in Industrie*, Bucharest 1974, pp. 55–56.

has been achieved mainly within the same enterprise and only exceptionally by transfers of production lines to other locations. More recently, however, the trend toward specialization has intensified, in part as a result of agreements with foreign partners on technical cooperation, as well as the conditions in world markets. In some industrial branches, progress in that direction has been slow. This applies, in particular, to the engineering subsector which, although commonly offering the best conditions for specialization and coordination, shows one of the heaviest plant and output concentrations and one of the lowest degrees of plant integration by international comparison.

Pricing of industrial goods

As in all centrally planned economies, prices are set by the authorities. They are uniform for any type of product, and, in any part of the country, and larger consumers do not enjoy any advantage over smaller ones. In practice, large consumers with delivery contracts are only charged the delivery price of the centrals' warehousing and distribution units, whereas the population which depends on retail outlets pays the higher retail price which covers the distribution cost and profit margin of the state warehouse and distribution company (ITA) and the retail stores.

The government's strategy has been dominated by long-term development strategy, emphasizing maximum use of domestic natural resources and the mobilization of the country's labor potential for industrial work (above). As a result, prices for some raw materials of the extractive industries were set at low levels. Farm prices were kept low in relation to industrial products. This may provide another explanation of why food processing and other industrial branches based on domestic supplies of agricultural materials showed a relatively larger decline in total industrial production than their physical output trends would suggest. In the past, prices for natural gas have been set too low relative to the price for coal, so that there was no incentive to increase the use of coal in power generation.

The vested interests of enterprises have entered into the price-setting process from another angle. Since their profit margins have been established on the basis of effective cost, enterprises have had an incentive to overstate planned costs, particularly on the price-setting of new industrial products, where such actions also provide a shield against inherent risks of new production, and thereby to inflate the real growth of gross industrial production. Since the chemicals and machine-building subsectors have generated many of the new products, this applies largely to them. In recognition of that possibility, the government has introduced, particularly since 1971 when the Law on Prices was put into force, measures to assess and adjust prices of products both before their introduction and after production has begun. These measures make it unlikely that overpricing of new goods is now an important source of distortion in the statistics.

The fact that the cost-price calculation, as used in the price-setting process, has not included any specific charges for fixed or total assets, except for 1974–76 when a production assets tax was introduced, has influenced enterprises to strive for unduly capital-intensive production and has not given adequate incentives for full use of these assets. Since the assets tax did not contribute to the expected extent to the better use of assets and to a realistic assessment of investment requirements, the government abolished this tax in 1976 and at the same time introduced a tax on benefits, which is not included in the production cost.

The last comprehensive round of price-resetting occurred during 1974–76 and was at least partly induced by the recent price changes in world markets. In these rounds, new prices were established for most industrial products. In the price-resetting process, adjustments were made for increases in raw material prices and for several wage increases and similar effects. In addition, those cases in which prices had been subsidized by the budget were abolished.

Quality and quality control

The production of quality industrial products has been a prime concern of Romania for years. This is not only underlined by the number of advanced technologies adopted in industrial production (through direct imports and joint ventures), but also by the continuous efforts to improve on them. Moreover, quality control is promoted through a complex system of standards and controls established at the institutional level and of incentives and penalties.

In many cases, Romania has gained and kept an international reputation for the quality of its products. Oil drilling equipment, equipment for the petrochemical industry, and tractors are only some examples where such a reputation is well established, and Romanian brandnames already speak for the quality of the relevant products. The success in the diversification of industrial exports further reflects this development.

Although the quality of some industrial products is comparable with international standards, the products may have to be sold at a discount in world markets to penetrate these markets. These products are not yet well established in world markets chiefly because sales support is insufficient, continuous marketing efforts are not made, and servicing facilities are insufficient.

There are still several industrial products, both consumer goods and investment goods, that have quality characteristics and other properties that make them acceptable only in more limited markets and sometimes at relatively low prices. The number of such products has been declining substantially in recent years, however, as a result of stricter measures to ensure and improve product quality.

In Romania, qualitative aspects of production are addressed in the plan and in quality control laws, the most recent of which was enacted in July 1977. The plan, in a separate chapter, establishes the share of quality products to be produced by industrial branches, centrals, and enterprises; new products and technologies; existing products to be improved; and standards to be applied; as well as those products that are to be taken off production. The targets set are binding, and compliance at the enterprise level is stimulated by granting premiums and by the possibility of penalties and other forms of punishment. Quality control is exercised by special Departments of Technical Quality Control at the ministries, centrals, and enterprises. These departments supervise the observance of technical specification and norms during all stages of the production process. They are subordinated to and cooperate with the General State Inspectorate for Quality Control, which has its own test facilities, and the Central Council of Workers Control, which is a RCP organ.

Although the institutional system set up to promote and control the quality of products is quite comprehensive, it is somewhat rigid. It is probably its rigidity and the required strict coordination of the entities involved that make it difficult to improve quality on a continuous basis and beyond the established targets. Also, as the prevailing incentive system is construed, it is still generally more important to achieve and overfulfill physical output targets than to concentrate on a continuous improvement of the quality of products.

Industry, Foreign Trade, and International Cooperation

Romania's impressive pace of industrialization is reflected in the rapid development and changing composition of its foreign trade.

Industrial imports and exports

Imports of industrial equipment, materials, and, since 1968, petroleum accounted for around 90 percent of total imports between 1950 and 1975 and over 90 percent of the absolute growth of imports during the period. Consequently, foreign exchange outlays rose steeply—from only US$0.2 billion in 1950 and about US$0.6 billion in 1960 to almost US$5.0 billion in 1975 (all expressed in current dollars).

To pay for these rising import requirements, which increasingly came from western industrialized economies and from developing countries providing essential raw materials and petroleum, Romania had to expand its commodity exports greatly and to shift from its traditional export base of raw materials and food items to higher-value processed commodities. Through energetic efforts, at times by suppressing domestic demand, and by taking advantage of every possible market opportunity abroad, Romania succeeded in boosting its industrial exports from very low levels in the 1950s and early 1960s to US$1.7 billion in 1970 and US$4.9 billion in 1975 (Tables SA6.11 and SA6.12). Industrial exports contributed about 92 percent of the absolute growth of total exports during 1960–75, but, as industry is defined in Romania, industrial exports also constitute a significant, though rapidly declining, proportion of unprocessed and semiprocessed materials. The share of these kinds of materials in total industrial exports was 62 percent in 1960, but has been about 45 percent since 1970. Exports of equipment goods and consumer manufactures totaling about US$240 million in 1960, US$44 million in 1970, and US$1.7 billion in 1975, expanded at almost equal rates, each representing about 20 percent of total industrial exports in 1960 but about 27 percent in 1975. The share of finished manufactures in total exports increased from about 10 percent in 1950 to 51 percent in 1970 and 55 percent in both 1972 and 1973. In 1974 and 1975, however, the share of manufactured goods declined to 50 percent, mainly because of increased prices of petroleum products and raw materials.

Although available information reveals little about the actual direction of exports by product, western industrialized markets appear to remain the main destination of unprocessed and semiprocessed materials, opening themselves up only slowly to finished manufactured exports, mostly of consumer goods. In equipment goods, the Romanian export assortment has been generally more limited to buyers in industrial market economies, largely because of the relatively small share of sophisticated equipment and the shortage of servicing facilities. Export restrictions on licensed product lines also contributed. Notable exceptions were machinery and equipment for mining and basic chemical productions, for which Romania has developed some well-established markets in advanced industrialized countries.

Because of the limitations imposed on the export of finished manufactured goods to western industrial countries, exports of these products remained confined to socialist countries for a long time. In more recent years, however, additional outlets were opened up in developing countries to help compensate for the growing imports of raw materials and petroleum supplied from this group of countries. Trade agreements with developing countries helped to increase Romanian exports to about $1.0 billion in 1975, equivalent to one-fifth of total exports of industrial goods. By comparison, an estimated 50 percent of total industrial exports is normally destined to other countries in the Council of Mutual Economic Assistance (CMEA) and about 30 percent to industrial market economies.

The trade flows between Romania and western market economies described above explain the trade deficits with these countries. This feature and the problems of trade financing are discussed in Chapter 7. Brief reference should also be made to Romania's thus far considerable surpluses with socialist and developing countries.

The value of industrial exports, which according to the Romanian definition of industry also includes exports of mining products, fuels, and electrical energy, represented in 1975 about 17 percent of total gross industrial output expressed in 1963 comparable prices (Table SA6.13). This contrasts with shares of 11 percent in 1970 and 5 to 10 percent during the 1950s and 1960s and appears to indicate a substantial rise in the export intensity of Romanian industry. Among the major individual branches of industry, fuels and chemicals, ferrous metallurgy, and engineering goods appear to export larger shares of their respective productions than industry as a whole.

The most important contributors to the growth of industrial exports between 1960 and 1975 have been the engineering subsector, chemicals, ferrous metallurgical products, and food products (Table SA6.12). Engineering goods contributed over 25 percent of the absolute growth of industrial exports between 1960 and 1975, and in 1975 they represented about 26 percent of total industrial exports. In engineering goods, Romania was able to expand export sales of equipment used in the petroleum industry, also machine tools, tractors, and, as official statistics indicate, ships and naval equipment. In tractors, exports accounted for an exceptionally high share of total production—over 70 percent in 1975 with the amount of imported products needed for production reduced to less than 5 percent. Tractors probably represent the best success story of any industrial product of Romania. Of basic domestic design and engineering, Romanian tractors have well-established markets throughout the world, including western industrialized economies. Other examples are oil drilling, mining, and petrochemical equipment.

Chemical products, including refined petroleum products, accounted for about 20 percent of the absolute growth of industrial exports between 1960 and 1975, and in 1975 they represented about 23 percent of total industrial exports. Excluding petroleum products, the subsector contribution to the growth of industrial exports during 1961–75 was 13 percent and its share in 1975 was 12 percent. Exports of the subsector included caustic soda, carbide, synthetic rubber products, and nitrogenous fertilizers. Export shares in relevant production volumes of 1975 were close to 20 percent for tires, about 33 percent for chemical fertilizers, close to 40 percent for caustic soda, and exceeded 50 percent for carbide. Except for caustic soda, the export shares of the other products mentioned have increased during the past decade.

In iron and steel products, the export of finished rolled products and pipes contributed approximately 10 percent of the absolute growth of industrial exports between 1960 and 1975, with about the same share of exports in 1975. The export share of the production of finished rolled products was about 14 percent in 1975, and it has declined significantly in recent years. The export share of steel pipes was about 26 percent in 1975, but this too has declined significantly in recent years. Romania remains a substantial net exporter of pipes, however. This is not the case for finished rolled products, in which Romania has been a net importer for years. But import surpluses have been declining in recent years because of increasing domestic production (Table 10.9).

Processed food products have become an important earner of convertible foreign exchange, with outlets abroad concentrated in western European countries. They accounted for 9 percent of the absolute increase of industrial exports in 1961–75, and their share in total industrial exports was 10 percent in 1975. Chief exports have been canned fruits and vegetables and meat preserves.

Although textiles and clothing contributed only 1.8 percent and 3.4 percent, respectively, to total industrial exports in 1975, both commodity groups stand out because of their steep export growth. From an export volume of

Table 10.9. *Source of Supply for Iron and Steel Products*
(thousands of tonnes)

	1965	*1970*	*1975*
Finished rolled products			
Production	2,347	4,504	6,810
Export	342	1,278	1,003
Import	1,076	1,361	1,570
Pipes			
Production	586	767	1,151
Export	235	300	295
Import	81	106	72
Total ferrous production in raw steel equivalents	3,426	6,517	9,545
Net exports	—	97	—
Net imports	456	—	145

Source: Information supplied by the Romanian authorities during discussions with the authors.

US$8 to US$9 million each in 1960, textile exports grew to US$89 million in 1975 and clothing exports to US$166 million. Exports were directed increasingly to the European Economic Community (EEC) countries. Romania's growing penetration of the EEC market led to an agreement between Romania and the EEC in November 1976, regulating eleven different textile exports from Romania to the EEC from January 1, 1976 until 1978. Individual quotas granted to Romania were calculated from the average level of supplies during the preceding three years (1973–75). Romania's trade volume by commodity groups and selected individual commodities is shown in Tables SA6.11 to SA6.16.

Cooperation agreements and joint ventures

In recent years, Romania has become a strong advocate of international economic and technical cooperation, and it has extended the scope of cooperation to countries and institutions throughout the world. This new orientation represents an important change from the past, when international collaboration was far more limited, focusing particularly on other CMEA countries. This new orientation is significant for industry in Romania, since it provides numerous opportunities and challenges, notably improved access and exposure to advanced technologies and knowledge, additional sources of raw material and energy supplies, and expanded markets abroad for its products and own technologies.

On the whole, Romanian cooperation with foreign companies has intensified markedly in the past few years, both within Romania itself and in developing and industrial nations. It was in these countries, however, that Romanian efforts clearly made the greater headway. This is reflected in the rapid increase of various forms of cooperation activities, including partnerships in the construction of industrial units, cooperation in geologic exploration and prospecting, setting up joint production and commercial ventures, and the more general fields of technical assistance and consulting. Cooperation agreements and joint ventures are discussed more extensively in Chapter 7.

The 1971–75 Plan and Current Development Issues in Industry

Like the previous plans, the past five-year plan, covering 1971–75, was overfulfilled in terms of growth of industrial output. This is a remarkable achievement considering that, during this period, there were problems resulting from flood damages, as well as increasing supply constraints and much higher import costs for primary energy and other important industrial inputs. Flexibility in the use of labor, which is inherent in the Romanian system, has also helped to facilitate the outcome of the plan, since labor could be mobilized easily to fulfill and overfulfill plan targets. In addition, there is a production incentive system aimed to achieve outputs over and above the established targets, and the individual targets are set to stimulate overfulfillment of the targets.

Achievement of planned output targets varied among subsectors. Plan targets were exceeded by a great margin in ferrous metallurgy, engineering, lumber, and wood processing, as well as in light industries, with the notable exception of food processing. In ferrous metallurgy, including the mining and dressing of ferrous ores, the largest annual expansion rates were in the output of rolled steel products (middle and thick sheets, 21.1 percent a year; thin sheets 18.1 percent) and in steel alloys (16.0 percent a year). Domestic supplies of iron ore have declined since 1971. In the engineering subsector, above-average increases in output of electrical engineering products (18.7 percent a year) and electronics (26.8 percent) are higher than in most mechanical engineering products, including transport equipment, and in metalworks. The better-than-planned performance of the wood processing industry mainly results from diversification and the related increases in the output of chipboard and particle board (14.1 percent a year) and of furniture (12.1 percent a year). Although timber production declined, better use was made of low-grade timber and wood waste. In light industries, where rapid substitution of chemical fibers and leather substitutes for traditional materials was emphasized, output grew particularly in ready-made garments and knitwear, a large part of which was destined for export.

As Table 10.10 shows, some industrial subsectors lagged behind planned output targets. These include electric power and fuels, chemicals, and food processing. In fuels, planned targets were not achieved, mainly because of the delays in bringing new coal mines into production. In power, the underfulfillment of the planned targets may have resulted from the measures adopted to save gas and oil. The lagging performance of the chemical subsector, compared with planned targets, is related both to unexpected major repairs and overhauls that became necessary during 1971–75 and to problems in commissioning new plants.

Table 10.10 also shows that labor productivity increases in industry remained a little below expectations. Effective costs of production, expressed per thousand lei of commodity output, could not be reduced to the planned extent. There were several reasons for this, the most important of which

Table 10.10. *Indicators of Industrial Achievement during the 1971–75 Plan*

Indicator	*Five-year plan*	*Actual achievement*
Indexes, 1975 (1970 = 100)		
Gross industrial output	169–176	184.7
Labor productivity in industry	142	137
Reduction of effective costs of production per 1,000 lei of commodity output	11–12	9.2
Average annual rates of growth, 1971–75 (percent)[a]		
Total socialist industry	*11.0–12.0*	*13.1*
Electric power	10.8–11.8	9.8
Fuels	6.0– 7.1	5.0
Ferrous metallurgy[b]	9.0– 9.9	11.3
Nonferrous metallurgy[b]	9.0–10.4	9.9
Engineering and metalworking	14.1–15.6	18.4
Chemicals	16.2–17.5	15.9
Construction materials	12.8–14.2	9.8
Lumber and wood processing	2.8– 3.5	6.2
Food processing	9.3–10.4	8.0
Other light industries	8.9–10.1	13.4

a. In gross output. These percentage rates differ slightly from the rates shown in Table SA6.1 due to the exclusion of industrial production of non-industrial units (training schools, design and research institutes, etc.).

b. Including mining and dressing of ores.

Sources: Communiqué Regarding on the Fulfillment of the Unified National Plan for Social and Economic Development of the Socialist Republic of Romania during the 1971–75 Period. (Bucharest: Publishing Office for Political Literature, 1976.)

were higher import costs in production; the effect of the price adjustments in 1974 and 1975; and the introduction of the production fund tax of 6 percent in 1973.[9]

From the industrial performance during the past five-year plan and from specific findings presented in other parts of this study, it seems clear that the level of Romanian industrialization involves much more complex planning in the longer-term than before, requiring corresponding adjustments. In addition, there are problems related to the changing conditions in world markets to which the country has been increasingly exposed. One of the

9. This tax was withdrawn on January 1, 1977. See Appendix G.

important issues facing industry is the adequate supply of energy, including hydrocarbons for chemical processing, and of other raw materials and intermediates. Because of the level reached in industrial development, industry has increasingly depended on imports, and this has implications, not only for the cost structure and competitiveness of some industrial products, but also for the future path of industrial development in the country, since these conditions are expected to be accentuated in the future.

These developing conditions call for particular attention to specific courses of action, so that Romanian long-term growth will not be constrained. These are discussed further below. The government recognizes these problems, and, in the context of the 1971–75 and 1976–80 Plans, has undertaken or is undertaking specific measures to address many of them.

(a) More rational use of scarce industrial materials. To meet this objective may require abandoning certain production lines, processes, and projects that make extensive use of materials or that consume very great amounts of energy (for example, electrolytic smelting). A critical review of programs designed to increase the use of low-grade domestic materials may also be appropriate; this would have to be done with a view to minimizing the cost-push in industry.

(b) Rationalization of industrial operations. This must be done at both the enterprise and branch levels to achieve a fuller and more economic use of capital and labor. This would control costs in industry and would promote those industrial activities in which Romania has clear competitive advantages in the long run. Prices that better reflect economic scarcities would provide guidance about the directions to be selected. This applies, in particular, to the planning process. In actual operations, however, where the price regulator is less important than in market economies, it would be necessary to improve the current system of efficiency control. The following specific improvements may be appropriate and should be considered.

(i) Improved allocation of labor to achieve higher levels of equipment use and labor productivity. This may be achieved by reorganizing enterprises to separate labor-intensive operations from capital-intensive process lines, by plant division, or by some reallocation of labor among industries;

(ii) Improved material flows and better use of space;

(iii) Increased industrial specialization, partly by reallocating production lines among existing enterprises.

(c) Appropriate incentives to improve the quality of industrial products and to make Romanian products more competitive in markets abroad. To be effective, specific measures would have to provide financial incentives for enterprises. Because of Romania's dependency on imports of energy,

Table 10.11. *Indicators of Planned Growth in Gross Industrial Production (in Comparable Prices), 1976–80*

Industry	*1980 planned index (1975 = 100)*	*Average annual growth (percent)*
Total industry	*162–170*	*10.2–11.2*
Electrical power	128–145	5.1– 7.7
Fuels	139–149	6.8– 8.3
Ferrous and nonferrous metallurgy	173–181	11.6–12.6
Engineering and metalworking	175–181	11.8–12.6
Chemicals	203–215	15.2–16.5
Construction materials	154–161	9.0–10.0
Lumber, pulp and paper, and wood processing	125–132	4.6– 5.7
Food processing	147–155	7.7– 9.2
Other light industries	147–152	8.0– 8.7

Source: Law (no. 4) on the Adoption of the Unified National Plan of Economic and Social Development of the Socialist Republic of Romania for 1976–80, *Official Bulletin of the Socialist Republic of Romania*, no. 65 (July 7, 1976).

industrial equipment, and materials and the ensuing need to develop an adequate volume of exports, achieving higher quality industrial outputs is one of the most urgent tasks.

The 1976–80 Development Plan and Prospects until 1990

The current five-year plan continues the past industrialization strategy, with particular attention to expanding basic industries and technologically advanced secondary industries. Industrial investments of 580.5 billion lei (in comparable prices) are planned. Total industrial output is to grow by 10.2 to 11.2 percent a year, which is about one percentage point less than the target set for the previous five-year period (Table 10.11). The largest output growth is to be achieved in the chemical, engineering, and metallurgical subsectors, whereas the output of electrical energy, fuels, construction materials, and light industries is planned to grow below the rate of industry as a whole.[10]

10. A more detailed discussion of the 1976–80 industrial sector targets is given in Appendix E.

If the implied branch coefficients (Table 10.12) for 1976–80 are compared with the actual developments during 1971–75, it is seen that chemicals and metallurgy have been given much greater emphasis in the current five-year plan, whereas engineering industries are now expected to contribute comparatively less to industrial growth than previously. The latter is explained by the need for a more adequate structure of this subsector, taking into account the domestic requirements and export provisions. Food processing has been given greater attention than in the previous plan period. This is obviously also true of fuels, where substantial increases in coal production are foreseen (Table SA6.17).

Labor productivity increases in industry are planned to range on the average between 8.5 percent and 9 percent annually, but no data are published on industrial subsectors. The question of labor productivity is a priority target during this plan period, since the period largely coincides with the planned gradual reduction of the work week to forty-four hours. No information has yet been provided on how much additional labor is anticipated to be absorbed by the various branches of industry.

Gross industrial production is planned to rise about 8.1 to 9.1 percent a year during 1981–90, compared with a plan target of 10.2 to 11.2 percent a year during 1976–80. In social product, industry's share is expected to increase from 67 percent in 1975 to about 71 percent in 1980. By 1990 the

Table 10.12. *Coefficients of Industrial Growth*

Industry	*1971–75 Plan (actual values)*	*Industry*	*1976–80 Plan (target values)*
Engineering	1.25	Chemicals	1.25–1.26
Chemicals	1.13	Engineering	1.06–1.08
Total industry	*1.00*	Metallurgy	1.06
Metallurgy	0.88–0.93	*Total industry*	*1.00*
Construction materials	0.88	Construction materials	0.94–0.95
Electrical energy	0.86	Food processing	0.89–0.91
Food processing	0.78	Other light industries	0.89–0.90
Lumber, pulp and paper, and wood processing	0.74–0.84	Fuels	0.85–0.87
Fuels	0.70	Electrical energy	0.79–0.85
		Lumber, pulp and paper, and wood processing	0.77

Sources: Table SA6.18 and World Bank calculations.

Table 10.13. *Planned Growth of Industry (at comparable 1963 prices), 1975, 1980, and 1990*

Industry	1975		1980		1990	
	Volume (billions of lei)	*Percent*	*Volume (billions of lei)*	*Percent*	*Volume (billions of lei)*	*Percent*
Electrical energy	15.8	2.7	20– 23	2.1– 2.3	—	—
Fuels	21.1	3.6	29– 31	3.1	—	—
Metallurgy	62.8	10.7	109–114	11.4–11.5	—	—
Engineering and metalworking	190.2	32.4	333–344	34.5–35.1	825–977	39.7–40.8
Chemicals	66.3	11.3	135–143	14.2–14.3	312–455	15.0–19.0
Construction materials	18.2	3.1	28– 29	2.9	—	—
Lumber, pulp and paper, and wood processing	34.6	5.9	43– 46	4.5– 4.6	—	—
Food processing	76.9	13.1	112–119	18.8–11.9	—	—
Other	101.0	17.2	141–149	14.8–14.9	—	—
Gross industrial production	*586.9*	*100.0*	*950–998*	*100.0*	*2,100–2,400*	*100.0*

Sources: Anuarul Statistic, various issues; Law (no. 4) on the Adoption of the Plan for 1976–80; *Directives of the Eleventh Congress of the Romanian Communist Party Concerning the 1976–80 Five-Year Plan and the Guidelines for Romania's Economic and Social Development over the 1981–1990 Period* (Bucharest: Meridiane Publishing House, 1975); and World Bank calculations.

contribution of industry to Romania's social product would be approximately 78 to 80 percent.

Assuming full achievement of the output targets for 1976–80, Romania would see a further concentration of industrial production in heavy industry, with the metallurgical, engineering, and chemical branches reaching a combined share in total industrial output of about 60 percent. The contribution of fuel and electrical energy to total industrial output would continue its relative decline. This trend reflects the growth of imports of primary energy that would make it necessary to rationalize the use of primary energy, mainly by reducing less economical uses of fuels or industrial feed stocks and by cutting down waste. Along with the overproportionate growth of output of heavy industries, the share of light industries will further decline, affecting industries in both food processing and consumer goods manufacturing (Table 10.13).

As indicated in the guidelines of the RCP for Romania's economic and social development over the 1981–90 period, heavy industries will continue to be emphasized strongly after 1980. The chemical and machine-building industries are envisaged to remain the leading growth sectors of industry. Steel output is expected to reach 25 to 27 million tons a year by 1990 to support an engineering subsector that would be growing at 9.5 to 11 percent during the 1980s. Together, the engineering and chemical branches of industry are expected to increase their share in gross industrial production from about 44 percent in 1975 to 55 to 60 percent in 1990.

As indicated earlier in this chapter, the economic growth of Romania will require further imports of energy and raw materials that, combined with changing conditions in world markets, will require a certain element of flexibility in the planning process for industry. The uncertainty involved will no doubt cause periodic revisions of established plan targets, making long-term planning more indicative in many respects than in the past. Recent measures designed to reduce specific consumption in industries reflect concern for increasing efficiencies of industrial assets. The planned industrial expansion also considers the cost and availability of primary energy and other raw materials, but adjustments might be necessary in the planning process. This may make the current planning system and Romania's industrial organization flexible enough to respond to the requirements and challenges of changing conditions in foreign markets. The prospects and problems facing the Romanian economy are assessed in more detail in Chapter 16.

11

The Agricultural Sector

Agriculture is a basic branch of the Romanian economy and plays a major role in the economic growth of the country. Between 1950 and 1975 social product from agriculture more than tripled, social product for each agricultural worker rose five times, and national income from agriculture more than doubled. In view of the principle characteristics of Romania's economic development, however, these increases in production, which have assured an expanding food base for a population growing at 1 percent a year, have been smaller than the rapid industrial growth, and the relative contribution of agriculture to the economy has declined. In 1938 agriculture employed almost 80 percent of the labor force and contributed the major share of the national income: that is, 38 percent compared with industry's share of 31 percent (Table 11.1). In the postwar period, industrial growth soon overtook agriculture as the principal source of national income. In 1950 agriculture accounted for 28 percent of national income[1] (compared with industry's share of 44 percent) and 26 percent of social product; by 1975 its share of national income and social product had fallen to 16 and 13 percent, respectively. This change in the structure of output shares, however, was not matched by an equally rapid change in the structure of the labor force, so that agriculture, with some 38 percent of the labor force in 1975, was only overtaken by industry in the last plan period as the major source of employment. Considering that in 1975 over half of Romania's population lived in rural areas, it is clear that, despite the progress in industrialization, the agrarian roots of the economy persist.

The importance of agriculture to the economy, however, goes beyond

1. Not only because of poor agricultural production resulting from war devastation (Table SA7.4), but also because of the large decrease in relative prices of agricultural goods.

le 11.1. *Agriculture's Share of the Economy, by Indicator*
centage)

	Country totals								
Indicator	*1938*	*1950*	*1955*	*1960*	*1965*	*1970*	*1973*	*1974*	*1975*
or force[a]	—	74	70	65	57	49	42	40	38
ional income[b]	38	28	37	33	29	19	19	16	16
al product[b]	30	26	30	25	22	17	16	14	13
ed assets	—	19	17	15	14	12	12	12	11
orts	—	55	43	36	35	27	29	27	23

Shares shown for 1938, 1950, and 1955 based on shares reported for 1930, 1948, and 1956, ectively.
Data for 1970, 1973, and 1974 according to methodology in force in 1974.
urce: *Anuarul Statistic al Republicii Socialiste Romania* (Bucharest: Directia Centrala de Sta- a, published yearly).

its being a sizable employer of labor; it is also important in its contribution to foreign trade, both as a direct earner of foreign exchange and insofar as its growth saves imports of food and industrial inputs. In spite of its relatively small contribution to national income in recent years, agriculture during the fifth plan period accounted for, on the average, somewhat more than a quarter of total exports and 30 to 35 percent of convertible currency earnings. Thus, quite apart from providing direct inputs from agriculture to industry, the agricultural sector has paid for a significant, if declining, proportion of the imported inputs needed for industry. Furthermore, since agriculture has been a source of an investable surplus for the rest of the economy through the effective price differences in the terms of trade between agriculture and industry, the industrialization program itself has depended to some extent on the level and stability of the growth of agriculture. In addition, agriculture has been a source of labor for the growth of industry and related sectors, a labor pool gainfully employed within agriculture until alternative employment opportunities have been established. The labor force in agriculture declined from 6.2 million in 1950 to 3.8 million in 1975, whereas the labor force in the nonagricultural sectors increased from 2.2 to 6.4 million. More than half of the growth of employment in nonagricultural sectors since 1950 has been filled by former agricultural workers who have either moved to urban centers or who have assumed nonfarm employment in rural areas. This movement of labor from agriculture was encouraged by the relatively low income in the sector. Despite measures introduced during the 1971–75 Plan, the income remains at least 10 percent below those in other sectors.

Despite its importance in the economy, Romanian agriculture remains significantly below its potential. Although the introduction of modern technologies has accelerated in recent years and although productivity has grown, both the present level of productivity and the degree of stability of production growth remain at low levels relative to the potential of the sector.[2] For this reason, production growth has very often fallen behind the targets set in the plan, a fact that attests to the difficulty of applying planned production methods in a sector still too vulnerable to fluctuations in weather and other conditions. To avoid these shortfalls and instabilities, successive attempts have been made to secure greater control over production, partly by institutional change to expand the socialization of agriculture, partly by improving infrastructure in the sector, in particular irrigation, and partly by expanding mechanization and by using improved inputs, including new seed varieties and chemical fertilizers.

Institutional Development and Planning

Romania's present agricultural structure has evolved gradually with the socialization of the country. The transformation proceeded in phases beginning in 1945 with various forms of organization involving differing degrees of social ownership during the transition period. The gradations in degree of socialization persist today in the differences between state agricultural units and the cooperative farms.

Development of agricultural institutions

The first moves to reorganize the agricultural sector in the immediate postwar period involved land reform designed to redistribute estate-owned land, about 10 percent of the total agricultural area, partly among peasant families and partly among newly created state farms. By 1950, 9.2 percent of arable land had been allocated to state farms, whereas 88 percent remained as private farms; land not in large estates in 1945 had been divided into about 20 million small tracts (averaging about 0.5 hectare), with each family operating many small and fragmented fields. This reform, along with the institution of compulsory delivery quotas, eliminated the kulaks, a wealthier class of peasants. These measures, however, were preliminary to the socialization of agriculture.

2. A graphic expression of this fact was given by President Ceausescu's statement to the conference on agriculture in February 1975.

The first attempts at collectivization were in 1949. Difficulties were encountered in establishing large-scale cooperative farms during the first few years because of lack of material resources and peasant unwillingness to give up land ownership, and because the organization of collectives proved too complex for a peasantry that lacked the organizational and managerial experience required to operate large farms efficiently. Consequently, the peasants were encouraged to group themselves into agricultural associations in which individual land ownership was retained, but land was pooled within the association, and remuneration was according to labor input. The associations served as an intermediary form of organization during the 1950s and, at their peak in 1959, accounted for some 30 percent of the total arable land area. Although the drive toward collectivization continued through this period, by 1959 collectives accounted for only 27.3 percent of all arable land, whereas private farms still accounted for 26.0 percent (Table 11.2).

The final move toward collectivization came between 1958 and 1962. During this period, peasants, both in private farms and in the agricultural associations, were persuaded to form agricultural producer cooperatives (CAP's), which became the dominant form of organization after 1962. By 1965 the associations had withered to insignificance, and private farm ownership had fallen to about 9 percent of all agricultural land. During the same period, there was also some marginal growth in the amount of land under the ownership of state units (IAS), resulting, for example, from land reclamation and from some transfer from private ownership. After the mid-1960s, as shown in Table 11.2, there was little change in the distribution of land, but the structure of the sector had been consolidated through a reduction in the number of farming enterprises. Between 1965 and 1972 the number of IAS's declined from 721 to 215, subsequently increasing to 391 in 1975.

Table 11.2. *Ownership of Agricultural and Arable Land, 1950–75*
(percentage)

	Agricultural land			*Arable land*			
Kind of ownership	*1955*	*1965*	*1975*	*1950*	*1955*	*1965*	*1975*
State units	25.5	30.2	30.1	9.2	13.7	20.0	21.1
Cooperatives	6.4	60.8	60.5	2.8	8.2	75.3	74.2
Agricultural associations	2.8	0.4	—	—	4.0	0.1	—
Individual farms	65.3	8.6	9.4	88.0	74.1	4.6	4.7

Source: Anuarul Statistic, various issues.

These changes have been associated with efforts to reorganize IAS's, where appropriate, into industry-like complexes, in which state enterprises and their individual farm units have been separated and reassigned to form enterprises specializing in only one activity. The number of specialized IAS's for pigs, poultry, and grain production has increased over the past decade, but production of other livestock has generally remained in mixed farms because of its strong dependence on land for pasture and fodder. The number of CAP's also fell, from 4,680 in 1965 to 4,419 in 1975. Other notable developments during this period were the establishment of closer cooperation between CAP's and IAS's and the creation of Intercooperative Associations (ICA's) under which CAP's pool resources for large-scale investment in dairying, beef fattening, pigs, and other production activities.

Production units

At present, farming operations in Romania, which are under the overall control of the Ministry of Agriculture and Food Industry, are carried out by four types of production units.

(a) State agricultural units (IAS's). These include state agricultural enterprises and other state units such as research stations, seed farms, greenhouse enterprises, and others responsible for leasing pasture and meadowland to private farmers and cooperatives. The IAS is a state-owned enterprise worked by state employees and managed by a director appointed by the Department for State Agriculture in the Ministry of Agriculture. In keeping with the territorial organization of planning and administration, the director also reports to the trust of IAS's at the judet level, as well as to the Workers Council of the enterprise. Each IAS has one or several separate farm units specializing in the production of crops or livestock as a mechanization unit (Table SA7.11 and Figure 11.1).

(b) Agricultural producer cooperatives (CAP's) and small holdings operated by cooperative farm members. Land, buildings, and other property on CAP's are owned collectively by members. In addition, members are allotted a small area for their personal use (an average of 0.15 hectare for each member in 1975), may own some livestock and farm buildings, and may also use CAP land once the CAP harvest cycle has been completed. Like the IAS's, each CAP usually has several farm units. CAP's, however, do not have farm machinery except what is needed for hauling materials and performing other work around farm buildings. Mechanized field operations are carried out under contract with machine tractor stations (SAM's).

The general assembly of the cooperative approves production, financial, and investment plans that later must be submitted to the General Directorate

Figure 11.1. *Organization of the State Agricultural Enterprise (Farm)*

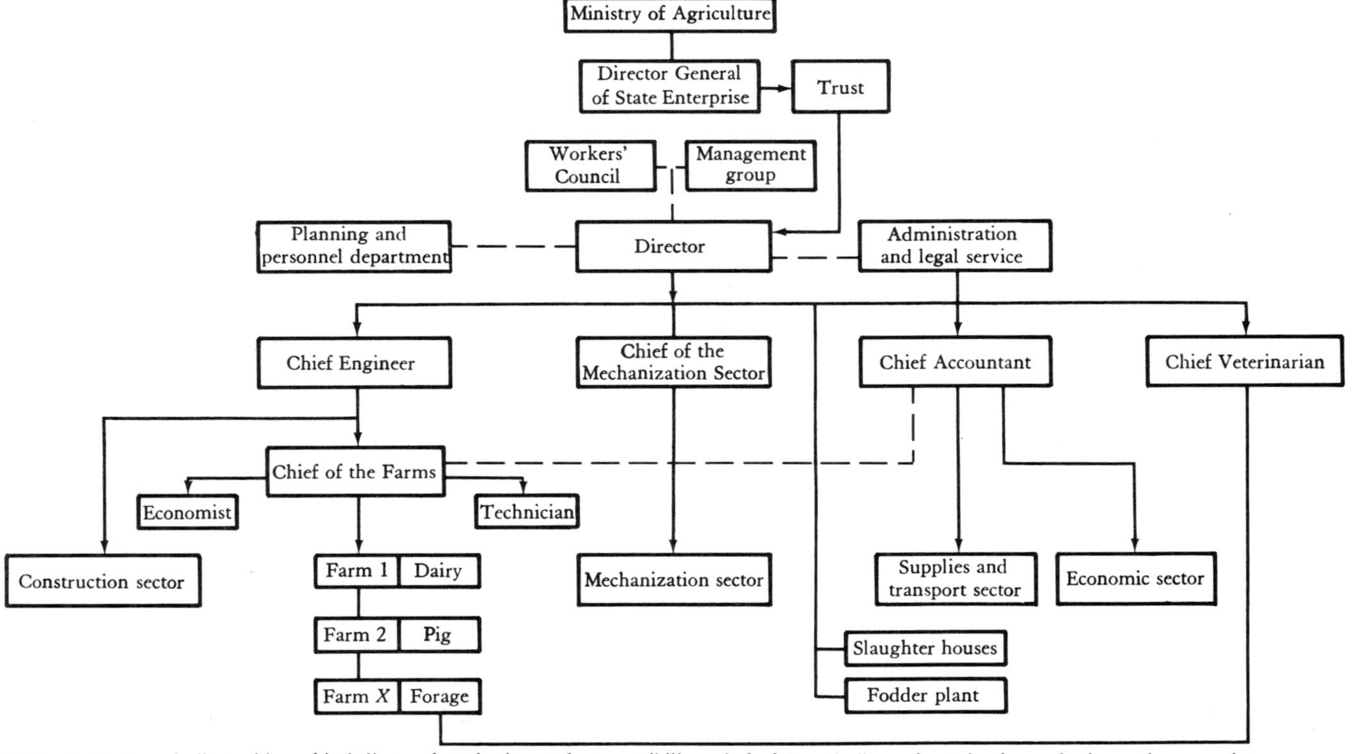

Note: Solid lines indicate hierarchical lines of authority and responsibility; dashed lines indicate channels of consultation and cooperation.

of Agriculture of the district for approval. The general assembly also must approve major contracts with suppliers, agricultural mechanization enterprises, and other cooperatives, and must decide how income is to be divided. All working adults, sixteen to sixty-two years old, are cooperators and members of the General Assembly (Table SA7.12 and Figure 11.2).

At a national level, the cooperatives are organized under the National Union of Production Cooperatives (NUPC). The NUPC was founded in 1966 by a congress of cooperative farms to look after the interest of CAP's and to help implement agrarian policies of the government. It undertakes social welfare programs for its members, administers the pension fund, provides legal services, and reviews all contracts between CAP's and centrals for marketing and input supplies. The NUPC has representatives at the judet level who participate in agricultural planning and decisionmaking, and it operates five training centers for members throughout the country. It directs all nonagricultural activities of its members and approves their employment in nonfarm jobs. A national congress is held every five years to discuss national policy objectives in agriculture and how CAP's can contribute to their achievement.

(c) Inter-cooperative associations (ICA's). Formed by several CAP's, these groups carry out large-scale factory-like production of livestock products, vegetables, and other greenhouse products. In 1975 there were 230 ICA's, mostly large-scale units to produce livestock. Typically they have little land and depend almost entirely on purchased feed and other material inputs. Capital required to establish ICA's is provided by CAP's and other participating units, either from their own resources or from loans from the Bank for Agriculture and Food Industry (BAFI). The ICA's are operated by state employees working for wages and are managed by a director, along with an administrative council made up of delegates elected by the general assemblies of member CAP's. Each ICA has a president elected from the presidents of the constituent CAP's.

(d) Individual farms. Farms consist of small areas, located mainly in mountainous regions where large-scale mechanized farming operations are difficult.

The station for agricultural mechanization (SAM), which is used to bring large-scale mechanization to the cooperatives, is an enterprise closely bound to the cooperatives, but separate from them. Romania has 743 SAM's, about one for every six CAP's and 12,000 hectares of agricultural land. They are supervised and coordinated by thirty-nine agricultural mechanization trusts (AME's) at the judet level. SAM's perform, through annual contracts, almost all mechanical work associated with crop and livestock production for CAP's

Figure 11.2. *Organization of an Agricultural Producer Cooperative*

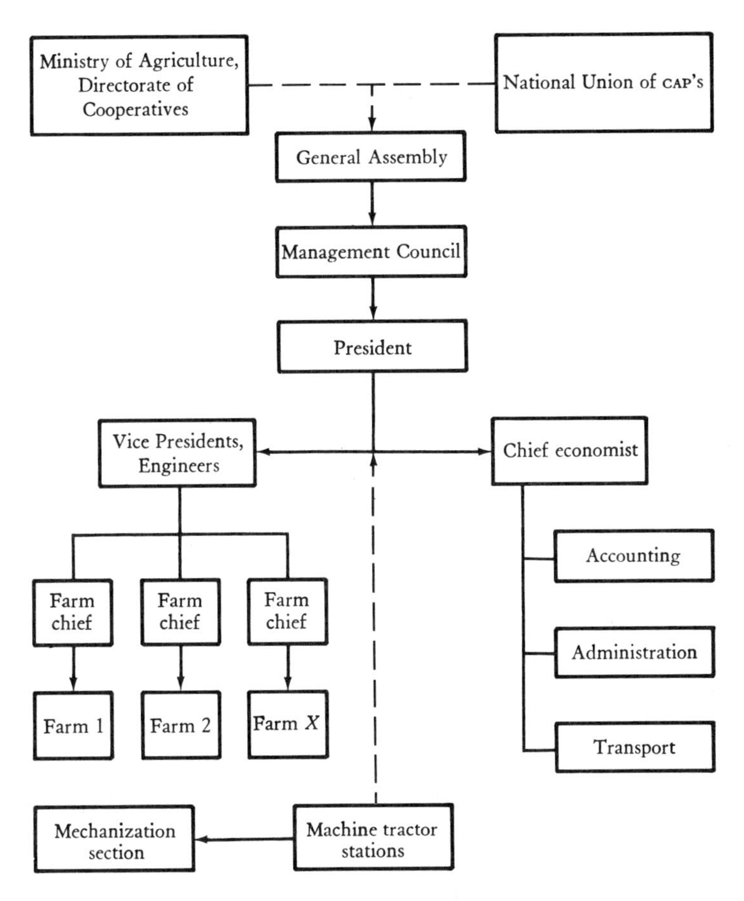

Note: Solid lines indicate hierarchical lines of authority and responsibility; dashed lines indicate channels of consultation and cooperation.

and maintain machinery. They haul input supplies and products and perform mechanical operations for irrigation. They also perform some work for private farmers (Table SA7.13).

Overall responsibility for production and marketing agricultural products, including processing and distributing some fruits and vegetables at retail levels, as well as for supplying agriculture with production inputs and services, is vested in the Ministry of Agriculture and Food Industry (MA). The MA is composed of departments, general directorates, directorates, centrals, trusts, and enterprises (Figures 11.3 and 11.4). The four departments are:

(a) Department of State Agriculture, with one central responsible for operating poultry enterprises and thirty-seven trusts at the judet level responsible for the operations of IAS's.
(b) Department of Land Reclamation and Agricultural Construction, which has institutes and trusts responsible for design and construction of irrigation, drainage, flood protection, and erosion control projects.
(c) Department of Food Industry, which has eight centrals that supervise the enterprises of processing and marketing meat, milling and baking, milk, sugar, fish, tobacco, oil-seeds, and beer (and all other alcoholic beverages), and one central for the complex of activities in the Danube Delta. These centrals supervise operations of food processing enterprises distributed throughout the country and market their produce.
(d) Academy of Agriculture and Forestry Sciences, which is responsible for all agricultural research and the production and distribution of improved seeds, plants, and breeding animals.

Other important centrals include:

(a) Central for mechanization of agriculture and production of equipment, which has one trust located in each of the thirty-nine judets (agricultural mechanization trusts, AME's). They supervise the operation of SAM's and plan for manufacturing agricultural machinery and spare parts.
(b) Central for exploitation of land reclamation systems, which has eighteen enterprises located in judets.
(c) Central for marketing cereals and production of feeds, which has several feed-mixing enterprises and thirty-nine enterprises located in judets and responsible for grain marketing.
(d) Central for vegetables and fruits, which comprises one trust directing and supervising processing enterprises, another trust super-

vising greenhouse enterprises, and thirty-nine enterprises at the judet level collecting and marketing vegetables and fruits.

(e) Central for wine and vineyards, which has several enterprises marketing grapes and processing wine and related products.

(f) Trust for textile crops, which has enterprises responsible for marketing and processing flax, hemp, and cotton.

(g) Trust called Protetan, which transforms nonfood livestock by-products into animal feed.

Marketing centrals of the MA are responsible for purchasing, grading, processing, storing, and marketing agricultural products. Marketing centrals usually have district enterprises and centers, which organize the collection, transport, and delivery of farm products to collection or delivery depots throughout the country. Agricultural products are moved from the depots to processing centers, and later are distributed to domestic and export agencies. Individual farmers and members of CAP's sell farm products produced on personal plots in peasant markets and to marketing centrals under contracts.

All sales of IAS's move directly to state marketing enterprises at prices established in advance by law. CAP's make contracts with marketing centrals to deliver specified quantities of farm products at prices fixed by law. They deliver a large part of their production to state marketing enterprises to fulfill obligations to SAM's. Penalties fixed by law are specified for unfulfilled contracts. Prices of farm products sold by individual farmers and members of cooperatives in peasant markets are permitted to fluctuate within certain limits specified by People's Councils.[3] Contract prices received by CAP's have been substantially higher than sale prices received by IAS's since 1973. Sale prices received by private farmers and CAP's for farm products not covered by contracts, however, are generally lower than contract prices. Foreign trade enterprises (under the MA, among which are Romagrimex, Fructexport, Prodexport, and Vinexport) purchase agricultural products for export. Foreign trade in grains, however, is planned and supervised by an organization named Agro-Export of the Ministry of Foreign Trade and Economic Cooperation.

The channel for, and administrator of, all investment funds provided to the agricultural sector from state funds is the Bank for Agriculture and Food and Industry (BAFI), established in 1968. Before then, financing in agriculture had been done by a department of the National Bank of Romania, except for investments in IAS's, which were carried out by the

3. Price ceilings are established for fruit and vegetables, but not for meats.

Figure 11.3. *Organization of the Ministry of Agriculture and Food Industry*

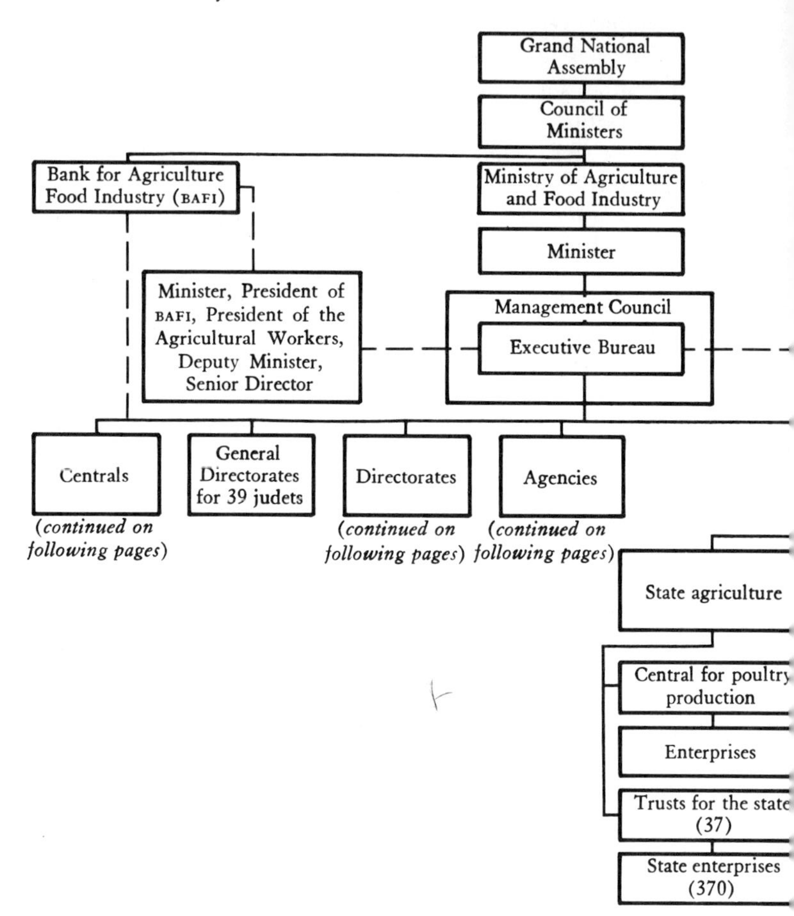

Note: Solid lines indicate hierarchical lines of authority and responsibility; dashed li[nes] indicate channels of consultation and cooperation.

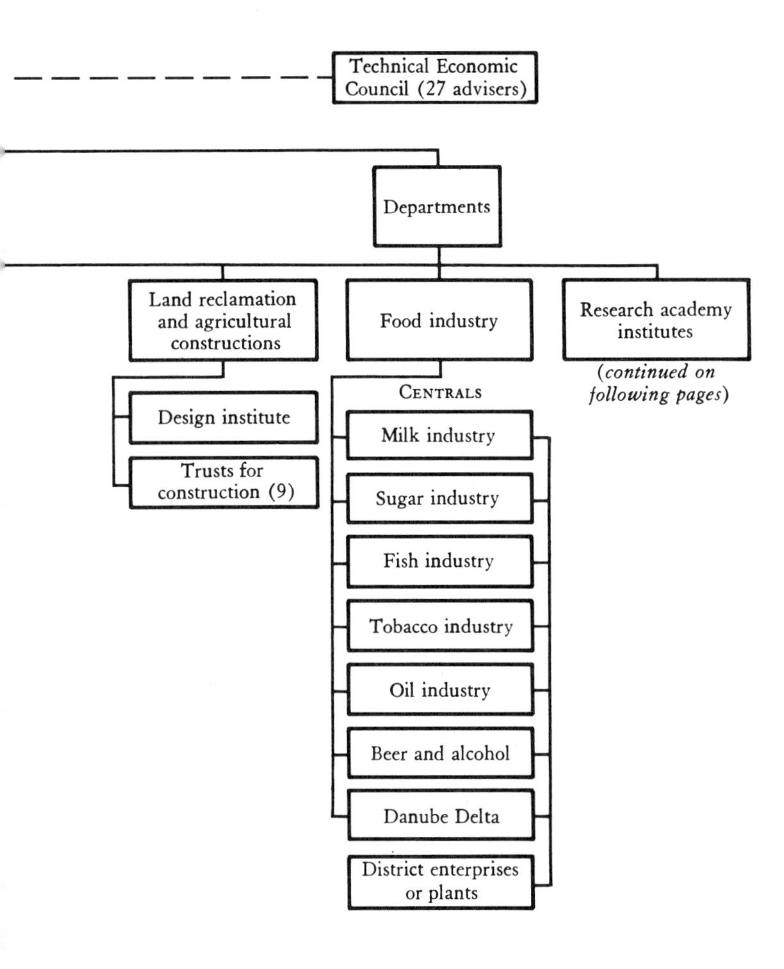

(*continued on following pages*)

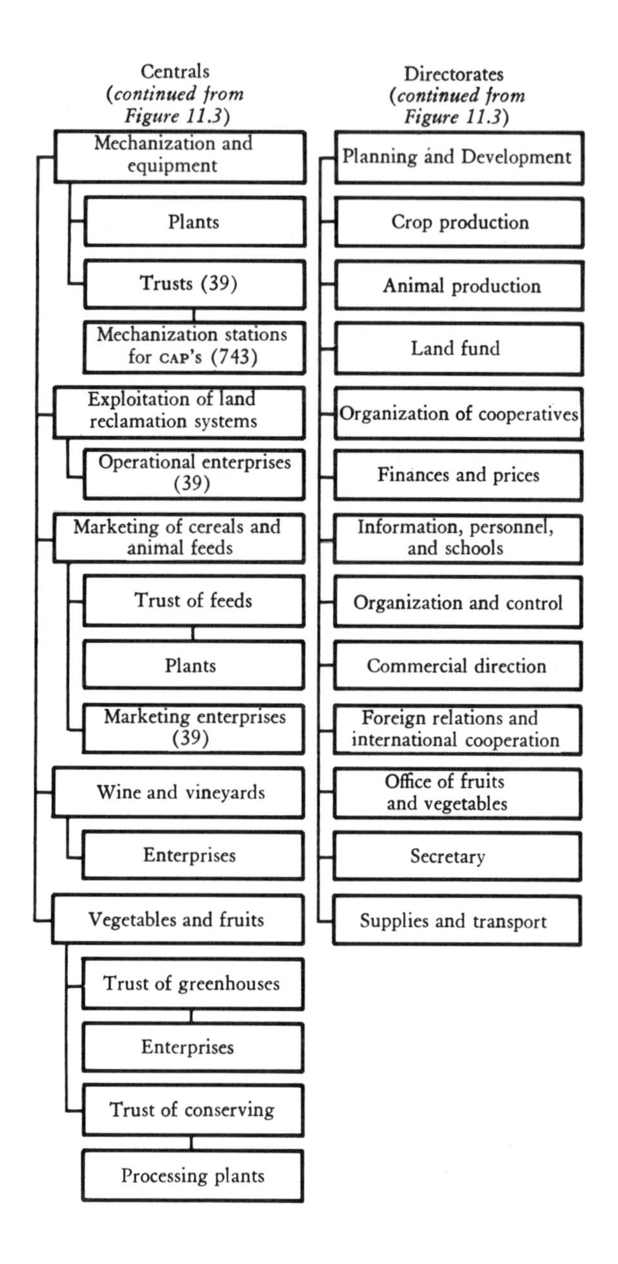

Centrals
(*continued from*
Figure 11.3)
Mechanization and equipment
Plants
Trusts (39)
Mechanization stations for CAP's (743)
Exploitation of land reclamation systems
Operational enterprises (39)
Marketing of cereals and animal feeds
Trust of feeds
Plants
Marketing enterprises (39)
Wine and vineyards
Enterprises
Vegetables and fruits
Trust of greenhouses
Enterprises
Trust of conserving
Processing plants
Directorates
(*continued from*
Figure 11.3)
Planning and Development
Crop production
Animal production
Land fund
Organization of cooperatives
Finances and prices
Information, personnel, and schools
Organization and control
Commercial direction
Foreign relations and international cooperation
Office of fruits and vegetables
Secretary
Supplies and transport

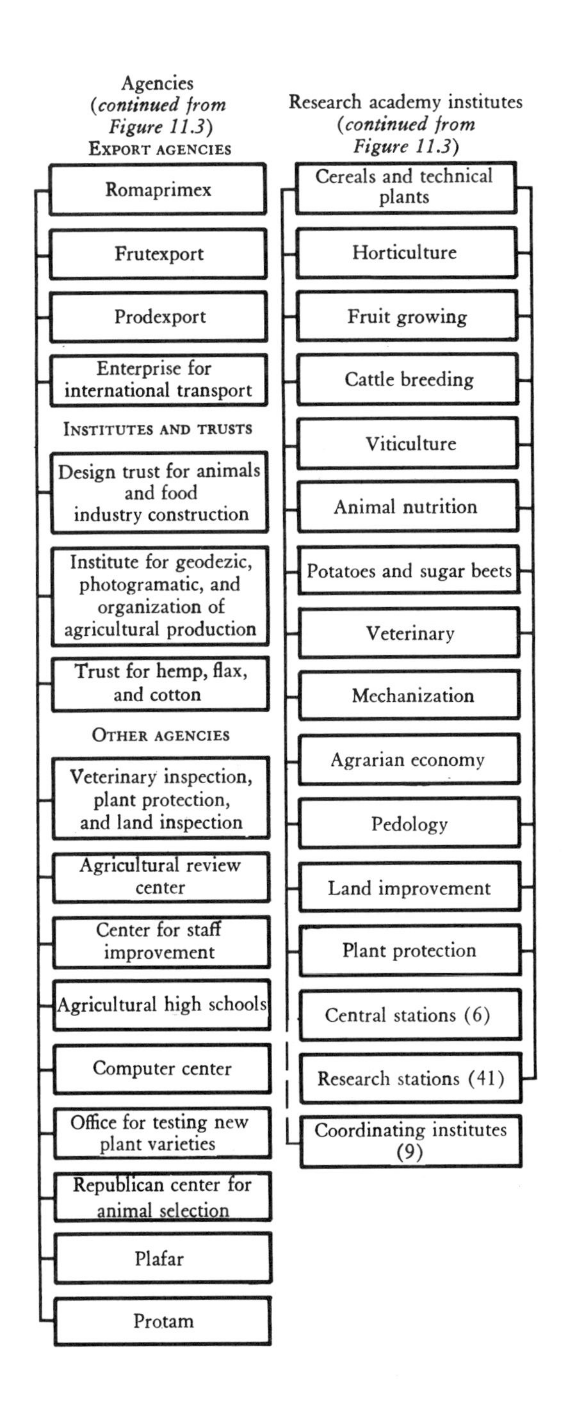

Agencies
(*continued from*
Figure 11.3)
EXPORT AGENCIES
Romaprimex
Frutexport
Prodexport
Enterprise for international transport
INSTITUTES AND TRUSTS
Design trust for animals and food industry construction
Institute for geodezic, photogramatic, and organization of agricultural production
Trust for hemp, flax, and cotton
OTHER AGENCIES
Veterinary inspection, plant protection, and land inspection
Agricultural review center
Center for staff improvement
Agricultural high schools
Computer center
Office for testing new plant varieties
Republican center for animal selection
Plafar
Protam
Research academy institutes
(*continued from*
Figure 11.3)
Cereals and technical plants
Horticulture
Fruit growing
Cattle breeding
Viticulture
Animal nutrition
Potatoes and sugar beets
Veterinary
Mechanization
Agrarian economy
Pedology
Land improvement
Plant protection
Central stations (6)
Research stations (41)
Coordinating institutes (9)

Figure 11.4. *Organization of the Ministry of Agriculture and Food Industry at the Judet Level*

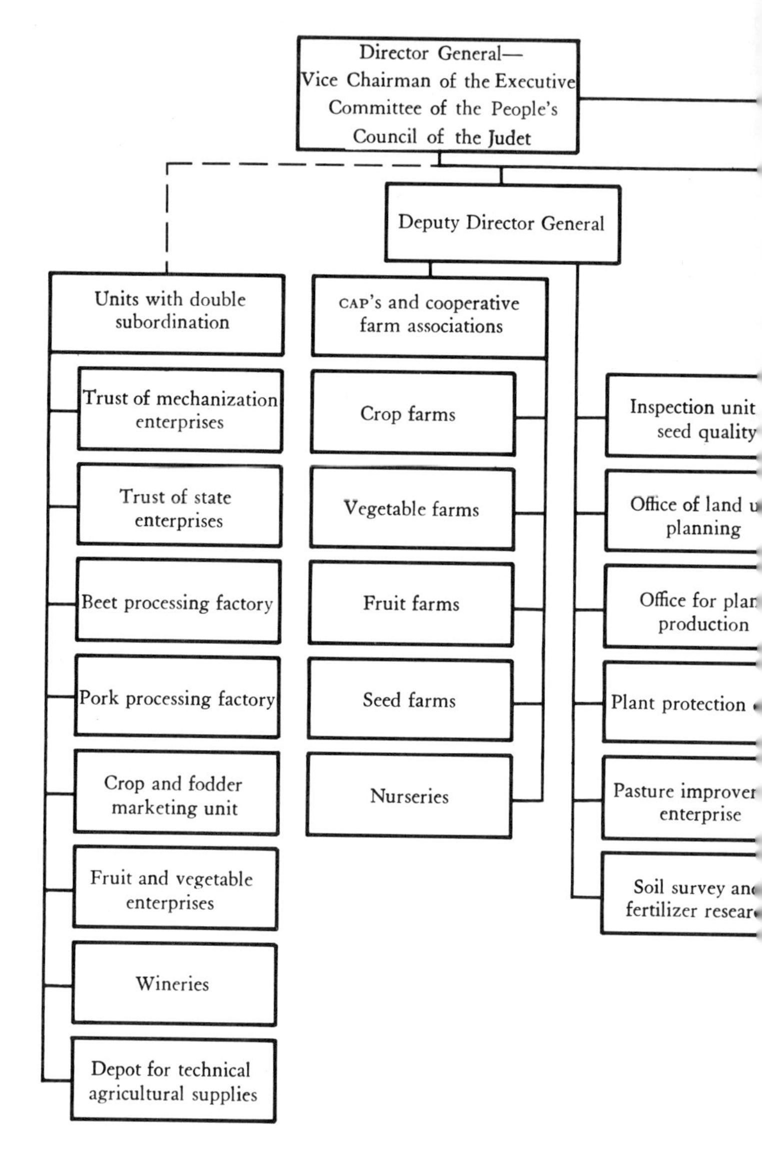

Note: Solid lines indicate hierarchical lines of authority and responsibility; dash indicate channels of consultation and cooperation.

Inspection and control group for agriculture and food industry

Deputy Director General

- Office for animal production
- Veterinary inspections
- Office for animal selection and reproduction
- Livestock raising and fattening farms
- Livestock raising complexes

Deputy Director General

- Office of plan preparation and monitoring
- Office for fruit marketing and conservation
- Office for norms and labor remuneration
- Office for investments and contracts
- Office for financing and accounting in CAP's
- Office for financial guidance and control in CAP's
- Office of land improvement and agricultural constructions
- Administration and bookkeeping
- Agronomist's house

Investment Bank. Details of the functions are given in Appendix H on the banking structure.

Agricultural planning

In agriculture, the planning process begins at the farm level under guidelines issued by the judet agricultural bodies within the framework of the national plan. IAS's and CAP's draw up tentative plans for production, investment, financing, employment, and the like, taking into account indicators that must be followed during the planning period. Plans are submitted to judet agricultural bodies, where they are reviewed before being sent to the MA, which aggregates the proposals into a first draft plan for submission to the State Planning Committee (SPC). After reviewing the plan for agriculture along with plans for other sectors and after making the necessary adjustments and correlations at the national level, the five-year plan and annual plan must be approved by the Grand Assembly before becoming law. Plans then move back to IAS's and CAP's through the MA and Judet Directorates for Agriculture. Plan targets in production and investments are established for individual farm units. Marketing centrals also participate in this planning process.

Several different criteria (indicators) are used to make decisions concerning resource use and investment projects. Agro-industry projects, in particular, require justification of their location. These projects must fit into a scheme of "territorial systematization," meaning that the location of the project must fit into the system or network envisaged by the overall national economic plan of development.

Trends in Agricultural Production

Although crop yields have fluctuated widely from one year to the next, the overall expansion of agricultural production has been considerable during the past two decades. Since 1955 gross agricultural production has almost doubled, growing at a compound annual rate of 2.9 percent from 1955 to 1975. The annual growth rate accelerated from 1.6 percent during 1955–65 to 4.2 percent during 1965–75. As total population increased slightly less than 1 percent annually, agricultural output per capita rose 2.0 percent annually, providing the basis for higher levels of food consumption per capita and larger agricultural exports. Agricultural exports are a significant proportion of total output, although the data available are not sufficient for precise calculation. In 1974 total agricultural exports, expressed in the foreign prices obtained, were 6.5 billion lei valuta, equivalent to 32.3 billion lei. In the same year, gross agricultural production was 91.2 billion lei, expressed in domestic prices. As no data are available on the relation between internal and external prices, the exact percentage of exported production cannot be calculated. It appears, however, that the share of production exported has been increasing over time.

Gross agricultural production has not increased at a steady pace; despite fluctuations from year to year, it has moved upward from one plateau to another with technological advances. For example, annual production averaged about 20 percent more in 1959–61 than in 1954–56; it increased to another level in 1966–70, about 50 percent higher than in 1954–56, and then increased to a record level in 1971–75 of 96 percent above 1954–56. The reasons for this pattern cannot be determined precisely, but a major reason is cyclical changes in weather affecting crop yields. The changing organization of farming units and the uneven growth in the supplies of fertilizer and other current inputs and in mechanization of farming operations have both contributed to upward spurts in total agricultural output.

Livestock production has grown at a higher rate and has varied less from year to year than crop production. Total livestock output increased 4.0 percent annually from 1955 to 1971–75, whereas total crop output increased by 2.1 percent. Livestock production has increased in relative importance, accounting for 43 percent of total agricultural production in 1975, compared with 31 percent in 1955. This is shown in the following figures for agricultural production, which are from *Anuarul Statistic*, various issues. Data for 1955 and 1960 reflect 1955 prices; for 1965 and after, they reflect 1963 prices.

	1955	*1960*	*1965*	*1970*	*1974*	*1975*
Crops	68.9	65.3	63.2	58.8	58.5	57.0
Livestock products	31.1	34.7	36.8	41.2	41.5	43.0

Gross agricultural production increased steadily each year during 1971–75, and in 1975 it was three times larger than in 1950. National income from agriculture, however, reached a record high in 1972, thanks to exceptional weather conditions, and declined slightly during 1973–75 because of poor climatic conditions. Both gross agricultural production and national income from agriculture were higher during each of the 1971–75 plan years than any of the five-year periods since 1950. Although gross production steadily improved, national income did not again reach the 1972 level, despite increased inputs, because of unfavorable weather during 1973 and 1974 and because of excessive rains and floods during 1975. The overall improvement in productivity and incomes was achieved mainly from scale economies resulting from reorganization and specialization and through increased use of fertilizers, farm machinery, improved supplies of feed, and an expansion in the irrigated area.

The composition of inputs used in agricultural production has changed greatly during the past two decades, as fixed assets (farm machinery, buildings, and the like) more than tripled, whereas the number of farm workers declined by 36 percent. Fertilizer use increased from only 22,000 tonnes (active substance) in 1955 to 929,000 tonnes in 1975. Irrigated areas increased from only 43,000 hectares in 1950 to 1.5 million hectares at the end of 1975. Land reclamation programs helped to increase the arable area from 9.4 million hectares in 1950 to 9.7 million hectares in 1975.

The productivity of Romanian agriculture has increased greatly in the past two decades, as shown by the growth of national income from agriculture for each worker and per hectare of agricultural land. Land productivity increased more than 50 percent from 1955 to 1975, whereas labor productivity increased by 100 percent. But average output for each unit of fixed assets has declined slightly, because investments have grown more rapidly than production and because capital goods have been substituted for land and labor. Annual net production for each agricultural worker was almost two-and-one-half times larger in 1971–75 than in 1954–56—a compound annual rate of 5.5 percent. National income from agriculture was 18 billion lei larger each year between 1971 and 1975 than between 1954 and 1956 (Table 11.3). Growth of labor productivity has supplied a surplus that im-

Table 11.3. *Annual Average Gross Agricultural Production, Material Expenses, and National Income from Agriculture, 1954–56 and 1960–65 to 1971–75*

Item	*1954–56*	*1960–65*	*1966–70*	*1971–75*
Values (billions of lei)				
Gross production	47	57	71	89
Material expenses	18	22	31	43
National income	29	35	40	46
Index (1954–56 = 100)				
Gross production	100	121	151	189
Material expenses	100	122	172	239
National income	100	121	138	159
Composition (percentage)				
Gross production	100	100	100	100
Material expenses	38	39	44	48
National income	62	61	56	52

Sources: Anuarul Statistic, various issues (for percentages) and Nicolae Ceausescu (speech delivered to the Congress of the People's Councils) *Scinteia* (February 5, 1976).

proved incomes of agricultural workers and supplied capital for agriculture and other sectors.

Crops

The major changes in the use of arable land in the past two decades include a reduction of the area devoted to cereals from 7.2 to 6.2 million hectares (largely because of the substitution of alternative crops for oats) and a corresponding increase in the cultivation of fodder crops and soybeans for the livestock industry and, to a lesser extent, pulses, vegetables, sugar beets, sunflower, and flax. Despite about a 14 percent reduction in the area under cereals for grain from 1954–55 to 1971–75, total grain production increased by 64 percent, as yield per hectare almost doubled (Table 11.4). Annual growth rates in yields per hectare were especially high for wheat and barley (4.3 percent) and for maize (2.5 percent), but were low for oats. Rising yields per hectare have more than offset declines in areas under wheat, barley, and maize; only the production of oats has declined. Total grain production for each person of the total population increased from 520 kilograms in 1954–55 to 711 kilograms in 1971–75, an average higher than in most other European countries.

Livestock

Expansion of all kinds of livestock production since 1955 has contributed to an annual growth rate of 4.3 percent in total livestock production. Romanian statistics show that total meat production more than doubled from 1954–56 to 1971–75; egg production increased 196 percent, milk increased 73 percent, and wool 55 percent. Pork production rose 154 percent, substantially more than other meats. Productivity, as measured by production for each animal, has increased for all livestock products. Growth in the number of cattle has been slow, only about 1.0 percent a year. But the number used as draft animals has declined, and most cattle now are kept almost exclusively for milk and meat production (Table 11.5).

Instability of crop production

Romania's weather conditions are variable. Crop yields and total crop production fluctuate widely from one year to the next, as in other countries with a similar climate. One measure of these fluctuations is the difference between actual yields per hectare and total crop production that would have resulted with computed straight-line upward trends based on actual data for 1954–73. For example, total crop production was 19.6 percent above the computed trend line in 1955, but 16.8 percent below in 1956. It was 21.2

Table 11.4. *Percentage Changes and Compound Annual Growth Rates in Crop Area, Yield, and Production, by Crop, 1954–55 to 1971–75*

	Percentage changes			*Percentage annual growth rates*		
Crop	*Area*	*Yield*	*Production*	*Area*	*Yield*	*Production*
Grains	−14	90	64	−0.8	3.3	2.5
Wheat and rye	−15	133	97	−0.8	4.3	3.5
Barley	−12	133	103	−0.7	4.3	3.6
Oats	−75	15	−71	−7.2	0.7	−6.5
Maize	−5	63	54	−0.3	2.5	2.2
Rice	67	−20	34	2.6	−0.9	1.5
Technical crops	61	—	—	2.4	—	—
Sunflower	66	68	172	2.6	2.7	5.2
Sugar beets	70	64	179	2.7	2.5	5.3
Tobacco	42	12	62	1.8	0.6	2.5
Flax for fiber	108	25	160	3.8	1.1	4.9
Flax for oil	186	63	366	5.4	2.5	8.0
Hemp	−52	75	−15	−3.6	2.9	−0.8
Potatoes	14	16	35	0.7	0.8	1.5
Vegetables	96	13	119	3.4	0.6	4.0
Fodder crops	96	—	—	3.4	—	—
Perennials for hay	130	46	245	4.3	1.9	6.4
Annuals for hay	−66	26	−36	−4.0	1.2	−2.2
Green feed	291	11	750	7.1	0.5	11.3
Silage	1,009	1	990	12.8	0.1	12.7
Root crops	84	117	299	3.1	4.0	7.2

— Not applicable.
Source: Computed on a twenty-year basis from *Anuarul Statistic*, various issues.

percent above the trend line in 1957, but 21.8 percent below in 1958. Similar wide variations have occurred for wheat, maize, sunflower, sugar beets, and potatoes. In most years, high yields for some crops do not offset low yields for others, causing total crop production to vary almost as much as yields of individual crops. For example, in 1970, yields of all major crops were substantially below computed trend lines, whereas in 1972 all were considerably above.

Yearly variation in rainfall is the major factor causing crop yields to fluctuate widely. Although there may be enough rainfall in July and August to obtain fairly high yields in some years, lack of rainfall often causes low

Table 11.5. *Livestock Production and Numbers, 1954–56 and 1971–75*

Livestock	1954–56 average	1971–75 average	Changes, 1954–56 to 1971–75: Percentage increase	Changes, 1954–56 to 1971–75: Percentage average annual growth
Production				
Milk (millions of hectoliters)	24.5	42.3	73	2.9
All meat (thousands of tonnes)	821.5	1,853.0	126	4.4
Pork (thousands of tonnes)	344.6	875.3	154	5.0
Eggs (millions)	1,570.7	4,644.3	196	5.9
Wool (thousands of tonnes)	19.8	30.6	55	2.3
Numbers[a]				
Cattle (thousands)	4,635.5	5,678.1	22	1.0
Hogs (thousands)	4,469.5	8,087.9	81	3.2
Poultry (millions)	30.0	62.9	110	4.0
Sheep (millions)	10.7	14.1	32	1.5

a. On hand at beginning of year.
Source: Anuarul Statistic, various issues.

yields and complete crop failure in some areas. Flood damage resulting from excessive rainfall, such as during late June and early July of 1975, also causes crop production to vary from year to year. Land reclamation programs to provide better flood protection, irrigation, and drainage should gradually reduce wide yield fluctuations and should raise yields to higher levels.

Wide variations in crop yields from year to year make it difficult in some years for Romania to supply domestic fodder requirements and to meet export targets for some agricultural products. Large reserve stocks of grains and other crop products need to be maintained for years when yields are low. Land reclamation programs, by helping to stabilize crop yields, reduce the need for and the cost of maintaining large carry-over stocks. They also could reduce the need for feed imports and reductions in livestock product exports and foreign currency receipts. In 1973 and 1974, when crop yields declined because of below-average weather conditions, Romania had to import some feedgrains and protein meals to meet its requirements for livestock feed, which was needed to achieve its export targets for livestock products.

Table 11.6. *Gross Agricultural Production, by Zones, 1967 and 1973*

			Change, 1967–73		*Percentage distribution of gross agricultural production*	
	Thousands of lei per hectare					
Zone	*1967*	*1973*	*Percentage increase*	*Percentage average annual growth*	*1967*	*1973*
Zone I	5.6	7.5	34	5.0	48	51
Zone II	4.6	5.4	17	3.0	28	27
Zone III	4.2	4.6	10	1.8	24	22
Total or average	4.9	6.1	24	3.6	100	100

Source: Computed from data reported in *Anuarul Statistic* showing percentage compositions of gross value of agricultural production and hectares of arable land by judet.

Regional changes

Gross agricultural production has increased more in the plains region (zone I) than in the foothills (zone II) and in the mountain and tableland (zone III) region in recent years. Between 1967 and 1973 gross agricultural production per hectare of agricultural land increased by 34 percent in zone I compared with 17 percent in zone II and only 10 percent in zone III. Expansion of the agricultural area of each region increased agricultural production slightly. Gross agricultural production increased at an annual rate of 5 percent in zone I, 3 percent in zone II, and only 1.8 percent in zone III (Table 11.6). As a result, the share of gross agricultural production accounted for by zone I increased from 48 percent in 1967 to 51 percent in 1973, whereas the shares of both zones II and III declined.[4]

Changes by types of production units

Agricultural production has been increased more by IAS's than by CAP's in the past decade. Gross agricultural production of IAS's rose 77 percent and that of CAP's 35 percent from 1965 to 1975 (Table 11.7). Although land area in different kinds of production units has not changed significantly since 1962, the use of fertilizer and other inputs has increased much more on

4. Total crop production was 7.1 percent above the long-term trend line in 1967 and 7.7 percent below in 1973. Therefore, the data cited above probably understate changes in the distribution of agricultural production among regions that would have occurred with average weather conditions.

Table 11.7. *Gross Production, Area, Fertilizer, and Investment of State Agricultural Enterprises and Agricultural Producer Cooperatives, 1965, 1970, and 1975*

Item	*1965*	*1970*	*1975*	*1975 ÷ 1965*
State agricultural enterprises (IAS's)				
Index of gross agricultural production (1960 = 100)	181	233	320	1.77
Agricultural area (thousands of hectares	2,077	2,089	2,058	.99
Arable area (thousands of hectares)	1,627	1,667	1,658	1.02
Irrigated area (thousands of hectares)	104	232	432	4.15
Fertilizer consumption (thousands of tonnes)	133	205	252	1.89
Total investment (millions of lei)	3,014	4,731	5,429	1.80
Yield of wheat and rye (kilograms per hectare)	2,777	1,995	2,548	.92
Yield of maize (kilograms per hectare)	2,671	3,341	3,525	1.32
Agricultural producer cooperatives (CAP's)				
Index of gross agricultural production (1962 = 100)	119	119	161	1.35
Agricultural area (thousands of hectares)	8,994	9,033	9,047	1.01
Arable area (thousands of hectares)	7,387	7,274	7,229	.98
Irrigated area (thousands of hectares)	116	431	977	8.42
Fertilizer consumption (thousands of tonnes)	123	379	583	4.77
Total investment (millions of lei)	2,811	4,111	4,778	1.70
Yield of wheat and rye (kilograms per hectare)	1,818	1,344	2,000	1.10
Yield of maize (kilograms per hectare)	1,758	2,024	2,738	1.56

Source: Anuarul Statistic, various issues.

IAS's than on CAP's. Investments per hectare also have been much larger on IAS's than on CAP's. In 1975, 26 percent of the arable land on IAS's was irrigated compared with only 14 percent on CAP's. Crop yields per hectare have been about 30 percent higher on IAS's than on CAP's. Yields and gross agricultural production have also increased more on IAS's than on CAP's, because the former have a larger share of their land in the most fertile areas. In 1973, 28 percent of the arable land in zone I was in IAS's compared with only 15 percent in zone II and 11 percent in zone III (Table 11.8). In addition, management practices have been improved more on IAS's than on CAP's in the past decade, and the use of fertilizer and other inputs and capital investments for buildings, mechanization, and livestock have been increased at higher rates on IAS's than on CAP's and individual farms. It appears that the marginal productivity of capital inputs has been higher on CAP's than on IAS's. There are, therefore, opportunities to greatly increase the productivity of CAP's by expanding the irrigated area and by providing additional capital inputs.

Table 11.8. *Production of Selected Crops, by Kind of Production Unit, 1975*
(thousands of tonnes)

Production unit	*All cereals*	*Oil seeds*[a]	*Sugar beets*	*Potatoes*	*Vegetables*
Total state agricultural units	3,546	161	14	196	448
	(23.2)	(20.0)	(0.3)	(7.2)	(17.8)
State agricultural enterprises	3,382	159	10	172	114
	(22.1)	(19.7)	(0.2)	(6.3)	(4.5)
Other state units	164	2	4	24	334
	(1.1)	(0.3)	(0.1)	(0.9)	(13.3)
Agriculture producer cooperatives	9,836	646	4,888	1,104	991
	(64.4)	(80.0)	(99.7)	(40.7)	(39.4)
Members of CAP's	1,480	—[b]	2	970	909
	(9.7)	(—)[b]	(—)[b]	(35.7)	(36.1)
Individual farms	404	—[b]	1	446	170
	(2.7)	(—)[b]	(—)[b]	(16.4)	(6.7)
Total	15,266	807	4,905	2,716	2,518

Note: Percentage figures given in parentheses.
a. Sunflower and others.
b. Less than 1,000 tonnes, or 0.1 percent.
Source: Anuarul Statistic, various issues.

Considering their small share of the arable land, individual farmers and members of CAP's account for large shares of the total production of crops and livestock. For example, in 1975 members of CAP's produced almost 10 percent of the cereals, 36 percent of the potatoes, and 36 percent of the vegetables, although they operated only 8 percent of the arable land (Table 11.9). Individual farmers produced 16 percent of the potatoes and 7 percent of the vegetables. Members of CAP's and individual farmers usually produce labor-intensive crops that have a high value of output per hectare.

Individual farmers and members of CAP's are especially important in livestock production. In 1975, CAP members produced 33 percent of the meat, 38 percent of the milk, 31 percent of the wool, and 48 percent of the eggs, whereas individual farmers produced 13, 20, 12, and 14 percent, respectively (Table 11.10). Grazing of cattle and sheep on state-owned pasture and meadowland is a major source of feed for livestock produced by individual farmers. In addition, individual CAP members may use CAP land for grazing

Table 11.9. *Selected Livestock Products, by Kind of Production Unit, 1975*

Production unit	*Total meat (thousands of tonnes)*	*Pork (thousands of tonnes)*	*Total milk (thousands of hectaliters)*	*Wool (thousands of tonnes)*	*Eggs (millions)*
Total state agricultural units	601	369	6,612	6,367	1,566
	(29.1)	(38.6)	(14.9)	(20.2)	(28.9)
State agricultural enterprises	561	354	6,322	5,386	1,512
	(27.2)	(37.0)	(14.2)	(17.1)	(27.9)
Other state units	40	15	290	981	54
	(1.9)	(1.6)	(.7)	(3.1)	(1.0)
Agriculture producer cooperatives	515	225	12,365	11,620	486
	(25.0)	(23.5)	(27.8)	(36.8)	(9.0)
Members of CAP's	688	279	16,753	9,861	2,624
	(33.3)	(29.1)	(37.7)	(31.3)	(48.5)
Individual farms	259	84	8,691	3,684	736
	(12.6)	(8.8)	(19.6)	(11.7)	(13.6)
Total	2,063	957	44,421	31,532	5,412

Note: Percentage figures given in parentheses.
Source: Anuarul Statistic, various issues.

Table 11.10. *Percentage Distribution of Arable Land, by Zone, 1975*

	IAS'S	CAP'S[a]	*Individual farms*
Zone I	28.1	70.3	1.6
Zone II	14.8	79.1	6.1
Zone III	11.5	77.7	10.8
All zones	21.1	74.2	4.7

a. Includes CAP private plots.
Source: Anuarul Statistic, various issues.

after the winter wheat harvest. Livestock production has been an important way of using family labor of individual farmers and CAP members who otherwise might not be employed.

Changes by region

Land in zone I, where agricultural output has grown most rapidly, apparently has been more responsive to improved technology than land in zones II and III. It is not known how fertilizer and other inputs have been distributed among regions, but increases probably have been greatest in zone I. Expansion of the irrigated area has been mainly in zone I, and this probably accounts, in large part, for the very large increases in agricultural production in this region. The annual growth rate in total agricultural output of 5 percent in zone I from 1967 to 1973 is impressive, especially since weather conditions were less favorable in 1973 than in 1967. The priority placed on upgrading technology and on investments to expand agricultural production in zone I appears to have been a wise policy from the standpoint of maximizing output growth.

Sources of growth in agricultural production

The following discussion of sources of growth in agricultural output and productivity deals with the country as a whole, since detailed data by regions are not available.

RESEARCH AND EDUCATION. Romania's well-developed programs of agricultural research and education have made important contributions to higher crop yields and productivity of livestock. Higher quality seeds, particularly for sunflower, hybrid maize, and wheat, and better breeds of livestock distributed by the Academy of Agricultural and Forestry Sciences have helped raise output and productivity levels, although there still is much room for improvement. Increases in livestock productivity have resulted from better breeds of animals and from improved feeding and related practices. Technically trained agriculturalists stationed on IAS's and CAP's to supervise farming operations are given detailed guides to follow in carrying out land preparation, planting, cultivating, and harvesting.

Agricultural education in Romania has been organized into a national system, coordinated by the Ministries of Agriculture and of Education, to provide training for specialists and skilled workers for the agricultural sector. The structure of formal education can best be divided into two branches: instruction for new personnel and for staff already employed. The former category starts with agricultural gymnasiums, or high schools, where students are exposed to a wide range of agricultural activities, as well as being given an opportunity to specialize. One group of these graduates proceeds directly to production complexes as skilled workers, while another portion continues to agricultural universities. Agricultural universities and institutes are dispersed throughout the country. The MA determines the numbers of experts needed in future years and thereby finalizes the number of seats available in the various disciplines. Postgraduate programs are also maintained at these institutions.

A varied refresher program is conducted for all levels of workers in the agricultural sector. The MA organizes eight-week review courses that are compulsory for all expert staff every five years. Similarly, short courses are given annually for experts and skilled workers to pass down knowledge to lower-level staff from research institutions, as well as to provide opportunities to discuss mutual problems. The Center for Management Training within the University of Economics and Political Science arranges two-year advanced training courses for management staff already in the field. In addition, the MA coordinates special weekly radio and television broadcasts designed to reach the basic educational needs of CAP members. Since the CAP's are equipped with television sets, the chief engineer organizes CAP members to view or hear the broadcasts and leads discussions based on the central topic of each program. Finally, in each CAP, courses are held to improve the skills of members during the winter.

FERTILIZER. Increased use of fertilizer has been an important factor contributing to higher crop yields. Fertilizer consumption increased from only 22,000 tonnes in 1955 to 929,000 tonnes (plant nutrients) in 1975 or from only 2 kilograms per hectare of arable land in 1955 to 95 kilograms per hectare in 1975 (Table 11.11). About 60 percent is used for grains, 5 percent for

Table 11.11. *Fertilizer Consumption, by Active Substance*
(thousands of tonnes)

Active substance	*1955*	*1960*	*1970*	*1971*	*1972*	*1973*	*1974*	*1975*
Nitrogen	10	25	367	431	421	420	480	572
Phosphate	7	47	203	180	173	242	299	314
Potash	5	3	24	22	45	53	35	43
Total	22	75	594	633	639	715	814	929
Kilograms per hectare of arable land	2	8	61	65	66	74	84	95

Source: Anuarul Statistic, various issues.

sugar beets, 5 percent for sunflower, 3 percent for potatoes, 3 percent for vegetables, and 24 percent for other crops. Use of fertilizer on grains may have increased by about 300,000 tons from 1955 to 1975, enough to increase total grain production 3 million tons, assuming a yield/response ratio of 10 kilograms of grain per kilogram of plant nutrients. Total grain production averaged about 8 million tonnes in 1954–56 compared with 15 million tonnes in 1971–75. Thus, larger applications of fertilizer appear to account for a large share of the increase of 7 million tons in total grain production.

LAND RECLAMATION AND IRRIGATION. Romania has long experience in building minor flood control and drainage structures, but large-scale construction of irrigation and flood control facilities is a recent development. Irrigated area increased from only 185,000 hectares in 1961 to 1.4 million hectares in 1975 or from only 1.9 percent of the arable area to 15 percent (Table 11.12). The objectives of irrigation include prevention of crop failure or reduced yields in years of low rainfall, higher yields in years with average rainfall, and increased double-cropping. Most irrigation projects also incorporate flood damage and drainage control. Most of the irrigated area is in southern and eastern parts of the country where rainfall is only 350 to 500 millimeters annually and varies widely from one year to the next.

Expansion of irrigated areas, together with improved flood control and drainage structures, have been important reasons for increased crop production. Most studies of crop production increases made possible by irrigation, flood control, and drainage facilities, along with improved cultural practices, show that crop production can be more than doubled over several years. Crop production for each hectare has doubled for the area placed under irrigation since 1955 and was equal to about 10 percent of total crop production in 1973. Of course other inputs required to make effective use of

Table 11.12. *Irrigated Area, by Crop, 1961 and 1975*

Crop	Thousands of hectares		Percentage of area irrigated	
	1961	*1975*	*1961*	*1975*[a]
Wheat	23.7	210.0	0.8	8.8
Maize	45.7	428.0	1.3	13.0
Sunflower	4.0	56.8	0.9	11.1
Sugar beets	5.4	55.9	3.1	22.7
Potatoes	2.4	15.8[b]	0.8	5.3
Vegetables	50.4	128.4	27.9	57.6
Lucerne and clover	—	181.2	—	24.9
Pasture and meadow	—	25.8	—	0.6
Vineyards	—	19.2	—	5.9
Orchards	—	10.6	—	2.5
Other crops	53.0	292.8	—	—
Total	184.6	1,424.2	1.9	14.8

a. Percentage of total arable area, excluding minor crops and pastures.
b. Data for 1972.
Source: Anuarul Statistic, various issues.

irrigated land were also provided, although not all in the quantities necessary for best results.

FARM MECHANIZATION. One of the most significant developments in Romanian agriculture during the past two decades has been rapid mechanization of many farm operations, because over 2.5 million workers moved from agriculture to jobs in other sectors (Table 11.13). By substituting capital for labor, mechanization has permitted the removal of large numbers of workers from agriculture without reducing output.

Most seed-bed preparation, cultivating, and harvesting still were carried out by animal-drawn implements in 1955, but numbers of farm machines have increased greatly in recent years (Table 11.14). Almost all field operations for producing crops now are mechanized. Much hand labor still is used to produce sugar beets, potatoes, tobacco, fruits, and vegetables, however, so there is still room for further mechanization. Romania has about 560,000 horses, which are used mainly for hauling operations, but also for some field work in hilly areas. Much land has been changed from producing feed for draught animals to producing livestock and other agricultural products for human use. About one million horses were used for draught purposes in the early 1950s, and many cattle were also once used for draught purposes. Therefore, a reduction in the number of draught animals has been

Table 11.13. *Labor Force in Agriculture and Other Sectors, 1954–75*
(thousands of workers)

	1954	*1960*	*1965*	*1970*	*1975*
			Actual numbers		
Agriculture	6,377	6,233	5,477	4,849	3,837
Other	2,770	3,305	4,207	5,026	6,314
Total	9,147	9,538	9,684	9,875	10,150
			Changes in numbers		
		1954–60	*1960–65*	*1965–70*	*1970–75*
Agriculture		−144	−756	−628	−1,012
Other		535	902	819	1,288
Total		391	146	191	276

Source: Anuarul Statistic, various issues.

an important source of feed for expanding dairy, beef, pork, and egg production. Draught animals will not be totally eliminated, however; terrain and the quality of rural roads necessitate their continued use.
agriculture increased from an annual average of 2.6 billion lei in 1955–59

CAPITAL INVESTMENTS. Capital investments have played an important role in increasing agricultural output and productivity. Total investments in agriculture increased from an annual average of 2.6 billion lei in 1955–59 to 15.4 billion lei in 1971–75 (Table 11.15). Investments for mechanization have been very large, making possible increased agricultural production with fewer workers. Investments for land reclamation became increasingly important in the 1960s. Agriculture's share of total investments in the economy increased from 15.2 percent in 1955–59 to almost 19 percent in

Table 11.14. *Numbers of Selected Farm Machines, Selected Years, 1955–75*

Machine	*1955*	*1970*	*1973*	*1974*	*1975*
Tractors	23,033	107,290	116,513	116,816	119,533
Mechanical cultivators	7,787	29,346	34,594	33,736	34,391
Chemical fertilizer spreaders	—	14,504	13,718	12,783	12,251
Tractor-drawn combines	46	43,916	33,222	28,438	20,209
Self-propelled combines	1,489	1,325	7,197	12,245	17,912
Combines for silage	—	7,129	9,117	9,130	9,445

Source: Anuarul Statistic, various issues.

1960–65. It decreased to 14.0 percent in 1971–75 and is planned to be 11.6 percent during 1976–80, with total investment expected to increase by about 50 percent.

The ratio of agricultural investment to the gross value of agricultural production has risen steadily from only 5.3 percent in 1955–59 to 17.3 percent in 1971–75. Similarly, the ratio of agricultural investment to national income from agriculture rose from only 8.5 percent in 1955–59 to 33.4 percent in 1971–75. The ratio of agricultural investment to output of the sector, however, has not reached as high a level as the ratio for other sectors. For, of the total economy, the ratio of investment to national income (Romanian methodology) was 31.4 percent in 1973. The fact that Romania has invested a large share of its current output in future production has contributed to high economic growth rates in agriculture, as well as in other

Table 11.15. *Investment in Agriculture during Plan Periods, 1955–59 to 1976–80, Compared with Total Investments and Agricultural Production*

	Annual averages				
Item	*1955–59*	*1960–65*	*1966–70*	*1971–75*	*1976–80*[a]
Agricultural investment (billions of lei)	2.65	7.11	10.31	15.39	23.2
Total investment (billions of lei)	17.42	37.89	66.16	109.80	200.0
Agriculture's share of total investment (precentage)	15.2	18.8	15.6	14.0	11.6
Gross value of agricultural products (billions of lei)	49.6	57.2	71.1	89.2	115–130
National income from agriculture (billions of lei)	31.0	35.0	40.0	46.0	60–68
Ratio of agricultural investment					
To gross value of agricultural production	5.3	12.4	14.5	17.3	20.0–17.8
To national income from agriculture	8.5	20.3	25.8	33.4	38.3–34.1

a. Plan estimates.
Source: Anuarul Statistic, various issues.

sectors. Investments in agriculture include certain items (for example, silos, stores, and certain buildings), which in certain countries are not classified as such. Major infrastructural projects, such as irrigation and greenhouses, have been responsible for the recent higher level of agricultural investment.

EMPLOYMENT. Between 1950 and 1975 the labor force in agriculture declined from 6.2 million to 3.8 million: that is, from 74 percent of the total labor force to 38 percent (Chapter 7). Only limited information is available on employment in each type of enterprise. Total personnel in agriculture increased from 219,200 in 1950 to 484,200 in 1975, when 252,000 were IAS employees and 126,383 were SAM employees. Between 1960 and 1975, the years for which figures are available, employees on IAS's rose from 224,000 to 252,000 whereas the equivalent figures for SAM's were 44,500 and 126,000 (Table SA7.11 and SA7.13). Similar figures for CAP's are not available; the published statistics represent the size of CAP membership by number of families, which was 3.9 million in 1962 and 3.4 million in 1975 (Table SA7.12).

Foreign Trade

Romania's trade in agricultural products has increased greatly in the past two decades, although less than in nonagricultural products, as might be expected with the emphasis placed on industrial growth in Romania. Exports of agricultural products (including forestry) rose from about 700 million lei valuta in 1950 to 6.5 billion in 1974, whereas imports increased from 285 million lei valuta to 4.7 billion in 1974 (Table 11.16). Despite the decline in agriculture's share of total exports from 55 percent in 1950 to 27 percent in 1974, agriculture's growing trade surplus (from 412 million lei in 1950 to almost 2.2 billion lei valuta in 1973 and 1.8 billion in 1974) has become increasingly important for financing imports for industrialization. Moreover, an increasing share of the growing trade surplus for agricultural products has been in convertible currency—a development that also has contributed to industrial growth.

Exports

Romania exports a wide variety of agricultural products (Tables 11.16, 11.17). Exports of processed foodstuffs have risen much more than raw materials for foodstuffs and other purposes. Items that have shown large increases in export value since 1965 include meat and meat products, cereals, sugar, vegetable oils, wine and alcoholic beverages, and fresh vegetables and potatoes. Exports of processed foodstuffs amounted to over half the total value of agricultural exports in 1974, compared with 39 percent in 1965.

Table 11.16. *Exports, Imports, and Trade Balances for Agricultural and Other Products, Selected Years, 1950–74*
(millions of lei valuta)

	1950	*1960*	*1965*	*1970*	*1973*	*1974*
Agricultural products[a]						
Exports	697	1,542	2,337	2,952	5,293	6,504
Imports	285	699	832	1,808	3,051	4,725
Balance	412	844	1,506	1,144	2,242	1,779
Total trade						
Exports	1,274	4,302	6,609	11,105	18,576	24,226
Imports	1,461	3,887	6,463	11,761	17,418	25,563
Balance	−187	415	146	−656	1,158	−1,337
Agriculture's share						
Exports	55	36	35	27	28	27
Imports	20	18	13	15	18	18

a. Includes forestry products and assumes sugar exports in 1973 at 1972 value.
Sources: External Trade of the Socialist Republic of Romania (Bucharest: Ministry of Foreign Trade and Central Statistics Office, 1973) and *Anuarul Statistic*, various issues.

The total value of agricultural exports increased by 12.0 percent annually from 1965 to 1974, compared with an annual growth rate in gross agricultural production of 4.4 percent annually. Thus, it appears that an increasing share of total agricultural output has been exported. Some of the rise in the total value of exports, however, has resulted from rising export prices and from the growing share of processed products. The shift in the composition of agricultural exports to include a larger share of processed foodstuffs has been stimulated by their rising export prices compared with those of raw materials.

Major changes in agricultural exports, measured in volumes, are indicated by the following figures for 1965 and 1974, in thousands of tonnes:

	1965	*1974*
Meat and meat products	61	132
Edible animal fats	19	52
Edible vegetable oils	33	165
Tinned vegetables	11	61
Fresh vegetables	137	185
Wines	43	90
Other alcoholic beverages	9	17
Refined sugar	34	107

Table 11.17. *Exports of Agricultural and Forestry Products*
(millions of lei valuta)

Product	*1965*	*1970*	*1971*	*1972*	*1973*	*1974*	*1[illegible]*
Foodstuffs							
Meat and meat products	219	271	323	442	762		
Dairy products	45	56	104	95	89		
Vegetables and potatoes	62	115	182	210	256		
Fruits (fresh, dried, and processed)	177	180	170	179	192		
Sugar	16	20	6	179	—		
Vegetable oils	55	206	278	219	298		
Wine and alcoholic beverages	180	265	316	342	361		
Others	165	232	265	128	559		
Subtotal	919	1,345	1,644	1,794	2,517	3,673	2,[illegible]
Raw materials for foodstuffs							
Cereals	308	131	240	354	734		
Live animals	79	245	242	390	372		
Seeds	26	48	47	56	28		
Others	97	77	73	282	206		
Subtotal	510	501	602	1,082	1,340	1,245	1,[illegible]
Other raw materials							
Sawn wood	499	576	626	651	840		
Wooden cases and plywood	121	121	123	133	139		
Pulp and paper	52	147	141	144	163		
Others	236	262	260	258	294		
Subtotal	908	1,106	1,151	1,186	1,436	1,586	
Grand total	*2,337*	*2,952*	*3,397*	*4,062*	*5,293*	*6,504*	

Note: Breakdown of totals not available for 1974 and 1975.
Sources: External Trade of the Socialist Republic of Romania and *Anuarul Statistic*, various is

Cereal exports have not changed significantly, fluctuating around an annual average of about 700,000 tonnes since 1960. Most of Romania's increased grain production has been used to expand the output of animal products, following a decision made in 1970 to forego foodgrain exports whenever necessary to ensure adequate supplies for livestock.

Romania has traded more with western European and North American countries in recent years. The share of agricultural exports going to non-CMEA countries increased from only 35 percent in 1960 and 40 percent in

1965 to 74 percent in 1973. Thus, convertible foreign exchange earnings have risen considerably. Large-scale, factory-like farm units for producing meat products, vegetables, and other agricultural products have been expanded to increase export earnings.

Imports

Agricultural imports consist mainly of raw cotton, crude leather, citrus fruits, cocoa, and other products not produced in the country in sufficient quantities (Table 11.18). Much of the growth in the total value of agricultural imports since 1965 has resulted from higher import prices. Nevertheless, agricultural imports as a share of total imports declined from 20 percent in 1950 to 18 percent during 1974. Growth of agricultural imports has

Table 11.18. *Imports of Agricultural and Forestry Products, 1960 and 1970–74*
(millions of lei valuta)

Product	*1965*	*1970*	*1971*	*1972*	*1973*	*1974*[a]
Foodstuffs						
Meat and meat products	—	27	138	120	25	
Fish and fish products	39	77	69	63	51	
Citrus fruits	15	23	36	46	54	
Sugar	—	90	117	76	74	
Alcoholic beverages	21	21	34	48	63	
Others	80	119	67	42	133	
Subtotal	155	358	461	395	400	587
Others						
Fodder (feeds)	35	68	79	157	467	
Live animals	1	19	5	9	42	
Raw cotton	302	388	434	480	529	
Wool	26	34	34	39	97	
Crude leather	61	152	115	217	290	
Cocoa	18	25	27	25	54	
Tobacco	9	13	29	14	14	
Pulp and paper	35	95	126	159	180	
Others	190	656	685	690	978	
Subtotal	677	1,450	1,534	1,790	2,651	4,138
Grand total	*832*	*1,808*	*1,995*	*2,185*	*3,051*	*4,725*

a. Breakdown for each item not available.
Sources: External Trade of the Socialist Republic of Romania and *Anuarul Statistic*, various issues.

been mainly from non-CMEA countries. Agricultural imports from non-CMEA countries accounted for 82 percent of the total from all countries in 1973 compared with about 46 percent in 1965.

Romania increased its imports of soybeans and protein meals greatly in 1973, and they also were large in 1974. Romanian authorities stated that these were necessary to meet production and export targets for livestock products when feedgrain production was lower than planned. One source states that Romania's imports of protein meals increased to 600,000 tonnes for the year beginning July 1, 1973, and to 1 million for the year beginning July 1, 1974, compared with 300,000 tonnes for the year beginning July 1, 1972.

Development Prospects and the Five-Year Plan for 1976–80

The 1976–80 Five-Year Plan provides for gross agricultural production to increase by 28 to 44 percent (5.1 to 7.6 percent annually) over that of the previous plan. Actual gross agricultural production averaged 25 percent larger in 1955–59 than in 1950–54 and 15 percent larger in 1960–65 than in 1955–59 (Table 11.19). It increased by about 25 percent from one plan period to the next during the last two plan periods. Therefore, an increase of 28 percent in 1976–80 over 1971–75 would be close to the actual achievement of the last plan (1971–75), whereas an increase of 44 percent would require a greatly accelerated growth of agricultural production. Gross agri-

Table 11.19. *Gross Agricultural Production: Period Averages and Percentage Changes from Preceding Period, 1950–54 to 1976–80*

Periods	*Annual averages (1950 = 100)*[a]	*Percentage change from previous period*
1950–54 (1st 5-year plan)	122.7	—
1955–59 (2nd 5-year plan)	153.0	24.7
1960–65 (3rd 6-year plan)	176.4	15.3
1966–70 (4th 5-year plan)	219.2	24.3
1971–75 (5th 5-year plan target)	269.2	36–49
1971–75 (actual)	275.3	25.6
1976–80 (6th 5-year plan)[b]	334–369	28–44

a. Actual averages except plan averages for 1971–75 and 1976–80.

b. Law (no. 4) on the Adoption of the Unified National Plan of Economic and Social Development of the Socialist Republic of Romania for 1976–80, *Official Bulletin of the Socialist Republic of Romania*, no. 65 (July 7, 1976).

Source: Anuarul Statistic, various issues.

cultural production increased at an annual rate of 2.0 percent during 1955–65 and 4.4 percent during 1965–75. Thus, the lower limit of the planned annual increase in gross agricultural production of 5.1 percent is more or less the same as the rate achieved during the past decade, but the upper limit of 7.6 percent annually exceeds growth rates ever achieved previously.

1976–80 Plan

Targets have been set for livestock numbers and individual products with lower and upper limits. By the end of 1980 the number of livestock is planned to reach 7.5 million head for cattle, 12 to 13 million for swine, 19 to 19.5 million for sheep and goats, and 50 to 57 million for egg-laying poultry. Production targets for various products call for increases from 1971–75 to 1976–80 of 35 to 51 percent for cereals, 32 to 49 percent for sunflower, over 50 percent for most other major crops, 41 to 52 percent for all meats, and 37 to 47 percent for milk (Table 11.20). These targets

Table 11.20. *Production Targets for Major Agricultural Products, 1976–80*

(thousands of tonnes, unless otherwise specified)

Product	Annual average 1976–80	1976–80 compared with 1971–75 (percent)	Actual, 1971–75
Cereals	20,000–22,360	135–151	14,804
Sunflower	1,000– 1,133	132–149	760
Sugar beets	8,600– 9,354	181–197	4,757
Soybeans	545– 575	246–260	221.0
Flax for fiber	300– 322	324–348	92.5[a]
Potatoes	4,600– 4,800	157–166	2,927
Field vegetables	4,200– 4,316	165–169	2,549
Fruit and grapes	3,800– 4,000	166–173	2,295
Meat (thousands of tonnes, live weight)	2,500– 2,687	141–152	1,768
Milk (millions of hectaliters)	58– 62	150–161	39
Eggs (millions)	6,000– 6,500	129–140	4,642
Wool	42– 47	138–153	30

a. Flax average is low because of 1975 floods.

Sources: Law (no. 4) on the Adoption of the Plan for 1976–80; *Communiqué Regarding the Fulfillment of the Unified National Plan for Social and Economic Development of the Socialist Republic of Romania during the 1971–75 Period* (Bucharest: Publishing House for Political Literature, 1976); and *Anuarul Statistic*, various issues.

Table 11.21. *Yield Targets for Agricultural Products, 1976–80*

Product	*Annual average, 1971–75 (kilograms per hectare)*	*Target, 1976–80 (kilograms per hectare)*	*Percentage increase*
Wheat and rye	2,210	3,000– 3,150	36–43
Maize	2,680	3,500– 3,800	31–42
Sunflower	1,450	2,000– 2,140	38–48
Sugar beets	22,140	34,000–36,000	54–63
Field vegetables	11,250	19,000–20,000	69–78

Sources: Directives of the Eleventh Congress of Romanian Communist Party Concerning the 1976–80 Five-Year Plan and the Guidelines for Romanian Economic and Social Development over the 1981–90 Period. (Bucharest: Meridiane Publishing House, 1975) and *Anuarul Statistic*, various issues.

may be compared with projected production in 1980, assuming continued annual growth rates from 1954–55 to 1971–75. Production of sunflower and eggs would exceed targets set for 1976–80, but growth rates for other products would have to exceed those during the past two decades to achieve their targets. But production of most agricultural commodities has grown more rapidly during the past decade than during the one before that. Continuation of growth rates of the 1965–75 period would mean achieving the lower 1976–80 plan targets for most agricultural products.

The 1976–80 Plan calls for yields per hectare and livestock production for each animal to increase greatly. For example, according to Directives, yields of major crops are expected to be 30 to 78 percent higher than those during 1971–75 (Table 11.21). Fertilizer use (active substance) is projected to rise to 250 to 280 kilograms per hectare of arable land, vineyards, and orchards in 1980 compared with 95 kilograms in 1975. Approximately 1.2 million hectares of additional land will be irrigated, bringing the total close to 3.0 million hectares in 1980. Drainage will be improved on 1.1 million hectares, erosion control measures will be carried out on about 1 million hectares, and the arable area will be increased by 125,000 hectares during 1976–80.

Planned investment in agriculture during 1976–80 will total 116 billion lei. Planned annual investment in agriculture will average 23.2 billion lei in 1976–80 compared with 15.4 billion in 1971–75 and 10.3 billion in 1966–70 (Table 11.22). Agriculture's share of total investment will con-

Table 11.22. *Distribution of Investment in Agriculture, by Kind of Enterprise and Subsector*

Enterprise or subsector	1960	1961–65	1966–70	1971–75	1976–80
	Annual averages (billions of lei)				
			Enterprises		
Agricultural production cooperatives, total	1.5	3.0	3.3	4.5	7.4
Own funds	1.0	2.2	2.2	2.0	4.3
Loans	0.5	0.8	1.1	2.5	3.1
Stations for agricultural mechanization (state budget)	1.5	1.4	1.4	2.3	4.0
State agricultural enterprises					
Total	1.5	2.5	3.8	4.8	3.7
State budget	1.0	2.0	3.2	4.1	3.2
Retained profits	0.5	0.5	0.5	0.5	0.5
Subtotal of above	4.5	6.9	8.7	11.4	15.1
Other	0.4	0.4	1.6	3.9	8.1
Total	4.9	7.3	10.3	15.3	23.2
			Subsectors		
		1971–75[a]		1976–80[a]	
Land reclamation		4.6 (32.7)		7.8 (33.6)	
Mechanization		3.4 (22.7)		6.5 (28.0)	
Vegetable production		1.5 (10.0)		3.2 (13.8)	
Animal production		4.4 (29.3)		4.9 (21.1)	
Other		1.1 (7.3)		0.8 (3.5)	
Total[b]		15.0		23.2	

a. Figures in parentheses are percentages of total investment.
b. Totals exclude investments for silos and farm storage and other building facilities.
Source: Data supplied by Romanian authorities during discussions with the authors.

tinue to decline, however, from 15.6 percent in 1966–70 and 14 percent in 1971–75 to 11.6 percent in 1976–80.

Investment plans for 1976–80 put greater emphasis on improving productivity of CAP's and SAM's than in previous plan periods. This policy shift toward CAP's, which account for 75 percent of the arable land, is a step in the right direction for realizing higher plan targets. Available data indicate that investments for CAP's will be 64 percent higher and those for SAM's will be 74 percent higher in 1976–80 than in 1971–75. Investments for

IAS's, however, which have been relatively large in recent years, will be reduced. Data also show that investments for land reclamation, mechanization, and vegetable production will be increased greatly and that those for animal production will be increased slightly in 1976–80 compared with 1971–75. The number of tractors of various types is expected to increase in 1975 by 70,000 tractors, some for replacement and some for additional operations.

The most important projected change in agriculture is a large improvement in labor productivity resulting from substitution of capital for labor. The labor force in agriculture is expected to decline to about 3 million in 1980, compared with 4.0 million in 1975, and to account for only 27 to 28 percent of the total labor force in 1980 compared with 38 percent in 1975. About 700,000 of the 1 million nonagricultural jobs to be created during 1976–80 will be filled by workers leaving agriculture. If the number of agricultural workers declines by 25 percent from 1975 to 1980 as planned and if gross production increases by 30 percent, gross production for each agricultural worker will increase 73 percent. The 1976–80 Plan envisages that real incomes of all workers will be 18 to 22 percent higher in 1980 than in 1975. In 1977 it was announced that this target had been revised to allow an increase of 30.2 percent in real wages by 1980. The plan also stated that real incomes of workers on CAP's and private farms were to rise by 20 to 29 percent over the plan period, and this figure was also increased to 30 percent in 1977. At the same time, changes in pensions for workers throughout the economy were announced (Chapter 9).

Perspectives to 1990

The Directives also include guidelines for economic and social development until 1990, calling for intensive development of agriculture. Gross agricultural production in 1986–90 is projected to be 50 to 80 percent larger than in 1971–75, with livestock products accounting for 50 percent of the total in 1986–90, compared with 40 percent in 1971–75. Total irrigated area will increase to 5 million hectares in 1990 (about half of all arable land and virtually all of the irrigable land) and fertilizer use to 300 to 325 kilograms per hectare (active substance). Cereal production is projected to rise to 28 to 30 million tonnes, averaging more than one tonne for each person. Yields per hectare are expected to rise greatly (Table 11.23).

Livestock numbers and production for each animal are also projected to increase greatly. For example, the number of pigs is expected to increase by 36 to 48 percent by 1980 and 105 to 127 percent by 1990 over the number in 1975 (Table 11.24). Large increases are also expected for cattle, sheep, goats, and poultry. Livestock will be fattened to heavier weights, thereby increasing meat production. Productivity for each animal will approximately

Table 11.23. *Yield Targets for Agricultural Products, 1990*

Product	*Annual average, 1971–75 (kilograms per hectare)*	*Target, 1990 (kilograms per hectare)*	*Percentage increase*
Wheat and rye	2,210	3,700	67
Maize	2,680	5,300– 5,800	98–116
Sunflower	1,450	2,300– 2,400	59– 66
Sugar beets	22,140	42,000–45,000	90–103
Flax for fiber	1,886	5,800– 6,000	207–218
Field vegetables	11,250	23,000–24,000	104–113

Source: Data supplied by Romanian authorities during discussions with the authors.

double from recent levels. In 1990 in IAS's, milk production for each cow is expected to average 3,300 to 3,500 liters annually; wool production for each sheep, 4.5 to 4.7 kilograms; and eggs for each laying hen, 200 to 240. In the CAP's, the respective figures are 2,200 to 2,400 liters, 3.3 to 3.7 kilograms, and 180 to 210 eggs.

Assessment of development prospects

Romania has great potential for expanding agricultural production. It should be able to increase gross agricultural production 28 percent in 1976–80 over 1971–75, as called for by the lower target of the five-year plan, if average weather conditions prevail. If Romania is able to fulfill plan stipulations for irrigating an additional 1.2 million hectares and to put into effect farming practices required for higher yields on this area, it should be able to move gross agricultural production closer to the upper targets.

Table 11.24. *Increase Targets for Livestock, 1980–1990*

Livestock	*Actual 1975*	*Targets 1980*	*Targets 1990*	*Percent increase from 1971–75: 1980*	*Percent increase from 1971–75: 1990*
		(millions of head)			
Cattle	6.1	7.5	10–11	23	63– 80
Pigs	8.8	12–13	18–20	36–47	104–127
Sheep and goats	14.3	19–19.5	20–22	32–37	40– 54

Sources: Law (no. 4) on the Adoption of the Plan for 1976–80; *Directives of Eleventh Congress of the Romanian Communist Party*; and *Anuarul Statistic*, various issues.

Table 11.25. *Average Annual Crop Yields and Fertilizer Use, by Kind of Farm, 1971–75*
(kilograms per hectare)

Item	Kind of farm		
	IAS's	CAP's	IAS/CAP's
Wheat and rye	2,873	2,115	136
Maize	3,388	2,672	127
Sunflower	1,747	1,378	127
Sugar beets	20,934	22,159	94
Potatoes	18,335	11,509	159
Lucerne	6,190	3,851	161
Fertilizer used on arable land[a]	132	65	203

a. Kilograms of active substance per hectare.

CROPS. Crop yields could be raised by increased use of improved seeds, fertilizer, and herbicides to control weeds and by better seedbed preparation, cultivation, and harvesting practices. Only enough herbicides were available in 1974 to control weeds on wheat planted on IAS's. The expansion in supplies of these inputs planned for 1976–80 should raise crop yields throughout the country. There undoubtedly is great potential for raising yields by more effective control of weeds and more timely performance of field operations. The planned expansion of farm machines on SAM's should improve field operations and should contribute to higher yields on CAP's.

Crop yields on IAS's are generally 25 to 60 percent higher than on CAP's (Table 11.25), largely because of the use of better seeds, more fertilizer, and other chemicals and better field operations. Also, a larger share of the land is irrigated on IAS's than on CAP's. Romania now plans to upgrade farming practices on the CAP's, however, and to irrigate more of their land. It should be possible to increase their crop yields by 25 to 50 percent by following agronomic practices similar to those now used on IAS's, so that CAP production will be close to the IAS level.

Comparison with neighboring countries also suggests that Romania has not been fulfilling its potential. Crop yields are lower in Romania than in other eastern European countries (Table 11.26). Differences in soil fertility and climatic conditions account for some of the differences, but its lower crop yields are undoubtedly partly caused by lower applications of fertilizer, poorer seeds, and less effective weed control. Fertilizer use is less than half that of nearby countries. Romania's plans to increase fertilizer use from an average of 95 kilograms (active substance) in 1975 to 250 to 280 kilograms

Table 11.26. *Crop Yields and Fertilizer Use in Eastern European Countries*
(kilograms per hectare)

	Crop yields, 1971–73 average				
Country	*Wheat*	*Maize*	*Sugar beets*	*Potatoes*	*Fertilizer used*[a]
Romania	2,220	2,681	23,096	12,008	65
Bulgaria	3,457	4,137	35,556	13,282	156
Czechoslovakia	3,554	4,229	34,090	14,953	272
German Democratic Republic	4,017	2,835	28,701	17,386	388
Hungary	3,218	3,840	31,576	10,628	196
Poland	2,708	2,977	31,020	17,520	205

a. Active substance per hectare of arable land in 1972.
Source: Food and Agricultural Organization of the United Nations, *Yearbook of Agricultural Production* (Rome: United Nations, 1974).

in 1980 per hectare of arable land, vineyards, and orchards should help much to increase yields, provided better seeds and other improved cultural practices are also introduced. Experimental trials made by research stations of the Academy of Agriculture and Forestry Sciences reinforce these conclusions. It will be especially important to improve farming practices on irrigated land. Some crops now under irrigation have been damaged by plant diseases and insects, so there may be much room for increasing yields on land already irrigated by upgrading farming practices.

Currently, Romania's seed industry has facilities for growing, cleaning, grading, drying, and storing only about 200,000 tonnes of the 600,000 tonnes of seeds used annually to grow wheat, maize, barley, sunflower, soybeans, and other field crops. It especially needs to expand seed-drying capacity. The provision of improved seed-handling facilities should enable Romania to increase yields of cereals and oilseeds 10 to 20 percent by using new varieties developed by the Academy of Agricultural and Forestry Sciences and thereby to reduce present high-seeding rates. Because germination rates are uncertain, seeding rates for cereals are often high, causing plant population to be too dense and lodging in fields where high germination rates occur. Additional seed-handling facilities are especially needed to use new monogram sugar beet hybrids, which have potential to increase yields about 18 percent. Romania also needs better seed-handling facilities to expand its exports of superior hybrid sunflower seed to the United States and hybrid corn and other seeds to European countries. It also needs to improve storage capacities for crops after harvest. The 1976–80 Plan gives priority to silo construction and modernization of on-farm storage.

The realization of increases in the crop yields described above will require improved farming practices, and the potential for increased crop yields may overstate yield gains under field conditions, since tests are made under ideal moisture conditions. Nevertheless, prospects for continued yield increases at rates achieved in the past decade appear good, because of plans to expand the irrigated area and to increase the use of improved seeds, fertilizer, and other inputs.

LIVESTOCK. Romania can expand beef, sheep, and milk production from its 4.5 million hectares of pasture and meadowland. Approximately 2 million hectares of state-owned land, located mainly between the arable low plains of zone I and the forested areas of zones II and III, could profitably be improved by clearing encroaching shrubs and trees, building access roads and stock water facilities, fencing, seeding, and fertilizing. Controlled grazing practices to prevent overstocking and to improve vegetative growth will be required to maximize livestock production. Pasture and meadowlands could be used to raise more cattle and lambs for fattening by specialized feeding enterprises.

Larger investments for development of pasture livestock could yield relatively high returns. A program to develop pastures was begun in 1972 involving expenditure of 300 to 400 million lei annually. In 1975 the amount was increased to 1.2 billion lei, which was enough to carry out minor improvements on 400,000 hectares. Financing is provided outside the state budget, largely by grazing fees of 30 lei a year for bovines and 10 lei for each sheep and by charges made for cutting pastures for hay. Unimproved pastures produce about 5,000 kilograms of green forage per hectare, but improved pastures produce three times as much. It is estimated that the cost of improving native pasture in mountain areas requires investments of 7,000 to 8,000 lei per hectare. Annual operating costs would be additional.

Little arable land is used for perennial hays and almost none for pasture in crop rotations. In 1971–75 roughage feed (fodder) crops accounted for 16 percent of the arable area, but only half was in perennial hays and almost none in rotation pasture. Agronomists believe that sound crop rotations for hay and pasture, involving more perennials such as lucerne and clovers, are required to conserve soil structure and fertility, to control insects and diseases, and to raise the protein content of roughage feeds. Field experiments also show that yields of maize, sunflower, and wheat increase substantially when these crops are grown on land right after perennial crops. About half of the 1.6 million hectares in fodder crops are annuals for hay, green feed, silage, and root crops harvested for barn feeding. Much of the cost of labor and capital could be saved by permitting livestock to harvest a larger share of their feed from perennial pastures instead of relying so heavily on harvesting roughage feed crops for barn feeding.

Achievement of the high targets set for livestock products depends on expanding total feed production and increasing the efficient use of feed. Roughage, as well as feed grain production, will need to average 45 to 50 percent more during 1976–80 than during 1971–75. A doubling of the area used to grow hay, green feed, silage, and root crops during the first two decades was made possible by reducing the area of grain cereals. Further reduction of the area in grain and expansion in the area of fodder crops will probably be necessary to produce the roughage required to achieve targets set for milk and beef production. Also, double-cropping of forage crops will help to meet these targets.

Despite much progress in recent years, there still is much room for upgrading the genetic quality of livestock breeds and for improving livestock/feed conversion ratios. The upward trend in output for each animal unit can be expected to continue. Shortage of grain concentrates, particularly high-protein meal, however, will be a major problem in achieving better balanced feeding rations and improving livestock/feed conversion ratios. Feedgrain shortage may also be an important constraint to achieving the high production targets for livestock products.

Romania is planning to establish many more large-scale, factory-like livestock enterprises to produce pork, beef, dairy products, poultry, and eggs, based mainly on purchased feed. Supplies of feed to private farmers and to members of CAP's will be increased, according to Romanian authorities, even though the number of large-scale livestock enterprises increases. Private farms and members of CAP's accounted for 46 percent of the meat, 57 percent of the milk, 43 percent of the wool, and 62 percent of the eggs produced in 1975. It is expected that total livestock production by individual farmers and CAP members will be maintained and perhaps increased, but large-scale units will account for an increasing share of national production. Factory-like livestock enterprises use feed more efficiently than small-scale production by private farmers and members of CAP's. But the latter probably use much poorer quality feed, which otherwise would be wasted.

Prospects for achieving a large increase in livestock production are good, but the targets, calling for doubling the number of cattle and pigs from 1971–75 to 1990, will require great efforts for achievement. They will require much more rapid increases in feed production and improvements of feed conversion ratios than have occurred during the past two decades.

12

The Construction and Housing Sectors

THE CONSTRUCTION PROCESS, by its very nature, is an important element in investment, and, since Romania bases its economic strategy upon a high rate of investment, it is not unexpected to find this sector playing such a crucial role in the development of the Romanian economy. It is, in fact, the third largest sector in terms of both national income and social product, as shown by the following 1975 data from *Anuarul Statistic*, in percentages based on current prices.

	Sector			
Item	*Industry*	*Construction*	*Agriculture*	*Transport and telecommunications*
Social product	64.7	8.6	13.3	4.2
National income	56.2	7.6	16.0	5.8

Total social product increased at an average annual rate of 9.8 percent between 1950–75, whereas construction social product[1] increased at an average annual rate of 11.5 percent. Similarly, national income increased at 9.7 percent a year with the construction element growing at 11.3 percent a year.

Performance of the Construction Sector

The scale of the growth of construction output can be seen more clearly in Tables 12.1 and 12.2. The increases in the early 1950s were large but mainly reflected progress from an underdeveloped base and large investments,

1. Construction social product includes construction work, capital repairs, and geologic and drilling operations.

Table 12.1. *Construction, 1950–75*

(billions of comparable 1963 lei)

Item	*1950*	*1955*	*1960*	*1965*	*1970*	*1971*	*1972*	*1973*	*1974*	*1975*
Construction social product	5.1	12.7	20.7	33.0	54.8	59.7	64.4	67.3	71.0	76.7
Construction national income	2.1	4.7	9.1	12.4	21.8	23.9	25.9	27.3	28.8	31.4
Construction output[a]	4.4	10.5	17.1	26.4	44.3	47.9	51.3	54.9	56.7	61.7
Construction work[b]	2.9	7.3	12.2	21.1	34.7	38.2	41.3	44.3	45.6	50.9

a. Includes construction work plus capital repairs.

b. Includes building, installation, and mounting of equipment in the socialist sectors.

Sources: Anuarul Statistic al Republicii Socialist Romania (Bucharest: Directia Centrala de Statistica, published yearly). *Investitii-Constructii in Republica Socialista Romania* (Bucharest: Central Statistics Office, 1966); and World Bank estimates.

Table 12.2. *Average Annual Growth Rates in Construction*
(percentage)

Item	*1951–55*	*1956–60*	*1961–65*	*1966–70*	*1971–75*
Social product	20.2	10.2	9.8	10.7	6.9
National income	16.9	14.3	6.4	12.0	7.6
Output	19.1	10.1	9.1	10.9	6.9
Work	20.3	10.8	11.5	10.5	7.9

Source: Anuarul Statistic, various issues.

including those for drilling and exploration. As the 1950s continued, some construction works were hampered by shortages of lumber and cement, both of which were required for export to obtain scarce foreign exchange for machinery imports. By the 1960s these constraints began to disappear, and, as the state diverted an increasing proportion of national income into investment, construction continued to grow very rapidly. The 1970s have also seen significant growth rates for the sector, but at a slower pace. This has not occurred because of slower investment growth, but because construction's share in investment has been reduced. This is discussed further below.

Tables SA8.1 and SA8.2 detail construction work by branches since 1960. As expected, the patterns follow the general development strategy. Over 50 percent of all construction is in industry, and between 80 and 90 percent of industrial construction is in the producer goods sector (group A). Not only does industry have the greatest share, but it has also shown a consistent growth rate throughout the period. The producer goods sector took the lead in the early 1960s, but consumer goods expanded rapidly toward the end of the decade, and both have continued to expand in the 1970s.

In general, the productive sector, together with housing, has accounted for the bulk of construction work. In 1960 the productive sector accounted for 74.8 percent of construction work, with housing taking a further 13.3 percent. By 1975 the productive sector had increased its share to 77.5 percent, and housing accounted for 12.3 percent.

Construction output in the socialist sector (that is, construction work plus capital repairs) is given in Tables SA8.3, SA8.4, and SA8.5, by category of output rather than by branch of economy. The average growth rates over the past fifteen years are the same for the economy as a whole and for both construction work and output, but construction output growth has been lower in the past five years, suggesting that capital repairs have declined relative to new construction. An explanation for this is that the average age of buildings has declined, and, as a result, capital repairs have decreased in importance relative to the rapidly increasing new construction.

Economic Efficiency in Construction

In 1950 the construction sector was labor-intensive, unmechanized, and relatively unsophisticated. By 1975 the picture had changed substantially. The sector is now much more mechanized and conscious of efficiency.

The biggest transformation has been in mechanization, which is part of a general policy of modernization and increased efficiency (Table 12.3). In 1955 only 22.9 percent of earth work and 37.7 percent of digging was done mechanically; by 1975 the respective figures were 90.6 and 91.7 percent. This, however, does not give the full picture. Fixed assets in construction have also been growing as a proportion of total assets (Table 12.4). They grew quickly in the first few years of the 1950s, but slowed down toward the end of the decade. In the 1970s their growth has been especially fast, with a 19.5 percent increase recorded in 1975 alone. Except for the 1950s, construction investment has had a similar growth (Table 12.5).

The statistics published on capital and labor in construction and the sector's output indicate the sector's development and its efficiency over the past twenty-five years. Between 1950 and 1970 the proportion of the labor force working in construction in both the socialist sector and the whole economy increased at a steady rate from 2.2 to 7.8 percent. The growth of investments and fixed assets proceeded at a less regular pace. Rapid growth of fixed assets between 1951 and 1955 was followed by a much smaller growth rate for the following five-year period, reflecting the period of economic consolidation that occurred during the second plan period. With the renewed industrialization after 1960, fixed assets expanded more rapidly again: 10.6 percent a year between 1960 and 1965. The fact that social product in construction increased more rapidly than national income and that the capital-output ratio increased throughout the plan period suggests that the infusion of labor and capital in the period was not fully

ble 12.3. *Mechanization in the Construction Sector, Kind of Work, 1955–75*

rcentage of work performed with mechanical means)

ind of work	1955	1960	1965	1970	1971	1972	1973	1974	1975
rth work	22.9	50.6	80.7	86.7	87.3	88.2	87.1	89.6	90.6
Digging	37.7	62.9	84.6	88.7	88.9	89.3	90.7	91.4	91.7
Transport	—	75.2	89.7	92.8	92.9	94.7	94.3	95.6	95.3
ncrete work	—	—	—	73.5	75.5	77.5	82.8	85.9	86.2
nding of sets	—	—	65.6	84.2	85.0	85.5	86.4	87.5	88.5

Source: Anuarul Statistic, various issues.

Table 12.4. *Fixed Assets in Construction, 1950–75*
(1950 = 100)

Item	*1950*	*1955*	*1960*	*1965*	*1970*	*1971*	*1972*	*1973*	*1974*	*1975*
Fixed assets in construction	100	396	477	791	1,376	1,560	1,851	2,033	2,318	2,769
Fixed assets in entire economy	100	125	161	223	337	368	398	433	478	534
Construction as percentage of total	0.7	2.2	2.0	2.4	2.7	2.9	3.1	3.2	3.3	3.5

Average annual rates of growth of fixed assets	*1951–55*	*1956–60*	*1961–65*	*1966–70*	*1971–75*
In construction	32.0	3.8	10.6	11.7	15.0
In total economy	4.6	5.2	6.7	8.6	9.6

Source: Anuarul Statistic, various issues.

effective and that greater output could only be obtained by a more-than-proportionate increase in inputs. This trend appears to have been reversed in the 1961–65 plan period, when national income from construction grew more rapidly than construction, and the incremental capital-output ratio (ICOR) for construction fell to 1.36 (Table 12.2 and Figure 12.1).

The developments between 1971–75 were somewhat different. As Table 12.2 shows, production increased at an average annual real rate of 7 to 8 percent. Fixed assets meanwhile grew at 15 percent a year, significantly faster than the productive sector average of 9.6 percent. Construction's share in fixed assets increased from 2.7 percent in 1970 to 3.5 percent in 1975, and its share of investment increased from 4.8 to 5.6 percent. The manpower position exhibited a different trend. In 1971 and 1972 there was an initial surge in the construction labor force (Table SA8.6), but after that it rapidly became more difficult to recruit construction workers. In absolute numbers, total occupied population and employees in construction dropped between 1972 and 1975. The response was to increase capital investment and to introduce modernized technology, particularly in 1974 and 1975, to maintain production growth. Some of the effects of this are shown in Table SA8.6. The capital-labor ratio in construction increased by 52.3 percent between 1972 and 1975, which was the same as the economy average. The capital/output ratio, however, rose by 18 percent as against the economy average of 13 percent, and output for each worker increased by 24 percent, only two-thirds of the economy average of 35 percent. In 1971–75 the ICOR in construction increased to 2.69 from 1.36 during the previous five years, whereas the ICOR for the total productive sector fell from 4.15 to 3.03. The picture then showed some labor unavailability, for which it was only possible to substitute capital at an increasing cost.

Role of construction in the investment process

Although an integral part of the investment process, the importance of construction has been diminishing over the past twenty-five years (Table SA8.8). This can be explained by examining the way in which efficiency has increased in the sector. The design cost of each project is determined by valuing the cost of materials, labor, design, and the like. Thus, increased efficiency in construction is reflected, over time, in a reduced share of construction in the design cost of projects and hence in the share of construction in investment.

Still, this is unlikely to account wholly for the fall. Because productivity of investment is a critical concept in which the opportunity cost of consump-

Figure 12.1. *Relation between Capital, Labor, and Output in the Construction and Productive Sectors, 1950–75*

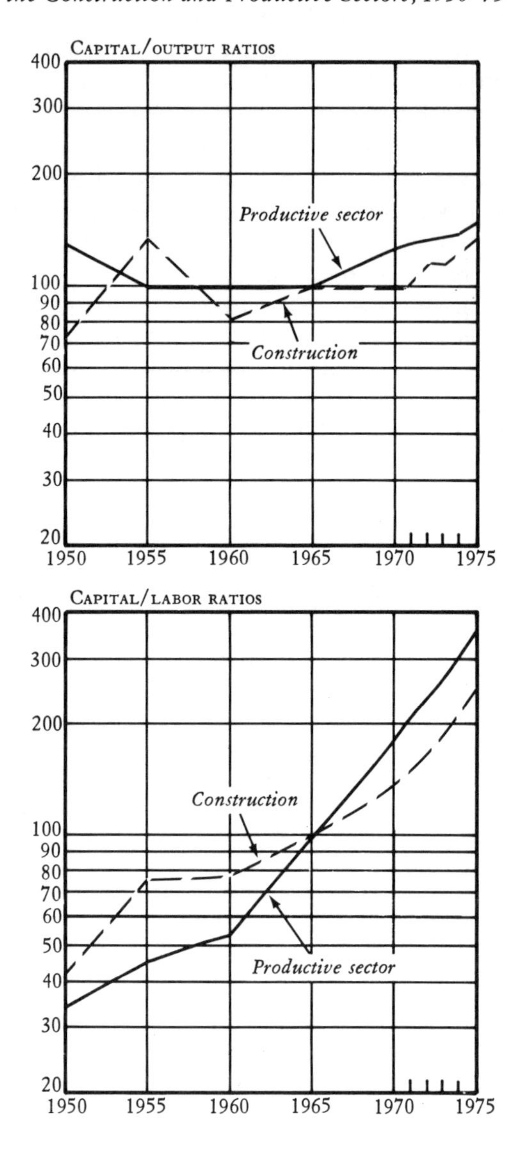

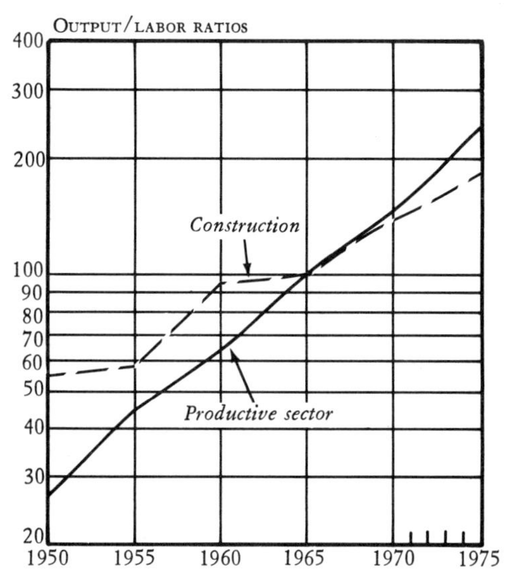

Output/labor ratios
400
300
200
100
90
80
70
60
50
40
30
20
1950
1955
1960
1965
1970
1975
Construction
Productive sector

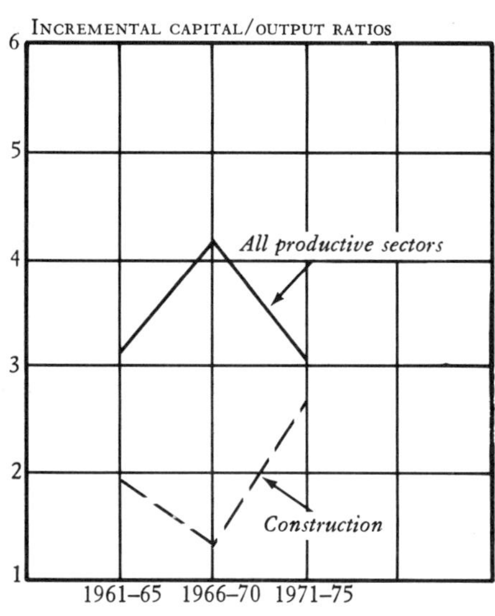

Incremental capital/output ratios
6
5
4
3
2
1
All productive sectors
Construction
1961–65
1966–70
1971–75

Table 12.5. *Investment in Construction, 1950–75*

Item	Investment in 1959 prices (millions of lei)			
	1950	*1955*	*1960*	*1965*
Total investment in the economy	5,633	13,466	24,615	44,857
Construction investment	369	292	531	1,931
Construction as percentage of total	6.5	2.2	2.2	4.3
	Average annual rate of growth			
	1951–55	*1956–60*	*1961–65*	
Total investment	18.9	12.8	12.7	
Construction investment	−4.6	12.7	29.5	

Source: Anuarul Statistic, various issues.

tion foregone is high (and with accumulation at 33 percent of national income in Romania, this can be assumed to be the case), it is very much in society's interest to maximize that productivity. The productivity of investment, for the most part, depends on the productivity of machinery and equipment rather than on the amount of construction. Therefore, to minimize the ICOR, construction costs should be minimized in each investment project.

After the price restructuring that began in 1973, raw material prices were increased to reflect the new higher world prices, and it became even more necessary to minimize the material inputs used in construction. Even with increased costs, it would have been possible for fixed-price values of construction to fall, thus explaining the particularly large changes in construction's share in 1974 and 1975. Some evidence is available to back up this hypothesis. In 1974, for example, the proportion of material expenditures in construction social product, in current prices, increased suddenly from 61.6 to 63.1 percent, having been stable for the previous three years. The state has been trying to minimize material inputs in construction, and this is discussed further below.

Organizational Structure and Planning System of the Construction Sector

Organization

Description of the organizational structure in construction is complex because of the various enterprises that are responsible to ministries, People's

Investment in 1963 prices (millions of lei)						
1965	*1970*	*1971*	*1972*	*1973*	*1974*	*1975*
44,659	74,790	82,617	91,717	99,231	112,457	130,640
1,826	3,595	4,290	4,448	4,148	5,652	7,317
4.1	4.8	5.2	4.8	4.2	5.0	5.6

Average annual rate of growth	
1966–70	*1971–75*
10.8	11.8
14.5	15.3

Councils, and cooperative unions. Construction activities are organized in terms of the final product (for example, a factory or school), as well as in terms of the form of activity (a building or installation). Since republican projects are the responsibility of ministries, they are built by construction enterprises or centrals responsible to ministries. Sociocultural projects and housing are the responsibility of People's Councils, and so they are built by units of the People's Councils. Similarly, services to the population are the responsibility of cooperatives, and so cooperatives maintain and make minor repairs on private housing units as well as building them. Figure 12.2 shows the structure of the construction industry.

In terms of output, the ministerial construction enterprises and centrals are the most important. Seven ministries[2] have their own construction enterprises that do certain specialized work for their ministries, and, in addition, there is the Ministry of Industrial Construction, which is the only one that specializes only in construction work. The Ministry of Industrial Construction undertakes a broader range of activities for different branches of the national economy: chemicals and petrochemicals, metalworking, machine-building, light industry, the food and agro-industry.

There is also a network of construction enterprises at the district level. There is one building trust or enterprise under each People's Council[3] in

2. Ministry of Transport and Telecommunications (all transport and telecommunications constructions); Ministry of Electric Power (power and hydro power); Ministry of Metallurgical Industry (siderurgical construction); Ministry of Mining, Petroleum, and Energy (mining construction only); Ministry of Agriculture and Food Industry (land and hydro improvement projects only); Ministry of Forestry and Construction Materials (forestry and roads); and Ministry of Chemical Industry.

3. The Municipality of Bucharest has one central under its responsibility.

Figure 12.2. *Organization of the Construction Industry*

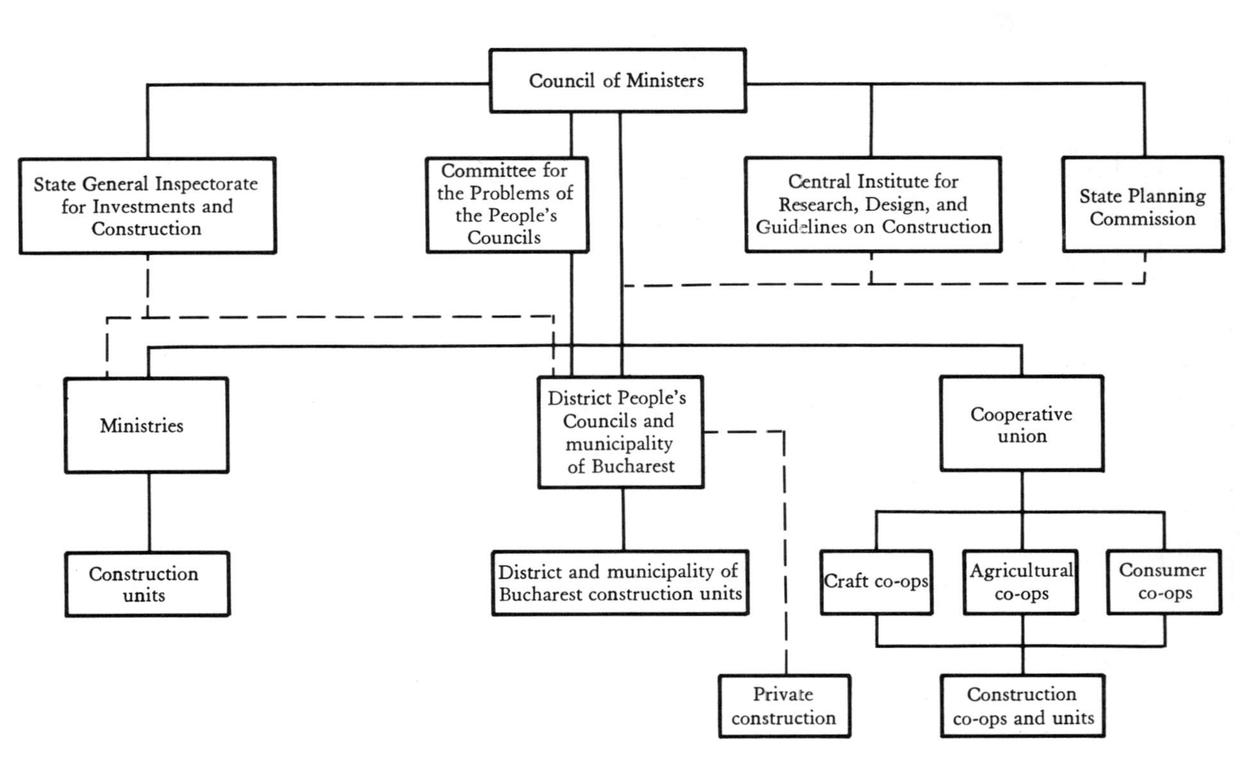

Note: Solid lines indicate hierarchical lines of authority and responsibility; dashed lines indicate channels of consultation and cooperation.

each district with direct responsibility to the Executive Committee. These units undertake all the construction work for which the People's Councils are responsible: that is, all sociocultural schemes (education, health, and so forth), housing, and local industrial projects.[4]

Construction work is also carried out in the cooperative sector in various ways. The craft cooperatives include cooperatives that specialize in construction alone. The aim is for each cooperative union to include just one construction cooperative.[5] These co-ops, each of which includes a number of specialized workshops, do three types of construction. First, they provide such services to the population as general household repairs (heating, sanitation, electrical, structural) and, in some cases, home-building; second, they do maintenance and repairs for both state and cooperative enterprises; and third, they implement investment projects for co-ops. In the rural areas, such activities are usually carried out by construction workshops, which are part of agricultural or consumer co-ops, rather than by specialized cooperative enterprises.

There is also a small amount of construction work carried on outside the state and cooperative sectors, but it has no distinct organizational structure. Since 1948 private construction enterprises have been phased out or have been brought into the co-op sector, and now most private construction work is on an individual basis, the most important part of which is housing constructed by private individuals for their own use.

There are many organizational frameworks within the construction sector, and differences even permeate industrial ministries. For example, the Ministry of Industrial Construction includes twenty-one trusts: fourteen of them are construction trusts that are territorially organized, three are installation and assembly trusts again territorially organized, and four are specialized trusts.[6] Each trust is directly responsible to the ministry only while remaining an independent self-administering unit with a legal entity. Each is comprised of units that are categorized by geographical position or specialization, and each unit has at least three building sites under its jurisdiction.

Other ministries have one construction central for each broad specialization, and, within each central, the enterprises are divided in terms of area and specialization. For example, within the Ministry of Transport and

4. These are usually small, consumer-oriented, and depend on local raw materials.

5. Bucharest, because of its size, has two: one specialized in construction, the other in installation.

6. These are the Insulation for Industrial Workers Trust, Specialized Works Trust, Assembly of Chemical Equipment Trust and Installation, and Automation Trust.

Telecommunications there is a construction central that includes construction enterprises for railways, river transport, telecommunications, and road construction. This central includes ten enterprises (six of which are regional railway construction enterprises) plus the Bucharest railway sites.

Despite independence as administrative units, the central and trusts rely on the ministry for certain services. The ministry will coordinate the activities of all centrals, particularly in the areas of training[7] and planning. In addition, each ministry has at least one design institute that draws up the technical specifications for each construction project.

The line of authority from the ministries and the People's Councils goes to the Council of Ministers, but there are several other centralized bodies also responsible to the Council of Ministers, but with a degree of authority over the ministries, the People's Councils, and in some cases also the cooperatives. First, there is the State General Inspectorate for Investments and Construction (SGIIC), whose functions are inspection for compliance with building laws, setting norms in construction,[8] and technical planning of large projects for the state sector only.

Second, there is a more scientific and technical institution concerned with building techniques in general, which is called the Central Institute for Research, Design, and Guidelines on Construction (CIDGC). It promotes the state's technical policy in construction, as well as in technical and economic efficiency. One aim of the organization is to coordinate research and development. It deals with general matters, such as the adoption of mechanized equipment, as well as more specific problems, such as how to reinforce buildings against seismic interference. Its other responsibility relates to design, and, through its subordinate institutes, it draws up standardized models that are fully designed and specified. In drawing up guidelines, it elaborates standards, norms, and instructions that become compulsory for the sectors and that are also consistent with the priorities of the construction sector. The CIDGC priorities are all related to the more economic use of resources. The chief ones are to minimize raw material inputs (especially steel); to minimize the use of manpower and the time taken to complete construction work; and to minimize the use of energy, both in the construction and in the use of the final output. These priorities are discussed below.

The CIDGC is subordinated to the Council of Ministers, as is the SGIIC. It has specific responsibilities toward units below it. All ministries have their own research and design institutes, which draw up the detailed designs

7. See Chapter 8 on human resources.

8. Among the norms is the requirement that all new construction meet approved seismic standards.

for the projects for which they are responsible. These research and design institutes are independent and cooperate with the CIDGC, which approves their plans, research, and designs for standard models.

These two institutions cover the whole state sector, but there is another that only affects the district construction enterprises. The Committee for the Problems of the People's Councils (CPC) is a centralized body to coordinate the technical activities of the People's Councils, including certain functions related to construction. It is much more a coordinator than a controller, and it is involved in standardizing the design of dwellings and in implementing physical planning.

Planning

The planning process in construction is, in essence, no different from that in other sectors, but, because construction is a derived activity in the investment planning process, there tends to be a slightly different timing.

The State Planning Committee's (SPC's) role in construction planning is twofold: it welds ongoing projects to new investments and is also responsible for calculating and maintaining the material balances for approximately fifty of the most important raw materials (for example, steel, cement, asbestos, aluminum, and so forth). To draw up the annual construction plan, the SPC begins by compiling lists of investments and establishing for both ongoing and new projects the volume of investment that has to be implemented. From this is determined the volume of investment by ministry (which implements the project) and, for the whole economy, the requirements for raw materials, labor, and equipment.

Meanwhile, at the micro level, the enterprises will be drawing up their own provisional plans. They are aware of the ongoing projects and are informed of the major projected investment programs. In addition, the five-year plan will have provided general guidelines on their expected levels of production. They will then draw up their plan proposals, establishing the indicators for the volume of production, labor productivity, salaries, numbers employed, and material expenditures for each 1,000 lei of output.

At this point (usually July or August), they contract with supplying enterprises for the necessary raw materials; the enterprises' demands being based on plan and material consumption norms. In addition, contracts are also made between the construction enterprises and the beneficiaries.

The enterprise plans are then sent to the relevant ministries who aggregate them, incorporate them into their own plans, and pass them on to the SPC. The SPC reconciles these proposed plans with its own macro plans, ensuring that all projects are consistent with the five-year plan. The plan is then disaggregated down to the ministry and from there to the enterprise.

The planning process for the five-year plan is essentially the same. Detailed account is taken, however, only of the major investment projects that will require a significant time to complete and for which the technico-economic documentation is prepared.

The procedure so far has only specifically described planning at the republican level. At the local level, however, the methods are the same, except that the enterprises pass on their plans to the People's Councils, who incorporate them into their own regional plans. In the same way, plans of the cooperative sector are forwarded to the cooperative unions. One difference exists, however: because the cooperatives are responsible for providing construction materials to private individuals, they are required to assess private demand when drawing up their plans.

Other construction, undertaken by the population, is regulated. It requires a permit from the People's Council indicating that it complies with the physical planning regulations. Thus, there is some degree of control over the operations, and the cooperatives are made aware of the expected demand for materials.

In recent years, there have been attempts to improve the quality of construction planning. This has led to the establishment of the Center for Organization and Cybernetics in Construction (COCC), which is a responsibility of the Ministry of Industrial Construction. The COCC works on a project in which all the key information on a given construction job, including its critical path, is fed into a computer. Thus, at any given time, it can provide an updated portfolio of construction work. From this, it can also calculate the implied demands for construction materials in detail and can help to draw up material balances. The project has advanced rapidly and should improve the efficiency of the construction industry. Planning and control systems already have been established covering the most important 10,000 out of 15,000 construction projects.

Other institutional arrangements

FINANCE. The financial arrangements, like the planning system, are slightly different in the construction sector. Whereas industrial and other enterprises hold bank accounts with the National Bank and agricultural enterprises hold theirs with the Bank for Agriculture and Food Industry (BAFI), construction enterprises hold bank accounts with the Investment Bank (IB).

Payment for construction is not made in advance, but monthly after performance. During the month, IB, taking into account the enterprise's production plan, advances credits to cover expenses incurred within that month. Monthly, the beneficiary reviews the work completed by the constructor and, if it is found satisfactory, authorizes IB to release the funds for the work performed. In this way, the construction enterprise repays the bank's credit.

In addition, IB gives credits for purchasing raw and other materials, as well as for seasonal financing. The interest rate is 2 percent. The bank assesses a rate of 12 percent when there is a failure to repay the credit. Credits for construction by CAP's and agricultural state farms is extended to them by BAFI. Strict penalties are imposed on delays both in delivery of materials and in completion of construction work.

Cooperatives maintain their accounts at the National Bank and they are not granted credit. For large investments (over 100,000 lei), however, credit can be extended to the handicraft cooperatives by IB. If in financial need, a cooperative can obtain loans from a central fund established by the Central Union of Co-ops, to which all co-ops contribute. Actual payment for construction work for the cooperatives is the same as for state enterprises.

LABOR FORCE IN CONSTRUCTION. Once again the construction sector does not fit into a conventional pattern. Unlike other countries where the construction labor force is temporary and on a project-to-project basis, in Romania, it has permanent status, in that all workers have contracts. In practice, however, the construction labor force fluctuates. A proportion of the labor is, in fact, seasonal. For example, cooperative agricultural workers are on contract with construction cooperatives for a certain period when not needed for agricultural work. In addition, the labor force tends to have a large turnover, particularly of unskilled workers. Some of them leave the construction enterprises to work on the completed project. Although the average wage in this sector is higher than that in any other sector, it had not been adequate to compensate for the nature of the work. In mid-1977 wages were adjusted to reflect the working conditions better.

Recruitment does not occur centrally or at site level but at unit level. Workers are expected to be mobile within a unit (either regional or specialized) and may be required to move their residence at regular intervals. Housing, however, is always provided.

To overcome some of these problems, training is provided for skilled and unskilled workers on all levels. The result is intended to be greater mechanization, learning of different skills, and greater productivity, leading to higher wages and more job satisfaction. In practice, it is also likely to lead to more highly specialized workers who end up tied to the construction industry.

EXTERNAL WORKS. Responsibility for construction work outside the country has been consolidated in a foreign trade enterprise called ARCOM, which was subordinated in mid-1977 to the Ministry of Foreign Trade and International Cooperation. It has undertaken various construction works, such as housing, refinery, and other plant building, in such countries as West Germany, Libya, Iraq, Lebanon, Sudan, and Syria. In general, the designs and technical knowledge are Romanian, but materials are usually supplied by the country itself, and local subcontractors are often used. There are some other ministries that undertake construction activities abroad, such as the Ministry of Mining, Petroleum, and Geology for oil drilling; the Ministry of Electrical Energy for hydro and thermal power plants; and the Ministry of Transport and Telecommunications for roads. Administratively, ARCOM acts like any other foreign trade enterprise and fits into the planning system accordingly. It exports construction services.

Present Position of and Prospects for Construction

As already noted, construction work grew at an average annual rate of 10.4 percent between 1960 and 1975. Although no precise plan targets are available, there is every indication that this rapid growth rate will continue and even increase between 1976 and 1980. For example, the 1977 Annual Plan requires an increase in construction work of 20.4 percent over 1976, and it has been estimated that between 1976 and 1980, the plan target is for an annual average rate of increase of some 15 percent. As a result, there is extra pressure on the industry, not only to produce efficiently, but also to attain its growth targets.

To evaluate the efficiency of the construction sector, the following criterion is used: construction is considered efficient if it imposes no constraints on the growth of the economy or is not constrained in its own growth by the supply of inputs under its control. Furthermore, it should not contribute to waste of resources through "overdimensioning" and "overfinishing."

First, the role of construction in the investment process cannot be fully evaluated, because detailed data on plan targets and achievements are not available. But it can be said that, until very recently the construction sector has met the requirements of the economy with generally increasing efficiency and that it has imposed no constraints upon economic growth.

Construction work was sluggish, however, in 1976 and also in 1977 before the earthquake. This may mean that the sector could not meet plan targets because of limitations in its capacity or in the capacity of enterprises delivering equipment and materials to it. Also, another limiting factor appears to be the shortage of construction workers. These factors affect the pace of construction work and project completion. Since construction accounts for 40 percent of total investment, the performance of the construction sector explains, to some extent, the overall shortfall of investment in 1976 and 1977.

Two additional important problems exist in the sector: the provision on time of designs and documentation for projects by the design institutes and the improved distribution and organization of personnel on building sites. The 1971–75 Communiqué on the plan's fulfillment highlighted the "delay in the elaboration of technical and economic documentation" as a deficiency which "affected the efficiency of investments and resulted in the delay of some production capacities." Similar difficulties were acknowledged in the 1976–80 and 1977 Plans. To correct them and to secure better-qualified personnel, wages in the design industry have been recently increased. The plans have also called for better organization, particularly at the site level.

Although the problems discussed above are characteristic of a rapidly growing sector, they show construction emerging as a constraint to the economy. This also explains the disproportionate attention given to the sector in the 1977 Plan. The situation has been aggravated by the additional requirements for construction following the earthquake. As explained further in Chapter 16, some of those additional requirements have been met through compulsory and voluntary work by the population. The government is also accelerating the introduction of more capital-intensive technology in the construction sector and is taking measures to improve quality. One important example of the latter is that the major responsibility for quality control was switched from on-site supervisors to the manufacturers of construction materials. This was accomplished by increasing the prefabricated component of construction works.

With regard to the second criterion discussed at the beginning of this section, there are indications that construction has been overfulfilling its role. Problems of works that are "overdimensioned" and "overfinished" were pinpointed in the 1971–75 Five-Year Plan, which also specified that appropriate action was to be taken by the Council of Ministers. The 1971–75 Communiqué on the plan's fulfillment reported on that action. There are indications, alluded to in the 1977 Plan, that there are still "overdimensioning and architectural exaggerations" in construction works.

One of the government's most important proposals affecting the sector is that material expenditures in construction should be cut by 30 percent by 1980. This reflects concerns about both overdimensioning and excessive consumption of inputs. Reductions in the consumption of materials and use of labor may be required for several reasons, for example, materials may have been used wastefully or else are in short supply. There is a strong concern for the former, since some construction methods have not completely eliminated waste of materials and labor. It was mentioned in Chapter 6 that a raw material constraint is already starting to hit the economy. Furthermore, the CIDGC is producing standardized designs where main priority is a minimal use of materials, especially steel and cement, the latter especially because of the large consumption of energy required for its production.

Overview of the Housing Sector

Two policy objectives have combined to increase the requirements for housing: improvements in the standard of living and industrial urbanization. These demands for housing are balanced by the economic constraints limiting the supply. Over 90 percent of housing cost is made up of construction, and, as neither construction capacity nor raw material inputs are limitless, there is a permanent tradeoff between housing and other construction projects, particularly between productive investments. The problem is not only to equate supply and demand in absolute quantities, but also in terms of quality and geographic distribution.

These situations are very real in Romania particularly since, as discussed above, the construction sector has been underfulfilling its targets in the first two years of the current five-year plan. For an annual rate of population growth of 1 percent, 66,000 dwellings a year[9] must be built to maintain the present per capita housing stock. Added to this are the tasks of replacing and maintaining the present stock (40 percent of which was built before 1944), meeting any local shortages that may develop from urbanization, and improving the living standards of those already housed.

In quantitative terms, the present housing stock provides an average of 0.978 dwelling for each family,[10] implying a deficit of 150,000 dwellings. The target of one dwelling for each family is at present achieved only in the rural areas, where in 1976 there were 1,019 dwellings for each 1,000 families.[11]

9. This is equal to the average number of dwellings completed a year in 1971–75 from direct state centralized and cooperative funds.

10. Based on an estimated housing stock of 6.7 million dwellings and 6.85 million family units in 1975.

11. A family is permitted to own one house plus a vacation residence, and, consequently, an average of over one is required before the deficit will be eliminated.

Structure

There are essentially two forms of housing in Romania: that built by the state and that built by private individuals for their own occupation. State-built housing can be sold or rented and is built by enterprises directly subordinated to the People's Councils. The People's Councils themselves are responsible both for the rental and sale of the dwellings that are financed by direct state funds.[12]

According to law, accommodations can be rented by any citizen. Priority is determined according to a classification of the population into seven categories, such as workers, employees transferred from one sector to another, and so forth. Within each category, such factors as levels of incomes and number of dependents are considered. Rents are determined by law and reflect the size of the housing and the income of the highest wage-earner in the family.[13] Rented accommodations are mainly in urban areas (75 percent of those built in 1975 were in urban areas); those in rural areas are usually located close to a major economic project, such as a dam or mine.

Apartments built by the state may also be purchased by private citizens, either with their own funds or with a loan from the state through the Savings and Consignment Bank. The size of the loan is limited by the number of rooms in the apartment, and the terms are determined by the level of income at the time of purchase;[14] the minimum down-payment

12. In certain cases, enterprises allocate funds for state-owned dwellings and are then permitted to administer them themselves.

13. Rents are determined by income and by the size of the apartment. The following rental rates are in lei per square meter:

	Income (lei)				
Area	*Up to 800*	*801–1,100*	*1,101–1,300*	*1,301–1,600*	*Over 1,600*
Floor space	1.80	2.20	2.40	2.50	2.70
Annex (halls, closets, etc.)	0.72	0.88	1.00	1.00	1.00
Porch, locker	0.36	0.44	0.50	0.50	0.50

14. The maximum loans are: 41,500 lei for a one-room apartment, 64,000 for two rooms, 81,000 for three rooms, 91,500 for four rooms, and 105,000 for five rooms. The calculation of rooms includes living rooms plus bedrooms, but excludes bathrooms and kitchens. Interest rates are 3 to 5 percent for the long-term loans up to 50,000 lei and are 6 percent for larger loans. Downpayments may be financed by short-term loans of up to five years at 8 percent. The effect of income on the terms is illustrated below:

	Income		
	Less than 1,500 lei	*1,500–2,000 lei*	*More than 2,000 lei*
Minimum advance payment (percentage)	20	25	30
Repayment period (years)	25	20	15

Table 12.6. *Investment in Housing, 1950–75*
(millions of lei)

Investment	*In 1959 prices* 1950	1951–55	1956–60	1960–65
Investment in national economy				
Total investment	6,304	61,916	100,180	199,692
Housing investment	706	6,260	15,654	23,068
Percentage of total	11.2	10.1	15.6	11.6
Investment in socialist sector				
Total investment	5,663	57,713	88,152	187,656
Housing investment	150	2,704	5,421	12,059
Percentage of total	2.6	4.7	6.1	6.4
Investment in social sector from central state funds				
Total investment	5,561	56,712	84,538	173,748
Housing investment	150	2,693	5,411	12,059
Percentage of total	2.6	4.7	6.4	6.9
Investment outside socialist sector				
Total investment	641	4,203	12,028	12,036
Housing investment	556	3,556	10,233	11,009
Percentage of total	86.7	84.6	85.1	91.5
Source of funds for housing construction				
State assistance	—	—	—	—
Population funds only	556	3,556	10,233	11,009
Nonsocialist sector housing as percentage of total housing	78.8	56.8	65.4	47.7

Source: Anuarul Statistic, various issues, and data provided by Romanian authorities during discussions with the authors.

must be 20 percent of the value of the purchase. This type of loan is only available for purchases from the state. Individuals may buy old properties, but they must purchase any mortgage obligation, and the terms may not be changed. Loans of up to 35,000 lei are available to construct private dwellings. Loans are also available for individuals who wish to purchase the housing that they rent. The terms of these loans are 6 percent, with five to ten years for repayment. State-built dwellings are rarely, if ever, available for purchase in rural areas.

Privately built houses are found mainly in rural areas; 76 percent of those built in 1975 were in rural areas. Building permits are required from the

In 1963 prices							
1965–70	*1970*	*1971*	*1972*	*1973*	*1974*	*1975*	*1971–75*
330,797	79,990	88,388	97,539	105,657	119,665	137,731	548,980
31,423	7,859	7,993	8,380	9,602	11,482	13,362	50,819
9.5	9.8	9.0	8.6	9.1	9.6	9.7	9.3
314,479	74,790	82,617	91,717	99,231	112,457	130,640	516,662
16,642	2,994	2,587	2,963	3,741	4,745	6,680	20,707
5.3	4.0	3.2	3.2	3.8	4.2	5.1	4.0
297,349	71,082	78,507	87,533	95,074	108,597	125,957	495,668
16,603	2,973	2,553	2,937	3,696	4,717	6,626	20,529
5.6	4.2	3.3	3.4	3.9	4.3	5.3	4.1
16,318	5,200	5,771	5,822	6,426	7,208	7,091	32,318
14,784	4,865	5,415	5,417	5,861	6,737	6,682	30,112
90.6	93.6	93.8	93.0	91.2	93.5	94.2	93.2
2,775	1,954	2,542	2,655	3,401	3,297	3,525	15,420
12,009	2,911	2,873	2,762	2,460	3,440	3,157	19,692
47.0	61.9	67.7	64.6	61.0	58.7	50.0	59.3

physical planning department of the People's Councils. Otherwise, this category of housing is unplanned. Credits are available to assist in building houses and in purchasing materials.

Performance

The government's concern to improve the housing situation of the population is evident. Investment in housing increased by 11.3 percent a year in constant prices between 1966 and 1975 (Tables 12.6 and 12.7). The housing stock grew at an average rate of 2.4 percent a year over the same

Table 12.7 *Average Annual Percentage Rates of Growth of Investment in Housing 1951–55 to 1971–75*

	In 1959 prices			In 1963 prices		In co... para... pric...
Investment	*1951–55*	*1956–60*	*1961–65*	*1966–70*	*1971–75*	*1951-*
Investment in national economy						
Total investment	18.2	13.6	11.3	11.2	11.5	13.
Housing investment	19.3	20.6	3.1	8.3	11.2	12.
Investment in socialist sector						
Total investment	18.9	12.8	12.8	10.9	11.8	13.
Housing investment	39.5	15.3	12.5	−0.9	17.4	16.
Investment in socialist sector from state centralized funds						
Total investment	18.7	12.1	12.4	11.3	12.1	13.
Housing investment	39.5	15.3	12.5	−1.0	17.4	16.
Investment outside socialist sector						
Total investment	11.8	22.3	−5.6	17.2	6.4	10.
Housing investment	10.4	24.4	−5.0	17.9	6.5	10.

Source: Anuarul Statistic, various issues.

period, which is higher than the population growth rate (Table 12.8). In terms of allocating investment funds, housing has had a relatively high share, varying from 15.6 percent of all investment in 1956–60 to 9.3 percent in 1971–75. Around 6 percent of the total investment in the socialist sector has been for housing using state-centralized funds.

Over the past decade, the structure of the housing stock has altered significantly in response to specific policy measures, with the share of urban dwellings increasing from 37.3 percent in 1965 to 43.3 percent in 1975, whereas urban population increased from 33.7 to 43.2 percent. By 1975 urban and rural areas both had an average of 3.2 persons for each dwelling.

Table 12.9 also indicates the success of the housing program, despite what had seemed to be a low growth rate. Overall, the average number of persons for each dwelling has been falling steadily. The decline has been

Table 12.8. *Estimate of Housing Stock, 1965–75*
(millions of dwellings)

Year	*Total*	*Urban*	*Rural*
1965	5.3	2.0	3.3
1966	5.4	—	—
1970	5.9	2.4	3.6
1974	6.53	2.79	3.75
1975	6.7	2.9	3.8

Sources: 1966, 1966 Population Census; 1974, *Current Trends and Politics in the Field of Housing Building and Planning* (Bucharest, 1976). Other figures are World Bank estimates using new housing data and current stock.

steadiest in rural areas; whereas heavy migration to the cities, a fall in new housing during 1965–70, and a sudden increase in the birth rate (Chapter 8) caused higher density.

As Tables 12.10 and SA8.7 show, in 1975 new urban housing comprised 81.7 percent of the total; in 1965 it was 45.3 percent. Along with changes in the structure of housing, financing patterns altered. State loans were introduced in urban areas, and these were used to purchase 27.3 percent of the new housing in 1975. State-constructed apartments for rent increased from 27.1 percent in 1965 to 51.6 percent in 1975, whereas self-constructed, self-financed housing fell from 72.9 percent in 1965 to only 21.1 percent in 1975 in both urban and rural areas.

The average size of new houses was also increasing, as shown in Table 12.11. Between 1965 and 1970 the increase applied to both urban and rural areas, except for those houses financed from state-centralized and cooperative funds. Table 12.12 shows that the size of dwelling has also been increasing in terms of the numbers of rooms.

Table 12.9. *Average Number of Persons for Each Dwelling, 1965, 1970, and 1975*

Year	*Total*	*Urban*	*Rural*
1965	3.66	3.27	3.88
1970	3.44	3.51	3.38
1975	3.17	3.17	3.17

Source: World Bank estimates.

Table 12.10. *Housing Turned over to Occupancy, by Source of Finance, 1965, 1970, and 1975*
(percentage of total number of actual housing units)

Source of finance	*1965*	*1970*	*1975*
Total from state funds	27.1	42.7	51.6
Urban	25.9	41.9	49.3
Rural	1.1	0.8	2.3
Total with state aid	—	17.8	27.3
Urban	—	17.8	27.3
Rural	—	—	—
Total from own funds	72.9	39.5	21.1
Urban	14.4	10.3	5.1
Rural	58.5	29.2	16.0

Other attempts have been made to tailor new housing to the demands of the population, for example, providing housing for single persons. Between 1970 and 1975, over 240,000 new units were completed, adding a stock of about 60,000 units available for single people in 1970 (Table 12.13).

Since 1965, the share of dwellings with three or more rooms has increased, whereas that of one-room dwellings has fallen substantially (Table 12.12). Thus the average cost of a housing unit has risen; between 1965 and 1975 this increase in costs is estimated to be about 70 percent. At the same time, improvements in the finishing of the dwellings and the provision of additional comfort have increased the cost of each square meter by 59 perecnt during 1965–75 (Table 12.14).

Achievements, 1971–75, and planned targets, 1976–80

Between 1971 and 1975, 751,896 new dwellings were occupied, an increase of 16.1 percent over the 1966–70 plan period. In terms of units completed, output did not grow consistently, and in no year exceeded the 1965 level (Table 12.12). In terms of living space, however, a continuing improvement took place. Of the 522,000 new dwellings planned (Table 12.15), a target of 98 percent were built, mainly because of underfulfillment of dwellings purchased with state assistance. Unplanned housing achieved 76 percent of its 1966–70 level.

In terms of annual plans, dwellings financed by state-centralized and cooperative funds fulfilled their targets in three out of the five years, and in no year was achievement less than 98 percent. Those purchased with state loans did not meet their targets in any year and in 1974 achieved only 73.5 percent of the planned level. Dwellings for single persons were introduced

Table 12.11. *Average Size of Dwellings Turned over for Occupancy, Urban and Rural, by Sources of Funding, 1965, 1970, and 1975*

(square meters)

Area and year	Total			From state, centralized, and cooperative funds			With state assistance			With own funds		
	Total area	Living space	Ratio	Total area	Living space	Ratio	Total area	Living space	Ratio	Total area	Living space	Ratio
All areas												
1965	—	25.9	—	—	31.1	—	—	—	—	—	23.9	—
1970	58.3	31.3	1.86	44.4	24.4	1.82	69.6	32.5	2.14	68.2	38.3	1.78
1975	69.1	33.7	2.05	62.0	29.1	2.13	72.4	34.4	2.10	82.1	43.9	1.87
Urban												
1965	—	28.8	—	—	31.2	—	—	—	—	—	24.4	—
1970	55.1	28.5	1.93	44.3	24.3	1.82	69.6	32.5	2.14	74.1	38.9	1.90
1975	67.6	31.9	2.12	61.9	28.9	2.14	72.4	34.4	2.10	95.7	47.5	2.01
Rural												
1965	—	23.9	—	—	28.6	—	—	—	—	—	23.8	—
1970	65.7	37.7	1.74	48.6	26.9	1.81	—	—	—	66.1	38.0	1.74
1975	75.9	41.4	1.83	63.0	32.0	1.97	—	—	—	77.8	42.8	1.82

— Not available.

Source: Anuarul Statistic, various issues.

Table 12.12. *Housing Put into Occupancy, by Number of Rooms and Sources of Funds, 1965–75*

(number of dwellings)

Item	*1965*	*1970*	*1971*	*1972*	*1973*	*1974*	*1975*
Total	*191,988*	*159,152*	*147,023*	*135,969*	*149,128*	*154,345*	*165,431*
	(100.0)	*(100.0)*	*(100.0)*	*(100.0)*	*(100.0)*	*(100.0)*	*(100.0)*
One room	57,116	26,548	16,972	14,654	16,770	10,605	14,952
	(29.8)	(16.7)	(11.5)	(10.8)	(11.2)	(6.9)	(9.0)
Two rooms	85,080	83,935	78,510	69,897	79,931	78,552	83,148
	(44.3)	(52.7)	(53.4)	(51.4)	(53.6)	(50.9)	(50.3)
Three rooms and over	49,792	48,669	51,541	51,418	52,427	65,188	67,331
	(25.9)	(30.6)	(35.1)	(37.8)	(35.2)	(42.2)	(40.7)
			From State Centralized and Cooperative Funds				
Total	*51,973*	*68,016*	*52,416*	*48,541*	*57,649*	*65,227*	*85,352*
	(100.0)	*(100.0)*	*(100.0)*	*(100.0)*	*(100.0)*	*(100.0)*	*(100.0)*
One room	6,334	14,849	6,759	4,985	6,556	6,367	8,974
	(12.2)	(21.8)	(12.9)	(10.3)	(11.4)	(9.8)	(10.5)
Two rooms	30,973	39,065	33,028	30,895	37,710	42,795	51,141
	(59.6)	(57.4)	(63.0)	(63.6)	(65.4)	(65.6)	(59.9)
Three rooms and over	14,666	14,102	12,629	12,660	13,383	16,065	25,237
	(28.2)	(20.8)	(24.1)	(26.1)	(23.2)	(24.6)	(29.6)

	From Funds of the Population with State Help						
Total	—	*28,279*	*36,010*	*37,326*	*42,924*	*41,909*	*45,153*
	(—)	(*100.0*)	(*100.0*)	(*100.0*)	(*100.0*)	(*100.0*)	(*100.0*)
One room	—	1,642	1,056	977	2,562	1,400	1,625
	(—)	(5.8)	(2.9)	(2.6)	(6.0)	(3.3)	(3.6)
Two rooms	—	16,459	20,760	18,787	23,247	17,956	19,886
	(—)	(58.2)	(57.7)	(50.3)	(54.1)	(42.9)	(44.0)
Three rooms and over	—	10,178	14,194	17,562	17,115	22,553	23,642
	(—)	(36.0)	(39.4)	(47.1)	(39.9)	(53.8)	(52.4)
	From the Population's Funds						
Total	*140,015*	*62,857*	*58,597*	*50,102*	*48,555*	*47,209*	*34,926*
	(*100.0*)	(*100.0*)	(*100.0*)	(*100.0*)	(*100.0*)	(*100.0*)	(*100.0*)
One room	50,782	10,057	9,157	8,691	7,652	2,838	4,353
	(36.3)	(16.0)	(15.6)	(17.3)	(15.8)	(6.0)	(12.5)
Two rooms	54,107	28,411	24,722	20,215	18,974	17,801	12,121
	(38.6)	(45.2)	(42.2)	(40.4)	(39.0)	(37.7)	(34.7)
Three rooms and over	35,126	24,389	24,718	21,196	21,929	26,570	18,452
	(25.1)	(38.8)	(42.2)	(42.3)	(45.2)	(56.3)	(52.8)

Note: Percentage figures are given in parentheses.
Source: Anuarul Statistic, various issues.

Table 12.13. *Units for Single People Financed from State Centralized and Cooperative Funds and Put into Occupancy, 1970–75*

Item	*1970*	*1971*	*1972*	*1973*	*1974*	*19*
Number	21,907	21,306	26,717	34,793	56,384	80,
Total area (thousands of square meters)	203	184	273	335	527	[illegible]
Inhabitable area (thousands of square meters)	108	96	138	173	277	[illegible]
Equivalent number of conventional apartments of 30 square meters inhabitable area	3,593	3,184	4,584	5,768	9,214	12,

Source: Anuarul Statistic, various issues.

into thc plan in 1974 and, in that year, overfulfilled it by 13.4 percent. The 1975 target was set at double that of the previous year, but only a 42.4 percent increase was made.

The initial targets for 1976–80 (Table 12.16) represented a 9.6 percent annual increase in dwellings financed from state-centralized and cooperative funds over 1971–75, which would not seem to be too taxing a target. Those financed with state assistance are planned to increase by 134 percent, which is 18.5 percent a year. The target increase in state-constructed dwellings is 59 percent, or 9.7 percent a year, and, in light of previous experience, would seem attainable. In 1977, however, the authorities decided to increase the plan target by 190,000 dwellings, of which 30,000 would be constructed to replace dwellings damaged by earthquake. This is a substantial increase, but it can probably be realized given the priority the government attaches to housing. Enough private individuals are expected to take out loans to purchase the new apartments to meet this goal. If this does not happen, though, the new dwellings will be rented out by the state.

Hostel accommodations for single persons are planned to increase by 24 percent over 1971–75. The revised plan target in 1976–80 is 272,500. Self-constructed housing is planned to increase to 250,000–300,000 from a 1971–75 level of 239,389. This requires a reversal in the downward trend (Table 12.12).

A housing program of 3 to 3.5 million new dwellings is envisaged for 1976–90 to meet projected requirements and to eliminate the housing shortage. This is certain to happen, since by 1980 the number of dwellings will equal the number of families. If the initial targets of the 1976–80 Plan are fulfilled, the housing stock should reach 7.7 to 7.8 million dwellings;

Table 12.14. *Costs and Sources of Funds for Housing Brought into Use, 1965 and 1970–75*

Item	*1965*	*1970*	*1971*	*1972*	*1973*	*1974*	*1975*
Fixed assets brought into use for the construction of housing (millions of lei)	5,205	7,573	7,756	8,080	8,960	11,193	12,965
From state funds and with state assistance	3,066	4,662	4,883	5,318	6,500	7,753	9,808
Built from the population's funds	2,139	2,911	2,873	2,762	2,460	3,440	3,157
Total constructed area (thousands of square meters)							
From state funds and with state assistance	3,528	5,189	5,229	5,686	6,570	7,401	9,256
Built from the population's funds	4,071	4,287	4,065	3,608	3,516	3,569	2,869
Cost per square meter of total constructed area (lei)							
From state funds and with state assistance	869	898	934	935	989	1,048	1,060
Built from the population's funds	525	679	707	766	700	964	1,100
Living space (thousands of square meters)							
From state funds and with state assistance	1,583	2,685	2,603	2,711	3,087	3,497	4,404
Built from the population's funds	2,210	2,405	2,230	1,963	1,921	1,942	1,534
Cost per square meter of living space (lei)							
From state funds and with state assistance	1,937	1,736	1,876	1,962	2,106	2,217	2,227
Built from the population's funds	968	1,210	1,288	1,407	1,281	1,771	2,058
Number of houses brought into use							
From state funds and with state assistance	50,959	99,888	91,610	90,451	106,341	116,350	142,832
Built from the population's funds	70,056	62,857	58,597	50,102	48,555	47,209	34,926
Cost per house (lei)							
From state funds and with state assistance	60,166	46,672	53,302	58,794	61,124	66,635	68,668
Built from the population's funds	30,533	46,311	49,030	55,128	50,664	72,867	90,391

Source: Anuarul Statistic, various issues.

Table 12.15. *Plan Targets and Achievements in Housing, 1971–75*
(number of dwellings)

Source of finance	1971–75		1971		1972	
	Planned	*Actual*	*Planned*	*Actual*	*Planned*	*Actu*
Total planned	*522,000*	*512,507*	*93,000*	*88,426*	*93,600*	*85,6*
From state centralized and cooperative funds	272,000	309,185	50,000	52,416	49,500	48,5
From funds of population with state assistance	250,000	203,322	43,000	36,010	44,100	37,3
Dwellings for single persons	Unplanned	219,504	—	21,306	—	26,7
Self-financed	Unplanned	239,389	—	58,597	—	50,1

Sources: *Anuarul Statistic*, various issues; Annual Plans for 1971–75; and Law (no. 10) of 19 on the Adoption of the Five-Year Plan for 1971–75 for the Economic and Social Development of Socialist Republic of Romania, *Official Bulletin of the Socialist Republic of Romania*, year 6, 129 (October 21, 1971).

if the number of families increases by 1 percent, it will reach 7.2 million by 1980; with a 2 percent increase, it will be 7.5 million. Thus, there should be at least 1 dwelling for each family. This does not necessarily mean that the shortage will be eliminated, since the urbanization and regional policy may create a geographic imbalance. Also some allowance has to be made for the deterioration of old houses.

Source of finance	1973		1974		1975	
	Planned	Actual	Planned	Actual	Planned	Actual
al planned	*110,000*	*100,573*	*117,300*	*107,136*	*133,280*	*130,505*
m state centralized nd cooperative funds	61,000	57,649	60,300	65,227	85,150	85,352
m funds of popula- ion with state ssistance	50,000	42,924	57,000	41,909	48,130	45,153
ellings for single ersons	—	34,793	49,700	56,384	110,800	80,304
-financed	—	48,555	—	47,209	—	34,926

Table 12.16. *Plan Targets, 1976–80*

From state centralized and cooperative funds	339,000
With state assistance	476,000
Total	815,000
Self-financed	250–300,000
Dwellings for single persons	200,000

Source: Law (no. 4) on the Adoption of the Unified National Plan of Economic and Social Development of the Socialist Republic of Romania for 1976–80, *Official Bulletin of the Socialist Republic of Romania*, no. 65 (July 7, 1976).

13

The Transport Sector

BROADLY SPEAKING, Romania has a fairly well-developed and evenly distributed transport network, which provides access to all major centers of economic activity.

Government Strategy and Policy

Government strategy for the transport sector during the past twenty years has focused more on modernization of the main elements of this system (especially the railroads) than on extension, contrary to the experience in most other developing countries. In 1950, for example, the railway system was 10,853 kilometers long. This was equivalent to a high density of 45.7 kilometers per 1,000 square kilometers. By 1975 the system had increased by less than 200 kilometers, to 11,039 kilometers—a density of 46.5 kilometers per 1,000 square kilometers. The road system amounted to about 76,000 kilometers in 1950, most unpaved. By 1975 it had increased by some 2,000 kilometers.[1] This marginal increase in the length of the road system is in marked contrast with developments over the same period in high-income

1. The public road network is classified by administrative function as shown below:

Class of road	*1971*	*1975*	*"Modernized" 1975*[a]
National	12,896	12,918	10,193
District	26,123	26,334	2,924 (District and Village)
Village	36,698	38,697	
Total	75,717	77,949	13,117

a. Modernization basically consists of asphalting roads according to certain specifications, which are described in the text.

developing countries. The railways and highways of Romania are shown on the maps on pages 306 and 307.

With a good existing national railway system, the government has preferred to invest in upgrading the system. The alternative to this was rapid modernization of the road system in the postwar decades and financing roads are still gravel or earth surfaced and cannot be considered to be all-authorities felt it would have consumed scarce resources (including foreign exchange) that were better used in more directly productive sectors. The increasing sophistication of the economy, however, has created pressures to modernize the road system. As a result, a highway modernization program was begun in 1956 to upgrade 13,000 kilometers of the national road network. By 1975, 20 percent of the national roads still remained to be modernized: that is, paved with asphalt. A second highway modernization program for 27,000 kilometers of the district roads was initiated in 1968; by 1976, 20 percent had been completed. Although progress in the road modernization programs has been steady, about two-thirds of the country's roads are still gravel or earth surfaced and cannot be considered to be all-weather.

The relatively low emphasis on road development can be best understood within a broader view of Romanian transport strategy. The national transport system is viewed as an integrated system in which each transport mode complements and does not compete with the others. The declared objective in 1950–70 had been to integrate the different modes so that, together, they meet the transport service requirements of the economy at minimum resource cost, particularly of energy consumption. To use the existing railway system as much as possible and to reduce energy consumption, trucking was generally restricted to small distances. This practice actually also reflects the limited infrastructure (vehicles and modernized roads) available at that time. A more planned distribution of transport service was initiated in 1971, when, based on past experience, it was decided that in principle all transport of goods under 50 kilometers would be by road and the remainder by rail and water. This policy was based on the premise that fuel consumption for each ton-kilometer of road freight transport was higher than that of rail and water and also that rail transport was cheaper and more efficient. This focus on the railway as the mainstay of the transport system was a common feature of the policy of all the eastern European socialist countries other than Yugoslavia. Since 1975, the distribution of goods traffic between railways and roads has not been so restricted, but is determined more systematically by studying, for each case, the distance the goods must travel when using alternative modes, all costs of loading and unloading, the tariff cost, and fuel savings.

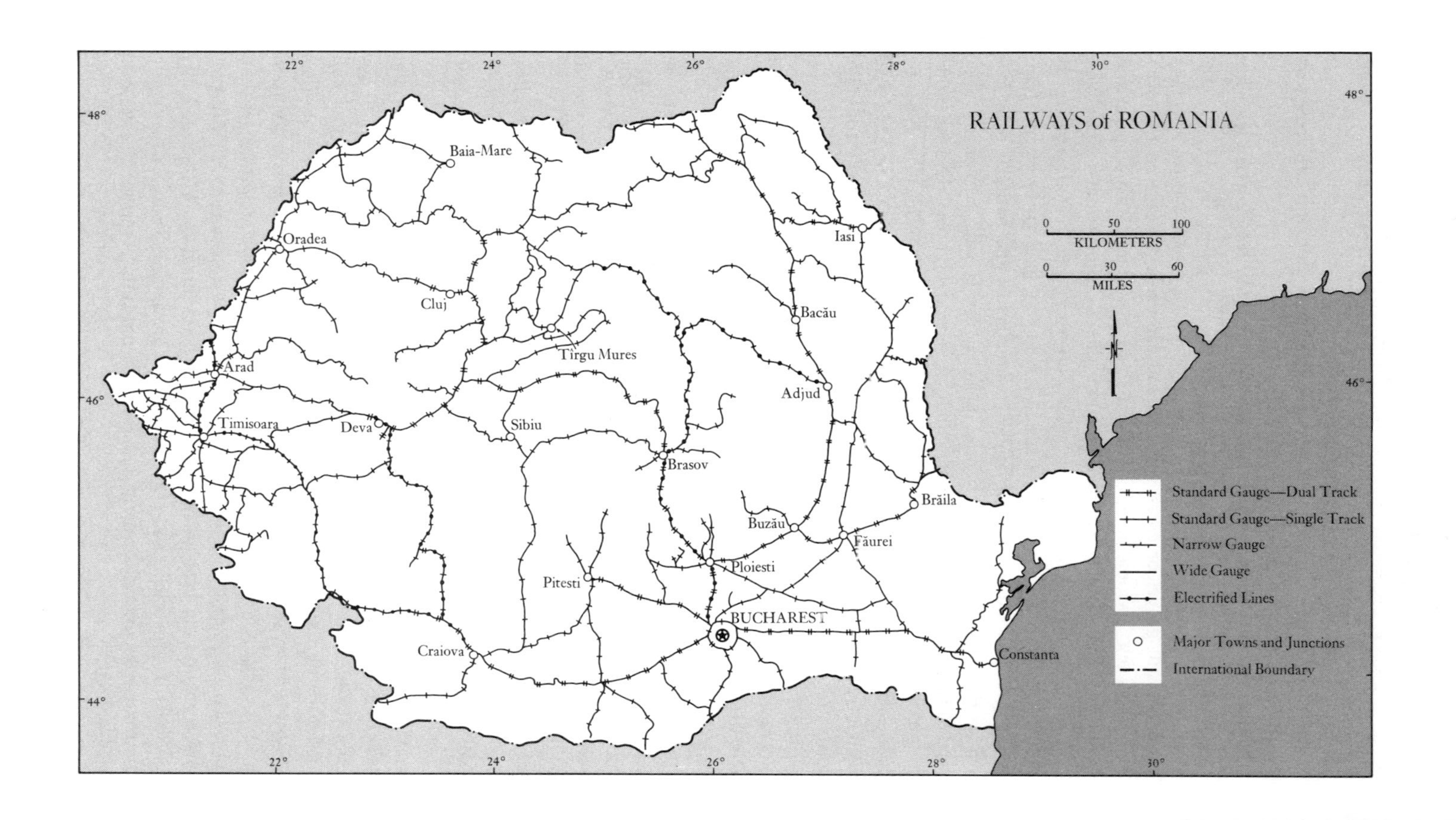
RAILWAYS of ROMANIA
0
50
100
KILOMETERS
0
30
60
MILES
N
Standard Gauge—Dual Track
Standard Gauge—Single Track
Narrow Gauge
Wide Gauge
Electrified Lines
Major Towns and Junctions
International Boundary
Baia-Mare
Oradea
Cluj
Iasi
Bacău
Tîrgu Mures
Arad
Adjud
Timisoara
Deva
Sibiu
Brasov
Brăila
Buzău
Făurei
Ploiesti
Pitesti
BUCHAREST
Craiova
Constanta
22°
24°
26°
28°
30°
48°
46°
44°

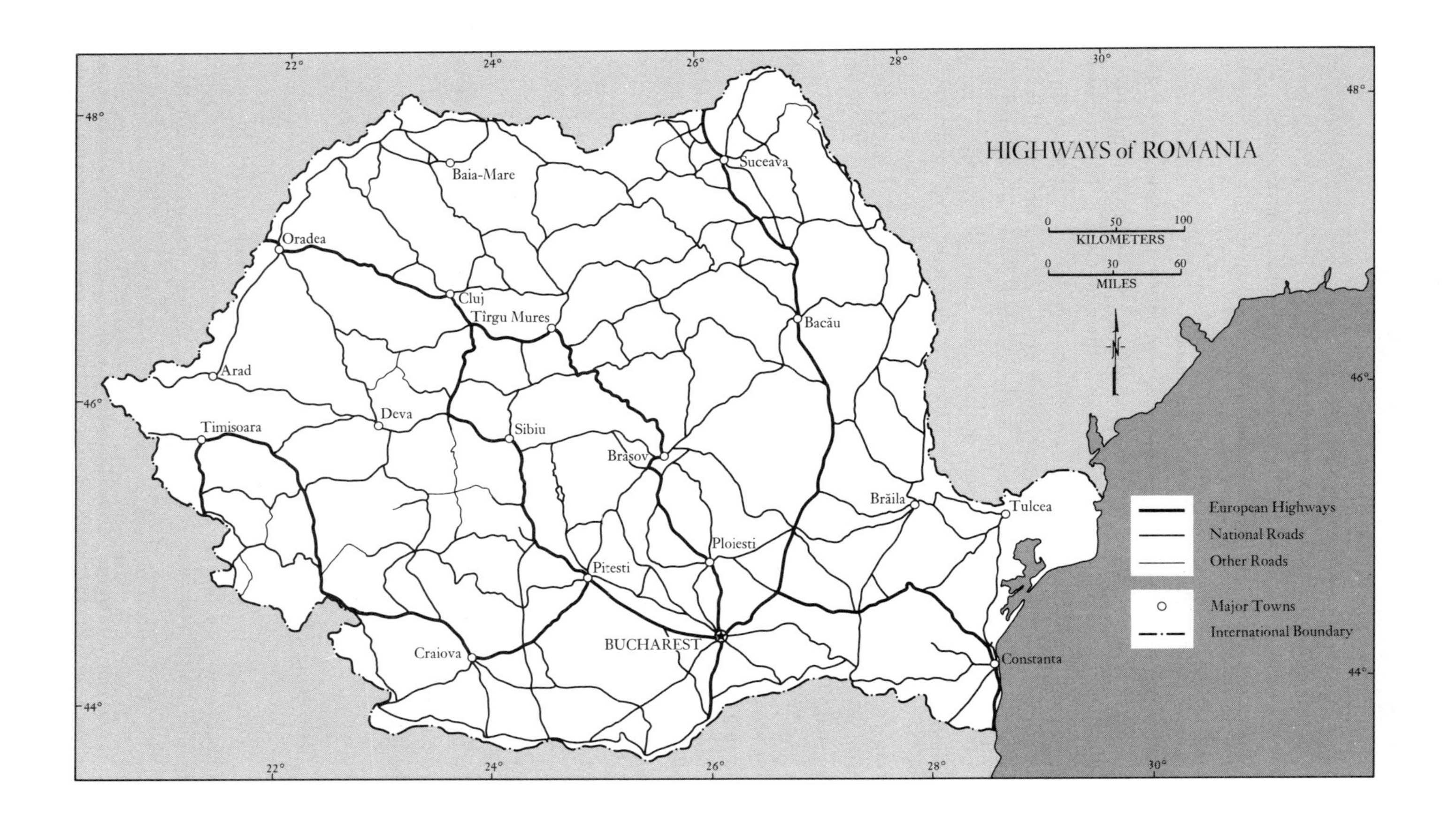
HIGHWAYS of ROMANIA
0
50
100
KILOMETERS
0
30
60
MILES
European Highways
National Roads
Other Roads
Major Towns
International Boundary
Baia-Mare
Suceava
Oradea
Cluj
Tîrgu Mures
Bacău
Arad
Deva
Timisoara
Sibiu
Brasov
Brăila
Tulcea
Ploiesti
Pitesti
BUCHAREST
Craiova
Constanta
22°
24°
26°
28°
30°
48°
46°
44°

The dominance of average cost considerations in transporting goods inevitably leads to a continuing emphasis on railway development. The distance limitation on trucking was based primarily on the desire to use an existing railway system.[2] It is questionable whether rail transport is generally more efficient than trucks for distances under 200 kilometers for loads other than bulk and generally for mineral or similar loads. The quality of door-to-door service (resulting also in less damage and pilferage), much greater speed, and frequency of deliveries (which lead to lower stocks and working capital requirement) are all factors, which, when appropriately considered, might involve lower total distribution cost. Finally, competition is possible only if each mode has some spare capacity, and this is an advantage when transport demands fluctuate, for example, during bumper crops, emergencies, and so forth. The criteria used to determine investment priorities in the sector appear to have met Romania's internal transport requirements, but the country's expanding trade and tourist links with western countries require that these investment priorities be reconsidered. The government is now doing this. For example, effective export competition requires service quality that in some cases may be possible only by using trucks. Bottlenecks in tourist traffic also already are developing during the high season, particularly in the Black Sea area.

In pursuing the policy objectives to conserve energy and to reduce pollution, the government recently has sought to use the inland waterway network more intensively. The Danube River, for example, flows for 1,075 kilometers through or along the borders of Romania, yet river transport plays a very small role in the country's transport system: some 0.9 percent in tonnage and less than 3 percent in ton-kilometers. It is confined mainly to bulk transport to and from industrial complexes along the Danube. Improvement of other rivers would require large investments in dams and locks to make them navigable. In the absence of other objectives, such as irrigation or flood protection, such investments are usually only justified for large traffic volumes.

The Role of the Sector in the Economy

During 1951–75 the transport of goods by all modes increased at an average annual rate that was considerably higher than that of the social product, but the growth of passenger traffic lagged. Annual growth rates

2. The only high-income nonsocialist country with a similar distance limitation on trucking is New Zealand, where the policy is admittedly to limit competition with the railway.

Table 13.1. *Average Annual Growth Rates of Social Product and Transport Sector, 1951–55 to 1971–75*

(percentage)

Item	*1951–55*	*1956–60*	*1961–65*	*1966–70*	*1971–75*
Social product	13.2	7.2	9.5	8.7	10.5
Total goods transport					
Tonnes	12.8	15.1	12.6	10.9	9.4
Tonnes per kilometer	12.9	7.2	13.3	16.3	9.1
Total passengers					
Number	16.2	1.1	8.6	9.7	11.4
Passengers per kilometer	8.6	−1.3	7.4	8.8	10.1

a. Includes only public transport and excludes the transport by enterprises and Peoples' Councils, which represents about 60 percent of total automobile transport.

Source: Anuarul Statistic al Republicii Socialiste Romania (Bucharest: Directia Centrala de Statistica, published yearly).

in the transport sector have varied over each five-year plan period, but, as illustrated in Table 13.1, they mostly outpaced the increase in social product. The share of the transport sector in the value of social product has remained at around 3.8 percent.[3] The sector's increasing contribution, though, to national income—from 3.9 percent in 1950 to 5.2 percent in 1975—indicates a substantial reduction in material expenditures and implies rising productivity.

As indicated, the modernization effort has concentrated almost exclusively on railways, with relatively little emphasis on road transport. Investments in railways have financed a continuous effort to reduce energy use through electrification and to increase the capacity of each line by improved signalling, the double-tracking of some lines, and the expansion and modernization of the locomotive and rolling stock fleet. For example, the share of goods traffic moved by diesel and electric locomotives increased from 1 percent in 1960 to 96.0 percent in 1976. The investments have been spread selectively throughout the system to develop the local handling capacity required by increasing volumes of economic activities and to avoid creating serious bottlenecks on specific routes.

3. Published national income statistics do not provide separate data for the transport and telecommunications sectors. The share of the telecommunications subsector, however, has been small (approximately 10 percent), and variations in it would not affect the main trends in the transport sector or change substantially the relative magnitudes. The shares given are an estimate for the transport sector only. Also, pre-1970 national income statistics excluded passenger transport.

Investments in the road system have consisted primarily of modernizing the national road system and, only secondarily, the district road system, as illustrated in Table 13.2. The increase of about 2,000 kilometers of local roads between 1971 and 1975 is mainly the result of opening roads that were initially constructed by industrial and mine enterprises to public traffic, rather than of construction of new roads for public use.

Overall, investments in the transport sector have remained at about the same share of total and socialist sector investment: approximately 9 to 9.5 percent and 10.5 percent, respectively, except for the Second and Third Five-Year Plans (1955–60 and 1961–65), during which they were significantly lower. The resource allocation to the transport sector appears low by international comparison, even more so, since it includes investments for ocean shipping vessels, buses, and trucks, which in most other countries are considered private rather than public investment. More detailed information on the sector investment over each of the five-year plan periods and for 1971–75 is given in Table 13.3. All sector investments are undertaken by the socialist sector from state central funds.

The investment program has led to a large increase in fixed assets. Despite a quadrupling of fixed assets during 1950–75, however, fixed asset formation in the transport sector lagged behind that of the economy at large, particularly in the 1960s. Despite a greater emphasis during the Sixth Five-Year Plan, the sector's share of total fixed assets in the economy has shown a small decline (Table 13.4).

The growth of the sector has been accompanied by substantial increases in the number of people employed: from 136,000 in 1950 to over 400,000 in 1975. The share of the sector in the national labor force has been remarkably steady (Table 13.5).

Table 13.2. *Modernization of the Road System, 1956–75*
(kilometers)

Kind of road	*1956*	*1960*	*1965*	*1970*	*1975*
Total roads	*76,142*	*76,154*	*75,898*	*75,879*	*77,949*
Modernized	3,625	5,883	8,508	11,091	13,117
National roads	9,682	10,573	11,514	12,167	12,918
Modernized	3,246	5,147	6,788	8,688	10,193
District and communal roads	66,460	65,581	64,384	63,712	65,031
Modernized	379	736	1,720	2,403	2,924

Source: Anuarul Statistic, various issues.

Table 13.3. *Investment in the Transport Sector*
(billions of lei)

Item	*Five-year plan investment*					*Annual investment, 1971–75, 1963 lei*				
	1959 lei			*1963 lei*						
	1951–55	*1956–60*	*1961–65*	*1966–70*	*1971–75*	*1971*	*1972*	*1973*	*1974*	*1975*
1. Total investment in the economy	61,916	100,180	199,692	330,797	548,980	88,388	97,539	105,657	119,665	137,731
2. Total Socialist sector investment	57,713	88,152	187,656	314,479	516,662	82,617	91,717	99,231	112,457	130,640
3. Total transport sector investment	5,797	7,511	16,239	31,627	49,888	8,247	8,902	9,023	10,290	13,426
4. Line 3 ÷ line 1	9.4	7.5	8.1	9.6	9.1	9.3	9.1	8.5	8.6	9.7
5. Line 3 ÷ line 2	10.0	8.5	8.7	10.1	9.7	10.0	9.7	9.1	9.2	10.3

Source: Anuarul Statistic, various issues.

Table 13.4. *Formation of Fixed Assets in the Transport Sector, 1950–75*
(1950 = 100)

Item	*1950*	*1955*	*1960*	*1965*	*1970*	*1971*	*1972*	*1973*	*1974*	*197*
Fixed assets in entire economy	100	125	161	223	337	368	398	433	478	534
Fixed assets in transport	100	118	131	177	264	287	309	333	368	414
Transport share of total (percent)	13.7	13.0	11.1	10.9	11.7	12.2	12.0	12.0	12.0	12.1

Source: Anuarul Statistic, various issues.

The constancy of the ratios of transport employment to total employment hides a dramatic employment reallocation from railroads to road transport. Disaggregated data show that the railroad's share of 76 percent of total transport employees in 1950 had declined to 44 percent by 1975, whereas that of road transport increased from 4 to 46 percent in the same period.

The Transport System

The mainstay of the transport system is the 11,039-kilometer railway network, which carried 90 percent of all tonne-kilometers in 1950 and still carried 82 percent in 1975.[4] In spite of the geophysical configuration of the country, no point is very far from one of the 1,441 railway stations. Present railway operations reflect a long tradition and thorough staff experience. The weakest link in the country's transport system is the 100-year-old, 1,800-meter-long single-line railway bridge across the Danube near Cernavoda. Nearly all the general and dry bulk cargo handled in the port of Constanta (averaging over 50,000 tonnes a day) passes over this bridge. Any interruption in service over this bridge would seriously impede transport flow to the ports, since there is no other rail connection to Constanta. Because of policies that have restricted road transport, it would not be possible to handle any large additional volume of freight diverted from rail. A new railway bridge across the Danube is the highest priority in Romania's

4. For a qualification on the relative shares of the transport modes see the footnote to Table 13.6.

able 13.5. *Employment in the Transport Sector, 1950–75*
ousands)

Item	*1950*	*1955*	*1960*	*1965*	*1970*	*1975*
otal employment						
1. Total economy	2,123.0	2,948.4	3,249.2	4,305.3	5,108.7	6,300.8
2. Transport sector	135.5	198.7	209.3	288.1	340.7	402.2
3. Line 2 ÷ line 1	6.4	6.7	6.4	6.7	6.7	6.4
orkers						
4. Total economy	1,222.9	1,967.9	2,284.1	3,109.9	3,838.9	4,993.8
5. Transport sector	94.7	148.4	166.9	241.2	299.4	367.7
6. Line 5 ÷ line 4	7.7	7.5	7.3	7.8	7.8	7.4

Source: Anuarul Statistic, various issues.

railway transport system and is included in the current five-year plan, as discussed below.

Romania's road system is over 78,000 kilometers long, but because road transport only started to attain some importance in the early 1960s, it carried less than 12 percent of total ton-kilometers moved by all modes of transport in 1975. There is only one 100-kilometer expressway (between Bucharest and Pitesti) and 264 kilometers of four-lane highways. Most of the local or district roads are not built to provide all-weather service, and old wooden bridges restrict the weight of trucks on many of these roads. This results in high-cost hauling by tractor-drawn carts, which operate on national and district roads where they create serious traffic hazards to faster moving traffic.

The other transport modes contribute only marginally to the total output of the sector. The share of transport of petroleum and gas by pipeline, for example, is small and has been almost constant over the years (2.2 percent of tonnage, 3.6 percent of ton-kilometers in 1975). Information on the role of the aviation subsector, until recently a military operation, is not available, but it is still negligible. Domestic maritime transport is limited to small volumes of transshipments from the Constanta port to the ports near the Danube Delta. And, as already discussed, river transport carries limited cargo and negligible passenger traffic. The share of the various modes of transport of goods and passengers during 1950–75 is shown in Tables 13.6, SA9.1, and SA9.2. The subsector's growth rates are given in Table SA9.3.

Although an important amount of Romanian exports and imports crosses its frontiers by land, the bulk of trade is handled through its ports on the Black Sea. The country's major port, Constanta, located about 225 kilometers

Table 13.6. *Structure of Transport of Goods and Passengers, by Mode, 1950–75*

Mode	*1950*	*1960*	*1970*	*1975*
	Goods transport			
Millions of tonnes rail	35.1	77.5	171.3	228.3
Percent	91.8	54.7	40.2	34.2
Billions of tonne-kilometers	7.6	19.8	48.0	64.8
Percent	89.4	87.6	85.2	82.0
Millions of tonnes road	1.0	56.6	239.8	418.8
Percent	2.7	40.0	56.4	62.7
Billions of tonne-kilometers	0.04	0.94	5.2	9.3
Percent	0.5	4.1	9.1	11.8
Millions of tonnes river	1.1	1.9	3.4	6.1
Percent	2.9	1.4	0.8	0.9
Billions of tonne-kilometers	0.67	0.87	1.35	2.08
Percent	7.9	3.8	2.4	2.6
Millions of tonnes pipelines	1.0	5.6	11.3	14.5
Percent	2.6	3.9	2.6	2.2
Billions of tonne-kilometers	0.19	1.02	1.84	2.85
Percent	2.2	4.5	3.3	3.6
	Passenger transport			
Millions of passengers rail	116.6	214.8	328.3	366.9
Percent	90.8	74.6	47.6	31.0
Billions of passenger-kilometers	8.16	10.74	17.79	22.38
Percent	95.1	88.0	69.2	54.1
Millions of passengers road	11.3	71.8	359.4	814.2
Percent	8.8	25.0	52.0	68.8
Billions of passenger-kilometers	0.39	1.42	7.86	18.92
Percent	4.5	11.7	30.5	45.7
Millions of passengers river	0.56	1.16	1.91	2.31
Percent	0.4	0.4	0.3	0.2
Billions of passenger kilometers	0.02	0.04	0.08	0.11
Percent	0.2	0.3	0.3	0.3

Note: Published statistics include maritime transport, which distorts completely the shares of the various transport modes. Because of the long distances (over 10,000 kilometers) of maritime transport, its share is published as 45 percent or even more than that of the railways. Moreover, the maritime statistics refer only to the oceangoing fleet under Romanian flag, making the statistics as published even more meaningless. The same is true for aviation statistics, but the distortion in this case is negligible because of low volumes.

Source: Anuarul Statistic, various issues.

east of Bucharest, handles about 90 percent of the country's seagoing trade and can accommodate tankers of 80,000 dead weight tons[5] and bulk carriers of 55,060 dead weight tons. The port's capacity is being expanded to handle oil tankers of 150,000 dead weight tons and bulk carriers of 100,000 dead weight tons. Dry cargo, other than bulk cargo, is still handled conventionally at Constanta; only 10 percent of the general goods cargo is unitized by palletization, preslinging, or containerization. The small volume of container traffic that is handled at the two container berths has to be loaded and unloaded in the port, since only about twenty railway stations have the facilities to handle containers. Nor is the trucking fleet geared to maximizing the economy of door-to-door container traffic. The commercial river ports of Galati and Braila, which are 150 kilometers and 170 kilometers, respectively, from the mouth of the Danube, handle the remaining 10 percent. These two ports can accommodate seagoing vessels of only about 12,000 dead weight tons because of the great alluvial deposits at the Danube mouth which limit the access of the vessels with a draught above 7 meters. Work is underway to allow vessels of more than 25,000 dead weight tons to enter the Danube. Tulcea, located 73 kilometers from the mouth of the Danube, is a small port where both sea and river vessels can be handled, and it is meeting the needs of local enterprises, as well as of the sea fishing fleet. Finally, there are some twenty-five river ports located along the 1,075 kilometers of the Danube that flows within Romanian territory. All seaports and half of the river ports have both rail and road connections. Nearly all land transport to and from the port is by rail, except for crude oil.

Table 13.6 illustrates four points:

(a) Contrary to the situation in nearly all other countries, the railways over the years have held their dominant position in terms of ton-kilometers of traffic, even though annual growth since 1965 has been only half that of road transport;[6]

(b) Even by the early 1960s, road transport surpassed rail transport in terms of tonnage moved, as a result of a road modernization program that started in 1956; in terms of ton-kilometers, however, its share remains very modest because of the limits on haulage distances;

(c) Recent annual growth of passenger road transport is five times that

5. Dead weight tonnage is the weight in long tons that a vessel can carry when fully laden.

6. There was a relatively strong reduction in the dominance of railways in 1975 over 1974. There are two plausible explanations: it may have resulted from interruptions from the 1975 floods or it was easier and quicker to restore temporarily road connections than rail connections.

of railways in numbers of passengers carried and four times in passenger-kilometer output;

(d) The relative role of both river and pipeline transport has remained constant and nearly negligible over the years.

Transport of goods by commodity groups

During 1951–75 the tonnage of commodity groups transported by the two main transport modes changed substantially. The share of agricultural, wood, and related products carried by rail has been halved to 16 percent and reduced to about one-third (10 percent) in general road transport (during the shorter period 1956–73 for which such statistics are available for this mode and excluding the transport within enterprises). The most striking development in the increase of tonnage hauled by road is the volume of quarry and ballast products, which, in 1972, accounted for 62 percent of total road tonnages, up from 40 percent in 1956 (Table 13.7). The unusually

Table 13.7. *Transport of Goods by Commodity Group, Railways and Road, 1972*

	Tons		*Ton-kilometers*	
	Railways	*Road*	*Railways*	*Road*
Total (thousands)	*193,740*	*276,173*	*53,280*	*5,738*
	Percentage of total			
Petroleum and petroleum products	8.8	1.0	8.9	1.7
Coal	10.7	0.2	6.4	0.1
Coke	1.6	—	1.3	—
Ferrous and nonferrous metal product, machinery, and equipment	7.8	1.7	9.8	8.6
Wood products	7.3	0.8	7.2	2.0
Firewood	1.5	0.9	1.2	1.5
Quarry and ballast products	23.1	62.7	13.9	30.2
Building materials	9.7	7.4	7.8	6.8
Cereals	3.1	3.4	2.9	5.8
Sugar beets	1.4	0.6	0.8	1.0
Products of light and chemical industry	5.4	1.4	6.9	6.8
Foodstuffs	3.9	4.4	4.3	10.7
Other	15.7	15.5	28.6	24.8

Source: Anuarul Statistic, various issues.

high volume of quarry and ballast products carried by road may be explained if the transport of contractors' materials is included in the reported transport of volume of goods. These products also account for the largest share of railway tonnage, but have not varied much from the 1975 share of 20.5 percent. A detailed breakdown of the transport of goods by commodity groups is given in Tables SA9.4 and SA9.5. The ton-kilometer figure shows that road transport, as in many countries, is important for moving higher-value goods, for example, chemical products, processed foodstuffs, machine goods, and so forth.

Operation of the Transport System

Responsibility for all transport modes other than aviation and pipelines is vested in the Ministry of Transport and Communications. Aviation has a separate department subordinated to the Council of Ministers, and pipelines are the responsibility of the Ministry of Mining, Petroleum, and Geology.

Organization and management

The organization of the Ministry of Transport and Communications is shown in Figure 13.1. In principle, the role of the officers and staff of the Ministry's headquarters is limited to planning, coordination, design, administration, and budgeting. For construction and actual transport operations, much authority is delegated to centrals and to the enterprises within them. Separate departments exist in the Ministry for railway, sea, and river transport.

On lower administrative levels, there is one General Directorate for post and telecommunications, a Directorate of Highways, and several other Directorates. Further, there are four centrals that report directly to the Minister: one for construction of civil works other than roads (Chapter 12), one for major repairs and overhaul of locomotives and rolling stock, one for road transport operations, and one for major repairs and overhaul of motor vehicles. These centrals are subdivided into a number of enterprises. On the same administrative level, but not responsible directly to the Minister, there are seven centrals within the Department of Railways. Each of these is responsible for railway operations within the seven geographic regions of the railway network. These centrals are not further subdivided into enterprises. There are also several transport enterprises that do not form part of any central, but are under the Department of Sea and River Transport and the Directorate of Highways. The broad principle behind this horizontal form of organization is that centrals and enterprises have their own revenues and thus can be financially self-supporting, except for

Figure 13.1. *Organization of the Ministry of Transport and Telecommunications*

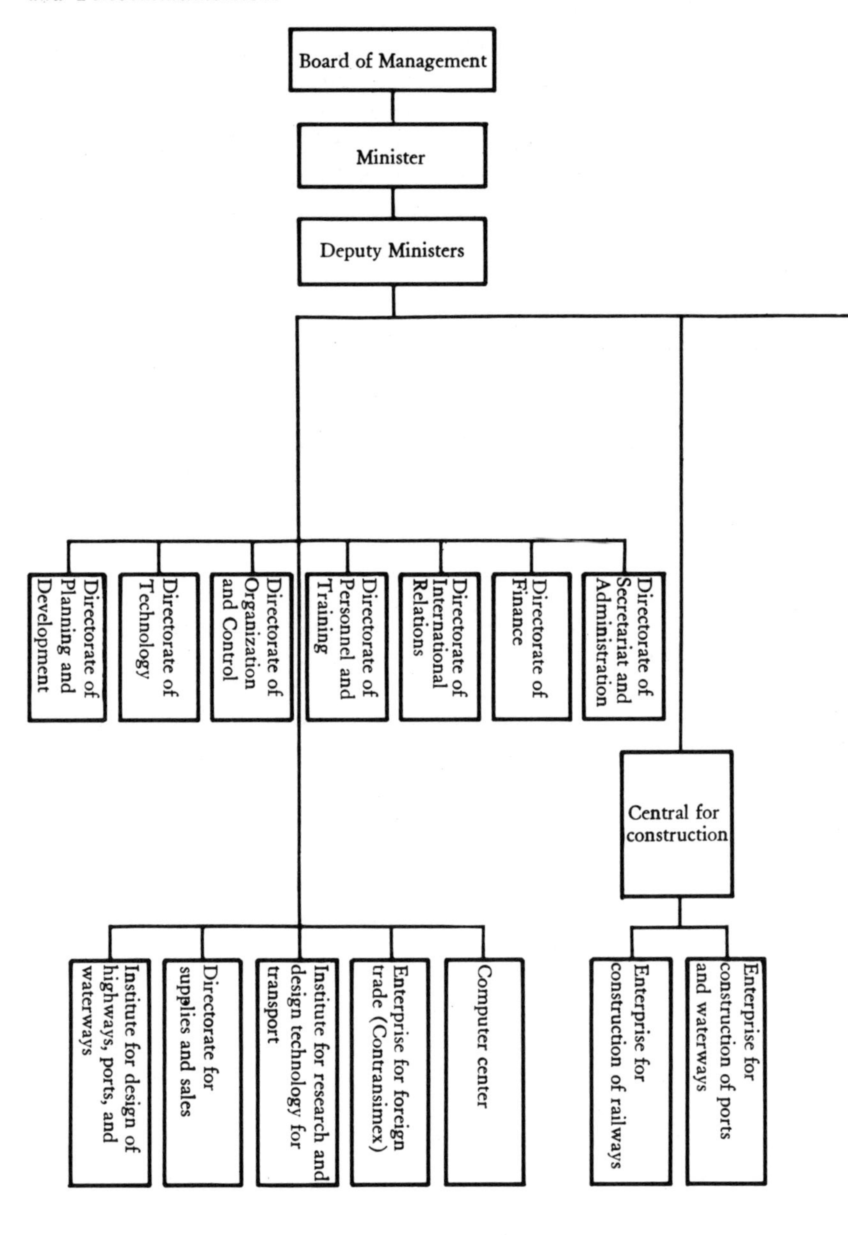

(continued on following page)

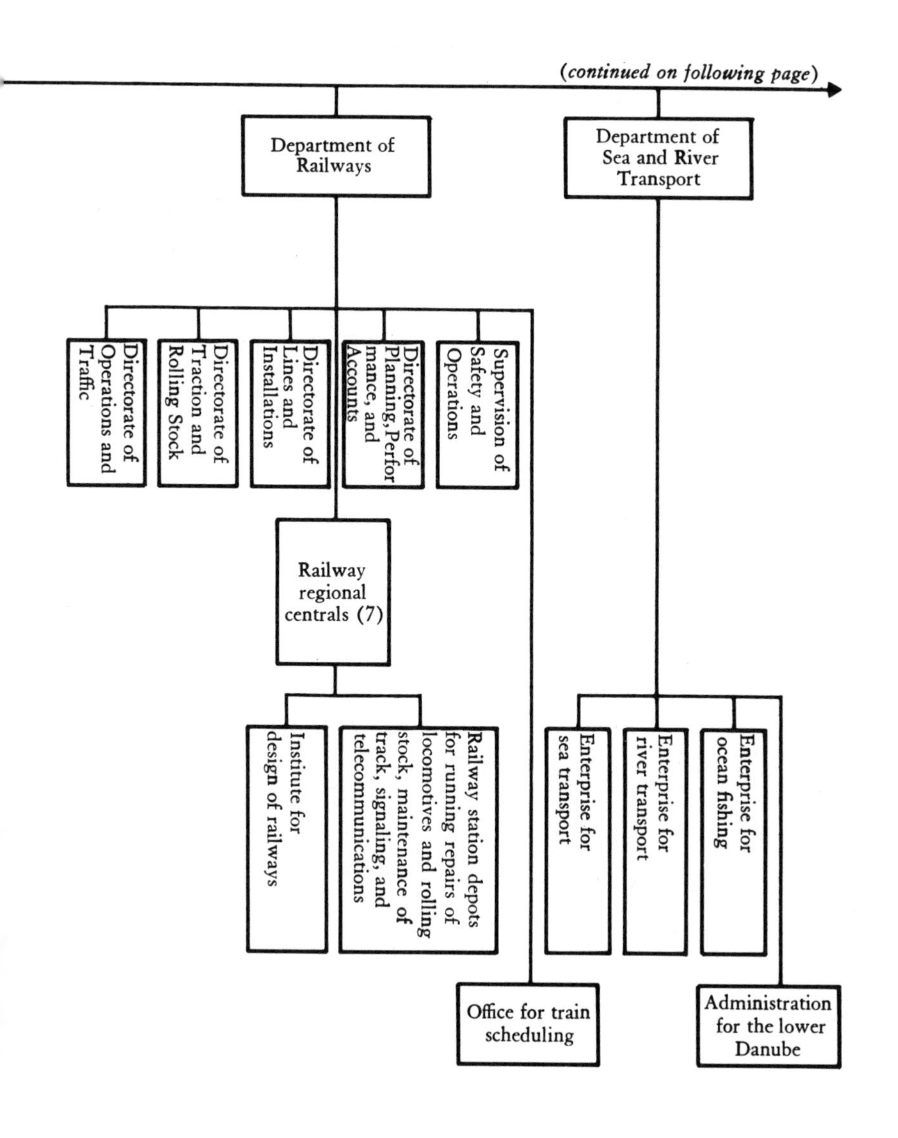

Figure 13.1 *Continued*

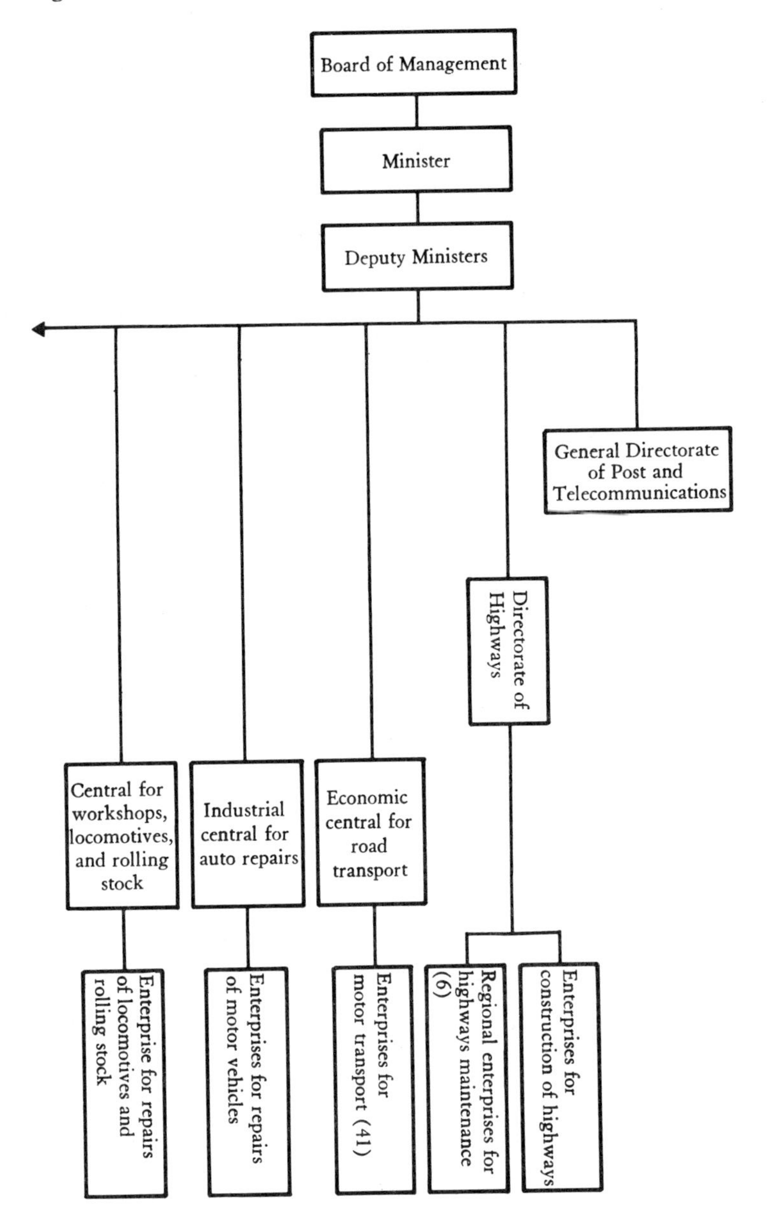

highway enterprises and the administration for the lower Danube, which are financed by the state budget.

All intercity passenger public transport is the responsibility of the Ministry of Transport and Communications. In the larger municipalities, public transport by trams, buses, trolleys, and taxis is the responsibility of the particular municipal administration. The subway line being constructed in Bucharest, however, will be administered by an enterprise responsible to the Ministry of Transport. The districts are responsible for maintaining district and communal roads and bridges, as well as for maintaining national roads within the boundaries of the capitals of the districts and municipalities. Funds for this purpose, however, are very limited compared with needs. In 1975, for example, they amounted to 1,013 million lei, a significantly lower figure than all previous allocations in the 1970s, and amounted to 2.5 percent of the district government's expenditures, which also was considerably less than a peak allocation of 5.5 percent of expenditures in 1970 (Appendix B).

Planning and coordination

The planning process in the transport sector follows the basic planning principles discussed in more detail in Chapter 3. The demand for transport, as for the construction sector, is a derived demand. This leads to a somewhat longer and more complex process of reconciling the demands of the economic sectors for transport with the physical capacities and expansion plans of transport enterprises at the micro level and with the allocation of investment funds.

As in other sectors, planning for new transport projects originates both at the micro level, through the enterprises, and at the macro level, through the State Planning Committee (SPC). Project proposals are submitted by the enterprises first to the centrals, where they are reviewed, and then to the Ministry of Transport and Telecommunications. Following technical reviews by the respective Directorates within the Ministry, they are further reviewed and coordinated by the Ministry's Directorate of Planning against the background of various other studies, one of which calculates the demand for transport services of the forty-five most important commodities. This study is undertaken by the Ministry in collaboration with the SPC. For these commodities, the minimum economic cost of meeting transport demand for various distances by each transport mode (or combination of modes) is calculated by computer. Important nonquantifiable factors, however, such as quality of service and speed, which affect the real social cost of transport, are not reflected in the computer inputs.

At this stage of review and coordination, new investment proposals that seem justified at the macroeconomic level are submitted by the Ministry to the SPC. The iterative process of further plan modifications and reconciliations for transport is no different from that of other sectors. When a total investment has to be reduced, however, supporting sectors of the economy, such as transport, are usually reviewed first, rather than the directly productive sectors. Planning is also undertaken at the district level, mainly for road and bridge maintenance, and these are incorporated into the local budget considered by the Ministry of Finance in drawing up the financial plans of the district.

Transport sector planning is based on planned or expected annual average traffic volumes rather than on seasonal peak volumes, since the general policy is to avoid investing resources in excess capacity in the transport sector. This policy has at least two advantages: it frees resources for effective use elsewhere within the economy and it can spur efficiency in transport enterprises by making them try to maximize transport output with the capacity available. The risk of this planning premise is that serious congestion may occur at times, even though the transport of nonseasonal commodities is fairly well spread over the year and is monitored monthly. Congestion seems to develop during two periods: harvest time and the last two months of the year when enterprises are involved in an all-out effort to meet or to exceed their annual targets. On the railways, for example, congestion has developed at such times because of too few wagons and limited capacity on certain lines. Since most decisions on the choice of transport modes for commodities are made far in advance and are reflected in the plan, there is usually little surplus capacity and flexibility to adjust, not only during harvest time if crops are larger than expected, but also during bad weather if road transport is adversely affected.

Efficiency, costs, and quality of construction in transport

The railway system's productivity can be illustrated from such indicators as passenger kilometers and tonne-kilometers per kilometer of track. These were at 2.0 and 5.9 million, respectively, and are among the highest in Europe. The number of employees (eighteen employees per kilometer) is also high compared with other railways. To a large extent this reflects the unusually large number of stations, which are usually less than 6 kilometers apart, and the volume of night traffic, which requires three shifts for operational employees. The number of traffic units (that is, tonne-kilometers plus passenger kilometers moved for each employee) amounts to 490,000 for each employee. This compares quite favorably with other railways and reflects again the very high average traffic density. More specifically, labor productivity measured in ton-kilometers more than tripled during 1950–75.[7]

Train punctuality, although still good, is deteriorating because, with up to eighty trains daily, some single lines are reaching their saturation point. The average daily haul for passenger trains is 485 kilometers. Commercial speeds are 70 to 75 kilometers per hour for rapid trains and 45 kilometers per hour for local trains on main lines. On branch lines, commercial speeds are only 30 kilometers per hour, reflecting the very large number of stations. It seems doubtful whether much local train traffic is economic compared with bus service. The national average distance for passenger traffic is also low, about 60 kilometers, reflecting the large number of passengers traveling only short distances. Whether, under Romanian conditions, it is important and economically beneficial to increase passenger train speeds up to 160 kilometers per hour on main lines, as intended, needs very careful examination, particularly since higher speeds become increasingly energy intensive.

The average daily haul for freight trains is 340 kilometers, with an average distance for freight traffic of 285 kilometers. Turnaround time for railroad cars is good, but, after declining to 3.6 days in 1960, it gradually increased to 3.8 days by 1975. No data on train load factors are available, but assuming an average load factor of 75 percent caused by partially empty return trips, average travel distance a day for railroad cars would be about 100 kilometers and average speeds would be about 26 kilometers per hour. In view of this, the intended increase in maximum running speeds for freight trains to 100 kilometers per hour might have little effect on the total turnaround time of railroad cars.

In road transport, trucks have an economic life of six to seven years; and buses, of seven to eight years. Trucks travel an average of 50,000 kilometers per year. This is quite low and reflects the short average hauling distance (22 kilometers) and the proportionately large and unproductive waiting time for loading and unloading. The average distance traveled may be low also because hauls to railway stations are made on unsatisfactory roads. Based on incomplete information, trucking rates are estimated to be very expensive. Since average hauling distance for railway freight is 284 kilometers, or thirteen times the average road haul, it is not surprising that movements by rail are proportionately cheaper.

The actual construction of transport infrastructure projects is the responsibility of the centrals and the large number of their enterprises that work

7. In a productivity index with 1950 = 100; 1960 was 142; 1970, 254; and 1975, 342.

within specific geographic regions. The design institutes within the Ministry also control construction work. The construction site activities are supervised by the beneficiaries of the works and through the autocontrol of the construction enterprises. Prices are stabilized during the planning and design stage. There appears to be a tendency to pressure designers and construction enterprises to squeeze costs to a bare minimum. Since final prices are allowed to deviate only 5 percent from contracted prices, there is a danger that design standards or construction specifications may be compromised when it appears that works cannot be properly built for the contracted prices. With planning, design, construction, and supervision under the same Ministry, it is also likely that pressure to reach physical targets (for example, kilometers completed) leads to reduced quality.

"Modernization" of national roads means, in practice, surfacing existing roads with asphalt concrete pavement, 6 to 7 meters wide. Shoulders are 1 meter wide. This is inadequate both for safety and drainage, but with the low volume of traffic on many road sections, this is not always inappropriate. For the district roads, paving is generally 5.5 to 6.0 meters of asphalt concrete with 1 meter of untreated shoulders. Local roads are improved by "light asphalt paving." For all three categories, however, quality of paving, drainage, shoulders, and the like needs to be improved to correspond better to the volume of traffic.

Energy consumption of the sector

Official statistics indicate that the transport sector is not as energy intensive as in many other countries. There are several reasons for this: the dominance of the railway system, restriction of trucking to short distances, the low level of private automobile ownership, and restrictions on fuel availability for official car use. Energy consumption by the transport sector and its share in total domestic energy consumption for 1970 and 1975 are shown in Table 13.8. The absolute decline in consumption in 1975 over 1970 can be attributed to the rationing measures introduced after the oil price crisis,[8] whereas the relative decline of the sector results from the substantial increase in the consumption of the industrial sector. Nevertheless, the energy consumption share of the sector is very low, compared, for example, with 15

8. Cars for general official use and for cooperative and public organizations were allotted a maximum of 180 liters of gasoline per month; those of higher level government personnel, 400 liters; and privately owned cars, 40 to 60 liters. In 1975 restrictions on gasoline use by privately owned cars were rescinded.

Table 13.8. *Energy Consumption of the Transport Sector*
(millions of tonnes of oil equivalent)

Item	*1970*	*1975*
1. Consumption of total economy	38.7	52.1
2. Consumption of transport sector	2.4	2.2
3. Line 2 ÷ line 1	6.1%	4.3%

Source: Table SA10.4.

percent in the United Kingdom in 1973. This may also result from definitional differences, however.

Information on long-term trends in energy consumption by the different transport modes is not available. It can be approximated, though, by using another country's fixed coefficients of energy consumption for each transport mode. This seems a reasonable approach, because energy intensiveness by mode usually does not differ much from country to country. The distribution of energy consumption in Romania by transport mode[9] is shown in Table 13.9.

The figures in Table 13.9 show the increasing amounts of energy consumed by road traffic; it now absorbs almost 29 percent of the sector's total energy consumption, despite its relatively small share in traffic. Romania cannot save much energy by shifting traffic from road to rail, since the bulk of long-haul traffic already goes by rail. In the United Kingdom, 75 percent of road freight traffic is moved on hauls under 40 kilometers. The Romanian

9. The coefficients used are for the United States and are from "Energy in the Transportation Sector" by William E. Mooz (Santa Monica Rand Corporation, 1973). They were used to calculate the average energy intensiveness of various freight modes in 1960–68. The energy intensiveness used in British Thermal Units (BTU's) is given below (. . . not applicable):

	Freight mode (per tonne-kilometer)	*Passenger mode (per passenger-kilometer)*
Waterway	310	. . .
Rail	465	1,624
Pipeline	1,147	. . .
Truck	1,488	. . .
Bus	. . .	1,054

All road passenger traffic was assumed to be by bus. The difference in BTU per ton-kilometer for railways and trucks appears to be smaller than World Bank experience suggests, a factor that would understate the energy intensiveness of the road system in the table. Door-to-door road routes, however, are shorter than road-rail-road routes, which is an important factor in considering the energy consumption for shorter distances.

Table 13.9. *Energy Consumption by Transport Mode, 1950–75*
(percentage)

	1950 Shares[a]		*1960 Shares*[a]		*1970 Shares*[a]		*1975 Shares*[a]	
Transport of goods								
Railways	89.0	88.0	88.0	76.0	85.0	69.0	82.0	6
Roads	0.4	2.0	4.0	12.0	9.0	24.0	12.0	2
Rivers	8.0	5.0	4.0	2.0	2.0	1.0	3.0	
Pipelines	2.0	5.0	4.0	10.0	3.0	6.0	3.0	
Transport of passengers								
Railways	95.0	97.0	88.0	92.0	69.0	78.0	54.0	6
Roads	5.0	3.0	12.0	8.0	31.0	22.0	46.0	3

Note: Aviation is not included, but its share is marginal.
a. The first figure represents share in total ton-kilometer or passengers-kilometer, respectiv the second represents share in total energy consumption.
Source: Derived from Tables SA9.1 and SA9.2, according to text footnote 10.

situation is very similar. The relative efficiency of passenger traffic by road is also shown.[10]

The 1976–80 Plan

The 1976–80 transport sector plan is designed to implement stated government policies with a renewed emphasis on energy conservation. It also emphasizes improvements in the productivity of the transport modes within existing capacities and calls for more intensive use of the Danube and of interior waters.[11] Any proposed development of road transport is linked closely with that of the other modes so that road distance traveled is minimized. Total investments in the transport sector will amount to 95.3

10. A weighted average of the energy intensity of the sector in the transport of goods was 473 BTU per ton-kilometer in 1950, 532 in 1960, 577 in 1970, and 606 in 1975, an increase of about 1 percent a year during 1950 to 1975. Converted to ton-miles, the 1960 and 1965 averages for Romania were 858 and 890 BTU's, respectively, compared with 1,288 and 1,346 BTU's, respectively, for the United States. The differences reflect the different importance of each transport mode in each country.

11. When allowance is made for the greater distances involved in transport by inland waterway, there is little difference in direct energy intensiveness between rail and inland waterway transport. (In the United States waterway routes are an average of 38 percent more circuitous than rail routes.) N. Seymer, *Intermodal Comparisons of Energy Intensiveness in Long Distance Transports* (London: Programme Press, 1976).

Table 13.10. *Railway and Road Growth Indicators, 1976–80*
(1975 = 100)

	Initial plan indicators					Revised plan indicators for 1980 as a percentage of 1975[a]
	1976	*1977*	*1978*	*1979*	*1980*	
Railway traffic						
Tonnage	106	113	120	127	134	122.6
Ton-kilometers	106	111	119	126	133	122.1
Passenger-kilometers	105	109	113	117	122	116.2
Road transport						
Tonnage	105.8	109.9	118	124.1	130.4	125.6
Ton-kilometers	110.8	117.1	123	129.9	136.7	121.4
Passenger-kilometers	115.0	125.0	137.2	164.7	180.2	132.2

a. All annual indicators for 1976–80 have been revised downwards as of 1977.
Source: Ministry of Transportation; data provided during discussions with the authors.

billion lei, or 9.5 percent of total plan investment, which is about double the amount included in the 1971–75 Plan. The growth indicators for rail and road goods transport are given in Table 13.10.

Specific goals

No breakdown of the total investment in the transport sector is available, but it is likely that the railways have been allotted the dominant portion (about 40 percent of total as in the 1971–75 Plan) and that allocations for road investments will be about 10 percent of the total. A major project to be undertaken is a new bridge across the Danube (above). The Plan also includes the complete elimination of steam traction, addition of over 800 kilometers of electrified rail track; addition of 430 kilometers of double track (bringing double track to 22 percent of the system by 1980), increased motive power and rolling stock[12] and improved technical condition of rail

12. The additions include 900 to 982 diesel and electric locomotives, 17,000 to 18,330 freight cars, and 1,500 to 1,625 passenger cars. It is not clear, however, what portion of these would be replacements and what portion would increase capacity.

network to allow speeds up to 160 kilometers per hour for passenger trains and up to 100 kilometers per hour for freight trains.

Very large amounts are to be spent on expanding the port of Constanta and on building the planned 62-kilometer Black Sea canal. The canal is designed to carry barge traffic between the Danube River and the Constanta port and to handle 100 million tonnes annually.[13] The Black Sea canal project is estimated to cost more than 20 billion lei, the major part of which is to be spent during the 1976–80 plan period to procure construction equipment. Its construction involves widening and deepening a 40-kilometer stretch of irrigation canals and building a new canal for the rest of the distance. Although the total volume of goods transported by river will increase sixfold after the canal is completed, the share of river transport will remain modest.

As for other transport modes, a significant expansion is envisaged for the fleet of river barges (70 percent) and for international maritime transport, since the government aims to transport 80 percent of all seagoing trade under the Romanian flag by 1990. By 1980 it intends to add 107 to 117 seagoing vessels with a capacity of 2.5 million dead weight tons, in addition to the present capacity of about 1 million dead weight tons. No new roads are planned. For the national road network, completion of the modernization program will be emphasized, but what is planned is still very modest considering the growth of road transport over the past five years.[14]

Assessment

The Five-Year Plan is based on exhaustive studies of requirements for transport services by major sectors and commodities, but these studies have not been published. It is not possible, therefore, to make a well-founded analysis of the plan, but certain general observations can be made. The growth indicators for the internal transport of goods (5.5 to 6 percent a year) are surprisingly low when compared with the growth of social product (10 to 11 percent a year) and of industrial output (10.2 to 11.2 percent a year). Only in two of the previous five-year plan periods did the transport of goods (in tons and ton-kilometers) grow at a lower rate than social product (Table 13.1), and, even in those cases, the maximum deviation was not more than 1 to 1.5 percentage points, or about 13 percent lower. The

13. This would mean about 300,000 tonnes a day; it would require large lock complexes to handle such volumes.

14. The Plan includes the modernization of only 1,100 to 1,261 kilometers of roads carrying heavy traffic, and light asphalt paving will be applied to 10,000 to 10,795 kilometers of roads carrying light traffic.

downward revision of the indicators accentuates this situation. Thus, it is difficult to reconcile the difference between the plan's growth estimates of transport of goods and that of social product. Initial excess line capacity on the railways has now been largely eliminated, and indications are that the railways are being used close to capacity, requiring a continuous program of increasing line capacity, locomotives, and rolling stock. There is evidence of strains on the capacity of the system.

One explanation for the lower growth of goods transport, which has been advanced by the authorities, is that the difference would be partially offset by an increase of own-account truck transport by the various industrial and construction enterprises as well as by a more efficient use of transport modes (above). But, considering that road transport is still at most 12 percent of total traffic volume in ton-kilometers, it would require a very large growth of the own-account trucking fleet to absorb the difference. Also, an analysis of disaggregated growth targets indicates that planned road transport growth is about half that experienced over the 1971–75 period, whereas that of rail is about the same.

Another explanation given is that, because of regionalization, the average length of a trip will shorten, since production is now closer to consumption areas. Detailed data to assess this are not available. First, such developments will depend on the spatial distribution of all industries. Although production outputs may be closer to consumption areas, production inputs of usually larger volumes than outputs may have to travel longer distances. Second, if the government's regionalization policy results in a wider and more equal spread of industrial activities, and thus of economic growth over the country, then local road transport over district and village roads will become much more important, and this will have to be reflected in the plan indicators.

Although the prevailing policy of squeezing road investments to a minimum is compatible with current objectives in the allocation of resources, it may prove more costly in the long run, since the geometric and engineering standards applied for road modernization are below modern standards. Newly built roads have uneven surfaces, low embankments and inadequate drainage, and they show pavement failures at an early stage. This is not the result of a lack of knowledge on the part of the highway engineers, but of insufficient funds to meet kilometer targets and the use of engineering practices that are not always appropriate.

The government's aim to transport 50 percent of all seagoing trade under Romanian flag by 1980 and to increase capacity from 1 to 3.5 million dead weight tons through local shipbuilding is ambitious. First, because of physical constraints, it will be difficult to construct all vessels domestically within the five-year plan periods. Therefore, the fleet would have to be expanded partly by purchasing vessels abroad. Second, the United Nations Committee on Trade and Development (UNCTAD), reflecting other developing countries' preferences, has advocated a 40-40-20 strategy for carrying foreign trade cargoes: that is, the bulk of the cargoes is to be shared by the trading countries and 20 percent is to be carried by vessels of third parties.

The foreign exchange expenditure saved by expanding the domestic fleet can also be overstated, as experience shows elsewhere. Even in domestic construction, some foreign currency is required for shipbuilding. Part of fuel, repairs, other consumables, and crews' expenditures would have to be paid for abroad in foreign currencies. And part of the savings of foreign currency will be offset, since payments for harbor and other dues, paid now in foreign currencies by foreign-flag vessels, will be paid in local currency by Romanian vessels. Third, Romanian ports are located often at the end of the routes; this, together with unbalanced port traffic, is likely to lead to relatively low load factors.

A final point addresses the issue raised earlier on the importance of cost considerations in developing the different transport modes in Romania. It appears that consideration is being given to creating "transport units," to which shippers would present their transport needs at any given time. These transport units would then decide how to best meet these demands and by what mode of transport. Their decisions would no longer be restricted by road haul distances and would help to reduce empty return trips. Such a system would have several advantages. It would introduce other factors than cost alone (above), such as greater flexibility, quality of service, and speed of deliveries in determining what mode of transport should be used. Experiments along these lines would be very worthwhile.

14

The Energy Sector

ROMANIA IS ENDOWED WITH NUMEROUS SOURCES of primary energy (Chapter 1), whose development has been closely linked with the energy requirements of the national industrialization and development effort. The government's strategy has been to use its most productive domestic resources as fully as possible. For a considerable time, energy self-sufficiency was attained. The country's industrialization gradually outgrew the resource base, however, and, in 1972–73, Romania passed from a net surplus to a net energy deficit. A net deficit in crude oil and oil products developed in 1975–76 and has continued since then.

Energy Strategy

The government's policies for developing energy resources during 1950–75 were articulated in three documents: the electrification plan for 1951–60; the Directives of the Eighth Congress of the Romanian Communist Party (RCP) for 1960–65; and the Directives of the Ninth Congress of the RCP for 1966–70.

The government's policy in its electrification plan and directives during 1951–65 had two main objectives: to increase domestic energy production to meet the rapidly increasing industrial and other fuel and power require-

Note: This chapter constructs and discusses Romania's current and projected energy resource balance. No sector discussion similar to those in earlier chapters is undertaken, because of insufficient data for all ministries involved in this sector. Even in this study, estimates and projections have required many assumptions because of limited information and should be regarded as being an approximate order of magnitude rather than a fixed quantity. Inaccuracies are undoubtedly present because of the use of aggregated production figures and average calorific values for conversion of energy sources to heat equivalents, but they are not considered serious enough to invalidate the overall situation described.

ments, including a national electrification program, and to develop an energy infrastructure in terms of personnel, research, study, and design institutes and enterprises to exploit energy resources.

The demand for energy had already increased substantially by 1965; total fuel consumption had increased threefold over 1950 levels and electric power consumption ninefold. Large investments, amounting to about 40 percent of total industrial investment, were undertaken during that period to expand the energy base and the country's electrification. Production targets were largely fulfilled. For electric power, a 340 percent increase in installed capacity brought capacity to nearly 3,300 megawatts in 1965. During that year, exports of electrical energy were approximately 300 megawatts more than imports (Table SA10.1).

The most important objectives of the 1965–75 Plans were:

(a) To increase output of primary energy to cover the economy's requirement as much as possible from internal resources, primarily coal and hydropower;
(b) To intensify efforts to conserve hydrocarbon resources and to direct their use to petrochemical production;
(c) To increase efficiency in the utilization of plant capacity and also in the consumption of users; and
(d) To expand oil and gas exploration, particularly in offshore areas.

These plan themes also underlie present government strategy. Since the oil crisis of 1973, they have been confirmed in an energy decree ordering more specific measures to develop the energy base and a more effective use of fuels and energy. The decree was issued in November 1973. Measures included the increased use of primary sources with low calorific levels to generate electricity; increased efforts to recover waste heat in industrial processes; and improved efficiency in energy use in industry, construction, transport, agriculture, and other socioeconomic activities. They also provided for acceleration of construction of nuclear power plants, gasoline rationing, and controls on space heating. The implementation of these measures immediately following the oil crisis appears to have been successful, as evidenced by the decreased demand for energy in the economy in 1974–75 (Tables SA10.1 and SA10.2).

Energy Management

There is no single ministry of energy in Romania; responsibility for energy production is divided among five ministries as follows:

Ministry	*Area of Responsibility*
Mines, Petroleum, and Geology (Ministry of Mines)	Extraction of oil, natural gas, anthracite, coking coal, coal, lignite, bituminous shale
Electric Power	Electrical energy
Chemical Industry	Petroleum refining and petrochemicals
Metallurgical Industry	Coke and coke-oven gases, coal-tar
Forestry Economy and Construction Materials	Wood

The State Planning Committee (SPC) coordinates energy planning, on a sector-by-sector basis.

The Ministry of Mines, Petroleum, and Geology is subdivided into directorates dealing with oil and gas, coal, geologic prospecting, technical development, planning and finance, training, investment, and international cooperation (Figure 14.1). All exploratory work for minerals and fuels is carried out by the General Directorate of Geology, which hands over proven, economically exploitable deposits to other departments of the Ministry. The Ministry is responsible for primary production of mineral fuels and for the operation of specialized facilities, such as natural gas processing plants and oil and gas pipelines. Products such as crude oil, natural gas liquids, natural gas, coal, and lignite are handed over to the end-users, who pay the Ministry at fixed prices. The Ministry is responsible for delivering natural gas to the ultimate consumer; it also exercises a control function by ensuring that individual consumers do not exceed their planned rate of consumption.

The Ministry of Electric Power (Figure 14.2) is responsible not only for operating power stations and for distributing electric energy from the national to the retail level, but also for designing and building thermal and hydroelectric generating facilities and transmission lines; for demand forecasting for electrical energy; and for arranging for international connections and electrical energy imports and exports. The Ministry of Electrical Energy obtains coal and natural gas for its thermal generating plants from the Ministry of Mines and fuel oil from the Ministry of Chemical Industry.

The Ministry of Chemical Industry receives from the Ministry of Mines all crude oil, natural gas liquids (extracted by the Ministry of Mines from associated gas), and a portion of the natural gas output for processing into refined petroleum products and petrochemicals. The Ministry of Chemical Industry, in turn, sells its output on both domestic and international markets.

Figure 14.1. *Organization of the Ministry of Mines, Petroleum, and Geology*

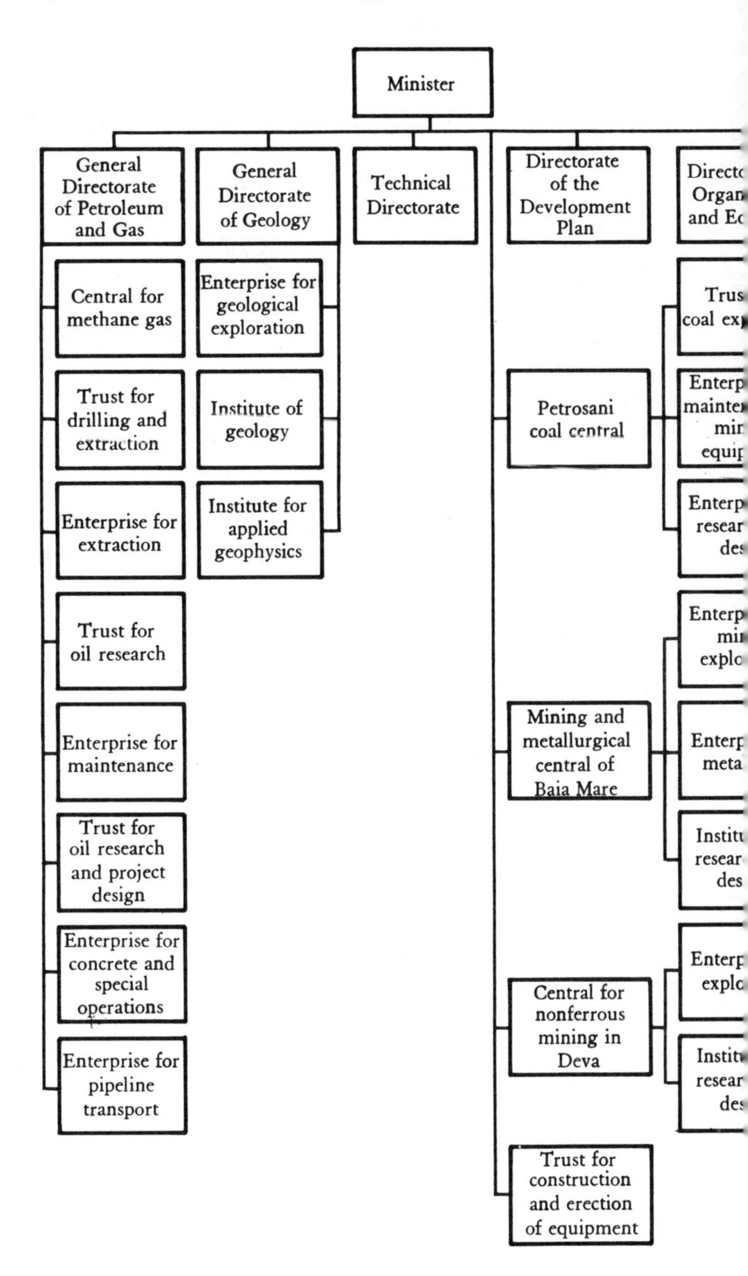

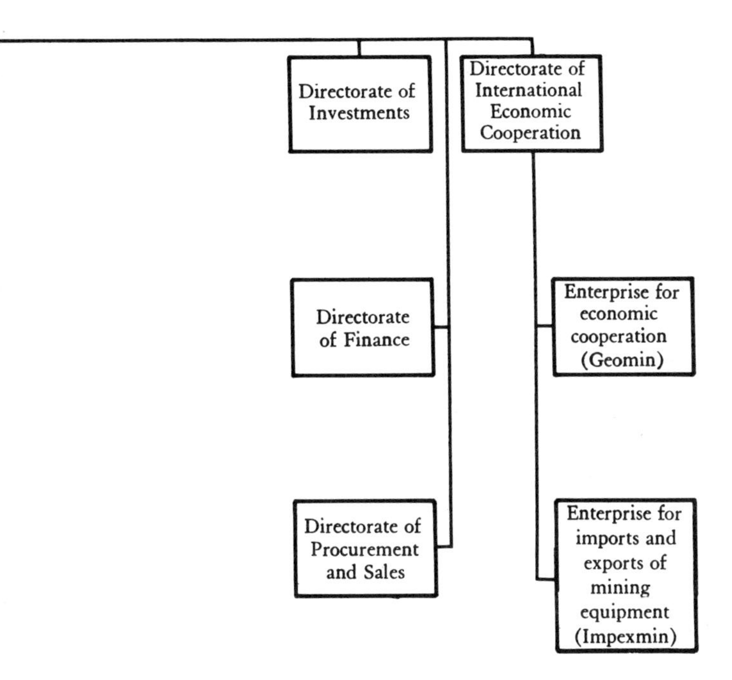
Directorate of Investments
Directorate of International Economic Cooperation
Directorate of Finance
Enterprise for economic cooperation (Geomin)
Directorate of Procurement and Sales
Enterprise for imports and exports of mining equipment (Impexmin)

Figure 14.2. *Organization of the Ministry of Electrical Energy*

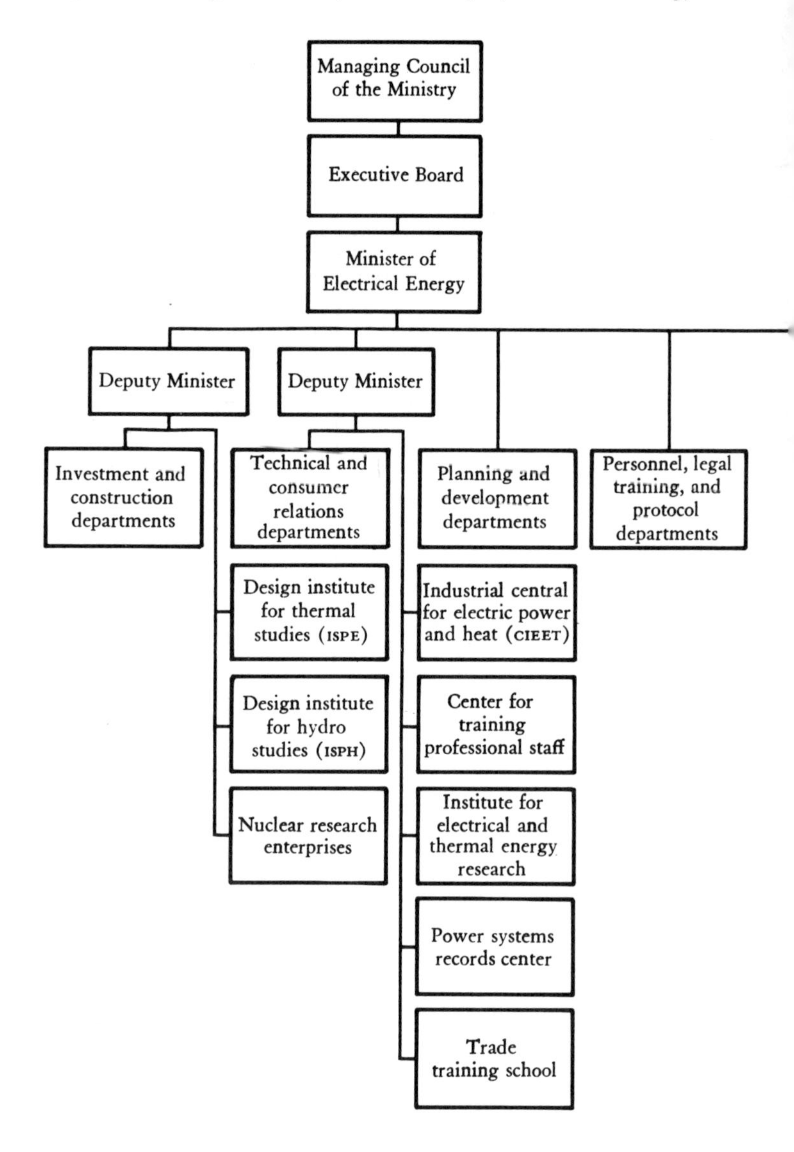

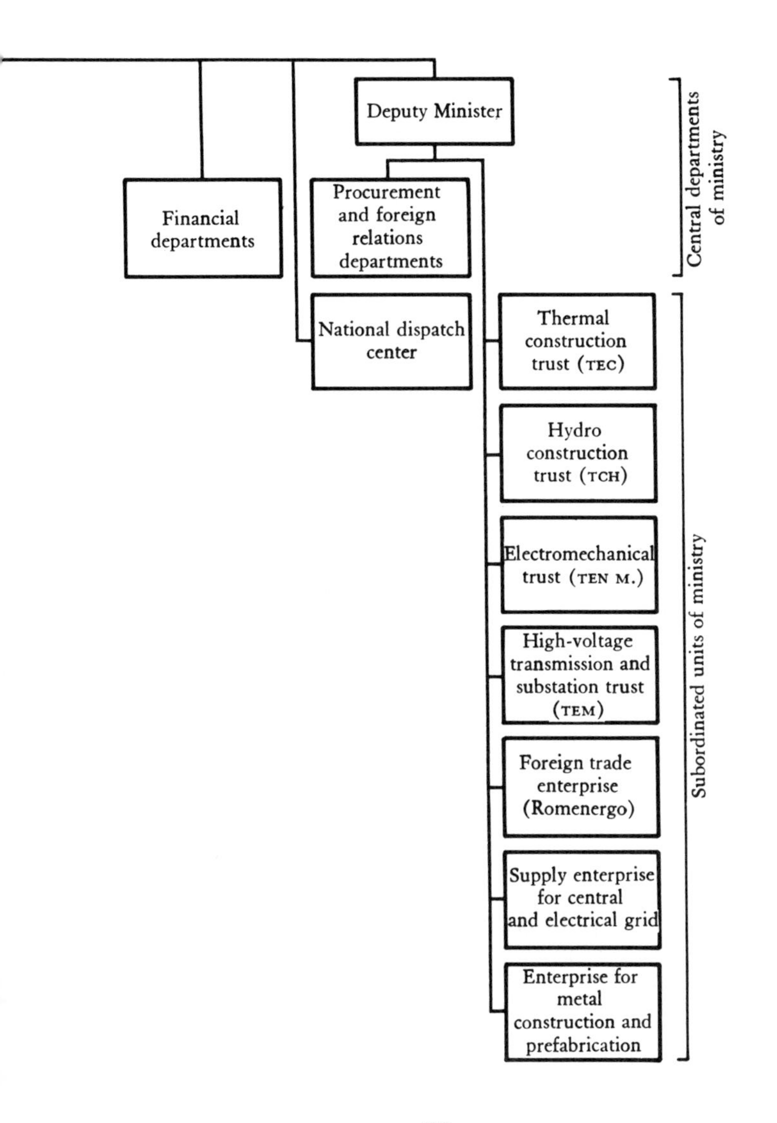
Deputy Minister
Financial departments
Procurement and foreign relations departments
National dispatch center
Thermal construction trust (TEC)
Hydro construction trust (TCH)
Electromechanical trust (TEN M.)
High-voltage transmission and substation trust (TEM)
Foreign trade enterprise (Romenergo)
Supply enterprise for central and electrical grid
Enterprise for metal construction and prefabrication
Central departments of ministry
Subordinated units of ministry

Similarly, the other two ministries listed above are responsible for the production and marketing of the products in their areas of authority.

Even though the production activities of the ministries are coordinated by the Plan according to the same principles as in most of the other sectors, the dispersion of responsibilities among so many agencies has led to difficulties in administering the diverse measures to reduce energy consumption and to improve efficient use. The 1973 oil crisis accentuated the need for more effective coordination in these areas and the Permanent Commission for the Coordination, Guidance, and Control of Fuel, Electric, and Thermal Power Consumption was established for that purpose in November 1973.

Supply and Demand of Energy Resources

The primary energy sources of Romania are crude oil, natural gas (both associated and nonassociated), coal, anthracite, coking coal, lignite, brown coal, bituminous shale, and hydropower, as shown on the map on page 339. Wood has played a small but significant part in the past as a domestic fuel, particularly in the countryside. There are important hydropower resources, and there is a geothermal potential that could be used for space heating.

Petroleum and natural gas

Romania was one of the earliest countries to produce crude petroleum,[1] and crude oil and petroleum products were important export commodities before World War II. During the war, the existing fields were severely damaged by overproduction, and many of the installations were destroyed. Despite a vigorous rehabilitation and development program, crude oil production did not surpass the 1938 level until 1952. Oil and gas are found in four areas in Romania, the most important of which is around Ploiesti. Except for this area, most of the fields are small and scattered and have thin reservoir sands at depths of 2,000 meters or less, as well as very complex geologic structures, many of which are of the salt diapir type. Geologic conditions, combined with the advanced state of depletion of many of the

1. Romanian crude oil is, for the most part, medium-gravity low-sulfur brown or black oil of asphaltic or napthenic type with a specific gravity of 0.82 to 0.88. Some deposits contain light-colored paraffinic oils with a lower specific gravity of 0.75 to 0.82. There are some heavy viscous black crude oils with a specific gravity greater than 0.88.

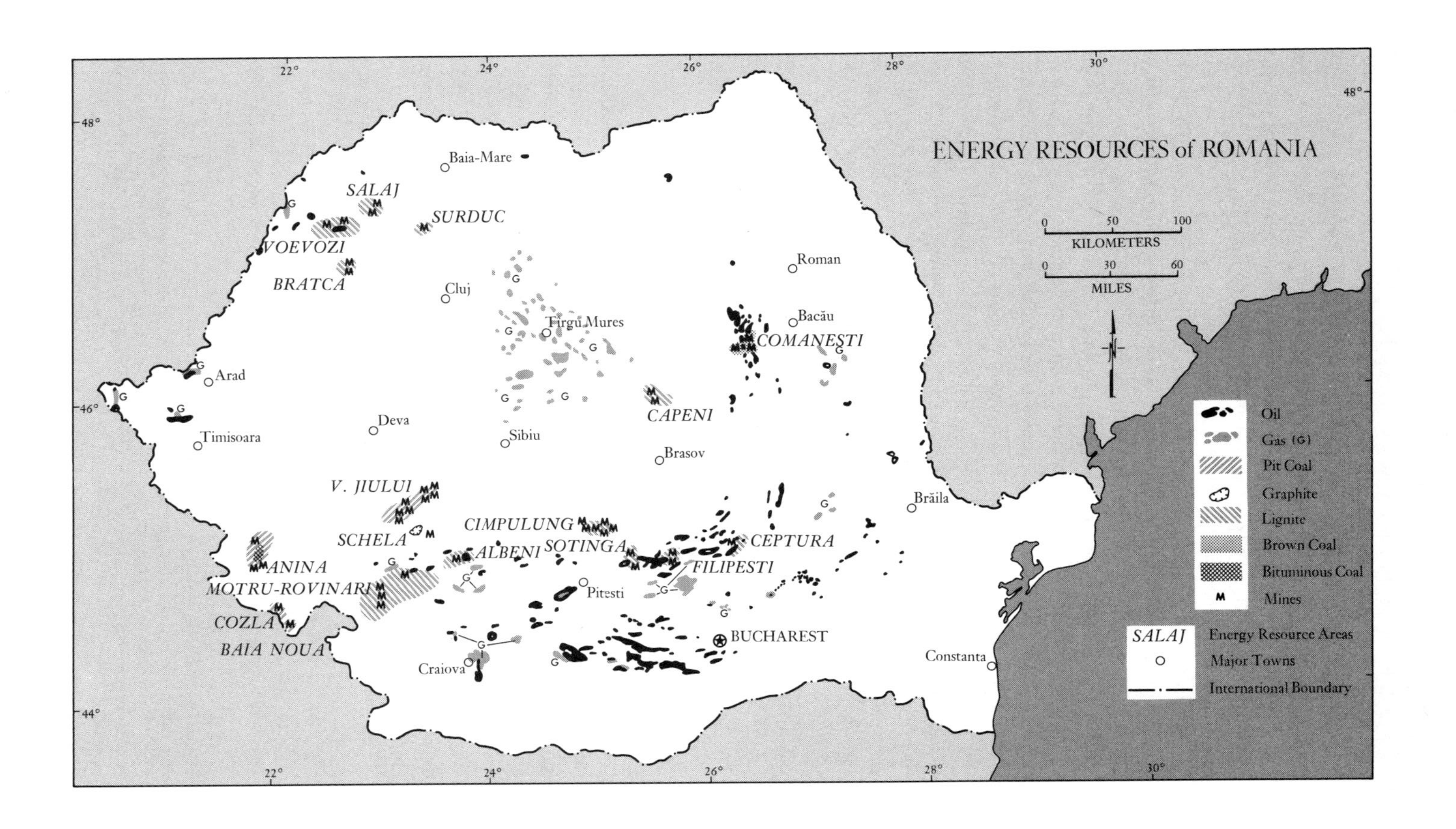
ENERGY RESOURCES of ROMANIA
0
50
100
KILOMETERS
0
30
60
MILES
Oil
Gas (G)
Pit Coal
Graphite
Lignite
Brown Coal
Bituminous Coal
Mines
SALAJ
Energy Resource Areas
Major Towns
International Boundary
Baia-Mare
Cluj
Tirgu Mures
Arad
Timisoara
Deva
Sibiu
Brasov
Roman
Bacău
Brăila
Constanta
Pitesti
Craiova
BUCHAREST
SALAJ
SURDUC
VOEVOZI
BRATCA
V. JIULUI
SCHELA
ANINA
MOTRU-ROVINARI
COZLA
BAIA NOUA
CIMPULUNG
ALBENI
SOTINGA
FILIPESTI
CEPTURA
COMANESTI
CAPENI
22°
24°
26°
28°
30°
48°
46°
44°

larger oil fields, tend to lower the productivity of each well and to raise production and transport costs. There is evidence that the individual productivity of most of the wells is low, about 10 tons a day or less, although their producing life is long.

Within the arc of the Carpathian Mountains lies the Transylvanian Basin. Between sixty and seventy nonassociated gas fields are located there, with multiple sand reservoirs at depths of around 3,000 meters. The gas is apparently high quality, almost pure methane, and has been extensively exploited, especially since 1960, when production began to climb rapidly.

No figures on oil and gas reserves are published by the Romanian government. Based on the nature and history of the oil fields and the present oil production levels, it is likely that known producible reserves are approximately 100 to 200 million tonnes,[2] which would presumably be produced over twenty years or more. It is not possible to calculate natural gas reserves on the basis of available information, but present restrictions on new gas connections indicate some sort of resource constraint, since by 1976 the supply of natural gas to the petrochemical industry had not reached 3 billion cubic meters annually, out of a total production of 33 billion cubic meters a year. As a working hypothesis in this chapter, reserves of about 500 billion cubic meters have been assumed.

Coal and related substances

Several geologic periods of coal formation in Romania have resulted in a range of coal fuels, grading from anthracite through steam coal, brown coal, lignite to the so-called bituminous shales. Coking coal in exploitable quantities is limited to the southwestern part of the country, principally in the area of Petrosani. The calorific value of these coals is variable, but averages 3,600 to 4,700 kilocalories per kilogram, or little more than half the value of imported coal. This low value results from the high ash content, ranging from 10 to 37 percent by weight.

Lignite deposits are distributed widely throughout the country, but many

2. Oil reserves were estimated by taking existing production levels and assuming that they would decline exponentially over twenty-five years from 1980 to a level of 1 million tonnes annually. The amount of oil to be produced during this period was totaled to give a figure of present producible reserves. The exponential rate of decline is a common feature of oil and gas production, especially in older and more mature fields. The period over which the decline takes place was estimated based on the known production history of the Romanian oil fields and the physical properties of the oil reservoirs. Allowance was made for discovery of some new reserves during the decline period. The reserve estimate is, by its nature, no better than an educated guess and should be regarded as giving a reasonable order of magnitude rather than a precise figure. Gas reserves were estimated in a similar manner.

are of little economic value because the reserves are contained in many thin seams (up to fifteen in some places), and in some areas the geology is very complex. The principal economically exploitable deposits of lignite are in Oltenia, in the district of Gorj near the town of Tirgu Jiu. There are two principal deposits, Motru, which is mined principally underground, and Rovinari, which is mined principally by open-cast strip mining. The geology of these deposits is less disturbed than that of many others in the country, but is nevertheless quite complex. The lignite has a calorific value of between 1,600 and 1,970 kilocalories per kilogram or about one-quarter that of good steam coal. The moisture content is around 43 percent and the ash content around 36 percent. It is susceptible to spontaneous combustion in storage unless the stockpile is rolled and compacted. Owing to its low calorific value, it is uneconomic to transport lignite any great distance from the mine, and the greater part is consumed in large thermal power stations near the mines.

The so-called "bituminous shales" occur in association with some coal deposits in the Anina-Oravitsa region. They contain 76 to 85 percent ash and have a calorific value of about 1,000 kilocalories per kilogram. Nevertheless, experiments have been carried out to prove whether or not they can be used as fuel in thermal power generating plants, and a rising production is expected, as discussed below. The geology of these deposits is reported to be as complex as that of the coals with which the shales are associated. That the Romanian government should contemplate mining such a low-grade fuel under difficult geologic conditions demonstrates its policy to maximize the use of domestic energy resources.

Official estimates of reserves of these resources are given in Table 14.1. It is not known whether these are recoverable reserves or known geologic reserves. If the latter, the mineable reserves will be considerably less. No figures of mineable reserves of bituminous shales are given, but they must be about 200 million tonnes to justify the proposed scale of development.

Table 14.1. *Coal Reserves*
(thousands of tonnes)

	Proven	*Probable*	*Possible*
Anthracite	14,000	1,275	8,018
Coking coal (huila)	18,712	325,612	52,724
Bituminous coal	39,029	711,285	85,192
Lignite and brown coal	360,411	386,620	68,107

Source: Ministry of Mines, Petroleum, and Geology; data provided during discussions with the authors.

Hydropower

The hydropower resources of Romania are estimated to be 12,300 megawatts, capable of generating 37,000 gigawatt-hours a year from some 630 sites. Only 75 percent of this is regarded as economically feasible for development at the present time, the remaining 25 percent being described as "technically feasible." Also, Romania's five plants on the Danube River, which are being constructed in cooperation with other countries on the river, should produce 2,400 megawatts and 12,300 gigawatt-hours a year. By 1975, 37 percent of the economically feasible hydrocapacity had been developed, and the government expects the full potential to be tapped by 1985.

Radioactive materials

No information is available on the existence of radioactive minerals, but, given the complex nature of Romanian mineral deposits, uranium may be present as a minor constituent, as in many other parts of the world. One radioactive fuel rod bundle has been fabricated and is now being tested, but whether this contains uranium mined in Romania is not known.

Wood and other vegetable fuels

Wood is still quite widely used in Romania as a domestic fuel for cooking. It is assumed that the availability of wood for fuel is limited and that it will stabilize at somewhat over 3 million tonnes annually on a sustainable yield basis. Other materials, such as maize stalks and corncobs, are used for domestic fuel in rural areas, but no estimate of the quantities involved is available. Romania does possess some peat deposits, but these are apparently not considered to be economically exploitable.

Geothermal energy

Exploration for deep oil reservoirs has shown the existence of widespread aquifers containing water over 100°C. The depth of these aquifers and the cost of pumping water from them, combined with the relatively low temperatures, indicate that economic power generation from geothermal sources is unlikely.

Consumption and production of energy

Energy demand in Romania has risen dramatically over the past twenty-five years as a result of the policy of rapid industrialization, from about 6.8

Table 14.2. *Internal Energy Consumption, by Major Sectors, 1970–75*

Sector	1970 Amount (tonnes of oil equivalent)	1970 Percent	1975 Amount (tonnes of oil equivalent)	1975 Percent	Growth, 1970/75 (percent)
Industrial consumption	30,614	79.2	43,394	83.3	42
Nonindustrial consumption	8,080	20.6	8,699	16.7	6
Agriculture	1,430	3.7	1,771	3.4	24
Transport and telecommunications	2,358	6.1	2,240	4.3	–5
Space heating (homes, offices, and so forth)	4,252	11.0	4,688	9.0	10
Total	*38,654*	*100.0*	*52,093*	*100.0*	*35*

Note: This table is extracted from Table SA10.4, in which an official percentage distribution of total energy consumption has been applied to estimates of total energy consumption. Total energy consumption has been estimated from Romanian data available in *Anuarul Statistic*, official data submitted to the United Nations, and from World Bank project appraisals. Calorific values used for conversion of different energy sources to heat units in this chapter are as follows:

Natural gasoline, 11.4 million kilocalories per metric tonne
Crude petroleum, 10.6 million kilocalories per metric tonne
Natural gas (dry), 8,150 kilocalories per cubic meter
Hydropower, 2,380 kilocalories per kilowatt-hour
Coal (Romanian), 4,150 kilocalories per kilogram
Coal (imported), 8,000 kilocalories per kilogram
Metallurgical coke, 7,500 kilocalories per kilogram
Lignite and brown coal, 1,785 kilocalories per kilogram
Wood, 2,800 kilocalories per kilogram
Bituminous shale, 1,000 kilocalories per kilogram

million tonnes of oil equivalent[3] in 1950 to about 52.1 million tonnes of oil equivalent in 1975 (Tables SA10.1, SA10.2, and SA10.3). Growth of energy consumption by nonindustry uses is considerably below the average growth of energy in the whole economy. This is illustrated in Table 14.2 for 1970–75, for which some disaggregated information is available.

The energy demand in Romania before 1950 was met predominantly by oil and oil products (Tables SA10.1 and SA10.2), and the country

3. Tonnes of oil equivalent. A unit of energy measurement, expressed in metric tons (tonnes); 1 tonne = 1.1 tons.

exported crude oil until 1959. The development of heavy metallurgical industries, primarily iron and steel, necessitated increased production of coke and coking coal, and, since domestic resources were limited and of poor quality, imports of these fuels rose rapidly from 1955. By 1960 supplies of natural gas from the Transylvanian Basin became increasingly important, and by 1965 this became the largest single energy source in the Romanian economy. Present consumption of natural gas is 33 billion cubic meters annually; this figure includes both associated and nonassociated gas, but not gas reinjected into the reservoirs for secondary recovery or pressure maintenance. This gas consumption is equal to more than 25 million tonnes of crude oil and represents the major source of primary fuel in Romania at the present time. In 1975 total domestic energy production amounted to 50.260 million tonnes of oil equivalent, imports to 8.819 million tonnes of oil equivalent, and exports to 6.989 million tonnes of oil equivalent. The changing structure in the contribution of primary energy resources is illustrated in Table 14.3. This table also shows that Romania had to increase gas production above previously anticipated levels to meet both the growing industrial energy and the shortfalls in other sectors.

To avoid a rapidly increasing energy deficit and to mitigate the implications of the oil crisis for the Romanian economy, swift action was taken. The emergency decree published on November 18, 1973 (above) set guide-

Table 14.3. *Anticipated and Actual Energy Production from Various Sources, 1965 and 1975*

	Directives[a]		*Actual*[b]
Form of energy	*1965*	*1975*	*1975*
Crude oil (millions of tonnes)	12.55	13.5–14	14.6
Associated oil-gas (thousand million cubic meters)	4	About 4.5	33.3 (associated oil-gas and methane gas combined)
Methane gas (thousand million cubic meters)	13.7	19–20	
Coal (millions of tonnes)	12	35–40	29.4
Nuclear energy (millions of tonnes cubic centimeters)	—	About 2	—
Hydropower (terawatt-hours)	1.0	10	8.7

a. *Directives of the Ninth Congress of the Romanian Communist Party*; draft *On Power Resources and the Country's Electrification in the 1966–1975 Period.* (Bucharest: Meridiane Publishing House, 1965.)

b. *Anuarul Statistic*, various issues.

lines for accelerated development of indigenous energy resources and for cuts in specific consumption of energy in each sector of the economy, together with stringent restrictions on private consumption through gasoline rationing. The price of motor fuels for the private consumer was raised from 2.50 to 4.50 lei per liter for premium gasoline and from 1.75 to 4.30 lei per liter for regular-grade gasoline. These measures only had a marginal effect on the consumption of energy in the economy as a whole, since the growth of the energy deficit was reduced only slightly during 1974 and 1975. In any case, the potential for reducing consumption in the private sector is very limited. The scope for reducing specific consumption in industrial production processes cannot be easily estimated because of a lack of detailed data relating to energy use before the oil crisis.

Foreign trade aspects

Historically, Romania has exported crude oil and refined products since the late 1800s. To avoid the early depletion of indigenous crude oil reserves, crude oil exports were ended in 1959, and crude oil imports began in 1968. Exports of refined products increased steadily from 1950 until 1968, when they amounted to 5.6 million tonnes, after which they declined to 4.9 million tonnes in 1973. In 1974 and 1975 exports of petroleum products rose again to 6.5 and 6.2 million tonnes, respectively (Table 14.4), as a result both

e 14.4. *Production, Domestic Consumption, and Export and Import*
il and Oil Products, 1970–76

Crude oil (thousands of tonnes)			Total of refined products (thousands of tonnes)				
Production[a]	*Import*	*Domestic consumption*	*Production*	*Export*	*Domestic consumption*	*Export (thousands of U.S. dollars)*	*Import (thousands of U.S. dollars)*
13,759	2,291	16,050	15,835	5,370	10,465	123,083	24,000
14,176	2,858	17,034	16,647	5,368	11,279	143,000	36,633
14,483	2,873	17,356	17,059	5,096	11,963	137,811	47,920
14,642	4,143	18,785	18,568	4,938	13,630	275,694	106,056
14,839	4,538	19,377	18,866	6,502	12,364	535,271	434,668
14,945	5,085	20,030	19,791	6,176	13,615	—	—
15,052	8,475	23,527	23,133	7,842	15,291	603,000[b]	605,000[b]

ncludes a small amount of production of by-products from natural gas wells.
Planned.
rce: Data provided by the Romanian authorities during discussions with the authors.

of crude oil imports and of restricted domestic consumption. The government's objective is to increase export of oil products embodying higher value-added, such as synthetic rubber and fibers, vehicle tires, drugs, and insecticides.

An increasing reliance on imported metallurgical coke and washed coal for coking has also developed as growth of demand, especially in metallurgy, is outrunning the availability of local resources to sustain it. Another reason for the increasing imports is the low quality of Romanian coals; they have poor coking qualities and a high ash content. During the past fifteen years, imports of these raw materials increased from about 1 million tonnes in 1960 to about 5 million in 1975.

Finally, in the electric power sector, international power connections exist with Hungary at 220 kilovolts, with Czechoslovakia at 400 kilovolts, through the USSR, with Bulgaria at 220 kilovolts, and with Yugoslavia at 400 kilovolts. Of the country's electricity production of 1975, about 7 percent was exported, principally to Czechoslovakia in payment for plants supplied earlier. Since imports of electricity are small, they are not relied upon.

The 1976–80 Plan

The Plan's goals[4] confirm the country's long-term energy policy articulated in the mid-1960s, namely:

(a) Maximum reliance on domestic production of primary energy resources;
(b) Priority in the development of coal, hydroelectric, and nuclear power, while using hydrocarbons as long as possible as raw materials for the chemical industry;
(c) Greatly increased use of indigenous solid fuels having low calorific value (lignite and bituminous shales).

Consumption

Total domestic energy consumption in 1980 is estimated to increase to 78 million tonnes of oil equivalent, as illustrated in Figure 14.3, Table SA10.4,

4. The Law of the Plan makes no direct reference to the increasing energy deficit in that period.

Figure 14.3. *Energy Consumption by Sector for 1975 and Forecast for 1980*

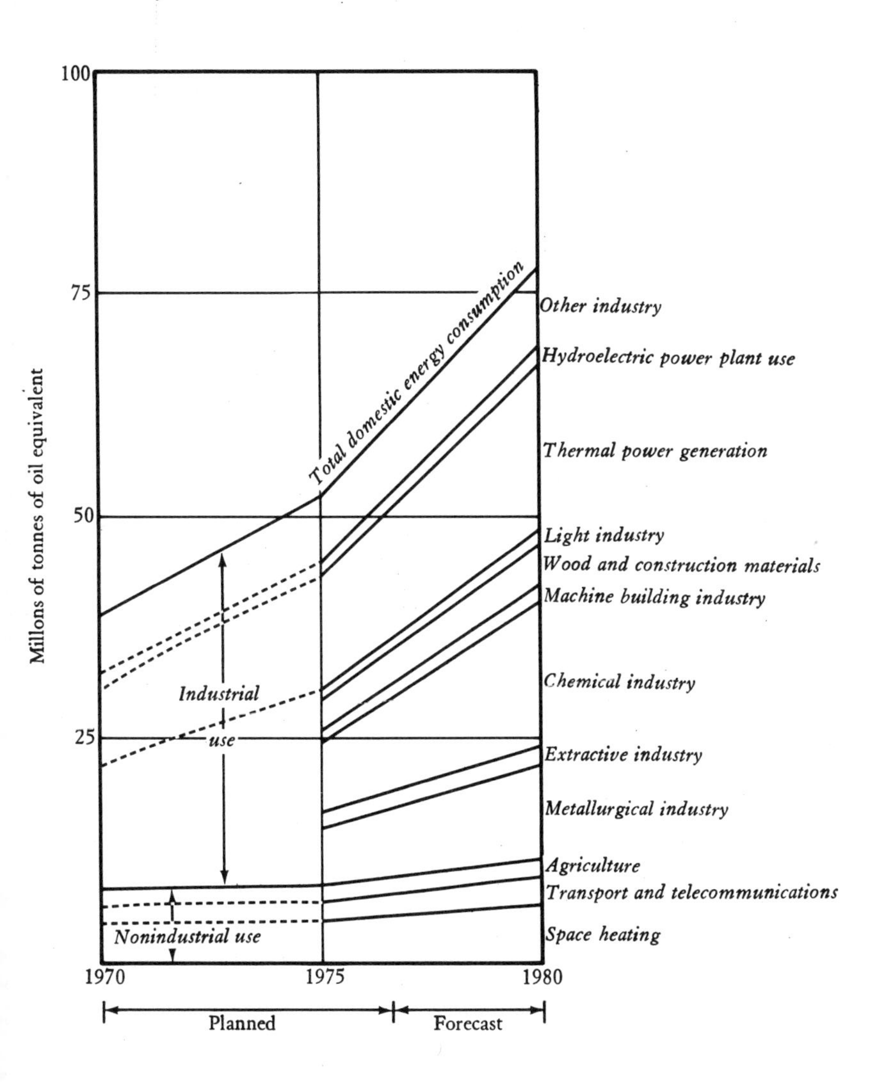

Note: Dashed lines represent World Bank estimates; solid lines represent actual data.

and the figures below, which are World Bank estimates using percentage distributions published by the Romanian government.

	1975	*1980*
Total	52.1	78.0
Industrial sector	43.4	66.4
Nonindustrial sector	8.7	11.6

The internal energy consumption will expand substantially because of a planned massive expansion of metallurgical and petrochemical industries and thermal power generation (Figure 14.3). Iron and steel production is forecast to increase from about 9.5 million tonnes in 1975 to 17 million tonnes in 1980, necessitating imports of around 7 million tonnes of coking coal or metallurgical coke in 1980. Petroleum refining capacity is planned to increase from its 1976 level of 23 million tonnes of primary distillation capacity to 38 million tonnes in 1980.

The projected domestic consumption estimates are conservative, since they allow for substantial targeted reductions in energy consumption in the industrial sector, amounting to 11.4 million tonnes of "conventional fuel" (coal equivalent)[5] and also for a substantial targeted recovery of waste heat, amounting to 6.7 million tonnes of conventional fuel.[6]

Production

The 1976–80 Plan includes specific production targets for four energy sources (Table 14.5). It is evident that most of the increases in energy

5. The targets for reduction of industrial energy consumption (in percentage of 1975 levels) are given below (n.a., not applicable):

Subsector	*Fuel*	*Electric power*
Mining extractive industry	23	1– 2
Metallurgical industry	14	10–11
Machine-building industry	26	18–19
Chemical industry	11.5	20–22
Wood and construction material industry	13	5– 6
Light industry	14.8	13–14
Food industry	13.8	12
Consumption in electric power plants	n.a.	7.5 (at least)

Source: Ioan Herescu, "Development of the Power Base," *Revista Economica*, July 16 and 23, 1976).

6. The target for recovery of waste heat amounts to 5 million tonnes of crude oil equivalent. Because of the inadequacy of the World Bank's present information, however, it is impossible to measure energy utilization in individual industries. The targets for recovery of waste heat were increased in 1977, but the total effect of the expected increased recovery on the energy balance is marginal.

Table 14.5. *Plan Targets for Energy Resources, 1976–80*

Resource	*1976*	*1977*	*1978*	*1979*	*1980*
Electric energy (terawatt hours)	57.5	63.1	65–67.7	70 –73.4	75–78.8
Coal, net (millions of tonnes)	29.6	33.5	38–40.7	45.5–48.2	53–56.6
Petroleum extracted (millions of tonnes)	14.7	14.8	15.1	15.3	15.5
Methane gas extracted (billions of cubic meters)	26.8	27.8	26.8	26.8	26.8

production in the five years will come from coal[7] and from electric energy production.[8] Crude oil production is planned to increase very slightly above current levels and to remain at about 15 million tonnes a year. Most of the fields are in an advanced state of depletion, and much of the present production is obtained by secondary recovery methods from partially or nearly depleted oil fields. Any increases in production are expected to come from more advanced secondary and tertiary recovery programs, such as the one recently announced that would allow recovery of an additional 2 million tonnes, rather than from new discoveries. This is so despite the existence of an active exploration program that includes drilling exploratory wells to depths of 8,000 meters. Important new oil and gas reserves may be discovered on the continental shelf of the Black Sea, where the first exploratory wells are now being drilled. Given the time required to develop offshore reserves, however, any offshore production is unlikely to have a significant effect on the availability of gas and oil in Romania during 1976–80.

The Plan permits new gas connections only to the petrochemical industry,

7. For coal production, the 1976–80 Plan includes three targets: (a) For coal and anthracite, a production level of 9.4 million tonnes by 1980 versus 7.5 million tonnes in 1975, (b) For bituminous shales, production to begin during the plan period and to reach 2.5 million tonnes by 1980; and (c) For lignite and brown coal, production to rise very rapidly from 20 million tonnes in 1975 to 47 million tonnes by 1980.

8. The developing structure of electric energy production has been projected as shown below (in percentages):

	1975	*1980*	*1985*
Hydroelectric plants	17	18.4	20.7
Nuclear plants	0	0	7.3
Thermoelectric plants using coal	29.4	44.0	57.6
Thermoelectric plants using gas and fuel oil	52	33	8.7
Waste heat recovery	1.6	4.6	5.7

Source: Herescu, "Development of the Power Base."

and production is expected to be held at a constant level to conserve reserves. Other energy resources have only limited potential. For example, geothermal energy is still at the experimental stage and will not affect energy production during the plan period. The availability of wood and other vegetable fuels is limited to somewhat over 3 million tonnes annually on a sustainable yield basis, as determined by the national program to conserve and develop forestry resources. The government's own schedule for the operation of the first nuclear facility has been pushed to the early 1980s.

With regard to hydropower, it is expected that by 1980, 57 percent of the economically feasible hydrocapacity will have been developed (versus 37 percent in 1975), generating about 14 terawatt-hours. Thermal power generation should increase to about 61 terawatt-hours. The production of thermoelectric power under the management of the Ministry of Electrical Energy, however, is expected to consume a total of 19 million tonnes of oil equivalent by 1980 (Table SA10.4), almost a quarter of total domestic energy consumption. This also demonstrates the strong dependence of the subsector on coal and lignite production.

It is evident that the economy's requirements for energy during the five-year plan, and as discussed later during the longer-term as well, will be for thermal and hydrogenerated electric power and coal lignite production (Figure 14.4). An increase in the production of lignite of the targeted size can only come, however, from a rapid growth of open-cast mining in the Rovinari area and other areas of Oltenia, and the whole planned program is geared to a very tight delivery schedule for new equipment. The development of new mines is also integrated with the construction of new power stations to burn the lignite. The open-cast mining system uses electrically powered mobile bucket-wheel excavators of German design, largely manufactured in Romania in cooperation with a West German firm. These are very large pieces of equipment, the largest in use in Romania, with a mining capacity of 2,000 cubic meters per hour. A delay of six months in commissioning a new excavator would result in a loss of production of around 1.5 million tonnes of lignite. This is equal to about 250,000 tonnes of oil, which would presumably have to be made up in oil imports, or an equivalent amount of production elsewhere in the economy would be lost. It is thus apparent that any substantial delays in delivering and commissioning new mining machinery or the new power stations to burn the lignite will have other economic repercussions. A setback in implementing the lignite production targets already occurred in 1976, when not only did production not increase, but, because of delays in commissioning new plants, it reached only about 95 pecrent of 1975 levels, which in turn were below 1974 levels.

Figure 14.4. *Net Primary Energy Consumption, 1950–80*

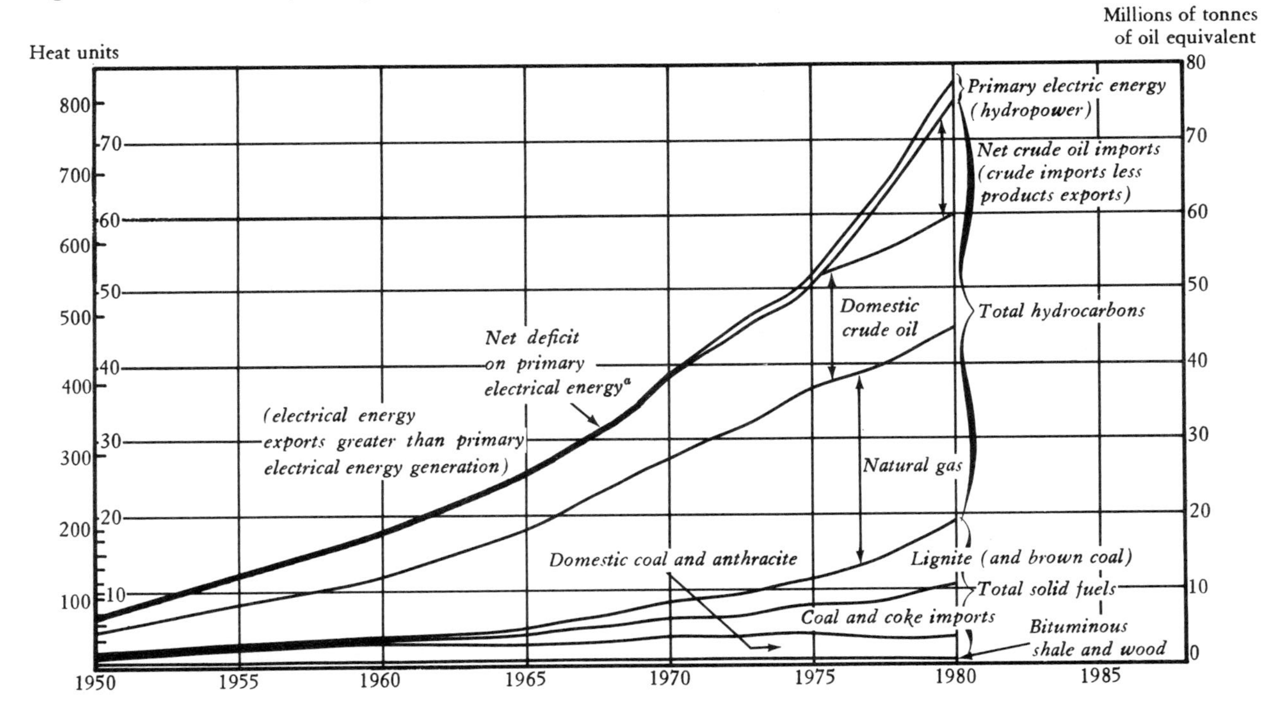

a. That is, electrical energy exports greater than primary electrical energy generation.

Energy balance in 1980

Romania's energy requirements and projected production of energy resources are outlined in Table 14.6. Production levels assume successful target implementation of the 1976–80 Plan. Oil imports are based on a historical relation of primary petroleum products to primary distillation capacity during 1970–75. Projected to 1980, an estimated 36 million tonnes of crude oil will be required for the targeted refining capacity (above), requiring importation of about 20.5 million tonnes of crude oil in 1980.

Romania imports the bulk of its coke and coal requirements from the USSR, Poland, and Czechoslovakia, with lesser amounts from the Federal Republic of Germany and the United States. Crude oil is imported principally from Iran and Iraq, with lesser amounts from Libya and Algeria. The actual prices paid for these imports are not known, nor can reliable forecasts be made of the 1980 price levels of these commodities. Nevertheless, if coke and coking coal are assumed to be worth US$50 per tonne on the same basis, the Romanian economy will have an external cost of about US$2.3 billion for energy imports in 1980 (in constant 1976 prices). Crude oil imports alone are expected to increase from about 14 percent of imports from convertible areas in 1975 to about 33 percent in 1980. Such substantial increases would obviously further strain Romania's already limited available convertible currency and would create additional pressure to improve export performance to pay the energy bill.

Table 14.6. *Energy Requirements and Production in 1980*
(millions of tonnes of oil equivalent)

Energy source	*Production*	*Exports*	*Supply available for local consumption*	*Total domestic consumption*	*Energy deficit = imports*
Solid fuels	12.6	—	12.6	19.3	6.7
Hydrocarbons	40.9	5.2	35.7	56.3	20.6
Electrical energy (hydropower)	2.9	0.6[a]	2.3	2.4	0.1
Total	*56.4*	*5.8*	*50.6*	*78.0*	*27.4*

a. Includes exports of electrical energy from plants burning solid fuels and hydrocarbons. When these are taken into account, no energy deficit in hydropower is anticipated, and the deficits for the subgroups, solid fuels, and hydrocarbons will be slightly higher.

Source: Rounded from Table SA10.2.

Figure 14.5. *Net Primary Energy Production for 1965–75 and Forecast for 1975–80*

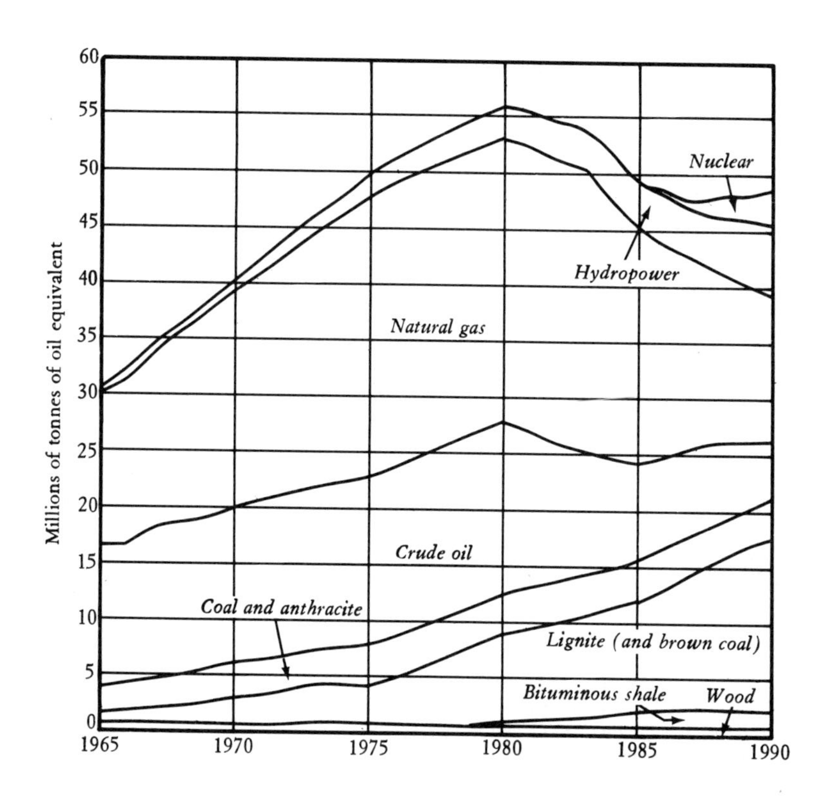

To secure the long-term supply of key energy resources, the government recently moved swiftly in two large commercial ventures. First, an agreement was made with Kuwait to invest US$1.25 billion, including the construction of a refinery in the Black Sea and securing oil for it to meet demands of the Romanian market, as well as to export products with a high value added. Second, an investment is to be made in a U.S. mine operation that would provide Romania with about 27 million tonnes of high-grade metallurgical coal over ten years, half of it at cost.[9] The reported total value of this transaction would be approximately US$2 billion.

Long-Term Energy Requirements and Resources

The data and discussion in this section are taken from a long-term forecast of Romania's energy supply and demand for 1980–90, which was carried out by the World Bank to see whether the energy deficit is likely to reverse after 1980. As illustrated in Figure 14.5, this study indicates that Romania's energy deficit would actually worsen in the long run (after 1980), in the face of a demand increasing at least at a constant rate, but with a declining primary energy production. Romania's long-term energy position is shown by the following World Bank estimates, in millions of tonnes of oil equivalent.

	1985	*1990*
Total production	50	49
Total consumption	109	154
Domestic energy shortfall	59	105

This forecast is based on an assumed growth in total consumption of domestic energy resources of 7 percent a year.[10] The assumptions on the supply of energy resources are more complex and are discussed below. The

9. The indicated current price for that coal was US$63 a tonne.

10. Consumption was estimated by establishing the historic relation between the growth of gross national product (GNP) and energy consumption in Romania; the overall energy demand was growing at about 7.5 percent. For planning purposes, the government is projecting a 7 percent annual growth of energy demand in the 1976–80 Plan, the difference probably being accounted for by government's plan to reduce specific energy consumption across the whole spectrum of industry, and to institute a large program of waste heat recovery. Allowing for the possibility of success in this policy, the growth rate of 7 percent has been used for the long-term estimates. Even with the expected lower economic growth rate in the 1980s and with increased conservation that might reduce the present rate of increase of energy consumption to 5 percent a year, the main conclusions derived from these estimates would remain.

Figure 14.6. *Forecast of Energy Consumption and Production to 1990*

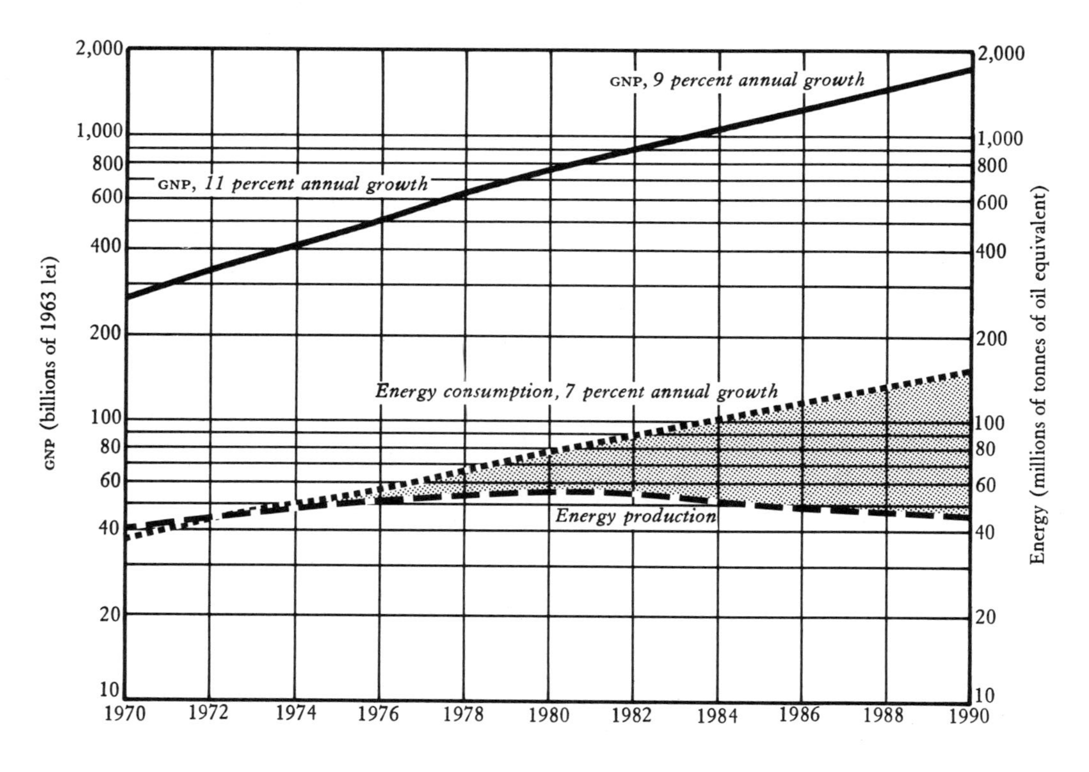

estimates of primary energy production up to 1995, by energy source and also in thermal equivalent of tonnes of oil equivalent, are given in Figure 14.6 and Table SA10.5.

The long-range production forecasts for crude oil and natural gas represent an estimate on what is likely to happen based upon the known history and characteristics of the Romanian oil and gas fields. As already noted, no information on oil and gas reserves is publicly available. Also, no production targets are available beyond 1980. Although the forecasts in this section could easily be incorrect by as much as 20 percent either way, or even more in the later years, the overall conclusion drawn from them could only be invalidated by large new oil and gas discoveries, which could yield some 50 million tonnes of oil equivalent by 1990. This would not affect the short-run conclusions, however, because of the lead time necessary to develop production on this scale. Although discoveries of new oil and gas fields on such a scale are possible, it seems unlikely that they could be made on the land and must therefore depend on the success of offshore exploration in the Black Sea. Production of this order of magnitude—equal to 1 million barrels of crude oil a day or 5,700 million cubic feet of natural gas a day—would imply recoverable reserves on the order of 1,000 million tonnes or 7.3 billion barrels of crude: that is, more than four times the total amount of crude oil produced from the Ploiesti region up to 1968. Discovery of such extensive reserves in the relatively restricted area of the Romanian continental shelf appears unlikely.

Long-range planning, therefore, indicates a further shift in the primary energy supply from natural gas and petroleum to lignite. Production is planned to rise rapidly and to stabilize at 115 million tonnes in 1990. Reserves are sufficient to maintain this level of production for more than thirty years, during which time lignite will be the principal fossil fuel resource of Romania. It will account for about 40 to 43 percent of primary energy production in 1990–95. A new source of energy, nuclear power, should also be providing a substantial contribution by 1995—approximately 6 million tonnes of oil equivalent (or about 13 percent of primary energy production in that year), almost equal to that of hydropower and natural gas.

Environmental Considerations

The planned shift from petroleum-based fuels to lignite in the Romanian economy will have an important environmental impact. The principal lignite mining area is in the district of Gorj in the southwestern part of the country, the open-cast mines are located in the Rovinari coal field, and the underground lignite mines are situated in the Motru area, some 15 kilometers west of Rovinari. Both coal fields are located near the Jiu River and its tributaries, and, in fact, it has been necessary to dam and divert the river to develop open-cast mining on the anticipated scale. The area to be mined is covered by good farming land in the Jiu valley, and there are numerous villages along the roads. It is estimated that by 1990, 30,000 hectares of prime agricultural land will have been used for industrial purposes, and ultimately one-half the total area of the district will have been mined. There are already serious problems with air and water pollution from sulfur dioxide, power station fly ash, and from coal dust in the rivers. Dewatering of the mines has led to a lowering of the groundwater table so that the water supply must be secured by special works.

Remedial measures to minimize the environmental consequences of large-scale mining and power generation are being undertaken. Soil from the mines and ash from the power stations are dumped in worked-out areas, and the land is leveled and replanted; high smokestacks are provided at the power stations to help disperse fumes; and electrostatic precipitators are to be installed to reduce the emission of fly ash. New housing is being provided for those displaced by mining operations, and villages are being provided with deeper water wells. Nevertheless, the dislocations and environmental damage resulting from the rapid development of lignite mining are obvious and undeniable.

Outside the mining areas, the shift from natural gas to lignite as the prime domestic and industrial fuel has already led to severe atmospheric pollution in the towns and cities. This is particularly noticeable at certain times of the year in the Danube plain, when atmospheric temperature inversions are common. It appears that no smokeless solid fuel is available even in Bucharest, which shares the common problem of urban air pollution.

Atmospheric pollution will also be increased by the change from low-sulfur domestic crude oil to the high-sulfur heavy oil imported from the Persian Gulf area. Although some of the sulfur content of lighter petroleum distillates is removed and recovered in the refining process, the sulfur content of the heavy fuel oil is not removed.

To prevent atmospheric pollution in urban areas from becoming worse during the current five-year plan, countermeasures are planned. Some relief could be obtained through continually providing the housing sector (which represents only a very small proportion of total energy consumption in Romania) with electricity from thermoelectric stations, natural gas, and smokeless fuel, as well as through better consumption of solid fuels in industrial premises.

15

The Tourism Sector

ROMANIA IS ENDOWED WITH A WIDE VARIETY of tourism assets. Along its 245-kilometer coast on the Black Sea are many wide beaches covered with fine sand, and the Danube Delta, stretching over 4,300 square kilometers, shelters a wealth of flora and fauna.

In the center of the country, the Transylvanian plateau is encircled by the Carpathian Mountains, with summits of over 2,000 meters and picturesque valleys. Conveniently located near Bucharest, the scenic Prahova Valley in the southern Carpathians is the seat of Romania's oldest mountain resort area, starting with the towns of Sinaia, Predeal, and Busteni. The Carpathian Mountains also contain numerous fresh- and saltwater springs and lakes, with mineral water originating in faults at various depths. There are more than 120 resorts for balneoclimatic therapy, some of them specializing in geriatric treatment.

Romania has a rich history with interesting archaeological remains and many treasures of medieval art. The monasteries of Bucovina in Northern Moldavia, whose exterior walls are wholly covered with sixteenth-century frescoes, have drawn special attention from Unesco and are probably the most distinctive monuments of Romanian art.

The tourist assets of the country might not have been realized, however, had the Romanians not developed a rather advanced tourism infrastructure to accommodate an increasing flow of domestic and foreign visitors. Romania is located on the international roads which connect northern and western Europe with the Balkan Peninsula and the Middle East and can easily be reached by air, rail, and road as well as on ships going down the Danube or landing at Constanta on the Black Sea. Accommodations of all types are being built— from deluxe hotels to mountain chalets and camping sites—and a range of holiday arrangements can now be organized through the network of tourist offices and agencies controlled by the Ministry of Tourism.

Government Policy

The government's recognition of the importance of tourism in the economy is rather recent and is marked by three major developments in the early 1970s: the formation of a Ministry of Tourism charged with the responsibility for formulating and coordinating tourism policy; the institution of the sector as "productive" in the national accounts as of 1971; and the establishment of most of the fifteen tourism offices around the world to promote actively the tourism attractions of the country.

The thrust of the Romanian tourism strategy is to develop higher-yield, higher-quality, and more diversified tourist facilities. Accommodation capacity is allocated to local and foreign tourism based on contracts signed with trade unions and foreign travel agencies in the fall of the year preceding the tourist season and on projections of the flow of independent tourists and their modes of transport. If actual demand by foreign tourists exceeds that planned, it is met, where necessary, by adjusting the allocation of facilities among local and foreign tourists, not only because of the need for the foreign exchange brought in by foreign tourists, but also because of the desire to satisfy foreign tourist demands. To control better the amount of foreign tourism and to make it compatible with the planned growth of the sector, various measures have encouraged organized group tourism under the auspices of various agencies of the Ministry of Tourism.

Of all regulations concerning international tourism, the foreign exchange rate and related regulations are expected to have the most important effect on demand. They favor organized tourism, which is more compatible with the planned nature of the economy. On October 2, 1974, the tourism rate of exchange was revalued by 17 percent to lei 12:US$1 (from lei 14.38:US$1), increasing the spread between the tourism rate of exchange and the conversion coefficient for foreign trade transactions. Officially, this revaluation was undertaken to achieve a purchasing power parity for tourist services in Romania and western Europe. There is not yet enough information to study the effect of this move on the foreign demand for tourism services, but it is reasonable to assume that the revaluation of the tourist rate would adversely affect the number of tourists who have to exchange their currencies in Romania. Organized group tourism would not be affected, because these tourism services are paid for in advance in foreign currencies. To compete effectively with other areas in southern Europe whose tourism assets are equally attractive, the authorities have also maintained competitive tariffs, and the implicit exchange rate of the package deals offered has been favorable and closer to the official trading rate. When demand is relatively inelastic, however, as with tourists visiting for a health cure or some other specific reason, the revaluation may have increased the economic returns to the government.

Since the average daily expenditures of individual tourists are higher than those of tourists in organized tours, the government has encouraged individual tourists in the country. At the same time, compulsory currency exchange regulations for individual tourists (amounting to US$10 a day per capita, or the equivalent in other currencies) discouraged tourists not wishing to purchase accommodations.

Importance of the Tourism Sector

Although international tourism has made a definite and increasing contribution to the national foreign exchange earnings, its overall effect on the balance of payments is still very small. As shown in Table 15.1, foreign exchange earnings from international tourism have increased from US$27.9 million in 1967 to US$188 million in 1975. The share of convertible currencies in these earnings was US$21 million in 1967 and US$134 million in

Table 15.1. *Effect of Tourism on the Balance of Payments, 1967 and 1971–75*
(millions of U.S. dollars)

Item	*1967*	*1971*	*1972*	*1973*	*1974*	*1975*
Relations with all areas						
Receipts from international tourism	27.9	76.9	96.0	134.4	152	188
Payments connected to Romanian tourism abroad[a]	2.0	15.3	24.9	38.8	53	47
Net effect	25.9	61.6	71.1	95.6	99	141
Relations with convertible area only						
Receipts from international tourism	21.0	51.8	68.0	96.2	102	134
Payments connected to Romanian tourism abroad[a]	0.1	9.4	17.2	21.5	22	19
Net effect	20.9	42.4	50.8	74.7	80	115

a. Includes promotional and other government expenditure to bring foreign tourists to Romania.

Source: Ministry of Finance; data provided during discussions with the authors.

1975, or slightly over two-thirds of the total, an average annual increase of 26 percent throughout 1967–75. When compared with earnings from merchandise exports, however, the contribution of the sector is small and has actually declined in relative terms to less than 5 percent of export earnings in convertible currencies in 1975 from 6 percent in 1971. This reflects Romania's reliance on industrial exports to finance the import program.

Similarly, the importance of the sector in the economy, as measured by allocations of investment funds (one-tenth of 1 percent) and its share of total employment, is small. Total sectoral investment in 1971–75 amounted to 5.1 billion lei, or less than 1 percent of investment. The average number of people employed directly by the Ministry of Tourism and its subsidiaries amounts to about 54,000 or an insignificant five-tenths of 1 percent of total employment.[1] No information is available on the sector's contribution to national income, but presumably it would also be minute.

Organization of the Tourism Sector

The Ministry of Tourism, through its thirty-nine district offices or various subsidiaries, owns about two-thirds of all lodging establishments considered suitable for international tourists, as shown in Table 15.2. The Ministry coordinates the activities of the various agencies that own assets in the tourism sector.

The highest tourism policymaking body in the Ministry is the Management Council, a collective body of thirty-nine members from all ministries and agencies concerned directly or indirectly with tourism (Figure 15.1). The Policy Council, whose members are appointed by the Council of Ministers, defines the broad guidelines and leaves responsibility for more detailed policy formulation to an Executive Board. The Minister of Tourism presides over both the Policy Council and the Executive Board. Except for Bucharest, Brasov, and the seaside, the Ministry's district offices are responsible for administering local tourism assets and facilities.

Demand for, and Supply of, Tourism Services

Foreign tourism remains the minor component of tourist traffic in Romania. Of a total of 33.5 million tourist nights spent in 1975 (Table SA11.1), a full 72 percent was spent by Romanian tourists; of the re-

1. A strong seasonal variation exists with a maximum of 73,000 employees in the peak season.

Table 15.2. *Ownership of Lodging Establishments, 1975*

	Ownership						
	Ministry of Tourism	*Ministry of Internal Trade*	*Judet Popular Councils*	*Central Union of Consumer Coopera-tives*	*Central Economic Office Carpati-* BTT-MAI	*Trade unions*	*Total*
All lodging establishments	*1,786*	*58*	*114*	*211*	*203*	*27*	*2,399*
Hotels	431	29	62	23	50	1	596
Motels	19	4	—	24	—	—	47
Villas	60	4	—	—	126	—	190
Establishments for rest and treatment	1,043	—	38	—	9	25	1,115
Inns	2	2	4	32	1	—	41
Chalets	153	11	3	37	6	—	210
Camping	78	8	7	95	11	1	200
Establishments for international tourism	587	7	5	40	113	—	752
Hotels	385	4	4	2	50	—	445
Motels	16	—	—	6	—	—	22
Villas	52	—	—	—	56	—	108
Establishments for rest and treatment	56	—	—	—	—	—	56
Inns	2	—	1	9	—	—	12
Chalets	19	2	—	—	1	—	22
Camping	57	1	—	23	6	—	87

Source: Ministry of Tourism; data provided during discussions with the authors.

Figure 15.1. *Organization of the Ministry of Tourism*

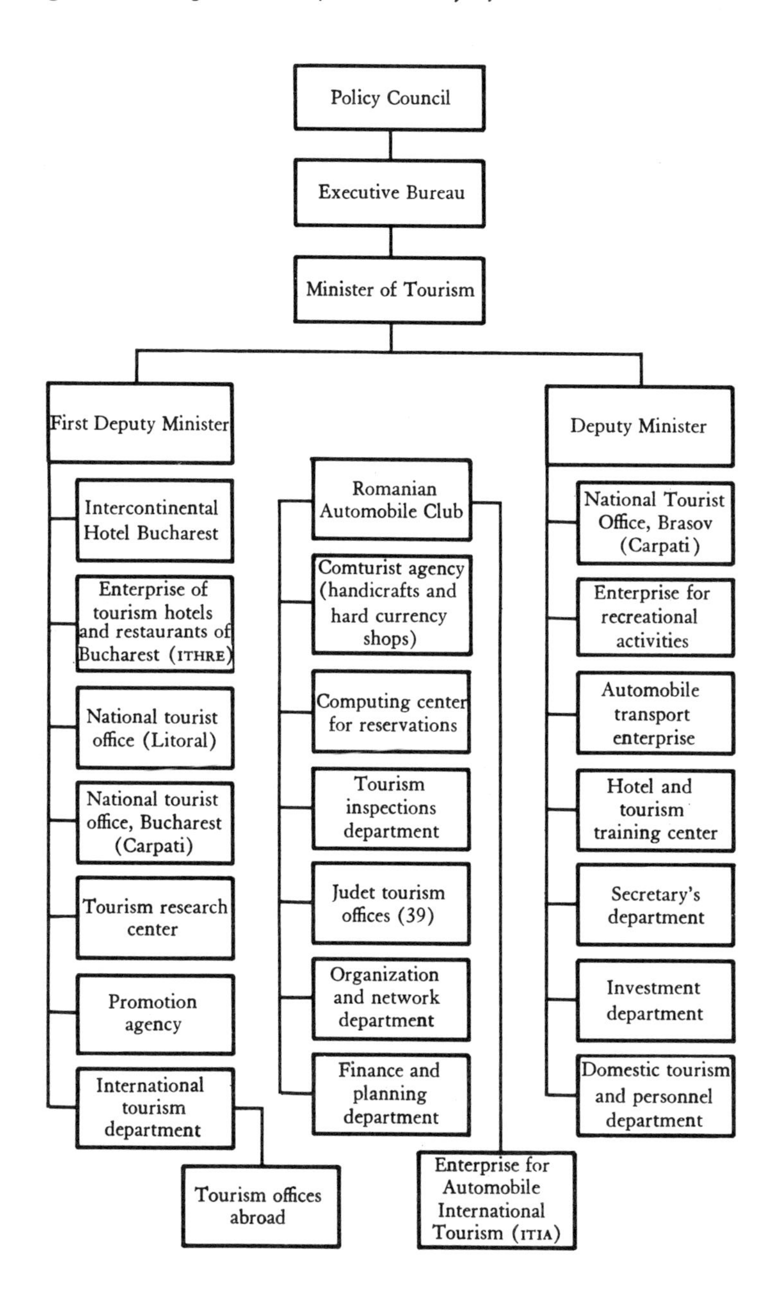

Table 15.3. *Foreign Tourist Arrivals in Romania, by Origin, 1965 and 1970–75*

	1965		*1970*		*1971*	
	Thousands	*Percentage*	*Thousands*	*Percentage*	*Thousands*	*Perce- age*
Tourists from socialist countries	475.0	70.3	1,911.2	83.5	2,213.3	81.
Organized tourism	105.9	15.7	218.8	9.6	215.5	7.
Tourists from nonsocialist countries	200.7	29.7	378.3	16.5	513.1	18.
Organized tourism	76.7	11.3	206.0	9.0	290.1	10.
Total tourist arrivals	675.7	100.0	2,289.5	100.0	2,726.4	100.
Organized tourism	182.6	27.0	424.8	18.6	505.6	18.

Note: Includes tourists in transit and border visitors.
Source: Ministry of Tourism; data provided during discussions with the authors.

mainder, 3.7 million nights (11 percent) were spent by tourists from socialist countries and 5.7 million (17 percent) by tourists from nonsocialist countries. The number of foreign tourists visiting Romania peaked in 1974 at 3.8 million and has been declining since, but the total tourist nights spent in the country have been increasing steadily.

Foreign tourism

Over 3.2 million foreigners visited Romania in 1975 (Table SA11.2). This is a very high figure considering the fact that only 120,000 foreigners arrived in 1961, 675,000 in 1965, and 2.3 million in 1970. These figures, however, and the very high growth rates they suggest (average annual growth of more than 50 percent between 1961 and 1965, 28 percent between 1965 and 1970, and about 7 percent between 1970 and 1975), reflect very different situations, depending on whether the foreigners came from socialist or nonsocialist countries. As shown in Table 15.3, socialist countries have been numerically the most important source for visitors to Romania. These high figures conceal the fact, however, that a great proportion of visitors from socialist countries were in Romania either in transit (1.2 million out of 3.2 million in 1974) or as border visitors. Only slightly more than 10 percent of them were members of organized tours who made arrangements for their stay through agencies of the Romanian Ministry of Tourism. The numbers of visitors from nonsocialist countries, on the other hand, increased at an average annual growth rate of 13.4 percent

1972		*1973*		*1974*		*1975*	
Thousands	*Percentage*	*Thousands*	*Percentage*	*Thousands*	*Percentage*	*Thousands*	*Percentage*
2,297.4	79.1	2,769.2	82.9	3,181.5	83.2	2,575.2	80.3
240.7	8.3	281.6	8.4	335.0	8.8	361.9	11.3
606.0	20.9	573.1	17.1	643.7	16.8	630.7	19.7
337.5	11.6	352.2	10.5	369.0	9.6	423.9	13.2
2,903.4	100.0	3,342.3	100.0	3,825.3	100.0	3,205.9	100.0
578.2	19.9	633.8	18.9	704.0	18.4	785.8	24.5

between 1965 and 1970 and about 11 percent between 1970 and 1975. Only a marginal proportion of these were in transit (4,100 in 1974), and since 1970 more than half of them have made arrangements for their stay through agencies of the Ministry of Tourism. The frequency of such arrangements has increased in the most recent years, possibly in response to the 1974 policy measures (above).

The statistics on tourist nights provide a truer picture of foreign tourism, however, and here the predominance of visitors from nonsocialist countries is strongly evident. Foreign-organized tourism accounted for about 80 percent of registered tourist nights, and, of this, 67 percent was from nonsocialist countries. Among the nonsocialist countries, the Federal Republic of Germany is by far the most important source of tourists (Tables SA11.1 and SA11.3).

Domestic tourism

Domestic tourism has increased substantially with growing income levels in Romania (Chapter 9). Measures have been taken to obtain higher occupancy during off season by offering domestic tourists discount prices and the accommodations used by the international tourists during the peak season.[2] For this reason, legislation has been adopted to spread holidays

2. About 70 percent of foreign tourists visit the Black Sea, most of them during the summer.

more evenly throughout the year. Particular emphasis is placed on promoting health and spa resorts that are open all year and tourism in the hinterland. As a result, Romanian tourists account for about 95 percent of tourist traffic in health and spa resorts, 85 percent in mountain resorts, and 84 percent in the other localities. Another trend is the Romanian tourists' growing sophistication as their own incomes have increased. They are now asking for better accommodations, better means of transport, and access to all the best resorts.

Visits abroad have increased, too: from 321,200 Romanians traveling to other countries in 1972 to 477,000 in 1975 (Table SA11.4). The increase has been particularly substantial for tourists going to neighboring socialist countries, except Yugoslavia. Tourism to nonsocialist countries decreased slightly between 1972 and 1975 and represented less than 10 percent of Romanian tourism abroad in 1975.

Supply of Tourist Facilities and Services

In 1975 there were 2,399 lodging establishments with about 86,000 rooms and 279,000 beds in Romania. Only 747 of these establishments, with about 59,000 rooms and 159,000 beds, however, offered standards suitable for international tourists. The distribution of this capacity between types of establishments and tourist areas is shown in Table SA11.5. As far as the regional distribution of capacity is concerned, the striking feature is the concentration at the seaside. In 1975 the Black Sea coast accounted for more than half of the total supply of beds and two-thirds of the beds suitable for international tourists.

The 1971–75 Plan provided for the establishment of facilities with 35,000 beds, of which about half were located at the seaside. The average cost per bed was about 70,000 lei at the seaside, 115,000 lei in the mountain resorts, and 150,000 lei in spa and health resorts. (All costs are in 1963 prices and do not include cost of land and infrastructure, such as power, water, and sewerage.) As in other sectors, Romanian policy has minimized the foreign exchange component of investments in the tourism sector. It never exceeds 20 to 25 percent for first-class accommodations and 30 percent for deluxe accommodations.

The data provided by the Ministry of Tourism on utilization of the capacity during 1970–75 (Table SA11.6) suggest a definite improvement, not only for the sector as a whole, with bed-occupancy rates increasing from 67.1 percent in 1970 to 76.7 percent in 1975, but also for each single form of accommodation. In comparing capacity utilization with other countries, these figures have to be interpreted with great prudence, however, as they measure capacity utilization only during the period when accommodation is available to the public and do not reflect the strong seasonal element affecting the tourist industry, particularly at the seaside.

To get a more accurate picture of the situation, specific bed-occupancy rates in the main tourist areas are computed in Table SA11.7, and these take into account the fraction of the year in which the various lodging establishments are open. They show interesting disparities, both among tourist areas as well as among forms of accommodation. Although annual capacity utilization for the whole country was 40.8 percent (36.6 percent in establishments for international tourists), it was only 24.8 percent (25.7 percent in establishments for international tourists) at the seaside, where most of the lodging establishments are closed except for the four-month summer season. In health and spa resorts, mountain resorts, and other localities, however, capacity utilization on an annual basis was estimated at 67.5 percent, 56.4 percent, and 53.5 percent, respectively (65.0 percent, 62.4 percent, and 64.2 percent in establishments for international tourists). This reflects the importance of rest and treatment in domestic tourism, as well as the efforts of the government in encouraging off-season tourism. Further improvements in the utilization of facilities are still required, though.

Another area needing much improvement is the quality of tourist services. The sector was expanded initially without a parallel intensive effort to develop a human resource infrastructure to meet the quality requirements of international tourists. As a result, service and managerial performance in the sector have lagged. Corrective actions have been taken, but their effect is still limited in relation to the large need for improvements. The most concerted effort to meet middle-level manpower requirements has been undertaken since 1971 under a United Nations Development Plan (UNDP) training project. About 15 percent of the permanent employees in the sector have attended intensive training or refresher programs under this project. The requirements for qualified higher-level technical and managerial staff in the sector, however, have not been addressed systematically yet.

Costs, Tariffs, Profits, and Control

The principal categories of costs in the tourism industry in 1974 and 1975 are broken down in Table 15.4. Overhead and depreciation account for more than 60 percent of the total. The high figures for repair and maintenance reflect the fact that most of the hotels have had to be completely renovated in recent years to improve the quality of their services. In other accounting systems, such expenditures may be handled as investments.

Tariffs are established centrally by the Ministry of Tourism and are

Table 15.4. *Principal Categories of Costs in the Tourism Industry, 1974 and 1975*
(percentage)

	Hotel industry[a]		Restaurants and public food supply[b]	
Cost category	*1974*	*1975*	*1974*	*1975*
Wages and social security contributions	18.7	19.0	45.9	46.6
Overhead	48.7	46.0	23.6	24.7
Reparation and maintenance (major works)	25.6			
Reparation and maintenance (minor works)	1.9			
Rents[c]	1.8			
Trips of official delegations	0.12			
Heat, light, water, power, and other overhead	19.3			
Transport			12.5	13.0
Depreciation	13.1	14.0	7.9	6.7
Administration and management	8.2	6.9	6.6	6.3
Promotion	3.1	—	0.3	—
Other costs	8.2	14.1	3.2	2.7

a. Includes only hotels depending on the Ministry of Tourism.

b. Includes many restaurants or establishments that do not belong to the Ministry of Tourism and cater to the needs of the local population as much as those of foreign tourists.

c. Rents are charged only for lease of premises that do not belong to the Ministry of Tourism.

Source: Ministry of Tourism; data provided during discussions with the authors.

subject to a periodic review to take into account trends in international tourism prices. In recent years, the government has raised tariffs for non-organized tourism to compare with average international prices, whereas tariffs for organized group tourism have been kept at a lower level to maintain their competitive advantage. Tariffs for domestic tourism involve a different set of criteria and may vary with those for international tourism.

Profitability has improved in recent years for deluxe and first-class hotels, which have benefited from an increase in capacity utilization and from the influx of foreign tourists who are charged full international rates. Second-class hotels, however, registered a decrease in their profitability as increased costs, particularly in wages, could not be compensated for by increased costs in domestic tariffs or in capacity utilization. The distribution of profits in the hotel industry is subject to very detailed rules. Since 1974 half of the profits have been forwarded to the national budget, about 15 percent have been retained to increase working capital; 18 percent have been transferred to the centralized investment fund of the Ministry of Tourism; about 4 percent have gone to the staff's compensation fund, to the repair and modernization fund, and to the special equipment fund; and the rest has been for miscellaneous provisions.

The Ministry of Tourism exercises a very strict control over all lodging establishments. In addition to auditing the accounts of individual units, the Ministry also assesses the efficiency of operations using several techno-economic indicators:

(a) Expenditure in lei per U.S. dollar of foreign exchange earned. The objective is to reduce the ratio for this indicator. Targets have changed substantially in recent years as a result of the devaluation of the U.S. dollar. Although a few years ago an expenditure of 20 lei per-dollar-earned was considered satisfactory, the objective now is to spend only 12 lei per dollar earned; in the peak season it seems possible to spend even less. Until recently, the tourism sector outperformed all other sectors working for exports in this respect. It now seems, however, that this advantage over other sectors is narrowing.

(b) Ratio of receipts (or profits) to the average value of fixed invested capital, as expressed in lei. The objective is to maximize this ratio. Achievement of the target established for this indicator is monitored even more closely than the first.

The 1976–80 Plan

The 1976–80 Plan provides for the creation of 46,300 beds, a 23 percent increase over the target in the 1971–75 Plan, which is already rather a large program. The total cost of the planned investment in the tourism sector for 1976–80 is 5 to 6 billion lei. Although this represents a 27 percent increase over the expenditure of the previous plan period, the share of the sector in total planned investment continues to be insignificant, about one-half of 1 percent. These allocations reflect the strong emphasis on industrialization in Romania's development strategy, as well as the government's desire for a gradual and controlled development of the sector during the plan period. A case could be made, however, for allocating more resources to a sector

Table 15.5. *Investment in the Hotel Industry, 1971–75 and 1976–80 Plans*

Location of hotels	1971–75 Plan: Millions of lei	1971–75 Plan: Percentage	1976–80 Plan: Millions of lei	1976–80 Plan: Percentage
Seaside	2,494	48.8	867	15.4
Spa and health resorts	579	11.3	1,315	23.5
Mountain resorts	417	9.7	1,527	27.2
Other tourist itineraries	1,538	30.2	1,906	33.9
Total	*5,108*	*100.0*	*5,615*	*100.0*

Source: Ministry of Tourism; data provided during discussions with the authors.

that has earnings in convertible currencies.[3] To look at one rough comparison: although in recent years investment in tourism has represented less than 1.5 percent of investment in industry, the convertible currency earnings of the tourism sector were almost 20 percent of those in industry.

The case for allocating more resources to the sector, however, cannot be based exclusively on the generation of additional net foreign exchange earnings. The data publicly available are not sufficient to establish the profitability of additional investment in tourism, and a more detailed analysis, based on occupancy rates, tariffs, and operational and investment costs, is needed before any conclusions can be reached in this respect.

As shown in Table 15.5, the 1976–80 Plan represents a radical change of emphasis in the regional distribution of investment. Only 15.4 percent of the planned investment will be allocated to the seaside; mountain resorts will receive 27.2 percent; spa and health resorts, 23.5 percent; and other towns along tourist itineraries the biggest relative share, 33.9 percent. This new emphasis on the hinterland has not only been stimulated by the problems of seasonality and lower occupancy rates encountered in the seaside, but by studies showing that tourist demand is becoming more diversified, with a greater proportion of tourists expressing interest in organized tours to different parts of the country. Diversification is also seen as a way to prevent a reduction in the average length of stay of foreign tourists—and possibly to increase it. The 1976–80 Plan will also emphasize the creation of high-quality accommodations. Quality standards will be reinforced throughout the country, and many investments will upgrade existing capacity to meet international tourism standards.

Foreign tourist arrivals are expected to increase at an average annual

3. In the past five years, these earnings have more than doubled.

Table 15.6. *Foreign Tourist Arrivals, 1974–75, and Projections, 1980*
(thousands)

	1974	*1975*	*1980*	*Average annual growth rate, 1975–80 (percent)*
Tourists from socialist countries	3,181.5	2,571	3,630	7.2
Tourists from non-socialist countries	643.7	635	770	3.9
Organized	369.0	428	555	5.4
Nonorganized	274.7	207	215	0.8
Total	*3,825.3*	*3,206*	*4,400*	*6.5*

Source: Ministry of Tourism; data provided during discussions with the authors.

rate of 6.5 percent, reaching 4.4 million in 1980 (Table 15.6). The growth rate is estimated to be about 7 percent for tourists from socialist countries and only 4 percent for those from nonsocialist countries, representing an increase from 635,000 in 1975 to 770,000 in 1980. The rather moderate growth rates in all categories, with organized tourism having a slight edge over the others, reflect the deliberate policy choices discussed earlier. The growth estimate for tourists from socialist countries has been reduced from a previous higher level (4.7 million by 1980), possibly to eliminate the favorable balance Romania has been enjoying with its partners in the Council for Mutual Economic Assistance (CMEA) in this area. Also, the estimates have not been adjusted to account for the effect of the earthquake on foreign tourism. The earthquake in March 1977 occurred at the beginning of the period when foreign reservations are confirmed. By May 1977 it was clear that over two-thirds of the expected foreign tourists had changed their holiday plans because of the earthquake.

The Romanians give higher priority to providing better and more diversified services to increase daily expenditures and are interested in increasing tourists from nonsocialist countries. Assuming that no substantial increase in the average stay of foreign tourists is to be achieved, increased daily expenditures per capita, particularly for tourists from nonsocialist countries, should play a very important role in achieving the objective assigned by the 1976–80 Plan, that of doubling gross foreign currency earnings from international tourism.

Longer-term Plans

For the 1980s the only projected expansion so far is in tourist-bed capacity. The increase planned for 1981–85 is 100,000 beds, with another 120,000 planned for 1986–90. This is quite an ambitious plan of expansion, especially if it means continuing a strategy directed toward developing higher-yield and higher-quality tourist facilities. If successful, it could more than double the sector's contribution of foreign exchange and could create new employment opportunities within the economy. Of course, domestic tourism would also benefit from such a policy but the underlying assumptions regarding domestic occupancy rates and the like are not available.

Notwithstanding the positive aspects of the sector's potential, even a doubling in activities by 1990 would have slight effect on its economic importance. And although every effort should be undertaken to make the fullest use of the national tourism assets, the potential contribution of the sector, particularly as an earner of foreign exchange, should not be overrated. It can provide a considerable sum of foreign exchange to finance the development effort, but it cannot be relied upon as a stable or major foreign exchange earner, because it is dependent on international economic conditions and is potentially volatile. Perhaps the latter characteristic is recognized by the government and explains why neither the annual nor the five-year plan includes any references to the sector. Faster and more expanded growth is not likely because of two major constraints: such sector growth would encounter strong competition from tourist services in neighboring Balkan states and would counteract the desire of the authorities for an orderly and controlled growth of tourism to ensure compatibility with plan objectives.

PART FOUR

Conclusion

16

Development Prospects

ROMANIA'S ACHIEVEMENTS HAVE SHOWN that in the 1950s and 1960s, a strong base was created for the rapid fulfillment of the economic and political goals of the country. During the 1960s the momentum of economic growth was more firmly established, and the long-term perspectives were more clearly defined.

Perspective Prognosis to 1990

The 1970s have been planned as the decisive period in the achievement of Romania's long-term development objectives. The economy is to move from a state of underdevelopment to one of economic strength. Industrial strength, in particular, is expected to be solidified, with 1990 as the target for Romania's economic parity with other eastern European economies. A per capita income of US$2,500 to US$3,000 is projected (in 1963 prices). Economic performance in 1971–75 was reviewed in Chapter 6; the record was one of the most successful in Romania's economic history. Growth targets were ambitious, but on average they were overfilled. Macroeconomic targets of the perspective and current five-year plans are reviewed in this chapter. (The 1976–80 plan targets and objectives for the major sectors were discussed in earlier chapters.)

The perspectives to 1990 were established by the Eleventh Congress of the Romanian Communist Party (RCP) in 1974 in its Directives for the 1976–80 Five-Year Plan and its guidelines for socioeconomic development in 1981–90.[1] The plan targets are given in Table 16.1. These figures were

1. *Directives of the Eleventh Congress of the Romanian Communist Party Concerning the 1976–80 Five-Year Plan and the Guidelines for Romania's Economic and Social Development over the 1981–90 Period.* (Bucharest: Meridiane Publishing House, 1975.)

Table 16.1. *Plan Targets for 1976–90*
(1990 vs. 1975)

Economic indicator	*Growth (percentage)*
National income	250–280
Gross industrial production	250–300
Gross agricultural production	50–80[a]
Investment in National Economy (five-year average)	
1975–90 vs. 1961–75	630
1981–90 vs. 1971–80	More than 100
Distribution of national income	
Consumption fund	68–70
Accumulation fund	30–32
Volume of foreign trade	200[b]
Real incomes per capita	216–252
Real remuneration	170–190
Volume of retail sales	190–240[c]

a. 1986–90 over 1971–75.
b. In 1975 prices.
c. In current prices.
Source: Directives of the Eleventh Congress of the Romanian Communist Party.

based on 1974 data and will be modified depending on the outcome of the 1976–80 Five-Year Plan.

A large, if slightly lower, share of resources are targeted for investment, mainly industry. The high growth rates of heavy industry will continue their momentum, furthering this sector's pivotal role and its contribution to Romania's social product, which should be 78 to 80 percent by 1990. Within this framework, the guidelines provide high growth rates for the engineering and chemical industries, whose contribution to gross industrial production will rise from 44 percent in 1975 to almost 50 percent in 1980 and to 55 to 60 percent by 1990. An ambitious program to develop the power resources is envisaged (Chapter 14) to meet the requirements of industrialization, coupled with an intensive drive to save energy, which is intended to contain energy consumption to about double the 1975 levels in face of a more than tripling expansion of national income.

In agriculture, emphasis will be placed on intensive development, with priority given to:

(a) The livestock subsector, whose share in total agricultural production is targeted to rise to 50 percent by 1990;
(b) Irrigation, reaching 5 million hectares by 1990, or about half of the country's arable land;

Figure 16.1. *Annual Plan Target, 1971–90*

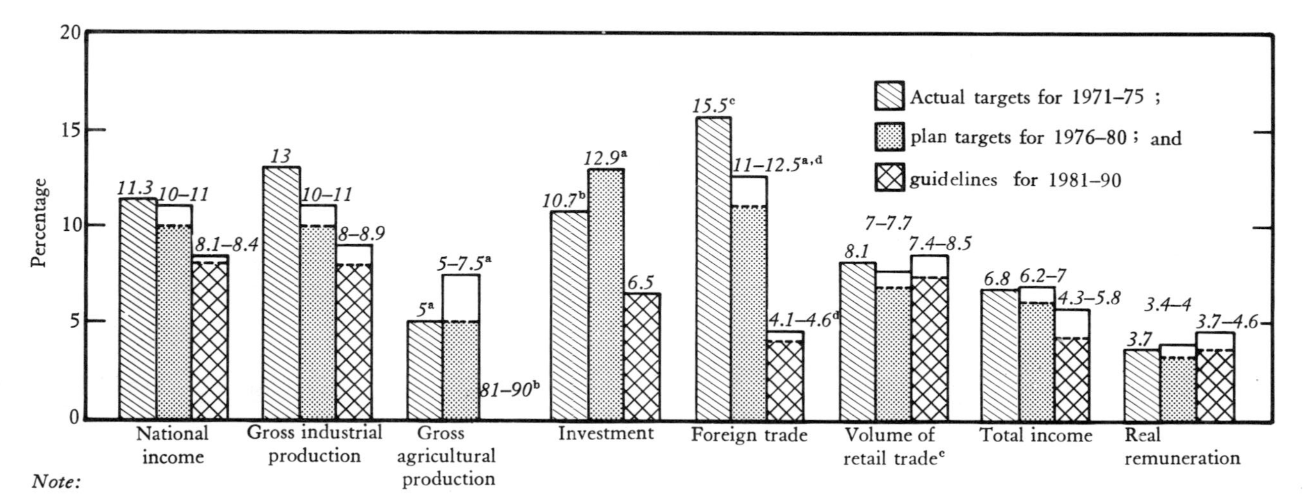

Note:

a. Five-year averages.

b. Gross agricultural output (annual average) in 1986–90 is expected to be 1.5 to 1.8 times larger than the annual average of 1971–75.

c. Current prices.

d. In 1975 prices.

Sources: Data for 1971–75 from *Anuarul Statistic*; for 1976–80, from Law (no. 4) on the Adoption of the Plan for 1976–80; and for 1981–85, from the *Directives of the Eleventh Congress of the Romanian Communist Party*.

(c) Mechanization; and
(d) Increased application of chemicals, reaching 300 to 325 kilograms per hectare by 1990 (compared with 115 kilograms in 1975).

With intensive mechanization, the bulk of Romania's manpower is expected to be released for the industrialization drive, leaving only about 12 to 15 percent of the labor force in the agricultural sector by 1990.

Improvements in both the quality and quantity of consumption are planned. Real incomes per capita are projected to increase annually by 5 to 6 percent from 1975 to 1990, and real remuneration is planned to be 1.7 to 1.9 times bigger at the end of the period. By 1990 provision of social funds (pension, health, recreation, and so forth) will have reached the level at which it accounts for 30 to 32 percent of the population's total income. The most important improvements in standard of living would be a reduced workweek (44 to 46 hours by 1980, and 40 to 42 hours by 1990) and more and improved housing. Because of the earthquake, however, the program to reduce the workweek was postponed, to begin in 1978 instead of 1977 and to end by 1982 instead of 1980.

The perspective prognosis is divided into two distinct periods with considerably different plan targets as shown by Table 16.2 and Figure 16.1.

Table 16.2. *Plan Targets and Achievements, Comparable 1963 Prices*
(lei, unless otherwise indicated)

Item	*1971–75 actual (1975 versus 1970)*	*1976–80 Directives (1980 versus 1975)*	*1976–80 Plan (1980 versus 1975)*	*1976–90 Perspective (1990 versus 1975)*
Social product	165	147–154	150–157	3.5–3.8x
National income	171	154–161	161–168.5	3.5–4.0x
Industrial production, gross	184	154–161	162–170	1.9x[a]
Agricultural production, gross[b]	125	125–134	128–144	7.3x[c]
Investments in national economy[b]	166	165–172	183.4	3.1x[a]
Volume of foreign trade[b,d]	206	172–180[e]	190–201[e]	300x[e,f]
Exports[b,d]	213	175–185[e]		
Imports[b,d]	200	160–170[e]		
Average number of employees	123.3	116–119	116–119.2	

(table continues on the following page)

Table 16.2. *Continued*

Item	*1971–75 actual*	*1976–80 Directives*	*1976–80 Plan*	*1976–90 Perspective*
Labor productivity (present work week)				
In industry	136	138–142	150–153.8	
In construction	146	150–156	150–156.9	
In railways	127	120–126	120–127.3	
Cut in material expenditures per 1,000 lei of marketable output in national industry	90.8	93– 93.5	90.5– 91.5	
Total real incomes	146	135–137	135–140	
Real incomes per capita	139			216–252
Remuneration fund		151–155		
Real remuneration	120	118–120	118–122	170–190
Real incomes of peasantry per capita	120	120–125	120–129	
Volume of retail sales[d]	148	140–145	145–147.5	2.96–3.4
Services to population	169	161–168	161–168.6	
Distribution of national income:				
Consumption fund (percent)	66	66– 67	66– 67	68–70
Accumulation fund (percent)	34	33– 34	33– 34	30–322

a. 1986–90 vs. 1971–75.
b. Five-year averages.
c. 1975–90 vs. 1971–75.
d. Current prices.
e. In 1975 prices.
f. 1990 as against 1975.

Sources: Anuarul Statistic al Republicii Socialiste Romania (Bucharest: Directia Centrala de Statistica, published yearly). Law (no. 4) on the Adoption of the United National Plan of Economic and Social Development of the Socialist Republic of Romania for 1976–80. *Official Bulletin of the Socialist Republic of Romania*, no. 65 (July 7, 1976); *Directives of the Eleventh Congress of the Romanian Communist Party.*

The high growth of 1971–75 is planned to continue its momentum throughout the 1970s under the current five-year plan, but with a lower growth rate in the 1980s. In absolute terms, though, the planned growth is still very substantial.

The 1976–80 Plan

Some of the planned levels of output for 1975, for example, in agriculture, that were used as the base for the Directives for the 1976–80 Plan were too high because of the subsequent flood damage. National income is planned to grow at an annual average real rate of 10 to 11 percent, which is only fractionally lower than the actual level achieved for 1971–75. Social product is expected to grow at 8.4 to 9.4 percent,[2] gross industrial production at 10.2 to 11.2 percent, and gross agricultural production at 5.0 to 7.6 percent. Except for agriculture, these are slightly lower than the levels previously achieved. Total investment, on the other hand, is planned to increase its rate of growth from 11.5 to 12.7 percent.

The volume of foreign trade (valued in 1975 prices) is planned to double over the period, following a doubling in prices during 1971–75. The Directives indicate that exports are planned to grow faster than imports, and an overall trade surplus is expected by 1980, especially with the convertible area. This will permit Romania to pay off a significant portion of her convertible currency foreign debt.

The indicators of the standard of living once again show rates of growth lower than those for the productive sectors, as would be expected with such a high reinvestment ratio. Until their recent revision, however, the rates were similar to those achieved in the previous plan. Total real incomes per capita are now planned to increase annually at about 7.2 percent versus an initial target of 6.2 to 7.0 percent, real wages at 5.4 percent versus the 3.4 to 4.1 percent initially planned, the real income per capita of the agricultural workers at 3.7 to 5.2 percent, and the growth of the consumption fund 8 percent.

The overall picture for 1976–80 appears to show an even more intensive industrialization drive. National income is to grow at a faster rate than social product, indicating a reduction, on average, of material inputs for each unit of output in the productive sector. Industry is still leading the way with high growth rates accounted for by large and increasing doses of investment. About 75 percent of the growth of the sector would come from increased investment, and 2,400 new plants are expected to become operational during the plan period. The policy for the past twenty years has been that the only way to achieve a multilaterally developed socialist society is through rapid industrial growth; the 1976–80 Plan continues that policy with chemicals and mechanical engineering as the major growth sectors.[3]

As a result of this growth, the structure of the economy will change further. By 1980, for example, the share of industry in social product is ex-

2. The planned lower growth rate of social product compared with national income indicates the expected decline in the portion of material expenditures because of increased efficiency in production.

3. Chapter 10 and Appendix E contain more detailed discussions of the plan for the industrial sector.

pected to increase to 69 percent from the 1975 share of 68 percent. Perhaps more important is the role of foreign trade. It is estimated that, in 1975, exports reached the high level of 27 percent of national income. By 1980 this is planned to increase to approximately 30 percent, involving Romania more deeply in world economy.

The 1981–90 perspective

The picture for the 1980s is somewhat different. Although the indexes of the standard of living continue to grow at a constant rate, the macro targets indicate a slight slowdown in the growth rate. The annual growth of national income during the decade is planned to be 8.1 to 8.4 percent, which, although lower than before, is still very high compared with the rest of the world. Similarly, growth of gross industrial production will drop to 8.0 to 8.9 percent a year from the 10.2 to 11.2 percent of the 1976–80 Plan. The growth of investment is more difficult to calculate, since data are provided only in five-year totals, but the size of the scaledown can be seen in the figures for total investment for 1976–80, which are 1.834 times larger than those of 1971–75; in 1981–90 there will be twice as much investment as in 1971–80. One estimate shows that the 1976–80 annual average growth rate of 12.7 percent is likely to be cut in half. This is consistent with the fact that the consumption fund will increase its share in national income to 68 to 70 percent for the whole 1976–90 period, which in turn implies that by 1990 the share will be even greater, and it can be assumed that by then the growth of real incomes will be close to that of the national income.[4] The targets for trade show a similar reversal of a previous trend. Trade volume for 1976–80 is planned to be twice that of 1971–75, whereas the total volume in 1990 is only three times that amount. In other words, the increase in trade over 1971–80 in absolute terms will be the same as over the entire 1981–90 period. It is estimated that with this slowdown in the rate of growth, exports will be reduced to 28 percent of national income by 1990 from 30 percent in 1980.

Additional development objectives

Both the 1976–80 Plan and the long-term perspectives indicate problems that Romania anticipates and also some directions in which the policies are intended to take the economy:

4. It is anticipated that in 1990 the real incomes will grow more than national income. Because of the relatively low growth rate of real income between 1976 and 1980, however, real incomes will increase by a smaller percentage than national income over the whole period, 1975–1990.

(a) Improving equity in regional development;
(b) Encouraging scientific and technological development;
(c) Improving work efficiency and product quality; and
(d) Reducing consumption of energy and raw materials.

The details of the plan given above are all macro growth targets, but since the late 1960s, regional development has also been a priority (Chapter 6). This priority has not been reduced as development continues, but instead has increased. It is also now being linked with a new development objective: town development and redevelopment.

The Directives devote a complete section to the "Development of Counties and Economic and Social Planning," where it states:

> The process of a balanced economic and social development of all counties and of physically planning of the territory will grow more marked under the next five-year plan, favorable conditions being ensured to a general raising of the civilization standards in all regions and a growing material level and spiritual standard of the whole people.[5]

Not only is a high growth rate desirable, but it is also essential that the benefits be distributed to all sectors. As before, the main instrument of regional equalization is industrial investment, with particular emphasis on the less-developed judets. The 1976–80 Plan envisages a further regional redistribution of industry, stating that by 1980 there should be no judet whose gross industrial output is less than the 10 billion lei in comparable prices. Of the forty judets of Romania, sixteen would have production levels between 10 to 15 billion lei, twelve between 15 to 25 billion lei, eight between 25 to 50 billion lei, and in only four judets (Brasov, Galati, Prahova, and the municipality of Bucharest) would the value of gross industrial output exceed 50 billion lei.[6] The highest average annual growth rates of production (15 percent and more) would be achieved in the industrially less-developed judets of Bistrita-Nasaud, Salaj, Tulcea, Vaslui, Covasna, Botosani, Vrancea, Gorj, and Ialomita. Industrial investment is not, however, the government's only instrument of regional equalization. As a departure from previous policy, the five-year plan also establishes the prerequisites for making each judet self-sufficient in meat and eggs.

As part of the general policy of regional development, the first stage of the National Program of Physical, Urban, and Rural Planning will be implemented. Under this program, big city growth will continue to be controlled, and a more rational geographic distribution of the population will

5. *Directives of the Eleventh Congress of the Romanian Communist Party.*

6. For distribution of judets by industrial outputs in earlier periods, see Table 6.9 and discussion in the text.

be effected by developing a network of towns and urban centers throughout the country. A total of 400 to 500 of these centers is planned for 1976–90, about 120 of them during 1976–80. The economic activities and viability of each town center would depend on its comparative advantage.

Another theme that recurs throughout the literature on the plans is that of the technicoscientific revolution that is to take place in the coming years. For example, the preamble to the 1976–80 Plan Law states:

> To obtain the objectives assigned it is planned to broaden the contribution made by Romanian scientific and technological research and development to resolution of the problems raised by fulfillment of the plan, so that the 1976–80 Five-Year Plan may be characterized as a Five-Year Plan of the technical and scientific revolution in all sectors of the national economy.[7]

Science will have several roles.[8] First, it is considered to be a major way to increase economic efficiency. Second, it is to have a leading role in creating new products and techniques to help Romania develop and utilize industrial processes that can compete with the most developed countries of the world. Emphasis is given to developing new products using local raw materials and technology.[9] Finally, it has a significant role in the search for and utilization of raw materials and energy resources.

For at least the past decade, all Romanian plans have emphasized the same problems: efficiency and quality. The 1976–80 plan is no exception, and in fact both these problems appear more critical now than when they were first raised.[10] The Directives point out that:

> Under the 1976–80 Five-Year Plan an essential target, besides the fast rate of development of material production, is the growing efficiency, the raising to a high qualitative level of the whole economic and social activity. This calls for firm activity to raise labor productivity, cut down production costs, improve the quality of products and better use the fixed assets of all material and financial resources of the country. Special attention will be paid to the cutting down of material expenditures.[11]

The increased seriousness of the problem has emerged at a time when growth has been the prescribed goal. Many of the expanding industries have been supplying internal markets and have been protected by tariff

7. Law (no. 4) on the Adoption of the Plan for 1976–80.

8. See also discussion on scientific and technological research in Appendix K.

9. For example, in 1976–80 over 85 percent of new or modernized technologies are to be achieved on the basis of Romanian knowledge.

10. Reduction of material expenditure for each unit output has now become a compulsory target, but there are difficulties in achieving it.

11. *Directives of the Eleventh Congress of the Romanian Communist Party.*

walls and by import restrictions.[12] At the same time, planned targets and prices have not necessarily been conducive to creating the optimal technical or economic methods of production. This suggests that inefficiencies have remained in some production processes despite planners' exhortations to the contrary. With enterprises striving to meet high growth targets, efficiency has suffered in some cases.

Various exhortations throughout the plan documents show awareness of these problems. The full use of existing capacities and fixed assets emerges as a major priority and one which, in a planned economy, should not be too difficult to achieve. Improving product quality, however, is a more difficult task. It cannot only be legislated, but it requires the creation of conditions engrained in the system to induce improvements in quality.

The final theme that runs through the plan is reducing the consumption of energy and raw materials. Chapter 14 indicated that the days of energy self-sufficiency are now past. Although Romania has a wide range of mineral resources, they are insufficient to supply the needs of the country. As a result, the plan consistently emphasizes the need to minimize raw material and energy inputs in all sectors and to maximize the internal output of both.[13] It is planned that until 1990 national income will increase 3.5 to 3.8-fold, whereas consumption of primary energy will about double. To accomplish this, priority has been given to "those subbranches and highly technical equipment that use less power," and the energy consumption of existing processes is to be reduced. The 1976–80 Plan also calls for reducing consumption of material expenditures by 90 billion lei.[14]

Major Issues and Problems

Romania is now in a transition stage, having become a net importer of energy resources in the early 1970s. It is expected to rely heavily on imports of raw materials and crude oil to attain its future growth targets. Although endowed with a wide variety of energy resources including crude oil, natural gas, coal, lignite, and hydropower, reserves of these are not adequate to meet the domestic energy requirements arising from the government's strategy of a rapidly growing industrial sector. Likewise, the

12. Actual tariffs have been low, but physical restrictions on imports have implied effective protection of many products.

13. This is consistent with the continuing general policy of import substitution wherever possible.

14. Sector and product specific targets have been discussed in Chapters 10 and 12 on the industrial and construction sectors.

demand for resources arising from the expansion and diversification of industrial output have now outgrown the country's resource base. The resource gap is being met by increasing imports of raw materials, such as metals and energy resources.

As a consequence, the scenario of Romania's future economic development is changing dramatically. Its investment policies will depend more and more on expanding foreign trade. To sustain its present growth momentum and the structure of its industrialization program, its manufactured goods will have to penetrate world markets much more deeply. A greater integration into the world economy will also introduce the complication of an unpredictable foreign trade sector, with its uncharted effect on a previously totally planned economy.

If all plans are fulfilled, Romania will have "taken off" and become an industrialized economy by 1990, on a level with many other countries considered to be developed. By then the consumption fund will have increased its share in national income to approximately 70 percent. Despite continuing policies of import substitution, Romania is expected to remain a trading nation with a ratio of exports to national income of about 28 percent. The major exports are expected to be chemicals and machinery and imports to be mainly fuels and other raw materials.

To use resources fully, the present plan is very tight in that the margins for error or underfulfillment are small. With the economy becoming more complex and with the number of linkages among sectors and with other economies increasing, unplanned disturbances are likely to set off reverberations through many sectors, making the planning process more difficult. In principle, each plan provides reserves to offset the effect of some external circumstances. For example, as shown in Chapter 3, the material balances include such plan reserves. The effect, though, of a major catastrophe (such as the recent earthquake and the flood in 1975) cannot be anticipated, and these are likely to have longer-term effects on the economy, requiring some adjustments in the implementation of the plan.

This study has identified difficulties that are emerging in the industrial, construction, transport, and energy sectors and their potential effects on overall growth, but it has also noted that the government recognizes these problems. From past experience, it will probably adapt measures to achieve the main objectives of the five-year plan. The implications of these constraints, as well as requirements for their elimination, are discussed below.

With domestic resource mobilization already at sustained higher levels, the major challenges facing the Romanian economy are:

(a) To increase economic efficiency in resource utilization and to improve product quality;

(b) To contain imports to planned levels to achieve sufficient export penetration of world markets for sustaining the targeted high growth rates;
(c) To develop the adaptability of the economic sectors to respond to world market changes and to offset the vulnerability of the economy to external economic oscillations.

Efficiency and product quality

It is apparent that the government has long recognized the need to increase efficiency in resource use and to improve product quality. But it has also been shown that despite progress, there is much room for further improvement. Some of the internal problems can be regarded as constraints that can be removed through the present planning and administrative system. For example, improvements in the accuracy of the planning and monitoring powers and corresponding changes in resource allocation could alleviate such potential problems as labor shortages in construction or in the rapidly growing sectors. Similarly, corrective actions in the industrial sector, such as increasing specialization in plants to reap the benefits of economies of scale, might be undertaken relatively easily.

But there are other problems whose resolution is more difficult. For example, product quality and maximizing returns on investments are important objectives. Product quality will be a major factor in determining Romania's capacity to become a significant exporting nation and to compete with established firms in these fields. But the indicators of the system that are used to evaluate and to reward performance will have to emphasize in much greater measure the quality of performance along with volumetric achievements. Another area of potential improvement in resource utilization is in the country's criteria for selecting projects, as noted in Chapter 3.

External sector issues

The internal problems described above assume greater importance when their effect on foreign trade performance is considered. The improvements in economic performance that are required to eliminate the problems of quality and efficiency can be built into the domestic plan and can be made gradually without providing fundamental obstacles to fulfilling objectives. These issues must be solved more quickly in the trade sector, however, if plans are to be implemented. Foreign trade has become a crucial sector in the economy, both in terms of absolute size and relations with the other sectors, and the fulfillment of the foreign trade plan is essential to reaching the main targets of the five-year plan.

The plan expects an increase in the export ratio to more than 30 percent by 1980, and, even with a minor reduction to about 28 percent by 1990, the plan implies an increase in the volume of trade by 300 percent by 1980 over 1975 levels. The visible problems in the external sector are, of course, twofold: containing imports to planned levels and promoting sufficient exports to achieve targets.

The review of 1971–75 showed that imports of all raw materials increased more rapidly than all the output indexes, with the share of fuel and raw materials increasing from 43 percent of all imports in 1970 to 52 percent in 1975. With the economy moving into a deficit position in the resource field, unless the growth of raw material inputs is reduced, the rapid growth rates in industrial production and national income are going to necessitate a continuing growth in imports.

Evidently, the Romanians are fully cognizant of this; a more economical use of raw materials, coupled with efforts to find additional resources at home and abroad and to produce more synthetic substitutes at home, are all major priorities in the plan. Nevertheless, the targets, such as the 8.5 to 9.5 percent cut in material expenditure for each 1,000 lei of marketable output in industry between 1975 and 1980, are quite high. If they are not met, imports will grow faster than planned, and efforts to contain them under these circumstances to planned levels could hold production back for lack of imports or could lead to deteriorating product quality if domestic substitutes of insufficient quality are used.

The import substitution policy is in fact broader than indicated above, since there are efforts to produce as much as possible within the country. In some cases, such as the production of certain consumer goods, the decision to establish a domestic industry is taken even if the ground rules using the trading rate of US$1 = 20 lei are not met and if the initial cost of the goods implies a higher rate. The policy is that in the long run, any process must be efficient: that is, infant industries may be protected in the short run. Import substitution on a massive scale has been reinstituted since the 1975 floods, and this will undoubtedly continue in the aftermath of the earthquake.

The more serious problem, however, is likely to be on the export side. In 1975 prices, total exports are required to grow at an average annual rate of about 12 to 13 percent until 1980, and then at an average rate of some 6 to 7 percent until 1990. Three sectors in particular are expected to lead this expansion: machinery and equipment, chemicals, and (to a lesser extent) industrial consumer goods. The official documents allow some deductions about the growth of the main industrial sectors. By 1980 chemicals and machinery and equipment are expected to increase their share in total exports to 50 percent compared with 38 percent in 1975, and this will increase further to about 60 percent by 1990. An annual growth rate of approximately 20 percent is estimated until 1980 and after that a lower rate of slightly under 10 percent. Industrial consumer goods are projected to grow at about 15 percent a year until 1980 and 10 percent thereafter.

The size of these increases can be seen from the fact that exports in constant prices will be 90 to 101 percent higher in 1980 than they were in 1975,[15] and three times higher by 1990. In absolute figures, exports are predicted to increase from US$5.3 billion to US$8.0 to US$9.0 billion in 1980 (in 1975 prices). Such an increase will not be easy to achieve in terms of output. But it will be even more difficult to sell this quantity of goods on the world market, especially since, even under favorable circumstances, the international economy is not expected to grow more than 5 to 6 percent a year. In other words, Romanian trade would be growing faster than world trade and would compete with others' shares in the world market. This could lead to retaliation and quota restrictions.

The greatest problem is likely to be in the field of machinery and equipment in convertible areas, where Romania will have to compete with such countries as West Germany, the United States, the United Kingdom, and France. To break into the market substantially, Romania will have to produce exceptionally high-quality equipment and to deliver it expeditiously, because these two elements probably are more important than others, including price. So far, Romania has a relatively limited number of capital goods that have successfully penetrated the convertible markets. Because of inadequate marketing and support services, several products with competitive quality have to be sold at discount prices, whereas in other products, substantial efforts have to be made to raise the quality level to that of world competition. For oil drilling equipment, for example, which is a quality product, Romania had the equipment available when the world shortage occurred. But it would have been more difficult to sell such amounts of equipment if, for example, American drills had been available at that time. If Romania has made an inroad into the markets, it is likely to be uphill work to increase, or even to maintain, its stake.

15. This target refers to the volume of trade in 1976–80 compared with 1971–75.

Certain avenues around these problems are being sought. One is to increase bilateral trade agreements,[16] and the second, in some ways complementary, is to move toward more trade with the developing world. In 1975 about 18 percent of trade was with developing countries, and by 1980 it is planned to increase to 30 percent. Almost half of the increase in trade will be with the developing countries between 1976 and 1980. They may have less stringent demands for sophisticated machinery and equipment and are likely to pay for them with raw materials, which is precisely what Romania requires. The group of developing countries, however, now includes most of the oil producers who have recently been very demanding about the quality of the goods they buy and have tended to purchase products from the developed economies.

Other problems exist in the field of machinery and equipment. At present, the greatest advances are being made in import substitutions. The purchasing of licenses has been a means of achieving that. Some licenses and patents, however, specifically exclude the possibility of exporting in competition with the mother firm.[17] If Romania is to obtain a permanent role in the world market for machinery and equipment, it will have to develop a technology that can compete in specific fields.

Responsiveness to world economic conditions

In the world market there are constant changes in requirements and demands. If Romania is to be successful, it must be responsive to these changes and use a flexible planning system. In this sense, the planning system would have to encourage more diversified production to satisfy the demands of world customers of producer and consumer goods. Decentralized decision-making along with a system of incentives would develop initiative in identifying and satisfying these demands.

The lower flexibility of the Romanian system also handicaps it to a certain degree in facing the cyclical trends of the world economy, particularly in chemicals and machinery. A slump in the world economy will hurt the country's exports to convertible currency areas and will affect total exports which are expected to retain a rather high share of about 28 percent of national income by 1990. Most imports will be raw materials and intermediate products rather than finished goods, so any containment of imports in

16. Amounts indicated in such agreements are targets, and their fulfillment, therefore, remains to be seen.

17. A good example is the recently signed agreement with Citroen.

the face of adverse exports will directly limit the level of production. Furthermore, as noted above, the linkages in the economy are becoming more extensive, and any disruptions will have far-ranging effects on the economy. Until recently, factors outside the country had little effect on Romania's economy. But Romania's increasing trade interaction with the world economy will increase the domestic economy's dependence on world market oscillations, and these new conditions are outside of the economy.

Economic Effect of the March 1977 Earthquake

The economy was dealt a severe blow on March 4, 1977, when a violent earthquake occurred in the east of the country, centered in the judet of Vrancea. The effects of the earthquake were most severe in the vicinity of Bucharest, and it killed 1,570 people, injured 9,300, and caused damage valued by the government at US$2 billion. A large proportion of the damage was to fixed assets, mainly buildings, and, of the US$1.4 billion damage to buildings, US$1 billion was to housing. The damage to fixed assets in the productive sector was relatively small, and foregone production and destruction of inventories were estimated at approximately US$500 million. The earthquake also had a substantial effect on the country's balance of payments prospects; government projections suggest that this effect will be approximately US$630 million during 1977 and 1978, consisting of US$350 million in lost exports (lost orders, production losses, and diversion of production to the domestic economy), US$250 million in additional lost imports, chiefly machinery and equipment for the construction sector, and about US$30 million in lost tourist receipts.

Immediately after the earthquake, the government began clearance and reconstruction work and was very successful in overcoming the immediate effects. Debris was cleared, housing was found for most of those left homeless, chiefly by giving them priority for new housing, and most enterprises were returned to full production within a few weeks. To deal with the substantial longer-term effect, the government instituted a comprehensive reconstruction program, which is planned to permit both the effect of the earthquake to be eliminated by 1980 and the targets of the 1976–80 Plan to be met. The two major components of the reconstruction program are the accelerated expansion of the construction sector and those industrial branches supplying equipment and materials to the sector and the construction of an additional 200,000 houses during 1976–80 to replace the housing destroyed by the earthquake and also to ease the housing constraint more quickly than previously anticipated. The resources for the additional tasks during this plan period are expected to be secured from three sources. The first source is the greater efforts of the population, with compulsory and unpaid work initially on all Sundays and later on one Sunday each month, voluntary work, deferred reduction in the working week, financial contributions from workers, and utilization of the army for reconstruction work. The second source is savings of production expenditures obtained from improving production efficiency, which is now expected to be greater than originally anticipated. The final source is external borrowings to finance those imports not paid for by intensified export efforts.

Although the government has stated clearly its determination that the earthquake will not prevent the implementation of plan targets on schedule, it is also clear that the earthquake has made this achievement more difficult. In the external sector, the earthquake adds to the difficulties, referred to earlier, in meeting foreign trade targets. In the domestic sector, the earthquake also accentuates several difficulties. First, the reconstruction program imposes additional tasks on the construction sector, which has been operating close to its capacity and, in particular, has been finding recruitment of additional labor difficult (Chapter 12). Although the reconstruction program will provide additional fixed assets and material resources in the sector, they must be complemented by increases in the labor force. Second, the government's plans to maintain the plan targets and to neutralize the effects of the earthquake can be put into effect only by mobilizing more resources, both by increasing the efforts of the labor force and by securing additional savings of production expenditures through greater efficiency. This chapter has identified improvements in efficiency as targets that have been difficult to fulfill in the past. In view of this, further acceleration in the rate of improving efficiency may be difficult, although the recasting of plan targets has been made on the basis of the improved performance in this area during the first two years of the plan period. Furthermore, not all of the savings from this source can be channeled into additional investment and production. Some must be allocated to the consumption fund, to provide the goods and services required for the higher increase in the standard of living announced in July 1977.

World Bank Projections of the Balance of Payments

The discussion so far has outlined the main issues and challenges facing the economy in meeting the 1976–80 and perspective plan targets. The rest of the chapter illustrates the convertible balance of payments constraint and Romania's possible convertible debt posture by projections made by the World Bank under different growth assumptions. The model used for all projections in this chapter is the World Bank's revised minimum standard model.[18]

As a starting point, the ideal situation of the full implementation of the government targets is presented. Where these targets have not been stated directly or openly, they have been deduced from official documents. Two runs of the model were obtained: one based on the additional assumption that the trade surplus to be established by 1980 to pay off the foreign debt would be maintained until 1990 and the other assuming that after 1980 imports would increase faster than exports, almost eliminating the trade surplus by 1990. Total trade has been assumed to increase by 11.2 percent in 1976–80[19] and to triple by 1990, according to the plan. Trade with the convertible areas is assumed to increase in 1976–80 with exports reaching 57 percent and imports 55 percent of the total by 1980. The same shares are assumed for 1990.

The results derived from these assumptions are summarized in Table 16.3. If these external sector targets were to be implemented fully, the outstanding convertible debt at the end of 1975 would be eliminated by 1981. Under the first model run, notable surpluses amounting to about 8 percent of exports would begin accumulating after that year, leading to a fast buildup of reserves and substantially expanding Romania's capacity to extend credit to other countries.

Alternatives for Development

It is clear that Romania is facing a period of challenge. It is trying to open new markets in many areas where competition is already well established. Under these circumstances, attainment of all the current medium- and long-term targets will be difficult. This raises the question of other viable alternatives that may exist for Romania to pursue its development strategy. Two such alternatives are explored below, along with their implications and the feasibility of their implementation. The first is based on the assumption that the implementation of the high growth targets is an

18. A word of caution is in order on the use of the World Bank model. It has been formulated to meet general and standardized World Bank needs. The logic of the structure of its equations is not necessarily appropriate for this economy. It is used, however, to obtain a general framework of reference, and the results, even if found generally meaningful, should be interpreted with caution.

19. Exports have been assumed to increase by 12.1 percent a year during the same period and imports by 10.4 percent.

Table 16.3. *Convertible Balance of Payments, 1975, and Projections, 1980 and 1985*
(millions of U.S. dollars in current prices)[a]

Item	Actual 1975	Estimates 1980	1985 (a)	1985 (b)
Exports[b]	2,839	8,603	16,151	15,950
Imports[b]	2,950	7,709	14,768	15,688
Trade balance	−111	895	1,383	262
Net factor services	−149	−68	334	127
Balance of current account	−261	827	1,717	389

Note: Column (a) presents the results of the first model run, and (b) the results of the second.

a. World Bank price indexes.

b. The real growth rates used for exports and imports for the two model runs are as follows:

	1976–80 (percent) (a)	1976–80 (percent) (b)	1981–1985 (percent) (a)	1981–1985 (percent) (b)
Exports	13.5	13.5	6.0	6.0
Imports	11.5	11.5	6.5	6.9

Source: World Bank estimates.

absolute necessity for the country to achieve stated objectives by 1990. If export targets to convertible areas are not achieved in 1976–80, substantial funds can be borrowed from external markets to finance the export shortfall so that both the investment program and the import of technology will not be affected. The second assumes that in the event of such export reversals, the government will trim some of its growth targets and finance externally only a small proportion of import requirements, rather than substantially increase dependence on the international capital markets to finance its growth, which is not part of government policy.

External resources

If the export targets to convertible areas are not achieved in 1976–80, the question arises as to how much possible leeway may exist for the government to borrow in the international capital markets, without jeopardizing its creditworthiness, to meet its energy and raw material requirements and to sustain the presently planned import program.

The results of several runs of the model indicate that reduction in exports of as much as 20 percent of present targets can be reasonably accommodated through international borrowing. That is, assuming an annual export growth rate to the convertible areas of close to 11 percent in 1976–80 (versus 13.5 percent assumed with a previous run), which marginally betters the 1971–75 performance, and a similar import rate, the debt service ratio will reach a trough in 1982 at about 9.5 percent, 24 percent in 1989, and 26 percent in 1990. Debt service to total debt outstanding will continue to be high, with about 25 percent reflecting the built-in assumptions in these projections that the bulk of borrowing will be medium term (eight years for repayment with up to two years grace period).

Such rather large-scale dependence on the international capital markets to finance growth is possible, but given past experience, is not likely. First, the government is on record to reduce substantially its external debt by the early 1980s. Second, if exports grow slowly, Romania would probably, as in the past, place stringent controls on imports. In 1975, for example, when reduced exports caused by the flood reduced convertible currency carnings, imports were permitted to increase only US$5 million more than in 1974. The same policy is in force in the period after the earthquake to make up for foregone exports and to save foreign exchange required to replace damaged and destroyed capital stock.

Import restrictions

The second alternative, which is more realistic, is for Romania to limit imports to the level of exports or to even lower levels to allow for debt repayment. Such a policy would lead to the desired balance of payments. Some long-term implications, however, need to be highlighted.

Substituting local technology for foreign can only be done to a limited extent. Substantial restrictions on the import of modern technology could affect the country's future capacity to penetrate international markets. Also, the substitution of foreign technology, to the extent it can be undertaken, can be accomplished only with higher costs. If these are sufficiently high, they could affect the growth of income, given the fact that the current domestic savings effort can be considered the highest that can be realistically achieved.

Because these factors potentially can constrain the achievement of Romania's growth targets and long-term objectives, it is possible that the government would favor financing a small proportion of its import requirements by borrowing in the international capital markets. The revised minimum standard model illustrates quantitatively the implications of the arguments above and establishes what the respective convertible debt and creditworthiness ratios would be.

More specifically, two alternative sets of real growth rates of exports to convertible currency areas in 1976–80 have been used, 8.5 and 10 percent a year. It has also been assumed that the government will contain imports within half a percentage point of export growth rates (9 and 10.5 percent, respectively). For 1981–85 the substantially reduced growth of the volume of trade anticipated by the government is reflected in three assumptions. First, the annual growth of exports and imports has been assumed to be 5.5 and 6 percent, respectively. It is also assumed that the bulk of borrowing will be medium term (eight years for repayment with up to two years grace period) and that reserves will increase annually at the rate of US$30 million. Table 16.4 summarizes the results derived from those assumptions.

These are not unreasonable growth scenarios. Actual export performance in 1976 indicates that the growth of exports over 1975 to convertible currency areas was within the assumed range above. It is difficult to predict whether these scenarios will be implemented. They imply certain trends, yet, in an economy like Romania's, where trade is a public monopoly, good projections require not just a good trend estimate but, more important, second guessing the preferences of the planners.

Table 16.4. *Convertible Balance of Payments, 1975, and Projections, 1980 and 1985*
(billions of U.S. dollars in current prices)[a]

Item	*Actual 1975*	*1980*		*1985*	
		(a)	*(b)*	*(a)*	*(b)*
Exports	2.84	6.7	7.2	12.3	13.2
Imports	2.95	7.0	7.5	12.5	14.3
Trade balance	−0.11	−0.3	−0.3	−1.1	−1.1
Net factor services	−0.15	−0.3	−0.3	−0.7	−0.7
Balance of current account	−0.26	−0.6	−0.6	−1.8	−1.8

Note: Column (a) presents the results of the first model run, and (b) the results of the second.

a. World Bank price indexes weighted per assumptions on composition of Romania's trade:

	1975	*1980*	*1985*
Exports	100	144	200
Imports	100	143	200

Source: World Bank estimates.

Irrespective of which growth scenario will be implemented, certain conclusions can be derived about Romania's development prospects. Its growth rate will remain quite high by international standards, and, by maintaining its present momentum, Romania will be among the more developed of the high-income developing countries in the 1980s. This growth will be attained with continuing government emphasis on utilizing the country's own resources and a large local investment effort and on more effective use of human, capital, and natural resources. Finally, for Romania to attain its growth targets and its plans to create a competitive industrial economy, it will have to attract foreign resources and to secure loans to support its development efforts.

Creditworthiness

The organization of economic activity in Romania, the pursuit of a development strategy involving high investment and savings rates, the country's major efforts to expand exports, and its debt management policies suggest that Romania is now creditworthy. Under the assumptions of the estimates above, the debt service ratio remains easily under manageable proportions, about 20 percent, although at generally higher levels than in 1971–75. Because of the built-in assumptions on the terms of borrowing, the proportions of annual debt service to total debt outstanding is expected to continue to be relatively high, about 20 to 29 percent.

PART FIVE

Appendixes

A

The Council of Ministers

Prime Minister
Deputy Prime Ministers (12), of whom the following five have double functions:
Deputy Prime Minister and Minister of Home Trade
Deputy Prime Minister and President of State Committee of Planning
Deputy Prime Minister and Minister of Agriculture and Food Industry
Deputy Prime Minister and President of the Council of Coordination of Consumer Goods Production in the Whole Economy
Deputy Prime Minister and Minister of Foreign Trade and International Cooperation
Minister of Foreign Affairs
Minister of National Defense
Minister of Internal Affairs
Minister of Finance
Minister of the Technical and Material Supply and the Control of the Fixed Assets Administration
Minister of Metal-working Industry
Minister of Machine Building Industry
Minister of Chemical Industry
Minister of Electric Power
Minister of Mines, Petroleum, and Geology
Minister of Industrial Construction
Minister of Forestry and Construction Materials
Minister of Light Industry
Minister of Education and Training
Minister of Tourism
Minister of Transport and Telecommunications
Minister of Labor
Minister of Health

Minister of Justice
Minister of Youth Problems
President of the National Council for Science and Technology
President of the Council of Socialist Culture and Education
President of the Committee for the Problems of the People's Councils
President of the State Committee for Prices
President of the National Council of Waters
Presidents of Social Activity Units (2): the General Union of Romanian Syndicates and the National Union of Agricultural Cooperatives
President of National Council of Women
State Secretaries (4): State Planning Committee, Foreign Trade (2), Chemical Industry
First Vice-Presidents (2): Council for Economic and Social Organization and Committee for People's Council
Department Directors (2): State Agricultural Department and Food Industry

B

Judet Government and Its Financing

In 1968 Romania was reorganized into thirty-nine judets (districts) and the Municipality of Bucharest. Each judet is intended to be, as far as possible, an integral economic and administrative unit. In general, the physical size and the population of all the judets are the same (in practice the largest is only twice the size of the smallest, and the most populous has a population only twice that of the least), and the long-run aim is that each judet should attain the same level of economic development.

System of Judet Government

Administratively each judet is independent. It is governed by representatives who are elected every five years and who form a People's Council; an Executive Committee is elected within the Council. This Council is not subordinated to any ministry, since it is directed and controlled by the Great National Assembly (Figure B.1). At this level of government, the party and the executive posts within the People's Council are held by the same persons "in order to provide a unified effort."

Towns and communes are also managed by People's Councils, which are elected every two-and-a-half years. The term town is self-explanatory. The commune is a basic unit of administrative and territorial organization. It comprises the total rural population in a limited territory, which is unified by some common economic or sociocultural interests. It may comprise one or several villages. The term does not in any way describe or imply a particular form of communal ownership, and a commune could include private farms, agricultural producer cooperatives (CAP's), and state units. These town and commune People's Councils are directly responsible to the judet

People's Council. They form a direct link, free from interference from any other agencies.

Figure B.1. *Organization of a Regional Government*

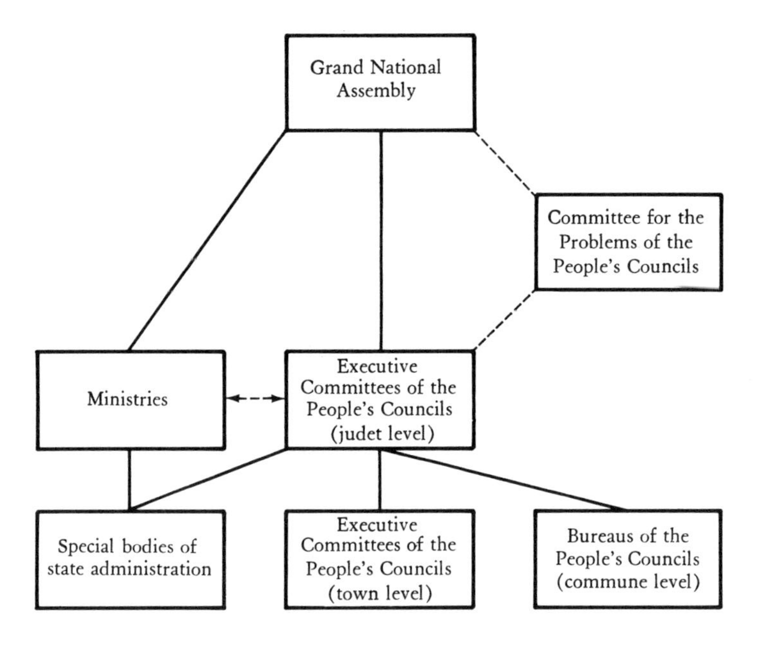

Note: Solid lines indicate hierarchical lines of authority and responsibility; dashed lines indicate channels of consultation and cooperation.

Local government, like central government, is based on the principle of democratic centralism. The people are consulted, but decisions are approved by People's Councils. Consequently, People's Councils have a twofold function. First, they are expected to assist in the decisionmaking process by expressing the views of the population under their jurisdiction, and second, they are responsible for implementing the resulting policies.

The basic function of the People's Councils is to solve local problems in accordance with national interests. With regard to the Romanian Communist Party (RCP) and state policy, as it affects the local level, the People's

Councils organize the implementation of development plans, analyze the economic and sociocultural issues affecting their territory, and propose solutions. At the same time, they organize, monitor, and control all activities for implementing the local socioeconomic plan and the local budget. They are responsible for overseeing the utilization of the productive capacities, the organization of labor and its regional distribution, and the implementation of the plan by all economic units, irrespective of their level of authority. They are also responsible for monitoring and controlling all agricultural production and for supplying goods and services to the population.

The People's Councils of the districts also have the broader function of drawing up the plans for the districts. They present a comprehensive plan directly to the State Planning Committee (SPC). The plan includes not only the items for which the People's Council is directly and uniquely responsible, such as housing, but all economic activities in its territory. These include activities where the responsibilities are shared, such as education and health, and also those where the responsibility rests solely at the ministry level, such as the output of republican industrial units. Consequently, drawing up a district plan that assures that the activities of the centrally subordinated units are consistent with those of the local units and with all ministry plans is a major task of coordination.

The system of planning at this local level is not different from that in other parts of the economy. Given the guidelines drawn up by the RCP, the local plan is assembled from the bottom. At each stage, cooperating and supplying agencies are consulted, and agreement is reached before aggregating to the next level. Consequently, for example, a new school will have to be agreed upon at the local level and with the Ministry of Education before the plan is finalized. It must be consistent with both the planning criteria of the judet and of the ministry. Thus, efficient planning relies heavily on permanent coordination between all levels and agencies.

As a result, when the local plan is submitted to the SPC, it is internally consistent. The only adjustments that have to be made will be to obtain the macro balance and the desired local distribution (although the local distribution will have partly been considered by coordination with the ministries). When the plan is finalized by the SPC and is approved by the National Assembly, it is then disaggregated again to the local level to be implemented.

The work of the People's Councils invariably involves cooperation with ministries in fields such as education and health. Similarly, when a republican project involves several agencies, for example, an industrial platform, the People's Council will contribute the basic municipal services, manpower, and equipment for its implementation. At times, combined financing schemes also are used for such matters as water supply. Overlapping with ministries is inevitable, but it appears that a spirit of cooperation prevails, and the difficulties and petty rivalries are overcome.

Although all People's Councils are independent and autonomous, a central body exists called the Committee for the Problems of the People's Councils (CPPC), which coordinates the technical activities of each judet. The CPPC is a permanent body of representatives of the People's Councils. Its president is a member of the Council of Ministers. The People's Councils are not responsible to the CPPC; it is there only for orientation and control.

The CPPC ensures that national policy is uniformly implemented by all People's Councils. It has special departments dealing with the problems of organizing and supervising local state administration, communal and housing administrations, and, finally, the physical planning of the territory.

Financing Judet Government

The local governments have usually depended heavily on central state budget subsidies to finance the activities for which they bear primary responsibility. Although they have their own revenues, which are different from those of the central budget, in most cases these revenues have been insufficient to meet expenditures. In 1968, for example, the share of revenues generated within the judet in local budgetary revenues was only 43 percent. As part of the overall reform measures undertaken in 1969 to increase economic efficiency and to improve administration, subsidies to the central state budget were reduced, whereas the self-financing capacity of the local governments was increased by tightening financial controls and by allowing the local governments the tax on the wages of employees working in the state sector and the turnover tax on the production of the economic units under local administration.

Along with the more traditional tax instruments (Table B.1) and such other local taxes as motor vehicle licenses, fees, building taxes, and stamp fees, the revenues of the local governments increased substantially after 1969, reaching a peak of 85 percent of total revenues in 1973. But they have declined precipitously since 1975, increasing relative dependence on state budget subsidies to the pre-1969 levels. Most of this decline is explained by a drastic reduction in the earnings from turnover taxes and other payments from the local units, which mainly results from organizational measures, such as changes in the enterprises distributing natural gas from local to republican status and also from the repricing exercise.

On the expenditure side, the local governments have allocated increasingly

Table B.1. *Revenue and Expenditure of Local Budgets, 1971–76*

Item	1971	1972	1973	1974	1975	1976
			Billions of lei[a]			
Revenue[b]	26.9	29.0	29.8	33.3	41.9	46.6
Expenditure	25.5	27.5	28.6	31.9	40.2	44.3
Balance	*1.4*	*1.5*	*1.2*	*1.4*	*1.7*	*2.3*
			Percentage of total			
Revenue						
Own income	83.5	81.6	85.0	76.3	56.5	56.5
Turnover tax	30.9	29.2	31.3	27.7	13.8	
Regularization tax	0.5	0.5	0.5	0.4	0.1	
Share in profits of economic units	15.8	14.5	15.5	12.4	9.9	
Taxes on cooperatives, public organizations' income, and on income of members from cooperatives	2.9	3.0	3.3	3.2	2.4	
Taxes from the population	19.4	19.6	20.8	20.3	17.5	
Other income	16.5	18.4	15.0	23.7	43.5	43.5
Expenditure						
Financing of state economic units and organizations	2.5	2.6	2.1	5.4	9.1	10.1
Municipal services	8.1	7.7	5.2	4.8	3.2	3.3
Maintenance of roads and bridges	5.2	5.3	4.0	3.0	2.5	2.7
Agriculture	8.5	8.1	8.2	7.6	6.6	6.4
Social welfare and cultural activities	54.4	53.0	54.3	52.1	45.3	46.7
Other	21.3	23.3	26.2	27.1	33.3	30.8

a. Excluded are local budget surpluses that are remitted to the state budget. These were, in 1971, lei 2.1 billion; 1972, lei 1.8 billion; 1973, lei 2.2 billion; 1974, lei 0.6 billion.

b. Includes state transfers.

Source: Anuarul Statistic al Republicii Socialiste Romania (Bucharest: Directia Centrala de Statistica, published yearly).

Table B.2. *Self-Financing of Expenditures, by Judet, 1971 and 1975*

Percentage of self-financing	*Number of judets*	
	1971	*1975*
Less than 50 percent	8	9
50–75 percent	12	15
More than 75 percent	20	16

larger portions of these revenues to finance state economic enterprises as well as local investments. This is reflected in the increase in this category of expenditures since 1974. The importance of municipal services and maintenance of roads and bridges is declining, and the impression is that allocation to these categories of expenditures is residual. The effect of the diminishing funds is reflected in the limited road maintenance (Chapter 13).

The budgeted amounts for the judets and the city of Bucharest are included annually in the Law for Adoption of the State Budget and are usually realized. An analysis of the 1971 and 1975 budget laws (Table B.2) suggests that an increasing proportion of judets have had less revenue from their own means to finance expenditures in 1975 than in 1971. Dependence on republican budget subsidies to local government has increased.

C

Industrial Organization

UNDER THE ROMANIAN SYSTEM OF CENTRALIZED ECONOMIC PLANNING, central authorities make all major production and investment decisions following a reconciliation process in which targets and objectives have been discussed and modified between the various levels of the institutional hierarchy. Central authorities also fix prices and control the activities of the enterprises. Industrial products are marketed by organizations outside the industrial enterprises. Progress toward production and investment targets and achievement of predetermined efficiency criteria is monitored daily, weekly, monthly, and quarterly at different levels of authority. The scope for individual decisionmaking in allocating resources is thus strictly limited to achieving centrally determined targets and norms.

Industry is organized at the republican, the local, and the cooperative levels. Republican industry is developed, operated, and controlled by a hierarchic structure that is made up of the Council of Ministers, industrial production ministries, ministries of trade, central economic synthesis organs[1] and other central authorities, and the industrial centrals and producing enterprises. Local industry is subordinated to the forty current district People's Councils. Local and republican industry together constitute the "state industry." Industrial cooperatives, finally, have their own, different organizational structure. Their roof organization is the Central Cooperative Union. Figure C.1 is a schematic of the hierarchy in industrial decisionmaking.

In republican industry, which in Romanian terms comprises all industrial activities of national interest, the organizational structure consists of three

1. State Planning Committee, Ministry of Finance, National Bank and other Banks, Ministry of Labor, Ministry of Technical-Material Supply and Fixed Assets Administration, Foreign Trade Ministry, State Committee for Prices, the National Council for Science and Technology, and the Central Statistical Office.

Figure C.1. *Organization of an Industrial Ministry*

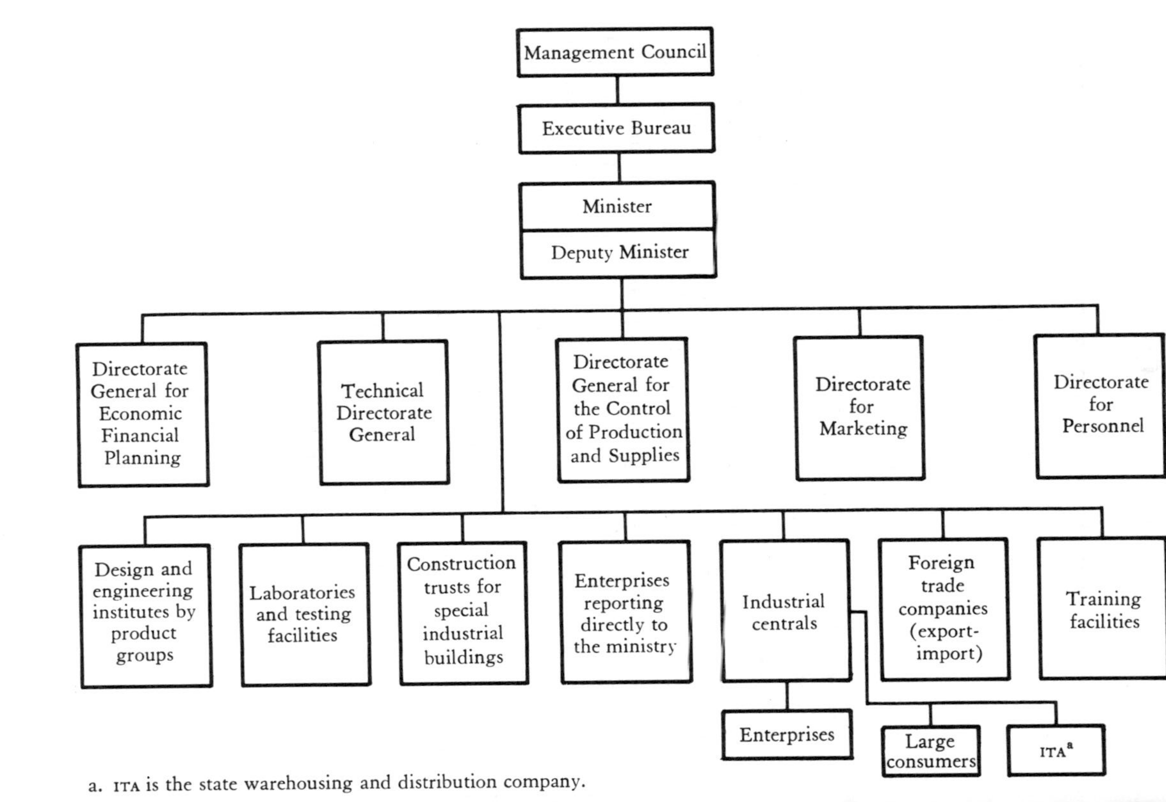

a. ITA is the state warehousing and distribution company.

stages, with the industrial production ministry (there are eight in all)[2] at the top, industrial centrals in the middle, and the production enterprises at the bottom.

Ministries

The ministry is responsible for the overall performance of the subsector; coordinates its activities through other central organs with the rest of the economy; translates national economic objectives into specific physical, financial, and efficiency targets for its subordinated industries; and approves specific investments (Appendix E). The ministry, through its design and technological engineering institutes and construction trusts, is also responsible for designing and executing industrial projects. Moreover, it usually has testing facilities for goods produced in the subsector and in research and development facilities. Most industrial ministries, in collaboration with the Ministry of Foreign Trade and International Cooperation, also control pertinent foreign trade operations through foreign trade enterprises under their jurisdiction.

Industrial Centrals

Industrial centrals are autonomous economic units that are comprised of many enterprises. They were first formed in 1969 as one of the measures to decentralize decisionmaking and other economic planning, supply, sales, and control functions. Previously, enterprises had been under the direct control of the subsector directorates of each ministry. These subsector directorates were abolished, and most enterprises in manufacturing, mining, and construction were combined into the centrals or industrial associations that are intended to help manage their constituent enterprises by taking some functions of the enterprises (supply, sales, and so forth), except production. About 217 centrals were formed, covering a work force of about 1.6 million people. These were subsequently reduced to 89 in 1973 to eliminate some duplication of effort and to foster both horizontal and vertical integration of industry subsectors and a concentration of effort in foreign trade. Further organizational changes increased their number to 112 in 1977.

2. The eight ministries are Ministry of Electrical Energy; Ministry of Mining, Petroleum, and Geology; Ministry of Metallurgical Industry; Ministry of Machine-building Industry; Ministry of Chemical Industry; Ministry of Forestry and Construction Materials; Ministry of Light Industry; and Ministry of Agriculture and Food Industry.

During the reorganization of the centrals in 1973, some noteworthy changes were introduced in the functions and responsibilities that could lead to more efficient development and execution of plans. In planning and finance, for example, responsibility has been decentralized from the ministries to the centrals for drawing up the production, finance, and investment plans, including striking material balances where appropriate, for the constituent enterprises. Also, the centrals are now the "titulars" of the plan within the realms of the ministries, which implies that they are directly responsible for fulfilling those respective plans. Finally, almost all product design and development functions are now concentrated in the centrals, in an attempt to forge better links between these functions and production. A typical organization chart of a central is given in Figure C.2.

Centrals may act as troubleshooters by shifting labor among their enterprises, allocating reserve funds, and providing technical support (engineering, design, testing) to enterprises in case of need. Centrals are usually also responsible for marketing products to large industrial consumers, and they maintain warehouses, which are often operated under subordinated warehousing enterprises. Smaller consumers of catalog items are supplied by state enterprises for supply and sales, known as Technical and Material Supply Units, which are scattered throughout the country.

Usually, several industrial enterprises are grouped into one industrial central. There are currently about 100 such centrals, each combining about ten production enterprises and over 10,000 employees. Actually, the number of enterprises under an industrial central varies substantially, ranging from about five for bearings to around forty in the knitting subsector. In one central, the number of employees can reach up to 100,000, as for example, in the cotton central.

Industrial centrals have been formed predominantly to coordinate similar production nationwide. Only where product characteristics were dissimilar, such as in food processing, are there several regional centrals in one subsector of industry. In most cases, the grouping followed the principle of horizontal integration. Only in mining and processing of ores are there a few examples of vertical integration.

The deputy general director of a central is usually also the director of the largest production enterprise of that central. The general director of the central is not appointed for a determined fixed term, and the position is not rotated among other directors of subordinated enterprises.

There are some exceptions to the above standard organizational structure of republican industry, however. There are some enterprises that are directly under the jurisdiction of a ministry and that have no industrial central. These enterprises are mostly highly specialized. In this context, the term

Figure C.2. *Organization of an Industrial Central*

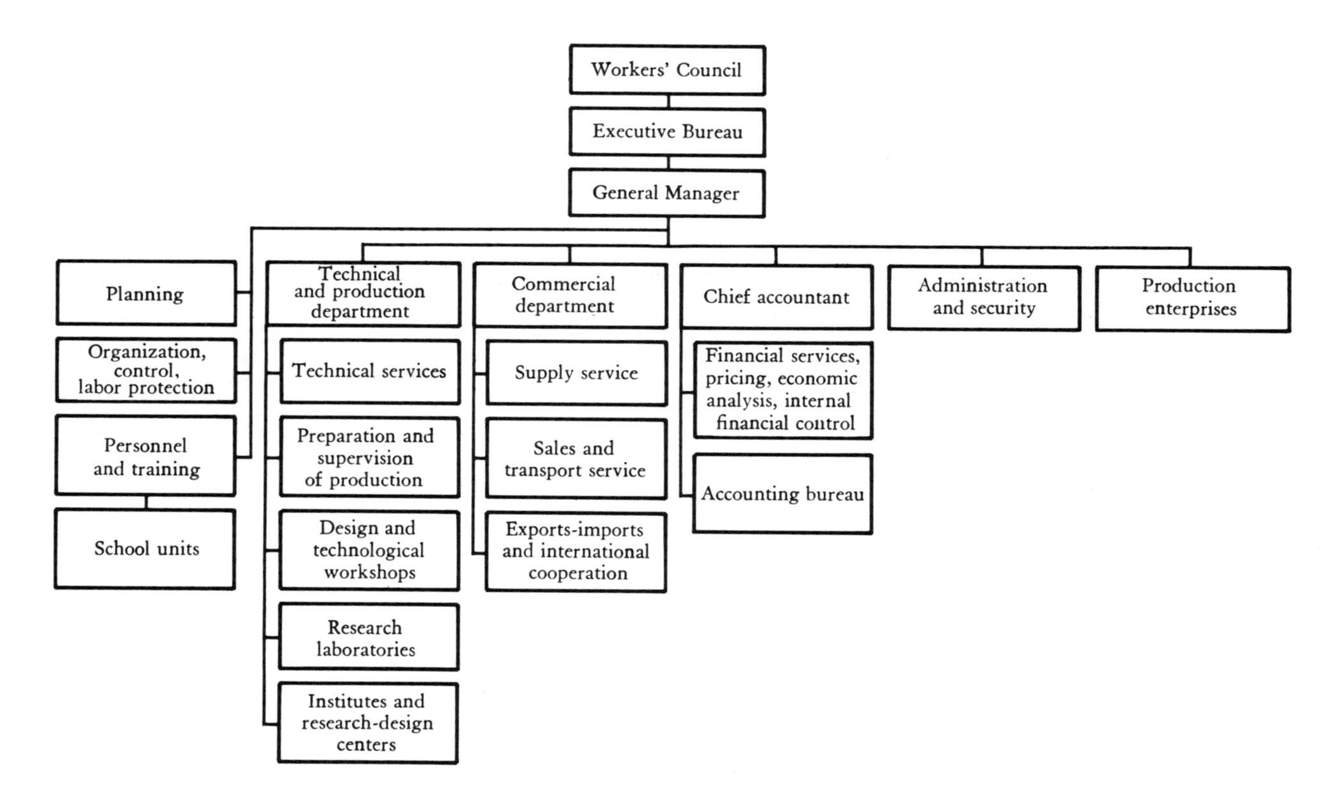

Figure C.3. *Organization of an Industrial Enterprise*

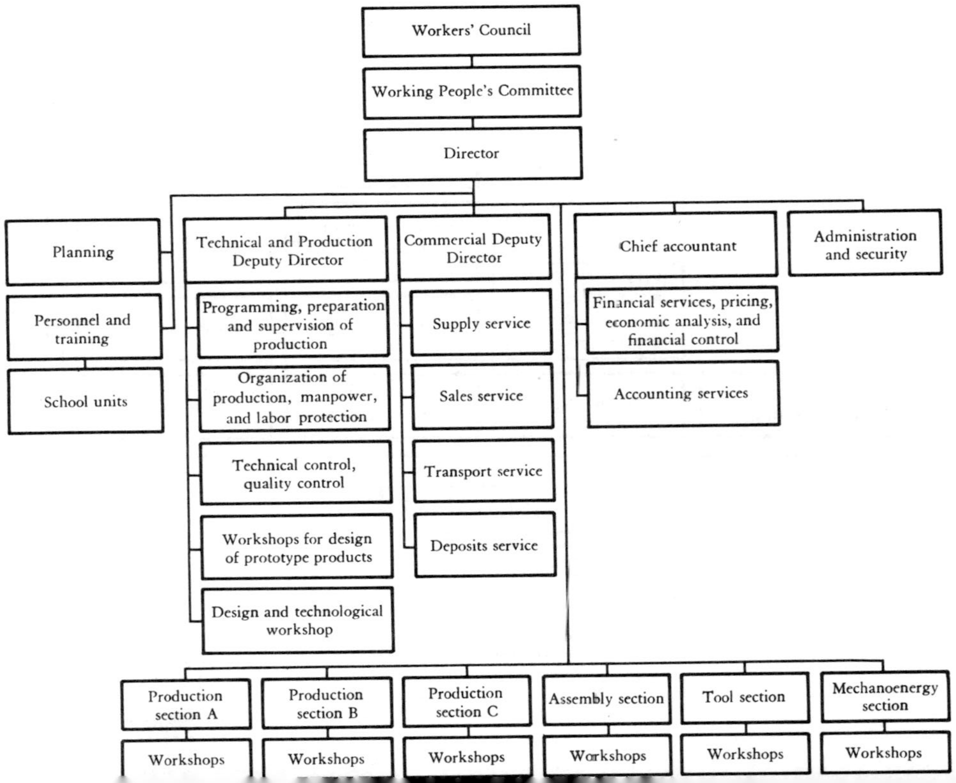

"trust" in Romania is not applied to industrial organizations, but to construction and agricultural enterprises only.

Industrial Enterprises

Industrial enterprises in Romania are organizations oriented primarily toward production, with limited autonomy and decisionmaking responsibilities outside production. Each enterprise has its own production plans based on the targets set by the industrial central and higher authorities, prepares separate financial statements, and may borrow from designated banks. Any substantive change in its organization, investment programs, production targets, or product mix, however, must be approved by the ministry and, in most cases, also by the Council of Ministers.

The highest decisionmaking power within an enterprise lies with the General Assembly, which elects the Workers' Council. The Workers' General Assembly normally meets twice a year to examine the operational results and to review the performance of the Working People's Council. This Council consists of elected representatives of workers and also of some members of the management and is chaired by the Manager of the enterprise. The General Manager is responsible for the day-to-day operations and for implementing planned targets. He is assisted by a team of directors, such as for planning and production, technical matters and investments, procurement and sales, and accounting (Figure C.3). The actual organization of an industrial enterprise may vary, however, according to the size of enterprise, expressed in total employment, and to the complexity of production. The Romanian system has five different organizational structures in enterprises.

D

National Accounting

IN ROMANIA, SOCIAL PRODUCT IS DEFINED as the total output of material production and productive services produced within the national economy. The productive sector comprises the subsectors in which material goods and services are produced, circulated, and distributed for final use. Subsectors in the nonproductive sector provide services to satisfy private and social needs, and their output is not included in the social product.[1] Productive and nonproductive activities are separated by function, and all activities producing goods and productive services are included within the productive sector, irrespective of whether the unit producing them is primarily categorized as productive or nonproductive. Therefore, the output of an economic unit is divided between the productive and nonproductive sectors, depending on the characteristics of the activities in the specific unit.

The social product is calculated by adding the value of the gross products of the subsectors of material production, including turnover tax. The gross product of industry is calculated as the sum of the gross output of all of the industrial enterprises. Gross industrial output includes value added in industry without deducting capital consumption and the value of inputs from outside industry and of inputs transferred from one industrial

1. Until and including 1970, the sector of material production comprised industry, agriculture, forestry, construction, transport of goods, telecommunications for the productive sector and trade (including restaurants, cafes, and so forth). The nonproductive sector included municipal services, dwelling rents, and other nonproductive services; education, culture, and art; science and scientific services; public health, social assistance, and physical culture; financial and insurance institutions; administration; and political and social organizations. In 1971 the following activities were included in the sector of material production: services rendered to agriculture by agricultural mechanization stations, veterinary services for agriculture, services for distribution of irrigation water, passenger transport and telecommunications serving the population and administrative and sociocultural units, services rendered by hotels, health resort enterprises, scientific research, computer centers, laundries, cleaning, dyeing, and photographic shops.

enterprise to another. This procedure thus involves substantial double-counting. In agriculture, the value of gross output is derived from separate calculations of the value of plant and animal production, as well as from agricultural services. Therefore, gross agricultural product includes not only inputs from other subsectors, but also a double-counting of the fodder and seed produced and used in agriculture. Gross output in construction is the value of all work performed in erecting and repairing buildings and structures, including the value of geologic prospecting and drilling work and work contributed by the population to constructing public buildings, roads, and bridges. In transport and telecommunications, gross output is the sum of gross receipts from transport and related services and from telecommunications services rendered to the public, to administrative and sociocultural units and to enterprises in other subsectors. In domestic trade, gross output is calculated as the difference between the sale and the purchase prices of traded commodities. The value of output in foreign trade is the value of exports at prices paid by the domestic foreign trade organizations to producers, minus the value of imported products at the prices paid by purchasers to the domestic foreign trade organizations. If imports (exports) exceed exports (imports) valued in foreign prices converted into lei at the official exchange rate, the value of this deficit (surplus) must be subtracted from (added to) the difference between imports and exports calculated at actual domestic prices. The goods and services that enter into the social product are valued at delivery prices, which include the turnover tax.

National income is measured by net material product, which is the sum of the net products of the subsectors of material production. The net product of a subsector is obtained by subtracting all material costs, including depreciation, from the gross product of the subsector. National income includes, therefore, wages and salaries, contribution to the social insurance, enterprise income, and the turnover tax. Compared with the traditional concept of national income, that in Romania excludes the net value of nonproductive services consumed by the population and the administration, but includes turnover taxes. The differences between the system of material production (SMP) and the United Nations system of national accounts (SNA) in terms of the makeup and utilization of national income are shown in Figures D.1 and D.2.

Figure D.1. *Production of National Income in the National System* (SMP) *and in the System of National Accounts* (SNA)

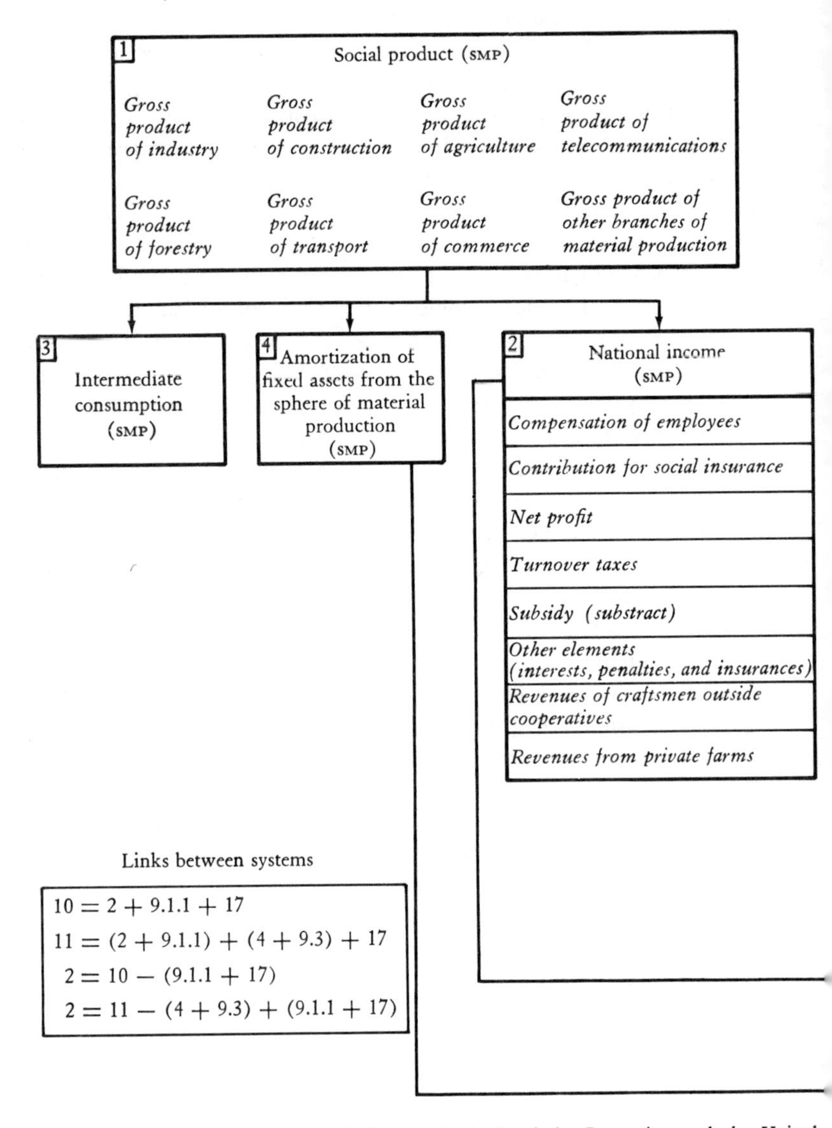

Note: SMP and SNA are, respectively, on the basis of the Romanian and the United Nations systems.

Source: Information provided by Romanian authorities during discussions with the authors.

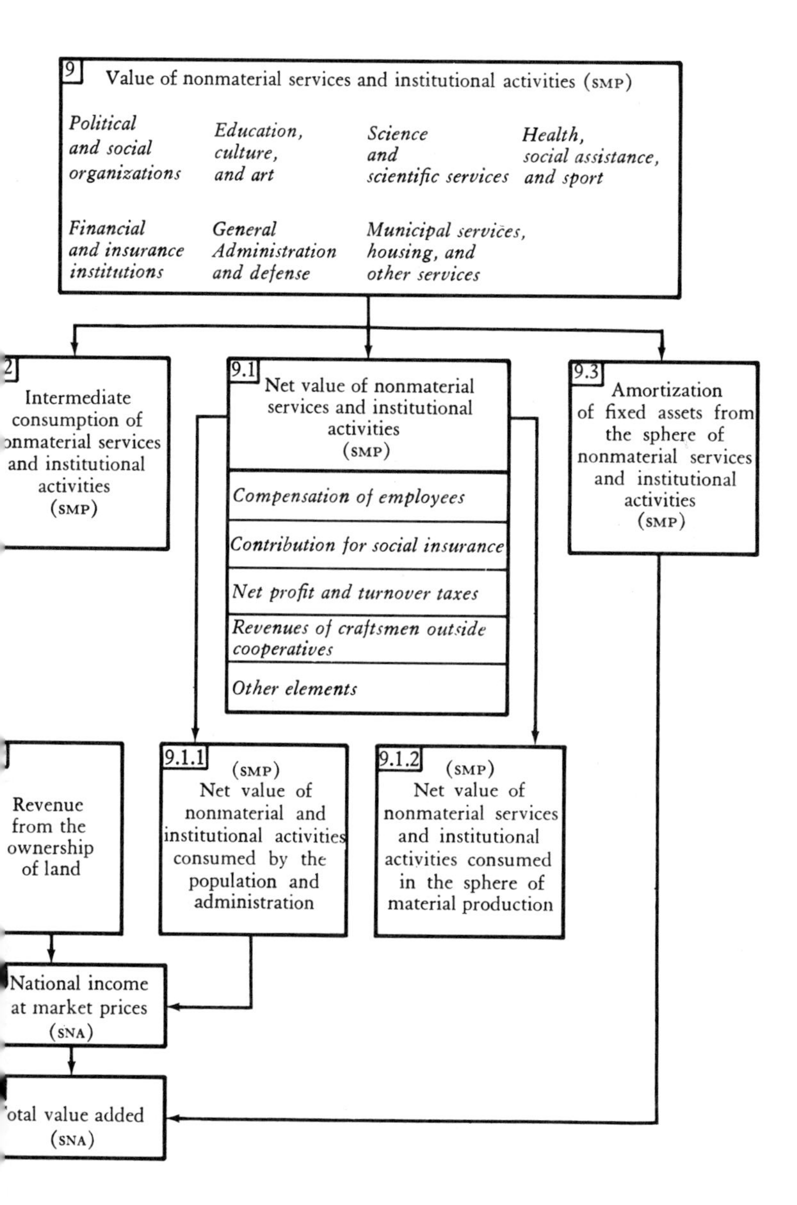
9
Value of nonmaterial services and institutional activities (SMP)
Political and social organizations
Education, culture, and art
Science and scientific services
Health, social assistance, and sport
Financial and insurance institutions
General Administration and defense
Municipal services, housing, and other services
2
Intermediate consumption of onmaterial services and institutional activities (SMP)
9.1
Net value of nonmaterial services and institutional activities (SMP)
Compensation of employees
Contribution for social insurance
Net profit and turnover taxes
Revenues of craftsmen outside cooperatives
Other elements
9.3
Amortization of fixed assets from the sphere of nonmaterial services and institutional activities (SMP)
Revenue from the ownership of land
9.1.1
(SMP)
Net value of nonmaterial and institutional activities consumed by the population and administration
9.1.2
(SMP)
Net value of nonmaterial services and institutional activities consumed in the sphere of material production
National income at market prices (SNA)
otal value added (SNA)

Figure D.2. *Use of National Income in the National System* (SMP) *and in the System of National Accounts* (SNA)

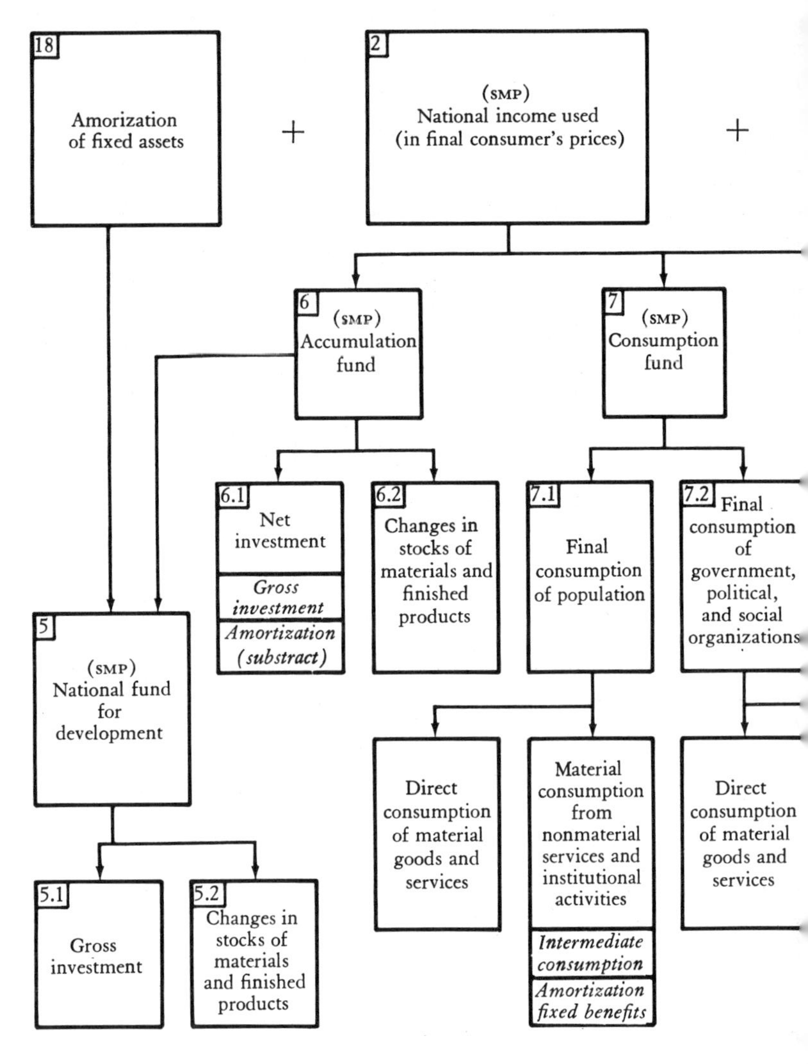

Note: SMP and SNA are, respectively, on the basis of the Romanian and the United Nations systems.

Source: Information provided by Romanian authorities during discussions with the authors.

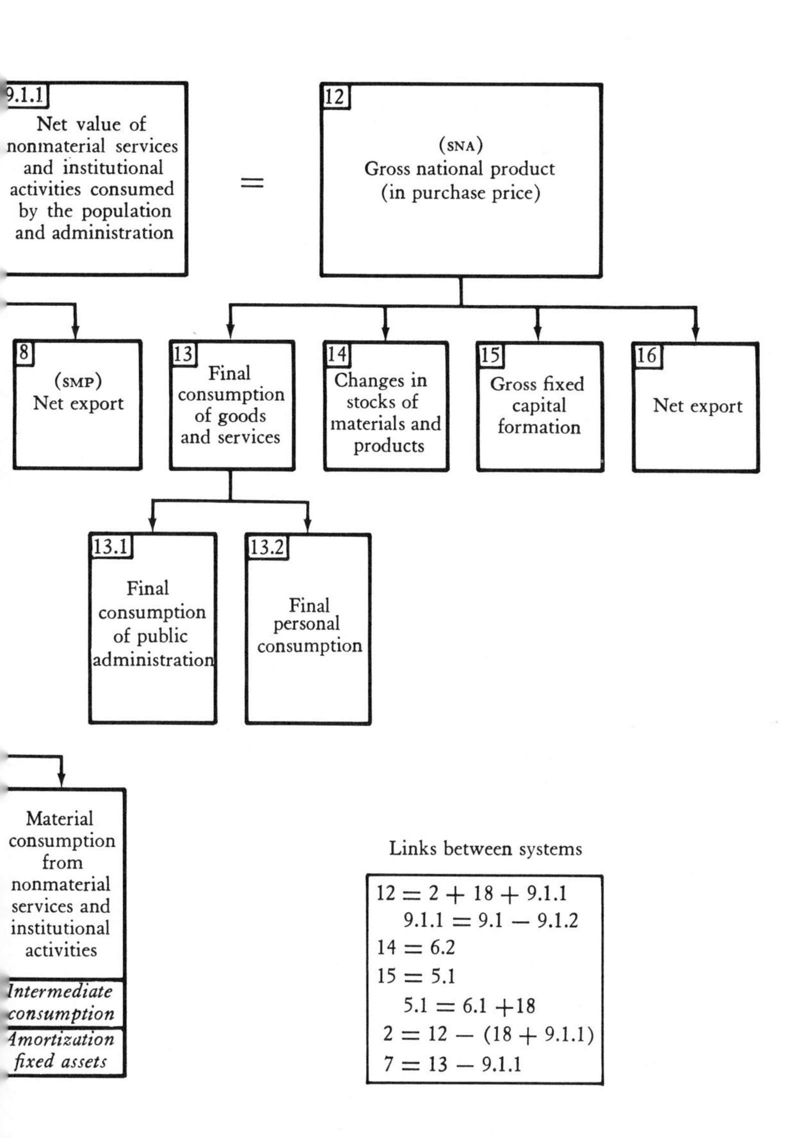

9.1.1
Net value of nonmaterial services and institutional activities consumed by the population and administration
=
12
(SNA)
Gross national product (in purchase price)
8
(SMP)
Net export
13
Final consumption of goods and services
14
Changes in stocks of materials and products
15
Gross fixed capital formation
16
Net export
13.1
Final consumption of public administration
13.2
Final personal consumption
Material consumption from nonmaterial services and institutional activities
Intermediate consumption
Amortization fixed assets
Links between systems
12 = 2 + 18 + 9.1.1
9.1.1 = 9.1 − 9.1.2
14 = 6.2
15 = 5.1
5.1 = 6.1 + 18
2 = 12 − (18 + 9.1.1)
7 = 13 − 9.1.1

E

Planning

THIS APPENDIX HAS SEVERAL PURPOSES: it examines the quantitative techniques used in the planning process; it discusses project selection criteria; it provides an example of an annual development plan; it updates the analysis in Chapter 6 by looking at economic performance in 1976 and the annual plan for 1977; and it looks at industrial targets for the 1976–80 plan period.

Quantitative Techniques

Mathematical economic models are used to establish a general reference and comparative framework in Romania's planning (Chapter 3). They are not used as extensively as in other eastern European economies, but there is a strong tendency to assimilate more and more of these models and their results in planning. The underlying sequence and logic in Romania's planning models is:

(a) Monosector and multisector simulation macroeconomic models to determine variants of the "final consumption vector" (which assists in formulating the targets of the five-year plans);
(b) An input-output table (27×27) to determine relations between subsectors and to check the material balances;
(c) Sectoral models to establish the direction of optimum development of production and investment of the sectors.

The use of these models in Romanian planning is reviewed below.

Long-term model

The basis for long-term forecasting and for determining the final demand is a set of three models. The initial model used is a monosector model,[1] with eight equations, seven variables, and three optional parameters. The model simulates the rate of accumulation and obtains values of the consumption fund, including the investment for the social and cultural sectors. On the basis of a time series for 1959–70, the model has been used to compute the optimum rate of accumulation for 1976–90.

This model has been extended to cover five sectors by using the production function approach to obtain long-run economic growth variants of the dynamics of national income, as well as of fixed assets and labor requirements for each sector.

The third model is an extension of the first and includes five policy variables linked to thirty-two equations.[2] This model has provided a good fit to the statistical data for 1960–72. It has been used in the preliminary draft of the 1976–80 Plan and also to establish many growth variants of the national economy for 1976–90. Finally, it is considered the central bloc of the simulation model in determining long-term growth process.

Medium-term model (input-output)

The use of input-output tables has had limited significance in Romanian planning so far. The obvious relevance of input-output models to Romanian planning problems, however, has resulted in extensive research efforts. The first input-output table was worked out in 1971 with data for 1970. The productive activity was distributed in seventy-four subsectors, each consisting of groups of similar products and services. The input-output table covered thirteen sectors of primary inputs and thirteen items of final demand. Some elements of that input-output table, as well as the input-output multipliers and import rates matrix, have been published.[3] To better use the information provided by the input-output table, a more aggregated table has been prepared (with thirty-six subsectors), which is

1. Emilian Dobrescu, *Correlation between Accumulation and Consumption* (Bucharest: Editur Politica, 1971).

2. I. Desmireanu, E. V. Topala, A. Camara, and S. C. Nita, "Model Macro-Economic Unisectoral Pentru Dezvoltaria Economei Nationale in Perioda 1976–1990," *Revista de Statistica* (March 1974).

3. M. Capata, *Balanta Statistica a Legatuziloz dintre Ramuzi* (Bucharest: Editur Politica, 1974); M. Capata, *Tipologia Economiiloz Nationale* (Bucharest: Editur Politica, 1976); E. Dobrescu, *Optimul Economiei Socialiste* (Bucharest: Editur Politica, 1976).

more appropriate to the classification of subsectors used in planning and statistical reports in Romania. Another matrix has also been built according to the criterion of organization pattern that covers only twenty-seven sectors and that corresponds to a large degree, but incompletely, to the structure of economic activity by ministries.

Another problem in applying input-output tables to planning in Romania has been the fact that rapid growth in the economy quickly outdates the technical coefficients derived from the table. This problem has led to recognition of the need for more efficient techniques in revising the tables. Efforts are being made to collect these data more efficiently from the enterprises to accelerate the updating process.

Sectoral model

Several sectoral models have been developed and used. These models are basically linear programming models.

(a) Agriculture sector model (long-term).[4] This is an optimization model, which maximizes the value of agricultural production while also satisfying the food requirements of the population. The model determines the growth of agricultural surplus, the required labor force, and volume and value of exports. It has been used to forecast the value of these parameters up to 1990.

(b) Optimization model for the oil refinery sector.[5] This model optimizes the production plans of five plants with thirty-five products in the short-, medium- and long-terms.

(c) Optimization model for constructing hydroelectric plants.[6] This model determines a program of planned growth of installed electric power. On the basis of given yearly investments and on estimated requirements for installed power, the model ranks needed construction of new plants according to the following criteria: cost of installed kilowatts, cost of produced kilowatt hour, and time required to recover investment.

4. State Planning Committee, *Modele Economico—Matematica De Prognoza De Permen Lung Pentru Optimizarea Structurii Productiei Agricole* (Bucharest: Agerpress, 1975).

5. V. Pescaru and V. Mierlea, "Model De Planificare Optima A Productiei In Subramura De Prelucrare A Titeiului."

6. State Planning Committee, "Program De Perspectiva Privind Constructia De Centrale Hidroelectrice in RSR."

(d) Optimization model for wood utilization. This model estimates the minimum amount of wood required to produce twenty-four wood products.

(e) Optimization models for chemical fertilizer for agriculture. There are three models for this subsector: an econometric model to estimate the internal fertilizer consumption; a dynamic programming model to analyze the structure of fertilizer production, required production capacity, and new locations and investments; and a linear programming model to distribute fertilizer regionally by the amount and types required for agriculture, as well as to determine the best location for new plants and to minimize investment and transport costs.

(f) Macroeconomic prediction model for developing research capacity during 1971–80. The model correlates the scientific research development with the general economic growth, and, on the basis of it, the efficiency of scientific research is ascertained, considering its contribution to the national income. The model also determines the priority fields in which Romanian science is to develop. The quantitative technique used is linear programming.

Romania is at present venturing into a detailed and integrated planning framework which uses most of the models already in use by the State Planning Committee (SPC) and certain ministries and also a few new ones. This will provide a more complete coverage for the economy and a more consistent aggregate planning framework.

The new models are divided into two categories: long-term and medium-term models. The long-term models include: (a) a model for human resources, which is based on population forecasting and determining the size of active population and on employment requirements; (b) a regional development model, which analyzes alternatives to reduce disparities among regions; and (c) an export-import model, which is still at a fairly aggregated stage.

For the five-year plans, the main focus in model formulation will be on input-output analysis. A lot of research is directed toward revising coefficients and toward incorporating a dynamic input-output model. Work is being undertaken on several models.

(a) A final demand model, which is to be derived from the long-term forecasting model. This model includes five components: individual consumers; social consumption; investment; increase in stocks; and exports. Using the final demand model and the input-output table, it is possible to obtain gross output levels;

(b) A model of inter-subsectors, which is the usual input-output model;

(c) A model for the investment and production funds;
(d) A model for human resources to determine manpower requirements (this will follow from the input-output model once it is made into a dynamic model);
(e) A foreign trade model, which will differ from the one described above, in that it will be more disaggregated;
(f) A model for staff training;
(g) A model of incomes of the population, which will be linked to the final demand model;
(h) A model of production cost and price trends.

In addition, there will be models for the key sectors: agriculture, energy resources, essential products, and a regional model, which will be more disaggregated than that mentioned above. These models will also be used to prepare the annual plans, but more disaggregation will be introduced.

Project Selection

Although the basic priorities for investment in the sectors is centrally established, detailed rules for investment criteria have been established to help determine the choice of projects as well as their size, the technologies applied, and other project characteristics according to 1969 law specifically concerned with investment policies and investment allocation criteria. These rules contain technical, economic and sociopolitical indicators and are the standard tool for designing and assessing projects. The approval of an industrial project is not based on the calculation of a single highly aggregated rate of economic return, but on many individual criteria that the project promises to meet. The main difficulties of such a methodology were discussed in Chapter 3. In the preparation and approval process, the criteria have different weights, which also may change over time, depending on the economic priorities. Moreover, these relative weights may change from project to project according to the priorities attached to them by the approving authorities. For example, a project might be approved because of its particular sociopolitical (national or regional) advantages, which are considered important enough to offset the temporarily less favorable economic efficiencies.

Criteria for project selection and investment

The standard criteria assessed during the selection and preparation process for investment indicate the general policy objectives pursued in industrial projects. There are three types of criteria: technical, economic, and sociopolitical. The technical criteria aim to ensure that technological processes and machinery and equipment are used that produce items comparable with similar products in world markets. Domestically developed technologies are used wherever they are comparable with international standards. The use of imported technologies and knowledge is encouraged, however, if it would lead to the development of new areas of industrial activity in Romania. Joint ventures are seen as the appropriate instrument for obtaining needed technology transfers and training.

The economic criteria are the decisive criteria in project selection and preparation. Depending on the kind of project and the prescribed approval procedures, up to seventeen categories of indicators must be submitted to the approving authorities. These include estimates of:

(a) Investment costs, expressed both in absolute totals and in specific costs per unit of output;
(b) Consumption of so-called "key" construction materials (steel, timber, cement, and so forth);
(c) Total and specific consumption of principal raw materials and intermediate products;
(d) Total and specific production costs, the latter normally expressed in lei per 1,000 lei of commodity output;
(e) Annual benefits (profits) and profit rates expected;
(f) "Pay-back period;"
(g) Employment and labor productivity;
(h) Efficiency of fixed assets;
(i) Efficiency of total assets in generating or saving foreign exchange;
(j) Indicators of capacity and factory space utilization.

The sociopolitical criteria mainly help to determine the geographic location of industry. They stress the principle of locating industries processing large volumes of raw materials close to where these materials are produced. This applies mainly to chemical industries, wood processing, and some food processing industries. Industries with large volumes of output (for example, fertilizers) and industries producing perishable products or products involving high transport costs are, however, located, in principle, near the centers of consumption. In addition industries requiring large quantities of electric power or water are located near such sources, industries that are heavy consumers of water and that require a large volume of transport are located along navigable waterways (iron and steel, organic dyestuffs, rayon), and technologically advanced industries (electronics, precision tools and instruments, and electrical engineering) are generally located where the necessary technological and scientific support (computers, research laboratories) is available. The productive units of the food industry are widespread, and their location is linked to sources of agricultural output. Attempts are being made to reduce the transport of raw materials and to bring fresh products, for example, vegetables and dairy and bakery products, closer to consumers. It appears that in the past, approval of investments has generally observed these established principles closely.

Apart from the principles mentioned above, sociopolitical criteria consider the effect of planned industrial projects on employment emphasizing maximum mobilization of labor and reduction of regional economic and social disparities. In particular, industries are being located in areas where industrialization is lagging. Another important aspect has been the utilization of female labor, particularly where, to date, extractive and heavy industries have created job opportunities predominantly for men. As a result, it has become a policy objective to establish light industries suitable for female labor (such as, electronics, textiles, clothing, shoes, and the like) in centers of heavy industries. On the whole, engineering and light industries have been used extensively to promote regional development, sometimes by first deciding to develop a specific place of limited economic growth opportunities and then by deciding on the type of industry to be set up. In this situation, the interests of the relevant local authorities and those of the industrial ministry could diverge, with the former wishing to set up industries where they want to promote development and the latter preferring to establish enterprises where other industries already exist.

These indicators provide an additional function when the project is implemented and in operation. They then form the basis for drafting the targets for the enterprise and provide the technical material to monitor and evaluate performance. The respective centrals and ministries are responsible for these functions.

Technical and economic indicators

Enterprises, industrial centrals, and other entities in charge of selecting and preparing projects have to prepare detailed project data to economically justify the project.[7] These data have to be submitted to the approving

7. Law (no. 72/1969) on Organization, Planning, and Execution of Investment Projects, *Official Bulletin of the Socialist Republic of Romania*, no. 154 (December 29, 1969), and Resolution (no. 900/1970) of the Council of Ministers on the Preparation and Execution of Investment Operations, *Official Bulletin of the Socialist Republic of Romania*, no. 75-76 (July 7, 1970).

authorities at least six months before the beginning of a plan year, to ensure that the project is integrated in the annual plan.

Information related to up to seventeen categories of indicators (listed below) is required. Apart from data on the project itself, quantitative information is required, which allows the project to be compared with other similar projects or enterprises in Romania and abroad. Moreover, a comparison has to be made with the average results attained by enterprises manufacturing similar products under the respective industrial ministry. Average indicators of the group of enterprises that produce similar products under the same ministry usually provide the data of the year preceding the application for project approval.

The principal indicators used to analyze and to select projects are detailed below.

INVESTMENT COST. This indicator is estimated on the basis of the available project documents and has to be presented as follows:

(1) Cost of construction and assembly (1,000 lei)
  (a) cost of construction (1,000 lei)
  (b) share of construction and assembly cost in total investment cost (percent)
  (c) share of construction cost in total investment cost (percent)
(2) Cost and volume of equipment (1,000 lei and in tonnes)
  (a) cost and volume of imported equipment (1,000 lei and in tons; 1,000 lei foreign exchange)
    (i) equipment imported from socialist countries (1,000 lei foreign exchange)
    (ii) equipment imported from capitalist countries (1,000 lei foreign exchange)
  (b) share of imported equipment in total equipment cost (percent)
(3) Other foreign exchange costs (1,000 lei foreign exchange). This category includes licenses, technical documents, knowledge, technical assistance, training of personnel abroad, spare parts, tools, instruments for initial outfitting, and so forth.
  (a) outlays in socialist countries (1,000 lei foreign exchange)
  (b) outlays in capitalist countries (1,000 lei foreign exchange)

TIMING OF PROJECT IMPLEMENTATION.
(1) Time between the start of project implementation and the start of operation of the entire capacity (months)
(2) Intermediate periods, if sections of the project are activated in stages
(3) Period between start of operations and the attainment of projected

levels of production, cost price, labor productivity, profitability, and so forth (months)

SPECIFIC INVESTMENT COSTS.

(1) Investment costs per unit of output (lei per tonne, piece, square meter, and so forth)
(2) Investment costs per 1,000 lei of community output,[8] when output is heterogeneous and cannot be expressed in physical or conventional units

CONSUMPTION OF PRINCIPAL CONSTRUCTION MATERIALS (lei per million lei of construction and assembly cost). This indicator applies to commodities such as metal, timber, cement, and so forth, for which material balances are established.

VALUE OF PRINCIPAL RAW MATERIALS AND INTERMEDIATE GOODS NEEDED FOR ANNUAL PRODUCTION (1,000 lei). For imported materials, the values and the duration of imports need to be specified. Plans to produce hitherto imported items in Romania must be indicated; if such plans do not exist, a reason for this is needed.

SPECIFIC CONSUMPTION OF PRINCIPAL RAW MATERIALS AND INTERMEDIATE GOODS PER UNIT OF OUTPUT (principal products only) (tonnes, kilograms, kilowatt-hours, and so forth per unit).

COST PRICE PER UNIT OF OUTPUT (lei per unit).

PRODUCTION COST PER 1,000 LEI OF COMMODITY OUTPUT.

(1) Total production cost expressed in terms of the enterprise's wholesale or estimated prices (lei per 1,000 lei)
(2) Material costs of production (lei per 1,000 lei)

TOTAL ANNUAL ACCUMULATION (NET INCOME). This indicator is the difference between the value of commodity output expressed in estimated prices or in the enterprise's wholesale prices (reduced by the amount of the com-

8. The annual value of commodity output is to be expressed in estimated or wholesale prices of the enterprise. For new products for which enterprise wholesale prices or estimated prices have not been established, the SPC or other authorized planning entities determine the wholesale price for the enterprise according to regulations.

modity turnover tax included in the wholesale price) and the commodity output expressed in terms of cost price:

(1) Annual profit (1,000 lei)
(2) Annual profit including equalization tax (1,000 lei)

PROFITABILITY.
(1) Ratio of annual profit to total cost price (percent)
(2) Ratio of annual profit plus annual equalization tax on total cost price (percent)

EMPLOYMENT. Total number of jobs created, broken down into number of skilled workers and number of basic workers.

LABOR PRODUCTIVITY (lei per worker and in tonnes, kilograms, square kilometers, and so forth per worker).

PERIOD OF RECOVERY OF INVESTMENT COST (PAY-BACK PERIOD).
(1) Based only on annual profits (years)
(2) Based on annual profits plus equalization tax (years)
(3) Based on net income (years)

EFFICIENCY OF FIXED ASSETS.
(1) The ratio of the value of annual gross output to the value of fixed assets, yielding the respective output (lei per leu of fixed assets)
(2) The ratio of the value of accumulation (annual profit, turnover tax, and equalization tax) to value of fixed assets (lei per leu of fixed assets)

EXPORT EFFICIENCY OF PRODUCTION or IMPORT SUBSTITUTION EFFICIENCY. This indicator is required only for enterprises producing commodities intended wholly or partly for exports or to substitute imports.

(1) Earnings or savings of foreign exchange in relation to cost price (lei per leu of foreign exchange)
(2) Earnings or savings of foreign exchange in relation to wholesale price of enterprise or estimated price (lei per leu of foreign exchange)
(3) Net annual contribution in foreign exchange lei
    (a) in relation to total foreign exchange lei per unit product exported (percent)
    (b) in relation to total investment (foreign exchange lei per leu invested)

(4) Period of recovery of foreign exchange cost of investment, including indirect costs from the net inflow (years)

EXTENSION OF PLANT PREMISES (hectares).

UTILIZATION OF CAPACITIES AND PRODUCTION AREAS (percent).
(1) In enterprise in charge of the project
(2) In the group of enterprises having comparable product mixes (same ministry)
(3) Extent of occupation of premises

Competences of approval of industrial projects

The level of the authority that approves a project is determined by the amount of investment involved in that project. All industrial projects fall into one of two categories. The following projects are approved according to one system.

(a) Extractive industries, including the processing of coal, oil, natural gas, and ores
(b) Ferrous and nonferrous metallurgy
(c) Production of refractory materials
(d) Engineering industries and metal processing
(e) Production, transmission, and distribution of electrical energy
(f) Chemical industry
(g) Pulp and paper industry
(h) Construction materials industry

Approvals for projects in the above category are given according to the following system.

(a) If the investment exceeds 70 million lei: the Council of Ministers;
(b) For investments less than 70 million lei: the industrial ministry concerned, the other central authorities, and the Executive Committee of the Popular Council concerned;
(c) For investments less than 30 million lei and provided such competences have been granted: industrial centrals and other organizations with statutory control over enterprises;
(d) For investments less than 10 million lei and provided such competences have been granted: industrial enterprises themselves.

For all industrial projects not listed above, there is a second system for approving projects.

(a) If the investment exceeds 50 million lei: the Council of Ministers;
(b) For investments less than 50 million lei: the industrial ministry concerned, other central authorities, and the Executive Committee of the People's Council concerned;
(c) For investments less than 30 million lei and provided such competences have been granted: industrial centrals and other organizations with statutory control over enterprises;
(d) For investments less than of 10 million lei and provided such competences have been granted: industrial enterprises themselves.

The 1976 Annual Development Plan[9]

Article 1. The Unified National Socioeconomic Development Plan of the Socialist Republic of Romania for 1976 is hereby adopted.

Item	*Absolute figures*	*Percent 1976/75 (estimate)*
1. Gross industrial production (billions of lei)	641.0	110.2
2. Gross agricultural production (billions of lei)	108.3–119.3	115–126.6
3. Volume of domestic movement of freight (billions of tonne-kilometers)	84.2	105.8
4. Value of investment in the national economy (billions of lei) (includes reserve for investment projects whose technical and economic indicators have not yet been approved)	159.5	119.4
5. Total value of foreign trade transactions (billions of foreign-exchange lei)	60.7	117.8
6. Retail sales of goods within the socialist commercial network (billions of lei)	154.8	110.0
7. Public services (billions of lei)	31.5	113.8
8. Average number of workers (thousands)	6,665	105.6
9. Productivity of labor within the national industrial sector (lei)	254,500	108.5
10. National income (billions of lei)	400.0	110.5
11. Total real per capita income (lei per month)	1,030–1,035	108–108.5

9. This is an informal World Bank translation of the 1976 Law of the Plan.

Article 2. The gross industrial product for 1976 will be 641 billion lei in comparative prices. The following levels will be attained with respect to the major industrial products:

Electric energy (billion kilowatt-hours)	57.5
Coal, net (millions of tonnes)	29.6
Petroleum, extracted (millions of tonnes)	14.7
Methane gas, extracted (billion cubic meters)	26.8
Steel (thousands of tonnes)	10,970
Fully finished rolled steel goods (thousands of tonnes)	7,800
Steel pipes (thousands of tonnes)	1,250
Lead (thousands of tonnes)	47
Zinc (thousands of tonnes)	55.4
Converter copper (thousands of tonnes)	40.3
Primary aluminum and aluminum alloys (thousands of tonnes)	206
Electric motors, 0.25 kilowatts and above (megawatts)	6,780
Electric and electronic measuring and control apparatus (billions of lei)	0.6
Electric and electronic automation equipment (billions of lei)	3.4
Electric and electronic computer equipment (billions of lei)	1.87
Computers (the equivalent of 120 KO computers)	58
Low-voltage electric apparatus (billions of lei)	3.29
Precision mechanics and optical equipment, hydraulic and pneumatic equipment and parts (billions of lei)	3.6
Metal cutting machine tools (billions of lei)	3.8
Tractors (thousands)	51.5
Trucks, motorized tractors, and dumptrucks (thousands)	36
Passenger cars (thousands)	60
Cross-country jeeps (thousands)	15
Utility vehicles (thousands)	11
Electric and diesel locomotives for arterial railways (units)	308
Oceangoing vessels (thousand dead weight tons)	350
River vessels (unit)	38
Basic macromolecular products (thousands of tonnes)	512.5
Synthetic rubber (thousands of tonnes)	146.5
Artificial fibers and filaments (thousands of tonnes)	65.5
Synthetic fibers and filaments (thousands of tonnes)	108.3
Tires (thousands)	4,425
Chemical fertilizer (100 percent active material) (thousands of tonnes)	2,280
Cement (equivalent 80 percent clinker) (thousands of tonnes)	14,000
Fiberboard and particle board (thousands of tonnes)	920

Wooden furniture (billions of lei)	10.8
Cellulose and semicellulose (thousands of tonnes)	636
Paper, cardboard, and pasteboard (millions of square meters)	8,769.0
(millions of tonnes)	765
Medicine (billions of lei)	3.6
Radio receivers (thousands)	860
Television receivers (thousands)	580
Electric appliances for household use (billions of lei)	1.6
Refrigerators (thousands)	375
Electric washing machines (thousands)	180
Household glassware (millions of lei)	705
Fine household ceramics (millions of lei)	333
Fabrics (billions of lei)	19.2
(millions of square meters)	1,066.7
Knitted products (millions of lei)	8,973
Ready-to-wear fabric clothing (billions of lei)	29.4
Footwear (millions of lei)	6,680
(millions of pairs)	102.87
Meat, total (thousands of tonnes)	945.4
Meat for processing and canning (thousands of tonnes)	278.5
Fish (thousands of tonnes)	189.6
Milk for direct consumption (thousands of hectoliters)	6,000
Butter (thousands of tonnes)	34.5
Cheeses (thousands of tonnes)	101.7
Edible oils (thousands of tonnes)	298
Margarine (thousands of tonnes)	21
Sugar (thousands of tonnes)	594
Sugar products (thousands of tonnes)	130
Canned fruits and vegetables and tomato paste (thousands of tonnes)	455.3
New wine (thousands of hectoliters)	6,840
Beer (thousands of hectoliters)	7,500

Article 3. The Council of Ministers will adopt specific measures to guarantee that concerned ministries as well as central and local authorities, centralized industrial units, and enterprises ensure the following:

(a) Steady expansion of production, with enough range and quality of products to satisfy the needs of the national economy; the over-achievement of plan targets for end-products that make more rational use of raw materials and intermediate products and for products whose sale to the public can be assured based on sale agreements and firm domestic and foreign orders;

(b) Optimal use of the production potential of the nation's industrial concerns through increased utilization of machinery, equipment, installations, and built-up industrial zones; increased shift coefficients; elimination of bottlenecks; regular supply of raw materials, intermediate products, and spare parts; and improved maintenance and repair of machinery, equipment, and installations;

(c) Acceleration in the modernization of production techniques and the assimilation of new products and technologies to increase substantially the technical and production efficiency levels and product quality and reliability;

(d) Improved production structure and increased utilization of raw materials and intermediate products through diversified production; increased the manufacture of products and models with high technological effectiveness; and reduced specific consumption of raw materials and intermediate products;

(e) Expanded effort to standardize and specialize production activities and to increase mutual cooperation among firms;

(f) Strict compliance with the schedules established to attain the design parameters for new investment projects.

Article 4. The following production levels will be attained for the principal agricultural products during 1976, assuming normal agricultural conditions throughout the year:

Agricultural product	*Total*	*Including State Agriculture Department*
Grain cereals (thousands of tonnes)	20,570	4,500
Grain wheat and rye (thousands of tonnes)	7,225	1,385
Grain corn (thousands of tonnes)	11,935	2,590
Sugar beets (thousands of tonnes)	7,200	—
Sunflowers (thousands of tonnes)	1,080	200
Beans (thousands of tonnes)	193	13.7
Soya (thousands of tonnes)	321	145
Flax for fiber (thousands of tonnes)	273	10.4
Hemp for fiber (thousands of tonnes)	192	—
Autumn potatoes (thousands of tonnes)	4,735	120
Field vegetables (thousands of tonnes)	3,950	143
Fruits (thousands of tonnes)	1,930	316
Grapes (thousands of tonnes)	1,642	340
Meat on the hoof (thousands of tonnes)	2,298	676.1
Cow's milk (thousands of hectoliters)	49,490	7,470
Wool (tonnes)	36,096	6,560
Eggs (millions)	5,845	1,853

Article 5. The total arable land under cultivation will cover a minimum of 9,741,000 hectares. Irrigated farms will cover 1,960,000 hectares, including 1,895,000 hectares of arable land.

Article 6. Livestock herds will reach the following levels by the end of 1976:

Kind of livestock	*Total*	*Including State Agriculture Department*
Cattle (thousands of head)	6,620	865
Cows and heifers (thousands of head)	3,273	360
Swine (thousands of head)	10,250	3,215
Sows (thousands of head)	1,000	316
Sheep and goats (thousands of head)	15,900	1,900
Egg-laying poultry (thousands of head)	47,530	11,700

Article 7. During 1976, the physical resources allocated to agriculture will be developed as follows:

(a) The agricultural sector will receive 14,000 tractors and 5,100 self-propelled combines, as well as miscellaneous agricultural machinery and equipment;

(b) An area covering 150,000 hectares will be irrigated, including 140,000 hectares in large perimeters and 10,000 hectares with local systems;

(c) Drainage works covering 215,000 hectares and erosion control measures for 144,000 hectares will be financed from state funds;

(d) The agricultural sector will receive 1,454,000 tons of chemical fertilizer (active material).

Article 8. To meet the goals of the plan pertaining to agricultural development, the Council of Ministers will adopt specific measures to make certain that the Ministry of Agriculture and Food Industry, the National Union of Agricultural Production Cooperatives, the Academy of Agricultural and Forestry Science, as well as district agricultural authorities, ensure the following:

(a) Maximum efficiency in the use of all agricultural and arable land, including land resulting from the reorganization of communes and land lying on the outskirts of villages and towns; full utilization of irrigated land; increase in agricultural and arable land through the execution of projects for reclamation of unproductive land; and the cultivation of temporarily idle land;

(b) Distribution of crops within the territorial boundaries based on the types of soil and the climatic conditions, as well as on the findings of agricultural production zoning studies; and granting of top priority to the cultivation of irrigated crops whenever such practice is economically justified to attain the design parameters for irrigation systems;

(c) Cultivation of vegetables under irrigation; production of increased quantities of early vegetables; and the construction of greenhouses and solariums to meet future local consumption needs of these products;

(d) Modernization of existing stands and the creation of new intensive and superintensive stands to increase fruit and vegetable production and to create the storage conditions required to ensure the supply of fresh vegetables to the public throughout the entire year;

(e) Expansion of the capacities of breeding greenhouses and increase of production capacities to cover global requirements for selected seeds, as well as planting stock specifically adapted to each agricultural production zone and its irrigation conditions; and application of specific technologies to each crop, production zone, and system of cultivation;

(f) Increase in livestock herds, improvement in selection and breeding activities, and reduction of losses caused by high mortality rates; increase in the number of livestock and poultry raised within the industrial sector; organization of sow maternity centers in communes to supply the public with hogs for raising and fattening; and construction of livestock installations in socialist districts satisfying the demand for milk and eggs in that district;

(g) Preparation of programs and establishment of technical and organizational parameters expressed on graphs kept on file by production units, which will ensure an increase in the average rate of livestock slaughter, particularly that of cattle and sheep;

(h) Expansion in feed production operations through an increase in the average yield per hectare, including the yields of natural pastures; use of all existing feed resources and design of new technologies to prepare feed through a rational use of all nutrients contained in feed resources; extended cultivation of feed crops, especially in irrigated perimeters; urgent completion of the harvesting machine system and mass production of feed using modern technology; and commissioning of all available facilities to produce high-yielding flours;

(i) Efficient management of mechanical resources, fertilizers, and other chemical materials used in agriculture;

(j) Introduction and expanded production, based on continuing research, of new varieties of cereals and industrial crops, seeds with high biological value, and upgraded animal breeds better adapted to the production zones in Romania.

Article 9. A total of 1.9 billion lei will be allocated for investment during 1976, to be used to create multipurpose reservoirs, pipelines, and catchments and to construct dams to protect villages and exposed farmland from the danger of flooding, as well as to regulate streams and rivers and to reinforce and protect river banks.

Article 10. In an effort to combat water and air pollution, the Council of Ministers will adopt special measures to make certain that all concerned ministries, central and local authorities, and centralized industrial concerns and enterprises ensure the construction and placement in operation of wastewater and gas treatment plants along with the respective investment facilities and the operation of these installations at required levels.

The National Council of Water Resources, concerned ministries, and other centralized and local authorities shall be responsible for overseeing the implementation of the portion of the plan regarding water resource management and the construction of wastewater treatment facilities at new industrial units and existing installations that do not presently have these facilities or whose treatment capacity is below the required level.

Article 11. The volume of timber and timber byproducts used within the economy during 1976 will reach 20,000,000 cubic meters. Furthermore, the 1976 Plan provides for the collection and most efficient use of timber felled in the course of forest hygiene operations and through tree care, clearing, and cutting of young stands of trees.

The Council of Ministers will take steps to guarantee that the Ministry of Forestry and Construction Materials and other plan administrators ensure the following:

(a) Strict adherence to the rules regarding multipurpose forest management and better organization of silvicultural and forestry operations;
(b) Creation of a total forested area of 57,700 hectares, 19,000 hectares of which will be used to grow special forest products used to produce cellulose wood, with resinous species accounting for 65 to 70 percent of the total forest area;
(c) Development of hunting and fishing activities in mountain waters and in specialized units, expansion of stands of fruitbearing shrubs, and harvesting of wild forest fruits;
(d) Execution of projects to regulate rivers and to reclaim unproductive

land to balance the water regime in hydrographic basins earmarked for the construction of hydroelectric plants and reservoirs and for environmental protection.

The Ministry of Forestry and Construction Materials, along with the Ministry of Equipment and Supplies and Fixed Capital Management Control, working in with plan administrators, will introduce a regime of "strict economy" in all sectors that consume wood.

Article 12. The Council of Ministers will ensure that concerned ministries, central and local authorities, government agencies, and enterprises, together with the National Council for Environmental Protection and the National Council on Water Resources carry out all tasks and implement all measures in the environmental protection program within the framework of the activities and resources provided for in the 1976 Development Plan.

Article 13. The total gross receipts generated by activities connected with public transportation in 1976 will be 28,835 million lei. The Council of Ministers will ensure that the Ministry of Transport and Telecommunications, working with the Ministry of Equipment and Supplies and Fixed Capital Management Control and Plan administrators take suitable measures to optimize connections between production and consumption centers; rational distribution of the volume of transport activities among the various transport media, including intensification of river transport along the Danube; improvement in the coefficients of utilization of the means of transport; increase in the degree of mechanization and automation in the transport sector; wider use of combined transport by modern technology, palletization, baling, containerization and transcontainerization; and reduction in industrial rail lines to the minimum required to increase transport efficiency.

The physical resources at the disposal of the transport sector will be expanded during 1976 by providing 137 diesel and electric locomotives, 5,000 freight cars, 320 passenger cars, more than 6,900 trucks, 1,500 trailers, 2,240 buses, oceangoing vessels amounting to a total of 289,000 dead weight tons, and 3 medium-sized airplanes. In addition, 286 kilometers of heavily traveled roads will be modernized, and 1,130 kilometers of roads carrying lighter traffic loads will be paved with a light asphalt coating.

Article 14. The total volume of investment in the national economy during 1976 will be 143.7 billion lei, including:

(a) 130.7 billion lei in government funds;

(b) 6.7 billion lei in funds supplied by public and cooperative associations, including 2.2 billion lei in government loans to agricultural production cooperatives;
(c) 6.3 billion lei in funds supplied by the public for projects partially dependent on money and labor contributions by the public, rural electrification, and housing construction with government assistance in the form of loans and labor.

The following sums of capital will be invested in the major sectors of the national economy during the year:

(a) 74.8 billion lei in industry (including the outfitting of drilling companies);
(b) 7.6 billion lei in construction;
(c) 17.2 billion lei in agriculture;
(d) 0.9 billion lei in scientific research and technological development;
(e) 14.7 billion lei in transport and telecommunications;
(f) 4.2 billion lei in trade, public food services, tourism, silos, and storage facilities;
(g) 4.4 billion lei in education, culture, and public health care;
(h) 12.8 billion in housing construction (including hostels for unmarried individuals);
(i) 4.1 billion lei in municipal services.

Article 15. A reserve fund of 15.8 billion lei is hereby established for investment projects whose execution is to begin sometime during 1976 but whose technical and economic indicators have not been duly approved as of December 1, 1975, as well as for other investment projects approved during implementation of the 1976 Plan. As the technical and economic indicators of these plans are approved, the SPC will secure funds and resources necessary for the volume of work to be performed in 1976, with a corresponding increase in plan indicators.

Article 16. A total of 355 major production units will be placed in operation during 1976: 300 industrial and 55 agricultural and installations for livestock raising and land reclamation.

Article 17. The Council of Ministers will adopt measures to guarantee that plan administrators, working with the SPC, the Ministry of Equipment and Supplies and Fixed Capital Management Control, ministries supplying machinery and equipment, and ministries with direct control over construction companies, as well as with the General State Inspectorate for Guidance and Supervision in Planning and Execution of Construction

Activities, the Committee on Problems of the People's Councils, and financing banks, ensure the following:

(a) Urgent preparation and subsequent approval of investment documents for projects scheduled to be executed in 1976 and for which no technical or economic indicators have been as yet approved to ensure final approval on or before June 30, 1976; general plan administrators are responsible for preparing all corresponding documentation according to the fixed schedule;
(b) Supply of equipment by the delivery deadlines specified in the contract, which themselves have been fixed considering the work schedules at new construction sites, as well as at construction sites whose operations have been left over from 1975, to ensure full implementation of all projects by the dates specified in the plan; general suppliers are responsible for delivery within the periods specified in the respective contracts, as well as for the quality of the equipment furnished by their own factories and by companies with which they collaborate;
(c) Execution of construction and installation according to investment project schedules, intensive use of construction equipment, increase in the degree of industrialization through application of optimal solutions, rational use of manpower, and increase in the shift coefficient at construction sites; general contractors are responsible for all construction and installation by their own companies, as well as for all work performed by their subcontractors;
(d) Training, in accordance with approved schedules, of the labor force in all new investment projects, by specialty and by trade; the timely organization and performance of technological experiments and tests to ensure placement in service of new facilities by the deadlines established in the plan; the ministries concerned, along with other central government agencies and enterprises benefitting from investment projects are responsible for executing these tasks.

Article 18. The value of new and redesigned products introduced into Romania's production sector for the first time in 1976 will represent a minimum of 11 percent of the total production value of the nation's manufacturing sector. The 1976 Plan includes a list of tasks related to the completion of 662 important scientific research and technological development facilities, the introduction and widespread use of 158 advanced technologies, and the introduction into the production cycle of 438 new and redesigned products, of which 220 are machines, items of equipment, apparatus, and installations and 218 are materials and consumer goods.

The Council of Ministers will take steps to guarantee that the National

Council for Science and Technology, in collaboration with plan administrators, will orient its efforts toward scientific research, technological development, and technical progress in the following directions:

(a) Amplification and intensification of activities connected with adopting new products to ensure a steady reduction in all types of imports throughout 1976 and thereafter; improvement in the structure of production; development of equipment required to execute investment programs; increase in the volume of exports; and diversification of the range of commodities placed on the domestic market to satisfy, as fully and as efficiently as possible, the needs of domestic consumers;
(b) Continuing improvement and wide-scale use of technologies ensuring efficient utilization of energy resources and high outputs at energy installations;
(c) An increase in the contributions made by technological research and development toward solving problems related to development of the country's raw materials by introducing into the economic cycle new reserves of useful minerals and better and more comprehensive use of these materials (including low-content substances) and wider use of wastes and all types of secondary materials; increase in the productivity levels of the labor force and reduction of physical waste during the production process through extended mechanization and automation; reduction in the specific consumption of coke, metal, wood, chemical products, building materials, and light industrial products; and broad application of new and improved techniques and technological processes;
(d) An increase in the contributions made by researchers to the improvement of working conditions and industrial hygiene and safety, public health care, and environmental protection.

Article 19. The Council of Ministers will make certain that the SPC, the Ministry of Equipment and Supplies and Fixed Capital Management Control, and the Ministry of Finance, working together with other concerned ministries, central government and local authorities, central agencies, and enterprises, take suitable steps to ensure more rational management of the physical resources allocated by the Plan and the application and enforcement of a strict "regime of economy," in particular through:

(a) Preparation and application of technologically justifiable consumption standards for all manufactured goods and constant revision and improvement in the norms and standards for consumption and storage of raw materials, intermediate products, fuels, energy, and packing materials with a view toward strict compliance, in all economic units, with duly approved norms and standards, down to the departmental and shop levels;

(b) Maximum conservation of metals through review and alteration of machinery and equipment designs, rational cutting of rolled metals, and reduction of losses during metallurgical processes;

(c) Intensification of the development and use in production of substitute materials with high economic efficiency and intensification of the collection and utilization of all types of wastes and recovery of secondary energy resources;

(d) Regular supplies according to production schedules and construction and installation work programs and strict adherence to all economic contracts formalized between two or more parties.

Article 20. The productivity of the country's labor force per employee for 1976 will be as follows:

(a) In national industry, 254,500 lei;
(b) In construction or installation, 102,500 lei;
(c) In railway transport, 547,700 conventional tonne-kilometers.

The number of persons employed in the economy will reach 6,655,000 during the year. A total of 315,750 skilled workers entering the production sector in 1976 will be trained in vocational, technical, and specialized secondary schools as well as through intensive, postsecondary qualification and specialization courses.

Article 21. The Council of Ministers will take measures to see to it that:

(a) The Ministry of Labor, the SPC, and plan administrators improve the organization of production and personnel in enterprises, at the departmental level, and at each work site and maintain the present ratio between the principal labor indicators and wages paid for labor performed;

(b) The National Council for Science and Technology and the SPC, working with plan administrators, adopt measures to introduce new technical discoveries and inventions and to ensure strict compliance with the program to assimilate new products and new technologies;

(c) The Ministry of Labor, the Ministry of Education, and the SPC prepare special programs to recruit, train, and continuously educate labor, by trade and by specialty. These programs will be carried out by ministries, central government agencies, economic units, and associations and socialist districts.

Article 22. Production costs for 1976. The maximum expenditure, per 1,000 lei of commodity production, in the national industry will be 906.5 lei and in state agricultural enterprises will be 980.0 lei. Maximum costs, per 1,000 convertible ton-kilometers, in railway transport facilities will be 131.7 lei.

The Council of Ministers will adopt measures to ensure that concerned ministries, central and local authorities, government agencies, and enterprises, working together with the Ministry of Finance and the banks, institute a rigid "regime of economy" to reduce the consumption of raw materials, intermediate products and packing materials, fuel, energy, labor costs, and overhead expenses and to eliminate all forms of waste.

Article 23. The tasks related to increasing labor productivity and to lowering production costs are minimal. Plan administrators will adopt specific measures to ensure that higher levels for these indicators are attained, based on the provisions of the plan and within the framework of special programs drawn up by concerned ministries, central agencies, and enterprises.

Article 24. The total volume of foreign trade for 1976, at current prices, will increase by 17.8 percent over the preliminary figures for 1975, with the revenue in foreign exchange generated by international tourism increasing by 7 percent.

The Council of Ministers will take measures to make certain that concerned ministries, central and local authorities, government agencies, and enterprises, working with the Ministry of Foreign Trade and International Economic Cooperation, the SPC, the Ministry of Finance and the banks ensure:

(a) Improvement in the range and quality of products for export to achieve higher levels of efficiency;
(b) Achievement of the level of integration scheduled for 1976 in relation to products assimilated and manufactured under license;
(c) Rational utilization of the foreign exchange allocated by the Plan to each ministry, central agency, and enterprise;
(d) Intensification of foreign market surveys to formalize contracts for exports and imports as provided for in the Plan;
(e) Intensification of negotiations with foreign allies to ensure compliance with agreements for cooperation and specialization as well as to

propose new measures designed to promote international economic collaboration.

Article 25. The national income for 1976 will be 10.5 percent higher than the preliminary figures for 1975, thereby ensuring the resources required for the national socioeconomic development fund along with a better standard of living for the people of Romania.

Article 26. The value of goods sold by retailers in 1976 will be 154.8 billion lei. To ensure a regular supply of goods to the Romanian public, the Council of Ministers will ensure that plan administrators, together with the Council for Coordination and Guidance of Public Supply and Service Activities, the Ministry of Light Industry, the Ministry of the Mechanical Engineering Industry, and other administrators charged with tasks related to market supply, adopt specific measures to:

(a) Diversify the range and improve the quality of products to be consumed by the Romanian public;
(b) Ensure a complete and regular supply of foods, textiles, footwear, furniture, household appliances and products, electric appliances and products, and children's articles in the quantities and assortments specified in the Plan;
(c) Distribute, by domestic trade authorities, commodities by district, with monthly targets set for basic products, to ensure a continuous supply of goods to retail outlets;
(d) Improve activities in the public food sector, through expanding production and diversifying culinary products to ensure that consumers receive high-quality food products and are protected against the effects of unhygienic conditions and practices;
(e) Improve the structure of commercial inventories, based on the program for resource allocation, to raise the standard of sales and supply of goods to the public.

Article 27. The value of services offered to the public in 1976 will be 31.5 billion lei. To satisfy public demand better, the Council of Ministers shall ensure that plan administrators, together with the Council for Coordination and Guidance of Public Supply and Service Activities, the Committee on Problems of the People's Councils, the Central Union of Artisans' Cooperatives, the Central Union of Consumer Cooperatives, the Ministry of Tourism, and other authorities entrusted with tasks within the service sector, adopt measures to:

(a) Broaden the range of services offered to the public;
(b) Rationally distribute service organizations throughout the country

and draw up a program for defining activities within the service network;

(c) Improve the quality of services offered and increase supervision within the sector.

Article 28. The total per capita real income of the population for 1976 will be between 8 and 8.5 percent higher than the preliminary figures recorded for 1975. The wage fund will reach the 173.3 billion lei mark. The average nominal monthly wage for 1976 will be 2,025 lei based on the provisions of the general wage increase, which was placed in force in 1975; real wages will increase by 8 to 8.7 percent compared with the preliminary figures for 1975.

The real income of the peasantry from work in agricultural production cooperatives and on individual farms, per gainfully employed person, will increase by 9 to 12 percent compared with the preliminary estimates for 1975.

Article 29. The physical resources available for education will increase, and measures will continue to be enforced to integrate production and research into the education sector. A total of 2,730 classrooms and 25,100 vacancies in boarding schools at the elementary, intermediate, secondary, and technical or vocational levels will be provided; new higher education facilities representing a total area of 42,940 square meters will be placed in service.

Article 30. The enrollment in kindergartens will increase by 31,400 pupils, and that of day-care centers will increase by 12,700, children's homes by 1,900, and nursery schools by 500.

Article 31. A total of 1,480 hospital beds will be made available, and new hospitals are earmarked for construction in the following areas: Pitesti, Curtea de Arges, Braila, Rimnicu Sarat, Nehoiu, Galati, Pascani, Slatina, Caracal, Rimnicu Vilcea, Craiova, and Bucharest.

Article 32. A total of 80,000 housing units will be built in 1976 with funds from the government, from cooperatives, and from the public, with 65,000 new units financed with a combination of private funds and state assistance in the form of loans and labor; 80,500 spaces in hostels for singles will be available for occupancy.

Article 33. In 1976 the water distribution network will be expanded by 535 kilometers, and the sewerage network will cover an additional 455 kilometers; the fleet of urban public transport vehicles will receive 1,615 additional pieces of equipment.

Article 34. The Council of Ministers, concerned ministries, central and local authorities, independent agencies, and enterprises are responsible for executing all Plan provisions and will adopt measures to ensure the regular attainment of the indicators specified therein.

Article 35. A breakdown and analysis of Unified National Plan indicators by individual plan administrators will be effected by decree of the Council of State. The indicators outlined in the present law may be modified during execution of the Plan only by enacting a new decree or law.

Article 36. Execution, in accordance with the appendix of the Unified National Socioeconomic Development Plan for 1974, adopted under the terms of Law No. 105/73, is hereby approved. This Law was enacted by the Grand National Assembly in its session of December 19, 1975.

Achievements during the 1976 Plan

The Communiqué on the fulfillment of the 1976 Annual Plan was published in *Scinteia* on February 6, 1977. The data given in it allow an assessment of Romania's achievements during 1976. Most of the data are aggregates, and, as a result, any conclusions drawn below should be considered as tentative.

Macro performance

The economy continued its rapid development in 1976. Although both the level and rate of growth of national income were achieved exactly (Table E.1) and a very strong performance was registered by the industrial sector, some sectors did not meet their plan targets.

Gross industrial production and gross agricultural production both reached target levels and achieved greater growth rates than planned;[10] these sectors are examined in more detail below. Investment was seriously below the planned level, increasing only 8.2 percent compared with a target of 19.4 percent. This would seem to be a poor performance even if the

10. Plan targets and achievements are not strictly comparable, since the targets are based on preliminary results for 1975 and achievements on actual results. In many cases, the actual results differ to some extent from the preliminary. Consequently, it is possible to achieve a planned level of output without attaining the planned rate of growth (or vice versa). Since Romanian targets are dynamic as well as absolute, an assessment of plan fulfillment should consider both measures.

ble E.1. *Macro Targets and Achievements, 1976*

Item	*Planned level*	*Achieved level*	*Planned percent-age growth*[a]	*Achieved percent-age growth*[b]
tional income (billions of lei)	400.0	400.0	10.5	10.5
oss industrial production (billions of lei)	641.0	661.0	10.2	11.5
oss agricultural production (billions of lei)	108.3–119.3	110.0	15.0–26.6	17.2
al investment in national economy (billions of lei)	159.5[c]	149.0	19.4[c]	8.2
eign trade (billions of lei)	60.7	60.8	17.8	14.5
ight transport	84.2	83.2	5.8	5.2
or productivity in industry (thousands of lei per employee)	254.5	257.2	8.5	8.8
mber of employees (thousands)	6,665	6,559	5.6	4.1
ialist retail sales (billions of lei)	154.8	154.6	10.0	8.6
using				
tate funds	80,000	67,381		
Vith state assistance	65,000	45,052		
Vith own funds	—	27,010		
al	—	139,443		
gle persons hostels	80,500	72,034		

Based on preliminary 1975 results.
Based on actual 1975 results.
Includes reserve for investment projects whose technico-economic indicators had not been fixed by December 1975.

savings accruing from the extensive project redesign carried out at the beginning of the year are considered. The trade position is less clear. In the absolute levels, the Plan was overfulfilled by 100 million lei valuta, but the growth rate was only 14.5 percent compared with a plan target of 17.8 percent. (This was because the preliminary result for 1975 understated actual performance by some 2 billion lei valuta.) Assessment is further complicated by the fact that the achieved level is in current prices, whereas the target is in predicted 1976 prices. Freight and passenger transport underfulfilled their targets, although the freight transport result may result from lower agricultural harvests rather than from any inadequacies in the transport sector. The increase in the number of employees in the economy was below target, and, partially as a result of this and also because of the excellent industrial performance, labor productivity in national industry surpassed its planned level.

The results relating to the living standards of the population were also less than planned. Socialist retail trade grew at 8.6 percent rather than at the 10 percent planned, and real remuneration increased at 6.1 percent, below the target of 8.0 to 8.7 percent. Average wages increased by 8.3 percent to 1964 lei per month, which fell short of the target of 2,025 lei. Retail prices grew somewhat less than expected, 0.9 percent, but not enough to compensate for the less-than-planned growth of nominal wages. Nevertheless, real incomes (which includes sociocultural expenditures of the state) grew at 9.5 percent. Since real incomes per capital were planned to increase by 8.0 to 8.5 percent and population growth was about 1 percent, the target was met.

In housing, achievements were only 78 percent of targets (Table E.1), and completion of single person's hostels was 9 percent below the planned level, a change from previous years when performance had been excellent. This shortfall in housing construction may explain why the 1977 planning targets were increased.

Industry

Targets for both gross industrial production and labor productivity in national industry were overfulfilled. The good performance of industry in overall terms contributed greatly to the fulfillment of the national income target. Table E.2 details targets and achievements and shows that the electronics industries led the way in both growth and overfulfillment.

Good performance was also obtained in pharmaceuticals and canned fruit and vegetables, but there was underfulfillment in chemical fertilizers, meat, and textiles. Both steel and cement were also below target, but this may reflect more the underachievement in investment and savings of material inputs throughout the economy than indicate poor performance in the subsectors.

In the energy sector, targets for both electrical power and extraction of methane gas were exceeded. The major weakness in the energy sector has been lignite production, which in 1976 was 5.2 percent below 1975 output, although the Plan had indicated a large expansion.

Agriculture

In 1976 agriculture recovered from its poor performance in 1975 when it was severely affected by floods. For many crops, record harvests were

Table E.2. *Selected Industrial Targets and Achievements, 1976*

Item	*Planned 1976*	*Achievement 1976*	*1976 achieved ÷ 1975 actual*
Electrical power (billions of kilowatt hours)	57.5	58.3	108.4
Net lignite (millions of tonnes)	—	18.2	94.8
Crude oil extracted (millions of tonnes)	14.7	14.7	100.8
Methane gas extracted (millions of tonnes)	26.8	29.8	110.5
Steel (millions of tonnes)	11.0	10.7	112.4
Cement (millions of tonnes)	14.0	12.5	108.9
Electrical household appliances (billions of lei)	1.6	1.7	118.4
Textiles (millions of square meters)	1,067	993	114.8
Meat (thousands of tons)	945	815	114.3
Butter (thousands of tons)	35.4	38	116.0
Cheese (thousands of tons)	101.7	115	120.0
Sugar (thousands of tons)	594	561	108.7
Canned fruit and vegetables	455	556	122.1
Electrotechnical and electronic automation equipment (billions of lei)	3.4	3.5	117.6
Low voltage electrical equipment (billions of lei)	3.2	3.6	123.3
Products of precision mechanics, optics, hydraulics, and pneumatic equipment, and elements (billions of lei)	3.6	3.7	112.4
Metal cutting machine tools (billions of lei)	3.8	3.8	119.3
Chemical fertilizer (millions of tonnes)	2.3	1.9	108.1
Pharmaceuticals (billions of lei)	3.6	3.9	127.4

obtained, and gross agricultural production grew by 17.2 percent. In spite of these increases, however, production only just exceeded the lower bound of the plan target, and, as Table E.3 shows, productivity for major crops and livestock products failed to reach their targets. The Communiqué attributed the shortfalls to unfavorable weather conditions at certain seasons, poor labor organization, and poor implementation of recommended technologies.

Table E.3. *Agricultural Achievements and Targets, 1966*
(thousands of tonnes or head)

Commodity	*Actual, 1975*	*Planned, 1976*	*Achieved, 1976*
Grain	15,266	20,570	19,794
Wheat and rye	4,912	7,225	6,779
Corn and sorghum	9,276	11,935	11,707
Sunflower	728	1,080	806
Sugar beet	4,905	7,200	6,900
Autumn potatoes	2,307	4,735	4,231
Field vegetables	2,392	3,950	3,313
Fruit	1,101	1,930	1,240
Grapes	1,182	1,642	1,493
Cattle	6,171	6,620	6,394
Cows and heifers	3,028	3,273	3,014
Pigs	8,813	10,250	10,192
Breeding sows	821	1,000	960
Sheep and goats	14,310	15,900	14,771

Conclusion

The year 1976 was planned as a year of high growth, to provide a firm foundation for fulfilling the five-year plan. The overall performance was good, with both industry and agriculture registering high growth rates, and foreign trade also increasing at a rapid rate. The shortfalls in investment and energy production indicate, however, the difficulties of maintaining the balanced momentum of the economy (Chapter 16).

The 1977 Annual Development Plan

The 1977 Annual Plan was approved by the National Assembly in November 1976. Following the earthquake of March 1977, the government announced that no changes would be made in the 1977 targets, although subsequent changes to the five-year plan have had some effect upon developments in 1977. These concern chiefly the revised targets for wages (Chapter 9 and Appendix I) and for housing.

In implementing the 1976–80 Five-Year Plan, 1977 was considered to be the "decisive year," and, in the RCP's resolutions on the Plan, three themes were emphasized:

(a) Elimination of unspecified inadequacies and shortcomings that apparently had appeared in economic activity;
(b) Energy conservation; and
(c) Reductions in consumption of materials, especially in construction, where the target for 1976–80 is to reduce by 30 percent the unit value of raw materials.

In recognition of the need to provide incentives for a better quality of work and products, the Plan refers in several places to the need to review and improve the remuneration of those involved in research and technological development and design work.

The Plan envisages that the momentum established in 1976 will continue and is consistent with the high targets established in the five-year period, which are given below in percentages computed on the basis of comparison prices.

Target	*Proposed growth compared with 1976*
Gross industrial production	10.5
Gross agricultural production	1.9–13.6
Volume of freight transport	3.0
Total investments in national economy	16.7
Volume of construction and assembly work	20.4
Total foreign trade volume	15.5
Socialist retail sales	8.4
Services for the population	12.5
Average number of personnel	4.6
Labor productivity in republican industry	9.2
Labor productivity in construction and assembly work	11.8
National income	11.3
Total per capita real income of population	5.9–6.3

Total investment will amount to 180.5 billion lei (in 1977 prices),[11] of which 163.9 billion lei will originate from state funds, 7.0 billion from the

11. Beginning with the 1977 Plan, values are to be expressed in current prices, rather than comparable prices. This will facilitate the continuation of price indexes. All values in the 1977 Plan are in 1977 prices.

funds of the cooperative and social organizations, and 9.5 billion from the funds of the population. The investment funds will be allocated as follows:

Sector	*Billions of lei*	*Percentage*
Industry	96.5	53.5
Construction	5.0	2.8
Agriculture	21.2	11.7
Scientific research and technological development	1.2	0.7
Transport and telecommunications	16.2	9.0
Commerce, restaurant industry, tourism, and storage bases	5.1	2.8
Education, culture, and health	6.0	3.3
Housing	18.8	10.4
Municipal services	6.4	3.5

A further sum of 2.8 billion lei is to be invested in environmental protection.

The Plan gives considerable emphasis to policies and actions to improve industrial performance. In particular, it states that efforts will be made to reduce the consumption of raw materials in industry and construction, to increase the use of waste materials and other secondary resources, and to improve the efficiency of use of raw materials to international standards. Specifically, the Central Committee of the RCP established the following targets for the remaining years of the current five-year plan:

(a) Achievement of a steel utilization coefficient of 85 percent in the production of rolled steel;
(b) Increase of the metal utilization in the manufacture of equipment to 85 to 95 percent;
(c) Development of processes leading to increased utilization of materials, including waste materials and other secondary resources;
(d) Development of solutions allowing a more effective utilization of energy and an important reduction in energy losses;
(e) Elaboration of programs and solutions in industrial constructions that lead to a savings of 30 percent in the use of materials. This is to be achieved by eliminating overdimensioning, using light-weight and cheaper materials that are produced domestically, and limiting deep foundations with reinforced pilings to special cases.

In anticipation of measures being implemented by industry and research and design institutes to comply with these targets, a target has been set of saving 3 to 4 million tons of steel and unspecified quantities of other basic industrial materials during 1977–80.[12] Although the policy of saving industrial materials had previously been implemented through special campaigns, the policy is now an integral part of the design of industrial products and construction.

Past objectives regarding improved utilization of industrial fixed assets and labor have been restated in the Plan. It calls for an increased utilization of capacity, a maximum use of factory space, improvements in organization of production, including cooperation with other industrial plants, and for a better allocation of labor, in part through shift work. References to improved quality of industrial products are scattered throughout the Plan, but, as in the case of the rationalization objectives, no specific measures are mentioned.

Nevertheless, the 1977 Plan aims to increase labor productivity in industry by 9.2 percent, a higher rate than the target set for 1976 (8.5 percent) and significantly above the average rate achieved during the Five-Year Plan of 1971–75 (6.4 percent). Gross industrial output is to increase by 10.5 percent in 1977 or at about the same rate as in the previous year.

Industrial Sector Targets for 1976 to 1980

Apart from the statement of quantitative production goals for a selected number of industrial commodities or commodity groups (Chapter 10), little is known about planned investments and major projects at the subsector level. The following paragraphs are based on the limited information available. Some of the information is only approximate and should be interpreted with care.

Chemical industries

Total investment allocated to this major subsector of industry amounts to about 120 billion lei, about 20 percent of the industrial investment planned for 1976–80. Among the projects to be implemented are new petrochemical complexes at Capul Idra and Teleajen for manufacturing basic products such as ethylene, propylene, styrene, benzene, and toluene; additional facilities at the Brazi and Timisoara petrochemical plants; a synthetic rubber plant within the Borzesti complex; fertilizer plants at

12. The resolution of the RCP of November 3, 1976 specifically mentioned copper, aluminum, and other nonferrous metals, cement, lumber, chemical products, electrical energy, and fuels.

Bacau, Arad, and Slobozia; the Giurgiu plant for sodium chloride products; facilities for manufacturing synthetic fibers and yarns at Cimpulung-Muscel and Roman; and plants for vehicle tires and other rubber products at Tirgu-Jui, Botosani, Zalau, Nassaud, Drobeta and Turnu-Severin.

To facilitate the rapid expansion of the petrochemical industry, new large refinery facilities will be put on-stream, nearly doubling the average primary distillation capacity available, from 59,000 tonnes per day throughput during 1971–75 to 104,000 tonnes per day during 1976–80. Total investment in refining is estimated at over 11 billion lei during the plan period. The largest single project is the refinery at Midia on the Black Sea, which has a planned capacity of 8 million tonnes a year (Table E.4).

In the chemical subsector, the planned expansion of production will rapidly increase the share of petrochemical products in total chemical output. Tentative estimates indicate that in 1980, some 60 percent of total output will be petrochemicals compared with approximately 40 percent in 1975. Particular emphasis is laid on expanded output of petrochemical base products, including polyethylene, polyvinyl chloride, and other plastic materials such as melamine (new), and of resins. In plastics alone, output is planned to raise from roughly 200,000 tonnes in 1975 to 800,000 tonnes in 1980. If this target can be accomplished, Romania's per capita production of plastics will be close to the 1975 average of France, and production will then not only eliminate the need for imports, but also probably leave surpluses for export. In synthetic resins, the current level of exports (about 59,000 tonnes in 1975) should rise significantly. Total investments in petrochemical base products are estimated to be about 10 billion lei during 1976–80, of which approximately three-quarters would be for capacities to produce plastics.

In synthetic and artificial fibers and yarns, the Plan calls for an increase in output from about 160,000 tonnes in 1975 to a range of 310,000 to 350,000 tonnes by 1980. During this period, new production lines will be opened up in polyamidic, acrylic, and polyester fibers. Fiber imports are planned to be replaced gradually by domestic production, whereas exports of synthetic fibers will increase over their current level of around 20,000 tonnes a year. Investments in synthetic fibers during 1976–80 are tentatively estimated to amount to about 8 billion lei. Information on total investment planned in this subsector of the chemical industry is not available.

Among the principal chemical production lines, the most rapid expansion will be in synthetic rubber, with total output reaching around 300,000 tons by 1980: that is, three times the volume of 1975. This growth is expected to be achieved largely by expanding existing plants, although some new production lines, such as for butylic rubber (a new product for Romania),

Table E.4. *Planned Expansion of Output of Principal Chemical Products*

Product	Actual,	Planned					Average annual percentage rate of growth
	1975	1976	1977	1978	1979	1980	
Chemical fertilizers (thousands of tonnes of nutrient substitute)	1,729	2,280	3,057	3,450–3,604	3,800–4,040	4,050–4,143	18.6–19.1
Synthetic polymer products (thousands of tonnes)	347	512.5	556	600–675	800–884	1,000–1,057	23.6–25.0
Synthetic and artificial fibers and yarns (thousands of tonnes)	159	173.8	184.1	190.9	210–233.1	310–348.7	14.3–17.0
Synthetic rubber (thousands of tonnes)	99	146.5	175	180–198.7	240–260	290–318	24.5–26.3
Tires (thousands)	3,703	4,425	4,875	5,000–5,115	5,200–5,460	7,500–7,855	15.2–16.2

Source: Information supplied by Romanian authorities during discussions with the authors.

will also be established. Although strengthening Romania's position as a net exporter of synthetic rubber, the planned increase in output is primarily to facilitate a rapid expansion of domestic tire manufacturing potential, as well as to allow a considerable diversification of outputs in other rubber products. Tires and other rubber products are major export items with exceptional growth records in recent years. The planned growth in their output is mainly to exploit further available export potential. In this context, Romania also plans to set up facilities to produce conveyor belts, which on grounds of the domestic market requirements alone would hardly be justified. Total investments in rubber and rubber products during 1976–80 are reported to be close to 3 billion lei.

In chemical fertilizers, investments of approximately 7 billion lei are expected to raise production levels from 1.7 million tonnes of nutrients in 1975 to a planned volume of about 4 million tonnes in 1980. Investment is concentrated on expanding existing plants at Craiova and Turnu Magurele and new plants at Slobozia, Arad, and Bacau. Romania is self-sufficient in nitrogenous fertilizers but depends on imports of phosphorus fertilizers. In nitrogenous fertilizers, Romania has also developed a strong position in exports (mainly urea), with shipments abroad accounting for over one-third of total production. Despite the planned increase in domestic fertilizer consumption to 11.0 to 11.5 million tonnes of nutrients between 1976–80, the country's export potential is not expected to decline. It could actually double if production increases as planned (Table E.5).

Table E.5. *Estimated Fertilizer Balance*
(thousand tonnes of nutrients)

Item	*1975*	*Annual average 1976–80*
Production	1,729	3,327–3,425
Export	650	1,027–1,225
Apparent or planned consumption	1,079	2,200–2,300

Steel industry

The output of raw steel is planned to increase from 9.55 million tonnes in 1975 to approximately 17 million tonnes by 1980. This growth is expected to be achieved by the further expanding existing capacities (at Galati, Hunedoara, Otelul Rosu, Cimpie Turzii, and Resita) as well as by developing a new integrated steel complex at Calarasi on the Danube.[13] Construction of the new steel complex began in 1977–78, with the first phase of development expected to be completed by about 1982. The initial size of the production facilities is said to be similar to the existing one at Galati, but provisions have been made for further expansion to over 10 million tonnes a year in the second half of the 1980s.

Because of the expected requirements of the major steel users in Romania, notably the engineering industry, the planned product mix is increasingly geared to high-value steels. In 1980 alloy and high-alloy steels will represent more than 13 percent of the total output of steel industry compared with 9 percent in 1975, whereas high-carbon, low-alloy steels are planned to reach a share of around 52 percent.

The output of finished rolled products is planned to increase to 11 to 12.3 million tonnes in 1980, which compares with about 6.8 million tonnes in 1975. The share of flat products in total production would increase from 50 percent in 1975 to approximately 55 percent in 1980.

In 1975 domestic supplies covered only about 20 and 50 percent of the respective industrial requirements of iron ore and metallurgical coke. The planned expansion of production is likely to increase further the dependence of the iron and steel industry on imports, despite efforts to utilize domestic low-grade ore. Published details do not indicate what contribution can reasonably be expected from domestic sources. In ferroalloys, the Plan envisages the creation of a domestic ferroalloy industry, with production expected to cover 60 percent of the requirements for ferromanganese and about 80 percent of those for ferrosilicon.

On the basis of the implied but unpublished plan parameters, Romania would increase its per capita steel consumption from 456 kilograms in 1975 to over 650 kilograms in 1980, at which level it would be comparable to the 1969 average of West Germany and more than that of Japan of the same year. In terms of output, the 1980 production level per capita can be compared with the 1973 average of West Germany.

Several factors might, however, contribute to curtailing these ambitious expansion plans, requiring implementation to be stretched over a longer period. Constraints may be imposed by limiting domestic raw material supplies to less than what is currently expected, which would then translate into even higher import requirements. But also in terms of demand for steel, factors may call for a slower expansion. One of these is related to the ambitious shipbuilding program envisaged during the plan period, which

13. The expectation that Calarasi would contribute to production during the current five-year plan appears overoptimistic, however.

experts consider unrealistic and hard to accomplish (Chapter 13). As a result, steel demand by the shipbuilding industry—a heavy steel user—may actually be smaller than currently anticipated. This would have considerable implications on the pace of capacity build-up and on the product mix of the steel industry. If the currently planned expansion of steel output would be maintained, however, Romania could become a fairly substantial net exporter of steel in the near future.

Mechanical engineering

Total investment allocated to the mechanical engineering subsector during 1976–80 is about 120 billion lei, representing 21 percent of total planned industrial investment. The funds are earmarked mainly to develop large engineering complexes, plants specializing in the manufacture of industrial equipment, and tractors, as well as to modernize existing capacities. The projects include heavy machine-building complexes at Iasi, Cluj, and Craiova; plants for technological equipment of the metallurgical, chemical, petroleum, and construction materials industry; and new shipyards for seagoing vessels at Tulcea and Mangalia. The Plan also envisages three new plants and a substantial expansion of the existing facilities to manufacture tractors and agricultural machinery. This will enable tractor production to rise from 50,000 units in 1975 to 70 to 80,000 units by 1980, of which about 55,000 units are for export. Also envisaged is an expansion of the shipyards of Constanta, Galati, and Braila (for seagoing vessels) and of several other yards (specializing on rivergoing vessels) during the plan period to reach about 1.1 to 1.2 million dead weight tons by 1980.

F

Stages of Economic Growth, 1950 to 1975

THE DEVELOPMENT OF THE ROMANIAN ECONOMY SINCE 1950 has not been an entirely smooth process; an examination of the distinct periods into which the twenty-five years can be broken identifies not only the internal and external constraints faced by the economy, but also the most important relations between sectors and their effect on economic growth.

The period between 1950 and 1975 can be divided into four sections:

(a) 1950–53, during which there was rapid growth of investment, industrial production, and national income;
(b) 1953–58, a period of slower growth, consolidation, and sizable annual fluctuations in the major economic indicators;
(c) 1958–65, during which the growth rate accelerated initially and an economic base for sustainable growth was completed;
(d) 1966–75, during which growth rates have been high and relatively constant.

The First Industrialization Drive, 1950–53

The period between 1950 and 1953 constituted the first industrialization drive, during which investment more than doubled and industrial output rose by almost 70 percent. The progress made in this period illustrates clearly the interdependence of sectors, the importance of foreign trade, and the priorities of industrialization policy, which are features of Romanian development throughout 1950–75. This period of rapid growth actually began in 1948, following a good harvest in 1947, which permitted a substantial increase in exports. In turn, the decline in food imports and rise in export earnings permitted larger imports of raw materials and intermediate goods so that the manufacturing industry could operate closer to capacity. The increase in agricultural production also generated a surplus, which could be channeled into investments. Investment rose from 6.3 to 14.6 billion lei, more than half of which was channeled into the producer goods sector, particularly fuels, metallurgy, and chemicals.

The rapid growth ended in 1953, when the difficulties in ensuring the proportionate growth of all sectors increased. There were two major reasons for the slowdown: one internal, the other external. First, the foreign trade balance could not be maintained. The growth of export goods, mainly petroleum, lumber, cement, and foodstuffs, could not be sustained to satisfy both internal requirements and exports, and by 1953 export growth was required to meet the reimbursement of credits for machinery and equipment imported since 1948. Second, the pace of industrialization created domestic imbalances. In particular, the division of national income between investment and consumption gave too few resources to consumption. Because of the disparity between rural and urban consumption levels, the increase in urbanization associated with industrialization required that consumer goods industries expand, even if no increase in the levels of rural and urban incomes was planned. Consumer goods industries received little investment, and the growth of agricultural production began to slow down, reflecting the low levels of investment in both state and private farms and the lack of incentives for private farmers to expand production. The distribution of investment gave few resources to not only consumer good industries but also to housing. Urban employment increased without a parallel increase in housing and urban services, thereby suppressing migration to towns.

Consolidation, 1953–58

These internal and external circumstances persuaded the Romanian Communist Party (RCP) to change its policies substantially to eliminate the disproportions in the economy while maintaining a considerable growth rate of industry and national income. During this period, the share of accumulation in national income was reduced, and investment outlays grew at a much slower rate (rising from 14.4 billion lei in 1953 to only 18.2 billion in 1958), with higher proportions given to housing, agriculture, and consumer goods. Investment in agriculture and consumer goods doubled between 1953 and 1955, although the effect on production levels did not materialize until later. Agricultural policies were also changed: procurement prices of animal products were raised; compulsory deliveries of cereals were reduced;

the acreage of cereals was increased at the expense of products for industrial use; and private farmers, who still accounted for most of marketed production, were given incentives to enter cooperatives and to increase production.

For heavy industry, the period was chiefly one of consolidation and preparation for further advance. Machine building and chemicals continued their high rates of growth, however; the growth of the former was maintained because imports of machinery were curtailed.[1] Projects were then completed and efforts were made to raise output by increasing labor productivity rather than by large increases in the labor force and capital for each worker. The annual growth of employment in the socialist sector was reduced to 2 to 3 percent compared with the 8 to 10 percent increases between 1950 and 1953, and most of the increase was directed to sectors that had been neglected previously. The accompanying decrease in the rate of urbanization also eased the housing shortage.

Renewed Industrialization, 1958–65

The period of consolidation ended in 1958, when the program of accelerated development, concentrating upon the expansion of heavy industry, was resumed. The RCP had planned to increase the growth rate in 1956 when the Second Five-Year Plan began, but political and economic circumstances in Romania and in Eastern Europe in general combined to prolong the period of consolidation. The five-year plan was abandoned in 1958 and was replaced by a six-year plan for 1960–65, in which the basis for a new expansion was laid out along the lines established at the RCP Plenum of November 1958.

The policies announced in 1958 were designed to lay the foundation for the stable and sustained development of the economy. They centered on an increase in the rate of accumulation and the renewed expansion of heavy industry, in particular the development of complex machine-building and chemicals industries based on the domestic metal, mineral, and fuel resources. An examination of achievements during the six-year plan, which to all intents and purposes matched the plan's targets, demonstrates the degree to which higher growth rates were achieved.

As Table 5.1 (Chapter 5) shows, the percentage of national income allocated to accumulation rose substantially during the plan period because of a rapid increase in investment. Between 1958 and 1962 investment

1. In 1957 they totaled 406 million lei, only 43 percent of the 1953 level.

doubled from 18.2 to 36.8 billion lei, an annual increase of 19 percent. Although the growth rate fell to 9 percent in the final two years of the plan, the marginal ratio of investment to national income was 44 percent during the plan. A higher percentage of total investment was allocated to the productive sector (80.5 percent in 1961–65 compared with 74.9 percent in 1956–60), and considerably more was allocated to industry.[2] Investment in agriculture also increased to finance collectivization, especially between 1958 and 1962, and to build up the productive capacity of state farms. Furthermore, in keeping with the decision to base further industrial expansion as much as possible on domestic resources, investment in mineral and metal prospecting rose sharply at the expense of crude oil. The share of the latter in total industrial investment declined rapidly throughout the postwar period (from 35 percent in 1951 to 14 percent between 1960 and 1965) as the limit to economic increases in production was reached. Another sector which suffered from the process of reallocation was housing, in which the share of funds fell from 15.6 percent in 1956–60 to 11.6 percent in 1961–65.

The distribution of investments by branch of industry mirrors the direction of industrialization outlined by the RCP, although the share of metallurgy does not fully reflect the change in priorities, because the Galati steel complex received insubstantial amounts of funds before 1963. The increase in chemicals is clear, as is the fact that the performance did not match plans, largely because of delays in constructing new chemical plants.

Between 1959 and 1965 economic growth was rapid, with national income increasing at about 9.1 percent a year. Industry, in particular, which grew at 14.5 percent a year, met most of its targets (except in those industries in which increments in production came from new plants) and overfulfilled by 7 percent its gross output target. This rapid growth not only resulted from increased investment, but also from increased factor productivity, particularly an accelerated growth of labor productivity, and from decreased comparable costs of industry, which fell at 3.9 percent a year compared with only 2.2 percent in the previous plan. As in the past, the agricultural sector had the least impressive growth rate, only 2 percent a year between 1959 and 1965; most of this growth came from the state farms. The poor harvest of 1961–62 was primarily responsible for the slowdown in the rate of growth of investment, through its impact on foreign trade. Between 1958

2. Because of the slowdown in industrial investment in 1964 and 1965, the five-year plan figures do not show fully the shift in investment allocation toward industry: in 1961–65, 46.5 percent of investment flowed into industry, compared with 44.9 percent in 1956–60.

and 1961 foreign trade was more or less in balance, the large increase in imports of capital goods (900 million lei in 1958 and 4 billion in 1959–1961) having been financed by a widely based increase in exports. After 1962, when export growth was lower than the 1958–61 increase of 70 percent, less foreign exchange could be spared to purchase machinery abroad. Indeed, in 1964 such outlays fell. It is important to realize, however, that foreign trade exerted a less determining influence on growth during these years. Internal growth, although eased between 1962 and 1964, was not cut back as much as during the first industrialization period for several reasons. First, Romania was able to replace some imports of machinery with domestic products, and the output of the domestic machine-building industry rose swiftly throughout the plan period.[3] Second, it was possible to raise exports of manufactures (for example, wood products, foodstuffs, and other consumer goods) to finance imports of raw materials to maintain full use of industrial capacity. This latter action was necessary because of the plan targets for new production of coke, iron ore, and some other metals could not be met. As a result of reallocating foodstuffs and consumer goods to external markets, the plan targets for the standard of living were not attained.

Self-Sustained Growth, 1966–75

The announcement in 1965 that the People's Republic was to be renamed the Socialist Republic of Romania indicated that, with the achievement of production goals in the 1960–65 plan and the completion of collectivization of agriculture, the RCP considered that the basis for a sustained drive toward socialism had been laid and that the first three five-year plans had largely succeeded in improving the uneven development of the economy. It also implied that stable growth could be maintained in the future.

The 1966–70 Plan envisaged a continued pattern of growth as in the 1960–65 Plan period, but at a somewhat lower rate. The proportion of national income allocated to the accumulation fund was planned to increase further, with investment projected to increase at 10.7 percent a year,[4] whereas the consumption fund was to grow at 7 percent a year. Approximately 56 percent of investment from centralized state funds was

3. In spite of this, the percentage of investment in equipment produced in Romania declined between 1960 and 1965, the result of the 4-billion-lei increase in machinery imports between 1958 and 1962.

4. The investment target was higher than the 1960–65 target but was significantly less than the actual growth of investment in the third plan period.

planned to go to industry, whose gross production was to increase by 10.7 to 11.6 percent a year, a significant deceleration of the previous plan's target and achievement. Once again, it was planned that the producer goods subsector would grow more rapidly than consumer goods, their respective growth rates projected at 11.2 to 12.1 and 9.9 to 10.5 percent. Within the producer goods sector, the growth rates of the leading sectors, chemicals and machine building, were to be particularly high, not only to meet internal demands but also to permit a large increase in their export. Although the growth of foreign trade was planned to be lower than in the previous plan period (the 1966–70 volume was to be 50 to 55 percent more than the 1961–65 figure), the target appears to have depended on hopes of large increases in the exports of chemicals and machinery and equipment rather than on the expansion of agricultural exports. The target for growth of consumer goods, which was high compared with previous plans, appears also to have anticipated substantial export growth as well as increases in domestic consumption. Agriculture was the one sector in which accelerated growth was anticipated; gross production was to increase by 26 to 32 percent compared with the previous five years.

The planned slowdown in the growth of production did not signal a redistribution of national income toward consumption. National income was projected to grow somewhat more slowly than between 1960 and 1965, at 8.5 percent a year. The targets for consumption also turned downward, the targets for both real wages and socialist retail trade[5] dropping below targets and achievements of the previous plan.

The plan gave special attention to two issues: regional development and increased efficiency of economic activities. During the first three plans, the major concern in allocating resources had been increasing the rate of reinvestment and the distribution of resources among sectors. In a country where transport and ancillary services for industry were underdeveloped and in short supply, logic demanded that investment be concentrated in existing centers to take advantage of economies of scale and existing services. As a result, regional inequalities of production and income had remained. The creation of an extensive industrial base and the easing of transport and other constraints enabled the government to pay more attention to a more equitable distribution of production among judets. The 1966–70 Plan emphasized the need for regional criteria to be followed in allocating investment, and the

5. Some fall in the growth of socialist retail trade was expected, since a significant part of its growth between 1960 and 1965 resulted from the completion of collectivization and the increase in marketed production of agricultural goods as peasant self-consumption declined.

1967 RCP conference subsequently approved measures for administrative and territorial reorganization to provide a framework for implementing regional policies (Chapter 3). The effects of regional policy are analyzed in Chapter 6.

The administrative and organizational reforms approved by the 1967 Plan represented not only attempts to improve regional planning and administration, but also a more general concern with efficient administration and planning. The Plan also emphasized the need for improved efficiency in production targets, reflecting the RCP's wish to move the economy away from an extensive development pattern to a more intensive path. These concerns resulted from the fact that, by the mid-1960s, the gains in productivity from mechanization itself had been largely obtained and that further economic growth would have to rely increasingly on deepening capital and on obtaining greater efficiency from existing inputs. Chapter 6 discusses the policies and performance during 1971 and 1975.

The actual pattern of growth during 1966–70 paralleled in many ways the achievements of the previous plan. Industry and investment overfulfilled their targets, whereas agriculture and retail sales fell short. Within industry, the producer goods sector registered substantially higher growth than planned, largely as a result of the rapid growth of chemicals and machine building. The overfulfillment of the investment target and the underfulfillment of consumption plans (in particular, those for incomes of the peasantry, which increased only 6 percent over the period compared with a target of 20 to 25 percent) led to a more substantial increase than planned in the proportion of national income going to the accumulation fund; over the plan period, the proportion was 29.5 percent.

Substantial changes occurred in the foreign trade sector. The volume of foreign trade rose by 75 percent in current prices. Imports rose rapidly in the first two years of the plan, especially from the convertible currency area, before slackening their growth; the major increases in imports were in machinery and equipment, fuels, and raw materials. In 1968, Romania began to import crude oil. Export growth failed to keep pace despite an average growth of 11 percent over the period. As a result, Romania ran a deficit of between 650 and 900 million lei valuta between 1967 and 1970, mostly with the convertible currency area and financed by suppliers and financial credits. This increased Romania's external debt. Growth in exports came largely from industrial consumer goods, minerals and metals, and machinery and equipment. The value of consumer goods exports, some of which were diverted from the domestic market, increased from 700 million to 2 billion lei valuta between 1965 and 1970: that is, from 11 to 18 percent of total trade. Exports of machinery and equipment increased from 18.5

percent of total trade in 1965 to 23 percent in 1970, but this increase, rapid though it was, was less than planned.

The most important feature of foreign trade during the period was the change in the regional structure of trade and the development of more extensive trading relations with developed and developing market economies. The changes reflected two major features of Romania's development strategy and economic position. First, they reflected the increasing inadequacy of Romania's domestic resource base. Despite the accelerated exploration for and exploitation of metals, minerals, or fuels during the 1960s, the pace of industrialization outran supplies in some cases and generated additional imports of those resources not found in Romania. To deal with this problem and to diversify the sources of supply, Romania expanded its trade with developing countries (Chapter 7) and, in particular, with the oil-producing countries to obtain metals and minerals and crude oil. Second, the changes (especially the development of trade with developed market economies) reflected the change of emphasis in Romania's industrial strategy. Further development of Romania's leading sectors—chemicals and machine building—required advanced technology, which could not be obtained from socialist countries. Therefore, between 1966 and 1970, Romania expanded its trade rapidly with the developed market economies, importing machinery and equipment largely in exchange for agricultural and industrial raw materials (Chapter 7).

In summary, the Romanian economy between 1966 and 1970 continued the pattern of growth established in the 1960–65 Plan and provided the basis for a renewed acceleration of growth during 1971–75. The economy during the latter period is examined in detail in Chapter 6.

G

Mobilization of Resources and Investment Finance

THIS APPENDIX PROVIDES ADDITIONAL DETAILS on the financing of investment and on the sources and expenditures of the central financial plan.

Centralized Financial Plan

The following information was provided by the Ministry of Finance during discussions with the authors:

Resources (funds)

Accumulation from benefits, turnover tax (tax on goods circulation)
- Benefits (exclusively tax on benefits)

Custom duties

Amortization

Incomes of state social insurance budget

Encashment of due rate from medium- and long-term credits granted to agricultural cooperatives and population

Tax on craftsmanship and on consumer cooperatives and enterprises of social organizations' incomes

Expenditures

Expenditures for financing objectives and actions achieved from social and economic development funds
- Expenditures for investments
- Building of dwellings, private property financed by Savings Bank credits
- Funds at the disposal of banks for medium- and long-term credits
- Expenditures to finance working capital
- Expenditures for state reserves

Expenditures for financing other objectives and actions concerning national economy
- Expenditures for economic activi-

(Table continues on the following page)

Resources (funds)	*Expenditures*
Tax on buildings and stamp tax of socialist sector	ties financed by budget
Tax on utilization of state property	Expenditures for science, actions connected with science, and geologic work
Other incomes from economic activities	Expenditures to cover price differences
Incomes achieved by state budgetary institutions	Funds from benefits of economic units
Tax on total wage fund	Expenditures for financing social-cultural actions
Agricultural tax paid by agricultural cooperatives	For education
Taxes on population	For culture and art
Other incomes	For health
Increased resources for short-term credit	For physical training and sports
Increase in deposits of population in Savings Bank used to grant credits for housing private property	For social assistance
Total resources	For state allocation for children
	For pensions and other categories (other than pensions for social insurance)
	Of state social insurance budget
	Expenditures for state security
	Expenditures for operating state administration, judicial bodies, and prosecutor
	Expenditures for other actions
	Increase of short-term credits
	Total expenditures

The System of Investment Finance

Investments in the Romanian economy are grouped according to the sector in which they are undertaken: that is, the socialist and private sectors. (The socialist sector is subdivided into the state and cooperative sectors.) The financing of these investments is grouped according to the origin of the funds and is often divided into state and other funds. State funds are further subdivided into centralized and noncentralized funds, as shown below:

State funds	*Other funds*
State budget	Cooperative and mass organizations' funds:
Republican budget	Agricultural cooperatives
Local budget	

(Table continues on the following page)

State funds	*Other funds*
Depreciation funds	Funds of the population for housing construction
Retained benefits	
Republican enterprises	
Local enterprises	
Bank credit	
Funds from liquidating fixed assets no longer in operation	
Other sources	

The preponderance of investments in the state sector is illustrated in the distribution during 1951–75 (Table G.1). Investment by the population is in housing, which is discussed in more detail in Chapter 12.

Financing Fixed Investment

The patterns of investment financing in Romania reflect the nature of the economic system. State funds finance most gross investment in the economy. Of these, the state budget plays the major role; it is the principal instrument for plan implementation. It mobilizes and allocates savings and investments in an economy that is under full administrative control, thus leaving a small intermediate role to the financial mechanism for investment purposes. As illustrated below, measures in 1969 attempting to redistribute the control and administration of the centralized funds were successful only initially. Recent data suggest that the substitution of fiscal flows by financial flows has not yet been accomplished to the extent desired.

The major change in investment finance was introduced in 1969 under a new law on investments (no. 72/1969, Chapter 3). This law was to decentralize investment decisionmaking in the economy by reducing the role of the budget in investment finance in favor of bank credit (Chapter 4), and of increased profits (benefits) retained by the firms for their minor investment and working capital needs, previously used almost fully by budgetary transfers. After some initial success in implementing these measures, the state budget has reestablished its dominance as the major source of investment finance (Table G.2).

Information on fixed investment by financing source for the economy during 1971–75 is given in Table G.3. Fixed investment increased by 57 percent, from 88 to 138 billion lei and has been mostly financed from budget and depreciation funds. The share of these in financing investment has been increasing, and in 1975 they accounted for almost 90 percent of the total. The share of all other sources has declined from 14.5 percent in 1971 to about 10.7 percent in 1975.

Table G.1. *Distribution of Gross Investment, 1951–55 to 1971–75*

Item	*1951–55*		*1956–60*		*1961–65*		*1966–70*		*1971–75*	
	(billions of lei)	*(percentage)*	*(billions of lei)*	*(percentage)*	*(billions of lei)*	*(percentage)*	*(billions of lei)*	*(percentage)*	*(billions of lei)*	*(percentage)*
Gross investment	61.9		100.2		199.7		330.8		548.9	
Socialist sector investment	57.7	93	88.2	88	187.7	94	314.5	95	516.5	94
State sector	56.6	91	84.0	84	171.2	86	294.1	89	490.0	89
Cooperative sector	1.1	2	4.2	4	16.4	8	20.3	6	26.6	5
Population	4.2	7	12.0	12	12.0	6	16.3	5	32.4	6

Source: Anuarul Statistic al Republicii Socialiste Romania (Bucharest: Directia Centrala de Statistica, published yearly).

ble G.2. *Distribution of State Centralized Funds*

Source	*1969*	*1970*	*1971*	*1972*	*1973*	*1974*	*1975*	*1976*
dget	59.3	40.7	44.5	45.3	46.4	48.2	55.2	53.0
preciation fund	34.8	34.8	35.0	34.4	35.1	34.7	33.0	34.0
ained benefits	2.5	14.4	14.5	16.7	16.6	14.4	10.3	12.5
nk credits	—	7.4	2.6	2.3	2.0	0.8	1.3	0.5
ner sources	3.4	2.7	3.3	1.3	—	2.0	—	—

ource: Table SA3.3.

Among state funds, the state budget is the main source of investment finance, and its significance has been increasing substantially, both in its share of total investment financing as well as among the state funds. In 1975 it provided for 49 percent of total investment financing, up sharply from 38 percent in 1971. Except for funds originating from depreciation charges, whose share has marginally increased the other three items, bank credit, retained benefits, and "other" have all declined. Investment financed by foreign borrowing is partly included in the amount reported for state budget financing and is not available separately.

Main Sources of Fixed Investment

There are three main sources of financing for fixed investments: the state budget, depreciation, and retained benefits.

State budget

The growth rate achieved by the Romanian economy during the past six years is the result of the government's ability to mobilize domestic resources. The chief instrument for mobilizing resources is a system of quotas and taxes on state enterprises, and the government seems to have used it with considerable effect to meet its need for investable capital. Most of the taxes are collected at the enterprise level. In 1950 government revenue amounted to 20 billion lei; twenty-five years later it was 239 billion lei. The experience of the past five years is particularly encouraging. Although 1971 was a year of slow growth in revenue, the rate of increase being just 4 percent, it accelerated markedly to 10.6 percent in 1972. An increase of 11.3 percent was targeted for 1973, but the actual result surpassed the planned objective. The total revenue obtained was 175.9 billion lei

Table G.3. *Fixed Investment by Financing Source, 1971–76*
(millions of lei)

	1971		*1972*		*1973*	
Financing source	*Amount*	*Percentage*	*Amount*	*Percentage*	*Amount*	*Perce[illegible] age*
Centralized state funds	75.7	85.5	83.4	85.5	91.0	86.[illegible]
State budget	33.7	38.1	37.8	38.8	42.2	40.[illegible]
Depreciation fund	26.5	30.0	28.7	29.4	31.9	30.[illegible]
Retained benefits	11.0	12.4	13.9	14.3	15.1	14.[illegible]
Bank credit	2.0	2.3	1.9	1.9	1.8	1.[illegible]
Other sources	2.5	2.8	1.1	1.1	—	—
Enterprises' own funds	2.8	3.2	4.1	4.2	4.1	3.[illegible]
Cooperative and mass organizations' funds	1.2	1.4	1.3	1.3	1.3	1.[illegible]
Agricultural cooperatives	2.5	2.8	2.4	2.5	2.4	2.[illegible]
Contributions of the population	0.4	0.5	0.5	0.5	0.5	0.[illegible]
Total socialist sector	82.6	93.4	91.7	94.1	99.2	93.[illegible]
Private investment	5.8	6.6	5.8	5.9	6.4	6.[illegible]
Total fixed investment	88.4		97.5		105.7	

Source: Anuarul Statistic, various issues.

instead of the planned level of 170.7 billion, and this implied a growth rate of 14.7 percent. In the following year the target was once again exceeded. The plan had aimed for an increase of 12.6 percent, but it turned out to be closer to 20 percent. The growth in revenue slowed down in 1975, but even though actual returns fell below expectations, the growth rate was only 2.3 percent less than the target and still a respectable 13.3 percent. By all accounts, this is an impressive performance, and it has made possible the absolute and proportional increase in the volume of resources devoted to investment.

As noted in Chapter 5, the structure of revenues has changed significantly, indicating the expansion and deepening of economic activities, as well as the effects of government measures to enhance the financial viability of the state enterprises. In 1950 revenues from turnover taxes were almost three

inancing source	1974 Amount	1974 Percent-age	1975 Amount	1975 Percent-age	1976 Amount	1976 Percent-age
tralized state funds	105.0	87.8	123.0	89.3	131.5	88.3
ate budget	50.6	42.3	67.9	49.3	69.7	46.8
epreciation fund	36.4	30.4	40.8	29.6	44.7	30.0
etained benefits	15.1	12.6	12.7	9.2	16.4	11.0
ank credit	0.8	0.8	1.6	1.2	0.7	0.5
ther sources	2.1	1.8	—	—	—	—
rprises' own funds	3.6	3.0	3.0	2.2	—	—
perative and mass organizations' funds	1.0	0.8	0.5	1.1	—	—
icultural cooperatives	2.5	2.1	2.8	2.0	—	—
tributions of the population	0.3	0.3	0.4	0.2	0.4	0.3
l socialist sector	112.5	94.0	130.6	94.8	141.2	94.8
ate investment	7.2	6.0	7.1	5.2	7.8	5.2
l fixed investment	119.7		137.7		149.0	

times the amount of the profits remitted to the budget by the enterprises. In 1975 profit payments were the largest single revenue source of the budget (Table SA5.1). In fact, if all types of payments to the budget by the enterprises are considered, they amounted in 1975 to about 61 percent of total revenue compared with 16 percent in 1950. The structure of revenues in 1950–75 is illustrated in Table G.4.

The declining share of turnover tax in total revenues should be expected. This tax is applicable only on consumer goods. Revenues from that tax are therefore determined by the volume of production of such goods, which has grown at a much slower rate than that of intermediate goods. The system of planning and dividing profits has changed substantially over the period, depending on the resource requirements of the economy. The levels and rates of profits have been influenced by the periodic price resettings,

Table G.4. *Structure of Budget Revenues, 1950–76*
(percentage)

Revenue source	*1950*	*1960*	*1970*	*1975*	*1976*
Turnover tax	42.6	31.0	30.4	17.7	17.6
Regularization tax	—	—	—	3.0	0.2
Profit payments of state enterprises and state economic operations	16.0	23.3	21.6	19.1	21.6
Production asset tax	—	—	—	16.2	16.8
Other quotas on state units	—	—	—	22.2	18.9
Duties and taxes from population	7.1	6.7	8.7	8.5	9.4
State social insurance payments	5.3	6.1	6.7	7.2	8.5

Source: Table SA5.1.

increase in wages, and related bonuses paid by the enterprises and various types of taxes discussed below. Profits have also been influenced by substantially increased production and improved efficiency, such as the reduced share of expenditures in the value of production. The exact distribution of profits of state enterprises differs from year to year. Generally about 65 percent is paid to the budget, 2 percent for bonuses, 20 percent for working capital purposes and for some minor investments, and the remainder for payment of credit obligations. Following the recent price resetting and new fiscal measures, the average profit range for all enterprises after the profit tax is planned to be 8 to 15 percent.

Tax revenues from the population have increased at about the same rate as total revenue, thus retaining almost a constant share of the total. The tax burden on the population appears to be light, about 4 to 5.5 percent of national income (Romanian methodology) or about 3 to 4.5 percent of gross national product (GNP). This must be viewed, though, as a nominal indicator, not particularly relevant to obtaining a measure of the effective incidence of taxation. The strict controls exercised by the state over the level and growth of individual and family earnings and on the prices of goods makes it even unnecessary to tax directly the population's income.[1]

Finally, depreciation funds have increased rapidly because of the expand-

1. This point is aptly illustrated by a 1977 measure to simplify the individual tax reporting and collection system. Salaried workers are now paid only their net salary, and their previous tax payments are aggregated and paid by the enterprises for which they work.

ing capital stock. This total is not publicly available and may or may not equal the amount of such funds devoted annually to investment, which is given further below. Until 1977 when new measures were introduced (below), depreciation was charged as long as capital goods were in service, even beyond their normal amortization period. Depreciation charges during the recognized economic life of an asset were allocated to the central and not kept by the enterprise. These funds were usually reinvested within the same industry, but not necessarily within the same firm. Thus, depreciation in the Romanian context was essentially a tax on capital that was earlier transferred to the enterprise cost free through the state budget. Depreciation charges extending beyond the recognized economic life of an asset were retained by the enterprise and could be used for small capital improvements or for working capital.

Romania's state tax system is discussed in detail below. The contribution of the various tax measures to the state budget in 1970–75 revenues is illustrated in Tables G.5 and G.6. Although state taxes play the major role in the mobilization efforts, the savings of the population and of the cooperatives as well as local levies provide some additional resources. These savings and other sources of fixed investment are also discussed below. Local levies have been discussed in Appendix B.

TURNOVER TAX. Until 1974 the turnover tax was the most important source of revenue for the government. This tax is added to the price of goods sold by producers to commercial enterprises to form the delivery price and is collected when goods are sold to the retail outlets. Since the 1974–76 repricing exercise, the turnover tax is quoted implicitly as the difference between the delivery price to the commercial enterprise and the production price. Before that, rates of turnover tax were quoted in different ways for different groups of products. In some cases, the rate was established as a proportion of the unit price at which the manufacturing enterprise sold its output to the commercial enterprise. In other cases, it was quoted as currently. The rates varied widely, although some of this variation is still maintained. Various items of food bore no tax; the rate was 10 percent or less on consumer durables, but it could be as high as 70 percent on alcohol, tobacco, and gasoline. Products made using waste materials and scrap were liable to half the actual tax rate. Turnover taxes are calculated on the invoice of each transaction. Considering what the tax obligations would be, enterprises pay the tax to the budget on different terms, varying from a daily basis up to quarterly. The turnover tax applies to both state enterprises and handicraft and consumer cooperatives. Rates for cooperatives, however, tend to be lower than in the state sector.

Table G.5. *Revenue and Expenditure of the State Budget, 1970–76*

(billions of lei)

Items of revenue or expenditure	*1970*	*1971*	*1972*	*1973*	*1974*	*1975*	*1976*
Total revenue	*133.3*	*138.6*	*153.4*	*176.0*	*210.1*	*238.6*	*254.5*
Turnover tax	40.5	44.0	45.1	48.0	46.0	42.1	44.9
Regularization tax	6.1	9.8	8.7	8.9	11.0	7.2	0.6
Benefit quotas from state enterprises	28.8	30.3	37.2	46.6	44.6	45.5	54.9
Tax on production fund and other taxes from socialist sector[a]	—	—	—	—	22.8	37.3	42.8
Other quotas from socialist units	n.a.	n.a.	n.a.	n.a.	37.4	53.0	48.1
Duties and taxes from population	11.6	12.9	13.9	15.4	17.4	20.2	23.9
Social security contributions of enterprises	8.9	9.6	10.3	12.4	14.4	17.2	21.6
Others	37.4	32.0	38.2	44.7	16.5	16.1	17.7
Total expenditure	*130.9*	*134.2*	*145.4*	*168.1*	*207.3*	*236.2*	*250.1*
Financing of the national economy	81.0	78.3	85.1	101.5	136.2	155.8	165.7
Investment[b]	32.2	36.0	40.3	44.8	53.5	78.1	

Other expenditure	48.8	42.3	44.8	56.7	82.7	77.7	
Financing of social and cultural expenditures	34.0	36.6	40.1	44.4	47.7	50.9	55.3
Education, culture, and art	10.2	10.8	11.4	12.0	12.8	13.8	15.5
Health	6.9	7.4	7.8	8.4	9.2	9.8	11.2
Social security and pensions	1.2	1.3	1.3	1.5	1.5	1.6	1.6
Physical education and sports	0.2	0.2	0.2	0.2	0.2	0.3	0.3
State subsidies for children	4.2	5.0	6.6	6.9	7.3	7.4	7.4
State social security	11.3	11.9	12.8	15.4	16.7	18.0	19.2
Defense	7.1	7.4	7.7	7.8	8.7	9.7	10.6
Administration and justice	2.5	2.6	2.6	2.7	2.7	2.7	3.0
Others	6.3	6.3	9.9	11.7	12.0	17.1	15.5

a. Contained in "Others" for years 1970–73.

b. Expenditure on state investment from state budget, plus expenditure on science and research. For 1975 and 1976 it includes customs duties as well.

Source: Anuarul Statistic, various issues.

Table G.6. *Annual Percentage Increases of Revenues of the State Budget, 1971–76*

Revenue source	*1971*	*1972*	*1973*	*1974*	*1975*	*1976*
Revenue, total	*4.0*	*10.6*	*14.7*	*19.4*	*13.6*	*6.7*
Turnover tax	8.6	2.4	6.6	−4.2	−8.0	6.7
Regularization tax	60.1	−11.7	2.9	23.5	−34.0	−99.2
Benefit quotas from state enterprises	5.1	22.7	25.4	−4.2	2.0	20.7
Tax on production fund and other taxes from socialist sector					63.5	10.9
Other quotas from socialist units					41.7	−9.2
Duties and taxes from population	10.8	10.8	10.9	12.8	16.0	18.3
Social security contributions of enterprises	7.4	7.3	20.5	15.6	19.0	25.6
Others		10.0	−1.0	24.4	−2.0	9.9

Source: Table G.5.

In the past, price adjustments have been infrequent, and turnover tax rates, which are fixed along with prices, have been quite stable. Thus, the revenue from this tax has risen with the increased sales of commodities. The recent price readjustment, however, affected both the rate structure and the significance of the turnover tax as a source of revenue, as illustrated in Table G.6. Broadly speaking, the turnover tax rates have declined, and the authorities have moved toward obtaining revenues from enterprise quotas.

TAXES ON EXCESS PROFITS. *Regularization tax.* The long period during which no price adjustments were made (1963–1974) affected the cost structure of many enterprises and their profitability. In 1970 it was decided to tax those products whose profit rate was too high (about 15 percent). The mechanism used to assess the tax was to establish a so-called "calculation price" for each product. The calculation price was computed using the average cost of the industrial subsector for the respective product or group of products, allowing for a normal profit level. This calculation price was less than the production price, and the difference between the two accrued to the budget as the regularization tax. This tax was imposed only when the product brought excessive profits within the industrial subsector rather than industrial enterprises. The adjustment of prices in 1974–76 has more

Table G.7. *Excess Profits Tax Rates*
(percentage)

Average annual profitability	*Tax rate*	*Average annual profitability*	*Tax rate*
15.01–17	3	29.01–31	51
17.01–19	15	31.01–33	57
19.01–21	23	33.01–35	54
21.01–23	30	35.01–37	57
23.01–25	35	37.01–39	59
25.01–27	40	39.01–40	61
27.01–29	44		

or less eliminated most gross asymmetrics between costs and prices and has reduced enterprise profits to normal levels. As a result, the tax was dropped when price adjustments for the products were effected.

Profits tax of 1977. Since major price adjustments are not made regularly and to prevent the accumulation of excessive profits by the enterprises in the future, a new tax on planned profitability exceeding 15 percent has been established as of January 1, 1977. The tax rates are given in Table G.7. They do provide an incentive to the enterprises to increase their profitability; all profits exceeding the planned level and arising from increased production or increased profitability will not be taxed. If the profit rate exceeds 40 percent, everything above 15 percent is siphoned to the budget.

BENEFIT (PROFIT) QUOTAS. Each enterprise contributes a portion of its profits to the state, and the aggregate total is one of the most important of revenues for the state budget. In fact, in 1976 it was expected to become the largest such source. The profit quota of an enterprise is fixed when the economic plan is prepared. It is determined by the plan and by deducting from the planned profit the amounts due by the enterprise, such as bonuses, self-financing, repayment of credit, and so forth. The difference is to be paid to the budget. During the plan period, payments from profits to the budget have the first claim on the firm's earnings. Bonus payments to workers, which are paid out of actual profits, are distributed only after the firm has met this primary and legal obligation. The profit quota has to be paid even if the enterprise fails to meet its plan targets. Handicraft and consumer cooperatives do not make benefit transfers to the state and instead pay a tax on their profits. The consumer cooperatives pay about 20 percent of their profits, whereas for the handicraft cooperatives, the tax is progressive by tranches from 25 percent for revenues exceeding profitability of 10 percent to 90 percent for revenues exceeding profitability of 20 percent, and the average rate is as high as 47 percent.

TAX ON PRODUCTION FUNDS. The tax on the production funds of an enterprise was introduced in 1974 but was withdrawn on January 1, 1977. It was a 6 percent levy on both the fixed and the working capital of the enterprise. The introduction of this tax implied substantial progress in eliminating the free use of capital and demonstrated a recognition by the authorities of the need for a more efficient use of capital. Although charge-free budgetary transfer continued during the imposition of the tax, for almost all investment activities, the tax was the equivalent to an interest charge on capital used by the enterprise and was paid by all units except those which were exempt because of financial difficulties. It was withdrawn purportedly because of administrative difficulties in evaluation and collection, but most likely because it reduced, if not eliminated, the established profitability of the larger enterprises within the revised price system.

TAX ON LAND USE (STATE OWNERSHIP). Since 1974, according to the Law on Lands, the socialist economic units, other than agricultural units, are obliged to pay an annual tax on their use of state land. These taxes are determined by certain economic criteria and are paid from profits. This tax is meant to stimulate the enterprises to use lands economically and to return to agricultural use as much land as possible. Besides the annual tax on land use, additional amounts are paid to release agricultural lands on which new investment projects are to be constructed, as well as to release temporarily lands occupied by building sites. These charges are included in investment costs.

OTHER TAXES AND PAYMENTS BY STATE ENTERPRISES. Most enterprises are subject to several other tax obligations, which are included under quotas from socialist units. Of these, the tax on buildings is the most significant. Also, all state enterprises make social security payments for their employees. These have grown steadily since 1970, but the expenditures of the state in this area have also expanded considerably partly because of an increase in the level of pension payments and partly because of the larger number of retired people. In 1977 a tax on the wage fund of enterprises was introduced ranging from 14.5 to 17.5 percent of the total wage funds. This is not actually a new tax, but consists of an administrative change wherein taxes on wages and salaries previously paid by the population will now be calculated and remitted to the budget by the enterprises. Employees would be paid their previous net salaries. This permits the employees to know their salaries better and simplifies accounting procedures.

DIRECT TAXES ON POPULATION. Revenues from direct taxes on the population have amounted up to 1977 to about 9 percent of total budget revenues. Until July 1977 a personal income tax was paid on wages and salaries if they exceeded 910 lei a month. The tax rates were slightly progressive, commencing at 10 percent and rising to a maximum of 45 percent. The overall average income tax was about 12 percent. Reduced rates were applied to families with dependents and to "decorated" employees. A change has also been introduced in the tax system affecting agricultural cooperatives. Until 1977 members of the agricultural cooperatives were taxed on their share of the cooperative's income, as well as on their earnings from the sale of produce grown on their private lots. The tax on the cooperative income was progressive, with average rates ranging from 6.5 to 16 percent. Incomes of private farmers and the private agricultural income of cooperative farmers were taxed at average rates ranging from 6 to 40 percent. The taxable income was determined by income norms per hectare and per animal. Writers, scientists, and artists pay a yearly tax on income earned ranging from 2 percent of income up to lei 2,400 to 21.3 percent on incomes of 120,000 lei. Craftsmen with their own workshops pay tax, as do professionals and others working on their own. Net taxable income is determined by deducting expenditures undertaken in attaining the gross income level. Finally, there are taxes or charges on property (on buildings, cars, and so forth), but these are not large.

In 1977 the previous income tax on cooperative farmers was paid by their cooperatives through a tax on land (per hectare), which is determined by the land's fertility and utilization, and through a tax on the portion of cooperative earnings which will be distributed to the farmers. This change was meant to increase land productivity and to encourage the cooperatives to retain a greater proportion of their earnings for their development fund, which is not taxed. Income taxes for private farmers and on income earned by cooperative farm workers working on their own plots have also been changed. They have been replaced by a tax on land, as in the case of the cooperatives.

TAXES ON FOREIGNERS AND JOINT VENTURES. Nonresidents are taxed 15 percent for amounts accruing from interest and commissions from commercial transactions, for services and staff training, for services as a consultant, and so forth; 20 percent on income from patents or licenses; and 25 percent on income from artistic and entertainment activities. Incomes from air or sea transport are taxed according to the quotas established by states that have such incomes. Profits of joint ventures operating in Romania are taxed annually at 30 percent. In some cases joint ventures may be exempted from taxation in the first year of operation, and may receive a 50 percent reduction in taxes for two subsequent years. An additional tax of 10 percent is imposed on the after-tax profits of joint ventures if the latter are transferred abroad. The tax applied to profits of joint ventures is reduced by 20 percent if profits are reinvested in Romania for at least five years.

Depreciation

The increases in depreciation funds have more than kept up with increases in state investments as a result of the rapidly increasing capital stock. Fixed assets are depreciated on the average in 21 years, but depreciation is charged as long as capital goods are in service, even beyond this normal amortization period. Depreciation charges over the recognized economic life of an asset are allocated to the central and are not kept by the enterprise. These funds are usually reinvested within the same industry but not necessarily within the same firm. Thus, in the Romanian context, depreciation essentially is a tax on capital earlier transferred to the enterprise cost-free through the state budget. Depreciation charges following the recognized economic life of an asset had, until 1977, been retained by the enterprise and could be used for small capital improvements or working capital. As of 1977, this "super depreciation" was abolished. The inventory value of fixed capital for depreciation purposes is understood to mean that for fixed capital existing as of December 31, 1964, the value established by a revaluation decreed by the Council of Ministers on that date, and that for fixed capital acquired or activated subsequently, the initial acquisition value.

Retained benefits

The use of retained benefits for investment purposes peaked in 1973–74 at 15 billion lei and subsequently declined. This decline is particularly significant, since measures were taken in 1970 to increase the financial resource requirements of enterprises for investment (and also working capital) and to reduce their complete dependence on budgetary transfers. In 1970 these transfers were reduced while at the same time the enterprises were allowed to retain a greater proportion of their profits, which were previously remitted to the state. This change was accommodated in the planning framework by introducing gross profit as a minimum plan target and by establishing rules for its distribution for financing working capital and some investment needs. The share of the gross profit of each enterprise paid to the state budget differed among enterprises, but at the minimum it was 10 percent. The amount of gross profits, working capital, and investments were still determined, however, by the plan targets and the respective ministries.

The effect of the new policy was immediate. In the year it was introduced, the various economic units retained about 38 percent of planned profits, compared with 10 percent in the previous one.

H

The Banking System

In Romania the banking system consists of the National Bank of the Socialist Republic of Romania, the Investment Bank, the Bank for Agriculture on Food Industry, the Romanian Bank for Foreign Trade, and the Bank for Deposits and Savings. All of these banks, except for the Romanian Bank for Foreign Trade, have branches and subbranches throughout the country.

The National Bank

The National Bank combines the functions of a central bank and a commercial bank. It is responsible for currency issue and organizes and coordinates the circulation of money and all activities connected with short-term credit. Together with the State Planning Committee (SPC), the Ministry of Finance, the Ministry for Material Supplies, and the specialized banks, it elaborates the drafts of the credit and cash plans of the economy and monitors their implementation. It organizes the granting of short-term credits on the basis of the approved plans and extends credits to the enterprises and economic organizations that have accounts with it. The specialized banks also hold accounts at the National Bank and may receive credits from it to supplement their own resources. All state economic units (except those in agriculture, construction, and foreign trade) are required to hold current accounts at the National Bank and to channel all transactions through these accounts. The Bank also is the main conduit for budgetary flows and, with the agreement of the Ministry of Finance, coordinates and monitors the collection of state revenues.

In the field of foreign relations, the National Bank participates in elaborating the balance of payments and monitors its planned execution. It establishes the rates of exchange in lei of the foreign currencies and organizes the exchange of foreign currencies. Finally, it concludes external financial contracts and payments of agreements.

The Investment Bank

The Investment Bank (IB) has a major and broad role in the economy, especially in industry. It is the channel for all sources of major domestic investment financing including budget allocations, depreciation funds, and share of planned benefits of enterprises allocated for investment. In 1973, IB also started to make credits on its own, although funds available for this purpose are still relatively small. IB administers and controls all investment funds (except for agriculture, food processing, silviculture, and forestry), however, and acts as the main fiscal agent of the government. The president of IB reports directly to the Minister of Finance, who has comprehensive authority in planning and financing all projects.

The IB is an organization with wide-ranging responsibilities in the implementation of projects. It plays a key role in the preparation, evaluation, procurement, execution, disbursement of investment funds, and supervision of all enterprises. For all projects, IB, together with other agencies of economic synthesis, reviews the technical and economic study before submission to the Council of Ministers for formal approval. Thereafter, IB ensures that the project is executed according to the approved plan. For each project, it will check all orders for equipment—domestic and foreign—before they are placed, will comment on any change in contracts, and can impose penalties on defaulting parties. Its inspectors check the appropriateness of equipment deliveries and whether the projects are progressing according to schedule. All local project-cost financing is channeled through and authorized by IB, which also keeps complete accounting records for each project until completion. IB has no legal authority to bring its views to bear directly on the management of an enterprise. In practice, however, IB can recommend necessary action to the Ministry of Finance, which, in turn, can act through the ministry concerned with the project.

The Bank for Agriculture and Food Industry

The Bank for Agriculture and Food Industry (BAFI) is an integrated bank established to finance production and investment in agriculture and agro-industries. The more important responsibilities of BAFI are:

(a) to act as fiscal agent for collecting and distributing budgetary funds;
(b) to grant short-term production credit;
(c) to approve investment proposals of state enterprises and cooperatives;
(d) to grant long-term investment credit;
(e) to maintain checking accounts and accept deposits;
(f) to exercise financial control over the execution of financial and investment plans;
(g) to cooperate with foreign and international organizations to finance investments in agriculture and agroindustries.

BAFI's operations are carried out by thirty-nine branches and fifty-seven subbranches. About 800 credit cooperatives also execute BAFI operations on a commission basis for small-scale lending. Institutions of national importance are served by the three operational departments in the head office: agro-industries, cooperative sector, and state sector.

One of BAFI's most important functions is that of financial agent for state long-term investments in agriculture and agro-industries. BAFI reviews and analyzes proposed development indicators, finances and extends credits for investments, supervises the procurement and use of the investment fund, and receives a commission of 5 percent of the investments channeled through it from the state budget.

BAFI makes both short- and long-term loans to the cooperative sector and to a limited degree to individual co-op members and private farmers. Short-term capital requirements of state enterprises are met by BAFI production credits. Long-term investments in state enterprises are normally financed from the state budget. Long-term lending to state agricultural enterprises started with a very limited scope under the "small mechanization program" and on a regional basis under projects financed by the World Bank (Sadova-Corabia Agricultural Credit Project, Flood Recovery Project, and Rasova-Vederoasa Project) and other projects. The shift from equity contributions to investment lending reflects a policy decision to require greater financial responsibility in the state agricultural sector.

In addition to controlling plan execution, BAFI intervenes even during project design whether it is financed from the state budget or from loan funds. The beneficiaries of investments draw up order notes, which are tendered to the designing institute to elaborate the project. The economic and engineering staff from BAFI provides advice both for the order notes and for the projects, with special attention paid to those criteria or indexes affecting economic efficiency. Once a plan is approved by BAFI, it is binding for both the client and BAFI. After approval, BAFI supervises the operations of borrowers and investors closely. Its inspectors visit clients regularly and report on conditions in the field. Delays and infractions in operations and project execution are penalized. In addition to the supervision activities carried out by BAFI branches, subbranches, and operational head office departments, there is a central supervision division, which ensures that this activity is performed properly.

Loans granted to agricultural cooperatives are primarily secured by "credit engagements" of borrowers who commit all present and future income to debt service and who are obliged to maintain all their revenue in BAFI accounts. In accordance with BAFI policy, short-term credit must not exceed 60 percent of production valued at selling prices. The law provides that in the case of a liquidity problem, BAFI's claims would have priority over other debts.

The total volume of BAFI financing rose from 149 billion lei (US$7.4 billion) in 1970 to 389 billion lei (US$19.0 billion) in 1975. Its structure remained relatively stable, with 80 percent being short-term production credit and the balance long-term investment financing.

The main sources of BAFI funds are statutory capital (800 million lei), the reserve fund representing accumulation of net profits (800 million lei), and special funds provided from the state budget based on the state's financial plan for agricultural investment targets. BAFI obtains short-term borrowings from the National Bank of Romania and accepts deposits from socialist organizations. BAFI pays 1.5 percent a year interest on these liabilities. Deposits have ranged between 4.0 and 5.1 billion lei over the past five years.

BAFI's net worth was 1,600 million lei on December 31, 1975. Because of its control over the accounts of its borrowers, surveillance of disbursements and loan proceeds, as well as detailed and rigorous inspections of operations at the project level, BAFI has had no reported loss from bad debt. In addition, BAFI does not run foreign exchange risk, since such operations are handled by the National Bank of Romania and by the Romanian Bank for Foreign Trade. Since its assets and liabilities are well protected against potential risks and given its close control of cost developments, BAFI is expected to remain in good financial condition.

The Romanian Bank for Foreign Trade

The Foreign Trade Bank executes all foreign payments and undertakes all other operations in foreign exchange. In addition to providing export finance and acting as the conduit for import credits, the Foreign Trade Bank operates an account to equalize the price of imports and exports with domestic prices. It has the right to issue commercial bills in favor of beneficiaries from abroad and may accept the issuing of bills of itself. All foreign trading firms operate their current accounts with the Foreign Trade Bank.

A main Bank activity is that of granting the Romanian foreign trade enterprises the credit facilities necessary to expand Romanian exports. At the end of 1975 the credits in lei granted to the foreign trade enterprises reached 9,662.2 million lei, as against 6,022.8 million lei at the end of 1970, representing an increase of 60.4 percent. A significant portion of the Bank's credits was to refinance the supplier credits extended by these enterprises to their customers abroad.

The Romanian Bank for Foreign Trade has concluded many agreements with foreign banks to facilitate further Romanian exports. In 1975 it monitored the implementation of 115 such agreements. By 1975 the network of correspondent banks had been extended to 1,055, in 110 countries of the world.

Finally, the Bank has entered into joint operations in four countries, forming the Anglo-Romanian, French-Romanian, German-Romanian, and Egypt-Romanian Banks, in which the Bank for Foreign Trade owns 50 percent of the capital.

The Bank for Deposits and Savings

This bank serves the banking needs of the population and accepts private lei deposits. It has an extensive network of branches and subbranches (about 1,800) in both urban and rural areas. In addition, there are 8,000 counters manned by part-time personnel in schools and enterprises throughout the country. Withdrawals and transfers can also be made through the post office. Both current and savings accounts are available, and both bear interest: 3.5 percent a year on sight deposits and 5 percent on term deposits. About 40 percent of these funds are lent to finance housing. The remainder are available to the National Bank to finance its own lending for working capital. Not all accounts at the Savings Bank are private accounts. In addition, some local and municipal accounts, together with the accounts of some social and religious organizations are held at the Savings Bank.

Resources of the Banking System

The banking system has expanded its resources rapidly almost doubling them in 1970–75 (Table H.1). The composition of these resources has also

ıble H.1. *Resources of the Banking System, 1960, 1970, and 1972–75*
ercentage)

Resources	*1960*	*1970*	*1972*	*1973*	*1974*	*1975*
nk's own resources	4.7	3.3	4.7	4.5	3.9	3.7
sources of the state budget	33.7	10.8	12.0	13.6	7.2	4.5
posits of the credit institutes with the National Bank	8.7	7.1	6.6	4.1	6.8	13.7
Bank for Agricultural and Food Industry	—	0.4	—	—	—	—
Romanian Bank for Foreign Trade	—	3.5	6.4	3.4	5.9	10.7
Investment Bank	6.9	1.4	0.2	0.7	0.9	3.0
Savings Bank	1.8	1.8	—	—	—	—
sources of enterprises, organizations, and institutions	23.5	29.2	26.2	25.6	32.0	29.6
sh in circulation	13.7	12.4	13.0	13.1	11.6	12.1
posits in the Savings Bank	5.1	22.1	23.6	24.9	24.1	25.5
Funds transferred to the state budget	4.7	18.7	16.9	14.9	12.6	11.5
her resources	10.6	15.1	13.9	14.2	14.4	10.9
tal (billions of lei)	—	94.0	117.0	136.0	160.0	170.0

ource: Data supplied by the Romanian authorities during discussions with the authors, except total in billions of lei, which is a World Bank estimate.

changed significantly, reflecting the fiscal measures decreed in 1969 and an increased marginal propensity to save by the population.

The budget used to be the dominant resource of the banking system. Following the 1969 measure, its role was reduced, and most recently its contribution has been only marginally significant. The enterprises' deposits with the banking institutions, however, have accounted for an increasing share of the resources of the banking system. This is the result of the larger financial authority that was devolved to the enterprises in 1970, through their retaining a larger percentage of planned profits to self-finance working capital needs and small investments and the requirement that all economic entities must keep their funds in bank accounts and make payments to each other through transfers.

The biggest relative increase, however, has been that of the savings deposits of the population in the Savings Bank. This development arose in response to a carefully planned new pattern of activity of the Savings Bank, which was introduced in the framework of the monetary reforms. The new activities included different interest rates and diversified schemes to encourage the population to be thrifty and to accumulate deposits for purchases requiring large down payments, such as apartments and cars. In its new role, the Bank has a substantial role not only in mobilizing resources, but also in transferring a substantial amount of them to the budget.

Monetary Instruments

The main objectives of monetary and credit policy are to provide enterprises with the required credit so that they can meet their plan targets and to provide sufficient liquidity in the economy, consistent with the availability of goods (Chapter 3).

Banks provide primarily short-run credit. At the end of 1975 total such credit outstanding was 170 billion lei (Table H.2), close to the planned level. The anticipated increase in the outstanding credit to assist enterprises affected by the flood did not materialize, since overall credit demand was lower than expected because of lower production levels. Also, some resources were channeled to the affected areas through the budget, which also reduced the need for short-term credit. The credit that is given for new investment or for extending and modernizing facilities amounts to self-financing by the enterprise, since it must generate the resources to repay its borrowing. Each item must have been cleared by the annual plan, however, and must have enough profitability to cover the repayment of the loan, which is usually granted for ten years. Investment credit is also available to offset frictional disturbances in the investment programs of the firms, for example, a level of disbursement higher than planned because of a change in the scheduling of a project. But this type of credit must be repaid by the end of the year. Although the government could make budgetary transfers on a quarterly basis, bank lending is more convenient and is expected to continue in the future, perhaps even on a somewhat larger scale.

The maturity for long-term credit is up to ten years (for agricultural cooperatives some credits are extended for up to twelve to twenty-five years) and for medium-term credits up to five years (Chapter 4). Investment credit is also available with one year maturity if any of the following conditions is met (article 100 of the Financial Law no. 9/1972):

(a) When an anticipated lag exists (which is foreseen in the enterprise's plan) between investment requirements and cash flow for investment purposes;
(b) When the investment plan for a specific year is exceeded, but this excess is also economically justified;

(c) When there is an unanticipated shortfall in the enterprise's funds for investment financing.

The largest percentage of bank credit operations is composed of short-term credit, chiefly to meet the needs of enterprises for working capital. On the average, 45 percent of the working capital requirements of the enterprises is financed by bank credit, whereas the working capital needs of new enterprises are met by the state budget. Bank credits are repaid from the profits of the enterprises or from other specific funds. The repayment period is twelve months, but it can vary for some subsectors of the economy. The National Bank extends credits to industry, trade, and transport. BAFI extends credit to agriculture, forestry, and food industry, and the Investment Bank to the construction sector. Foreign trade enterprises

Table H.2. *Money Supply, Cash in Circulation, Savings Deposits, and Short-Term Bank Credits, Selected Years*

Year	*Money supply*	*Cash in circulation*	*Savings deposits*	*Short-term bank credit outstanding*
		Millions of lei at end of year		
1973	...	17,793	33,869	131,270
1974	160,063	18,558	38,681	155,251
1975	176,384	21,379	44,925	170,162
1976	201,366	23,914	52,134	193,965
		Percentage annual average increase		
1961–65	9.2	9.1	38.3	10.0
1966–70	13.6	11.3	20.1	13.7
1961–70	11.3	10.2	28.9	11.8
1971–75	13.8	11.9	16.2	14.1
		Percentage annual increase		
1969	13.7	8.1	15.1	13.8
1970	24.4	4.9	9.7	26.0
1971	12.4	14.1	15.9	13.1
1972	11.4	14.9	15.4	10.4
1973	13.7	14.7	19.6	14.6
1974	17.7	4.3	14.2	18.3
1975	10.2	15.2	16.1	9.6
1976	14.2	11.9	16.0	14.0

Source: Data supplied by the Romanian authorities during discussions with the authors.

Table H.3. *Annual Interest Rates, 1970–74 and 1975*
(percentage)

Item	Kind of interest					
	Normal credits		*Special credits*		*Overdue credits*	
	1970–74	*1975*	*1970–74*	*1975*	*1970–74*	*1975*
Credits for working capital						
Industry, transport, services, research and development, and technical and material supply	2 and 5	5	10 and 12	7	10 and 12	12
Construction	2 and 5	2	—	4	12	12
Trade and related services	3	3	8	5	8	8
Foreign trade	4 and 5	5	—	7	8	10
Agriculture and related activities						
State units	4	4	10 and 12	6	12	12
Cooperative units	2 and 4	2	—	4	6	6
Agricultural mechanization stations	2 and 4	3	—	5	12	8
Members of cooperatives and private peasants	2	2	—	—	6	6
State and cooperative units for installment credits	3	3	—	—	—	—
Inventories for state reserves	2	2	—	—	—[a]	—[a]
Large-scale repair operations	3 and 4	4	—	—	—[a]	—[a]
Credits given to specialized banks	1.5	1.5	—	—	—	—
Special credits approved by Council of Ministers	0–5	2	—	—	—[a]	—[a]
Investment credit						
Fixed investment						
During execution	2	2	—	—	6	6

After termination	2–4	4	—	—	6	6
Small-scale mechanization	1	1	—	—	—[a]	—[a]
Misappropriation of funds	—	—	—	—	12	12
Financing of equipment						
Until planned installation	0.1	0.1	—	—	—	2
Installation delayed three months	—	—	—	—	6	6
Installation delayed six months	—	—	—	—	12	12
Failure to accumulate planned investment funds	12	12	—	—	12	12
Supply of materials for investment	0.1	2	—	—	6	6
Approved exceeding of investment plan	0.1	0.1	—	—	—	—
Agricultural cooperatives	1.5 and 2	3	—	—	5	6
Members of cooperatives and private peasants	3	3	—	—	10	10
Loans granted upon approval by Council of Ministers						
For inventories for modified investment plan and of sufficient retained earnings	4 and 5	4	—	—	12	12
For elimination of damage from calamities	—	2	—	—	12	12
Credits to the population						
Construction and purchase of dwellings	2–8	2–8	—	—	12	12
Installment credits	5	5	—	—	10	10
Interest rates on deposits						
Current account	1.5	1.5	—	—	—	—
Deposits in the Savings Bank	2–5	2–5	—	—	—	—
Deposits in foreign currency	2–5	2–5	—	—	—	—
Deposits of Savings Bank in National Bank	4.5	4.5	—	—	—	—

a. Interest rate on overdue credit that applies to the branch of the particular economic unit.

Source: Decree (no. 234/1974) of the State Council, *Official Bulletin of the Socialist Republic of Romania*, year X, no. 166 (December 26, 1974) and data supplied by the Romanian authorities during discussions with the authors.

engaged in exporting borrow from the Bank for Foreign Trade, repaying their debts once they receive payment from the foreign trading partner. The level of short-term credit in the economy is provided in the quarterly Credit Plan, drawn up by the National Bank with the Ministry of Finance, the other banks, and other agencies of economic synthesis.

The banking system also fulfills a complementary auditing function in supervising the financial activities of the enterprises. In recent years, credit policy has been strengthened as an instrument to improve the efficiency of the enterprises' financial operations. The Ministry of Finance and the National Bank were given sufficient authority to establish the financial direction of a firm, should it fail to meet its plan targets.

Changes in short-term credit determine changes in the money supply. The latter amounted in 1975 to 176 billion lei and in 1976 to 201.4 billion lei (Table H.2).

A new structure of interest rates (Table H.3) was introduced on January 1, 1975, replacing the one put in operation five years earlier. The new structure was intended to simplify the previously complex regulation of interest rates (Chapter 4).

I

Wages and Other Income

WAGES ARE DETERMINED BY A COMPLEX SYSTEM OF CRITERIA. In addition to regular wages, a worker may receive income through bonuses, seniority supplements, overtime pay, and other specialized payments.

Determination of Wages

Wages are determined by law in Romania. The quantity, quality, and social significance of performed work are the stated criteria according to which the structure, as distinct from the average level, of wages is established. The wage structure is viewed as a mechanism for achieving maximum economic efficiency in the allocation of labor, for providing material incentives to the labor force to increase productivity, and as a means of distributing income equitably.[1] The dominant feature of the distribution of income (Table I.1) is that until 1975, there was a large concentration of people with wages between 900 and 2,000 lei. Although the proportion of workers earning less than 900 lei has decreased and the proportion earning more than 2,500 lei has increased, this concentration was altered only in 1975. The compressed distribution is also revealed by the industrial structure of wages in Table SA1.15.

Wages are paid on a piece rate, time rate, or commission basis. In some cases the piece rate is independent of the level of individual output, in others it is a positive function of output; in some cases it applies to an individual, in others to a team of workers. Daily or monthly production norms are set for the technical, financial, administrative, and other workers

1. Law (no. 57) on Remuneration According to the Quantity and Quality of Labor, *Official Bulletin of the Socialist Republic of Romania*, no. 154 (December 16, 1971) and Decree (no. 188) of 1977.

Table I.1. *Income Categories, by Groups of Recipients, Various Years*
(percentage)

Group of recipients	*1970*	*1971*	*1972*	*1975*
Total employees (including workers)				
Less than 900 lei	7.0	6.1	5.5	—
901–1100 lei	20.3	18.2	17.4	—
1101–1300 lei	22.0	21.9	21.2	3.5
1301–1500 lei	15.7	16.1	16.2	16.8
1501–2000 lei	20.8	22.6	23.5	44.6
2001–2500 lei	8.2	8.8	9.5	25.8
Over 2500 lei	6.0	6.3	6.7	9.3
Workers only				
Less than 900 lei	8.0	6.8	6.1	—
901–1100 lei	21.9	19.4	18.3	—
1101–1300 lei	24.0	24.0	23.1	—
1301–1500 lei	17.0	17.4	17.5	—
1501–2000 lei	20.3	22.3	23.5	—
2001–2500 lei	6.1	7.0	7.9	—
Over 2500 lei	2.7	3.1	3.6	—

Note: Data are based on gross income.
Source: Data provided by the Romanian authorities during discussions with the authors.

who are paid on a time rate and for the sales and other personnel who are paid on a commission basis.

For determining wages, unskilled workers are differentiated according to whether they do "regular," "heavy," or "extra heavy" work. Also for each type of work there is a base and three additional remuneration levels among which workers are distributed on the basis of their performance and seniority. This entire structure varies among branches and subbranches which are grouped into fourteen categories. Table I.2 documents the structures for the two categories at the top and the two at the bottom of the wage hierarchy. The ratio of the highest wage (underground mines A —step III—extra heavy work) to the lowest wage (wood processing A and B—base—regular) is roughly 2:1.

Skilled workers in each of fifty-two networks are divided among four to seven categories according to their level of skill. Within these categories there is a base and three additional remuneration levels. Table I.3 lists all fifty-two networks, and Table I.4 documents the structures for the two groups at the top and the two at the bottom of the wage hierarchy. The ratio of the highest wage (underground mines—step III—skill category 5)

Table I.2. *Net Wage Structure in Four Industrial Categories of Unskilled Labor, 1974*
(lei per month)

Wage scale and level	*Wage levels by classification of duties*		
	Regular	*Heavy*	*Extra heavy*
Underground mines A			
Base	1,759	1,976	2,193
Step I	1,823	2,040	2,257
Step II	1,887	2,103	2,320
Step III	1,951	2,167	2,384
Underground mines B			
Base	1,581	1,798	2,002
Step I	1,645	1,861	2,078
Step II	1,708	1,925	2,142
Step III	1,772	1,989	2,206
Surface mines C, quarries—gravel pits, wood processing B for piece rates, and in organizations making no distinction between piece and time rates for determination of wages due, food B			
Base	1,295	1,367	1,438
Step I	1,316	1,387	1,459
Step II	1,336	1,408	1,479
Step III	1,357	1,428	1,499
Wood processing A and B for work under state supervision forestry operations B, local industry, construction materials B, food C			
Base	1,285	1,357	1,428
Step I	1,306	1,377	1,448
Step II	1,326	1,397	1,469
Step III	1,346	1,418	1,489

Source: Decree (no. 188) of 1977.

to the lowest wage (local industry—base—skill category) is 2.5:1. In addition to the regular skill categories, there is a specialist category that includes workers who perform a range of particularly complex operations. Although the wages are considerably higher for such specialists and taking them into consideration raises the ratio of highest to lowest wages among skilled

Table I.3. *Industry Categories of Skilled Workers*

Number	Scale and level
1.	Underground mines A.
2.	Underground mines B.
3.	Underground mines C.
4.	Underground mines D.
5.	Ferrous metallurgy A.
6.	Mechanical engineering, level AO, for piece rates.
7.	Ferrous metallurgy B.
8.	Drilling.
9.	Mechanical engineering, level A, piece rates.
10.	Mechanical engineering, level Ao, for work under state supervision.
11.	Mechanical engineering, level B, piece rates.
12.	Construction A, piece rates.
13.	Mechanical engineering, level A, for work under state supervision.
14.	Farm machine mechanics—for shopwork.
15.	Electric energy A.
16.	Chemistry Ao.
17.	Nonferrous metallurgy.
18.	Printing A.
19.	Surface mines A.
20.	Construction A, for work under state supervision.
21.	Mechanical engineering, level B, for work under state supervision.
22.	Electric energy B.
23.	Chemistry A.
24.	Petroleum A.
25.	Construction B, piece rates.
26.	Printing B.
27.	Tanning.
28.	Petroleum B.
29.	Chemistry B.
30.	Surface mines B.
31.	Glass.
32.	Wood processing, level A, piece rates.
33.	Forestry operations A.
34.	Electric energy C.
35.	Refractory materials.
36.	Construction materials A.
37.	Leather garments.

(Table continues on the following page)

Table I.3. *Continued*

38.	Food A.
39.	Construction B, for work under state supervision.
40.	Textiles.
41.	Wood processing, level B, piece rates.
42.	Surface mines C—quarries.
43.	Municipal services A.
44.	Food B.
45.	Wood processing, level A, for work performed under state supervision.
46.	Wood processing, level B for work under state supervision.
47.	Forestry operations B.
48.	Local industry.
49.	Municipal services B.
50.	Construction materials B.
51.	Food C.
52.	Silviculture.

workers to 2.8:1, their effect on the overall distribution among skilled workers is limited, since, by law, specialists are limited to 1 percent (and with special dispensation from the Council of Ministers to 2 percent) of an enterprise's skilled labor force.

The wage structures of skilled and unskilled workers overlap. The ratio of the highest wage paid to a (nonspecialist) skilled worker to the highest wage paid to an unskilled worker is only 1.4:1. The ratio of the highest wage paid an unskilled worker to the lowest paid skilled worker is 1.6:1. This suggests that at any given time, there are likely to be quite a few older unskilled workers earning more than skilled workers who are recent labor force entrants, since there is a positive relation between seniority and wage step and skill level. Formal training may be a partial substitute for experience: that is, a worker with more education can enter the wage structure at a higher skill level, but once he has entered, the progression from step to step and level to level is constrained by requirements of minimum time worked at each step. At least one year must be spent at the base level and two years at each of the higher steps.[2] Furthermore, during a year, no more than 40 percent of the total number of workers employed by each enterprise may be promoted to higher wage steps or levels.

The monthly wages of technical, financial, administrative, service, and guard personnel range from 1,290 lei, the national minimum, to 5,820 lei,

2. Reductions in the length of time in each step, in no case exceeding one-third of the requirement, can be granted under special circumstances.

Table I.4. *Net Wage Structures in Four Industrial Categories of Skilled Labor*
(lei per month)

Wage scale and level	*Classification categories*						
	1	*2*	*3*	*4*	*5*	*6*	*Spec[illegible]*
Underground mines A							
Base	1,938	2,180	2,430	2,767	3,124		3,5[illegible]
Step I	1,989	2,244	2,512	2,856	3,213		3,6[illegible]
Step II	2,053	2,308	2,588	2,945	3,302		3,7[illegible]
Step III	2,116	2,371	2,677	3,034	3,404		3,8[illegible]
Underground mines B							
Base	1,734	1,989	2,244	2,499	2,805		3,2[illegible]
Step I	1,798	2,053	2,308	2,575	2,907		3,3[illegible]
Step II	1,861	2,116	2,371	2,652	3,009		3,4[illegible]
Step III	1,925	2,180	2,435	2,728	3,111		3,5[illegible]
Construction materials B, Food C							
Base	1,459	1,540	1,622	1,703	1,816		1,9[illegible]
Step I	1,479	1,561	1,642	1,724	1,856		2,05[illegible]
Step II	1,499	1,581	1,663	1,754	1,897		2,1[illegible]
Step III	1,520	1,601	1,683	1,765	1,938		2,1[illegible]
Forestry operations B, local industry (specific activities)							
Base	1,459	1,540	1,622	1,703	1,785	1,897	2,0[illegible]
Step I	1,479	1,561	1,642	1,724	1,805	1,938	2,15[illegible]
Step II	1,499	1,581	1,663	1,744	1,826	1,979	2,21[illegible]
Step III	1,520	1,601	1,683	1,765	1,856	2,020	2,28[illegible]

Source: Decree (no. 188) of 1977.

the maximum wage for workers employed in state organizations. The wage structures of workers in these occupations varies among seven groups of subsectors, as illustrated for nine categories of professional or technical workers in Table I.5. For occupations such as technicians, the structure of wages overlaps considerably the wage structures of both skilled and unskilled workers. For higher paying occupations such as economists, chemists, and physicists, there is little overlap with unskilled workers.

The wages of management personnel depend primarily on the categorization of the enterprise in which the work is done, according to subsector group and grade of organization. The seven subsector groups in Table I.6

are the same as those in Table I.5. Some of the criteria for determining the grade of organization are the volume of output, complexity of production activities, and the percentage of output to be exported. For managers, the ratio of the highest basic wage to the lowest is 2.2:1. There is no overlap between the wage structures of management and unskilled workers, little between the structures of management and skilled workers, and somewhat more between the structures of management and professional or technical workers.

Supplementary Sources of Income

For workers at all levels, the basic wages paid average 88 to 95 percent of total remuneration, but for any individual, the proportion may be considerably less. The balance is accounted for by various forms of bonus payments and by increments to wages for uninterrupted employment or for work performed under extraordinary conditions.

Bonuses

The annual bonuses for the staff of commercial enterprises are paid out of profits. The bonus fund is a fixed percentage of planned profits; for the economy as a whole, it cannot represent more than 3 percent of planned profits. Enterprises that exceed planned profits may increase the bonus fund by as much as 16 percent of the increment; enterprises that fail to meet profit targets reduce the bonus fund 1 percent for each percentage point of underfulfillment. Failure to fulfill targets relating to other indicators of performance may also reduce the fund.

The planned bonus fund plus one-half of the increment for exceeding performance targets is distributed at the end of the year among all personnel in proportion to wage earnings, although as a reward for distinguished work performance, certain individuals may receive bonuses which, as a proportion of their annual wage, are 20 percent greater than those received by other workers. Similarly, individuals who have performed particularly poorly or who have committed disciplinary violations may be penalized by a reduced bonus. The remaining half of the increment to the bonus fund is distributed among those workers deemed to have the greatest responsibility for exceeding the targets. Personnel attached to financial ministries and other agencies responsible for coordinating the activities of the various subsectors of the economy receive bonuses based on the performance of their subordinate units taken as a whole. Personnel of other nonprofit organiza-

Table I.5. *Net Wage Ranges in Seven Industrial Categories of Professional and Technical Workers*
(lei per month)

	Remuneration category at base level and at highest grade			
	Engineer		*Economist, chemist, physicist*	
Branch group	*Ordinary*	*Chief*	*Ordinary*	*Chief*
Underground mining	3,170 4,220	3,325 4,620	2,415 3,170	2,840 3,640
Surface mining	2,640 3,480	2,640 4,020	2,415 3,170	2,640 3,640
Metallurgy and geological exploration	2,640 3,480	2,640 4,020	2,415 3,170	2,640 3,640
Mechanical and electrical engineering and railroad and air transport	2,415 3,170	2,640 3,640	2,310 3,030	2,520 3,480
Chemical, petroleum, agricultural, construction, wood processing, and shipping industries	2,310 3,030	2,520 3,480	2,220 2,895	2,415 3,325
Light industry, forestry, food processing, municipal services, and commerce	2,220 2,895	2,415 3,325	2,140 2,760	2,310 3,170
Light industry, food processing, local industry, and commerce	2,140 2,760	2,310 3,170	2,070 2,640	2,220 3,030
Construction materials, local industry, and commerce	2,070 2,640	2,220 3,030	2,020 2,520	2,140 2,895

Source: Decree (no. 188) of 1977.

tions receive bonuses, in proportion to wage level, from a fund that constitutes 1.5 percent of the regular wage fund.

In addition to the annual bonus fund, 1 percent of the planned wage fund is set aside for bonuses distributed throughout the year to reward outstanding achievements. There are also bonuses for employees responsible for innovations that increase labor productivity or that economize on raw materials, intermediate products, fuel, and energy. These are limited in value to 30 percent of the savings effected (50 percent in the case of highly

Branch group	*Remuneration category at base level and at highest grade*			
	Technician		*Planner, bookkeeper, statistician, commodity expert*	
	Ordinary	*Chief*	*Ordinary*	*Chief*
Underground mining	2,070	2,520	1,620	1,870
	2,640	3,480	1,980	2,310
Surface mining	1,920	2,220	1,620	1,870
	2,310	3,030	1,920	2,310
Metallurgy and geological exploration	1,870	2,140	1,620	1,870
	2,220	2,895	1,920	2,310
Mechanical and electrical engineering and railroad and air transport	1,820	2,070	1,620	1,870
	2,140	2,760	1,920	2,310
Chemical, petroleum, agricultural, construction, wood processing, and shipping industries	1,770	2,020	1,620	1,870
	2,070	2,640	1,920	2,370
Light industry, forestry, food processing, municipal services, and commerce	1,720	1,970	1,570	1,820
	2,020	2,520	1,870	2,220
Light industry, food processing, local industry, and commerce	1,670	1,920	1,545	1,770
	1,970	2,415	1,820	2,140
Construction materials, local industry, and commerce	1,620	1,820	1,545	1,720
	1,920	2,310	1,820	2,070

important materials) and are paid out of the wage fund of the enterprise, except when the innovation is applicable to several other enterprises, in which case the cost is born by a national fund established in the plan for that purpose. Similarly, personnel responsible for economizing on imports or producing exports in excess of targets are eligible for bonuses. Individual bonuses, which in total may not exceed three months wages, are awarded by the management of an enterprise with the consent of the trade union committee.

Table I.6. *Structure of Basic Wages of Management Personnel*

Grade organization of the enterprise	*Remuneration category for the position of manager, by branch group*						
	I	*II*	*III*	*IV*	*V*	*VI*	*VII*
Special	6,310	5,960	5,535	5,255	4,995	4,745	4,545
I	5,960	5,660	5,255	4,995	4,745	4,495	4,295
II	5,660	5,380	4,985	4,745	4,495	4,295	4,045
III	5,305	5,095	4,745	4,495	4,235	4,045	3,855
IV	4,845	4,595	4,235	4,045	3,855	3,640	3,485
V	4,350	4,105	3,855	3,640	3,485	3,330	3,190
VI	3,915	3,695	3,485	3,330	3,190	3,055	2,920

Source: Data provided by Romanian authorities during discussions with the authors.

Outstanding performance on the job is rewarded by bonuses; failure to fulfill assigned duties is penalized by reduced pay. Remuneration may be reduced by 1 percent of the basic wage for each percentage point of underfulfillment of plan target, to a maximum of 20 percent. If production shortfalls are made up, all or part of the penalty may be restored, depending on the effects of the shortfall on other producers, as well as the time required to remedy the situation. In cases where a worker's failure to fulfill plan targets or indicators results from situations outside the organization in which he is employed, no penalty is imposed. Such cases are:

(a) Failure to receive, as stipulated in supply contracts, raw materials, intermediate goods, or capital equipment that are inputs into the production process.
(b) Lengthy interruptions in an enterprise power supply.
(c) Failure of a contractor to complete new facilities on schedule.
(d) Natural disasters.

Other income supplements

Employees in all sectors receive increments to their monthly wages as a reward for uninterrupted service with their enterprise, according to the scale set out in Table I.7.

Employees working in jobs in which, despite safety precautions, there remains some risk of physical harm are entitled to an increment to their monthly wage, determined annually by the Council of Ministers. Workers in jobs characterized by difficult working conditions, for which recruitment of manpower is difficult, may benefit from increments of up to 15 percent of

Table I.7. *Pay Increment for Uninterrupted Employment*

Years of uninterrupted employment	*Base wage increase*[a] *(percentage)*
5–10	3
10–15	5
15–20	7
Over 20	10

a. Miners receive an increment for 1 to 5 years tenure; workers in organizations subordinate to the Ministry of Transport receive somewhat larger increments.

their base wage. A worker who, in addition to successfully performing his own job leads a team or brigade of workers, is entitled to an increment of up to 10 percent of his basic wage. Workers who perform overtime and who are not compensated by corresponding free time receive their basic wages plus 50 percent for the first two hours and plus 100 percent for subsequent hours. Wages for work on rest days or national holidays are also double the regular wage. Employees who work the night shift receive eight hours pay for seven hours work; if they work eight hours they receive a 15 percent increment to their wages.

Income Determination within Agricultural Units

The remuneration of the labor force within a state agricultural unit (IAS) is based on piecework. Contracts are concluded between the enterprise manager and the farm chiefs or between the farm chiefs and the chief of the work teams. The contract includes the worker's expected input, volume of produce, and the remuneration, which is calculated as a fixed value per tonne of production or a percentage per 1,000 lei of output. Throughout the year, workers receive monthly advance payments of about 80 percent of their total remuneration in the arable sector and 90 percent in the livestock subsector. At the end of the year, the remuneration is finalized based upon the level of production achieved. In addition, at the end of the year, the workers may receive bonuses out of profits realized from the overfulfillment of the plan. The economic and technical staff is remunerated monthly depending on the fulfillment of the plan of the enterprise at large. Overfulfillment of the plan will lead to additional compensation of up to 20 percent, whereas underfulfillment of the plan will reduce remuneration by up to 20 percent.

For the agricultural production cooperatives, wages are computed on the basis of production norms, but the remuneration is both in cash and in products at a ratio established under the plan. Overfulfillment of the planned output targets may lead to additional remuneration, up to 50 percent.

The agricultural production cooperatives ensure that their members receive a guaranteed monthly income, which varies by agricultural activities: 1,500 lei in the livestock sector and for workers employed in the irrigation sector and 1,200 lei in vegetable growing and fruit growing. This income is based on work norms of twenty-five working days a month. In farming, the farmers receive a guaranteed income of 40 lei for each working day, provided they meet their contractual obligations with regard to their input. If the cooperatives do not have enough funds to pay the guaranteed income, they may receive loans from the Bank for Agriculture and Food Industry (BAFI), without interest, reimbursable from the next year's income.

J

The Social Welfare System

ROMANIA, AS BEFITS A SOCIALIST COUNTRY, has a comprehensive social welfare system providing assistance to all members of society for education, health, pensions, insurance, and help to those in need. A caveat is needed concerning terminology. Apart from the general term "social welfare system," all terms used in this section are those used by the Romanians themselves. The Romanian concept of social assistance, however, is not the same as that used in countries such as the United Kingdom or the United States, and care should be taken when using such terms.

The full scope of the social welfare system is shown in Figure J.1. It shows that the state provides full educational, health, housing, and socio-cultural facilities to the whole population. These areas are discussed to a large extent in the text.

Social Insurance

In Romania's social policy, great importance is given to the social insurance system, since it is considered to be one of the means to improve the living standards of the working people and their families. The main program for old age, sickness, and injuries insurance is the state social insurance. Coverage is extended to all persons working on the basis of an employment contract in enterprises, institutions, associations, and other legal entities, as well as to their families and to youth being trained on-the-job as skilled workers. All persons insured under this program receive pensions and sickness pay.

The scheme is administered by the Ministry of Labor, and it is financed by contributions of the state enterprises, amounting to 15 percent of the wage fund. It has its own budget, which is a part of the state budget. At

Figure J.1. *Organization of the Social Welfare System*

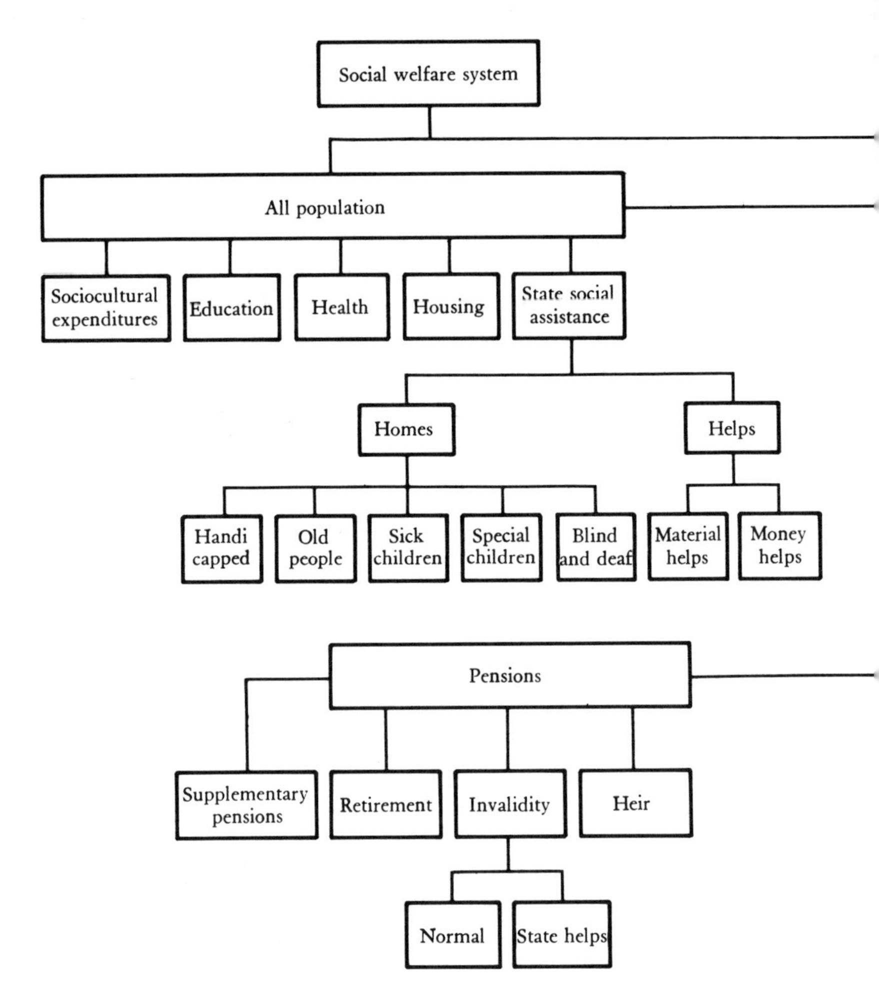

* Also available to nonstate employees.

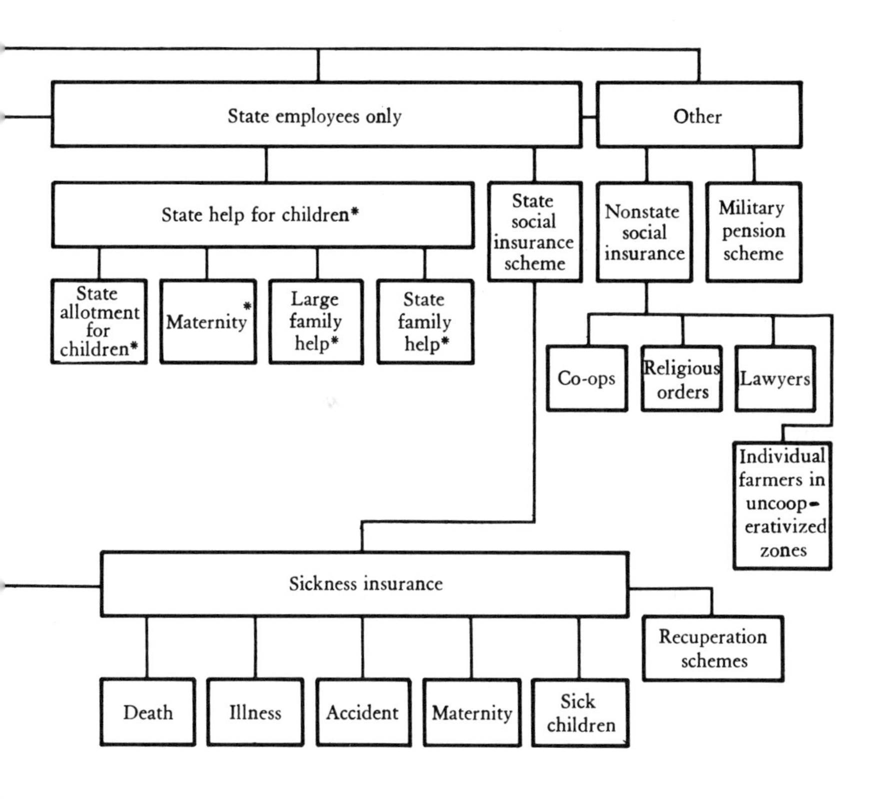
State employees only
Other
State help for children*
State social insurance scheme
Nonstate social insurance
Military pension scheme
State allotment for children*
Maternity*
Large family help*
State family help*
Co-ops
Religious orders
Lawyers
Individual farmers in uncoop-erativized zones
Sickness insurance
Recuperation schemes
Death
Illness
Accident
Maternity
Sick children

present, this program is yielding a surplus, which accrues to the state budget.

Pensions are the most important part of the scheme. The compulsory retirement age for men is sixty-two and for women is fifty-seven, but men may voluntarily retire at sixty and women at fifty-two if they fulfill the conditions of service time: that is, thirty years service for men and twenty-five for women. When they reach retirement age, both men and women may apply, if their employer concurs, to postpone their retirement up to another three years. Those who have been working under conditions classified as dangerous or heavy may retire earlier. A person qualifies for a pension only after ten years of employment. The actual level of pension is based on the level of salary and on the length of service. The salary used in the calculation is the average of the monthly wages in the highest five continuous years out of the past ten years of service. A man is entitled to a full pension after thirty years service and a woman after twenty-five years. In a woman's case, leave for raising children up to six years old is counted as employment time. Those who do not fulfill the service time condition for a full pension receive a reduced amount, according to the length of employment. For ten years of service, an employee receives a fixed pension amount, which in turn, is increased by a constant amount for each subsequent five-year period of service. Persons working for a longer time than is required to obtain a full pension receive, for each year of the first five surplus years, an extra 1 percent of the salary used in the calculation and, for each additional year, an extra 0.5 percent.

In addition to the pension granted by the state social insurance, persons working on the basis of an employment contract can receive a supplementary pension. They need to contribute, however, during their service period 2 or 4 percent (each individual determines the percentage) of their monthly wages, to establish the fund of supplementary pensions. Upon retirement, the supplementary pension is estimated as a percentage of the salary used in the calculation, according to the number of years of contribution and to the percentage of the wage contributed.

Invalidity pensions are also part of the state social insurance scheme. They are granted for the period of incapacitation.

Finally, the heir pension is granted to the children and spouse of a family if the deceased head of the household was a pensioner or was entitled to a pension. This pension is calculated as a percent of the pension of the deceased: that is, 50 percent if there is only one entitled heir, 75 percent if there are two, and 100 percent if there are three or more heirs.

Although all these pensions are rights, each individual must claim them. Any person who considers himself entitled to a pension applies to his employer, who fills up his pension form and submits it for verification to the Pension and Social Insurance Commission of the respective entity. The pension will be granted by the Pension Commission in the district where the beneficiary lives. The pensions are paid by the Ministry of Labor.

The amounts of the pensions are not permanently fixed. Each five-year plan provides for a general pension increase reflecting both the state's interest to increase the living standards of the working people and the increasing affluence of the national economy. The 1976–80 Plan, for example, provides for a 15 to 16 percent increase in the average real pension by 1980 over the 1975 level.

In addition to pensions, the social insurance scheme includes compensation for income loss of a wage earner who has to attend a sick person or someone requiring care because of sickness, accident, illness prevention, recovery from illness or accident, and child sickness.

Finally, the state social insurance scheme provides assistance during recovery from an illness. The scheme will pay a proportion of the cost for state employee to visit a recuperation clinic where he lives or at a health spa. The scheme will also pay the full cost of the medical attendance.

This network of social insurance provided by the state is for state employees only. Members of handicraft cooperatives, agricultural production cooperatives, or other professional associations (writers, musicians, artists, and so forth), lawyers, and the clergy of different religions receive pensions and sickness payments from their own schemes. In granting these pensions, the same basic principles apply. The state determines the minimum amounts of all payments, but no scheme is precluded from paying out larger amounts, depending upon the funds available. For cooperatives, the contributions are made by each cooperative to the Central Union of those cooperatives, which then becomes responsible for the pension payments.

State Social Assistance

The state social assistance is the basic state scheme for those who are unable to support themselves fully because of physical incapacity or for other reasons. The scheme is fully financed by the state budget and is administered on the central level by the Ministry of Labor and on the local level by the Executive Committees of the People's Councils.

Social assistance is extended to the following groups:

(a) To orphans and to those children whose healthy upbringing is not possible within their own families. These children are either sent to other families or to boarding schools, nurseries, and homes for preschool and schoolchildren;

(b) To mentally and physically handicapped persons as well as to institutions of social assistance;

(c) To the old aged population.

State Help for Children

Another element of the social welfare system is the state help for children, which once again predominantly applies to state employees. The most recent law governing this system is Law no. 246 of August 1, 1977. The most important part of this scheme is the state allotment for children. This allotment is granted monthly, and the amount depends on the number of children in the family, the level of the father's salary, and on whether he lives in an urban or rural area. An allotment is received for each child up to sixteen years old, with the amount growing progressively with the number of children. Workers in handicraft cooperatives and consumer cooperatives, as well as writers, artists, printers, sculptors and composers, members of the Bar Association, and employees of other social organizations also receive such allotments under the same conditions as for those employed on a contract basis, but the allotments are granted from the funds of these cooperatives or associations. Members of agricultural cooperatives have a special scheme of allotment for children.

In addition to the state help for children, the following benefits are also granted:

(a) A lump sum maternity benefit is given for the third and subsequent children in a family. This is available to all mothers, irrespective of whether they are or are not wage earners, and it is independent of family incomes;

(b) Monthly money help to mothers with five or more children up to eighteen years old;

(c) Monthly help to the wives of those in military service, if they are not wage earners or do not have other financial means for support.

Other Elements

There is, finally, a military pension scheme (IOVR), which is state run and financed but independent of the state or any other social insurance scheme. It provides pensions for war invalids, war orphans, war widows, and widows of war invalids.

State employees in Romania are part of a comprehensive noncontributory social welfare program. Cooperative workers have to pay for their own social insurance scheme from cooperative funds, but this is not very different from the situation of state employees, since their contributions come from the profits of the cooperative. The difference is, however, that the pensioners of the cooperatives will receive only their own funds back at most, whereas the pensioners of the state sector may receive pensions over and above their contributions as the country becomes more affluent.

Putting the system in perspective, it is more comprehensive than those in most nonsocialist countries. In few countries will employees receive a pension of 85 percent of salary without having made contributions, and then have this amount increased at 3 percent a year in real terms. Most people are well covered; a few are less well covered, although the few most likely will not be the most needy.

Private farmers not belonging to any cooperatives have been integrated into the pension scheme as of 1977 (Law no. 5 of June 30, 1977). Besides pensions for old ages, they now receive medicine free of charge when they are hospitalized or are under treatment at home. With the inclusion of this category of persons in the social insurance scheme, social assistance has now been generalized to cover all people.

K

Scientific and Technological Research and Development

SINCE 1969, ROMANIA HAS INTENSIFIED its research and technological development activities in an effort to support the socioeconomic development of the country with more indigenous technology. Especially in industry, research and development has been emphasized to help broaden the country's industrial base and to support the diversification and specialization of industry. Efforts have concentrated on the following general objectives:

(a) Expanding the raw material base and fully utilizing natural resources;
(b) Improving the existing technologies and developing new production technologies and the associated equipment;
(c) Improving the quality and diversification of production;
(d) Establishing export competitiveness;
(e) Increasing environmental protection and improving living conditions;
(f) Intensifying agricultural production.

The objectives of scientific research—technological development and introduction of technological progress—are included in the national plan for economic and social development and are coordinated, financed, and controlled through it. They are also closely linked with the specific targets for various activities of the economy, especially those concerning investment and production. The general coordination and guidance in these areas is provided by the National Council for Science and Technology (CNST), which is under the direct control of the Central Committee of the Romanian Communist Party (RCP) and of the Council of Ministers. Together with the State Planning Committee (SPC), the sector ministries, other state agencies, and the central research institutes and science academies, the CNST formulates the general research objectives and establishes the necessary fund and staff requirements within the annual five-year plans. The CNST coordinates the activity of some research and technological engineering institutes and finances some programs and products that are of special importance for the development of science and technology. In addition, the CNST collaborates with other central supervisory bodies and with the ministries concerned to coordinate activities of scientific and technological cooperation with other countries, and it initiates and concludes agreements on cooperation programs.

Each economic ministry has its own specialized research and technological engineering institutes, which are subordinated to the ministry, the industrial central, or enterprises. The employees in research activity and technological developments, including the planning and design departments, numbered about 76,000 in 1970 and 150,000 in 1975; this reflects the increased emphasis on Romania's own contribution to its development efforts in recent years. Expenditure for equipment and materials in research and development amounted to about 3.7 billion lei during the 1971–75 plan period compared with only 0.8 billion lei during the 1961–65 plan period. During 1971–75 the funds allocated to scientific research, technological development, and introduction of technical progress amounted to 25.3 billion lei, of which 83 percent were met by the industrial centrals and enterprises, and the remainder by the state budget. In 1975 the combined expenditure for manpower, equipment, and materials allocated to research and technological development was more than 1.3 percent of national income, and the salaries of those engaged in research are among the highest in the economy. These figures also indicate the stress now put on such activities in the Romanian economy.

The result of Romania's research and technological development has been quite impressive. Between 1960 and 1970, Romania introduced nearly 100 inventions and nearly 200 industrial installations of advanced technology, notably in industrial machinery and in mechanical equipment. Moreover, some 70 percent of the new industrial processes introduced during 1971–75 were of Romanian conception. Progress has been most rapid in machine building, where, through continuous adaptation and development, currently more than 80 percent of total output is based on Romanian technology. In chemical equipment, indigenous Romanian designs and processes constitute some 30 percent of the relevant output.

The direction of past industrial research and technological development for 1976–80 is as described below.

(a) In the extractive industries, activities focusing on the exploitation of reserves of coal, petroleum, and natural gas in great depths; identification of new sources of raw materials and their efficient exploitation; new technologies; more processing and mechanization; and automation of processing;

(b) In energy production, development of systems reducing the consumption of high-grade fuels and increasing the utilization of low-grade fuels, including bituminous shales; rational use of energy; development of complex automation; and creation of new equipment for hydroelectric power plants;

(c) In the metallurgical industries, development of new processes to produce high-quality steels; production, rolling, and heat treatment of steels; and reduction of the consumption of metals by improved technological processes;

(d) In the mechanical engineering industry, development of power-generating equipment; of equipment and installations for deep-sea drilling and exploration; of seagoing vessels of great capacity, of automated machine tools; and of new production lines to process plastics, and so forth;

(e) In the electrical equipment industry, development of new electric motors, computer equipment, electronic components, and automation means;

(f) In the chemical industry, development of new technologies for production of polyisoprene and polybutadiene rubber, for resins and varnishes used by the electrical engineering industry; diversification of the production of chemical fibers, pharmaceuticals, and herbicides; new chemical products; fertilizers; and the increased use of processed oil;

(g) In the construction materials industry, development of new technologies to manufacture cement, glass, reinforced elements, and masonry blocks of steamed porous concrete; expansion of plastics use in construction; and so forth;

(h) In the wood processing and paper industries, development of new processes to produce particle board, furniture, and low-weight paper and the use of new kinds of wood to produce cellulose;

(i) In light industries, development of new technologies to manufacture textile products from natural and synthetic fibers; production of new poromeric synthetic leathers and of leather substitutes; and improved use of the natural leathers, new glass, and products for industrial purposes and consumer goods;

(j) In the agricultural sector, production of new kinds of wheat, maize, and potatoes and of new hybrids of maize, sunflower, and other plants;

(k) In mathematics, physics, chemistry, and biology, basic applied research is given special attention both to encourage general science development, as well as to develop the economic sectors.

With the research and technological development programs to introduce modern technologies, special attention is paid to the engineering activities in the chemical sectors, machine building, and power for obtaining technologies and products that are competitive in the world markets.

Statistical Appendix

Table SA1.1. *Past and Projected Population, by Sex, 1948–2000*

Year	Total midyear population (thousands)	Male: Number (thousands)	Male: Percentage	Female: Number (thousands)	Female: Percentage	Annual growth rate (percentage)	Growth in five-year plan period (percentage)
1948	15,873	7,672	48.3	8,201	51.7		
1949	16,084[a]					1.3	
1950	16,311					1.4	
1951	16,464					0.9	
1952	16,630					1.0	
1953	16,847					1.3	6.2
1954	17,040					1.1	
1955	17,325					1.7	
1956	17,583[b]	8,550	48.6	9,033	51.4	1.5	
1957	17,829	8,680	48.7	9,149	51.3	1.4	
1958	18,056	8,799	48.7	9,257	51.3	1.3	6.2
1959	18,226	8,888	48.8	9,338	51.2	1.0	
1960	18,403	8,982	48.8	9,421	51.2	1.0	
1961	18,567	9,069	48.8	9,498	51.2	0.9	
1962	18,681	9,131	48.9	9,550	51.1	0.6	
1963	18,813	9,201	48.9	9,612	51.1	0.7	3.4
1964	18,927	9,262	48.9	9,665	51.1	0.6	
1965	19,027	9,315	49.0	9,712	51.0	0.5	
1966	19,141[c]	9,371	49.0	9,770	51.0	0.6	
1967	19,285	9,448	49.0	9,837	51.0	0.8	
1968	19,721	9,671	49.0	10,050	51.0	2.3	6.4
1969	20,010	9,820	49.1	10,190	50.9	1.5	
1970	20,253	9,945	49.1	10,308	50.9	1.2	
1971	20,470	10,057	49.1	10,413	50.9	1.1	
1972	20,663	10,157	49.2	10,506	50.8	0.9	
1973	20,828	10,244	49.2	10,584	50.8	0.8	4.9
1974	21,029	10,348	49.2	10,681	50.8	1.0	
1975	21,245	10,460	49.2	10,785	50.8	1.0	
1976	21,446	10,565	49.3	10,881	50.7	0.9	
1977[d]	21,559	10,627	49.3	10,933	50.7		
1980	22,311	11,018	49.3	11,294	50.7		5.0
1985	23,542	11,662	49.5	11,880	50.5		5.5
1990	25,019	12,435	49.7	12,584	50.3		6.3
1995	26,383	13,151	49.8	13,232	50.2		5.5
2000	27,872	13,928	49.9	13,944	50.1		5.6

a. January 25 census figure.
b. February 21 census figure was 17,489,450.
c. March 15 census figure was 19,103, 163.
d. January 5 census figure; preliminary data.
Sources: Anuarul Statistic al Republicii Socialiste Romania (Bucharest: Directia Centrala de Sta-
ca, published yearly); 1980–2000 figures from United Nations Secretariat, Department of Eco-
ic and Social Affairs, Population Division, "Selected World Demographic Indicators by Countries
0–2000." (United Nations: New York, May 1975); estimates represent the high variant.

Table SA1.2. *Principal Demographic Indicators, 1948–76*

Year	*Birth-rate (per 1,000 inhabitants)*	*Death-rate (per 1,000 inhabitants)*	*Rate of natural increase (percentage)*	*Infant mortality (per 1,000 live births)*	*Marriages (per 1,000 inhabitants)*	*Divorces (per 1,000 inhabitants)*	*Age structure of fertility*[a] *(percentage)*			*Year*
							Under 25	*25–39*	*Over 39*	
1948	23.9	15.6	8.3	142.7	11.2	1.12				1948
1949	27.6	13.7	13.9	136.3	11.6	1.33				1949
1950	26.2	12.4	13.8	116.7	11.7	1.47				1950
1951	25.1	12.8	12.3	118.1	10.3	1.23				1951
1952	24.8	11.7	13.1	104.7	10.2	1.41				1952
1953	23.8	11.6	12.2	96.3	10.4	1.30				1953
1954	24.8	11.5	13.3	88.8	12.1	1.68				1954
1955	25.6	9.7	15.9	78.2	11.4	1.80				1955
1956	24.2	9.9	14.3	81.5	11.7	1.66				1956
1957	22.9	10.2	12.7	80.9	11.4	1.86				1957
1958	21.6	8.7	12.9	69.4	11.7	1.96	46.2	51.7	2.1	1958

1959	20.2	10.2	10.0	75.5	10.7	1.69	47.9	50.1	2.0	1959
1960	19.1	8.7	10.4	74.6	10.7	2.01	48.5	49.4	2.1	1960
1961	17.5	8.7	8.8	69.4	9.7	1.80	49.9	48.0	2.1	1961
1962	16.2	9.2	7.0	58.8	9.9	2.04	49.3	48.4	2.3	1962
1963	15.7	8.3	7.4	55.2	9.3	1.92	49.1	48.5	2.4	1963
1964	15.2	8.1	7.1	48.6	9.0	1.86	48.4	49.3	2.3	1964
1965	14.6	8.6	6.0	44.1	8.6	1.94	47.6	50.1	2.3	1965
1966	14.3	8.2	6.1	46.6	8.9	1.35	47.8	49.9	2.3	1966
1967	27.4	9.3	18.1	46.6	8.0	—[b]	42.7	54.9	2.4	1967
1968	26.7	9.6	17.1	59.5	7.5	0.20	43.3	54.1	2.6	1968
1969	23.3	10.1	13.2	54.9	7.0	0.35	45.4	52.0	2.6	1969
1970	21.1	9.5	11.6	49.4	7.2	0.39	48.4	49.0	2.6	1970
1971	19.5	9.5	10.0	42.4	7.3	0.47	51.4	46.0	2.6	1971
1972	18.8	9.2	9.6	40.0	7.6	0.54	53.6	43.9	2.5	1972
1973	18.2	9.8	8.4	38.1	8.2	0.69	55.7	42.1	2.2	1973
1974	20.3	9.1	11.2	35.0	8.3	0.85	55.7	42.2	2.1	1974
1975	19.7	9.3	10.4	34.7	8.9	1.62	56.1	41.9	2.0	1975
1976	19.5	9.6	9.9	31.4	9.1	1.68	56.3	41.9	1.8	1976

a. Live births to mothers of ages shown.
b. Negligible, since the law covering divorce was modified.
Source: Anuarul Statistic, various issues.

Table SA1.3. *Age and Sex of Population and Dependency Ratios, Selected Years*

Item	*1948*	*1956*	*1966*	*1970*	*1971*
Total population[a] (thousands)	*15,873*	*17,489*	*19,103*	*20,253*	*20,470*
Male	7,672	8,503	9,351	9,945	10,057
Female	8,201	8,986	9,752	10,308	10,413
Percentage males	48.3	48.6	49.0	49.1	49.1
Age structure of total population					
Under 15 years		27.5	26.0	25.9	25.6
15–64 years		66.1	66.1	65.5	65.6
Above 64 years		6.4	7.9	8.6	8.8
Male					
Under 15 years		28.8	27.2	27.0	26.7
15–64 years		65.8	66.1	65.5	65.6
Above 64 years		5.4	6.7	7.5	7.7
Female					
Under 15 years		26.3	24.9	24.9	24.6
15–64 years		66.4	66.1	65.4	65.5
Above 64 years		7.3	9.0	9.7	9.9
Dependency ratio[b]					
Total		51.3	51.3	52.7	52.5
Male		52.1	51.3	52.6	52.3
Female		50.6	51.4	52.8	52.6

a. 1948, 1956 are census figures; the remainder are estimates for July 1.

b. Dependency ratio: $R = (x + y)/e$, where x = population under 15 years of age, y = population over 64 years, and e = population from 15 to 64 years.

Source: Anuarul Statistic, various issues.

Item	*1972*	*1973*	*1974*	*1975*	*1976*
Total population[a] (thousands)	*20,663*	*20,828*	*21,029*	*21,245*	*21,446*
Male	10,157	10,244	10,348	10,460	10,565
Female	10,506	10,584	10,681	10,785	10,881
Percentage males	49.2	49.2	49.2	49.2	49.3
Age structure of total population					
Under 15 years	25.4	25.2	25.1	25.2	25.4
15–64 years	65.6	65.6	65.5	65.2	64.8
Above 64 years	9.0	9.2	9.4	9.6	9.8
Male					
Under 15 years	26.4	26.2	26.2	26.2	26.4
15–64 years	65.7	65.7	65.6	65.4	65.0
Above 64 years	7.9	8.1	8.2	8.4	8.6
Female					
Under 15 years	24.4	24.2	24.1	24.3	24.4
15–64 years	65.5	65.5	65.4	65.0	64.6
Above 64 years	10.1	10.3	10.5	10.7	11.0
Dependency ratio[b]					
Total	52.4	52.4	52.7	53.5	54.3
Male	52.2	52.1	52.4	53.1	53.8
Female	52.6	52.6	53.0	53.8	54.7

Table SA1.4. *Population, by Rural and Urban Areas and by Sex, 1948–77*

		Urban population					*Rural population*				
Year	*Total population (thousands)*	*Male*	*Female*	*Total*	*Percentage of total population*	*Annual growth rate (percentage)*	*Male*	*Female*	*Total*	*Percentage of total population*	*Annual growth rate (percentage)*
1948	15,873	1,803	1,910	3,713	23		5,869	6,291	12,160	77	
1949	16,084										
1950	16,311										
1951	16,464										
1952	16,630										
1953	16,847										
1954	17,040										
1955	17,325										
1956	17,583	2,699	2,805	5,515	31.4		5,852	6,227	12,068	68.6	
1957	17,829			5,620	31.5	1.9			12,209	68.5	1.2
1958	18,056	2,812	2,914	5,726	31.7	1.9	5,987	6,343	12,330	68.3	1.0
1959	18,226			5,811	31.9	1.5			12,415	68.1	0.7
1960	18,403	2,914	2,998	5,912	32.1	1.7	6,067	6,424	12,491	67.9	0.6

1961	18,567	2,976	3,055	6,030	32.5	2.0	6,093	6,443	12,537	67.5	0.4
1962	18,681	3,016	3,094	6,110	32.7	1.3	6,115	6,456	12,571	67.3	0.3
1963	18,813	3,077	3,157	6,234	33.1	2.0	6,124	6,455	12,579	66.9	—[c]
1964	18,927	3,119	3,198	6,317	33.4	1.3	6,143	6,467	12,610	66.6	0.2
1965	19,027	3,169	3,249	6,417	33.7	1.6	6,147	6,463	12,610	66.3	—[c]
1966	19,141	3,650	3,671	7,344	38.4	(14.4)[b]	5,720	6,100	11,797	61.6	(−6.3)
1967	19,285	3,719	3,749	7,468	38.7	1.7	5,728	6,088	11,817	61.3	—[c]
1968	19,721			7,909	40.1	5.9			11,812	59.9	—[c]
1969	20,010			8,096	40.5	2.4			11,914	59.5	0.9
1970	20,253	4,101	4,157	8,258	40.8	2.0	5,844	6,151	11,995	59.2	0.7
1971	20,470			8,423	41.1	2.0			12,047	58.9	0.4
1972	20,663	4,258	4,332	8,591	41.6	2.0	5,898	6,174	12,072	58.4	0.2
1973	20,828	4,341	4,420	8,761	42.1	2.0	5,902	6,165	12,067	57.9	—[c]
1974	21,029	4,449	4,530	8,979	42.7	2.5	5,899	6,151	12,050	57.3	—[c]
1975	21,245	4,550	4,632	9,182	43.2	2.3	5,910	6,153	12,063	56.8	0.1
1976	21,446			9,403	43.8	2.4			12,042	56.2	—[c]
1977[a]	21,559	5,065	5,172	10,237	47.5	(8.9)	5,562	5,761	11,323	52.5	(−6.0)

a. January 5 census figures; provisional data.
b. Rural and urban definitions changed in 1966.
c. Less than ± 0.1 percent.
Source: Anuarul Statistic, various issues.

Table SA1.5. *Population, by Judet and Rural-Urban Areas, Selected Years*
(thousands)

Judet	*Total population*	*Urban*	*Rural*	*Percentage urban*
		1948		
Total Romania	*15,873*	*3,713*	*12,160*	*23.0*
Alba	361	43	318	11.9
Arad	476	94	382	19.7
Arges	449	56	393	12.5
Bacau	415	60	355	14.5
Bihor	536	102	434	19.0
Bistrita-Nasaud	234	20	214	8.5
Botosani	385	73	312	19.0
Brasov	301	95	206	31.6
Braila	271	95	176	35.1
Buzau	430	63	367	14.7
Caras-Severin	302	42	260	13.9
Cluj	520	170	350	32.7
Constanta	311	108	203	34.7
Covasna	157	20	137	12.7
Dimbovita	379	50	329	13.2
Dolj	615	115	500	18.7
Galati	342	101	241	29.5
Gorj	281	18	263	6.4
Harghita	258	26	232	10.1
Hunedoara	307	52	255	16.9
Ialomita	298	44	254	14.8
Iasi	432	114	318	26.4
Ilfov	699	45	654	6.4
Maramures	321	43	278	13.4
Mehedinti	305	46	259	15.1
Mures	461	82	379	17.8
Neamt	357	59	298	16.5
Olt	442	48	394	10.9
Prahova	558	150	408	26.9
Satu-Mare	313	62	251	19.8
Salaj	263	20	243	7.6
Sibiu	335	96	239	28.7
Suceava	440	73	367	16.6

Table SA1.5. *Continued*

Judet	*Total population*	*Urban*	*Rural*	*Percentage urban*
		1948 (continued)		
Teleorman	492	55	437	11.2
Timis	589	149	440	25.3
Tulcea	192	39	153	20.3
Vaslui	345	60	285	17.4
Vilcea	342	38	304	11.1
Vrancea	290	46	244	15.9
Bucharest	1,067	1,042	25	97.7
		1966		
Total Romania	*19,103*	*7,306*	*11,797*	*38.2*
Alba	383	132	251	34.5
Arad	481	188	293	39.1
Arges	530	135	395	25.5
Bacau	598	202	396	33.8
Bihor	586	251	335	42.8
Bistrita-Nasaud	270	50	220	18.5
Botosani	452	52	400	11.5
Brasov	443	300	143	67.7
Braila	340	140	200	41.2
Buzau	481	92	388	19.1
Caras-Severin	359	153	205	42.6
Cluj	630	314	316	49.8
Constanta	466	235	231	50.4
Covasna	177	55	122	31.1
Dimbovita	422	130	292	30.8
Dolj	691	197	494	28.5
Galati	474	180	294	38.0
Gorj	298	67	231	22.5
Harghita	282	89	193	31.6
Hunedoara	475	324	151	68.2
Ialomita	363	75	288	20.7
Iasi	619	180	439	29.1
Ilfov	757	76	681	10.0
Maramures	428	183	245	42.8
Mehedinti	310	78	232	25.2

(Table continues on the following page)

Table SA1.5. *Continued*

Judet	*Total population*	*Urban*	*Rural*	*Percentage urban*
		1966 (continued)		
Mures	562	183	379	32.6
Neamt	470	136	334	28.9
Olt	477	69	408	14.5
Prahova	701	392	309	55.9
Satu-Mare	359	106	253	29.5
Salaj	263	51	212	19.4
Sibiu	415	247	168	59.5
Suceava	573	147	426	25.7
Teleorman	521	91	430	17.5
Timis	608	274	334	45.1
Tulcea	237	66	171	27.8
Vaslui	432	80	352	18.5
Vilcea	369	81	288	22.0
Vrancea	351	68	283	19.4
Bucharest	1,452	1,435	17	98.8
		1975		
Total Romania	*21,245*	*9,182*	*12,063*	*43.2*
Alba	403	167	236	41.5
Arad	497	233	264	46.9
Arges	607	207	401	34.0
Bacau	686	268	417	39.1
Bihor	628	238	391	37.8
Bistrita-Nasaud	294	58	236	19.6
Botosani	492	107	385	21.7
Brasov	505	330	175	65.3
Braila	278	183	195	48.3
Buzau	524	113	411	21.5
Caras-Severin	378	177	197	47.4
Cluj	695	376	320	54.0
Constanta	544	328	226	59.2
Covasna	195	84	111	42.9
Dimbovita	463	158	311	33.7
Dolj	750	283	468	37.7
Galati	566	277	289	49.0

Table SA1.5. *Continued*

Judet	*Total population*	*Urban*	*Rural*	*Percentage urban*
		1975 (continued)		
Gorj	334	98	236	29.3
Harghita	315	117	198	37.1
Hunedoara	519	368	151	70.9
Ialomita	396	112	284	28.2
Iasi	736	284	452	38.6
Ilfov	811	110	701	13.6
Maramures	492	233	259	47.4
Mehedinti	330	119	210	36.2
Mures	617	255	361	41.4
Neamt	543	175	368	32.2
Olt	521	116	406	22.2
Prahova	793	411	383	51.8
Satu-Mare	392	141	251	36.0
Salaj	273	56	217	20.6
Sibiu	460	266	194	57.8
Suceava	652	181	471	27.7
Teleorman	543	143	400	26.3
Timis	650	311	339	47.9
Tulcea	263	80	183	30.5
Vaslui	484	122	362	25.2
Vilcea	408	99	309	24.3
Vrancea	388	93	295	24.0
Bucharest	1,707	1,707	—	100.0
		1976		
Total Romania	*21,559*	*10,237*	*11,323*	*47.5*
Alba	410	182	228	44.5
Arad	512	259	253	50.6
Arges	632	242	389	38.4
Bacau	668	281	386	42.1
Bihor	633	254	379	40.1
Bistrita-Nasaud	287	68	218	23.8
Botosani	451	118	334	26.1
Brasov	583	408	175	70.0
Braila	378	206	172	54.4
Buzau	508	126	382	24.9

(Table continues on the following page)

Table SA1.5. *Continued*

Judet	*Total population*	*Urban*	*Rural*	*Percentage urban*
		1976 (continued)		
Caras-Severin	386	192	193	49.9
Cluj	715	417	299	58.3
Constanta	609	409	200	67.1
Covasna	199	93	106	46.6
Dimbovita	493	182	311	37.0
Dolj	750	307	443	41.0
Galati	582	315	267	54.2
Gorj	349	113	236	32.4
Harghita	326	131	195	40.2
Hunedoara	514	369	145	71.8
Ialomita	373	125	248	33.5
Iasi	729	333	396	45.6
Ilfov	780	118	662	15.1
Maramures	493	240	253	48.7
Mehedinti	322	125	198	38.7
Mures	605	273	332	45.2
Neamt	532	184	348	34.6
Olt	519	131	387	25.3
Prahova	817	441	376	53.9
Satu-Mare	394	155	239	39.3
Salaj	264	64	201	24.2
Sibiu	482	292	189	60.7
Suceava	634	192	442	30.3
Teleorman	523	151	372	28.8
Timis	697	370	327	53.1
Tulcea	254	91	163	35.8
Vaslui	437	125	312	28.7
Vilcea	414	117	297	28.3
Vrancea	370	102	268	27.6
Bucharest	1,934	1,934	—	100.0

Source: Anuarul Statistic, various issues.

Table SA1.6. *Total Population, Population of Working Age, Active Population, and Participation Rates, by Sex and Rural-Urban Areas, Selected Years, 1948–76*

Item	*1948*	*1956*	*1960*	*1965*	*1970*	*1975*	*1976*
Total population[a] (thousands)	*15,873*	*17,583*	*18,403*	*19,027*	*20,253*	*21,245*	*21,446*
Rural population	12,160	12,068	12,491	12,610	11,995	12,063	12,042
Male	5,869	5,852	6,067	6,147	5,844	5,910	
Female	6,291	6,227	6,424	6,463	6,151	6,153	
Urban population	3,713	5,515	5,912	6,418	8,258	9,182	9,403
Male	1,803	2,699	2,914	3,169	4,101	4,550	
Female	1,910	2,805	2,998	3,249	4,157	4,632	
Population of working age[b]		*11,560*		*12,510*	*13,264*	*13,845*	*13,902*
As a percentage of total population		65.7		65.7	65.5	65.2	64.8
Rural		7,640		7,894	7,441		
Male		3,660		3,830			
Female		3,980		4,064			
Urban		3,920		4,616	5,823		
Male		1,930		2,300			
Female		1,990		2,316			
Active population (thousands)		*10,449*	*9,538*	*9,684*	*9,875*	*10,150.8*	*10,227*
Participation rates (percentage of working-age population)				*77.4*	*74.4*	*73.3*	*73.6*

a. Except for 1948, figures are for July 1.
b. Defined as those between the ages of 15 and 64, inclusive.
Source: Anuarul Statistic, various issues.

Table SA1.7. *Regional Distribution of Urbanization, Selected Years, 1930–77*

	All judets	1930 Number of judets	1930 As percentage of total population	1948[a] Number of judets	1948[a] As percentage of total population	1956[a] Number of judets	1956[a] As percentage of total population
Group I	Less than 25 percent urban	32	78.15	30	70.23	23	52.25
Group II	25–50 percent urban	7	17.20	9	23.05	14	36.36
Group III	More than 50 percent urban	1	4.65	1	6.72	3	11.39
	Total population	40	14,280,729	40	15,872,624	40	17,489,450
		1966[a]		*1973[b]*		*1977[a]*	
Group I	Less than 25 percent urban	11	24.42	9[c]	19.88	4[d]	8.53
Group II	25–50 percent urban	23	45.10	24[c]	55.66	25[d]	55.18
Group III	More than 50 percent urban	6	20.18	7[c]	24.46	11[d]	36.29
	Total population	40	19,103,163	40	20,827,525	40	21,559,416

a. Census figures.

b. Population on July 1st.

c. Group I: Bistrita-Nasaud, Botosani, Buzau, Ilfov, Olt, Salaj, Vaslui, Vilcea, and Vrancea. Group II: Alba, Arad, Arges, Bacau, Bihor, Braila, Caras-Severin, Covasna, Dimbovita, Dolj, Galati, Gorj, Harghita, Ialomita, Iasi, Maramures, Mehedinti, Mures, Neamt, Satu-Mare, Suceava, Teleorman, Timis, and Tulcea. Group III: Brasov, Bucharest, Cluj, Constanta, Hunedoara, Prahova, and Sibiu.

d. Group I: Bistrita-Nassaud, Buzau, Ilfov, and Salaj. Group II: Alba, Arges, Bacau, Bihar, Botosani, Caras-Severin, Covasna, Dimbovita, Dolj, Gorj, Harghita, Ialomita, Iasi, Maramures, Mehedinti, Mures, Neamt, Olt, Satu-Mare, Suceava, Teleorman, Tulcea, Vaslui, Vilcea, and Vrancea. Group III: Arad, Brasov, Braila, Bucharest, Cluj, Constanta, Galati, Hunedoara, Prahova, Sibiu, and Timis.

Sources: Anuarul Demografic al Republicii Socialiste Romania (Bucharest: Central Statistics Office and National Demographic Commission, 1974) and *Anuarul Statistic*, various issues.

Table SA1.8. *Population of Seven Largest Urban Areas, Selected Years, 1930–77,*

Population component	City and district							Total urban areas
	Bucharest (Bucharest)	*Brasov (Brasov)*	*Constanta (Constanta)*	*Craiova (Dolj)*	*Galati (Galati)*	*Iasi (Iasi)*	*Timisoara (Timis)*	
Population								
1930	639,040	59,232	59,164	63,215	100,611	102,872	91,580	3,051,253
1948	1,041,807	82,984	78,586	84,574	80,411	94,075	111,987	3,723,139
1956	1,177,661	123,834	99,676	96,897	95,646	112,977	142,257	4,746,672
1966	1,366,684	163,345	150,276	152,650	151,412	161,023	174,243	6,743,887
1973	1,528,562	193,086	185,737	188,333	191,111	202,052	204,687	7,939,061
1977	1,807,044	257,150	256,875	222,399	239,306	264,947	268,785	9,393,897
Composition of 1966 population								
Percentage born in city	37.49	28.80	29.59	30.18	36.21	32.69	30.24	41.01
Percentage born elsewhere	62.51	71.20	70.41	69.82	63.79	67.31	69.76	58.99
Percentage arrived								
Before 1920	3.19	1.19	2.09	1.83	2.30	2.03	4.10	2.12
1920–44	23.15	13.53	15.49	10.33	10.25	9.98	16.86	12.25
1945–59	21.79	32.44	25.93	22.79	16.84	22.76	23.17	21.26
1960–66	11.47	21.94	23.10	29.90	29.74	28.69	21.10	20.31
Unknown	2.91	2.10	3.80	4.97	4.66	3.85	4.53	3.05

Note: Excludes suburban areas.

Source: Anuarul Demografic al Republicii Socialiste Romania and *Anuarul Statistic*, various issues.

Table SA1.9. *Migration Balance, by Urban, Suburban, and Rural Areas, 1968–73*

Year	*Total arrivals*	*From urban areas*	*From suburban areas*	*From rural areas*
		Urban areas		
1968	166,907 (23.4)	66,578 (9.3)	8,776 (1.3)	91,553 (12.8)
1969	163,035 (22.3)	62,032 (8.5)	8,827 (1.2)	92,176 (12.6)
1970	168,674 (22.6)	58,547 (7.8)	9,690 (1.3)	100,437 (13.5)
1971	187,825 (24.6)	59,060 (7.8)	11,974 (1.5)	116,791 (15.3)
1972	191,419 (24.6)	58,314 (7.5)	11,236 (1.4)	121,869 (15.7)
1973	224,798 (28.3)	64,601 (8.1)	12,772 (1.6)	147,425 (18.6)
		Rural areas		
1968	102,301 (8.7)	26,181 (2.2)	3,854 (0.4)	72,266 (6.1)
1969	101,823 (8.5)	26,382 (2.2)	4,175 (0.3)	71,266 (6.0)
1970	110,211 (9.2)	28,367 (2.4)	4,569 (0.4)	77,275 (6.4)
1971	105,515 (8.8)	26,806 (2.2)	4,550 (0.4)	74,159 (6.2)
1972	127,996 (10.6)	32,927 (2.7)	5,164 (0.4)	89,905 (7.5)
1973	133,705 (11.1)	35,046 (2.9)	5,550 (0.5)	93,109 (7.7)

Note: Figures in parentheses represent number per 1,000 residents; minus figures represent net emigration.

Source: Anuarul Demografic al Republicii Socialiste Romania.

Total departures	*To urban areas*	*To suburban areas*	*To rural areas*	*Aggregate balance of migration*
		Urban areas		
96,799 (13.5)	66,578 (9.3)	4,040 (0.5)	26,181 (3.7)	70,108 (9.9)
91,707 (12.5)	62,032 (8.5)	3,293 (0.4)	26,382 (3.6)	71,328 (9.8)
90,381 (12.1)	58,547 (7.8)	3,467 (0.5)	28,367 (3.8)	78,293 (10.5)
89,593 (11.8)	59,060 (7.8)	3,727 (0.5)	26,806 (3.5)	98,232 (12.8)
95,301 (12.3)	58,314 (7.5)	4,060 (0.5)	32,927 (4.3)	96,118 (12.3)
103,426 (13.0)	64,601 (8.1)	3,779 (0.5)	35,046 (4.4)	121,372 (15.3)
		Rural areas		
177,484 (15.0)	91,553 (7.8)	13,665 (1.1)	72,266 (6.1)	—75,183 (—6.3)
175,038 (14.7)	92,176 (7.7)	11,596 (1.0)	71,266 (6.0)	—73,215 (—6.2)
187,936 (15.7)	100,437 (8.4)	10,224 (0.9)	77,275 (6.4)	—77,725 (—6.5)
203,994 (16.9)	116,791 (9.7)	13,044 (1.0)	74,159 (6.2)	—98,479 (—8.1)
225,549 (18.7)	121,869 (10.1)	13,775 (1.2)	89,905 (7.4)	—97,553 (—8.1)
252,530 (20.9)	147,425 (12.2)	11,996 (1.0)	93,109 (7.7)	—118,825 (—9.8)

Table SA1.10. *Net Migration, by Age Group, Urban and Rural Areas, 1968–73*

Age group (years)	1968 Absolute magnitude of net migration[a]	1968 Migrants per 1,000 residents[b]	1969 Absolute magnitude of net migration[a]	1969 Migrants per 1,000 residents[b]	1970 Absolute magnitude of net migration[a]
			Urban areas		
Less than 15	8,580	5.6	9,424	6.0	10,009
15–19	13,023	19.0	12,883	19.9	12,387
20–24	16,475	28.1	18,130	27.6	24,511
25–29	12,086	20.0	12,855	21.7	14,085
30–34	6,551	10.1	6,829	10.2	6,855
35–39	3,944	6.4	3,565	5.7	3,662
40–44	2,609	4.7	2,216	3.8	2,033
45–49	1,488	3.6	1,229	2.6	1,113
50–54	751	2.5	503	1.8	485
55–59	1,105	2.9	921	2.4	577
60 and over	3,496	4.3	2,773	3.3	2,576
Total	70,108	9.9	71,328	9.8	78,293
			Rural areas		
Less than 15	—8,833	—2.6	—9,173	—2.7	—9,726
15–19	—15,330	—15.4	—14,866	—14.0	—13,463
20–24	—17,746	—26.2	—18,858	—27.8	—24,272
25–29	—12,668	—17.3	—12,520	—18.3	—13,390
30–34	—6,696	—7.7	—6,526	—7.6	—6,428
35–39	—4,111	—4.6	—3,594	—4.1	—3,576
40–44	—2,728	—3.2	—2,241	—2.6	—2,062
45–49	—1,605	—2.5	—1,260	—1.7	—1,171
50–54	—797	—1.7	—523	—1.2	—496
55–59	—1,124	—1.7	—958	—1.4	—584
60 and over	—3,545	—2.2	—2,696	—1.6	—2,557
Total	—75,183	—6.3	—73,215	—6.2	—77,725

a. A minus figure indicates a net emigration.

b. Per 1,000 urban residents in upper portion of table; per 1,000 rural residents in lower portion.

Source: Anuarul Demografic al Republicii Socialiste Romania.

1970	1971		1972		1973	
Migrants per 1,000 residents[b]	Absolute magnitude of net migration[a]	Migrants per 1,000 residents[b]	Absolute magnitude of net migration[a]	Migrants per 1,000 residents[b]	Absolute magnitude of net migration[a]	Migrants per 1,000 residents[b]
			Urban areas			
6.2	13,784	8.5	9,659	5.8	11,754	7.0
20.6	14,120	24.1	13,807	23.3	13,402	22.8
32.9	29,690	37.3	31,444	39.3	41,517	52.0
24.1	16,736	28.2	16,833	26.8	24,035	35.0
10.2	8,778	13.0	8,446	12.7	10,843	16.6
5.9	4,937	7.7	4,721	7.2	6,240	9.3
3.4	3,064	5.0	3,139	5.1	3,769	6.1
2.3	1,733	3.3	1,938	3.6	2,683	4.8
1.7	837	2.7	1,110	3.2	1,588	3.8
1.5	1,170	3.1	1,218	3.6	1,129	3.8
2.9	3,383	3.7	3,803	4.0	4,412	4.5
10.5	98,232	12.8	96,118	12.3	121,372	15.3
			Rural areas			
—2.8	—13,424	—4.0	—10,404	—3.1	—11,969	—3.5
—11.9	—15,230	—12.9	—15,143	—12.7	—14,135	—11.8
—35.1	—29,902	—40.8	—31,538	—39.6	—40,598	—47.0
—20.8	—16,143	—26.4	—16,333	—27.6	—22,814	—40.1
—7.7	—8,472	—10.7	—8,188	—11.1	—10,053	—14.9
—4.1	—4,910	—5.7	—4,625	—5.5	—5,873	—7.1
—2.4	—3,194	—3.7	—3,265	—3.8	—3,660	—4.3
—1.5	—1,877	—2.3	—1,923	—2.4	—2,672	—3.3
—1.1	—842	—1.8	—1,105	—2.0	—1,568	—2.4
—0.9	—1,123	—1.8	—1,202	—2.2	—1,110	—2.4
—1.5	—3,362	—1.9	—3,827	—2.1	—4,373	—2.4
—6.5	—98,479	—8.1	—97,553	—8.1	—118,825	—9.8

Table SA1.11. *Structure of Occupied Population, by Major Sector, 1950, 1955, 1960, 1965, and 1970–76*

(thousands of persons and percentage of occupied persons[a])

Sector	*1950*	*1955*	*1960*	*1965*
Occupied population	8,377.2	9,362.6	9,537.7	9,684.0
Industry	1,000.7	1,222.9	1,440.2	1,862.9
	(12.0)	(13.1)	(15.1)	(19.2)
Construction	186.3	402.6	470.5	609.3
	(2.2)	(4.3)	(4.9)	(6.3)
Agriculture	6,208.7	6,511.0	6,233.1	5,476.5
	(74.1)	(69.5)	(65.4)	(56.5)
Transport	166.8	216.5	235.5	296.7
	(1.9)	(2.4)	(2.4)	(3.1)
Telecommunications	21.8	34.2	39.1	52.2
	(0.3)	(0.3)	(0.4)	(0.6)
Trade	205.8	308.4	322.1	386.4
	(2.5)	(3.3)	(3.4)	(4.0)
Municipal services, housing, and other nonproductive services	58.5	87.7	146.7	205.5
	(0.7)	(0.9)	(1.5)	(2.1)
Education, culture, and arts	191.4	203.4	252.1	341.1
	(2.3)	(2.2)	(2.7)	(3.5)
Science and scientific services	19.1	29.6	37.8	50.8
	(0.2)	(0.3)	(0.4)	(0.5)
Administration	142.1	140.0	110.8	98.8
	(1.7)	(1.5)	(1.2)	(1.0)
Public health	90.8	111.5	155.8	188.6
	(1.1)	(1.2)	(1.6)	(2.0)
Other services	67.6	76.9	76.7	96.4
	(0.8)	(0.8)	(0.8)	(1.0)

a. Percentages appear in parentheses.

Source: Anuarul Statistic, various issues.

1970	1971	1972	1973	1974	1975	1976
9,875.0	9,938.9	9,970.9	10,020.6	10,070.1	10,150.8	10,227.0
2,276.8	2,457.1	2,601.2	2,797.6	2,983.2	3,109.7	3,267.9
(23.0)	(24.7)	(26.1)	(27.9)	(29.6)	(30.6)	(31.9)
768.2	800.6	840.2	826.2	812.7	825.5	848.1
(7.8)	(8.1)	(8.4)	(8.2)	(8.1)	(8.1)	(8.3)
4,848.6	4,602.2	4,382.5	4,206.3	4,012.1	3,837.4	3,640.8
(49.1)	(46.3)	(44.0)	(42.0)	(39.8)	(37.8)	(35.6)
357.3	369.0	377.3	389.6	391.3	431.8	435.8
(3.7)	(3.7)	(3.8)	(3.9)	(3.9)	(4.3)	(4.3)
56.4	59.6	62.7	65.1	67.5	68.7	69.8
(0.6)	(0.6)	(0.6)	(0.6)	(0.7)	(0.7)	(0.7)
427.1	468.9	509.0	516.1	542.0	558.7	592.4
(4.3)	(4.7)	(5.1)	(5.2)	(5.4)	(5.5)	(5.8)
305.6	319.8	308.5	316.3	321.8	348.7	363.5
(3.0)	(3.2)	(3.1)	(3.2)	(3.2)	(3.4)	(3.5)
364.9	373.7	386.4	380.9	394.6	408.6	421.5
(3.7)	(3.7)	(3.9)	(3.8)	(3.9)	(4.0)	(4.1)
46.2	54.0	64.8	70.2	65.8	77.3	81.5
(0.5)	(0.6)	(0.6)	(0.7)	(0.7)	(0.8)	(0.8)
70.0	70.3	69.2	67.4	67.7	67.6	68.1
(0.7)	(0.7)	(0.7)	(0.7)	(0.7)	(0.7)	(0.7)
225.3	228.3	237.0	245.0	257.5	267.3	276.7
(2.3)	(2.3)	(2.4)	(2.4)	(2.5)	(2.6)	(2.7)
108.9	115.0	111.2	116.9	129.6	123.0	131.9
(1.1)	(1.2)	(1.1)	(1.2)	(1.3)	(1.2)	(1.3)

Table SA1.12. *Employment in the State Sector, by Professional Category, 1950, 1955, 1960, 1965, and 1970–76*

(thousands of persons and percentage of employment in the state sector[a])

Professional category	*1950*	*1955*	*1960*	*1965*
Total occupied population[b]	*8,377.2*	*9,362.6*	*9,537.7*	*9,684.0*
Total employment in the state sector[b]			3,208.4	4,234.0
Workers			2,212.5 (69.0)	3,018.7 (71.3)
Engineers				
Technicians				
Foremen				
Personnel with higher economic studies				
Personnel with secondary economic studies			550.6 (17.1)	700.3 (16.5)
Other personnel with higher studies				
Other personnel with secondary education				
Intermediate health personnel				
Office personnel			294.5 (9.2)	347.2 (8.2)
Attendants, watchmen, and the like			150.8 (4.7)	167.8 (4.0)

a. Percentages appear in parentheses.

b. End of the year.

Source: Anuarul Statistic, various issues.

1970	1971	1972	1973	1974	1975	1976
9,875.0	*9,938.9*	*9,970.9*	*10,020.6*	*10,070.1*	*10,150.8*	*10,227.0*
5,099.5	5,051.2	5,402.1				
3,867.8	3,793.0	4,089.1				
(75.8)	(75.1)	(75.7)				
110.3	114.3	122.8				
(2.2)	(2.3)	(2.3)				
170.0	161.2	170.8				
(3.3)	(3.2)	(3.2)				
50.2	51.4	54.9				
(1.0)	(1.0)	(1.0)				
51.8	63.0	67.9				
(1.0)	(1.2)	(1.3)				
122.7	138.2	145.1				
(2.4)	(2.7)	(2.7)				
182.1	200.4	207.3				
(3.6)	(4.0)	(3.8)				
199.6	205.8	212.8				
(3.9)	(4.1)	(3.9)				
59.1	57.7	59.8				
(1.2)	(1.1)	(1.1)				
170.6	150.7	152.6				
(3.3)	(3.0)	(2.8)				
115.3	115.5	119.0				
(2.3)	(2.3)	(2.2)				

Table SA1.13. *Average Annual Growth in Gross Output, Employment, and Productivity, by Major Economic Sector and Plan Period, 1950–75*

(percentage)

Item	Total economy[a]	Industry[b]	Construction[c]	Agriculture[d]	Transport and telecommunications[e]
			1951–55		
Gross output	13.2	15.1	19.1	10.1	18.5
Employment[f]	2.2	4.1	16.7	0.9	5.9
Labor productivity[g]	10.8	10.6	2.1	9.1	11.9
			1956–60		
Gross output	7.2	11.0	10.2	1.1	7.0
Employment	0.1	3.3	3.2	−0.9	1.8
Labor productivity	7.1	7.4	6.8	2.0	5.1
			1961–65		
Gross output	9.5	13.8	9.0	2.4	12.4
Employment	−0.1	5.3	5.3	−2.6	4.9
Labor productivity	9.6	8.1	3.5	5.1	7.1
			1966–70		
Gross output	8.7	11.9	10.9	1.9	9.0
Employment	0.1	4.1	4.7	−2.4	3.5
Labor productivity	8.6	7.5	5.9	4.4	5.3
			1971–75		
Gross output	10.5	13.0	6.9	6.4	11.1
Employment	0.2	6.4	1.4	−4.8	3.9
Labor productivity	10.3	6.1	5.3	11.5	6.9

a. Social product.
b. Gross industrial production.
c. Output of construction and assembly.
d. Gross agricultural production.
e. Social product in transport and telecommunications.
f. Occupied population in productive sectors.
g. Gross output per employed person.
Source: Anuarul Statistic, various issues.

Sector	*1950*	*1955*	*1960*	*1965*	*1970*	*1971*	*1972*	*1973*	*1974*	*1975*	*1976*
Total: all employees	*366*	*536*	*854*	*1,115*	*1,434*	*1,471*	*1,498*	*1,563*	*1,663*	*1,813*	*1,964*
Industry	371	565	887	1,160	1,432	1,461	1,482	1,549	1,660	1,823	1,942
Construction	420	581	877	1,183	1,555	1,608	1,648	1,734	1,925	2,111	2,203
Agriculture	259	426	731	1,009	1,327	1,372	1,408	1,488	1,543	1,737	1,934
Forestry	345	391	617	842	1,145	1,178	1,211	1,297	1,341	1,552	1,745
Transport	376	608	946	1,101	1,544	1,568	1,599	1,626	1,743	1,870	2,090
Telecommunications	353	491	792	1,032	1,239	1,250	1,262	1,332	1,368	1,490	1,737
Trade	350	440	724	964	1,277	1,332	1,345	1,382	1,436	1,523	1,735
Municipal services, housing, and other nonproductive services	320	493	778	1,013	1,243	1,282	1,327	1,390	1,464	1,580	1,757
Education, culture, and arts	386	503	875	1,089	1,445	1,471	1,503	1,583	1,663	1,784	1,976
Science and scientific services	385	657	1,018	1,228	1,592	1,679	1,703	1,756	1,810	2,024	2,201
Public health, social assistance, and physical culture	336	525	801	1,030	1,339	1,375	1,411	1,483	1,542	1,622	1,844
Total: workers	*325*	*502*	*800*	*1,047*	*1,333*	*1,371*	*1,401*	*1,467*	*1,570*	*1,725*	*1,867*
Industry	336	529	854	1,112	1,354	1,385	1,409	1,479	1,592	1,756	1,871
Construction	360	547	817	1,109	1,462	1,519	1,562	1,646	1,834	2,023	2,111
Agriculture	244	405	690	940	1,226	1,270	1,304	1,377	1,423	1,622	1,826
Forestry	202	363	603	843	1,098	1,126	1,151	1,220	1,284	1,444	1,648
Transport	332	538	851	1,006	1,452	1,478	1,525	1,576	1,684	1,822	2,040
Telecommunications	336	485	756	980	1,179	1,191	1,204	1,275	1,310	1,432	1,679
Trade	305	382	678	908	1,183	1,245	1,261	1,294	1,355	1,438	1,649
Municipal services, housing, and other nonproductive services	305	483	751	978	1,201	1,240	1,286	1,339	1,406	1,515	1,700

Source: Anuarul Statistic, various issues.

Table SA2.1. *Number of Schools, Enrollments, and Staff, by Level of Education, Selected Years, 1950/51–1976/77*

Level of education	*1950/51*	*1960/61*	*1965/66*	*1970/71*	*1971/72*	*1972/73*
Preschool						
Kindergartens	4,435	7,375	7,627	10,336	10,809	11,542
Enrollments	199,096	354,677	353,721	448,244	506,435	591,670
Teaching staff	5,826	12,533	13,579	18,887	20,174	23,224
Primary						
Schools	15,342	15,110	14,997	14,958	14,959	14,935
Enrollments	1,779,208	2,346,343	2,992,802	2,941,265	2,832,093	2,729,092
Teaching staff	67,146	93,794	130,035	137,786	138,092	137,456
General school						
Schools	15,332	15,076	14,965	14,927	14,925	14,899
Enrollments	1,777,987	2,346,322	2,987,240	2,934,051	2,823,749	2,720,199
Teaching staff	66,954	93,140	128,253	135,695	136,039	135,089
General school of art						
Schools	10	34	32	31	34	36
Pupils enrolled	1,221	12,556	17,774	19,198	20,200	20,859
Number enrolled from general school	—	12,535	12,212	11,984	11,856	11,966
Teaching staff	192	654	1,782	2,091	2,053	2,367

Secondary						
Lycées	343	587	589	831	909	921
Enrollments	93,255	251,144	371,724	505,891	502,236	505,223
Teaching staff	5,127	11,467	14,181	23,140	24,519	25,122
General lycées						
Lycées	224	562	556	577	578	532
Enrollments	59,903	241,539	359,836	383,056	368,817	349,980
Teaching staff	3,328	10,529	13,117	15,902	16,623	16,107
Specialized lycées						
Lycées	110	14	14	226	303	361
Enrollments	33,046	7,631	9,282	118,577	128,525	149,895
Teaching staff	1,710	510	453	6,489	6,938	8,051
Art lycées						
Lycées	9	11	19	28	28	28
Pupils enrolled	306	1,974	2,606	4,258	4,894	5,352
Number enrolled from general lycées	—	—	—	—	—	4
Teaching staff	89	428	611	749	958	964
Vocational						
Schools	546	519	441	403	409	435
Enrollments	99,257	127,224	182,391	195,941	210,364	228,845
Teaching staff	7,808	7,330	10,374	11,775	13,299	14,170
Apprenticeship at the job						
Pupils enrolled	—	—	—	85,731	95,877	101,999

(Table continues on the following pages)

Table SA2.1. *Continued*

Level of education	1973/74	1974/75	1975/76	1976/77	Percentage rates of growth of enrollments and staffs: 1950/51–1974/75	Percentage rates of growth of enrollments and staffs: 1965/66–1974/75
Preschool						
Kindergartens	12,438	13,289	13,537	13,600	—	—
Enrollments	704,940	770,016	812,420	825,028	5.8	9.0
Teaching staff	27,640	31,743	33,789	35,001	7.3	9.9
Primary						
Schools	14,761	14,761	14,695	14,591	—	—
Enrollments	2,742,818	2,889,946	3,019,776	3,125,584	2.0	—
Teaching staff	135,503	139,790	144,978	147,582	3.1	0.9
General school						
Schools	14,723	14,722	14,656	14,552	—	—
Enrollments	2,733,414	2,882,109	3,011,538	3,117,163	2.0	—
Teaching staff	133,108	137,405	142,373	144,973	3.0	—
General school of art						
Schools	38	39	39	39	—	—
Pupils enrolled	21,870	21,798	22,617	22,842	12.7	2.3
Number enrolled from general school	12,466	13,961	14,379	14,421	—	1.5
Teaching staff	2,395	2,385	2,605	2,609	11.0	3.3

Secondary						
Lycées	907	1,058	1,064	1,082	—	—
Enrollments	509,669	707,767	901,977	1,015,886	8.8	7.4
Teaching staff	25,128	31,766	41,617	46,447	7.9	9.4
General lycées						
Lycées	452	434	428	414	—	—
Enrollments	324,508	344,585	361,062	371,201	7.6	—
Teaching staff	14,823	14,818	14,539	15,261	6.4	1.4
Specialized lycées						
Lycées	427	596	608	640	—	—
Enrollments	179,628	357,444	535,181	639,011	10.4	50.0
Teaching staff	9,319	15,885	26,070	30,138	9.7	48.0
Art lycées						
Lycées	28	28	28	28	—	—
Pupils enrolled	5,655	5,738	5,734	5,674	13.0	9.2
Number enrolled from general lycées	122	—	—	—	—	—
Teaching staff	986	1,063	1,008	1,048	10.9	6.3
Vocational						
Schools	459	468	426	440	—	—
Enrollments	250,459	191,821	122,630	93,747	2.8	0.6
Teaching Staff	13,514	11,088	5,391	3,826	1.5	0.7
Apprenticeship at the job						
Pupils enrolled	103,032	66,611	31,356	25,564	—	—

Table SA2.2. *EducationalAttainment of the Population in Rural and Urban Areas, and by Sex, 1956 and 1966*

Years of schooling	1956 Thousands	1956 Percent	1966 Thousands	1966 Percent
Total population	17,489		19,103	
1–4	11,114	63.6	11,441	59.9
5–8	1,139	6.5	1,680	8.8
9–12	629	3.6	1,742	9.1
More than 12	214	1.2	328	1.7
Total		74.9		79.5
Males	8,503		9,351	
1–4	5,508	64.8	5,220	55.8
5–8	616	7.2	829	8.9
9–12	353	4.2	1,078	11.5
More than 12	153	1.8	221	2.4
Total		78.0		78.6
Females	8,986		9,752	
1–4	5,606	62.4	6,221	63.8
5–8	523	5.8	851	8.7
9–12	276	3.1	664	6.8
More than 12	61	0.7	107	1.1
Total		72.0		80.4
Total urban	5,474		7,462	
1–4	2,980	54.4	3,582	48.0
5–8	771	14.1	959	12.9
9–12	485	8.9	1,361	18.2
More than 12	191	3.5	292	3.9
Total		80.9		83.0

Table SA2.2. *Continued*

Years of schooling	1956 Thousands	1956 Percent	1966 Thousands	1966 Percent
Urban male	2,684		3,717	
1–4	1,423	53.0	1,583	42.6
5–8	408	15.2	476	12.8
9–12	269	10.0	814	21.9
More than 12	134	5.0	195	5.2
Total		83.2		82.5
Urban female	2,790		3,745	
1–4	1,557	55.8	1,999	53.4
5–8	363	13.0	483	12.9
9–12	216	7.7	547	14.6
More than 12	57	2.0	97	2.6
Total		78.6		83.5
Total rural	12,015		11,640	
1–4	8,134	67.7	7,859	67.5
5–8	368	3.1	721	6.2
9–12	144	1.2	380	3.3
More than 12	23	0.2	36	0.3
Total		72.2		77.3
Rural male	5,820		5,633	
1–4	4,085	70.2	3,636	64.5
5–8	208	3.6	353	6.3
9–12	85	1.5	263	4.7
More than 12	20	0.3	27	0.5
Total		75.6		76.0
Rural female	6,195		6,007	
1–4	4,049	65.4	4,223	70.3
5–8	160	2.6	368	6.1
9–12	59	1.0	117	2.0
More than 12	3	0.1	9	0.2
Total		68.9		78.5

Note: The age-group categories for years of schooling are mutually exclusive rather than cumulative: that is, for total population in 1956, 63.6 percent of the population had one to four years of schooling; an additional 6.5 percent of the population went on to finish five to eight years of schooling. In other words, 70.1 percent of the population had up to eight years of schooling.

Source: Population Census of Romania 1956, 1966.

Table SA2.3. *Number of Specialized Lycées and Their Enrollments, Graduates, and Staff, 1966/67–1976/77*

Kind of lycée	*1966/67*	*1970/71*	*1971/72*	*1972/73*
Lycées, total	182	226	303	361
Enrollments, total	35,643	118,577	128,525	149,895
Graduates, total	—	18,945	22,804	24,746
Teaching staff, total	2,119	6,489	6,938	8,051
Industrial lycées				
Lycées	61	74	134	193
Enrollments	5,329	36,836	48,616	70,994
Graduates	—	3,223	5,767	6,522
Teaching staff	455	2,224	2,495	3,660
Agricultural lycées				
Lycées	59	59	62	64
Enrollments	11,212	27,934	27,447	27,528
Graduates	—	5,621	5,992	5,905
Teaching staff	652	1,567	1,558	1,564
Forestry lycées				
Lycées	—	4	4	4
Enrollments	—	667	793	1,059
Graduates	—	68	30	66
Teaching staff	—	38	42	60
Economic lycées				
Lycées	43	41	48	45
Enrollments	8,762	30,439	28,008	26,156
Graduates	—	6,769	7,268	7,598
Teaching staff	438	1,322	1,332	1,176
Pedagogical lycées				
Lycées	19	46	46	46
Enrollments	10,340	22,114	22,634	22,692
Graduates	—	3,264	3,660	4,509
Teaching staff	574	1,280	1,471	1,544
Health lycées				
Lycées	—	2	9	9
Enrollments	—	587	1,027	1,466
Graduates	—	—	87	146
Teaching staff	—	58	40	47

Source: Anuarul Statistic, various issues.

Kind of lycée	*1973/74*	*1974/75*	*1975/76*	*1976/77*
Lycées, total	427	596	608	640
Enrollments, total	179,628	357,444	535,181	639,011
Graduates, total	27,065	25,696	33,383	—
Teaching staff, total	9,319	15,885	26,070	30,138
Industrial lycées				
Lycées	261	382	397	429
Enrollments	104,393	252,191	405,379	501,508
Graduates	7,298	9,239	16,889	—
Teaching staff	5,067	10,663	19,526	23,257
Agricultural lycées				
Lycées	65	93	98	91
Enrollments	28,773	50,318	64,790	62,180
Graduates	8,058	5,996	5,817	—
Teaching staff	1,586	2,311	3,095	2,989
Forestry lycées				
Lycées	5	5	5	8
Enrollments	1,495	1,747	2,146	4,479
Graduates	400	297	199	—
Teaching staff	70	92	118	215
Economic lycées				
Lycées	42	52	48	48
Enrollments	21,903	30,731	39,643	44,703
Graduates	5,790	5,837	5,993	—
Teaching staff	1,086	1,283	1,687	1,775
Pedagogical lycées				
Lycées	45	44	41	42
Enrollments	21,437	19,461	18,898	19,842
Graduates	5,378	4,176	4,052	—
Teaching staff	1,377	1,291	1,248	1,361
Health lycées				
Lycées	9	20	19	22
Enrollments	1,627	2,996	4,325	6,299
Graduates	141	151	433	—
Teaching staff	133	245	396	541

Table SA2.4. *Number of Vocational Schools and Their Enrollments, Staff, and Graduates, by Kind of Vocational Training, Selected Years, 1950/51–1976/77*

Kind of vocational training	*1950/51*	*1960/61*	*1965/66*
Schools			
Total	*546*	*519*	*441*
Mining	11	16	20
Electric power and electrical engineering	12	2	5
Metallurgy and engineering	264	72	57
Industrial chemistry	15	14	23
Timber industry	21	16	14
Light industry	40	63	31
Food industry	31	3	7
Agriculture and forestry	72	251	156
Transport and telecommunications	34	22	25
Building and building materials	13	32	48
Trade	26	28	27
Health	—	—	27
Other specialties	7	—	1
Enrollments			
Total	*99,257*	*127,224*	*182,391*
Mining	2,764	5,615	9,657
Electric power and electrical engineering	7,216	512	5,141
Metallurgy and engineering	45,626	32,493	41,650
Industrial chemistry	2,392	3,667	11,531
Timber industry	3,336	3,447	4,776
Food industry	4,174	458	3,438
Building and building materials	7,416	12,489	21,781
Agriculture and forestry	6,377	35,135	45,372
Transport and telecommunications	4,950	5,186	11,309
Trade	4,108	5,151	7,557
Health	—	—	2,522
Light industry	9,524	23,071	16,459
Other specialties	1,374	—	1,198

1970/71	1971/72	1972/73	1973/74	1974/75	1975/76	1976/77
			Schools			
403	*409*	*435*	*459*	*468*	*426*	*440*
21	20	21	25	25	25	26
13	13	16	17	17	17	18
61	69	83	98	109	118	129
20	19	21	21	22	23	23
20	20	20	26	27	26	25
27	27	23	27	39	37	37
7	7	8	12	10	14	11
94	94	94	90	88	60	62
32	33	34	34	35	34	40
51	48	53	52	57	50	43
31	33	36	38	38	21	26
25	25	25	18	—	—	—
1	1	1	1	1	1	—
			Enrollments			
95,941	*210,364*	*228,845*	*250,459*	*191,821*	*122,630*	*93,747*
10,735	8,601	10,410	11,398	8,238	4,921	3,463
5,789	6,447	7,116	7,006	4,924	2,720	1,594
58,649	70,549	81,377	94,885	75,986	52,852	42,159
13,571	15,303	16,195	17,091	11,707	6,688	3,355
5,662	6,111	7,157	9,295	6,964	4,407	2,940
4,419	4,648	4,973	4,913	3,229	1,940	1,377
26,114	26,233	29,260	29,545	21,122	9,072	5,635
21,367	19,487	18,398	17,805	11,008	5,073	5,099
16,669	18,591	19,992	20,475	13,791	6,964	5,969
6,846	7,881	8,669	9,306	7,463	3,679	3,047
5,096	4,798	3,657	1,122	—	—	—
20,665	21,152	20,775	26,807	26,997	24,125	19,109
359	563	866	811	392	189	—

(Table continues on the following page)

Table SA2.4. *Continued*

Kind of vocational training	*1950/51*	*1960/61*	*1965/6*
	Teaching staff		
Total	*7,808*	*7,330*	*10,374*
Mining	257	299	737
Electric power and electrical engineering	418	44	98
Metallurgy and engineering	3,885	2,063	2,381
Industrial chemistry	197	278	783
Light industry	743	1,450	950
Food industry	273	18	217
Building and building materials	193	644	1,277
Agriculture and forestry	621	1,790	2,290
Transport and telecommunications	646	321	601
Timber industry	148	225	243
Trade	325	198	331
Health	—	—	387
Other specialties	102	—	79
	Graduates		
Total	*24,783*	*30,236*	*60,774*
Mining	730	1,535	2,984
Electric power and electrical engineering	883	106	1,310
Metallurgy and engineering	9,578	6,060	12,556
Industrial chemistry	450	606	3,735
Timber industry	1,993	1,173	1,439
Light industry	3,290	4,431	6,759
Food industry	537	209	1,346
Building and building materials	881	4,195	8,325
Agriculture and forestry	1,045	8,860	15,403
Transport and telecommunications	3,993	954	3,257
Trade	1,068	2,107	3,310
Health	—	—	—
Other specialties	335	—	350

Source: Anuarul Statistic, various issues.

1970/71	1971/72	1972/73	1973/74	1974/75	1975/76	1976/77
			Teaching staff			
11,775	*13,299*	*14,170*	*13,514*	*11,088*	*5,391*	*3,826*
718	732	826	702	540	216	62
322	385	456	325	173	43	26
3,098	3,880	4,678	4,709	4,448	2,429	1,749
861	1,031	1,309	1,275	974	354	68
1,435	1,474	1,261	1,391	1,632	1,273	1,087
310	311	194	229	88	59	57
1,797	1,907	1,910	1,898	1,064	342	94
1,025	909	917	862	552	244	241
819	1,022	1,194	1,005	743	132	242
423	505	510	546	429	125	53
488	664	694	526	414	174	147
458	377	179	15	—	—	—
21	102	42	31	31	—	—
			Graduates			
68,492	*70,867*	*78,915*	*84,820*	*91,117*	*77,359*	
3,563	2,817	3,146	3,514	3,853	3,780	
1,423	2,308	2,112	2,295	2,142	2,188	
17,373	19,217	24,993	28,216	31,350	31,585	
4,742	4,341	4,938	5,477	5,518	5,318	
2,297	1,821	2,296	2,661	3,071	3,370	
7,953	8,823	8,572	9,941	12,096	12,264	
1,553	1,755	2,016	2,165	1,824	1,130	
9,658	9,207	11,202	10,885	12,633	6,013	
10,018	9,623	7,045	7,631	7,087	3,112	
4,965	5,316	6,075	6,749	6,636	6,406	
2,359	3,318	3,885	3,876	4,678	2,005	
2,468	2,229	2,330	1,118	—	—	
120	92	305	292	220	188	

Table SA2.5. *Number of Graduates, by Level of Education, 1950/51–1975/76*

School year	*General schools*	*Specialized lycées*	*General lycées*	*Art lycées*	*Vocational schools*
1950/51	81,987	4,690	8,339	185	24,783
1951/52	102,082	8,633	13,384	278	41,429
1952/53	113,477	7,190	11,678	158	49,464
1953/54	108,063	6,943	26,073	221	35,810
1954/55	107,719	5,061	17,626	268	28,252
1955/56	106,648	3,628	29,269	262	26,320
1956/57	99,383	1,593	29,309	164	25,727
1957/58	107,482	903	10,191	303	32,610
1958/59	116,698	527	30,731	243	30,880
1959/60	145,639	228	36,829	16	25,313
1960/61	182,216	—	46,550	247	30,236
1961/62	246,202	—	46,307	282	50,870
1962/63	329,739	815	55,274	331	45,056
1963/64	—[c]	1,616	62,266	348	65,166
1964/65	306,652	1,888	68,877	432	65,929
1965/66	304,671	2,402	78,283	547	60,774
1966/67	306,239	—	99,553	556	59,512
1967/68	300,730	1,121	25,663	529	70,291
1968/69	316,963	4,759	76,218	683	79,492
1969/70	338,478	11,124	82,613	742	78,535
1970/71	360,887[d]	18,945	81,344	759	68,492
1971/72	353,396[d]	22,804	79,446	881	70,867
1972/73	346,850[d]	24,746	83,839	1,065	78,915
1973/74	342,351[d]	27,065	87,112	1,268	84,820
1974/75	351,736	25,696	85,143	1,392	91,117
1975/76	367,045	33,383	47,822	1,368	77,359

a. With one to three years' duration.

b. Gradually absorbed in the general and specialized schools.

c. Transition from seven to eight years.

d. Subsequent years include enrollments for ten grades in these schools.

Source: Anuarul Statistic, various issues.

School year	*Appren-ticeship at the job*[a]	*Tech-nical schools*[b]	*Schools for foremen*	*Post-lycée special-ization*	*Two-year peda-gogical institute*	*Higher educa-tion*
1950/51		13,926				9,510
1951/52		23,304				7,555
1952/53		17,036				10,984
1953/54		20,780				12,379
1954/55		21,644				8,163
1955/56		2,715		487		11,274
1956/57		2,965	527	2,707	—	11,829
1957/58		1,780	3,190	2,320	203	12,047
1958/59		1,939	2,956	3,623	179	10,948
1959/60		2,988	3,335	4,178	587	10,896
1960/61		3,835	3,355	3,892	871	10,296
1961/62		3,429	6,671	8,383	701	11,114
1962/63		1,537	4,062	10,847	—	11,673
1963/64		7,567	6,563	7,344	—	14,269
1964/65		9,091	6,160	7,248	2,173	19,503
1965/66		8,334	4,996	7,551	1,732	22,589
1966/67		8,556	4,803	10,517	1,377	21,742
1967/68	796	5,588	6,464	10,603	1,063	22,852
1968/69	6,292	4,118	11,414	12,052	1,535	23,917
1969/70	13,303	521	9,064	16,719	1,744	24,471
1970/71	30,515	878	5,670	11,477	1,900	28,840
1971/72	33,858	87	6,687	10,461	766	35,149
1972/73	37,186	—	6,536	12,232	596	31,547
1973/74	40,041	—	7,341	15,335	287	30,301
1974/75	35,812	—	6,047	12,455	—	28,899
1975/76	24,446	—	7,399	11,362	—	30,839

Table SA3.1. *Growth of Social Product, National Income, and Gross National Product (in 1963 Comparable Prices), 1950, 1955, and 1960–76*

Year	*Social product*[a] *(lei)*	*Annual percentage growth rate*	*National income*[a] *(lei)*	*Annual percentage growth rate*	*Gross national product*[a] *(lei)*	*Annual percentage growth rate*
1950	83		35.4		43.1	
		13.3[b]		14.2[b]		13.6[b]
1955	155		68.0		81.6	
		7.2[b]		6.9[b]		7.3[b]
1960	219		94.9		116.2	
1961	244	11.4	104.4	10.0	128.9	10.9
1962	259	6.1	109.0	4.4	136.1	5.6
1963	281	8.5	119.7	9.8	148.5	9.1
1964	314	11.7	133.5	11.5	165.7	11.6
1965	344	9.6	146.2	9.5	182.5	10.1
1966	380	10.5	160.7	9.9	201.6	10.5
1967	417	9.7	172.8	7.5	218.7	8.5
1968	449	7.7	184.8	6.9	235.1	7.5
1969	484	7.8	198.6	7.5	252.7	7.5
1970	523	8.1	212.1	6.8	268.9	6.4
1971	584	11.7	240.7	13.5	304.9	13.4
1972	641	9.8	264.7	10.0	334.9	9.8
1973	708	10.4	293.0	10.7	370.6	10.7
1974	788	11.3	329.5	12.5	417.7	12.7
1975	864	9.6	361.9	9.8	460.2	10.2
1976	950	10.0	400.0	10.5	508.3	10.5

a. Using post-1970 methodology (Appendix D).

b. Annual average for the five-year period.

Source: Anuarul Statistic, various issues, and data supplied by Romanian authorities during discussions with the authors.

Table SA3.2. *Structure of Social Product, National Income, and Gross National Product, 1965–76*

(billions of 1963 comparable lei)

Item	*1965*	*1966*	*1967*	*1968*	*1969*	*1970*	*1971*	*1972*	*1973*	*1974*	*1975*	*1976*
Social product	344	380	417	449	484	523	584	641	708	788	864	950
Industry	188.8	210.3	236.8	262.1	289.8	324.7	360.6	400.3	456.9	517.3	571.5	633.2
Construction	33.0	34.8	40.7	45.7	48.3	54.8	59.7	64.4	67.3	71.0	76.7	83.3
Agriculture	76.3	87.5	89.0	86.3	89.0	83.9	101.5	109.1	109.9	112.9	116.6	135.9
Transport and telecommunications	16.7	18.2	20.1	21.9	23.3	25.3	27.5	29.5	32.0	34.2	39.5	42.0
National income	146.2	160.7	172.8	184.8	198.6	212.1	240.7	264.7	293.0	329.5	361.9	400.0
Industry	68.7	75.7	85.5	96.2	108.0	125.0	139.5	157.3	184.1	208.8	232.5	260.0
Construction	12.4	13.4	15.3	17.4	18.7	21.8	23.9	25.9	27.3	28.8	31.4	34.0
Agriculture	40.6	46.8	46.6	43.7	44.4	39.4	51.6	55.2	52.4	51.2	51.2	62.6
Transport and telecommunications	8.8	9.7	10.7	11.7	12.5	13.6	14.8	16.3	18.0	19.6	23.0	23.9
Nonproductive sector[a,b]	21.8	24.8	27.1	29.2	31.6	33.2	37.7	41.5	45.7	51.8	57.5	65.5
Housing[c]	7.0	7.3	7.6	7.9	8.4	8.8	9.2	9.6	10.0	10.4	10.7	11.1
Other nonproductive services	14.8	17.5	19.5	21.3	23.2	24.4	28.5	31.9	35.7	41.4	47.5	54.4
Depreciation[d]	14.5	16.1	18.8	21.1	22.5	23.6	26.5	28.7	31.9	36.4	40.8	44.7
Gross national product	182.5	201.6	218.7	235.1	252.7	268.9	304.9	334.9	370.6	417.7	460.2	510.2

Note: Post-1970 methodology is used (Appendix D). Gross national product = national income + nonproductive sectors + depreciation.

a. Excluding defense and other public organizations.

b. Calculated on the basis of labor force in the nonproductive sector.

c. Calculated as 5 percent of the housing stock.

d. Equal to the Depreciation Fund.

Source: Anuarul Statistic, various issues.

Table SA3.3. *Gross Investment in the National Economy, 1949–76*
(millions of lei)

Year	*Gross investment*	*Socialist sector: Total*	*Socialist sector: State sector*	*Socialist sector: Cooperative sector*	*Funds of the population*	*Gross investment by plan period*
			1959 prices			
1949	5,004	4,379	4,379	—	625	
1950	6,304	5,663	5,610	53	641	
1951	8,628	7,970	7,860	110	658	
1952	11,346	10,647	10,526	121	699	
1953	14,365	13,567	13,423	144	798	61,916
1954	12,992	12,063	11,769	294	929	
1955	14,585	13,466	13,061	405	1,119	
1956	16,710	15,195	14,813	382	1,515	
1957	16,420	14,238	13,734	504	2,182	
1958	18,214	15,648	14,947	701	2,566	100,180
1959	21,171	18,456	17,498	958	2,715	
1960	27,665	24,615	22,981	1,634	3,050	
1961	32,623	29,934	27,575	2,359	2,689	
1962	36,809	34,325	31,075	3,250	2,484	
1963	39,594	37,310	33,278	4,032	2,284	199,692
1964	43,489	41,230	37,762	3,468	2,259	
1965	47,177	44,857	41,545	3,312	2,320	

Table SA3.3. *Continued*

Year	Gross invest-ment	Socialist sector: Total	Socialist sector: State sector	Socialist sector: Cooper-ative sector	Funds of the popu-lation	Gross invest-ment by plan period
			1963 prices			
1965	47,014	44,659	41,477	3,182	2,355	
1966	51,649	49,246	45,970	3,276	2,403	
1967	60,236	57,526	53,686	3,840	2,710	
1968	67,256	64,573	60,406	4,167	2,683	330,797
1969	71,666	68,344	64,263	4,081	3,322	
1970	79,990	74,790	69,802	4,988	5,200	
1971	88,388	82,617	76,890	5,727	5,771	
1972	97,539	91,717	86,058	5,659	5,822	
1973	105,657	99,231	93,723	5,508	6,426	548,980
1974	119,665	112,457	107,251	5,206	7,208	
1975	137,731	130,640	124,797	5,843	7,091	
1976	149,006	141,233	134,808	6,425	7,773	
			1977 prices			
1976	151,567	142,793	136,001	6,792	8,774	

Source: Anuarul Statistic, various issues.

Table SA3.4. *Gross Investment in the Socialist Sector, by Branch of the Economy, Selected Years, 1950–76*
(millions of lei)

	1959 prices				*19* *pr*
Branch of the economy	*1950*	*1955*	*1960*	*1965*	*19*
Total	*5,663*	*13,466*	*24,615*	*44,857*	*44,*
Industry	2,751	7,685	11,828	22,321	22,
Producer goods	2,372	6,387	10,051	20,233	20,
Consumer goods	379	1,298	1,777	2,088	2,
Building	369	292	531	1,931	1,
Agriculture	583	1,828	4,894	8,283	7,
Forestry	74	159	209	263	
Transport	940	1,060	2,034	4,173	4,
Telecommunications	39	64	190	302	
Trade	147	364	736	1,222	1,
Municipal services, housing, and other nonproductive services	216	1,051	2,541	4,342	4,
Housing only	150	794	1,618	2,920	3,
Education, culture, and arts	193	412	720	825	
Education	88	234	440	692	
Culture and arts	105	178	280	133	
Science and scientific services	106	156	321	198	
Public health, social assistance, and physical culture	151	252	393	524	
Administration	77	43	157	284	
Other branches	17	100	61	189	

							1977
			1963 prices				*prices*
1970	*1971*	*1972*	*1973*	*1974*	*1975*	*1976*	*1976*
74,790	*82,617*	*91,717*	*99,231*	*112,457*	*130,640*	*141,233*	*142,793*
37,961	42,850	49,257	56,033	61,274	67,829	70,723	69,350
32,139	35,976	41,751	45,999	49,821	57,787	59,671	58,578
5,822	6,874	7,506	10,034	11,453	10,042	11,052	10,772
3,595	4,290	4,448	4,148	5,652	7,317	9,787	9,194
12,454	13,796	14,088	13,945	15,344	17,587	19,759	20,736
313	380	388	439	465	544	612	632
7,856	8,247	8,902	9,023	10,290	13,426	14,560	14,433
613	687	754	1,112	1,993	1,300	1,661	1,589
2,828	3,454	3,642	3,466	3,985	4,849	5,618	5,974
5,316	5,229	6,230	6,700	7,561	10,960	11,860	13,700
2,994	2,578	2,963	3,741	4,745	6,680	6,184	7,834
1,591	1,517	1,827	1,940	2,218	2,673	2,749	3,029
1,184	1,194	1,408	1,675	1,974	2,302	2,282	2,534
407	323	419	265	244	371	467	495
438	578	539	584	1,186	903	992	959
1,143	777	906	846	1,264	1,373	1,227	1,375
500	526	473	700	925	886	1,219	1,375
182	286	263	295	300	993	466	447

(Table continues on the following pages)

Table SA3.4. *Continued*

Branch of the economy	1959 prices				196 pric
	1950	1955	1960	1965	196
	Investments from state funds[a]				
Total	*5,561*	*13,090*	*23,219*	*41,645*	*41,54*
Industry	2,747	7,600	11,770	22,199	22,86
Producer goods	2,372	6,384	10,049	20,228	20,91
Consumer goods	375	1,216	1,721	1,971	1,94
Building	369	292	531	1,930	1,82
Agriculture	568	1,708	3,915	5,759	5,02
Forestry	74	159	209	263	25
Transport	940	1,060	2,030	4,173	4,08
Telecommunications	39	64	190	302	31
Trade	122	311	640	997	1,00
Municipal services, housing, and other nonproductive services	214	1,027	2,443	4,141	4,31
Housing only	150	797	1,618	2,920	3,13
Education, culture, and arts	187	361	569	705	70
Education	85	213	345	608	61
Culture and arts	102	148	224	97	9
Science and scientific services	106	156	321	198	19
Public health, social assistance, and physical culture	101	209	384	507	50
Administration	77	43	156	282	27
Other branches	17	100	61	189	18

a. Includes investment from the funds of enterprises.

b. Figures for 1976 are not exactly comparable with those of previous years because of min definitional changes, which affect agricultural investment figures the most.

Source: Anuarul Statistic, various issues.

1963 prices							1977 prices
1970	1971	1972	1973	1974	1975	1976	1976
Investments from state funds[a]							
71,082	*78,507*	*87,533*	*95,074*	*108,597*	*125,957*	*133,985*[b]	*135,065*[b]
37,506	42,319	48,733	55,468	60,828	67,330	70,232	68,839
32,104	35,931	41,697	45,946	49,793	57,743	59,612	58,515
5,402	6,388	7,036	9,522	11,035	9,587	10,620	10,324
3,579	4,257	4,410	4,118	5,635	7,301	9,770	9,177
10,267	11,380	11,794	11,688	12,924	14,935	14,621	15,343
313	380	388	437	465	540	609	629
7,850	8,239	8,884	9,004	10,273	13,391	14,542	14,412
613	687	754	1,112	1,993	1,300	1,661	1,589
2,491	2,997	3,054	2,860	3,563	4,421	5,159	5,473
4,964	4,880	5,831	6,347	7,396	10,646	11,524	13,322
2,973	2,553	2,937	3,696	4,717	6,626	6,114	7,746
1,406	1,318	1,596	1,698	1,954	2,336	2,359	2,580
1,094	1,075	1,268	1,517	1,770	2,096	2,102	2,317
312	243	328	181	184	240	257	263
438	578	539	584	1,186	903	992	959
990	668	820	774	1,158	1,127	1,035	1,146
483	518	471	699	922	736	1,018	1,153
182	286	259	285	300	991	463	443

Table SA3.5. *Investment in the Socialist Sector, by Judet (in 1963 Prices), 1965, 1970, 1975, and 1976*

Judet	*1965*	*1970*	*1975*	*1976*	*1965*	*1970*	*1975*	*1976*
	(millions of lei)				*(percentage of total investment)*			
Total	*44,659*	*74,790*	*130,640*	*141,233*				
Alba	454	989	1,780	2,280	1.0	1.3	1.4	1.6
Arad	626	1,062	2,342	2,131	1.4	1.4	1.8	1.5
Arges	1,702	3,050	5,402	4,612	3.8	4.1	4.1	3.3
Bacau	1,956	1,746	4,864	4,623	4.4	2.3	3.7	3.3
Bihor	1,075	1,804	2,621	2,774	2.4	2.4	2.0	2.0
Bistrita-Nasaud	128	372	643	775	0.3	0.5	0.5	0.5
Botosani	353	459	1,214	1,382	0.8	0.6	0.9	1.0
Brasov	1,007	2,536	5,568	5,424	2.3	3.4	4.3	3.8
Braila	1,393	1,501	2,672	2,968	3.1	2.0	2.0	2.1
Buzau	582	1,348	2,470	3,245	1.3	1.8	1.9	2.3
Caras-Severin	824	1,326	2,460	2,914	1.8	1.8	1.9	2.1
Cluj	1,327	1,868	3,366	3,580	3.0	2.5	2.6	2.5
Constanta	1,667	4,630	6,337	9,480	3.7	6.2	4.9	6.7
Covasna	130	540	919	1,034	0.3	0.7	0.7	0.7
Dimbovita	452	1,460	4,498	3,860	1.0	2.0	2.4	2.7
Dolj	2,347	2,688	3,505	3,654	5.3	3.6	2.7	2.6
Galati	2,680	4,258	5,899	6,285	6.0	5.7	4.5	4.5
Gorj	859	1,514	5,707	5,929	1.9	2.0	4.4	4.2
Harghita	339	907	1,189	1,124	0.8	1.2	0.9	0.8
Hunedoara	1,863	2,776	4,007	4,150	4.2	3.7	3.1	2.9
Ialomita	1,036	2,323	2,162	2,353	2.3	3.1	1.7	1.7
Iasi	892	1,635	2,682	3,449	2.0	2.2	2.1	2.4
Ilfov	1,037	1,941	2,955	3,916	2.3	2.6	2.3	2.8
Maramures	920	952	1,691	1,944	2.1	1.3	1.3	1.4
Mehedinti	606	1,740	1,271	1,312	1.4	2.3	1.0	0.9
Mures	1,698	1,427	2,643	2,498	3.8	1.9	2.0	1.8
Neamt	714	1,344	1,875	3,052	1.6	1.8	1.4	2.2
Olt	1,379	1,680	2,885	3,027	3.1	2.2	2.2	2.1
Prahova	1,631	2,704	5,869	6,277	3.7	3.6	4.5	4.4
Satu-Mare	264	656	1,093	1,150	0.6	0.9	0.8	0.8
Salaj	143	368	707	927	0.3	0.5	0.5	0.7
Sibiu	744	1,216	2,659	2,403	1.7	1.6	2.0	1.7
Suceava	813	1,139	1,918	1,910	1.8	1.5	1.5	1.4
Teleorman	1,653	1,100	2,626	2,698	3.7	1.5	2.0	1.9
Timis	909	2,085	3,743	4,256	2.0	2.8	2.9	3.0
Tulcea	414	838	1,647	2,521	0.9	1.1	1.3	1.8
Vaslui	340	662	1,399	1,632	0.8	0.9	1.1	1.2
Vilcea	347	1,521	2,690	2,611	0.8	2.0	2.1	1.8
Vrancea	401	689	1,136	1,423	0.9	0.9	0.9	1.0
Bucharest	6,956	11,935	19,524	19,648	15.6	16.0	14.9	13.9

Source: Anuarul Statistic, various issues.

Table SA3.6. *Financing of Investment, 1951–76*
(billions of lei)[a]

Source	Total 1951–55	Total 1956–60	Total 1961–65	Total 1966–70	1971	1972	1973	1974	1975	Total 1971–75	1976
					Sources of investment						
Socialist sector investment	57.7	88.2	187.7	314.5	82.6	91.7	99.2	112.5	130.6	516.6	141.2
State sector investment	56.6	84.0	171.2	294.1	76.9	86.1	93.7	107.3	124.8	488.7	134.8
Cooperative sector investment	1.1	4.2	16.4	20.4	5.7	5.6	5.5	5.2	5.8	27.9	6.4
Own investment of population	4.2	12.0	12.0	16.3	5.8	5.8	6.4	7.2	7.1	32.3	7.8
Total investment	*61.9*	*100.2*	*199.7*	*330.8*	*88.4*	*97.5*	*105.7*	*119.7*	*137.7*	*548.9*	*149.0*
					Sources of finance						
Centralized state funds					75.7	83.4	91.0	105.0	123.0	478.1	131.5
State budget					33.7	37.8	42.2	50.6	67.9	232.2	69.7
Depreciation funds					26.5	28.7	31.9	36.4	40.8	164.3	44.7
Retained benefits					11.0	13.9	15.1	15.1	12.7	67.8	16.4
Bank sources[b]					2.0	1.9	1.8	0.8	1.6	8.1	0.7
Other sources					2.5	1.1	—	2.1	—	5.7	—
Noncentralized state funds					2.8	4.1	4.1	3.6	3.0	17.6	2.5
Cooperative funds					3.7	3.7	3.7	3.5	4.2	18.8	6.8
Self-financing of population					5.8	5.8	6.4	7.2	7.1	32.3	7.8
Contributions of the population[c]					0.4	0.5	0.5	0.3	0.4	2.1	0.4
Total finance					*88.4*	*97.5*	*105.7*	*119.7*	*137.7*	*548.9*	*149.0*

a. For 1951–65, expressed in 1959 prices; for 1966–76, in 1963 prices.
b. Bank credit net of repayment.
c. Includes volunteer work by cooperatives and villages for socialist sector projects.
Source: Anuarul Statistic, various issues; data supplied by the Romanian authorities during discussions with the authors; and World Bank estimates.

Table SA3.7. *Structure and Evolution of Fixed Assets, by Major Sector, 1950–76*

Sector	Structure						
	1950	*1955*	*1960*	*1965*	*1970*	*1975*	*1976*
	Billions of lei						
Total	225.2	281.5	362.6	502.2	757.1	1,203.3	1,325.0
	Percentage of total						
Industry	19.8	24.2	27.7	31.8	35.9	41.6	42.2
Construction	0.7	2.2	2.0	2.4	2.7	3.5	3.9
Agriculture	19.0	16.6	14.9	13.5	11.5	11.4	11.2
Transport	13.7	13.0	11.1	10.9	11.7	12.1	12.1
Municipal services and other nonproductive services	31.2	28.3	28.4	25.2	24.8	19.7	18.9
Education, culture and arts, public health, and social expenditures	2.5	3.2	3.3	3.8	3.7	3.5	3.5
Other	13.1	12.5	12.6	12.4	9.7	8.2	8.2

Source: Anuarul Statistic, various issues.

Sector	*Average annual growth rate (percentages)*				
	1951–55	*1956–60*	*1961–65*	*1966–70*	*1971–75*
			Billions of lei		
Total	4.6	5.2	6.7	8.6	9.7
			Percentage of total		
Industry	8.8	8.1	9.7	11.3	12.9
Construction	31.4	3.2	10.7	11.2	15.5
Agriculture	1.8	2.9	4.6	5.2	10.0
Transport	3.5	1.9	6.3	10.2	10.4
Municipal services and other nonproductive services	2.6	5.3	4.2	8.3	4.7
Education, culture and arts, public health, and social expenditures	9.9	5.9	9.8	8.0	8.5
Other	3.6	4.8	7.0	3.4	6.0

Table SA3.8. *Socialist Retail Trade, 1960, 1965, and 1970–76*
(billions of lei, in current prices)

Retail commodity	*1960*	*1965*	*1970*	*1971*	*1972*	*1973*	*1974*	*1975*	*197*
Total	*41.4*	*67.6*	*96.7*	*105.9*	*112.4*	*121.3*	*134.1*	*145.6*	*159*
Foodstuffs	14.1	24.9	34.6	38.7	40.4	43.3	47.2	51.5	57
Public catering	4.3	7.9	12.9	14.7	16.0	17.5	19.4	20.4	22
Nonfood commodities, total	23.0	34.9	49.2	52.5	55.9	60.5	67.5	73.7	79
Textiles and footwear	11.9	17.6	24.5	25.7	27.9	30.5	33.6	35.7	n
Cosmetics and perfumes	0.3	0.5	0.8	0.9	1.0	1.2	1.3	1.5	n
Hardware, chemicals, and electrical	4.2	7.8	11.2	12.3	12.5	13.3	15.3	18.1	n
Tobacco, cigarettes, and matches	1.9	2.1	2.8	3.1	3.4	3.7	4.2	4.4	n
Stationery and books	0.8	1.5	2.0	2.2	2.2	2.4	2.3	2.5	n
Building materials	1.4	1.5	1.8	1.8	1.9	2.0	2.3	2.3	n
Furniture	1.0	1.9	3.2	3.4	3.6	3.5	4.4	5.0	n
Pharmaceutical	0.7	0.8	1.1	1.2	1.2	1.3	1.4	1.5	n

Source: Anuarul Statistic, various issues, and data provided by Romanian authorities during d cussions with the authors.

able SA4.1. *Volume of Foreign Trade, 1950–76*
nillions of lei valuta)

ear	*Total trade*	*Exports* FOB	*Imports* FOB	*Trade balance*	*Annual average growth rates for each plan period (percentages)*		
					Total	*Exports*	*Imports*
50	2,734.5	1,274.2	1,460.3	−186.1			
51	3,215.5	1,579.7	1,635.8	−56.1			
52	4,009.3	1,826.3	2,183.0	−356.7			
53	4,973.4	2,196.2	2,777.2	−581.0	14.2	14.7	13.7
54	4,543.7	2,216.0	2,327.7	−111.7			
55	5,301.4	2,530.2	2,771.2	−241.0			
56	5,075.3	2,660.7	2,414.6	+246.1			
57	5,416.4	2,465.7	2,950.7	−485.0			
58	5,700.2	2,810.0	2,890.2	−80.2	9.1	11.2	7.0
59	6,416.4	3,134.6	3,011.8	+122.8			
60	8,189.3	4,302.2	3,887.1	−415.1			
61	9,642.9	4,754.8	4,888.1	−133.3			
62	10,554.4	4,907.7	5,646.7	−739.0			
63	11,622.2	5,490.2	6,132.0	−641.8	9.8	9.0	10.7
64	13,009.2	6,000.4	7,008.8	−1,008.4			
65	13,071.9	6,609.2	6,462.7	+146.5			
66	14,396.2	7,116.9	7,279.3	−162.4			
67	17,648.6	8,372.1	9,276.5	−904.4			
68	18,465.2	8,811.4	9,653.8	−842.4	11.8	10.9	12.7
69	20,241.6	9,798.7	10,442.9	−644.2			
70	22,865.7	11,104.9	11,760.8	−655.9			
71	25,222.1	12,606.0	12,616.1	−10.1			
72	28,838.2	14,373.0	14,465.2	−92.2			
73	35,993.6	18,575.9	17,417.7	+1,158.2	18.4	19.0	17.7
74	49,789.2	24,225.8	25,563.4	−1,337.6			
75	53,095.4	26,546.9	26,548.5	−1.6			
76	60,798.4	30,504.5	30,293.9	+210.6			

ource: *Anuarul Statistic*, various issues.

Table SA4.2. *Exports, by Country of Destination, 1960, 1965, and 1970–76*
(millions of lei valuta)

Country	*1960*	*1965*	*1970*	*1971*	*1972*	*1973*	*1974*	*1975*	*1976*
Total exports	*4,302.2*	*6,609.2*	*11,104.9*	*12,606.0*	*14,373.0*	*18,575.9*	*24,225.8*	*26,546.9*	*30,504.5*
CMEA, total	2,833.2	4,226.4	5,669.6	6,111.1	6,877.2	8,456.9	8,849.0	10,289.9	11,743.4
Albania	11.7	18.5	18.7	26.9	30.6	39.6	55.1	42.7	46.8
Bulgaria	55.1	55.3	140.5	164.0	290.2	369.6	446.2	480.0	435.5
Cuba	—[a]	14.5	87.9	62.8	34.8	44.4	62.8	84.4	86.1
Czechoslovakia	375.8	571.5	790.9	734.8	825.2	1,091.0	1,183.8	1,162.1	1,368.8
German Democratic Republic	323.4	430.4	634.8	781.1	955.7	1,321.6	1,510.4	1,339.6	2,079.5
Hungary	252.1	230.7	377.8	430.0	357.2	519.5	498.9	872.7	994.5
Poland	125.2	269.7	425.3	497.4	501.6	930.7	982.3	1,012.3	1,156.0
U.S.S.R.	1,688.6	2,630.6	3,172.9	3,398.9	3,868.7	4,120.4	4,085.5	5,278.9	5,558.6
Other socialist countries, total	306.1	308.9	783.0	1,046.1	1,144.2	1,152.2	1,650.8	1,923.4	2,248.9
China	200.0	159.8	431.2	595.8	674.2	640.1	833.8	1,094.0	1,236.8
People's Republic of Korea	31.9	30.4	47.7	59.8	79.9	87.6	142.9	110.5	124.0
Yugoslavia	47.4	98.6	246.1	369.4	353.2	388.6	641.9	676.0	856.8
Vietnam	26.8	20.1	58.0	21.1	36.9	35.9	32.2	42.9	31.3
Developed market economies, total	873.1	1,531.6	3,284.5	3,992.6	4,549.0	5,980.2	9,455.4	8,225.0	9,406.5
Austria	94.2	145.8	329.4	297.6	284.2	449.8	732.0	597.9	685.6
Belgium	12.8	27.4	97.3	107.3	101.9	150.6	247.9	234.3	271.0
Canada	0.5	1.7	26.9	51.1	65.6	114.2	121.8	102.5	143.9
France	116.9	131.2	364.0	502.9	528.6	610.7	804.3	747.9	890.9

Italy	153.7	395.7	656.3	730.3	922.9	1,010.7	1,287.6	1,123.6	1,001.6
Japan	—[a]	83.5	33.3	53.6	95.1	123.6	279.1	253.7	224.7
Netherlands	19.3	40.4	130.5	181.9	223.8	410.9	750.7	594.6	781.2
Sweden	14.3	37.7	48.9	58.7	92.6	159.4	225.0	320.7	369.0
Switzerland	66.7	56.6	149.7	207.1	200.1	279.9	874.5	712.2	510.7
United Kingdom	89.5	183.2	306.9	304.9	367.4	479.9	1,203.6	624.2	745.3
United States	3.8	15.8	80.5	155.2	191.0	320.8	367.4	485.5	944.1
Developing countries, total	289.8	542.3	1,367.8	1,456.2	1,802.6	2,986.6	4,270.6	6,108.6	7,105.7
Algeria	—[a]	1.0	51.8	35.3	63.1	89.7	113.0	178.6	205.8
Argentina	12.9	6.7	1.1	10.1	12.8	3.7	36.7	170.5	50.5
Brazil	17.5	27.2	34.9	20.4	15.8	18.6	40.7	105.3	392.5
Egypt	53.5	101.8	138.4	116.5	172.3	163.5	540.8	367.2	346.5
Greece	23.7	49.1	172.0	165.6	159.8	337.3	281.1	416.9	681.0
India	69.3	40.5	96.1	85.6	101.7	131.2	231.9	331.9	215.1
Iran	0.7	3.7	200.6	160.7	164.8	246.0	368.8	811.2	928.1
Iraq	8.0	16.8	3.3	5.6	37.8	33.7	272.6	325.1	156.5
Israel	3.1	9.7	138.1	116.7	156.2	177.3	231.8	155.6	147.6
Jordan	5.4	7.6	13.4	17.3	16.9	23.8	41.9	95.3	207.6
Lebanon	37.3	47.2	105.2	167.6	233.6	235.6	375.2	384.0	342.9
Libya	0.3	19.0	87.2	83.6	96.0	221.1	381.1	582.0	565.8
Portugal	10.7	13.9	5.1	30.5	10.1	39.2	61.9	68.2	175.9
Spain	2.3	37.9	58.9	63.6	115.4	234.7	254.3	354.0	170.9
Syria	10.7	46.2	18.1	17.0	18.4	41.9	96.0	305.9	776.9
Turkey	7.5	18.6	55.2	22.2	15.8	40.2	129.2	227.5	519.7

Note: Romanian trade is categorized by country of payment. See footnote 8 in Chapter 7.
a. Less than 0.1.
Source: Anuarul Statistic, various issues.

Table SA4.3. *Imports, by Country of Origin, 1960, 1965, and 1970–76*
(millions of lei valuta)

Country	1960	1965	1970	1971	1972	1973	1974	1975	1976
Total imports	*3,887.1*	*6,462.7*	*11,760.8*	*12,616.1*	*14,465.2*	*17,417.7*	*25,563.4*	*26,548.5*	*30,293.9*
CMEA, total	2,640.4	3,718.5	5,758.8	5,931.5	6,566.3	7,082.8	8,401.1	9,864.8	12,161.6
Albania	4.4	15.1	20.6	30.4	38.4	40.9	52.9	38.5	58.1
Bulgaria	51.7	78.4	257.3	237.7	310.8	341.3	509.8	543.1	653.9
Cuba	—[a]	0.1	77.8	88.5	51.4	92.5	206.0	42.9	74.5
Czechoslovakia	383.1	417.5	951.3	896.0	963.5	986.9	1,046.9	1,284.6	1,316.2
German Democratic Republic	311.1	375.0	690.5	919.6	1,043.8	1,125.4	1,340.0	1,569.4	2,174.2
Hungary	154.6	168.6	286.6	408.8	407.2	461.8	628.4	730.8	981.9
Poland	138.5	222.4	460.8	431.0	521.1	567.1	845.6	1,060.3	1,574.6
U.S.S.R.	1,595.6	2,436.9	3,004.8	2,907.9	3,203.3	3,448.6	3,756.8	4,578.6	5,305.1
Other socialist countries, total	201.3	239.2	584.2	859.3	903.2	1,161.0	1,600.6	1,693.7	1,605.5
China	141.6	131.2	372.1	536.4	529.9	675.5	904.4	1,070.4	1,003.6
People's Republic of Korea	17.7	21.0	36.1	64.1	62.2	79.5	94.4	74.6	39.2
Yugoslavia	29.1	74.5	175.2	256.7	309.6	405.6	596.5	533.8	545.9
Vietnam	12.9	12.5	0.8	2.1	1.5	0.4	5.3	14.9	16.8
Developed market economies, total	885.4	2,087.7	4,534.0	4,880.6	5,767.7	7,212.1	12,108.5	10,762.3	10,516.1
Austria	59.2	143.2	356.7	364.6	373.0	452.3	645.2	894.9	940.2
Belgium	15.0	31.4	182.5	165.7	135.3	204.9	343.1	307.1	468.9
Canada	7.5	2.1	13.0	47.8	32.0	45.0	33.8	15.1	156.1
France	149.0	295.3	673.6	806.9	783.7	838.9	838.9	941.3	1,266.0

Italy	98.1	311.6	577.3	641.8	738.0	727.9	869.8	1,149.8	954.8
Japan	—[a]	106.0	160.6	214.8	248.0	390.1	745.5	835.4	680.7
Netherlands	23.6	56.5	190.7	188.3	155.4	306.6	657.0	424.5	485.6
Sweden	28.5	44.8	139.4	138.2	151.0	196.7	278.6	268.9	246.3
Switzerland	51.4	72.4	254.3	243.2	420.9	385.2	957.9	1,356.3	828.8
United Kingdom	106.5	263.4	592.9	689.9	788.6	634.9	1,441.9	879.2	823.3
United States	37.8	54.8	358.6	377.5	413.4	754.6	1,191.1	688.6	1,375.4
Developing countries, total	160.0	417.3	883.8	944.7	1,228.0	1,961.8	3,453.2	4,227.7	6,010.7
Algeria	—	5.2	26.4	59.0	126.3	73.0	302.5	229.8	8.4
Argentina	9.7	6.7	54.9	37.1	61.0	17.1	6.3	2.5	110.3
Brazil	7.3	30.5	31.1	36.2	14.7	53.0	72.1	162.2	245.3
Egypt	49.3	104.5	112.3	90.8	143.3	111.6	208.5	359.4	140.5
Greece	12.2	21.6	40.3	51.9	51.9	146.1	131.5	213.4	226.9
India	20.4	52.9	91.7	113.5	101.1	115.6	102.6	178.9	291.9
Iran	—	3.4	148.6	186.1	189.0	290.8	676.6	890.9	1,506.1
Iraq	0.2	0.9	—	—	0.7	39.6	168.6	34.8	855.6
Israel	9.9	11.4	59.9	62.2	47.5	67.0	136.3	142.7	68.3
Jordan	—	—	0.4	0.7	—	—	—	31.9	51.6
Lebanon	2.4	5.4	9.2	9.0	35.6	16.8	476.5	78.6	40.4
Libya	—	—	—	13.0	83.2	167.9	151.1	351.3	707.6
Portugal	3.7	10.3	11.1	10.9	12.9	11.7	23.7	30.3	40.5
Spain	4.1	28.3	52.1	40.9	68.5	92.2	149.7	181.8	127.4
Syria	5.0	58.3	5.8	7.0	9.7	26.1	73.3	96.6	37.2
Turkey	7.4	16.8	18.2	27.6	48.9	49.8	22.1	35.0	141.8

Note: Romanian trade is categorized by country of payment. See footnote 8 in Chapter 7.

a. Less than 0.1.

Source: Anuarul Statistic, various issues.

Table SA4.4. *Commodity Composition of Exports, 1950–76*
(millions of lei valuta)

Commodity	1950	1955	1960	1965
Total exports	*1,274.2*	*2,530.2*	*4,302.2*	*6,609.2*
Machinery and equipment	53.1	155.0	717.3	1,232.0
	(4.2)	(6.1)	(16.7)	(18.8)
Fuel, mineral raw materials, and metals	430.1	1,123.2	1,591.3	1,658.9
	(33.8)	(44.4)	(36.9)	(25.1)
Chemicals, fertilizers, and rubber	21.1	33.0	93.9	425.2
	(1.7)	(1.3)	(2.2)	(6.4)
Building materials	56.1	98.5	108.2	224.5
	(4.4)	(3.9)	(2.5)	(3.4)
Vegetables and animal raw materials	368.2	505.7	631.2	910.3
	(28.9)	(20.0)	(14.7)	(13.8)
Live animals	—[a]	0.9	0.3	1.3
	(—)[a]	(—)[a]	(—)[a]	(—)[a]
Unprocessed foodstuffs	147.8	319.4	403.1	509.6
	(11.6)	(12.6)	(9.4)	(7.6)
Other foodstuffs	180.7	262.4	508.2	918.9
	(14.1)	(10.4)	(11.8)	(13.9)
Industrial consumer goods	17.1	32.1	248.7	728.5
	(1.3)	(1.3)	(5.8)	(11.0)

Note: Percentage figures are given in parentheses.
a. Less than 0.1.
Source: Anuarul Statistic, various issues.

1970	1971	1972	1973	1974	1975	1976
11,104.9	*12,606.0*	*14,373.0*	*18,575.9*	*24,225.8*	*26,546.9*	*30,504.5*
2,534.5	2,911.6	3,575.5	4,538.9	4,984.4	6,722.4	7,841.4
(22.8)	(23.1)	(24.9)	(24.4)	(20.6)	(25.3)	(25.7)
2,512.9	2,552.7	2,368.0	3,216.3	5,308.0	5,911.9	7,343.4
(22.7)	(20.2)	(16.5)	(17.3)	(21.9)	(22.3)	(24.1)
778.4	1,031.7	1,181.8	1,352.7	2,714.5	2,857.0	2,526.3
(7.0)	(8.2)	(8.2)	(7.3)	(11.2)	(10.8)	(8.3)
285.4	335.4	418.0	610.3	723.2	772.0	921.3
(2.6)	(2.6)	(2.9)	(3.3)	(3.0)	(2.9)	(3.0)
1,130.7	1,208.0	1,234.0	1,500.1	1,733.9	1,665.1	1,968.5
(10.2)	(9.6)	(8.6)	(8.1)	(7.2)	(6.3)	(6.5)
4.2	1.6	1.4	0.3	3.7	4.9	9.8
(—)[a]	(—)[a]	(—)[a]	(—)[a]	(—)[a]	(—)[a]	(—)[a]
501.4	601.7	1,081.6	1,339.7	1,244.5	1,512.9	1,933.8
(4.5)	(4.8)	(7.5)	(7.2)	(5.1)	(5.7)	(6.3)
1,345.1	1,643.6	1,793.8	2,517.3	3,672.7	2,821.8	2,963.5
(12.1)	(13.1)	(12.5)	(13.6)	(15.2)	(10.6)	(9.7)
2,012.3	2,319.7	2,718.9	3,500.3	3,840.9	4,278.9	4,996.5
(18.1)	(18.4)	(18.9)	(18.8)	(15.8)	(16.1)	(16.4)

Table SA4.5. *Commodity Composition of Imports, 1950–76*
(millions of lei valuta)

Commodity	*1950*	*1955*	*1960*	*1965*
Total imports	*1,460.3*	*2,771.2*	*3,887.1*	*6,462.7*
Machinery and equipment	559.3	1,052.0	1,308.3	2,579.6
	(38.3)	(38.0)	(33.6)	(39.9)
Fuel, mineral raw materials, and metals	343.4	570.0	1,331.6	2,031.7
	(23.5)	(20.6)	(34.3)	(31.4)
Chemicals, fertilizers, and rubber	65.8	146.5	289.1	407.3
	(4.5)	(5.3)	(7.4)	(6.3)
Building materials	16.5	14.2	40.9	92.3
	(1.1)	(0.5)	(1.1)	(1.4)
Vegetables and animal raw materials	311.4	540.0	520.2	707.4
	(21.4)	(19.5)	(13.4)	(11.1)
Live animals	0.3	0.8	11.6	0.8
	(—)[a]	(—)[a]	(0.3)	(—)[a]
Unprocessed foodstuffs	9.3	215.6	85.9	54.5
	(0.7)	(7.8)	(2.3)	(0.8)
Other foodstuffs	4.9	116.2	98.8	155.4
	(0.3)	(0.2)	(2.4)	(2.4)
Industrial consumer goods	149.4	115.9	200.7	433.7
	(10.2)	(4.1)	(5.2)	(6.7)

Note: Percentage figures are given in parentheses.
a. Less than 0.1.
Source: Anuarul Statistic, various issues.

1970	*1971*	*1972*	*1973*	*1974*	*1975*	*1976*
11,760.8	*12,616.1*	*14,465.2*	*17,417.7*	*25,563.4*	*26,548.5*	*30,293.9*
4,739.1	5,315.1	6,670.3	7,337.7	8,698.3	9,213.7	9,636.5
(40.3)	(42.2)	(46.1)	(42.2)	(34.0)	(34.7)	(31.8)
3,578.6	3,813.7	3,843.0	4,826.9	8,209.5	10,153.2	12,409.3
(30.4)	(30.2)	(26.6)	(27.7)	(32.1)	(38.2)	(41.0)
788.3	679.9	806.6	1,119.7	2,586.7	1,721.1	2,066.7
(6.7)	(5.4)	(5.6)	(6.4)	(10.1)	(6.5)	(6.8)
181.2	1,155.3	162.8	183.2	237.5	296.4	345.7
(1.5)	(1.2)	(1.1)	(1.1)	(1.0)	(1.1)	(1.2)
1,187.4	1,101.3	1,502.0	2,113.3	2,686.0	2,223.8	2,211.0
(10.1)	(8.7)	(10.4)	(12.1)	(10.5)	(8.4)	(7.3)
18.9	5.5	9.0	42.3	44.4	23.8	40.9
(0.2)	(—)[a]	(0.1)	(0.2)	(0.2)	(0.1)	(0.1)
265.8	450.8	332.0	576.9	1,511.3	1,320.5	1,925.6
(2.3)	(3.6)	(2.3)	(3.3)	(5.9)	(5.0)	(6.4)
357.6	460.6	395.0	400.5	587.3	595.4	617.2
(3.0)	(3.7)	(2.7)	(2.3)	(2.3)	(2.2)	(2.0)
643.9	633.9	744.5	817.2	1,002.4	1,000.6	1,041.0
(5.5)	(5.0)	(5.1)	(4.7)	(3.9)	(3.8)	(3.4)

Table SA4.6. *Structure of Imports and Exports, by End Use, 1950–76*
(percentage)

End use	*1950*	*1955*	*1960*	*1965*	*1970*	*1971*	*1972*	*1973*	*1974*	*1975*	*1976*
Imports											
Capital goods	38	38	34	40	40	42	46	42	34	35	32
Raw materials	46	48	50	43	43	42	39	43	49	51	55
Fuels, minerals, and metals	24	21	34	31	31	30	26	28	32	38	41
Agricultural raw materials	22	27	16	12	12	12	13	15	17	13	14
Intermediate goods	6	6	9	8	8	7	7	8	11	8	8
Foodstuffs	0	4	2	2	3	4	3	2	2	2	2
Industrial consumer goods	10	4	5	7	6	5	5	5	4	4	3
Exports											
Capital goods	4	6	16	19	23	23	25	24	21	25	26
Raw materials	75	77	61	46	38	34	32	32	34	34	37
Fuels, minerals, and metals	34	44	37	25	23	20	16	17	22	22	24
Agricultural raw materials	41	33	24	21	15	14	16	15	12	12	13
Intermediate goods	6	5	5	10	9	11	11	11	14	14	11
Foodstuffs	14	11	12	14	12	14	13	14	15	11	10
Industrial consumer goods	1	1	6	11	18	18	19	19	16	16	16

Source: Anuarul Statistic, various issues, and data provided by Romanian authorities during discussions with the authors.

Table SA4.7. *Exports, by Commodity Group and Trading Area, 1975*
(percentage)

Commodity group	CMEA *countries*	*Other socialist countries*	*Developed market economies*	*Developing countries*
Total exports	*38.8*	*7.2*	*31.0*	*23.0*
Machinery and equipment	35.4	45.4	6.6	27.8
Fuel, mineral raw materials, and metals	18.8	23.0	33.4	12.5
Chemicals, fertilizers, and rubber	6.2	23.8	7.6	18.8
Building materials	3.1	2.9	2.1	3.8
Vegetable and animal raw materials	4.9	2.0	6.5	9.8
Live animals	—	—	—	0.1
Unprocessed foodstuffs	4.1	0.2	8.0	7.1
Other foodstuffs	7.9	0.7	15.6	11.6
Industrial consumer goods	19.7	2.0	20.3	8.6

Source: Data supplied by the Romanian authorities during discussions with the authors.

Table SA4.8. *Imports, by Commodity Group and Trading Area, 1975*
(percentage)

Commodity group	CMEA *countries*	*Other socialist countries*	*Developed market economies*	*Developing countries*
Total imports	*37.2*	*6.4*	*40.5*	*15.9*
Machinery and equipment	48.9	19.4	36.3	0.8
Fuel, mineral raw materials, and metals	35.2	29.5	31.8	68.3
Chemicals, fertilizers, and rubber	3.6	4.2	10.3	4.0
Building materials	1.0	2.4	1.4	0.1
Vegetable and animal raw materials	3.9	9.7	8.1	19.9
Live animals	0.1	—	1.6	—
Unprocessed foodstuffs	0.9	3.6	9.6	2.7
Other foodstuffs	2.2	10.5	0.8	3.0
Industrial consumer goods	4.3	20.7	1.6	1.1

Source: Data supplied by the Romanian authorities during discussions with the authors.

Table SA5.1. *Items of Revenue and Expenditure of the State Budget, 1950–76*
(millions of lei)

Item	*1950*	*1955*	*1960*	*1965*
Revenue, total	*19,965.3*	*44,486.7*	*58,170.9*	*96,953.7*
Turnover tax	8,510.2	17,247.7	18,015.0	28,701.2
	(42.6)	(38.8)	(31.0)	(29.6
Regularization tax	—	—	—	—
	(—)	(—)	(—)	(—
Profit payments of state enterprises and state economic organizations	3,189.4	6,696.8	13,532.9	20,683.4
	(16.0)	(15.1)	(23.3)	(21.3
Production asset tax	—	—	—	—
	(—)	(—)	(—)	(—
Other profit payments of state units	—	—	—	—
	(—)	(—)	(—)	(—
Duties and taxes from the population	1,420.5	3,841.8	3,919.0	5,672.2
	(7.1)	(8.6)	(6.7)	(5.9
State social insurance incomes	1,059.8	2,070.9	3,573.8	5,930.5
	(5.3)	(4.7)	(6.1)	(6.1
Expenditure, total	*19,073.2*	*42,915.7*	*55,422.5*	*93,057.3*
Financing of the national economy	10,009.1	26,460.4	35,658.6	63,494.6
	(52.5)	(61.7)	(64.3)	(68.2
Science	—	452.0	857.3	1,436.0
	(—)	(1.1)	(1.5)	(1.5
Financing of sociocultural activities	3,444.9	6,539.9	13,245.7	20,925.0
	(18.1)	(15.2)	(23.9)	(22.5
National defense	3,246.4	4,226.7	3,392.1	4,734.9
	(17.0)	(9.8)	(6.1)	(5.1
Organs of state power and administration, judicial organs, and organs of the procurator's office	1,491.9	1,391.1	1,734.8	2,285.2
	(7.8)	(3.2)	(3.1)	(2.5

Note: Percentage figures are given in parentheses.
Source: Anuarul Statistic, various issues.

1970	*1971*	*1972*	*1973*	*1974*	*1975*	*1976*
33,341.5	*138,629.6*	*153,382.2*	*175,972.1*	*210,111.2*	*238,553.3*	*254,527.8*
40,543.7	44,026.0	45,086.2	48,045.8	46,006.8	42,135.5	44,946.8
(30.4)	(31.8)	(29.4)	(27.3)	(21.9)	(17.7)	(17.7)
6,136.0	9,823.6	8,670.9	8,922.7	11,023.2	7,234.1	588.1
(4.6)	(7.1)	(5.7)	(5.1)	(5.2)	(3.0)	(0.2)
28,829.1	30,296.2	37,187.3	46,622.3	44,646.8	45,538.8	54,861.1
(21.6)	(21.9)	(24.2)	(26.5)	(21.2)	(19.1)	(21.6)
—	—	—	—	22,790.3	38,569.1	42,836.4
(—)	(—)	(—)	(—)	(10.9)	(16.2)	(16.8)
—	—	—	—	37,442.8	53,053.3	48,128.2
(—)	(—)	(—)	(—)	(17.8)	(22.2)	(18.9)
11,618.8	12,875.4	13,874.0	15,382.2	17,357.7	20,200.9	23,786.2
(8.7)	(9.3)	(9.0)	(8.7)	(8.3)	(8.5)	(9.3)
8,944.5	9,605.8	10,305.4	12,422.2	14,365.2	17,198.0	21,633.4
(6.7)	(6.9)	(6.7)	(7.1)	(6.8)	(7.2)	(8.5)
30,900.2	*134,237.4*	*145,432.3*	*168,090.7*	*207,322.0*	*236,168.6*	*250,147.6*
31,019.0	78,347.8	85,121.3	101,548.7	136,152.0	155,827.7	165,733.7
(61.9)	(58.4)	(58.5)	(60.4)	(65.7)	(66.0)	(66.3)
1,923.1	2,264.6	2,459.6	2,631.9	2,896.0	3,166.8	3,387.7
(1.5)	(1.7)	(1.7)	(1.6)	(1.4)	(1.3)	(1.4)
34,019.0	36,596.1	40,131.6	44,395.8	47,686.6	50,915.9	55,252.5
(26.0)	(27.3)	(27.6)	(26.4)	(23.0)	(21.6)	(22.1)
7,066.8	7,423.6	7,709.8	7,835.4	8,743.8	9,713.2	10,574.8
(5.4)	(5.5)	(5.3)	(4.7)	(4.2)	(4.1)	(4.2)
2,457.9	2,636.8	2,613.4	2,714.5	2,701.8	2,673.9	3,003.9
(1.9)	(2.0)	(1.8)	(1.6)	(1.3)	(1.1)	(1.2)

Table SA5.2. *Revenue and Expenditure of Local Budgets, 1950–76*
(millions of lei)

	1950	*1955*	*1960*	*1965*
Revenue, total[a]	*2,209.8*	*6,532.3*	*10,897.7*	*17,359.7*
Own revenue	771.4	2,804.0	5,177.2	5,754.0
	(34.9)	(42.9)	(47.5)	(33.1)
Turnover tax	—	—	—	—
	(—)	(—)	(—)	(—)
Regularization tax	—	—	—	—
	(—)	(—)	(—)	(—)
Profit payments of enterprises and state economic organizations	325.8	760.0	1,937.1	2,434.0
	(42.2)	(27.1)	(37.4)	(42.3)
Taxes on cooperatives and public organizations' incomes[b]	—	224.0	482.1	848.8
	(—)	(8.0)	(9.3)	(14.8)
Other payments of economic enterprises	119.3	349.4	726.0	601.0
	(15.5)	(12.5)	(14.0)	(10.4)
Duties and taxes from the population	96.3	266.9	417.3	792.0
	(12.5)	(9.5)	(8.1)	(13.8)
Tax on production funds	—	—	—	—
	(—)	(—)	(—)	(—)
Expenditure	*2,077.6*	*6,126.2*	*10,363.2*	*16,893.1*
Financing of economic enterprises and organizations	2.0	804.5	633.5	1,195.6
	(0.1)	(13.1)	(6.1)	(7.1)
Municipal services	46.2	369.9	543.5	790.0
	(2.2)	(6.0)	(5.2)	(4.7)
Road and bridge maintenance and repair	65.4	259.5	227.7	610.1
	(3.1)	(4.2)	(2.2)	(3.6)
Agriculture and zootechnics	222.8	415.4	606.9	1,058.2
	(10.7)	(6.8)	(5.9)	(6.3)
Sociocultural activities	1,180.1	2,890.1	5,520.3	8,990.8
	(56.8)	(47.2)	(53.3)	(53.2)

Note: Percentage figures are given in parentheses.
a. Including allocation from republican budget.
b. Until 1968 it included taxes on land of the agricultural cooperatives.
c. Less than 0.1 percent.
Source: Anuarul Statistic, various issues.

1970	1971	1972	1973	1974	1975	1976
26,005.9	*29,018.9*	*30,782.9*	*31,946.0*	*33,859.2*	*41,890.0*	*46,555.8*
19,198.2	22,433.8	23,636.5	25,322.5	25,426.5	23,672.7	26,301.8
(73.8)	(77.3)	(76.8)	(79.3)	(75.1)	(56.5)	(56.5)
6,978.0	8,326.7	8,762.9	9,326.5	9,212.4	5,787.8	6,018.3
(36.3)	(37.1)	(37.1)	(36.8)	(36.2)	(24.4)	(22.9)
60.1	140.8	136.6	141.1	115.9	58.6	4.5
(0.3)	(0.6)	(0.6)	(0.6)	(0.5)	(0.2)	(—)[c]
3,662.3	4,247.4	4,213.9	4,633.4	4,155.7	4,143.3	3,569.6
(19.1)	(18.9)	(17.8)	(18.3)	(16.3)	(17.5)	(13.6)
685.4	729.9	872.8	979.5	1,079.9	1,006.9	876.7
(3.6)	(3.3)	(3.7)	(3.9)	(4.2)	(4.3)	(3.3)
995.1	1,253.4	1,341.6	1,326.4	1,102.8	1,029.8	1,034.1
(5.2)	(5.6)	(5.7)	(5.2)	(4.3)	(4.4)	(3.9)
4,764.3	5,215.9	5,667.9	6,202.7	6,757.4	7,349.6	8,847.6
(24.8)	(23.3)	(24.0)	(24.5)	(26.6)	(31.0)	(33.6)
—	—	—	—	—	—	2,740.1
(—)	(—)	(—)	(—)	(—)	(—)	(10.4)
23,354.0	*25,475.7*	*29,321.2*	*30,710.9*	*32,455.7*	*40,158.4*	*44,294.3*
592.6	649.0	745.8	602.5	1,723.2	3,666.8	4,482.5
(2.5)	(2.5)	(2.5)	(2.0)	(5.3)	(9.1)	(10.1)
1,669.9	2,061.3	2,112.3	1,471.3	1,523.9	1,305.6	1,449.5
(7.2)	(8.1)	(7.2)	(4.8)	(4.7)	(3.3)	(3.3)
1,279.1	1,331.3	1,445.5	1,136.6	955.0	1,013.4	1,212.2
(5.5)	(5.2)	(4.9)	(3.7)	(2.9)	(2.5)	(2.7)
1,910.1	2,164.0	2,230.9	3,358.5	2,423.1	2,667.5	2,842.3
(8.2)	(8.5)	(7.6)	(7.7)	(7.5)	(6.6)	(6.4)
12,794.0	13,842.9	14,571.2	15,496.4	16,635.3	18,180.1	20,680.4
(54.8)	(54.3)	(49.7)	(50.5)	(51.3)	(45.3)	(46.7)

Table SA5.3. *Sociocultural Expenditure, 1960, 1965, and 1970–76*
(millions of current lei)

Item	*1960*	*1965*	*1970*	*1971*	*1972*	*1973*	*1974*	*1975*	*1976*
Expenditures from state budget	13,246	20,925	34,019	36,596	40,132	44,396	47,687	50,916	55,253
Education	3,496	6,533	9,235	9,842	10,418	11,044	11,782	12,893	14,463
Culture and arts	529	737	922	981	999	944	980	929	1,019
Health	2,955	4,795	6,930	7,386	7,817	8,434	9,178	9,853	11,182
Social assistance and pensions	990	884	1,250	1,279	1,318	1,509	1,548	1,600	1,648
Physical education and sports	10	66	187	204	212	192	236	275	333
Children's allowances	1,726	2,715	4,232	5,023	6,561	6,923	7,289	7,364	7,402
State social insurance	3,540	5,195	11,263	11,881	12,808	15,350	16,674	18,002	19,205
Local expenditure	5,520	8,991	12,794	13,843	14,571	15,496	16,635	18,180	20,680
Total	*18,766*	*29,916*	*46,813*	*50,439*	*54,703*	*59,892*	*64,322*	*69,096*	*75,933*

Source: Anuarul Statistic, various issues.

Table SA6.1. *Average Annual Percentage Growth Rates of Gross Industrial Production, 1951–55 to 1975–76*

Industrial subsector	*1951–55*	*1956–60*	*1961–65*	*1966–70*	*Plan, 1971–75*	*Actual, 1971–75*	*1975–76*
Total industry	*15.2*	*10.9*	*13.8*	*11.9*	*11.0–12.0*	*12.9*	*11.4*
Electric power	18.4	12.7	20.6	16.6	10.8–11.8	9.8	9.4
Fuels	13.3	7.6	8.1	6.0	6.0– 7.1	5.3	7.8
Ferrous metallurgy, including ferrous ores	8.8	19.8	11.4	12.3	9.0– 9.9	11.3	11.1
Ferrous metallurgy only	8.5	20.2	11.7	12.3	9.0– 9.9	11.5	11.6
Nonferrous metallurgy, including nonferrous ores	16.4	12.7	13.4	12.4	9.0–10.4	10.0	7.5
Engineering and metalworks	22.7	16.1	16.9	15.8	14.1–15.6	18.1	12.2
Mechanical engineering	22.3	21.0	16.1	15.9	14.1–15.6	19.8	13.0
Electrical engineering	28.4	19.8	26.1	20.4	14.1–15.6	21.8	10.4
Metalworks	25.6	11.8	17.0	19.6	14.1–15.6	13.8	11.0
Repairs and maintenance	19.4	6.2	13.4	6.4	14.1–15.6	7.3	12.0
Chemicals	24.0	17.5	25.5	21.4	16.2–17.5	15.8	16.3
Construction materials	20.3	10.2	16.0	13.0	12.8–14.2	10.0	14.3
Lumber and wood processing	12.7	8.0	13.1	6.5	2.8– 3.5	6.4	4.4
Wood processing only	12.7	11.7	15.1	9.0	n.a.	7.9	6.2
Pulp and paper	6.5	10.9	19.1	14.3	n.a.	9.1	9.7
Textiles	11.7	6.2	10.5	11.1	n.a.	12.1	16.4
Clothing	8.4	10.0	11.2	12.4	n.a.	17.1	11.4
Leather, furs, and footwear	11.3	7.6	10.2	9.5	n.a.	9.1	10.3
Food processing	11.1	7.1	8.5	6.5	9.3–10.4	7.4	9.8
Soap and cosmetics	17.6	4.3	8.5	9.3	9.3–10.4	10.7	11.4
Printing	16.0	10.8	14.8	7.1	9.3–10.4	1.7	8.3
Group A	16.8	12.8	15.7	12.9	9.3–10.4	13.7	11.6
Group B	13.1	8.4	10.5	9.8	9.3–10.4	11.1	11.8

Note: Data are calculated from index series of gross industrial production expressed in 1963 comparable prices.
Sources: Anuarul Statistic, various issues, and data supplied by the Romanian authorities during discussions with the authors.

Table SA6.2. *Structure of Gross Industrial Production, 1950–76*

(percentage)

Industrial subsector	1955 prices				1963 prices				
	1950	*1955*	*1960*	*1965*	*1965*	*1970*	*1974*	*1975*	*1976*
Electric power	1.9	2.2	2.5	3.2	2.6	3.2	2.7	2.7	2.6
Fuel	11.3	10.9	9.1	7.0	7.0	5.3	3.9	3.6	3.5
Coal and coke	3.3	2.7	2.5	1.9	1.9	1.6	1.3	1.2	1.1
Petroleum and methane gas	8.0	8.2	6.6	5.1	5.1	3.7	2.6	2.4	2.4
Ferrous metallurgy[a]	5.4	4.2	6.3	5.6	8.3	8.5	7.7	7.9	7.8
Ferrous metallurgy only	5.1	4.0	6.1	5.5	8.1	8.2	7.6	7.8	7.7
Nonferrous metallurgy[b]	2.1	2.3	2.1	2.1	3.2	3.3	2.7	2.8	2.6
Engineering and metalworks	13.3	18.8	24.0	28.3	21.2	25.0	30.5	32.4	33.3
Mechanical engineering	6.3	9.0	14.6	16.5	11.9	14.1	18.3	20.4	21.5
Electrical engineering	0.9	1.5	2.4	4.1	2.9	4.2	5.5	6.1	6.1
Metalworks	2.2	3.5	2.9	3.4	2.9	4.0	4.1	3.9	3.8
Repairs and maintenance	3.9	4.8	4.1	4.3	3.5	2.7	2.6	2.0	1.9
Chemicals	3.1	4.7	6.1	10.0	6.7	10.1	11.2	11.3	11.7

Construction materials	2.4	3.2	3.2	3.6	3.3	3.4	3.1	3.1	3.1
Lumber and wood processing	9.9	8.9	7.5	7.1	8.2	6.4	5.0	4.7	4.4
Wood processing only	5.5	5.1	5.1	5.3	5.9	5.2	4.3	4.1	3.9
Pulp and paper	1.3	0.9	1.0	1.2	1.2	1.4	1.2	1.2	1.1
Textiles	11.1	10.0	7.9	6.8	7.4	7.2	7.3	6.8	7.0
Clothing	7.5	5.9	5.6	5.0	4.2	4.3	5.2	5.1	5.0
Leather, furs, and footwear	4.0	3.5	2.8	2.4	2.4	2.1	1.9	1.9	1.9
Food processing	24.2	21.7	18.9	14.8	22.0	17.3	14.2	13.1	12.7
Other	2.5	2.8	3.0	2.9	2.3	2.5	3.4	3.4	3.3
Group A	53.0	55.8	62.9	70.0	65.2	70.5	71.0	72.3	72.5
Group B	47.0	44.2	37.1	30.0	34.8	29.5	29.0	27.7	27.5

a. Includes mining of ferrous ores.
b. Includes mining of nonferrous ores.
Source: Anuarul Statistic, various issues.

Table SA6.3. *Output of Selected Industrial Products, 1950–76*

Code	*Product*	*1950*	*1955*
01.03	Ferrous metallurgy[a]		
	Iron ore, 30–35 percent iron (thousands of tonnes)	392	63
	Pig iron (thousands of tonnes)	320	57
	Raw steel (thousands of tonnes)	555	76
	Rolled steel products, except tubes (thousands of tonnes)	402	49
	Steel tubes (thousands of tonnes)	58	6
01.04	Nonferrous metallurgy[b]		
	Aluminum and aluminum alloys (thousands of tonnes)	—	–
01.05.01	Mechanical engineering		
	Industrial steam boilers (units)	310	64
	(tonnes of steam per hour)	740	1,26
	Internal combustion engines (units)	4,853	12,36
	(thousands of horsepower)	179	72
	Metalworking machinery (units)	—	2,08
	(tonnes)	—	2,09
	Excavators (units)	—	
	Tractors (units)	3,469	3,50
	Grain combines (units)	50	–
	Diesel and electric locomotives (units)	—	–
	Motor lorries and motor tractors (units)	—	2,86
	Motor cars (units)	—	–
	Bearings (thousands)	217	1,66
01.05.02	Electrical engineering		
	Electric motors 0.25 kilowatts and over (thousands of kilowatts)	94	14
	Electric generators (1,000 kilovolts)	16	5
	Electric transformers 0.25 kilovolts and over (thousands of kilovolts)	205	30
	Radio sets (thousands)	40	8
	Television sets (thousands)	—	–
	Household washing machines (thousands)	—	–
	Refrigerators (thousands)	—	–
01.06	Chemicals		
	Soda ash, 100 percent (thousands of tonnes)	38	5
	Caustic soda, 100 percent (thousands of tonnes)	15	2
	Sulfuric acid, 100 percent (thousands of tonnes)	52	9
	Chemical fertilizers, 100 percent active substances (thousands of tonnes)	1	1

1960	1965	1970	1971	1972	1973	1974	1975	1976
1,460	2,479	3,206	3,467	3,361	3,234	3,265	3,065	2,835
1,014	2,019	4,210	4,382	4,890	5,713	6,081	6,602	7,415
1,806	3,426	6,517	6,803	7,401	8,161	8,848	9,549	10,733
1,254	2,347	4,504	4,763	5,230	5,833	6,253	6,810	7,305
338	586	767	825	880	902	973	1,151	1,213
—	9	101	111	122	141	187	204	207
183	232	648	533	568	298	615	641	528
260	662	2,992	2,823	2,555	3,884	4,255	6,139	6,821
35,276	49,998	95,035	102,136	137,259	166,081	182,686	202,161	210,287
2,603	4,751	9,442	10,239	12,319	13,964	15,353	17,467	17,886
4,441	7,163	14,138	15,058	15,988	20,547	24,834	28,267	29,889
6,420	11,433	23,156	26,578	31,101	35,987	42,474	56,746	65,297
127	465	732	658	693	983	1,162	1,210	1,325
17,102	15,836	29,287	30,400	34,883	38,800	44,550	50,003	53,911
5,500	5,012	1,179	1,317	2,060	2,903	5,315	5,659	5,198
10	110	265	266	286	311	343	334	247
8,383	14,306	35,018	35,164	36,100	34,903	31,547	35,965	33,875
1,200	3,653	23,604	29,602	38,501	60,210	67,507	68,013	71,107
4,553	13,572	24,487	26,115	28,355	31,094	50,257	70,577	72,660
559	1,255	2,834	3,397	4,136	4,682	5,465	6,521	6,265
83	295	747	523	482	913	976	1,479	2,234
1,577	4,138	8,775	9,779	11,108	16,396	18,284	15,973	15,434
167	323	455	484	527	623	602	712	791
—	101	280	300	324	397	451	512	548
38	75	131	131	141	152	162	178	199
11	125	135	192	196	222	279	332	376
180	350	582	601	665	677	807	693	814
74	233	330	344	380	383	444	566	673
226	541	994	1,047	1,162	1,311	1,358	1,448	1,555
71	293	895	1,082	1,200	1,242	1,410	1,729	1,869

(Table continues on the following pages)

Table SA6.3. *Continued*

Code	*Product*	*1950*	*195*[illegible]
	Phosphatic fertilizers (thousands of tonnes)	1	
	Nitrogenous fertilizers (thousands of tonnes)	—	
	Chemical fibers and yarns (thousands of tonnes)	2	
	Synthetic rubber (thousands of tonnes)	—	—
	Plastic and synthetic resins (thousands of tonnes)	0.4	
	Tires (thousands)	217	41[illegible]
	For motor vehicles (thousands)	74	1[illegible]
01.08	Construction materials		
	Cement (thousands of tonnes)	1,028	1,9[illegible]
	Bricks and ceramic blocks (millions)	371	6[illegible]
	Prefabricated concrete parts (thousands of cubic meters)	—	1[illegible]
01.09	Wood products		
	Plywood (thousands of cubic meters)	15	[illegible]
	Veneer (thousands of square meters)	1,265	4,2[illegible]
	Chipboard (thousands of tonnes)	—	—
01.10	Pulp and paper		
	Cellulose and semicellulose, 100 percent dryness (thousands of tonnes)	59	[illegible]
	Paper (thousands of tonnes)	86	1[illegible]
	Newsprint (thousands of tonnes)	30	[illegible]
01.11	Glass, porcelain, and crockery		
	Window glass of 2 millimeter thickness (thousands of square meters)	—	8,0[illegible]
01.12	Textiles		
	Cotton yarns (thousands of tonnes)	29	[illegible]
	Woolen yarns (thousands of tonnes)	13	[illegible]
	Cotton fabrics (millions of square meters)	148	2[illegible]
	Woolen fabrics (millions of square meters)	23	[illegible]
	Knitwear (millions of units)	13	[illegible]
01.14	Leather and footwear		
	Shoes (millions of pairs)	11.2	17[illegible]
	Leather shoes (millions of pairs)	8.7	10[illegible]
01.15.16	Other products		
	Meat (thousands of tonnes)	140	2[illegible]
	Meat products (thousands of tonnes)	10	[illegible]
	Butter (tonnes)	2,261	6,8[illegible]
	Sugar (thousands of tonnes)	87	1[illegible]
	Beer (thousands of hectoliters)	871	1,3[illegible]
	Soap (thousands of tonnes)	17	[illegible]

a. Includes mining of ferrous ores. b. Includes mining of nonferrous ores.

Source: Anuarul Statistic, various issues.

1960	1965	1970	1971	1972	1973	1974	1975	1976
52	127	244	245	313	361	404	404	493
19	166	647	827	874	854	980	1,292	1,331
4	21	77	95	100	116	159	159	179
—	31	61	71	73	83	92	99	95
12	75	206	251	274	302	283	347	465
743	2,492	3,444	3,419	3,393	3,901	4,296	4,526	5,083
337	1,222	2,457	2,647	2,946	3,249	3,517	3,703	4,115
3,054	5,406	8,127	8,523	9,212	9,848	11,195	11,520	12,548
627	1,027	1,705	1,750	1,733	1,944	1,954	1,833	1,686
219	895	2,284	2,811	3,243	3,414	3,704	4,150	4,658
68	200	246	244	243	249	263	269	275
11,772	24,512	49,989	53,173	54,732	56,011	59,865	66,096	71,885
31	124	204	265	330	382	467	535	578
91	233	445	453	456	482	574	575	610
140	244	431	447	457	480	514	518	549
44	52	53	53	53	53	53	44	77
18,817	28,805	45,215	60,399	63,854	66,445	68,251	66,757	71,003
52	78	109	121	130	144	157	145	165
19	25	36	38	41	46	49	51	56
248	319	437	482	531	571	612	591	677
32	41	63	70	74	83	94	96	105
41	78	140	169	189	208	226	204	246
30.2	42.6	65.8	71.4	78.9	85.4	90.8	86.9	95.7
19.6	29.0	40.4	41.9	45.4	50.2	54.8	51.6	54.9
270	308	425	418	490	584	671	714	815
48	59	104	118	137	141	160	181	212
12,591	21,753	30,713	29,514	32,499	34,327	30,320	33,003	38,273
391	402	377	484	520	628	516	516	561
1,633	2,665	4,375	4,951	5,051	5,621	6,480	7,449	7,625
37	46	42	44	45	54	64	55	53

Table SA6.4. *Size Structure of Subsectors of Republican Industry, 1960–75*

Industrial subsector	*Year* *(1)*	*Number of enter-prises* *(2)*	*Employ-ment* *(3)*	*Column 3 ÷ column 2* *(4)*
Fuels	1960	27	85,842	3,179
	1965	26	99,542	3,829
	1970	54	94,677	1,753
	1974	49	96,996	1,980
	1975	50	97,352	1,947
Ferrous metallurgy[a]	1960	18	67,465	3,748
	1965	17	67,010	3,942
	1970	19	84,611	4,453
	1974	20	95,100	4,755
	1975	23	104,720	4,553
Nonferrous metallurgy[b]	1960	17	33,323	1,960
	1965	18	58,991	3,277
	1970	19	62,571	3,293
	1974	25	73,091	2,924
	1975	26	74,334	2,859
Engineering and metalworks	1960	199	241,097	1,212
	1965	190	351,563	1,850
	1970	214	460,520	2,152
	1974	263	699,298	2,659
	1975	267	774,521	2,901
Chemicals	1960	57	45,856	804
	1965	63	82,398	1,308
	1970	65	118,246	1,819
	1974	70	150,246	2,146
	1975	69	161,809	2,345
Construction materials	1960	65	37,615	579
	1965	66	51,423	779
	1970	68	59,457	874
	1974	75	67,258	897
	1975	76	70,158	923
Wood exploitation and processing	1960	130	154,181	1,186
	1965	136	215,290	1,583
	1970	120	219,396	1,828
	1974	131	219,011	1,672
	1975	129	217,180	1,684

a. Including mining and dressing of ferrous ores.
b. Including mining and dressing of nonferrous ores.
Source: Anuarul Statistic, various issues.

Table SA6.4. *Continued*

Industrial subsector	*Year* *(1)*	*Number of enter-prises* *(2)*	*Employ-ment* *(3)*	*Column 3 ÷ column 2* *(4)*
Pulp and paper	1960	16	12,511	782
	1965	17	22,920	1,348
	1970	18	25,363	1,409
	1974	18	29,124	1,618
	1975	18	30,062	1,670
Glass and ceramics	1960	19	15,658	824
	1965	19	20,653	1,087
	1970	19	25,259	1,329
	1974	20	33,879	1,694
	1975	23	36,564	1,590
Textiles	1960	125	127,228	1,018
	1965	120	157,101	1,309
	1970	127	190,166	1,497
	1974	147	252,051	1,715
	1975	154	258,254	1,677
Leather, furs, and footwear	1960	36	33,783	938
	1965	34	41,416	1,218
	1970	35	54,615	1,560
	1974	38	64,547	1,699
	1975	38	64,971	1,710
Food processing	1960	207	79,346	383
	1965	262	125,926	481
	1970	263	103,902	395
	1974	248	118,868	479
	1975	250	120,843	483
Printing	1960	18	13,233	735
	1965	26	19,967	768
	1970	24	19,169	799
	1974	27	18,891	700
	1975	27	18,302	678
Total, republican industry	*1960*	*1,001*	*1,003,366*	*1,002*
	1965	*1,065*	*1,409,276*	*1,323*
	1970	*1,126*	*1,628,933*	*1,447*
	1974	*1,251*	*2,071,700*	*1,656*
	1975	*1,276*	*2,190,605*	*1,717*
Total industry, republican and local	*1960*	*1,658*	*1,241,025*	*748*
	1965	*1,572*	*1,648,401*	*1,049*
	1970	*1,731*	*1,996,803*	*1,154*
	1974	*1,699*	*2,564,972*	*1,510*
	1975	*1,731*	*2,690,614*	*1,554*

Table SA6.5. *Sector Allocation of Industrial Investment, 1950–76*
(millions of lei)

Industrial subsector	*1950*[a]	*1955*[a]	*1960*[a]	*1965*[a]	*1965*[b]	*1970*[b]
Total industry	*2,751*	*7,685*	*11,828*	*22,321*	*22,986*	*37,961*
Electric power	267	885	1,175	4,059	3,895	5,771
	(9.7)	(11.5)	(9.9)	(18.2)	(16.9)	(15.2)
Fuels	1,342	2,731	3,239	4,195	4,945	5,211
	(48.8)	(35.5)	(27.4)	(18.8)	(21.5)	(13.7)
Ferrous metallurgy[c]	184	667	812	2,618	2,665	3,406
	(6.7)	(8.7)	(6.9)	(11.7)	(11.6)	(9.0)
Nonferrous metallurgy[c]	66	565	480	1,542	1,571	1,120
	(2.4)	(7.4)	(4.0)	(6.9)	(6.8)	(3.0)
Engineering and metalworks	203	486	1,049	1,546	1,551	7,525
	(7.4)	(6.3)	(8.9)	(6.9)	(6.7)	(19.8)
Chemicals	91	497	1,521	2,787	2,820	4,284
	(3.3)	(6.5)	(12.9)	(12.5)	(12.3)	(11.3)
Construction materials	104	341	278	882	895	2,124
	(3.8)	(4.4)	(2.3)	(4.0)	(3.9)	(5.6)
Lumber and woodworking	110	531	855	1,365	1,335	1,697
	(4.0)	(6.9)	(7.2)	(6.1)	(5.8)	(4.5)
Pulp and paper	36	43	708	1,245	1,244	583
	(1.3)	(0.6)	(6.0)	(5.6)	(5.4)	(1.5)
Textiles	107	142	354	545	543	1,388
	(3.9)	(1.8)	(3.0)	(2.4)	(2.4)	(3.7)
Clothing	1	8	46	90	91	204
	(0.0)	(0.1)	(0.4)	(0.4)	(0.4)	(0.5)
Leather, furs, and footwear	17	21	86	107	105	157
	(0.6)	(0.3)	(0.7)	(0.5)	(0.5)	(0.4)
Food processing	143	573	989	958	945	2,438
	(5.2)	(7.5)	(8.4)	(4.3)	(4.1)	(6.4)
Soap and cosmetics	3	4	3	1	1	9
	(0.1)	(—)[d]	(—)[d]	(—)[d]	(—)[d]	(—)[d]
Printing	44	60	24	34	33	90
	(0.6)	(0.8)	(0.2)	(0.2)	(0.1)	(0.2)
Other	33	131	209	347	347	1,954
	(1.2)	(1.7)	(1.8)	(1.5)	(1.5)	(5.2)
Group A, producer goods	(86.2)	(83.1)	(85.0)	(90.6)	(91.0)	(84.7)
Group B, consumer goods	(13.8)	(16.9)	(15.0)	(9.4)	(9.0)	(15.3)

Note: Figures in parentheses represent percentage of total industry for year indicated.
a. In 1959 prices. b. In 1963 prices. c. Includes mining of ores. d. Less than 0.1 percent.
Source: Anuarul Statistic, various issues, and data supplied by Romanian authorities during discussions with the authors.

Industrial subsector	*1971*[b]	*1972*[b]	*1973*[b]	*1974*[b]	*1975*[b]	*1976*[b]
Total industry	*42,850*	*49,257*	*56,033*	*61,274*	*67,829*	*70,723*
Electric power	6,325	6,394	7,329	8,313 (13.6)	9,555 (14.1)	9,974 (14.1)
Fuels	5,619	5,981	6,427	7,558 (12.3)	9,257 (13.6)	10,111 (14.3)
Ferrous metallurgy[c]	3,025	3,154	4,297	6,216 (10.1)	7,671 (11.3)	7,550 (10.7)
Nonferrous metallurgy[c]	1,649	2,332	2,336	1,862 (3.0)	1,966 (2.9)	2,556 (3.6)
Engineering and metalworks	8,345	9,745	11,662	12,913 (21.1)	13,289 (19.6)	15,066 (21.3)
Chemicals	5,801	8,620	9,735	9,714 (15.9)	10,005 (14.7)	9,091 (12.9)
Construction materials	2,638	2,993	3,184	2,632 (4.3)	2,998 (4.4)	3,164 (4.5)
Lumber and woodworking	1,660	1,581	1,937	2,116 (3.5)	2,268 (3.3)	2,252 (3.2)
Pulp and paper	799	1,143	1,043	772 (1.3)	1,072 (1.6)	473 (0.7)
Textiles	1,882	2,178	2,549	2,399 (3.9)	2,395 (3.5)	2,499 (3.5)
Clothing	200	327	401	484 (0.8)	382 (0.6)	260 (0.4)
Leather, furs, and footwear	187	173	126	330 (0.5)	314 (0.5)	307 (0.4)
Food processing	2,797	2,891	2,967	4,145 (6.8)	4,443 (6.6)	4,952 (7.0)
Soap and cosmetics	16	13	41	43 (—)[d]	106 (0.2)	39 (—)[d]
Printing	84	74	82	147 (0.2)	120 (0.2)	90 (0.1)
Other	1,823	1,658	1,917	1,630 (2.7)	1,988 (2.9)	2,399 (3.4)
Group A, producer goods				(81.3)	(85.2)	(84.4)
Group B, consumer goods				(18.7)	(14.8)	(15.6)

Table SA6.6. *Size Distribution of Industrial Enterprises*

Item	Number of workers						
	Up to 200	*201–500*	*501–1,000*	*1,001–2,000*	*2,001–3,000*	*3,001–5,000*	*Over 5,000*
Number of enterprises							
1960	27.8	35.5	21.2	10.1	3.1	1.3	1.0
1965	17.0	30.8	25.6	17.1	5.1	2.9	1.5
1970	14.7	27.4	25.9	20.3	6.2	3.8	1.7
1975	10.0	20.6	24.0	24.5	10.5	6.9	3.5
Number of workers							
1960	5.2	18.4	22.9	21.8	11.7	7.5	12.5
1965	2.4	11.2	20.1	26.6	13.5	11.9	14.3
1970	1.8	9.2	18.4	28.2	14.7	13.4	14.3
1975	0.9	5.0	12.4	24.6	17.9	18.1	21.1
Fixed assets							
1960	27.8	35.5	21.2	10.1	3.1	1.3	1.0
1965	17.0	30.8	25.6	17.1	5.1	2.9	1.5
1970	14.7	27.4	25.9	20.3	6.2	3.8	1.7
1975	10.0	20.6	24.0	24.5	10.5	6.9	3.5
Gross industrial production							
1960	5.3	20.5	22.0	20.0	12.7	6.8	12.7
1965	2.2	12.9	20.9	24.3	13.8	11.6	14.3
1970	3.2	10.0	16.8	25.8	13.0	12.9	18.3
1975	1.7	6.0	10.4	20.0	16.6	18.7	26.6

Source: Anuarul Statistic, various issues.

Table SA6.7. *Composition of Gross Investment in Industry, 1950–76*

Industrial sector	1950	1955	1960	1965	1965	1970	1971	1972	1973	1974	1975	1976
	(millions of 1959 lei)				(millions of 1963 lei)							
Total industry	*2,751*	*7,685*	*11,828*	*22,321*	*22,986*	*37,961*	*42,850*	*49,257*	*56,033*	*61,274*	*67,829*	*70,723*
Group A	2,372	6,387	10,051	20,233	20,923	32,139	35,976	41,751	45,999	49,821	57,787	59,671
Group B	379	1,298	1,777	2,088	2,063	5,822	6,874	7,506	10,034	11,453	10,042	11,052
Construction works			5,784	10,487	10,756	17,183	19,673	21,726	24,119	24,594	26,186	27,246
Group A			4,951	9,543	9,809	14,471	16,780	18,579	19,689	20,236	22,126	23,264
Group B			833	944	947	2,712	2,893	3,147	4,430	4,358	4,060	3,982
Machinery and other equipment			3,882	8,175	8,188	15,446	16,959	21,428	25,820	30,282	34,714	35,623
Group A			3,030	7,163	7,200	12,652	13,392	17,471	20,821	23,774	29,204	29,146
Group B			852	1,012	988	2,794	3,567	3,957	4,999	6,508	5,510	6,477
Other investments[a]					4,042	5,332	6,218	6,103	6,094	6,398	6,929	7,854

a. Includes exploration, prospecting, expenditure for investment analysis, training of construction workers, expenditure for management, and supervision of project implementation.

Source: Anuarul Statistic, various issues.

Table SA6.8. *Investment per Job Created, by Industrial Subsector, 1951–55 to 1971–75*

(thousands of lei per job)

Industrial subsector	*1951–55*	*1956–60*	*1961–65*	*1966–70*	*1971–*
Total industry (average)	*123*	*263*	*221*	*424*	*37*
Electric power	870	5,366	674	5,536	13,07
Fuels	519	9,952[b]	1,769	—[c]	7,57
Ferrous metallurgy[a]	287	322	765	1,522	1,47
Ferrous metallurgy only	—	—	—	—	—
Nonferrous metallurgy[d]	451	186	290	802	8
Engineering and metalworks	39	58	72	172	1
Chemicals	130	337	350	514	7
Nonmetallic minerals	109	205	86	660	5
Construction materials	76	670	173	421	1,2
Lumber and wood processing	33	361	97	339	4
Pulp and paper	—[c]	405	388	571	7
Glass and ceramics	69	60	78	458	1
Textiles	28	61	79	136	1
Clothing	3	7	17	23	[illegible]
Leather, furs, and footwear	20	25	60	59	[illegible]
Food processing	71	567	140	446	4
Printing	92	63	65	—[c]	[illegible]
Other	263	128	851	981	6

Note: 1951–65 in 1959 prices, 1966–75 in 1963 prices.

a. Including mining and dressing of ferrous ores.

b. Reflecting mainly investments in petroleum development and exploitation.

c. Subsectors showing absolute declines in employment.

d. Including mining and dressing of nonferrous ores.

Sources: Anuarul Statistic, various issues, and World Bank calculations.

ıble SA6.9. *Increases in Industrial Employment during the Five-Year Periods ıce 1950, by Industrial Subsector*
ıousands)

Industrial subsector	*1951–55*	*1956–60*	*1961–65*	*1966–70*	*1971–75*
ɔtal industry	*270.8*	*170.9*	*420.4*	*390.4*	*736.1*
ectric power	5.1	0.8	18.4	4.4	2.9
ıels	24.0	1.4	11.0	−0.7	4.6
rrous metallurgy[a]	8.9	13.2	12.5	11.0	16.5
Ferrous metallurgy only	7.9	11.6	11.4	10.8	16.5
ɔnferrous metallurgy[b]	4.3	13.1	20.1	7.3	12.6
ıgineering and metalworks	65.6	53.8	113.7	140.4	365.8
ıemicals	16.8	15.1	37.4	44.3	57.0
ɔnmetallic minerals	1.5	1.3	2.3	1.9	2.7
ɔnstruction materials	20.9	2.3	21.4	17.7	11.8
ımber and wood processing	56.7	8.5	64.9	23.1	20.2
lp and paper	−0.1	4.3	11.5	4.2	6.2
ass and ceramics	2.1	5.1	5.4	5.6	14.1
xtiles	22.6	16.7	32.2	48.0	94.4
othing	9.4	15.4	23.8	35.9	60.7
ather, furs, and footwear	4.4	8.2	8.1	20.1	18.1
od processing	23.3	5.2	33.7	24.1	39.2
ap and cosmetics	−0.1	0.4	0.4	0.2	1.7
inting	4.7	2.9	3.0	−0.5	−1.1
her	0.7	3.2	0.6	3.4	8.7

ı. Including mining and dressing of ferrous ores.
ɔ. Including mining and dressing of nonferrous ores.
ource: Anuarul Statistic, various issues.

Table SA6.10. *Average Annual Growth Rates of Labor Productivity, by Industrial Subsector*

Industrial subsector	*1950–75*	*1965–75*	*1970–75*
Total industry	*7.9*	*6.8*	*6.4*
Electric energy	11.7	11.1	8.3
Fuels	5.6	5.2	4.3
Ferrous metallurgy[a]	8.3	8.4	8.1
Ferrous metallurgy only	8.2	8.3	8.0
Nonferrous metallurgy[b]	5.5	8.0	5.9
Engineering and metalworks	11.0	8.3	7.4
Chemicals	10.8	9.9	7.7
Construction materials	9.3	7.4	6.4
Lumber and wood processing	6.4	4.9	4.8
Pulp and paper	6.4	7.8	5.1
Textiles	5.5	5.2	4.6
Clothing	6.8	6.6	8.1
Leather, furs, and footwear	7.0	4.5	5.2
Food processing	4.5	3.0	3.2

Note: Labor productivity is defined as gross industrial production per employee.

a. Including mining and dressing of ferrous ores.

b. Including mining and dressing of nonferrous ores.

Source: Anuarul Statistic, various issues.

Table SA6.11. *Industrial Exports, by Commodity Categories, 1960–75*
(millions of U.S. dollars)

Year	*Equipment goods*	*Industrial materials*	*Consumer goods*	*Total industrial exports*	*Total exports*
1960	119.6	401.8	121.6	642.9	717.0
	(18.6)	(62.5)	(18.9)	(100.0)	
1965	205.3	533.2	241.8	980.3	1,101.5
	(20.9)	(54.4)	(24.7)	(100.0)	
1970	422.4	781.0	521.5	1,724.9	1,850.8
	(24.5)	(45.3)	(30.2)	(100.0)	
1971	485.3	841.8	607.5	1,934.6	2,101.0
	(25.1)	(43.5)	(31.4)	(100.0)	
1972	646.6	926.1	783.7	2,356.3	2,599.1
	(27.4)	(39.3)	(33.3)	(100.0)	
1973	913.2	1,324.8	1,133.2	3,371.3	3,737.6
	(27.1)	(39.3)	(33.6)	(100.0)	
1974	1,002.9	2,087.5	1,416.6	4,507.0	4,874.4
	(22.3)	(46.3)	(31.4)	(100.0)	
1975	1,352.6	2,234.8	1,335.7	4,923.1	5,341.4
	(27.5)	(45.4)	(27.1)	(100.0)	

Note: In accordance with the Romanian definition of industry, industrial exports also include electric energy, fuels, and other mining products (largely included in "industrial materials"). Percentage figures are given in parentheses.

Source: Ministry of Foreign Trade and International Cooperation; data supplied during discussions with the authors.

Table SA6.12. *Volume and Percentage of Industrial Exports, by Branch of Industry, 1960, 1965, 1970, and 1975*

(volume in millions of U.S. dollars)

Code	Industrial subsector	1960		1965		1970		1975	
		Volume	*Percentage*	*Volume*	*Percentage*	*Volume*	*Percentage*	*Volume*	*Percentage*
01.01–01.18	*Total industrial exports*	*642.9*	*100.0*	*980.3*	*100.0*	*1,724.9*	*100.0*	*4,923.1*	*100.0*
01.01	Electrical energy	0.6	0.1	6.7	0.7	28.1	1.6	44.8	0.9
01.02	Fuels[a]	175.6	27.3	143.9	14.7	128.9	7.5	550.3	11.2
01.03	Ferrous metallurgy[b]	66.2	10.3	111.0	11.3	223.7	13.0	486.8	9.9
01.04	Nonferrous metallurgy[b]	4.4	0.7	8.2	0.8	37.0	2.1	98.4	2.0
01.05	Engineering and metalworks	59.6	9.3	113.0	11.5	199.6	11.6	662.8	13.5
	Machine tools	1.0	0.2	4.8	0.5	11.5	0.7	51.9	1.1
	Ships and naval equipment	12.2	1.9	17.4	1.8	39.6	2.3	99.5	2.0
	Equipment for petroleum industry	14.7	2.3	39.6	4.0	44.7	2.6	143.4	2.9
	Equipment for chemical industry	1.5	0.2	13.5	1.4	8.2	0.5	39.4	0.8
	Equipment for cement industry	9.5	1.5	0.6	0.1	1.9	0.1	8.7	0.2

01.06	Chemicals	15.6	2.4	70.9	7.2	129.7	7.5	574.8	11.7
01.07	Nonmetallic minerals	0.2	0	0.8	0.1	1.7	0.1	8.7	0.2
01.08	Construction materials	18.0	2.8	37.4	3.8	47.6	2.8	155.3	3.1
01.09	Lumber and wood processing	91.7	14.3	129.5	13.2	134.5	7.8	213.9	4.3
01.10	Pulp and paper	1.7	0.3	8.7	0.9	24.5	1.4	56.2	1.1
01.11	Glass and ceramics	2.2	0.3	2.0	0.2	3.5	0.2	15.2	0.3
01.12	Textiles	8.8	1.4	12.0	1.2	27.7	1.6	89.1	1.8
01.13	Clothing	8.4	1.3	30.4	3.1	81.7	4.7	165.8	3.4
01.14	Leather and footwear	3.4	0.5	11.3	1.2	49.1	2.8	93.9	1.9
01.15	Food processing	80.2	12.5	120.4	12.3	186.1	10.8	474.8	9.6
01.16	Soap and cosmetics	0	0	0	0	1.0	0.1	13.5	0.3
01.17	Printing	2.7	0.4	2.6	0.3	5.0	0.3	3.7	0.1
01.18	Others[c]	103.6	16.1	171.5	17.5	415.1	24.1	1,215.1	24.7

a. Includes petroleum products.
b. Includes mining of ores.
c. Not elsewhere included.
Sources: Ministry of Foreign Trade and International Cooperation and *Anuarul Statistic*, various issues.

Table SA6.13. *Relation of Gross Industrial Production and Exports, 1970 and 19*

Code	Subsector of industry	1970		
		Gross industrial production[a] *(1)*	*Exports (2)*	*(2) ÷ (per cent (3)*
01.01–01.18	*Total industry*	*15,973.8*	*1,724.9*	*10.8*
01.01	Electrical energy	511.2	28.1	5.5
01.02+ 01.06	Fuels and chemicals	2,460.0	258.6	10.5
01.03	Ferrous metallurgy, including ferrous ores	1,357.8	223.7	16.5
01.04	Nonferrous metallurgy, including nonferrous ores	527.1	37.0	7.0
01.05+ 01.18	Engineering, metalworks, and other nontraditional activities	4,185.1	614.7	14.7
01.07	Nonmetallic minerals	31.9	1.7	5.3
01.08	Construction materials	543.1	47.6	8.8
01.09	Lumber and wood processing	1,022.3	134.5	13.2
01.10	Pulp and paper	223.6	24.9	11.1
01.11	Glass and ceramics	95.8	3.5	3.7
01.12	Textiles	1,150.1	27.7	2.4
01.13	Clothing	686.9	81.7	11.9
01.14	Leather and footwear	335.4	49.1	14.6
01.15	Food processing	2,763.5	186.1	6.7
01.16	Soap and cosmetics	31.9	1.0	0.[illegible]
01.17	Printing	48.1	5.0	10.4

a. Converted from volumes expressed in comparable 1963 prices at a rate of 20 lei per U.S. lar; subsector totals are approximations.

Source: Anuarul Statistic, various issues; Ministry of Foreign Trade and International Coop tion; and World Bank calculations.

Code	Subsector of industry	1975 Gross industrial production[a] (4)	Exports (5)	(5) ÷ (4) (percent) (6)
01–18	*Total industry*	*29,343.9*	*4,923.1*	*16.8*
01	Electrical energy	792.3	44.8	5.7
02+06	Fuels and chemicals	4,372.3	1,125.1	25.7
03	Ferrous metallurgy, including ferrous ores	2,318.2	486.8	21.0
04	Nonferrous metallurgy, including nonferrous ores	821.6	98.4	12.0
05+18	Engineering, metalworks, and other nontraditional activities	10,123.6	1,877.9	18.5
07	Nonmetallic minerals	88.0	8.7	9.9
08	Construction materials	909.7	155.3	17.1
09	Lumber and wood processing	1,379.2	213.9	15.5
10	Pulp and paper	352.1	56.2	16.0
11	Glass and ceramics	176.1	15.2	8.6
12	Textiles	1,995.4	89.1	4.5
13	Clothing	1,496.5	165.8	11.1
14	Leather and footwear	557.5	93.9	16.8
15	Food processing	3,844.1	474.8	12.4
16	Soap and cosmetics	58.7	13.5	23.0
17	Printing	58.6	3.7	6.3

Table SA6.14. *Trade Balances of Major Commodity Groups, 1950–76*
(millions of U.S. dollars)

Commodity group	*1950*	*1955*	*1960*	*1965*	*1970*
Machinery and equipment					
Exports	8.8	25.8	119.6	205.3	422.4
Imports	93.2	172.0	218.0	429.9	789.8
Balance	−84.4	−146.2	−98.4	−224.6	−367.4
Coverage (percent)	9.4	15.0	54.9	47.8	53.5
Fuels, mineral raw materials and metals					
Exports	71.7	187.2	265.2	276.5	418.8
Imports	57.2	98.4	221.9	338.6	596.4
Balance	14.5	88.8	43.3	−62.1	−177.6
Coverage (percent)	125.3	190.2	119.5	81.7	70.2
Chemicals, fertilizers, rubber					
Exports	3.5	5.5	15.6	70.9	129.7
Imports	11.0	24.4	48.2	67.9	131.4
Balance	−7.5	−18.9	−32.6	3.0	−1.7
Coverage (percent)	31.8	22.5	32.4	104.4	98.7
Building materials					
Exports	9.3	16.4	18.0	37.4	47.6
Imports	2.8	2.4	6.8	15.4	30.2
Balance	6.5	14.0	11.2	22.0	17.4
Coverage (percent)	332.1	683.3	264.7	242.9	157.6
Vegetable and animal raw materials (except those for food)					
Exports	63.1	84.4	105.2	151.9	189.2
Imports	52.0	90.1	88.6	118.0	201.1
Balance	11.1	−5.7	16.6	33.9	−11.9
Coverage (percent)	121.3	94.7	118.7	128.7	94.1
Raw materials for food production					
Exports	23.0	53.2	67.2	84.9	83.6
Imports	1.5	35.9	14.3	9.1	44.3
Balance	21.5	17.3	52.9	75.8	39.3
Coverage (percent)	15x	148.2	469.9	933.0	188.7
Foodstuffs					
Exports	30.1	43.7	84.7	153.2	224.2
Imports	0.8	19.4	16.5	25.9	59.6
Balance	29.3	24.3	68.2	127.3	164.6
Coverage (percent)	38x	225.3	513.3	591.5	376.2
Industrial consumer goods					
Exports	2.9	5.4	41.5	121.4	335.4
Imports	24.9	19.3	33.5	72.3	107.3
Balance	−22.0	−13.9	8.0	49.1	228.1
Coverage (percent)	11.6	28.0	123.9	167.9	312.6

Note: Coverage is defined as (exports/imports) × 100.
Source: Anuarul Statistic, various issues.

Commodity group	1971	1972	1973	1974	1975	1976
Machinery and equipment						
Exports	485.3	646.6	913.2	1,002.9	1,352.6	1,577.7
Imports	885.8	1,206.2	1,476.4	1,750.1	1,853.7	1,938.9
Balance	−400.5	−559.6	−563.2	−747.2	−501.1	−361.2
Coverage (percent)	54.8	53.6	61.9	57.3	73.0	81.4
Fuels, mineral raw materials and metals						
Exports	425.4	428.2	647.1	1,068.0	1,189.5	1,477.5
Imports	635.6	694.9	971.2	1,651.8	2,042.8	2,496.8
Balance	−210.2	−266.7	−324.1	−583.8	−853.3	−1,019.2
Coverage (percent)	66.9	61.6	66.6	64.7	58.2	59.2
Chemicals, fertilizers, rubber						
Exports	172.0	213.7	272.2	546.2	574.8	508.3
Imports	113.3	145.9	225.3	520.4	346.2	415.8
Balance	58.7	67.8	46.9	25.8	228.6	92.5
Coverage (percent)	151.8	146.5	120.8	105.0	166.0	122.2
Building materials						
Exports	55.9	75.6	122.8	145.5	155.3	185.4
Imports	25.9	29.4	36.9	47.8	59.6	69.6
Balance	30.0	46.2	85.9	97.7	95.7	115.8
Coverage (percent)	215.8	257.1	332.8	304.4	260.6	266.4
Vegetable and animal raw materials (except those for food)						
Exports	201.6	223.4	301.9	349.6	336.0	396.1
Imports	184.5	273.3	433.7	549.4	452.3	444.9
Balance	17.1	−49.9	−131.8	−199.8	−116.3	−48.8
Coverage (percent)	109.3	81.7	69.6	63.6	74.3	89.0
Raw materials for food production						
Exports	100.3	195.6	269.6	250.4	304.4	389.1
Imports	75.1	60.0	116.1	304.1	265.6	387.4
Balance	25.2	135.6	153.5	−53.7	38.8	1.7
Coverage (percent)	133.6	326.0	232.2	82.3	114.6	100.4
Foodstuffs						
Exports	273.9	324.4	506.5	739.0	567.8	596.3
Imports	76.8	71.4	80.6	118.2	119.7	124.2
Balance	197.1	253.0	425.9	620.8	448.1	472.1
Coverage (percent)	356.6	454.3	628.4	625.2	474.4	480.1
Industrial consumer goods						
Exports	386.6	491.6	704.3	772.8	861.0	1,005.3
Imports	105.7	134.6	164.4	201.7	201.4	209.5
Balance	280.9	357.0	539.9	571.1	659.6	795.8
Coverage (percent)	365.8	365.2	428.4	383.1	427.5	479.9

Table SA6.15. *Exports of Selected Industrial Commodities, 1960–76*

Code	*Industrial subsector*	*1960*	*19*
01.03	Ferrous metallurgy		
	Rolled steel products (thousands of tonnes)	318.6	34
	Steel pipes (thousands of tonnes)	151.0	23
01.04	Nonferrous metallurgy		
	Metals and alloys (thousands of tonnes)	16.0	2
	Rolled products (thousands of tonnes)	1.0	
01.05.01	Mechanical engineering		
	Machinery and equipment for the petroleum industry (millions of U.S. dollars)	14.7	3
	Equipment for the chemical industry (millions of U.S. dollars)	1.5	1
	Equipment for the cement industry (millions of U.S. dollars)	9.5	
	Tractors, includes units not fully assembled (thousands)	4,526	3,40
	Excavators (units)	36	9
	Mobile compressors (units)	137	18
	Machine tools for metal working (units)	704	1,67
	Bearings (thousands)	277	4,09
	Cars (units)	—	32
	Trucks (units)	555	2,54
01.05.02	Electrical engineering		
	Transformers (units)	2,522	3,97
	Electric motors 1 kilowatt and over (thousands of kilowatts)	192	37
01.06	Chemicals		
	Caustic soda (thousands of tonnes)	30.4	10
	Carbon black (thousands of tonnes)	16.6	[illegible]
	Carbide (thousands of tonnes)	23.3	5
	Chemical fertilizers (thousands of tonnes)	—	
	Urea, granulated (thousands of tonnes)	—	
	Synthetic rubber (thousands of tonnes)	—	[illegible]
	Tires with tubes and tubeless (thousands)	0.3	36
	Synthetic fibers (thousands of tonnes)	—	

1970	1971	1972	1973	1974	1975	1976
1,278.1	1,122.1	1,076.4	1,103.5	950.6	1,003.1	966.7
299.5	242.5	255.0	253.2	238.4	316.0	376.8
55.6	62.2	59.6	55.0	99.1	88.6	77.6
10.3	4.4	3.9	7.8	15.7	35.7	31.4
44.7	62.2	74.2	80.6	101.2	143.4	170.3
8.2	10.1	12.6	12.2	16.2	39.4	56.3
1.9	4.6	4.2	4.1	0.4	8.7	19.0
13,475	11,317	20,247	27,428	26,683	35,714	37,212
21	44	55	347	481	422	427
274	165	296	257	529	487	521
3,825	4,599	4,612	6,353	5,136	6,451	6,799
7,452	6,860	7,098	7,273	13,883	21,755	22,990
5,405	6,711	7,082	9,782	6,628	4,085	6,456
9,452	7,637	8,676	7,902	5,697	7.118	6,036
4,231	4,545	4,104	5,775	3,380	5,099	5,906
1,060	1,194	1,537	1,457	1,907	2,333	2,816
94.8	93.9	115.2	78.9	111.2	222.7	279.9
34.8	36.3	38.1	32.9	25.7	30.3	36.7
62.6	90.9	145.2	164.3	160.1	173.6	151.2
442.2	824.6	1,027.7	1,087.2	1,284.7	1,414.1	1,932.7
91.0	168.7	209.4	399.8	449.7	626.8	802.6
24.6	28.7	32.2	33.4	31.9	39.0	41.3
511.9	500.8	475.8	577.8	519.4	838.5	976.9
5.2	13.9	14.6	15.5	19.8	23.6	47.2

(Table continues on the following page)

Table SA6.15. *Continued*

Code	*Industrial subsector*	*1960*	*196*
01.08	Construction materials		
	Cement (thousands of tonnes)	959.2	1,538.
01.09	Wood products		
	Lumber, coniferrous (thousands of cubic meters)	867.8	1,413.
	Lumber, broadleaf (thousands of cubic meters)	360.9	563.
	Plywood (thousands of cubic meters)	23.5	112.
	Veneers (thousands of square meters)	3,311.5	5,526.
	Chipboard (thousands of square meters)	321.7	3,413.
	Furniture (millions of U.S. dollars)	10.3	41.
01.10	Pulp and paper		
	Paper (thousands of tonnes)	8.4	17.
01.11	Glass, porcelain, and crockery		
	Glass, 2-millimeter equivalent (thousands of square meters)	5,746.8	9,074
	Crystal ware and fine ceramics (millions of U.S. dollars)	2.2	2.
01.12	Textiles		
	Cotton fabrics (millions of square meters)	24.6	34.
	Garments (millions of U.S. dollars)	8.4	30.
	Knitwear (millions of U.S. dollars)	0.5	7.
01.13	Leather and footwear		
	Leather shoes (thousands of pairs)	644.9	3,085
0.115.16	Other products		
	Canned vegetables (thousands of tonnes)	2.3	11
	Tomato paste (thousands of tonnes)	3.3	8
	Canned fruits (thousands of tonnes)	65.8	86
	Sugar (thousands of tonnes)	76.7	34

Source: Anuarul Statistic, various issues.

1970	1971	1972	1973	1974	1975	1976
1,200.0	934.6	1,084.3	1,786.1	1,799.0	2,834.7	2,712.6
1,273.9	1,395.2	1,422.3	1,176.5	626.3	1,012.7	699.9
642.9	659.0	631.2	561.6	409.4	432.3	402.1
102.8	95.5	97.8	97.5	94.8	100.0	118.0
7,594.2	7,248.8	7,428.0	5,200.0	4,406.0	3,462.0	4,647.0
2,712.9	6,228.3	7,912.0	9,631.9	10,836.1	16,876.0	18,554.3
77.6	89.8	111.3	166.2	192.9	225.7	246.3
103.8	90.5	90.2	76.9	110.9	91.5	152.9
7,177.8	8,964.5	13,364.6	15,377.0	15,507.0	15,008.0	16,874.0
3.5	5.5	9.0	13.2	15.2	15.2	16.4
83.7	68.0	80.6	98.1	60.4	62.2	82.6
78.8	87.5	111.3	143.7	149.1	168.2	186.5
33.6	44.6	59.1	83.0	87.0	92.9	104.2
12,306.0	13,397.0	13,406.0	16,133.0	16,737.0	16,596.0	18,373.0
26.7	37.6	49.4	61.4	61.3	48.5	59.2
12.5	12.7	20.8	23.8	27.7	24.7	15.5
74.8	89.6	83.8	85.4	83.2	59.2	65.3
39.4	10.0	156.5	—	106.7	8.4	—

Table SA6.16. *Imports of Selected Industrial Commodities, 1960–76*

Code	*Industrial subsector*	*1960*	*1965*
01.03	Ferrous metallurgy		
	Iron ore (thousands of tonnes)	917.1	2,623.2
	Metallurgical coke (thousands of tonnes)	655.8	929.8
	Ferroalloys (thousands of tonnes)	25.3	52.6
	Rolled products (thousands of tonnes)	830.1	1,076.5
	Pipes (thousands of tonnes)	83.4	80.3
01.05.01	Mechanical engineering		
	Mining equipment (millions of U.S. dollars)	1.3	4.0
	Machinery and equipment for the petroleum industry (millions of U.S. dollars)	4.8	3.4
	Metallurgical equipment (millions of U.S. dollars)	1.6	2.6
	Machine tools for metal working (units)	1,469	713
	Equipment for the chemical industry (millions of U.S. dollars)	2.0	5.1
	Machinery for pulp, paper, and wood processing industry (millions of U.S. dollars)	2.3	4.3
	Equipment for the textile, garment, and knitting industry (millions of U.S. dollars)	2.5	7.5
	Lifting and transport equipment (millions of U.S. dollars)	4.5	7.5
	Road construction equipment (millions of U.S. dollars)	2.0	8.5
	Telecommunications equipment (millions of U.S. dollars)	4.9	6.0
	Buses (units)	151	127
	Cars, includes units not fully assembled (units)	1,186	11,880
	Bearings (millions of U.S. dollars)	2.3	4.7
01.06	Chemicals		
	Potassium fertilizers (thousands of tonnes)	4.0	13.3
	Natural rubber (thousands of tonnes)	9.3	19.2
	Synthetic rubber (thousands of tonnes)	9.2	5.1
	Tires, with tubes and tubeless (thousands)	204.1	100.1
01.08	Construction materials		
	Refractory materials (thousands of tonnes)	39.3	63.0
01.12	Textiles		
	Cotton fabrics (thousands of square meters)	2,976	18,606
	Woolen fabrics (thousands of square meters)	1,565	3,044
	Silk and synthetic fiber fabrics (thousands of square meters)	207	821
01.13	Leather and footwear		
	Rubber shoes (thousands of pairs)	817.9	77.3
	Leather shoes (thousands of pairs)	—	126.0

Source: Anuarul Statistic, various issues.

1970	1971	1972	1973	1974	1975	1976
6,267.8	6,939.4	7,614.8	9,501.0	10,001.8	10,878.7	11,740.0
2,416.5	2,434.5	2,495.7	2,965.0	2,573.5	2,537.2	2,816.0
102.0	120.8	118.4	151.2	153.5	175.2	223.3
1,360.6	1,411.5	1,200.4	1,193.9	1,293.7	1,570.4	1,940.1
106.2	90.8	130.2	140.2	101.6	82.0	101.0
13.9	11.9	9.4	11.1	31.1	41.7	56.8
4.9	2.6	3.7	2.3	6.3	7.7	7.8
10.4	23.6	36.3	77.6	121.3	99.2	83.3
3,416	4,978	5,738	5,466	5,959	5,195	395.9
31.3	80.1	169.6	175.6	212.0	133.7	98.4
8.8	26.9	32.4	15.8	20.2	42.7	12.6
14.0	23.6	45.2	42.4	56.2	48.7	50.9
30.4	32.8	37.9	31.9	57.6	87.1	116.7
18.5	26.9	31.2	29.7	30.2	34.6	50.1
15.1	15.4	23.6	30.2	47.5	49.6	65.3
396	517	438	515	456	460	659
11,451	3,937	9,114	1,293	2,598	3,898	4,069
8.9	11.8	15.9	20.4	19.5	23.6	27.3
29.9	34.2	58.6	59.8	64.7	91.9	109.5
37.1	26.9	47.5	54.1	50.4	41.3	68.5
11.3	13.5	13.9	16.9	21.7	18.2	23.8
46.8	61.7	63.3	64.7	55.7	54.8	43.4
83.8	87.5	84.4	84.3	100.1	94.7	112.4
29,612	21,218	22,343	28,815	41,982	37,297	26,701
3,950	3,195	5,321	3,762	6,669	4,842	1,102
2,799	3,712	4,858	5,702	6,493	3,706	1,801
146.0	156.0	395.0	313.5	630.0	144.0	—
214.0	445.0	565.0	768.0	312.8	479.0	693

Table SA6.17. *Planned Expansion of Selected Industrial Products during the 1976–80 Five-Year Plan*

Product	Actual	
	1975	*1976*
Electric energy (billions of kilowatt-hours)	53.7	58.3
Coal (millions of tonnes)	29.4	28.1
Crude oil (millions of tonnes)	14.6	14.7
Methane gas (billions of cubic meters)	27.0	29.8
Raw steel (thousands of tonnes)	9,549	10,733
Primary aluminum and aluminum alloys (thousands of tonnes)	204	207
Electric motors, 0.25 kilowatts and above (megawatts)	6,521	6,265
Tractors (thousands)	50.0	53.9
Trucks (thousands)	36.0	33.9
Electric and diesel-electric locomotives (units)	334	247
Sea-going vessels (thousands of deadweight tonnes)	296[a]	374
River vessels (units)	12[a]	13
Chemical fertilizers, 100 percent primary content tonnes)	1,729	1,869
Synthetic rubber (thousands of tonnes)	98.9	95.2
Chemical fibers and yarn (thousands of tonnes)	159	179
Vehicle tires (thousands)	3,703	4,115
Cement, 80 percent clinker equivalent (thousands of tonnes)	11.5	12.5
Chipboard and fiber board (thousands of tonnes)	826	895
Wood furniture (billions of lei)	10.1	10.9
Cellulose and semicellulose (thousands of tonnes)	575	610
Paper, cardboard, and pasteboard (thousands of tonnes)	649	693
Radio receivers (thousands)	712	791
Television sets (thousands)	512	548
Refrigerators (thousands)	332	376
Fabrics (millions of square meters)	866	993
Knitwear (millions of lei)	8,973[a]	—
Garments (billions of lei)	29.4[a]	—
Footwear (millions of pairs)	86.9	95.7
Meat (thousands of tonnes)	713	815
Edible oils (thousands of tonnes)	321	322
Sugar (thousands of tonnes)	516	561
Canned fruits and vegetables (thousands of tonnes)	455	556

Note: The choice of products shown is that of the law adopting the 1976–80 Plan.

a. 1976 Plan figure. No comparison is possible with earlier years because of change in unit of measurement.

Sources: Law (no. 4) on the Adoption of the Unified Naitonal Plan of Economic and Social Development of the Socialist Republic of Romania, *Official Bulletin of the Socialist Republic of Romania*, vol. 12, no. 65 (July 7, 1976) and *Anuarul Statistic*, various issues.

1977	Planned 1978	1979	1980	Average annual growth rate 1976–80 (percent)
63.1	65.0–67.7	70.0–73.4	75.0–78.8	6.8–7.9
33.5	38.0–40.7	45.5–48.2	53.0–56.6	12.5–14.0
14.8	15.1	15.3	15.5	1.2
27.8	26.8	26.8	26.8	−0.1
11,980	13,000–13,590	14,000–14,510	16,600–17,270	11.3–12.6
208	215–218	240–245	255–260	4.6–5.0
7,300	8,500–9,000	9,600–10,300	11,000–12,000	11.0–13.0
55.7	57.0–61.0	60.0–67.7	70.0–80.0	7.0–9.9
36.0	36.0–37.0	42.0–45.0	45.0–50.0	4.6–6.8
320	325–330	340–360	365–385	1.8–2.9
560	600–674	900–987	1,100–1,235	33–37
40	55–59	60–62	63–65	13.5–14.4
3,057	3,450–3,604	3,800–4,040	4,050–4,143	18.6–19.1
175.0	180.0–198.7	240–260	290–318	24–26
184.1	190.9	210.0–233.1	310.0–348.7	14.3–17.0
4,875	5,000–5,115	5,200–5,460	7,500–7,855	15.2–16.2
15.1	16.0–16.8	17.0–18.15	19–20	10.6–11.7
990	1,000–1,100	1,100–1,170	1,200–1,250	7.7–8.6
11.8	12.0–13.0	13.5–14.2	14.5–15.6	7.5–9.1
658	662	670–683	730–800	4.9–6.8
812	800–849	850–890	900–920	6.8–7.2
910	950–1,000	1,000–1,090	1,100–1,180	9.1–10.6
600	620–640	650–680	700–730	6.5–7.4
415	430–460	460–505	510–550	9.0–10.6
1,137	1,150–1,209	1,220–1,298	1,400–1,426	10.1–10.5
10,030	10,800–11,210	12,000–12,330	13,500–14,020	10.8–11.8
32.1	33.0–34.6	36.0–38.1	38.2–40.4	6.8–8.3
109.6	116.0–118.2	125.0–127.5	135.0–138.7	9.2–9.8
1,047	1,070–1,165	1,166–1,316	1,320–1,464	13.1–15.4
517	520–557	560–602	605–623	13.5–14.2
805	820–925	950–1,000	1,000–1,030	14.2–14.8
468	480	500	520	2.7

Table SA6.18. *Subsector Coefficients of Industry*

Industrial sector	*25-year growth, 1951–75*		*Industrial sector*	*Recent development, 1971–75*	
	Volume (1950 = 100)	*Sub-sector coeffi-cient*		*Volume (1970 = 100)*	*Sub-sector coeffi-cient*
Chemicals	11,200	5.3	Engineering and metalworks	230	1.25
Nonmetallic minerals	6,400	3.0	Nonmetallic minerals	221	1.2[illegible]
Engineering and metalworks	6,100	2.9	Clothing	220	1.2[illegible]
Electric energy	3,700	1.8	Chemicals	208	1.1[illegible]
Construction materials	2,500	1.2	Glass and ceramics	195	1.0[illegible]
Glass and ceramics	2,100	1.0	Textiles	177	0.9[illegible]
Nonferrous metallurgy	2,100	1.0	Ferrous metallurgy	171	0.9[illegible]
Ferrous metallurgy	2,000	1.0	Soap and cosmetics	166	0.9[illegible]
Pulp and paper	1,700	0.8	Construction materials	161	0.8[illegible]
Clothing	1,600	0.8	Nonferrous metallurgy	161	0.8[illegible]
Textiles	1,200	0.6	Electric energy	159	0.8[illegible]
Printing	1,100	0.5	Leather, fur, and footwear	155	0.8[illegible]
Soap and cosmetics	1,100	0.5	Pulp and paper	155	0.8[illegible]
Leather, fur, and footwear	976	0.5	Food processing	143	0.7[illegible]
Lumber and wood processing	926	0.4	Lumber and wood processing	136	0.7[illegible]
Food processing	700	0.3	Fuels	129	0.7[illegible]
Fuels	685	0.3	Printing	109	0.5[illegible]
Group A industries	2,900	1.4	Group A industries	190	1.0[illegible]
Group B industries	1,200	0.6	Group B industries	169	0.9[illegible]
Total industry	*2,100*	*1.0*	*Total industry*	*184*	*1.0*[illegible]

Source: Anuarul Statistic, various issues.

Table SA6.19. *Indicators of Regional Distribution of Industry, by Groups of Judets*

Indicator	*1967*	*1974*	*1976*
Industrial employment (all judets = 100)	100.0	100.0	100.0
Group I	6.7	9.0	9.6
Group II	48.9	51.0	51.3
Group III	26.6	24.0	23.6
Bucharest	17.8	16.0	15.4
Industrial employment (percent of total employment)	38.5	44.2	44.4
Group I	24.0	33.6	34.9
Group II	37.5	44.2	44.7
Group III	45.3	49.3	49.1
Bucharest	41.4	45.0	44.3
Gross industrial output (all judets = 100)	100.0	100.0	100.0
Group I	6.9	8.5	9.3
Group II	47.1	48.9	49.1
Group III	28.2	25.1	24.6
Bucharest	17.8	17.5	16.9

Note: Group I comprises the judets of Bistrita-Nasaud, Botosani, Buzau, Ilfov, Olt, Salaj, Vaslui, Vilcea, and Vrancea; Group II comprises the judets of Alba, Arad, Arges, Bacau, Bihor, Braila, Caras-Severin, Covasna, Dimbovita, Dolj, Galati, Gorj, Harghita, Ialomita, Iasi, Maramures, Mehedinti, Mures, Neamt, Satu Mare, Suceava, Teleorman, Timis, Tulcea; Group III comprises the judets of Brasov, Cluj, Constanta, Hunedoara, Prahova, and Sibiu; and Bucharest comprises the municipality of Bucharest.

Sources: Anuarul Statistic, various issues, and World Bank calculations.

Table SA6.20. *Indicators of Regional Distribution of Industry, by Industrial Subsector, 1965 and 1974*

(percentage of gross industrial production)

Industrial subsectors	*Year*	*Less than 5 percent*	*5–10 percent*	*10–20 percent*	*20–30 percent*	*More than 30 percent*	*Judet with more than 30 percent*
Fuels	1965	26	—	2	—	1	Prahova, group III
	1974	26	3	2	1	—	
Ferrous metallurgy[a]	1965	5	4	—	1	1	Hunedoara, group III
	1974	7	3	1	1	1	Galati, group II
Nonferrous metallurgy[a]	1965	9	1	2	—	1	Maramures, group II
	1974	10	2	1	1	1	Olt, group I
Engineering and metalworkers	1965	36	2	1	1	—	
	1974	35	3	1	1	—	
Chemicals	1965	34	4	1	1	—	
	1974	33	5	2	—	—	
Nonmetallic minerals	1965	10	3	1	—	1	Cluj, group III
	1974	17	1	—	1	1	Cluj, group III
Construction materials	1965	35	3	2	—	—	
	1974	33	5	2	—	—	

Wood exploitation and processing	1965	34	5	1	—	—	
	1974	35	5	—	—	—	
Pulp and paper	1965	9	3	5	—	—	
	1974	18	5	4	—	—	
Glass and ceramics	1965	35	—	3	2	—	
	1974	34	—	6	—	—	
Textiles	1965	35	3	1	—	1	Bucharest
	1974	35	4	—	1	—	
Clothing	1965	38	1	—	—	1	Bucharest
	1974	37	2	—	1	—	
Leather, furs, and footwear	1965	35	3	1	—	1	Bucharest
	1974	35	2	2	1	—	
Food processing	1965	39	—	1	—	—	
	1974	38	1	1	—	—	
Soap and cosmetics	1965	23	1	2	—	1	Bucharest
	1974	22	1	2	—	1	Bucharest
Printing	1965	37	1	—	—	1	Bucharest
	1974	37	2	—	—	1	Bucharest
Other subsectors	1965	37	1	1	1	—	
	1974	32	7	1	—	—	

a. Includes mining and dressing of ores.
Source: Anuarul Statistic, various issues.

Table SA6.21. *Indicators of Regional Distribution of Industrial Employment and Gross Industrial Output, by Judets, 1967 and 1975*

	Industrial employment (totals and district shares)		*Industrial employment as percentage of total employment*		*Gross industrial output (totals and district shares)*	
Judet	*1967*	*1975*	*1967*	*1975*	*1967*	*1975*
Total Romania	*1,799,800*	*2,802,100*			*n.a.*	*586.9 billion lei*
All judets	*100.0*	*100.0*	*38.5*	*44.5*	*100.0*	*100.0*
Alba	2.1	2.1	47.6	50.4	1.5	1.4
Arad	2.9	2.5	42.8	45.6	2.6	2.0
Arges	2.6	3.4	35.7	48.9	2.1	3.7
Bacau	3.3	2.8	44.4	45.4	3.8	2.8
Bihor	3.0	3.1	39.0	47.8	2.4	2.4
Bistrita-Nasaud	0.6	0.6	28.7	33.3	0.3	0.3
Botosani	0.6	0.7	23.9	31.4	0.7	0.6
Brasov	5.8	5.5	54.2	58.9	6.5	6.5
Braila	1.8	1.6	35.8	39.5	2.2	1.9
Buzau	1.0	1.5	28.4	40.3	1.0	1.5
Caras-Severin	3.0	2.2	52.2	50.3	3.0	2.0
Cluj	4.2	4.1	42.3	48.2	3.5	3.5
Constanta	1.7	1.9	19.6	24.9	2.1	2.2
Covasna	0.9	0.9	45.6	47.5	0.6	0.6
Dimbovita	2.1	2.6	49.2	53.5	1.7	1.9

Dolj	2.0	2.4	26.7	37.1	2.7	3.1
Galati	1.9	2.3	25.9	38.7	2.3	4.3
Gorj	1.4	1.4	42.8	40.4	0.9	1.0
Harghita	1.6	1.9	47.1	53.3	1.1	1.1
Hunedoara	4.8	3.3	51.1	51.3	5.7	3.7
Ialomita	0.5	0.8	11.5	23.6	0.6	0.9
Iasi	1.9	2.3	28.0	38.0	2.3	3.3
Ilfov	1.1	1.5	20.4	30.6	1.2	1.3
Maramures	2.4	2.1	45.4	47.9	2.1	1.3
Mehedinti	0.8	1.0	24.4	37.9	0.8	1.1
Mures	3.0	3.0	39.2	47.9	3.7	2.9
Neamt	2.1	2.3	46.1	51.5	2.5	2.7
Olt	0.6	1.4	16.7	36.8	1.1	2.3
Prahova	5.9	5.2	47.7	53.6	6.7	5.5
Satu-Mare	1.6	1.7	43.3	47.1	1.2	1.3
Salaj	0.5	0.7	31.2	39.2	0.3	0.3
Sibiu	4.2	3.7	55.3	58.6	3.7	3.6
Suceava	2.3	2.4	37.9	45.7	1.9	1.7
Teleorman	0.6	1.2	17.3	34.7	0.9	1.2
Timis	4.3	4.2	39.7	47.5	3.7	3.5
Tulcea	0.8	0.9	31.1	34.9	0.5	0.5
Vaslui	0.6	1.0	21.8	35.2	0.7	0.8
Vilcea	0.9	1.1	25.3	33.3	0.7	1.0
Vrancea	0.8	0.8	27.3	30.6	0.9	0.7
Municipality of Bucharest	17.8	15.9	41.4	45.3	17.8	17.6

Source: Anuarul Statistic, various issues.

Table SA6.22. *Relative Changes in Industrial Structure of Less-Developed Judets (Group I), by Year and Judet, 1965 and 1974*

(percentage of industry total)

Judet	*Year*	*Fuels*	*Ferrous metallurgy*	*Nonferrous metallurgy*	*Engineering goods*	*Chemicals*	*Non-metallic minerals*
Bistrita-Nasaud	1965	—	—	3.1	2.8	0.1	—
	1974	0	—	1.6	15.7	0.1	—
Botosani	1965	—	—	—	7.5	0.1	—
	1974	0.5	—	—	12.2	0.1	—
Buzau	1965	5.3	—	—	16.4	7.5	—
	1974	2.2	13.0	0	21.6	14.9	—
Ilfov	1965	14.6	—	—	15.2	2.0	—
	1974	3.8	—	—	23.9	2.8	—
Olt	1965	32.8	—	8.5	7.7	0.4	—
	1974	1.8	—	43.9	25.3	0.6	3.1
Salaj	1965	10.6	—	—	5.0	0.3	—
	1974	8.5	—	—	33.4	0.4	—
Vaslui	1965	—	—	—	36.8	0	—
	1974	—	—	—	36.7	0	—
Vilcea	1965	3.9	—	—	1.4	13.5	0.8
	1974	1.7	—	—	6.8	44.3	0.6
Vrancea	1965	—	—	—	2.7	2.5	—
	1974	0.2	—	—	6.9	4.7	—
Average of all judets of Group I	1965	7.5	—	1.3	10.6	2.9	0.1
	1974	2.1	1.4	5.1	20.3	7.5	0.4
Percentage shares of judets in national outputs	1965	8.4	—	2.7	3.6	3.3	2.3
	1974	4.3	2.5	32.5[a]	5.9	6.2	21.9

Judet	Year	Construction materials	Wood exploitation and processing	Pulp and paper	Textiles	Clothing	Food	Others
Bistrita-Nasaud	1965	3.2	48.8	5.5	0.9	1.9	31.8	1.9
	1974	4.4	31.2	3.9	10.8	2.3	25.7	4.3
Botosani	1965	0.9	3.7	0	13.8	11.6	56.9	5.5
	1974	2.9	2.4	0.1	16.0	28.2	31.2	6.4
Buzau	1965	2.5	13.8	—	0.6	10.9	41.3	1.7
	1974	4.2	4.3	—	1.1	10.0	19.2	9.5
Ilfov	1965	3.6	3.6	0.3	5.9	2.4	45.0	7.4
	1974	2.5	2.7	0.5	22.1	3.9	24.6	13.2
Olt	1965	1.3	3.3	—	0.3	2.7	40.5	2.5
	1974	1.4	1.2	—	2.5	1.3	12.7	6.2
Salaj	1965	8.0	23.2	—	0.2	5.7	44.0	3.0
	1974	7.2	15.5	—	7.1	4.0	21.7	2.2
Vaslui	1965	0.6	5.5	—	0.9	8.0	47.4	0.8
	1974	1.8	6.0	0	4.2	26.8	23.2	1.3
Vilcea	1965	1.9	31.0	—	0	1.7	35.4	10.4
	1974	2.9	11.9	0	0.2	1.8	17.2	12.6
Vrancea	1965	2.5	17.5	—	0.1	10.1	63.5	1.1
	1974	5.7	14.2	—	0.5	26.4	39.4	2.0
Average of all judets of Group I	1965	2.7	16.7	0.6	2.5	6.1	45.1	3.9
	1974	3.7	9.9	0 5	7.2	11.6	23.9	6.4
Percentage shares of judets in national outputs	1965	4.9	11.0	2.0	2.5	9.7	14.2	—
	1974	8.4	10.7	1.5	7.5	15.9	12.8	—

a. Slatina Aluminum Works.
Source: Anuarul Statistic, various issues.

Table SA7.1. *Indexes of Social Product, National Income, and Fixed Assets of Total Economy and Agriculture, 1950–76*
(1950 = 100)

	Social product		*National income*		*Fixed assets*	
Year	*Total*	*Agri-culture*	*Total*	*Agri-culture*	*Total*	*Agri-culture*
1950	100	100	100	100	100	100
1955	186	163	192	170	125	110
1960	263	171	268	169	161	127
1965	414	198	413	169	223	159
1970	629	218	599	164	337	213
1971	701	264	680	214	368	235
1972	771	283	748	229	398	254
1973	852	287	828	217	433	279
1974	947	293	931	213	478	302
1975	1,038	304	1,024	213	534	334
1976	1,145	353	1,132	261	588	361

Source: Anuarul Statistic, various issues.

Table SA7.2. *Agriculture's Share of Social Product, National Income, and Fixed Assets, 1938–76*
(percentage)

Year	*Social product*	*National income*	*Fixed assets*
1938	30.1	38.1	—
1950	25.7	27.8	19.0
1955	30.4	37.4	16.6
1960	24.5	33.0	14.9
1965	21.5	28.9	13.5
1970	16.5	18.5	11.5
1971	18.1	22.2	11.6
1972	17.1	21.2	11.6
1973	16.1	18.5	11.7
1974	14.1	15.9	11.5
1975	13.3	16.0	11.4
1976	14.3	18.3	11.2

Source: Anuarul Statistic, various issues.

Table SA7.3. *Indexes and Structure of Gross Agricultural Production, 1938–76*

Year	Index (1938 = 100)			Structure[a]		
	Total	Crops	Live-stock	Total	Crops	Live-stock
1938	100	100	100	100.0	69.7	30.3
1948	62	55	76	100.0	62.6	37.4
1950	74	65	94	100.0	61.4	38.6
1955	120	119	123	100.0	68.9	31.1
1960	126	118	145	100.0	65.3	34.7
1965	143	133	163	100.0	65.3	34.7
1965	143	133	163	100.0	63.2	36.8
1970	157	136	201	100.0	58.8	41.2
1971	186	172	219	100.0	62.3	37.7
1972	204	185	246	100.0	61.3	38.7
1973	206	179	265	100.0	58.7	41.3
1974	208	180	269	100.0	58.5	41.5
1975	214	181	287	100.0	57.0	43.0
1976	251	220	320	100.0	59.1	40.9

a. 1938–65 in 1955 prices; 1965–76 in 1963 prices.
Source: Anuarul Statistic, various issues.

Table SA7.4. *Land Use and Irrigated Area, 1938–76*
(thousands of hectares)

Land use	*1938*	*1950*	*1955*	*1960*	*1965*	*1970*
Arable	10,093	9,378	9,662	9,822	9,817	9,737
Pasture	2,703	2,852	2,693	2,814	2,945	3,002
Meadows	1,714	1,682	1,361	1,387	1,371	1,416
Vineyards	249	227	229	311	312	347
Orchards	247	184	167	213	346	428
Subtotal	15,006	14,324	14,112	14,547	14,791	14,930
Forest	6,476	6,446	6,483	6,403	6,378	6,315
Other	2,268	2,980	3,155	2,800	2,581	2,505
Total	*23,750*	*23,750*	*23,750*	*23,750*	*23,750*	*23,750*
Irrigated area	15	42	93	200	230	731

	1971	*1972*	*1973*	*1974*	*1975*	*1976*
Arable	9,732	9,716	9,662	9,708	9,741	9,760
Pasture	3,007	3,031	3,047	3,037	3,033	3,032
Meadows	1,421	1,424	1,431	1,423	1,414	1,404
Vineyards	345	339	335	332	329	327
Orchards	430	433	429	429	430	431
Subtotal	14,935	14,943	14,904	14,929	14,946	14,955
Forest	6,313	6,312	6,309	6,313	6,316	6,316
Other	2,502	2,495	2,537	2,508	2,488	2,479
Total	*23,750*	*23,750*	*23,750*	*23,750*	*23,750*	*23,750*
Irrigated area	957	1,144	1,254	1,395	1,474	1,729

Source: Anuarul Statistic, various issues.

Table SA7.5. *Area under Crops, 1954–76*
(thousands of hectares)

Crop	1954	1955	1956	1957	1958	1959
Grains						
Wheat and rye	2,653	3,150	3,066	3,123	3,113	3,107
Barley	438	390	300	303	292	289
Oats	435	385	339	352	311	299
Maize	3,302	3,265	3,571	3,722	3,645	3,554
Rice	15	19	17	15	17	27
Other	19	10	9	7	8	5
Subtotal	6,862	7,219	7,302	7,522	7,386	7,281
Pulses						
Peas	96	82	43	37	36	49
Beans	67	54	40	39	37	30
Soybeans	28	28	30	18	12	22
Other	8	5	4	5	6	6
Subtotal	199	169	117	99	91	107
Technical crops						
Flax for fiber	23	25	24	24	19	18
Hemp for fiber	59	58	55	48	44	37
Cotton	172	169	113	60	14	15
Sunflower	336	300	294	286	352	513
Flax for oil	30	28	33	34	24	26
Sugar beet	107	145	139	131	141	201
Tobacco	32	34	35	40	47	36
Chicory	1	1	1	1	1	2
Medicinal crops, and the like	18	17	15	12	9	10
Other	33	36	55	49	62	59
Subtotal	811	813	764	685	713	917
Potatoes, vegetables, and melons						
Potatoes	250	258	256	265	270	276
Vegetables	188	169	164	172	173	186
Melons and watermelons	20	23	20	24	26	22
Other	67	59	56	—	1	—
Subtotal	458	450	440	461	470	484
Fodder crops						
Perennials for hay	394	309	281	262	313	293
Annuals for hay	336	311	387	391	375	346
Annuals for green feed	59	62	68	66	57	76
Silage crops	26	30	36	41	68	116
Root crops	37	30	27	23	18	19
Subtotal	852	742	799	783	831	850
Seed crops and plants	33	29	24	27	21	36
Total	*9,215*	*9,422*	*9,446*	*9,577*	*9,512*	*9,675*
Intercropping, total[a]	*818*	*894*	*1,152*	*1,170*	*1,294*	*1,371*

Crop	1960	1961	1962	1963	1964	1965
Grains						
Wheat and rye	2,934	3,059	3,120	2,954	3,050	3,085
Barley	266	284	250	224	195	233
Oats	270	243	173	130	89	116
Maize	3,572	3,428	3,107	3,379	3,319	3,306
Rice	21	11	7	14	20	19
Other	3	4	7	8	20	7
Subtotal	7,066	7,029	6,664	6,709	6,693	6,766
Pulses						
Peas	91	89	152	139	94	99
Beans	29	28	24	39	41	27
Soybeans	25	10	8	8	5	6
Other	8	5	6	7	6	4
Subtotal	153	132	190	193	146	136
Technical crops						
Flax for fiber	22	28	29	30	25	23
Hemp for fiber	36	31	24	23	26	21
Cotton	—	—	—	—	—	—
Sunflower	480	439	427	464	467	462
Flax for oil	27	28	30	38	47	51
Sugar beet	200	172	155	178	190	190
Tobacco	22	28	38	41	40	38
Chicory	2	2	1	1	2	1
Medicinal crops, and the like	7	8	9	14	12	9
Other	71	59	44	42	50	38
Subtotal	867	795	757	831	859	833
Potatoes, vegetables, and melons						
Potatoes	292	293	298	319	306	298
Vegetables	190	181	182	204	195	181
Melons and watermelons	19	17	17	21	20	19
Other	—	—	—	—	—	—
Subtotal	501	491	497	544	521	498
Fodder crops						
Perennials for hay	371	363	396	458	550	566
Annuals for hay	350	365	340	293	257	234
Annuals for green feed	104	161	193	221	178	220
Silage crops	253	289	501	377	484	303
Root crops	19	28	49	32	20	16
Subtotal	1,097	1,206	1,479	1,382	1,489	1,339
Seed crops and plants	43	52	56	78	95	116
Total	*9,727*	*9,705*	*9,643*	*9,737*	*9,803*	*9,688*
Intercropping, total[a]	*2,217*	*2,493*	*2,287*	*2,688*	*2,703*	*2,300*

(Table continues on the following page)

Table SA7.5. *Continued*
(thousands of hectares)

Crop	1966	1967	1968	1969	1970	1971
Grains						
Wheat and rye	3,125	2,975	2,860	2,801	2,366	2,548
Barley	246	257	292	307	288	330
Oats	138	127	132	131	131	128
Maize	3,288	3,221	3,344	3,293	3,084	3,131
Rice	20	22	25	29	28	27
Other	4	2	4	2	4	2
Subtotal	6,821	6,604	6,657	6,563	5,901	6,166
Pulses						
Peas	119	119	111	97	106	96
Beans	28	44	39	39	49	62
Soybeans	17	49	49	54	79	147
Other	4	1	4	2	3	3
Subtotal	168	213	203	192	237	308
Technical crops						
Flax for fiber	29	32	34	35	36	40
Hemp for fiber	23	28	29	29	23	25
Cotton	—	—	—	—	—	—
Sunflower	468	481	520	533	604	548
Flax for oil	54	63	66	72	79	84
Sugar beet	194	176	185	188	170	178
Tobacco	38	39	36	36	34	39
Chicory	1	1	2	1	1	1
Medicinal crops, and the like	9	11	10	12	13	12
Other	93	50	47	50	45	42
Subtotal	858	881	929	956	1,005	963
Potatoes, vegetables, and melons						
Potatoes	306	315	316	305	286	290
Vegetables	195	185	217	223	225	227
Melons and watermelons	19	15	17	16	12	15
Other	1	1	—	—	—	—
Subtotal	521	516	550	544	523	532
Fodder crops						
Perennials for hay	586	705	741	798	733	767
Annuals for hay	218	189	163	135	145	165
Annuals for green feed	217	223	201	198	224	240
Silage crops	203	208	185	210	301	250
Root crops	20	14	13	17	20	27
Subtotal	1,244	1,339	1,303	1,358	1,423	1,449
Seed crops and plants	117	105	96	90	84	115
Total	*9,729*	*9,658*	*9,738*	*9,703*	*9,173*	*9,533*
Intercropping, total[a]	*2,169*	*1,948*	*1,664*	*1,466*	*1,368*	*1,238*

a. Beans, pumpkins, and potatoes.
Source: Anuarul Statistic, various issues.

Crop	*1972*	*1973*	*1974*	*1975*	*1976*
Grains					
Wheat and rye	2,565	2,391	2,429	2,386	2,429
Barley	327	314	403	442	410
Oats	121	105	85	70	45
Maize	3,196	2,957	2,963	3,305	3,378
Rice	27	23	23	22	21
Other	1	1	—	15	68
Subtotal	6,237	5,791	5,903	6,240	6,351
Pulses					
Peas	79	61	37	23	6
Beans	72	81	83	84	84
Soybeans	109	183	238	121	155
Other	2	1	1	1	1
Subtotal	262	326	359	229	246
Technical crops					
Flax for fiber	46	48	51	60	66
Hemp for fiber	25	27	32	32	33
Cotton	—	—	—	5	—
Sunflower	554	512	509	511	521
Flax for oil	83	84	82	83	85
Sugar beet	197	234	219	247	235
Tobacco	39	52	53	57	53
Chicory	1	1	1	1	1
Medicinal crops, and the like	19	16	20	24	26
Other	48	57	65	65	50
Subtotal	1,012	1,031	1,032	1,078	1,070
Potatoes, vegetables, and melons					
Potatoes	296	284	295	289	289
Vegetables	221	235	230	223	255
Melons and watermelons	16	13	12	13	13
Other	—	—	—	—	—
Subtotal	533	532	537	525	556
Fodder crops					
Perennials for hay	754	829	797	892	835
Annuals for hay	190	148	123	86	59
Annuals for green feed	253	278	243	169	159
Silage crops	256	437	382	231	240
Root crops	53	69	80	80	87
Subtotal	1,506	1,761	1,625	1,458	1,380
Seed crops and plants	107	109	112	110	106
Total	*9,657*	*9,550*	*9,568*	*9,639*	*9,709*
Intercropping, total[a]	*1,246*	*996*	*1,045*	*979*	*932*

Table SA7.6. *Area under Crops, by Kind of Production Unit, 1950–76*
(thousands of hectares)

Kind of unit	*1950*	*1955*	*1960*	*1965*	*1970*	*1971*
Total, state agricultural units	523	1,220	1,596	1,670	1,644	1,758
	(5.7)	(12.9)	(16.4)	(17.3)	(17.9)	(18.4
State agricultural enterprises	476	647	1,284	1,576	1,544	1,636
	(5.2)	(6.8)	(13.2)	(16.3)	(16.8)	(17.2
Other state units[a]	47	573	312	94	100	122
	(0.5)	(6.1)	(3.2)	(1.0)	(1.1)	(1.2
Total, agricultural producer cooperatives	43	804	3,200	7,564	7,092	7,332
	(0.5)	(8.5)	(32.9)	(78.0)	(77.3)	(76.9
Operated by CAP's	41	772	2,980	6,770	6,311	6,537
	(0.5)	(8.2)	(30.6)	(69.8)	(68.8)	(68.5
Operated by CAP members	2	32	220	794	781	795
	(—)	(0.3)	(2.3)	(8.2)	(8.5)	(8.4
Agricultural associations	—	358	3,142	14	1	1
	(—)	(3.8)	(32.3)	(0.1)	(—)	(—
Individual farms	8,576	7,060	1,797	446	443	450
	(93.8)	(74.8)	(18.4)	(4.6)	(4.8)	(4.7
Total	*9,142*	*9,442*	*9,735*	*9,694*	*9,180*	*9,541*

Note: Percentage figures are given in parentheses.
a. Area cropped by "other state units" is more than the arable area held by them.
Source: Anuarul Statistic, various issues.

Kind of unit	*1972*	*1973*	*1974*	*1975*	*1976*
ɔtal, state agricultural units	1,806	1,803	1,812	1,825	1,849
	(18.7)	(18.9)	(18.9)	(18.9)	(19.0)
State agricultural enterprises	1,668	1,643	1,633	1,637	1,657
	(17.2)	(17.2)	(17.0)	(17.0)	(17.0)
Other state units[a]	138	160	179	188	192
	(1.5)	(1.7)	(1.9)	(1.9)	(2.0)
ɔtal, agricultural producer cooperatives	7,412	7,305	7,316	7,366	7,409
	(76.7)	(76.4)	(76.4)	(76.3)	(76.2)
Ɔperated by CAP's	6,617	6,513	6,535	6,585	6,639
	(68.5)	(68.1)	(68.2)	(68.2)	(68.3)
Ɔperated by CAP members	795	792	781	781	770
	(8.2)	(8.3)	(8.2)	(8.1)	(7.9)
;ricultural associations	1	—	—	—	—
	(—)	(—)	(—)	(—)	(—)
lividual farms	446	451	458	458	461
	(4.6)	(4.7)	(4.7)	(4.8)	(4.7)
tal	*9,665*	*9,559*	*9,575*	*9,648*	*9,719*

Table SA7.7. *Crop Production, 1954–76*
(thousands of tonnes)

Crop	*1954*	*1955*	*1956*	*1957*	*1958*	*19*
Grains						
Wheat and rye	2,310	3,220	2,572	3,853	3,037	4,1
Barley	386	445	291	417	305	4
Oats	357	374	305	392	250	3
Maize	4,953	5,877	3,932	6,338	3,657	5,6
Rice	50	35	36	36	37	
Other	8	6	3	4	7	
Subtotal	8,064	9,956	7,139	11,041	7,293	10,3
Pulses						
Peas	68	75	28	31	23	
Beans	80	189	103	111	102	1
Soybeans	12	14	10	9	6	
Other	3	4	3	5	3	
Technical crops						
Flax fiber	26	45	46	50	28	
Hemp	130	144	129	121	92	1
Cotton	79	20	19	13	5	
Sunflower	281	277	223	255	286	5
Flax for oil	10	10	10	12	5	
Sugar beets	1,295	1,840	1,397	1,880	1,593	3,1
Tobacco	19	26	26	36	31	
Chicory	14	10	13	12	13	
Medicinal crops	4	5	5	7	6	
Other	5	6	5	51	25	
Potatoes, vegetables, and melons						
Potatoes	2,396	2,608	2,675	3,058	2,777	2,8
Vegetables	1,520	1,570	1,064	1,460	1,354	1,9
Melons	370	439	217	344	234	2
Fodder crops						
Perennials for hay	976	904	720	711	760	7
Annuals for hay	726	705	696	903	678	9
Annuals for green feed	536	798	564	597	508	7
Silage crops	287	377	341	709	1,108	1,9
Root crops	603	432	326	281	219	2

Crop	1960	1961	1962	1963	1964	1965
ains						
Vheat and rye	3,552	4,094	4,129	3,877	3,916	6,062
Barley	405	468	419	351	348	485
Dats	284	275	167	124	79	124
Maize	5,531	5,740	4,932	6,023	6,692	5,877
Rice	49	31	20	51	54	46
Dther	5	4	10	10	18	9
Subtotal	9,826	10,612	9,677	10,436	11,107	12,603
ses						
Peas	101	105	136	138	94	123
Beans	148	135	78	78	87	78
Soybeans	12	5	3	3	3	3
Dther	5	3	4	5	2	3
chnical crops						
Flax fiber	42	38	61	54	41	53
Hemp	105	89	68	66	74	72
Cotton	—	—	—	—	—	—
unflower	522	481	449	506	518	564
Flax for oil	10	12	12	18	24	35
ugar beets	3,127	2,678	2,006	2,114	3,375	3,013
Tobacco	15	18	26	40	42	34
Chicory	19	28	16	9	16	10
Medicinal crops	6	8	6	10	9	9
Dther	34	27	15	34	16	48
atoes, vegetables, and melons						
Potatoes	3,019	2,875	2,597	2,692	2,640	2,195
Vegetables	1,831	1,712	1,454	1,701	1,763	1,654
Melons	188	155	115	220	170	146
lder crops						
Perennials for hay	989	968	914	1,074	1,427	1,847
Annuals for hay	1,116	1,171	710	798	741	671
Annuals for green feed	1,222	2,218	2,005	2,921	3,015	3,970
ilage crops	4,601	5,231	5,971	5,790	5,835	3,296
oot crops	276	378	425	293	300	254

(Table continues on the following pages)

Table SA7.7. *Continued*
(thousands of tonnes)

Crop	1966	1967	1968	1969	19
Grains					
Wheat and rye	5,165	5,891	4,896	4,396	3,3
Barley	483	531	590	544	5
Oats	170	163	114	137	1
Maize	8,022	6,858	7,105	7,676	6,5
Rice	55	68	60	68	
Other	4	1	5	2	
Subtotal	13,899	13,512	12,770	12,823	10,0
Pulses					
Peas	163	183	76	106	
Beans	114	105	43	84	
Soybeans	20	41	47	51	
Other	2	1	2	2	
Technical crops					
Flax fiber	77	68	46	60	
Hemp	91	113	114	117	
Cotton	—	—	—	—	
Sunflower	671	720	730	747	
Flax for oil	38	39	30	37	
Sugar beets	4,018	3,523	3,621	3,480	2,
Tobacco	40	35	32	24	
Chicory	14	13	23	11	
Medicinal crops	10	9	6	8	
Other	63	62	41	57	
Potatoes, vegetables, and melons					
Potatoes	3,352	3,096	3,706	2,165	2,
Vegetables	2,176	2,000	2,296	1,963	2,
Melons	195	164	121	117	
Fodder crops					
Perennials for hay	2,293	2,561	2,122	2,882	2,
Annuals for hay	889	661	350	386	
Annuals for green feed	4,748	4,380	3,995	3,884	4,
Silage crops	4,187	3,124	4,019	3,866	3,
Root crops	371	269	302	420	

Source: Anuarul Statistic, various issues.

Crop	1971	1972	1973	1974	1975
ains					
Wheat and rye	5,661	6,099	5,528	5,048	4,912
Barley	789	838	730	916	952
Oats	161	111	102	91	57
Maize	7,850	9,817	7,397	7,440	9,241
Rice	66	45	50	53	68
Other	2	3	3	2	36
Subtotal	14,530	16,912	13,810	13,550	15,266
lses					
Peas	123	91	65	45	29
Beans	93	89	83	91	82
Soybeans	165	186	244	298	213
Other	3	1	1	1	1
chnical crops					
Flax fiber	94	82	73	101	114
Hemp	112	98	117	120	134
Cotton	—	—	—	—	—
Sunflower	791	850	756	681	728
Flax for oil	58	51	45	40	45
Sugar beets	3,975	5,581	4,380	4,947	4,905
Tobacco	30	38	38	39	40
Chickory	8	8	7	6	5
Medicinal crops	13	13	10	11	14
Other	14	17	26	—	—
atoes, vegetables, and melons					
Potatoes	3,783	3,672	2,644	4,119	4,716
Vegetables	2,581	2,544	2,779	2,955	2,518
Melons	145	146	131	149	160
lder crops					
Perennials for hay	2,584	2,561	3,158	3,094	3,913
Annuals for hay	512	574	450	430	325
Annuals for green feed	5,391	6,110	5,460	5,469	5,902
Silage crops	4,832	5,841	5,895	6,447	5,989
Root crops	860	2,230	1,990	2,899	2,355

Table SA7.8. *Crop Yields per Hectare, 1938–76*
(quintals)

Crop	*1938*	*1948*	*1950*	*1960*	*1965*	*197*
Grains						
Wheat and rye	13.1	9.3	8.0	12.1	19.7	14
Barley	7.2	5.8	6.1	15.2	20.9	17
Oats	7.1	6.6	5.4	10.5	10.7	8
Maize	10.6	6.2	7.4	15.5	17.8	21
Rice	25.6	14.4	20.9	23.9	24.5	23
Pulses						
Peas	9.8	7.1	5.7	11.0	12.5	14
Beans[a]	3.3	5.0	2.4	7.3	5.0	5
Soybeans	9.4	5.9	4.1	4.8	4.8	11
Fiber crops						
Flax	9.5	17.1	18.3	18.6	23.2	18
Hemp	27.6	24.5	18.9	28.7	34.1	33
Oilseed crops						
Sunflower seed	8.7	3.0	4.2	10.7	12.2	12
Flax	—	—	1.5	3.8	6.9	[illegible]
Castor seed	6.7	4.0	3.4	11.2	5.3	[illegible]
Poppy seed	5.7	3.4	1.5	4.5	4.5	[illegible]
Mustard seed	2.6	1.8	1.8	3.8	4.6	[illegible]
Other industrial crops						
Sugar beets	136.9	82.1	81.3	156.6	158.7	17
Tobacco	8.1	5.3	4.7	7.2	9.2	[illegible]
Chicory	153.0	45.0	—	86.0	99.6	9
Potaotes, vegetables, and melons						
Potatoes	82.6	39.1	69.5	102.8	72.9	7
Onions	51.7	28.2	45.6	72.1	63.9	5
Cabbage	98.6	49.5	79.8	159.9	135.5	14
Tomatoes	62.5	34.2	74.6	128.3	137.4	10
Green pepper	27.8	14.7	24.6	70.4	72.4	6
Garlic	12.3	—	18.3	27.3	21.6	2
Edible roots	—	30.2	54.9	96.2	96.5	8
Watermelons and melons	54.3	50.7	71.8	100.2	75.2	7
Fodder crops						
Lucerne	36.5	19.5	22.0	23.2	36.1	4
Clover	34.4	17.7	24.6	26.2	28.0	2
Vetch	—	9.5	12.7	24.6	29.0	2
Annuals for green feed	—	—	—	94.8	103.1	10
Plants used for silage	—	—	—	165.3	89.9	9

a. Presumably based on the area harvested for beans.
Source: Anuarul Statistic, various issues.

Crop	1971	1972	1973	1974	1975	1976
ains						
Wheat and rye	22.2	23.8	23.1	20.8	20.6	27.9
Barley	23.9	25.6	23.2	22.8	21.5	30.1
Oats	12.5	9.1	9.8	10.7	8.1	12.2
Maize	25.1	30.7	25.0	25.1	27.8	34.1
Rice	24.2	16.7	21.7	22.8	31.3	17.9
lses						
Peas	12.8	11.6	10.7	12.3	12.6	19.3
Beans[a]	6.2	5.7	6.4	6.2	5.8	5.6
Soybeans	11.2	17.1	13.4	12.5	17.6	13.7
ber crops						
Flax	23.4	17.7	15.2	19.6	19.0	30.0
Hemp	44.1	39.3	42.4	37.7	42.0	39.3
seed crops						
Sunflower seed	14.4	15.4	14.8	13.4	14.3	15.3
Flax	6.9	6.1	5.3	4.8	5.4	5.9
Castor seed	5.9	5.0	5.4	4.4	6.0	3.1
Poppy seed	3.0	3.7	4.0	4.3	2.4	5.5
Mustard seed	4.5	3.9	4.9	5.9	6.1	5.4
ner industrial crops						
Sugar beets	223.3	283.9	186.9	226.4	198.6	294.4
Tobacco	9.2	9.7	7.3	7.3	7.0	12.2
Chicory	86.4	73.8	85.9	52.0	50.6	31.5
atoes, vegetables, and melons						
Potatoes	128.9	121.9	92.0	137.4	89.1	159.2
Onions	67.9	72.8	71.6	77.2	59.4	81.2
Cabbage	191.0	189.7	182.0	195.0	163.2	243.4
Tomatoes	138.0	143.0	160.0	166.3	117.4	161.9
Green pepper	79.0	82.2	83.6	95.5	106.3	74.9
Garlic	28.9	25.9	27.1	27.5	26.7	27.0
Edible roots	110.1	103.5	108.9	108.6	90.3	147.0
Watermelons and melons	91.0	85.5	90.5	111.6	111.2	72.6
lder crops						
Lucerne	39.1	41.1	45.1	45.7	51.3	51.2
Clover	30.0	26.1	34.2	29.6	35.5	29.3
Vetch	30.3	28.8	28.1	—	—	—
Annuals for green feed	132.2	123.4	108.0	115.2	142.5	143.6
Plants used for silage	142.9	166.0	107.8	121.3	139.6	164.3

Table SA7.9. *Livestock Numbers at Beginning of Year, 1938–77*
(thousands)

	Cattle		Pigs		Sheep		Goats		
Year	*Total*	*Cows*	*Total*	*Sows*	*Total*	*Ewes and ewe lambs*	*Total*	*She-goats*	*Poultry*
1938	3,653	1,787	2,761	606	10,087	8,357	364	298	27,325
1951	4,502	2,200	2,197	242	10,222	7,945	498	417	17,610
1955	4,630	—	4,370	372	10,882	7,485	593	413	29,500
1956	4,800	1,950	4,950	369	11,120	7,935	598	413	33,000
1958	4,470	—	3,249	303	10,374	7,769	513	409	35,000
1959	4,394	—	4,008	496	10,662	8,581	446	356	35,000
1960	4,450	—	4,300	524	11,200	9,220	415	331	37,000
1961	4,530	2,240	4,300	545	11,500	9,300	404	332	38,000
1962	4,707	—	4,665	408	12,285	9,169	562	454	44,692
1963	4,566	—	4,518	395	12,168	8,991	550	465	34,150
1964	4,637	—	4,658	495	12,400	9,061	619	516	38,358
1965	4,756	—	6,034	552	12,734	9,274	744	592	39,910
1966	4,935	2,328	5,365	461	13,125	9,852	807	660	40,085
1967	5,198	—	5,400	485	14,109	10,471	828	685	43,966
1968	5,332	—	5,752	538	14,380	10,854	732	636	47,148
1969	5,136	—	5,853	566	14,298	10,813	632	554	47,618
1970	5,035	—	5,972	648	13,836	10,876	565	509	53,894
1971	5,216	2,625	6,359	682	13,818	10,655	536	478	54,333
1972	5,528	2,742	7,742	788	14,071	10,941	563	489	61,262
1973	5,767	2,838	8,785	881	14,455	10,968	534	465	64,496
1974	5,897	2,940	8,987	893	14,302	10,866	499	423	66,511
1975	5,983	2,997	8,566	825	13,929	10,620	443	400	67,672
1976	6,126	3,028	8,813	821	13,865	10,398	445	402	78,626
1977	6,351	3,014	10,193	960	14,331	10,590	444	385	91,503

Source: Anuarul Statistic, various issues.

Table SA7.10. *Livestock Production, 1938–76*

Year	Meat (thousands of tons, live weight)		Milk (thousands of hectoliters)		Eggs (millions)	Wool (tons)	Honey (tons)
	Total	Pork	Total	Cow			
1938	763	326	21,575	17,600	1,354	15,130	2,560
1950	644	214	22,930	18,930	1,100	15,600	2,520
1955	886	401	25,726	21,986	1,546	20,710	3,300
1956	818	326	23,628	20,553	1,766	19,503	3,240
1957	801	311	25,371	21,850	2,000	19,113	2,724
1958	852	312	28,136	24,580	2,002	19,562	4,370
1959	903	356	30,660	27,100	2,160	21,000	4,151
1960	969	376	32,420	28,620	2,355	21,850	4,040
1961	1,057	399	33,900	29,900	2,600	23,000	4,400
1962	1,036	412	31,630	28,000	2,568	24,200	6,125
1963	910	339	29,923	26,520	2,258	22,600	6,730
1964	1,102	469	30,210	26,600	2,456	24,779	6,851
1965	1,116	454	32,518	28,831	2,630	25,410	7,718
1966	1,265	503	37,381	33,336	2,814	26,072	8,833
1967	1,356	568	41,234	37,194	3,011	28,626	10,122
1968	1,297	566	38,334	34,577	3,113	30,583	8,052
1969	1,271	557	37,579	34,057	3,315	30,752	
1970	1,393	623	37,932	34,427	3,537	29,725	7,638
1971	1,555	710	38,494	34,851	3,984	28,670	11,829
1972	1,787	846	41,554	37,702	4,300	30,697	11,536
1973	1,934	920	43,683	39,864	4,655	31,037	11,123
1974	1,926	942	43,482	39,860	4,871	30,861	9,958
1975	2,063	957	44,421	40,990	5,412	31,532	7,585
1976	2,311	1,084	48,302	44,821	6,153	32,020	13,030

Source: Anuarul Statistic, various issues.

Table SA7.11. *Principal Indicators of State Agricultural Enterprises, 1960–76*

Indicator	*1960*	*1965*	*1970*	*1971*	*1972*	*1973*	*1974*	*1975*	*1976*
Number of units	560	721	370	215	364	369	370	391	392
Total employees (thousands)	224	301	292	298	297	288	245	252	270
Workers (thousands)	202	267	267	276	275	266	228	235	251
Agricultural area (thousands of hectares)	1,720	2,077	2,089	2,068	2,070	2,058	2,057	2,058	2,060
Arable area (thousands of hectares)	1,341	1,627	1,667	1,660	1,664	1,650	1,654	1,658	1,659
Fixed assets (millions of lei)	8,984	15,698	27,152	30,472	32,896	33,640	37,009	38,924	42,917
Investment (millions of lei)	1,516	3,014	4,731	4,487	4,746	4,372	5,007	5,429	6,238
Agricultural tractors									
In physical units	16,093	24,716	29,704	31,543	32,106	30,194	27,221	28,381	31,498
In terms of 15 horsepower	23,674	40,974	53,016	55,937	57,926	54,477	48,852	51,224	57,182
Gross agricultural production (1960 = 100)									
Total	100	181	233	263	286	297	285	320	367
Crops	100	172	193	233	246	240	209	232	255
Livestock	100	203	323	334	378	426	458	519	618
Production per hectare (quintals)									
Wheat and rye	17.6	27.8	20.0	28.4	29.9	32.4	27.0	25.5	32.6
Maize	18.8	26.7	33.4	33.7	37.3	33.7	28.1	35.3	40.4
Production per animal									
Milk per cow (liters)	2,730	2,957	2,855	2,544	2,419	2,574	2,367	2,329	2,819
Wool per sheep (kilograms)	2.5	2.9	3.3	3.1	3.2	3.3	3.3	3.5	3.3
Eggs per chicken (number)	115	184	215	226	225	225	213	217	223

Source: Anuarul Statistic, various issues.

Table SA7.12. *Principal Indicators of Agricultural Production Cooperatives, 1962–76*

Indicator	*1962*	*1965*	*1970*	*1971*	*1972*	*1973*	*1974*	*1975*	*1976*
Number of units	5,398	4,680	4,626	4,601	4,549	4,462	4,420	4,419	4,418
Families (thousands)	3,925	3,409	3,454	3,455	3,453	3,443	3,437	3,429	n.a.
Agricultural area (thousands of hectares)	9,085	8,994	9,033	9,041	9,025	8,991	9,025	9,047	9,055
Arable area (thousands of hectares)	7,677	7,387	7,274	7,258	7,219	7,166	7,198	7,229	7,239
Families per unit (number)	727	728	747	751	759	772	778	776	n.a.
Agricultural area per unit (hectares)	1,683	1,922	1,953	1,965	1,984	2,015	2,042	2,047	n.a.
Investment, total (millions of lei)	2,964	2,811	4,111	4,642	4,419	4,283	4,286	4,778	5,362
State granted credit	984	372	1,892	2,169	2,089	1,903	1,773	1,964	n.a.
Own funds	1,980	2,439	2,219	2,473	2,330	2,379	2,513	2,814	n.a.
Gross agricultural production (1962 = 100)									
Total	100	119	119	146	159	156	158	161	195
Crops	100	120	115	146	158	149	150	150	186
Livestock	100	116	140	146	165	190	197	214	234
Production per hectare (quintals)									
Wheat and rye	12.2	18.1	13.4	21.3	22.8	21.6	20.0	20.0	27.5
Maize	16.0	17.6	20.2	24.6	30.9	24.7	25.7	27.4	33.9
Production per animal									
Milk per cow (liter)	1,551	1,410	1,297	1,205	1,177	1,235	1,191	1,225	1,312
Wool per sheep (kilograms)	2.2	2.1	2.2	2.0	2.1	2.1	2.0	2.1	2.1
Eggs per chicken (number)	81	62	79	138	171	185	182	194	202

Source: Anuarul Statistic, various issues.

Table SA7.13. *Principal Indicators of Stations for Agricultural Mechanization, 1960–76*

Indicator	*1960*	*1965*	*1970*	*1971*	*1972*	*1973*	*1974*	*1975*	*1976*
Number of units	243	264	293	772	743	743	743	743	743
Total personnel	44,502	85,667	96,118	106,200	113,690	113,986	118,761	126,383	131,540
Personnel per unit	183	324	328	132	153	153	160	170	177
Fixed assets, total (millions of lei)	5,522	9,796	12,527	13,615	14,203	15,129	17,013	19,137	21,895
Investments, total (millions of lei)	1,467	941	1,534	1,934	1,661	1,699	2,943	3,185	3,629
Numbers of machines									
Agricultural tractors									
In physical units	26,598	55,439	75,710	80,425	80,529	82,638	86,532	88,461	91,448
In terms of 15 horse-power	39,562	90,128	128,621	139,027	141,038	143,971	152,278	158,086	163,410
Tractor-drawn ploughs	30,689	62,056	73,311	72,625	73,333	72,068	75,207	76,706	77,036
Mechanical cultivators	12,356	14,680	23,824	28,349	29,004	28,102	27,359	27,769	28,733
Chemical fertilizer spreaders	988	2,020	10,283	10,173	10,611	9,918	9,260	8,691	7,803
Mechanical sprayers and dusters	1,166	4,082	7,187	7,731	8,200	8,093	9,120	11,316	12,632
Tractor-drawn grain combines	8,428	23,058	33,615	30,213	26,401	26,507	24,053	17,337	14,244
Maize combines	30	24	1,583	1,586	1,363	1,529	1,528	1,513	1,430
Self-propelled combines	698	31	289	1,131	2,455	4,285	8,091	11,927	17,056
Combiner for silage plants	60	4,109	4,130	4,100	4,797	5,990	6,295	6,925	n.a.
Motor lorries and tankers	785	1,085	1,413	1,522	1,613	1,649	1,693	1,724	1,913

Work performed (thousands of hectares of standard-depth plowing), total	14,181	34,100	42,473	45,629	47,072	53,152	53,033	60,729	62,903
Plowing	4,726	7,604	7,868	7,488	6,950	8,718	7,708	8,252	7,091
Sowing	2,358	5,798	6,055	6,466	6,366	6,737	6,477	6,845	6,734
Hoeing	852	3,749	5,483	6,146	6,783	6,488	6,682	6,028	8,248
Cereal harvesting	576	1,541	1,723	1,870	2,059	1,996	2,094	2,041	2,229
Work performed for agricultural producer co-operatives (thousands of hectares of standard-depth plowing)	10,495	31,990	36,943	40,205	40,811	46,166	45,428	52,625	53,646
Average volume of work per average tractor in terms of 15 horsepower (hectares of standard-depth plowing)	442	401	339	333	343	368	347	391	383
Average volume of work per worker (hectares of standard-depth plowing	319	398	442	430	414	466	447	481	478

Source: Anuarul Statistic, various issues.

Table SA7.14. *Number of Agricultural Tractors and Machines, 1938–76*

Equipment	*1938*	*1950*	*1955*	*1960*	*1965*	*1970*
Agricultural tractors						
In physical units	4,049	13,713	23,033	44,194	81,356	107,29
In terms of 15 horsepower	4,858	16,746	30,488	65,290	132,982	184,77
Tractor-drawn plows	—	13,642	25,613	46,130	86,215	97,24
Mechanical cultivators	—	1,343	7,787	20,667	23,241	29,34
Rotary hoes	—	—	—	6,784	17,118	14,44
Mechanical seeders	—	6,350	12,454	33,948	65,964	54,52
Chemical fertilizer spreaders	—	—	—	3,182	4,363	14,50
Mechanical sprayers and dusters	—	—	—	2,864	5,417	10,71
Tractor-drawn grain combines	—	74	46	15,995	36,552	43,91
Maize combines	—	—	—	846	3,143	4,57
Self-propelled combines	—	44	1,489	1,582	292	1,32
Combiner for silage plants	—	—	—	920	7,716	7,12
Arable area per physical tractor (hectares)	2,493	684	420	222	121	9

Source: Anuarul Statistic, various issues.

Equipment	*1971*	*1972*	*1973*	*1974*	*1975*	*1976*
gricultural tractors						
In physical units	114,184	115,606	116,513	116,816	119,533	128,024
In terms of 15 horsepower	198,596	204,045	204,548	206,400	213,652	229,405
ractor-drawn plows	96,821	97,465	95,506	95,599	96,633	98,833
echanical cultivators	33,909	35,165	34,594	33,736	34,391	36,107
otary hoes	12,713	10,992	9,643	7,750	6,690	6,105
echanical seeders	50,711	49,238	43,436	43,672	46,462	44,117
hemical fertilizer spreaders	14,424	14,492	13,718	12,783	12,251	12,067
echanical sprayers and dusters	11,804	13,152	13,130	13,942	16,705	19,119
ractor-drawn grain combines	39,753	34,949	33,222	28,438	20,209	15,391
aize combines	4,465	4,308	4,148	3,528	2,956	2,644
lf-propelled combines	2,595	4,628	7,197	12,245	17,912	23,567
ombiner for silage plants	6,973	7,161	9,117	9,130	9,445	7,719
rable area per physical tractor (hectares)	85	84	83	83	81	76

Table SA7.15. *Chemical Fertilizer Used in Agriculture, by Kind of Production Unit*

(thousands of tons of active substance, unless otherwise indicated)

Unit and fertilizer	*1950*	*1955*	*1960*	*1965*	*1970*	*197*
All production units						
Nitrogen (N)	2.6	9.5	24.7	144.5	366.9	431.
Phosphate (P_2O_5)	1.6	7.1	46.8	110.1	203.2	179.
Potash (K_2O)	1.7	5.3	3.0	11.8	24.2	22.
Total	5.9	21.9	74.5	266.4	594.3	633.
State agricultural enterprises						
Nitrogen (N)	1.0	1.8	13.3	73.1	121.3	134.
Phosphate (P_2O_5)	0.7	1.8	32.0	54.0	71.8	62.
Potash (K_2O)	0.3	0.8	0.8	6.1	12.1	11.
Total	2.0	4.4	46.1	133.2	205.2	208.
Agricultural production cooperative						
Nitrogen (N)	0.1	1.2	8.4	66.0	239.7	290
Phosphate (P_2O_5)	0.1	0.9	10.8	52.0	127.5	113
Potash (K_2O)	—	0.3	1.1	5.2	11.7	10
Total	0.2	2.4	20.3	123.2	378.9	414
Other units						
Nitrogen (N)	1.5	6.5	3.0	5.4	5.9	6
Phosphate (P_2O_5)	0.8	4.4	4.0	4.1	3.9	4
Potash (K_2O)	1.4	4.2	1.1	0.5	0.4	0
Total	3.7	15.1	8.1	10.0	10.2	11
Total fertilizer use per hectare under crops (kilograms of active substance)[a]						
All agricultural units	0.6	2.3	7.6	27.1	61.0	65
State agricultural enterprises	3.7	6.4	34.9	81.9	122.5	124
Agricultural production cooperatives	0.9	3.1	6.8	18.0	56.5	62
Other units	0.4	1.8	1.7	6.2	6.4	6

a. Estimates obtained by dividing fertilizer use shown here by area under crops by type of pr[illegible] duction unit shown in Table SA7.6.

Source: Anuarul Statistic, various issues.

	1972	1973	1974	1975	1976
ll production units					
Nitrogen (N)	421.0	419.6	480.3	571.8	640.0
Phosphate (P_2O_5)	172.9	241.8	298.6	314.4	321.9
Potash (K_2O)	45.1	53.2	34.8	42.5	43.5
Total	639.0	714.6	813.7	928.7	1,005.4
tate agricultural enterprises					
Nitrogen (N)	124.1	115.4	118.0	143.9	155.9
Phosphate (P_2O_5)	54.0	79.1	81.5	90.8	93.5
Potash (K_2O)	22.4	24.3	13.9	17.3	15.0
Total	200.5	218.8	213.4	252.0	264.4
gricultural production cooperative					
Nitrogen (N)	265.1	264.8	314.3	365.8	419.6
Phosphate (P_2O_5)	109.8	151.7	195.3	197.3	206.8
Potash (K_2O)	20.2	24.9	17.3	20.2	24.2
Total	395.1	441.4	526.9	583.3	650.6
ther units					
Nitrogen (N)	31.8	39.4	48.0	62.1	n.a.
Phosphate (P_2O_5)	9.1	11.0	21.8	26.3	n.a.
Potash (P_2O)	2.5	4.0	3.6	5.0	n.a.
Total	43.4	54.4	73.4	93.4	n.a.
otal fertilizer use per hectare under crops (kilograms of active substance)[a]					
All agricultural units	65.8	73.7	84.1	95.4	103.4
State agricultural units	120.1	131.5	129.2	151.8	159.6
Agricultural production cooperatives	59.4	66.7	79.6	87.9	98.0
Other units	26.8	33.3	44.8	57.2	n.a.

Table SA7.16. *Irrigated Area, by Kind of Production Unit and Land Use, 1961–76*

Item	*1961*	*1965*	*1970*	*1973*	*1974*	*1975*	*1976*
			Thousands of hectares[a]				
Type of production units							
State agricultural units	—	104.4	231.5	357.1	395.0	432.1	469.
Agricultural production cooperatives	—	115.9	431.6	753.3	832.9	977.4	1,029.
Other	—	2.3	1.5	—	—	14.7	15.
Total arable area	—	222.6	664.6	1,110.4	1,227.9	1,424.2	1,513.
Land use							
Crops							
Wheat	23.7	8.8	48.5	192.6	221.2	210.0	225.
Maize or grain	45.7	57.5	156.5	219.5	251.2	428.0	454.
Sunflower	4.0	1.6	21.5	53.1	60.4	56.8	64.
Sugar beets	5.4	3.7	18.1	—	37.0	55.9	55.
Potatoes	2.4	2.5	10.8	—	—	—	–
Vegetables	50.4	57.7	116.6	118.0	117.5	128.4	134.
Lucerne and clover	—	35.2	100.5	140.7	153.1	181.2	175.
Other crops	53.0	45.9	165.3	334.4	329.3	292.8	334.
Total arable area	184.6	212.9	637.8	1,057.3	1,169.7	1,353.1	1,443
Pasture and meadow	—	5.0	11.6	19.4	19.4	25.8	28.
Vineyards	—	3.6	9.3	16.7	18.9	19.2	24.
Orchard	—	1.1	5.9	7.0	9.1	10.6	13.
Subtotal	—	9.7	26.8	43.1	47.4	55.6	66.
Total agricultural area	—	222.6	664.6	1,110.4	1,227.9	1,424.2	1,513

Item	1961	1965	1970	1973	1974	1975	1976
			Percentages of area[b]				
'ype of production unit							
State agricultural units	—	6.3	14.1	19.8	21.8	23.7	25.4
Agricultural production cooperatives	—	1.7	6.8	11.6	12.7	14.8	15.5
Other	—	0.2	0.1	—	—	1.2	1.2
Total arable area	—	2.3	7.2	11.6	12.8	14.8	15.6
,and use							
Crops							
Wheat	0.8	0.3	2.1	8.1	9.1	8.8	9.3
Maize or grain	1.3	1.7	5.1	7.4	8.5	13.0	13.4
Sunflower	0.9	0.4	3.6	10.4	11.9	11.1	12.4
Sugar beets	3.1	2.0	10.7	—	16.9	22.7	23.6
Potatoes	0.8	0.8	3.8	—	—	—	—
Vegetables	27.8	31.9	51.9	50.3	51.1	57.6	52.8
Lucerne and clover	—	—	16.6	21.4	24.5	24.9	—
Other crops	—	—	—	—	—	—	—
Total arable area	1.9	2.3	7.2	11.1	12.8	14.8	14.8
Pasture and meadow	—	0.1	0.3	0.4	0.4	0.6	0.6
Vineyards	—	1.2	2.7	5.0	5.7	5.9	7.6
Orchard	—	0.3	1.4	1.6	2.1	2.5	3.0
Subtotal	—	—	—	—	—	—	—
'otal agricultural area	—	1.5	4.5	7.5	8.2	9.5	10.1

a. At the end of crop year.

b. Computed by dividing data reported in this table by data reported in Tables SA7.4, SA7.5, and A7.6.

Source: Anuarul Statistic, various issues.

Table SA8.1. *Construction Work, by Subsector of the National Economy, 1960–76*
(millions of lei)

Subsector	1959 prices		1963 prices			
	1960	*1965*	*1965*	*1970*	*1966–70*	*1971*
Total	*11,895*	*20,478*	*21,086*	*34,735*	*148,131*	*38,247*
Industry	5,827	10,555	10,756	17,183	76,971	19,673
Group A	4,994	9,611	9,809	14,471	64,801	16,780
Group B	833	944	947	2,712	12,170	2,893
Building	44	115	124	419	1,096	325
Agriculture	1,414	3,047	3,094	5,650	20,914	6,696
Forestry	25	27	27	38	185	56
Transport	1,015	1,201	1,250	2,813	10,818	2,853
Telecommunications	123	151	169	326	1,318	372
Trade	448	668	701	1,674	5,547	2,022
Municipal services, housing, and other nonproductive services	2,162	3,817	4,025	4,393	22,143	4,237
Housing only	1,582	2,803	3,017	2,863	15,911	2,455
Education, culture, and arts	491	457	488	1,028	4,239	963
Education only	280	401	429	807	3,350	791
Culture and arts only	211	56	59	221	889	172
Science and scientific services	77	32	34	169	692	241
Public health, social assistance, and physical culture	192	215	225	749	2,428	470
Administration	70	113	111	246	1,101	286
Other	7	80	82	47	679	53

Note: Excludes repairs and maintenance.
Source: Anuarul Statistic, various issues.

Subsector	1963 prices					
	1972	1973	1974	1975	1971–75	1976
otal	*41,333*	*44,298*	*45,628*	*50,854*	*220,360*	*53,090*
dustry	21,726	24,119	24,594	26,186	116,298	27,246
Group A	18,579	19,689	20,236	22,126	97,410	23,264
Group B	3,147	4,430	4,358	4,060	18,888	3,982
uilding	282	210	449	197	1,463	236
griculture	6,744	6,945	6,517	6,733	33,635	7,032
orestry	54	50	74	68	302	89
ransport	3,070	2,976	2,721	3,468	15,088	3,568
elecommunications	419	568	539	521	2,419	542
rade	2,005	1,897	1,981	2,352	10,257	2,725
unicipal services, housing, and other nonproductive services	4,938	5,388	5,980	8,520	29,063	8,714
Housing only	2,790	3,509	4,360	6,247	19,361	5,723
ducation, culture, and arts	1,105	1,208	1,225	1,383	5,884	1,335
Education only	917	1,089	1,131	1,264	5,192	1,176
Culture and arts only	188	119	94	119	692	159
:iences and scientific services	184	154	217	233	1,029	247
ublic health, social assistance, and physical culture	498	452	709	705	2,834	696
dministration	224	245	543	403	1,701	607
ther	84	86	79	85	387	53

Table SA8.2. *Share of Construction Work, by Industrial Sector, 1960–76*
(percent)

Sector	1960[a]	1965[a]	1965[b]	1970[b]	1971[b]	1972[b]	1973[b]
Industry	49.0	51.5	51.0	49.5	51.4	52.6	54.4
Group A	42.0	46.9	46.5	41.7	43.9	45.0	44.4
Group B	7.0	4.6	4.5	7.8	7.5	7.6	10.0
Construction	0.4	0.6	0.6	1.2	0.8	0.7	0.5
Agriculture	11.9	14.9	14.7	16.3	17.5	16.3	15.7
Forestry	0.2	0.1	0.1	0.1	0.2	0.1	0.1
Transport	8.5	5.9	5.9	8.1	7.5	7.4	6.7
Telecommunications	1.0	0.7	0.8	0.9	1.0	1.0	1.3
Trade	3.8	3.3	3.3	4.8	5.3	4.9	4.3
Municipal services	18.2	18.6	19.1	12.7	11.1	11.9	12.2
Housing	13.3	13.7	14.3	8.2	6.4	6.8	7.9
Education, culture, and arts	4.1	2.2	2.3	2.9	2.5	2.7	2.7
Education	2.3	1.9	2.0	2.3	2.1	2.2	2.5
Culture and arts	1.8	0.3	0.3	0.6	0.4	0.5	0.3
Scientific research	0.6	0.2	0.2	0.5	0.6	0.4	0.3
Health	1.6	1.0	1.1	2.2	1.2	1.2	1.0
Administration	0.6	0.6	0.5	0.7	0.8	0.6	0.6
Other	0.1	0.4	0.4	0.1	0.1	0.2	0.2

a. In 1959 prices.
b. In 1963 prices.
Source: Anuarul Statistic, various issues.

Sector	1974[b]	1975[b]	1976[b]	Average annual rates of growth 1961–65	1966–70	1971–75	1961–75
Total				*11.5*	*10.5*	*7.9*	*10.0*
Industry	53.9	51.5	51.3	12.7	9.8	8.8	10.4
Group A	44.3	43.5	43.8	14.0	8.1	8.8	10.3
Group B	9.6	8.0	7.5	2.5	23.4	8.4	11.2
Construction	1.0	0.3	0.4	21.2	27.6	−14.0	10.6
Agriculture	14.3	13.2	13.2	16.6	12.8	3.6	10.9
Forestry	0.1	0.1	0.2	1.6	7.1	12.3	6.9
Transport	6.0	6.8	6.7	3.4	17.6	4.4	8.3
Telecommunications	1.2	1.0	1.0	4.2	14.0	9.8	9.3
Trade	4.3	4.6	5.1	8.3	19.0	7.0	11.3
Municipal services	13.1	16.8	16.4	12.0	1.8	14.2	9.2
Housing	9.6	12.3	10.8	12.1	−1.1	16.9	9.1
Education, culture, and arts	2.7	2.7	2.5	−1.3	16.1	6.1	6.7
Education	2.5	2.5	2.2	7.5	13.5	9.4	10.1
Culture and arts	0.2	0.2	0.3	−31.0	30.2	−11.7	−4.1
Scientific research	0.5	0.5	0.5	−16.1	37.8	6.6	7.2
Health	1.5	1.4	1.3	2.3	27.1	−1.2	8.8
Administration	1.2	0.8	1.1	10.1	17.3	10.4	12.3
Other	0.2	0.2	0.1	63.0	−10.6	12.6	18.0

Table SA8.3. *Index of Construction Output, by Category of Object, 1965–76*
(1960 = 100)

Category	*1965*	*1970*	*1971*	*1972*	*1973*	*1974*	*1975*	*1976*
Total	*181*	*311*	*340*	*364*	*391*	*406*	*444*	*473*
Industrial building and construction	218	382	427	482				
Agriculture and zoo technical buildings and					563	613	644	676
construction	191	282	278	290	310	249	215	264
Buildings for transport, telecommunications, trade, and sociocultural activities	172	450	426	446	403	441	517	563
Residential buildings	201	294	311	347	422	474	593	614
Roads	136	199	202	210	205	198	251	238
Railways	134	209	230	230	216	226	263	250
Supply networks and pipelines (includes sewerage)	201	251	287	361	345	326	392	388
Power distribution and telecommunications	213	371	406	429	448	452	480	480

Source: Anuarul Statistic, various issues.

Table SA8.4. *Shares of Construction Output, by Category of Object, Socialist Sector*

Category	*1960*[a]	*1965*[a]	*1965*[b]	*1970*[b]	*1971*[b]	*1972*[b]	*1973*[b]	*1974*[b]	*1975*[b]	*1976*[b]
Industrial building and construction	28.1	33.8	32.9	33.6	34.3	36.2	39.3	41.3	39.7	39.1
Agriculture and zoo technical buildings and construction	10.4	11.0	11.2	9.6	8.7	8.5	8.4	6.5	5.1	5.9
Buildings for transport, telecommunications, trade, and sociocultural activities	6.0	5.7	5.8	8.8	7.6	7.5	6.3	6.6	7.1	7.2
Residential buildings	11.6	12.8	13.3	11.3	11.0	11.4	12.9	13.9	16.0	15.5
Roads	8.7	6.6	6.2	5.3	4.9	4.8	4.3	4.0	4.7	4.2
Railways	4.5	3.3	4.5	4.0	4.1	3.8	3.3	3.3	3.6	3.2
Supply networks and pipelines (includes sewerage)	5.6	6.2	6.2	4.5	4.7	5.6	4.9	4.5	4.9	4.6
Power distribution and telecommunications	7.1	8.4	7.6	7.6	7.7	7.6	7.4	7.2	7.0	6.5

a. In 1959 prices.
b. In 1963 prices.
Source: Anuarul Statistic, various issues.

Table SA8.5. *Average Annual Rates of Growth of Construction Output, by Category of Object, Socialist Sector, 1961–65 to 1971–75*
(percent)

Category	*1961–65*	*1966–70*	*1971–75*	*1961–75*
Total	*12.6*	*11.4*	*7.4*	*10.4*
Industrial building and construction	16.9	11.9	11.0	13.2
Agriculture and zoo technical buildings and construction	13.8	8.1	−5.6	5.3
Buildings for transport, telecommunications, trade, and sociocultural activities	11.5	21.2	2.8	11.6
Residential buildings	15.0	7.9	15.1	12.6
Roads	6.4	7.9	4.7	6.4
Railways	6.0	9.3	4.7	6.7
Supply networks and pipelines (includes sewerage)	15.0	4.5	9.3	9.5
Power distribution and telecommunications	16.3	11.7	5.2	11.0

Source: Anuarul Statistic, various issues.

Table SA8.6. *Employment, Growth Rates, and Capital-Output-Labor Ratios in the Construction Industry, 1950–76*

Item	*1950*		*1955*		*1960*
Employment (thousands)					
Total occupied population	8,377.2		9,362.6		9,537.7
Occupied population in construction	186.3		402.6		470.5
Percentage in construction	2.2		4.3		4.9
Average number of employees	2,123.0		2,948.4		3,249.2
Average number of employees in construction	174.9		367.9		371.9
Percentage in construction	8.2		12.4		11.4
		Average annual rates of growth (percent)			
		1951–55		*1956–60*	
Total occupied population		2.3		0.3	
Occupied population in construction		16.7		3.1	
Average number of employees		6.8		2.0	
Average number of employees in construction		16.0		0.2	
Capital/output ratios[a] (1965 = 100)					
Construction	73		133		82
Total productive sector	129		100		94
Output/labor ratios[b] (1965 = 100)					
Construction	55		58		95
Total productive sector	27		46		64
Capital/labor ratios (1965 = 100)					
Construction	42		76		78
Total productive sector	34		46		54
Incremental capital/output ratios[c]					
Construction					
Total productive sector					

(Table continues on the following pages)

Table SA8.6. *Continued*

Item	*1965*	*1970*	*1971*
Employment (thousands)			
Total occupied population	9,684.0	9,875.0	9,938.9
Occupied population in construction	609.3	768.2	800.6
Percentage in construction	6.3	7.8	8.1
Average number of employees	4,305.3	5,108.7	5,374.5
Average number of employees in construction	512.5	682.5	714.2
Percentage in construction	11.9	13.4	13.3
	Average annual rate of growth (percent)		
	1961–65	*1966–70*	
Total occupied population	0.3	0.4	
Occupied population in construction	5.3	4.7	
Average number of employees	5.9	3.5	
Average number of employees in construction	6.6	5.9	
Capital/output ratios[a] (1965 = 100)			
Construction	100	99	102
Total productive sector	100	128	13[illegible]
Output/labor ratios[b] (1965 = 100)			
Construction	100	140	14[illegible]
Total productive sector	100	144	16[illegible]
Capital/labor ratios (1965 = 100)			
Construction	100	138	15[illegible]
Total productive sector	100	184	21[illegible]
Incremental capital/output ratios[c]			
Construction	1.93	1.36	
Total productive sector	3.11	4.15	

Item	1972	1973	1974	1975	1976
mployment (thousands)					
Total occupied population	9,970.9	10,020.6	10,070.1	10,150.8	10,227.0
Occupied population in construction	840.2	826.6	812.7	825.5	848.1
Percentage in construction	8.4	8.2	8.1	8.1	8.1
Average number of employees	5,629.6	5,829.6	6,024.6	6,300.8	6,558.8
Average number of employees in construction	746.2	739.5	715.1	736.4	749.2
Percentage in construction	13.3	12.7	11.9	11.7	11.4

	Average annual rate of growth (percent) 1971–75				
Total occupied population	0.5				
Occupied population in construction	1.4				
Average number of employees	4.3				
Average number of employees in construction	1.5				
ıpital/output ratios[a] (1965 = 100)					
Construction	117	117	126	138	
Total productive sector	133	137	140	150	
ıtput/labor ratios[b] (1965 = 100)					
Construction	151	162	174	187	
Total productive sector	179	198	223	242	
Capital/labor ratios (1965 = 100)					
Construction	170	189	220	259	
Total productive sector	239	270	313	364	
:remental capital/output ratios[c]					
Construction	2.69				
Total productive sector	3.03				

ι. Ratio of fixed assets to national income, in comparable prices.

ι. Ratio of national income to occupied population.

. Ratio of investment to increase in national income over the five-year period, in 1963 compar- : prices.

'ource: *Anuarul Statistic*, various issues.

Table SA8.7. *Housing Turned over to Occupancy, 1965–76*

Year	*Total*				*From state, centralized, and cooperative funds*			
	Number of dwellings		*Area (thousands of square meters)*		*Number of apartments*		*Area (thousands of square meters)*	
	Actual	*Conventional*	*Total*	*Inhabitable area*	*Actual*	*Conventional*	*Total*	*Inhabitable area*
				Total				
1965	191,988	165,599	—	4,968	51,973	53,864	—	1,616
1970	159,152	166,053	9,273	4,982	68,016	55,231	3,018	1,658
1966–70	647,668	688,541	40,332	20,657	297,135	281,421	17,804	8,444
1971	147,023	157,914	9,110	4,737	52,416	45,164	2,601	1,354
1972	135,969	151,175	9,021	4,536	48,541	43,823	2,692	1,315
1973	149,128	161,154	9,751	4,835	57,649	51,620	3,227	1,549
1974	154,345	172,067	10,443	5,162	65,227	59,998	3,809	1,799
1975	165,431	185,609	11,430	5,568	85,352	82,657	5,290	2,480
1971–75	751,896	827,919	49,755	24,838	309,185	283,262	17,619	8,497
1976	139,443	n.a.	n.a.	n.a.	67,381	n.a.	n.a.	n.a.

Table SA8.7. *Continued*

	With state assistance				*From own funds*			
	Number of dwellings		*Area (thousands of square meters)*		*Number of apartments*		*Area (thousands of square meters)*	
Year	*Actual*	*Conventional*	*Total*	*Inhabitable area*	*Actual*	*Conventional*	*Total*	*Inhabitable area*
				Total				
1965	—	—	—	—	140,015	111,735	—	3,352
1970	28,279	30,633	1,968	919	62,857	80,189	4,287	2,405
1966–70	36,042	41,663	2,746	1,250	314,491	365,457	19,782	10,963
1971	36,010	38,418	2,444	1,153	58,597	74,332	4,065	2,230
1972	37,326	41,925	2,721	1,258	50,102	65,427	3,608	1,963
1973	42,924	45,487	3,008	1,365	48,555	64,047	3,516	1,921
1974	41,909	47,350	3,065	1,421	47,209	64,719	3,569	1,942
1975	45,153	51,796	3,271	1,554	34,926	51,156	2,869	1,534
1971–75	203,322	224,976	14,509	6,751	239,389	319,681	17,627	9,590
1976	45,052	n.a.	n.a.	n.a.	27,010	n.a.	n.a.	n.a.

(Table continues on the following pages)

Table SA8.7. *Continued*

	Total				*From state, centralized, and cooperative funds*			
	Number of dwellings		*Area (thousands of square meters)*		*Number of apartments*		*Area (thousands of square meters)*	
Year	*Actual*	*Conventional*	*Total*	*Inhabitable area*	*Actual*	*Conventional*	*Total*	*Inhabitable area*
				Urban				
1965	77,433	74,264	—	2,228	49,804	51,796	—	1,554
1970	111,325	105,932	6,133	3,178	66,679	54,056	2,953	1,622
1966–70	386,934	386,999	24,159	11,611	289,411	273,304	17,305	8,200
1971	103,451	103,454	6,192	3,104	51,364	44,259	2,550	1,328
1972	97,797	102,735	6,407	3,083	47,363	42,725	2,627	1,282
1973	110,539	112,127	7,091	3,364	55,802	49,916	3,118	1,497
1974	115,558	120,982	7,668	8,629	62,516	57,322	3,645	1,719
1975	135,092	143,726	9,127	4,312	81,476	78,540	5,046	2,356
1971–75	562,437	583,024	36,485	17,492	298,521	272,762	16,986	8,182
1976	115,234	n.a.	n.a.	n.a	63,675	n.a.	n.a.	n.a.

Table SA8.7. *Continued*

Year	With state assistance				From own funds			
	Number of dwellings		Area (thousands of square meters)		Number of apartments		Area (thousands of square meters)	
	Actual	Conventional	Total	Inhabitable area	Actual	Conventional	Total	Inhabitable area
				Urban				
1965	—	—	—	—	27,629	22,468	—	674
1970	28,279	30,633	1,968	919	16,367	21,243	1,212	637
1966–70	36,042	41,663	2,746	1,250	61,481	72,032	4,108	2,101
1971	36,009	38,414	2,444	1,153	16,078	20,781	1,198	623
1972	37,326	41,925	2,721	1,258	13,108	18,085	1,059	543
1973	42,904	45,478	3,007	1,365	11,833	16,733	966	502
1974	41,909	47,350	3,065	1,421	11,133	16,310	958	489
1975	45,158	51,796	3,271	1,554	8,463	13,390	810	402
1971–75	203,301	224,963	14,508	6,751	60,615	85,299	4,991	2,559
1976	45,052	n.a.	n.a.	n.a.	6,507	n.a.	n.a.	n.a.

(*Table continues on the following pages*)

Table SA8.7. *Continued*

	Total				*From state, centralized, and cooperative funds*			
	Number of dwellings		*Area (thousands of square meters)*		*Number of apartments*		*Area (thousands of square meters)*	
Year	*Actual*	*Conventional*	*Total*	*Inhabitable area*	*Actual*	*Conventional*	*Total*	*Inhabitable area*
				Rural				
1965	114,555	91,335	—	2,740	2,169	2,068	—	62
1970	47,827	60,121	3,140	1,804	1,337	1,175	65	36
1966–70	260,734	301,542	16,173	9,046	7,724	8,117	499	244
1971	43,572	54,460	2,918	1,633	1,052	905	51	26
1972	38,172	48,440	2,614	1,453	1,178	1,098	65	33
1973	38,589	49,027	2,660	1,471	1,847	1,704	109	52
1974	38,787	51,085	2,775	1,533	2,711	2,676	164	80
1975	30,339	41,883	2,303	1,256	3,876	4,117	244	124
1971–75	189,459	244,895	13,270	7,346	10,664	10,500	633	315
1976	24,209	n.a.	n.a.	n.a.	3,706	n.a.	n.a.	n.a.

Table SA8.7. *Continued*

	With state assistance				*From own funds*			
	Number of dwellings		*Area (thousands of square meters)*		*Number of apartments*		*Area (thousands of square meters)*	
Year	*Actual*	*Conventional*	*Total*	*Inhabitable area*	*Actual*	*Conventional*	*Total*	*Inhabitable area*
				Rural				
1965	—	—	—	—	112,386	89,267	—	2,678
1970	—	—	—	—	46,490	58,946	3,075	1,768
1966–70	—	—	—	—	253,010	293,425	15,674	8,802
1971	1	4	—[a]	—[a]	42,519	53,551	2,867	1,607
1972	—	—	—	—	36,994	47,342	2,549	1,420
1973	20	9	1	—[a]	36,722	47,314	2,550	1,419
1974	—	—	—	—	36,076	48,409	2,611	1,453
1975	—	—	—	—	26,463	37,766	2,059	1,132
1971–75	21	13	1	—[a]	178,774	234,382	12,636	7,031
1976	—	—	—	—	20,503	n.a.	n.a.	n.a.

n.a. Not available.
a. Conventional apartments are defined as thirty square meters of inhabitable area.
Source: Anuarul Statistic, various issues.

Table SA8.8. *Structure of Investment in Construction, 1950–76*
(millions of lei)

Item	1959 prices			
	1950	1955	1960	1965
Total investment	5,663	13,466	24,615	44,857
Construction work	2,855	7,046	11,895	20,478
Construction as percent of total investment	50.4	52.3	48.3	45.7
	1963 prices			
	1965	*1970*	*1971*	*1972*
Total investment	44,659	74,790	82,617	91,717
Construction work	21,086	34,735	38,247	41,333
Construction as percent of total investment	47.2	46.4	46.3	45.1
	1963 prices			
	1973	*1974*	*1975*	*1976*
Total investment	99,231	112,457	130,640	141,233
Construction work	44,298	45,628	50,854	53,090
Construction as percent of total investment	44.6	40.6	38.9	37.6

Source: Anuarul Statistic, various issues.

Table SA9.1. *Transport of Goods, by Subsector, 1950–76*

Subsector	*1950*	*1955*	*1960*	*1965*	*1970*
Railways					
Thousands of tonnes	35,069	58,963	77,492	114,354	171,312
Percent	91.8	84.3	54.7	44.8	40.2
Millions of tonne-kilometers	7,598	14,675	19,821	30,981	48,045
Percent	89.4	91.6	87.6	86.5	85.2
Roads					
Thousands of tonnes	1,046	7,335	56,608	130,850	239,776
Percent	2.7	10.5	40.0	51.2	56.4
Millions of tonne-kilometers	42	272	936	2,533	5,156
Percent	0.5	1.7	4.1	7.1	9.1
River					
Thousands of tonnes	1,108	1,596	1,914	2,865	3,396
Percent	2.9	2.3	1.4	1.1	0.8
Millions of tonne-kilometers	669	648	865	1,222	1,346
Percent	7.9	4.0	3.8	3.4	2.4
Petroleum pipelines					
Thousands of tonnes	997	2,034	5,586	7,422	11,251
Percent	2.6	2.9	3.9	2.9	2.6
Millions of tonne-kilometers	189	430	1,019	1,057	1,841
Percent	2.2	2.7	4.5	3.0	3.3
Total					
Thousands of tonnes	*38,220*	*69,928*	*141,600*	*255,491*	*425,735*
Millions of tonne-kilometers	*8,498*	*16,025*	*22,641*	*35,793*	*56,388*

(Table continues on the following page)

Table SA9.1. *Continued*

Subsector	*1971*	*1972*	*1973*	*1974*	*1975*
Railways					
Thousands of tonnes	184,787	193,740	205,955	218,073	228,264
Percent	40.0	39.7	39.2	38.9	34.2
Millions of tonne-kilometers	50,840	53,280	57,103	61,618	64,803
Percent	85.0	84.9	84.8	84.7	82.0
Roads					
Thousands of tonnes	260,735	276,173	301,530	322,583	418,759
Percent	56.4	56.7	57.3	57.6	62.7
Millions of tonne-kilometers	5,496	5,738	6,003	6,446	9,290
Percent	9.2	9.1	8.9	8.9	11.8
River					
Thousands of tonnes	4,103	5,270	5,432	5,881	6,103
Percent	0.9	1.1	1.0	1.1	0.9
Millions of tonne-kilometers	1,286	1,564	1,727	2,012	2,077
Percent	2.2	2.5	2.6	2.8	2.6
Petroleum pipelines					
Thousands of tonnes	12,516	11,942	13,059	13,249	14,541
Percent	2.7	2.5	2.4	2.4	2.2
Millions of tonne-kilometers	2,171	2,226	2,514	2,586	2,848
Percent	3.6	3.5	3.7	3.6	3.6
Total					
Thousands of tonnes	*462,141*	*487,125*	*525,976*	*559,786*	*667,667*
Millions of tonne-kilometers	*59,793*	*62,808*	*67,347*	*72,662*	*79,018*

Subsector	1976	Average annual growth rate (percent) 1965–70	1970–75	Average distance (kilometers) 1970	1975
Railways					
Thousands of tonnes	238,047	8.4	5.9	280	284
Percent	33.8				
Millions of tonne-kilometers	67,556	9.2	6.2		
Percent	81.3				
Roads					
Thousands of tonnes	442,236	12.9	11.8	21.5	22.2
Percent	62.7				
Millions of tonne-kilometers	9,857	15.3	12.5		
Percent	11.9				
River					
Thousands of tonnes	6,740	3.5	12.5	396	340
Percent	1.0				
Millions of tonne-kilometers	1,859	2.0	9.1		
Percent	2.2				
Petroleum pipelines					
Thousands of tonnes	17,270	8.7	5.2	164	196
Percent	2.5				
Millions of tonne-kilometers	3,828	11.8	9.1		
Percent	4.6				
Total					
Thousands of tonnes	*704,293*	*10.7*	*9.4*	*132*	*118*
Millions of tonne-kilometers	*83,100*	*9.5*	*7.0*		

Note: Official statistical data for aviation include international traffic. These data are not shown in this appendix; because of the very low numbers involved, however, the effect on the percentage distribution is negligible.

Source: Anuarul Statistic, various issues.

Table SA9.2. *Transport of Passengers, by Mode, 1950–76*

Subsector	*1950*	*1955*	*1960*	*1965*	*1970*
Railways					
Passengers	116,551	251,690	214,823	262,093	328,328
Percent	90.8	92.6	74.6	60.3	47.6
Millions of passenger-kilometers	8,155	12,460	10,737	13,535	17,793
Percent	95.1	95.5	88.0	78.8	69.2
Road					
Passengers	11,294	19,257	71,757	170,149	359,388
Percent	8.8	7.1	25.0	39.2	52.0
Millions of passenger-kilometers	388	558	1,419	3,573	7,858
Percent	4.5	4.3	11.7	20.8	30.5
River					
Passengers	563	951	1,159	1,910	1,913
Percent	0.4	0.3	0.4	0.4	0.3
Millions of passenger-kilometers	16	34	41	65	76
Percent	0.2	0.2	0.3	0.4	0.3
Total					
Passengers	*128,408*	*271,898*	*287,739*	*434,152*	*689,629*
Millions of passenger-kilometers	*8,559*	*13,052*	*12,197*	*17,173*	*25,727*

Subsector	*1971*	*1972*	*1973*	*1974*	*1975*
Railways					
Passengers	338,002	361,467	367,147	377,805	366,881
Percent	45.3	43.8	40.8	38.0	31.0
Millions of passenger-kilometers	18,811	20,184	21,228	22,406	22,380
Percent	67.5	66.2	63.9	61.8	54.1
Road					
Passengers	404,978	461,261	530,609	613,739	814,215
Percent	54.3	55.9	59.0	61.8	68.8
Millions of passenger-kilometers	8,992	10,231	11,866	13,739	18,915
Percent	32.2	33.5	35.7	37.9	45.7
River					
Passengers	1,864	1,899	1,950	2,132	2,306
Percent	0.3	0.2	0.2	0.2	0.2
Millions of passenger-kilometers	83	90	93	101	106
Percent	0.3	0.3	0.3	0.3	0.3
Total					
Passengers	*744,844*	*824,627*	*899,706*	*993,676*	*1,183,402*
Millions of passenger-kilometers	*27,886*	*30,505*	*33,187*	*36,246*	*41,401*

(Table continues on the following page)

Table SA9.2. *Continued*

Subsector	1976	Average annual growth rate (percent) 1965–70	1970–75	Average distance (kilometers) 1970	1975
Railways					
Passengers	373,159	4.6	2.2	54	61
Percent	30.4				
Millions of passenger-kilometers	23,077	5.6	4.7		
Percent	55.1				
Road					
Passengers	850,459	16.1	17.8	22	23
Percent	69.4				
Millions of passenger-kilometers	18,668	17.1	19.2		
Percent	44.6				
River					
Passengers	2,253	0.1	3.8	40	46
Percent	0.2				
Millions of passenger-kilometers	101	3.1	6.9		
Percent	0.3				
Total					
Passengers	*1,225,871*	*9.7*	*11.4*	*37*	*35*
Millions of passenger-kilometers	*41,846*	*8.4*	*10.0*		

Note: Official statistical data for aviation include international traffic. These data are not shown but, because of the low numbers involved, the effect on the percentage distribution is negligible.

Source: Anuarul Statistic, various issues.

able SA9.3. *Average Annual Percentage Rates of Growth Transport Modes, 1951–55 to 1971–75 and 1951–75*

Mode	*1951–55*	*1956–60*	*1961–65*	*1966–70*	*1971–75*	*1951–75*
			Goods transport			
umber of tonnes	12.8	15.1	12.6	10.9	9.4	12.1
Rail	11.0	5.6	8.1	8.4	5.9	7.8
Road	48.0	50.0	18.2	12.8	11.8	27.0
River	7.6	3.7	8.4	3.5	12.4	7.0
Sea	1.7	−0.2	48.0	26.2	8.1	15.3
Air	18.5	−15.6	10.8	29.2	5.9	8.6
Pipeline	15.3	22.4	5.9	8.7	5.3	11.3
onne-kilometers	12.9	7.2	13.3	16.3	9.1	11.7
Rail	14.1	6.2	9.3	9.2	6.2	9.0
Road	45.0	28.1	22.0	15.3	12.5	24.0
River	−0.7	6.0	7.2	1.9	9.1	4.6
Sea	3.1	8.4	51.0	35.0	12.1	20.6
Air	24.6	−7.8	20.0	48.0	9.5	17.4
Pipeline	17.9	18.8	0.7	11.8	9.1	11.5
			Passenger transport			
umber of passengers	16.2	1.1	8.6	9.7	11.4	9.3
Rail	16.6	−3.1	4.1	4.6	2.2	4.7
Road	11.3	30.1	18.8	16.1	17.8	18.7
River	11.0	4.0	10.5	0.0	3.8	5.8
Air	26.7	9.3	13.4	18.0	10.5	15.4
assenger-kilometers	8.6	−1.3	7.4	8.8	10.1	6.7
Rail	8.8	−3.0	4.7	5.6	4.7	4.1
Road	7.5	20.6	20.3	17.1	19.2	16.8
River	16.3	3.8	9.7	3.2	6.9	7.9
Air	24.6	15.4	34.1	21.6	13.8	21.7

Source: Anuarul Statistic, various issues.

Table SA9.4. *Rail Transport of Goods, by Commodity Group, 1950–76*
(thousands of tonnes)

Commodity group	*1950*	*1955*	*1960*	*1965*	*1970*	*1971*
Petroleum and petroleum products	3,801	9,873	9,964	12,311	16,071	16,1[illegible]
Coal	3,013	4,255	6,631	10,220	18,813	19,4[illegible]
Coke	492	695	1,018	1,467	3,149	3,1[illegible]
Ferrous and nonferrous metal products, machinery, and equipment	1,585	2,338	5,502	8,483	14,062	14,4[illegible]
Wood products	3,983	5,616	7,115	11,550	14,547	14,6[illegible]
Firewood	3,048	3,187	3,607	2,695	2,706	2,7[illegible]
Quarry and ballast products	6,910	11,523	13,943	23,839	37,945	43,7[illegible]
Building materials	2,534	4,083	5,778	10,274	16,743	17,8[illegible]
Cereals	1,922	2,919	2,909	4,681	5,386	5,3[illegible]
Sugarbeets	537	1,187	2,685	2,141	2,031	2,2[illegible]
Products of light and chemical industries	633	730	1,949	4,452	8,650	9,1[illegible]
Foodstuffs	2,224	2,955	3,916	5,474	7,457	7,1[illegible]
Others	4,387	9,602	12,475	16,767	23,752	28,8[illegible]
Total	*35,069*	*58,963*	*77,492*	*114,354*	*171,312*	*184,7[illegible]*

Source: Anuarul Statistic, various issues.

Commodity group	1972	1973	1974	1975	1976	Average distance (kilometers), 1972
etroleum and petroleum products	17,065	18,481	19,686	21,312	23,644	277
oal	20,803	21,789	22,978	25,371	23,254	164
oke	3,045	3,784	3,351	3,593	3,577	236
errous and nonferrous metal products, machinery, and equipment	15,067	16,293	17,900	20,070	21,718	346
Vood products	14,173	14,530	15,236	15,469	14,880	272
irewood	2,832	2,435	2,324	2,161	1,687	226
uarry and ballast products	44,819	45,838	47,785	46,988	49,919	165
uilding materials	18,815	19,240	20,527	21,654	22,562	222
ereals	6,060	6,786	6,894	7,582	8,628	248
ugarbeets	2,648	3,390	2,750	3,056	3,194	157
roducts of light and chemical industries	10,344	11,193	14,086	15,204	17,168	354
oodstuffs	7,472	7,431	8,233	7,788	8,113	307
thers	30,597	34,765	36,323	38,016	39,703	—
otal	*193,740*	*205,955*	*218,073*	*228,264*	*238,047*	*248*

Table SA9.5. *Road Transport of Goods, by Commodity Group, 1956–76*

(thousands of tonnes)

Commodity group	*1956*	*1960*	*1965*	*1970*	*1971*	*1972*	*1973*	*1974*	*1975*	*1976*	*Average distance (kilometers), 1972*
Petroleum and petroleum products	40	254	958	2,546	2,429	2,828	3,490				35
Coal	114	241	554	538	692	563	529				13
Ferrous and nonferrous metal products, machinery, and equipment	182	716	2,289	3,558	4,944	4,767	5,336				103
Wood products	444	2,345	2,098	2,361	2,323	2,078	1,976				56
Firewood	893	2,796	1,865	2,864	2,919	2,571	2,402				33
Quarry and ballast products	3,629	28,674	73,518	150,153	164,065	173,237	187,920				10
Building materials	750	2,933	7,947	17,319	21,453	20,464	23,325				19
Cereals	584	2,946	7,178	6,938	7,685	9,505	10,278				35
Sugarbeets	143	963	1,216	1,102	1,333	1,715	2,289				32
Products of light and chemical industries	183	1,083	2,488	3,431	4,244	3,901	4,915				100
Foodstuffs	863	2,778	7,556	11,156	11,536	12,245	12,826				50
Others	1,162	10,879	23,183	37,810	37,112	42,299	46,244				—
Total	*8,987*	*56,608*	*130,850*	*239,776*	*260,735*	*276,173*	*301,530*	n.a.	n.a.	n.a.	*21*

n.a. Not available.

Source: Anuarul Statistic, various issues.

Table SA10.1. *Primary Energy Supply, 1950–75, and Projections to 1980*

Energy source	1950	1955	1960	1965	1970	1971	1972	1973	1974	1975	1980 planned forecast
					Solid fuels (thousands of tonnes)						
Domestic production											
Coal and anthracite	2,733		4,481	6,036	8,087	8,505	8,073	8,294	8,523	8,809	9,400
Lignite	811		3,145	5,461	14,044	13,792	16,557	17,716	20,001	19,916	47,090 (Lignite and brown coal)
Brown coal	349		537	598	704	654	641	654	683	660	
Bituminous shale	—		—	—	—	—	—	—	—	—	2,500
Wood[a]	2,137		2,138	2,288	2,385	2,203	2,583	3,673	3,064	2,800	2,850
Subtotal, domestic production	6,030		10,301	14,383	25,220	25,154	27,854	30,337	32,271	32,185	61,840
Imports											
Metallurgical coke	—		656	930	2,417	2,435	2,496	2,965	2,574	2,537	9,000 (all imports)
Coking coal	—		416	679	685	703	698	1,294	1,538	2,222	
Anthracite	—		—	27	43	40	56	62	334	198	
Subtotal, imports	—		1,072	1,636	3,145	3,178	3,250	4,321	4,446	4,957	9,000
Total, solid fuels (net domestic consumption)	6,030		11,373	16,019	28,365	28,332	31,104	34,658	36,717	37,142	70,840
					Petroleum (thousands of tonnes)						
Domestic production											
Crude oil	5,047		11,500	12,571	13,377	13,793	14,128	14,287	14,486	14,590	15,100
Natural gas liquids[b]	153		288	381	382	383	355	355	353	355	420
Subtotal, domestic production	5,200		11,788	12,952	13,759	14,176	14,483	14,642	14,839	14,945	15,520

(Table continues on the following pages)

Table SA10.1. *Continued*

Energy source	*1950*	*1955*	*1960*	*1965*	*1970*	*1971*	*1972*	*1973*	*1974*	*1975*	*1980 planned forecast*
Imports											
Crude oil	—		—	—	2,291	2,858	2,873	4,143	4,538	5,085	20,480
Subtotal, imports	—		—	—	2,291	2,858	2,873	4,143	4,538	5,085	20,480
Exports											
Crude oil[b]	100		—	—	—	—	—	—	—	—	—
Gasoline	1,350		2,305	1,273	647	588	578	610	1,106	1,464	620
Kerosene	700		836	451	144	69	67	8	17	4	8
Gas oil	800 (Gas oil and Fuel oil combined)		1,286	1,979	2,548	2,620	2,374	2,195	2,378	2,024	2,230
Fuel oil			1,229	1,639	1,532	1,541	1,615	1,715	2,656	2,258	1,750
Lubricating oil	—		211	294	349	358	355	314	308	307	320
Bitumen	—		81	106	45	47	31	9	5	10	9
Paraffin wax	—		20	20	19	16	14	11	10	7	9
Petroleum coke	—		14	52	67	110	48	65	19	97	54
Liquefied petroleum gases[b]	—		—	—	31	20	12	6	—	—	—
Subtotal, exports	2,950		5,982	5,814	5,382	5,369	5,094	4,933	6,499	6,171	5,000
Net domestic consumption[c]	2,250		5,806	7,138	10,668	11,677	12,307	13,907	12,935	13,924	31,000
Natural gas (millions of cubic meters)											
Domestic production[d]	3,422		10,530	17,695	25,309	27,013	28,012	29,546	30,440	33,306	33,027
Exports[b]	—		204	200	200	200	200	195	205	194	200
Net domestic consumption	3,422		10,326	17,495	25,109	26,813	27,812	29,351	30,235	33,112	32,827

Electrical energy (millions of kilowatt-hours)										
Domestic production (hydropower)[e]	169	397	1,005	2,773	4,495	7,343	7,547	8,476	8,711	13,000
Imports[e]	—	—	265	28	64	411	251	785	502	500
Exports[e]	—	28	577	2,334	3,247	3,561	3,552	2,892	2,918	2,800
Net domestic consumption	169	369	693	467	1,312	4,193	4,246	6,369	6,295	10,700

a. Firewood figures from *Anuarul Statistic*, various issues, and World Bank estimate of wood burned as industrial fuel.

b. United Nations Statistical Office, *Statistical Papers*. "Series J, World Energy Supplies," New York: United Nations.

c. Includes internal refinery consumption, which averaged around 9 percent from 1965 to 1975 but is assumed to be reduced to 5 percent by 1980.

d. Sum of "Gaz Metan" and "Gaze de Sonda" in *Anuarul Statistic*, various issues.

e. World Bank, "Appraisal of the Riul Mare-Retezat Hydropower Project in Romania," report no. 1103-RO. (A restricted circulation document) (Washington, D.C., March 1976, processed.)

Table SA10.2. *Primary Energy Supply, 1950–75, and Projections to 1980*
(thousands of tonnes of oil equivalent)

Energy source	*1950*	*1955*	*1960*	*1965*	*1970*	*1971*	*1972*	*1973*	*1974*	*1975*	*1980 planned forecast*
Solid fuels											
Domestic production											
Coal and anthracite	1,070		1,754	2,363	3,166	3,330	3,161	3,248	3,337	3,449	3,680
Lignite	137		530	920	2,365	2,323	2,788	2,983	3,368	3,354	7,930 (Lignite and Brown coal)
Brown coal	58		90	101	118	110	108	110	115	111	
Bituminous shale	—		—	—	—	—	—	—	—	—	236
Wood	565		565	604	630	582	682	970	809	740	753
Subtotal, domestic production	1,830		2,939	3,988	6,279	6,345	6,739	7,311	7,629	7,654	12,599
Imports											
Metallurgical coke	—		464	658	1,710	1,723	1,766	2,098	1,821	1,795	6,730 (Metallurgical coke and Washed coal and anthracite)
Washed coal and anthracite	—		314	533	550	560	569	1,023	1,412	1,826	
Subtotal, imports	—		778	1,191	2,260	2,283	2,335	3,121	3,233	3,621	6,730
Total, solid fuels (net domestic consumption)	1,830		3,717	5,179	8,539	8,628	9,074	10,432	10,862	11,275	19,329

					Hydrocarbons					
Domestic production										
Crude oil	5,047	11,500	12,571	13,377	13,793	14,128	14,287	14,486	14,590	15,100
Natural gas liquids	165	310	410	411	425	430	441	441	452	452
Natural gas	2,631	8,096	13,605	19,459	20,808	21,538	22,717	23,404	25,608	25,393
Subtotal, domestic production	7,843	19,906	26,586	33,247	35,026	36,096	37,445	38,331	40,650	40,945
Imports										
Crude oil	—	—	—	2,291	2,858	2,873	4,143	4,538	5,085	20,480
Natural gas	—	—	—	—	—	—	—	—	—	—
Subtotal, imports				2,291	2,858	2,873	4,143	4,538	5,085	20,480
Exports	—	—	—							
Crude oil	100	—	—	—	—	—	—	—	—	—
Natural gas	—	157	154	154	154	154	150	158	149	154
Petroleum products	2,850	6,133	5,849	5,374	5,310	5,074	4,908	6,482	6,182	5,008
Subtotal, exports	2,950	6,290	6,003	5,528	5,464	5,228	5,058	6,640	6,331	5,162
Total, hydrocarbons supply	7,843	19,906	26,586	35,538	37,884	38,969	41,588	42,869	45,735	61,425
Net domestic consumption, hydrocarbons	4,893	13,616	20,583	30,010	32,420	33,741	36,530	36,229	39,404	56,263
					Electrical energy					
Domestic production (hydropower)	38	89	226	623	1,009	1,649	1,695	1,903	1,956	2,919
Imports	—	—	59	6	14	92	56	176	113	112

(Table continues on the following page)

Table SA10.2. *Continued*

Energy source	*1950*	*1955*	*1960*	*1965*	*1970*	*1971*	*1972*	*1973*	*1974*	*1975*	*1980 planned forecast*
Exports	—		6	126	524	729	800	798	649	655	629
Net primary electrical energy supply	38		83	159	105	294	941	953	1,430	1,414	2,402
Total primary energy production	9,711		22,934	30,800	40,149	42,380	44,484	46,451	47,863	50,260	56,463
Total energy imports	—		778	1,250	4,557	5,155	5,300	7,320	7,947	8,819	27,322
Total energy exports	2,950		6,296	6,129	6,052	6,193	6,028	5,856	7,289	6,986	5,791
Total domestic energy consumption	*6,761*		*17,416*	*25,921*	*38,654*	*41,342*	*43,756*	*47,915*	*48,521*	*52,093*	*77,994*

Source: Table SA10.1.

Table SA10.3. *Secondary Energy Supply, 1950–75, and Projections to 1980*

Energy source	1950	1955	1960	1965	1970	1971	1972	1973	1974	1975	1980 planned forecast
Thermal electric energy[a] (millions of kilowatt hours)	1,944	4,017	7,253	16,210	32,315	34,959	36,096	39,230	40,586	45,009	59,550
Metallurgical coke (thousands of tonnes)	72	144	820	1,135	1,070	1,108	1,134	1,321	1,851	2,277	8,500[b]
Refined petroleum products (thousands of tonnes)											
Liquefied petroleum gases	12	43	77	108	207	223	228	247	243	251	400
Gasoline	1,502	2,635	2,792	2,458	2,786	3,017	3,135	3,361	3,450	4,048	4,000
Kerosene	736	1,362	1,289	965	969	1,050	1,093	1,024	979	1,018	2,000
Gas oil	731	1,626	2,376	3,600	5,049	5,277	5,116	5,597	5,432	5,511	14,600
Fuel oil	1,681	4,037	3,824	3,773	4,249	4,371	4,759	5,431	6,054	5,989	10,000
Lubricating oil	125	165	317	491	606	600	642	648	653	600	1,500
Bitumen	92	132	249	341	537	565	580	604	584	610	1,000
Paraffin wax[c]	11		32	34	37	38	40	40	38	39	44
Petroleum coke[c]	20		31	103	198	241	205	210	215	221	396
Unallocated					1,197	1,265	1,267	1,406	1,217	1,504	
Total, refined products	4,910		10,987	11,873	15,835	16,647	17,059	18,568	18,866	19,791	33,940
Crude oil, processed[d] (thousands of tonnes)	5,100		11,788	12,952	16,050	17,034	17,356	18,785	19,377	20,030	36,000

(Table continues on the following page)

Table SA10.3. *Continued*

Energy source	1950	1955	1960	1965	1970	1971	1972	1973	1974	1975	1980 planned forecast
Apparent domestic consumption of refined petroleum products (thousands of tonnes)											
Liquefied petroleum gases	12		77	108	176	203	216	241	243	251	400
Gasoline	305		487	1,185	2,139	2,429	2,557	2,751	2,345	2,584	3,380
Kerosene	36		453	514	825	981	1,027	1,016	963	1,014	1,992
Gas oil	1,612 (gas oil and fuel oil combined)		1,090	1,621	2,501	2,657	2,742	3,402	3,054	3,487	12,370
Fuel oil			2,595	2,134	2,717	2,830	3,144	3,716	3,398	3,731	8,250
Lubricating oil	125		106	197	257	242	287	334	345	293	1,180
Bitumen	92		168	235	492	519	549	595	579	600	991
Paraffin wax	11		12	14	18	22	27	30	29	32	35
Petroleum coke	20		17	52	131	131	157	146	196	124	342
Unallocated					1,209	1,265	1,230	1,399	1,212	1,499	
Total apparent domestic consumption[e]	*2,213*		*5,005*	*6,060*	*10,465*	*11,279*	*11,936*	*13,630*	*12,364*	*13,615*	*28,940*

a. Taken from tables of industrial production in United Nations Statistical Office, *Statistical Yearbook* (New York: United Nations, 1975), which differ from tables of electrical balance.

b. Estimate based on planned steel production, assuming direct imports of coke are eliminated in favor of imports of coking coal for blending with local production.

c. United Nations Statistical Office. *Statistical Papers*. "Series J, World Energy Supplies."

d. Sum of crude oil and natural gas liquids produced, and imported crude oil.

e. Actual figures for consumption of products, excluding internal refinery consumption and losses.

Sources: Anuarul Statistic, various issues; Law (no. 4) on the Adoption of the Unified National Plan of Economic and Social Development of the Socialist Republic of Romania for 1976–80, *Official Bulletin of the Socialist Republic of Romania*, no. 65 (July 7, 1976); and data provided by the Romanian authorities during discussions with the authors, except as noted.

Table SA10.4. *Internal Energy Consumption, by Sector, 1970, 1975, and 1980*
(thousands of tonnes of oil equivalent)

Sector	*1970*	*1975*	*1980*
Industrial use			
Metallurgical industry	n.a.	6,251	10,529
Extractive industry	n.a.	1,719	2,028
Chemical industry[a]	n.a.	7,814	16,378
Machine-building industry	n.a.	1,354	2,028
Wood and construction materials	n.a.	3,438	4,446
Light industry	n.a.	1,146	1,716
Production of thermoelectric power	9,006	12,764	18,796
Hydroelectric power	657	1,771	3,120
Other industrial use	n.a.	7,137	7,331
Subtotal	30,614	43,394	66,372
Nonindustrial use			
Agriculture	1,430	1,771	2,262
Transport and telecommunications	2,358	2,240	3,042
Space heating	4,252	4,688	6,318
Subtotal	8,040	8,699	11,622
Total domestic energy consumption	*38,654*	*52,093*	*77,994*

n.a. Not available.

a. Including energy-bearing raw material.

Source: World Bank estimates; subtotals for 1970 and 1975 from Ioan Herescu, "Development at the Power Base," *Revista Economica* (July 16 and 23, 1976).

Table SA10.5. *Primary Energy Production, 1980, 1985, and 1990*

Energy source	*1980*	*1985*	*1990*
Hydropower (millions of kilowatt-hours)	13,000	19,000	29,000
Crude oil and natural gas liquids (thousands of tonnes)	15,520	8,800	5,200
Natural gas (millions of cubic meters)	33,021	27,000	16,500
Coal and anthracite (thousands of tonnes)	9,400	9,400	9,400
Lignite and brown coal (thousands of tonnes)	47,090	59,147	93,147
Bituminous shale (thousands of tonnes)	2,500	15,000	15,000
Wood (thousands of tonnes)	2,850	3,030	3,030
Nuclear energy (millions of kilowatt-hours)	—	—	13,368
Thermal equivalent (thousands of tonnes of oil equivalent)			
Hydropower	2,919	4,266	6,511
Crude oil and nautral gas liquids	15,520	8,800	5,200
Natural gas	25,393	20,760	12,700
Coal and anthracite	3,680	3,680	3,680
Lignite and brown coal	7,930	9,960	15,686
Bituminous shale	236	1,415	1,415
Wood	753	800	800
Nuclear energy	—	—	3,000
Total	*56,431*	*49,681*	*48,992*

Source: World Bank estimates.

Table SA11.1. *Number of Tourist Nights, by Country of Residence and Tourist Area, 1975*
(thousands)

Country	*Seaside*	*Spa and health resorts*	*Mountain resorts*	*Other localities*	*All areas*
Romanian tourists	5,724.1	7,641.5	2,775.8	11,962.3	28,103.7
Foreign tourists	6,462.6	363.9	550.6	2,304.1	9,681.2
Socialist countries	2,659.1	41.1	156.4	1,018.0	3,874.6
Bulgaria	9.3	0.7	9.2	137.2	156.4
Czechoslovakia	1,399.2	3.7	15.4	124.7	1,543.1
German Democratic Republic	402.9	4.5	67.4	119.9	594.7
Hungary	79.9	21.9	15.9	187.5	305.2
Poland	610.8	3.9	8.2	118.4	741.3
U.S.S.R.	147.7	4.0	36.2	231.7	419.6
Yugoslavia	7.7	2.4	2.5	76.8	89.4
Other socialist countries	1.5	—	1.6	21.8	24.9
Nonsocialist countries	3,803.5	322.8	394.2	1,286.1	5,806.6
Austria	80.1	3.0	3.8	64.5	151.4
Belgium	183.6	1.6	23.8	48.4	257.4
Canada	1.3	0.9	1.4	14.2	17.8
Denmark	118.3	20.0	11.8	33.8	183.9
Finland	100.5	110.2	5.3	33.0	249.0
France	245.8	4.0	16.3	147.0	413.1
Germany, Federal Republic of	2,139.5	83.8	140.3	254.9	2,618.5
Greece	2.2	5.1	1.3	53.4	62.0
Israel	13.9	26.6	32.9	75.6	149.0
Italy	101.2	7.6	12.9	168.8	290.5
Netherlands	186.2	1.5	48.4	64.0	300.1
Norway	81.4	0.7	1.6	13.0	96.7
Sweden	144.8	24.9	11.5	23.8	205.0
Switzerland	68.6	2.1	2.5	34.5	107.7
United Kingdom	218.5	10.0	33.2	62.5	324.2
United States	15.7	6.1	25.2	103.7	150.7
Other nonsocialist countries	101.9	14.7	22.0	91.0	229.6
Total, all tourists	*12,186.7*	*8,005.4*	*3,326.4*	*14,266.4*	*37,784.9*

Source: Ministry of Tourism, *Capacitati de cazare si utilizarea lor in anul 1975*, June 1976.

Table SA11.2. *Number of Foreign Tourist Arrivals, by Country of Residence, 1972–76*
(thousands)

Country	*1972*	*1973*	*1974*	*1975*	*1976*
Socialist countries	2,297.4	2,769.2	3,181.5	2,575.2	2,623.0
Bulgaria	303.7	312.5	380.5	460.1	476.2
Czechoslovakia	576.4	632.9	597.8	572.8	477.1
German Democratic Republic	126.6	142.8	178.9	199.9	182.6
Hungary	235.0	335.6	360.6	369.1	447.6
Poland	237.6	353.4	431.2	477.4	477.8
U.S.S.R.	231.4	285.0	333.2	317.6	325.9
Yugoslavia	582.4	701.4	893.9	170.9	227.2
Other socialist countries	4.3	5.6	5.6	7.4	8.6
Nonsocialist countries	606.0	573.1	643.7	630.7	545.7
Australia	1.8	1.8	2.2	2.0	2.2
Austria	29.2	29.3	29.3	19.2	21.3
Belgium	15.8	16.1	14.7	19.0	19.3
Canada	4.2	3.7	4.2	4.2	3.8
Denmark	12.8	11.1	13.1	11.2	8.8
Finland	6.7	9.8	18.9	25.2	25.6
France	38.3	46.6	55.0	45.7	41.9
Germany, Federal Republic of	267.4	205.0	239.6	206.5	148.6
Greece	5.9	7.3	8.7	24.1	27.1
Israel	9.7	14.1	15.3	13.1	9.6
Italy	52.5	52.3	51.0	46.2	37.6
Japan	2.5	2.3	3.0	3.5	4.0
Lebanon	3.1	2.7	2.8	2.7	2.5
Netherlands	23.3	25.2	24.0	31.9	29.5
Norway	5.1	4.0	5.2	8.6	4.8
Spain	5.2	7.9	10.3	9.0	4.5
Switzerland	13.3	11.5	15.8	12.4	10.4
Sweden	13.5	14.9	18.3	20.5	20.5
Turkey	7.1	9.2	12.7	17.1	21.3
United Kingdom	41.8	44.9	37.2	37.5	36.1
United States	24.0	22.9	28.3	35.2	28.1
Other nonsocialist countries	22.7	30.7	34.2	35.9	38.2
Total	*2,903.4*	*3,345.9*	*3,861.7*	*3,409.6*	*3,168.7*

Note: Includes tourists in transit and border visitors.
Source: Ministry of Tourism; data supplied during discussions with the authors.

Table SA11.3. *Regional Distribution of Foreign Tourist Nights, 1974–76*
(thousands)

Region	From socialist countries	From nonsocialist countries	Total
1974			
Seaside	1,766.5	3,040.0	4,806.4
Spa and health resorts[a]	—	371.9	371.9
Mountain resorts[a]	80.7	214.1	294.8
Cruises	—	48.4	48.4
Hunting	—	12.5	12.5
Bucharest	195.0	281.9	476.9
Other localities	281.7	533.3	815.0
Miscellaneous	—	24.5	24.5
Total	*2,323.9*	*4,526.6*	*6,850.5*
1975			
Seaside	1,931.8	3,546.2	5,478.0
Spa and health resorts[a]	—	373.9	373.9
Mountain resorts[a]	120.2	264.5	384.7
Cruises	—	24.1	24.1
Hunting	—	—	—
Bucharest	252.8	324.8	577.6
Other localities	221.2	567.9	789.1
Miscellaneous	—	4.0	4.0
Total	*2,526.0*	*5,105.4*	*7,631.4*
1976			
Seaside	1,468.8	2,355.0	3,823.8
Spa and health resorts[a]	0.6	348.8	349.4
Mountain resorts[a]	73.5	201.7	275.2
Cruises	—	25.7	25.7
Hunting	—	—	—
Bucharest	182.0	267.3	449.3
Other localities	224.9	701.2	926.1
Miscellaneous	—	—	—
Total	*1,949.8*	*3,899.7*	*5,849.5*

Note: Includes organized tourism only.

a. Classification between spa and health resorts, on the one hand, and mountain resorts, on the other, might not necessarily be the same as in other tables.

Source: Ministry of Tourism; data supplied during discussions with the authors.

Table SA11.4. *Number of Romanian Tourists Abroad, by Country, 1972–76*

Country	*1972*	*1973*	*1974*	*1975*	*1976*
In socialist countries	244,455	409,912	509,582	415,734	414,308
Bulgaria	51,229	145,805	197,024	158,144	139.935
Czechoslovakia	19,607	27,017	33,559	26,594	28,196
German Democratic Republic	17,127	25,017	28,602	26,537	30,026
Hungary	82,882	126,800	145,366	102,866	103,931
Poland	18,177	15,584	24,507	18,314	22,937
U.S.S.R.	36,609	55,584	65,637	75,094	79,591
Yugoslavia	18,824	13,974	14,917	8,185	9,692
In nonsocialist countries	67,004	66,405	62,055	42,585	45,290
Austria	5,384	5,837	5,999	3,052	4,060
Belgium	1,416	1,257	1,040	1,356	1,028
Canada	399	407	337	390	708
Denmark	829	681	493	1,125	360
Finland	592	432	465	973	342
France	7,423	7,728	6,975	4,188	5,035
Germany, Federal Republic of	21,816	23,882	21,280	13,795	11,090
Greece	2,451	2,313	1,509	1,459	3,802
Israel	7,629	5,582	4,288	3,070	3,196
Italy	7,559	7,950	8,050	4,227	4,400
Netherlands	924	947	1,051	981	1,099
Sweden	1,010	1,013	1,009	756	673
Switzerland	2,171	2,037	2,148	1,565	1,635
Turkey	3,256	2,467	3,291	1,799	3,619
United Kingdom	1,962	1,978	1,989	1,451	1,775
United States	2,283	1,894	2,131	2,402	2,468
In other countries[a]	9,766	10,141	16,544	18,957	21,391
Total	*321,225*	*486,458*	*588,181*	*477,276*	*480,989*

a. Not allocated between socialist and nonsocialist countries.
Source: Ministry of Tourism; data supplied during discussions with the authors.

Table SA11.5. *Capacity of Accommodation, by Region and Kind, 1975*

Region and accommodation	*Lodging establishments*		*Rooms*		*Beds*	
	Total	*Number for interna-tional tourists*	*Total*	*Number for interna-tional tourists*	*Total*	*Number for interna-tional tourists*
Seaside	558	353	42,619	38,733	145,268	107,126
Hotels	255	253	37,664	37,344	79,278	78,621
Villas	71	66	1,701	1,389	3,665	2,887
Establishments for rest and treatment	194		3,254		8,763	
Inns						
Camping	38	34			27,414	25,618
Lodging with the inhabitants					26,148	
Spa and health resorts	435	63	11,913	3,138	31,609	8,343
Hotels	14	12	1,690	1,647	3,117	3,011
Motels	1	1	38	38	76	76
Establishments for rest and treatment	404	43	10,129	1,416	24,005	3,891
Inns	1	1	37	37	80	80
Chalets	8		19		112	
Camping	9	6			1,499	1,285
Lodging with the inhabitants					2,720	
Mountain resorts	322	45	5,409	2,083	15,115	4,967
Hotels	18	16	1,748	1,688	3,675	3,568
Motels	2	2	64	64	129	129
Villas	15	14	102	100	271	267
Establishments for rest and treatment	246		2,951		7,790	
Chalets	39	11	544	231	2,472	735
Camping	2	2			478	268
Lodging with the inhabitants					300	

(Table continues on the following page)

Table SA11.5. *Continued*

Region and accommodation	Lodging establishments: Total	Lodging establishments: Number for international tourists	Rooms: Total	Rooms: Number for international tourists	Beds: Total	Beds: Number for international tourists
Other localities	1,091	286	26,475	15,315	87,413	39,011
Hotels	311	164	17,295	14,084	3,471	27,213
In Bucharest	35		4,735		8,864	
Motels	44	19	1,144	622	2,435	1,317
Villas	104	28	874	221	2,735	823
Establishments for rest and treatment	271	13	4,563	135	11,421	300
Inns	40	11	515	177	1,383	489
Chalets	170	6	2,084	76	7,966	297
Camping	151	45			15,454	7,487
Lodging with the inhabitants					8,992	
Boarding schools					2,308	1,085
Country total	*2,406*	*747*	*86,416*	*59,269*	*279,405*	*159,447*
Hotels	598	445	58,397	54,763	120,785	112,413
Motels	47	22	1,246	724	2,644	1,522
Villas	190	108	2,677	1,710	6,671	3,977
Establishments for rest and treatment	1,115	56	20,897	1,551	51,979	4,191
Inns	41	12	552	214	1,463	569
Chalets	215	17	2,647	307	10,550	1,032
Camping	200	87			44,845	34,658
Lodging with the inhabitants					38,160	
Boarding schools					2,308	1,085

Source: Ministry of Tourism, *Capacitati de cazare si utilizarea lor in anul 1975*, June 1976.

Table SA11.6. *Capacity Utilization (Bed Occupancy Rates) In Period when Accommodation Can Be Provided, 1970–75*

Accommodation	*1970*	*1971*	*1972*	*1973*	*1974*	*1975*
Hotels	73.7	76.6	75.7	76.3	78.7	80.2
Motels	49.5	50.1	59.7	54.1	55.1	53.4
Villas[a]	73.2	82.1	82.7	83.8	86.1	84.9
Chalets	29.9	22.1	25.2	27.8	30.2	33.3
Inns	34.0	44.2	48.9	52.4	46.2	46.8
Camping	50.1	47.8	54.4	53.4	62.3	69.8
Total	*67.1*	*69.8*	*71.5*	*72.6*	*75.7*	*76.7*

a. Includes establishments for rest and treatment.

Source: Ministry of Tourism; data provided during discussions with the authors.

Table SA11.7. *Capacity Utilization (Bed Occupancy Rates), by Region and Kind of Accommodation, 1973*

Region and accommodation	Average number of days on which accommodation can be provided (A)		Capacity utilization during period of time given in (A) (percentage) (B)		Capacity utilization over the whole year (percentage)	
	All establishments (1)	Establishments for international tourists (2)	All establishments (3)	Establishments for international tourists (4)	All establishments (3) × (1) ÷ 365 (5)	Establishments for international tourists (4) × (2) ÷ 365 (6)
Seaside	127	129	71.3	72.8	24.8	25.7
Hotels	134	134	74.5	74.5	27.4	27.4
Motels	105	105	79.6	79.6	22.9	22.9
Establishments for rest or treatment	156	135	87.7	83.9	37.5	31.0
Camping						
Bungalows	120	120	48.4	48.4	15.9	15.9
Tents already installed	91	91	76.9	76.9	19.2	19.2
Space for tourist tents	94	93	51.0	62.0	13.1	15.8
Spa and health resorts	287	310	85.8	76.5	67.5	65.0
Hotels	351	350	72.5	72.4	69.7	69.4
Motels	365	365	82.0	82.0	82.0	82.0
Establishments for rest or treatment	293	350	88.4	81.9	71.0	78.5
Inns	365	365	33.4	33.4	33.4	33.4
Chalets	228	—	26.9	—	16.8	—
Camping	128	131	52.8	52.3	18.5	18.8
Mountain resorts	296	310	69.6	73.5	56.4	62.4
Hotels	328	328	78.1	77.6	70.2	69.7
Motels	308	308	61.3	61.3	51.7	51.7
Villas	365	—	64.9	—	64.9	—

Table SA11.7. *Continued*

Region and accommodation	*Average number of days on which accommodation can be provided (A)*		*Capacity utilization during period of time given in (A) (percentage) (B)*		*Capacity utilization over the whole year (percentage)*	
	All establishments (1)	*Establishments for international tourists (2)*	*All establishments (3)*	*Establishments for international tourists (4)*	*All establishments (3) × (1) ÷ 365 (5)*	*Establishments for international tourists (4) × (2) ÷ 365 (6)*
Establishments for rest or treatment	282	—	75.6	—	58.4	—
Chalets	311	350	39.0	38.8	33.2	37.2
Camping	67	67	96.7	96.7	17.8	17.8
Other localities	290	304	67.3	77.1	53.5	64.2
Hotels	348	348	78.2	79.3	74.6	75.6
In Bucharest	350	n.a.	74.5	n.a.	71.4	n.a.
Motels	235	258	51.8	58.2	33.4	41.1
Villas	356	—	71.4	—	69.6	—
Establishment for rest or treatment	245	210	77.7	89.8	52.2	51.7
Inns	283	259	54.3	64.0	42.1	45.4
Chalets	293	318	24.4	46.4	19.6	40.4
Camping	135	128	59.0	69.9	21.8	24.5
Country total	*205*	*179*	*72.6*	*74.6*	*40.8*	*36.6*
Hotels	200	190	76.3	76.4	41.8	39.7
Motels	245	268	54.1	60.0	36.3	44.1
Villas	185	105	72.9	79.6	36.9	22.9
Establishments for rest or treatment	260	220	84.4	82.7	60.1	49.8
Inns	289	273	52.4	58.6	41.5	43.8
Chalets	296	337	27.8	41.7	22.5	38.5
Camping	108	111	53.4	59.3	15.8	18.0

n.a. Not available.

Source: Ministry of Tourism, *Capacitati de cazare si utilizarea lor in anul 1973*, June 1974, and World Bank calculations.

References

Anuario Estadístico de España (Annual Statistics of Spain). Madrid: Instituto Nacional de Estadistica, 1976.

Anuarul Demografic al Republicii Socialiste Romania (Annual Demographic Data of the Socialist Republic of Romania). Bucharest: Central Statistics Office and National Demographic Commission, 1974.

Anuarul Statistic al Republicii Socialiste Romania (Annual Statistics of the Socialist Republic of Romania). Bucharest: Directia Centrala de Statistica (Central Statistics Office), published yearly.

Capata, M. *Balanta Statistica a Legatuziloz dintre Ramuzi (Statistical Balance and Relations between Sectors)*. Bucharest: Editur Politica, 1974.

Capata, M. *Tipologia Economiiloz Nationale (Model of the National Economy)*. Bucharest: Editur Politica, 1976.

Ceaucescu, Nicolae. "Report Concerning Measures for Perfecting the Management and Planning of the National Economy and for Improving the Administrative and Territorial Organization of Romania." Report delivered to the National Conference of the Romanian Communist Party, Bucharest, December 6, 1967. Bucharest: Meridiane Publishing House, 1967.

Ceausescu, Nicolae. Statement to the conference on agriculture, February 1975.

Ceausescu, Nicolae. Speech delivered to the Congress of the People's Councils. *Scinteia* (February 5, 1976).

Ceausescu, Nicolae. Speech delivered to the Plenary meeting of the Central Committee of the Romanian Communist Party, Bucharest, November 23, 1976.

Communiqué Regarding the Fulfillment of the Unified National Plan for Social and Economic Development of the Socialist Republic of Romania during the 1971–75 Period. Bucharest: Publishing Office for Political Literature, 1976.

Current Trends and Policies in the Field of House Building and Planning. Bucharest, 1976.

Data supplied by Romanian authorities during discussions with the authors.

Decree (no. 188) of 1977.

Decree (no. 234/1974) of the State Council. *Official Bulletin of the Socialist Republic of Romania*, year 10, no. 166 (December 26, 1974).

Desmireanu, I., E. V. Topala, A. Camara, and S. C. Nita. "Model Macroeconomic Unisectoral Pentru Dezvoltaria Economei Nationale in Perioda 1976–90." ("A

Single-sector Macroeconomic Model for the Development of the National Economy in the 1976–90 Period"). *Revista de Statistica* (March 1974).

Directives of the Central Committee of the Romanian Communist Party on the Perfecting of Management and Planning of the National Economy in Keeping with the Conditions of the New Stage of Romania's Socialist Development. Bucharest: Agerpres, October 1967.

Directives of the Eleventh Congress of the Romania Communist Party Concerning the 1976–80 Five-Year Plan and the Guidelines for Romanian Economic and Social Development over the 1981–90 Period. Bucharest: Meridiane Publishing House, 1975.

Directives of the Ninth Congress of the Romanian Communist Party on Power Resources and the Country's Electrification in the 1966–75 Period; draft. Bucharest: Meridiane Publishing House, 1965.

Directives of the Tenth Congress of the Romanian Communist Party Concerning the 1971–75 Five-Year Plan and the Guidelines for the Development of the National Economy in the 1976–80 Period; draft. Bucharest: Meridiane Publishing House, 1969.

Dobrescu, Emilian. *Correlation between Accumulation and Consumption.* Bucharest: Editur Politica, 1971.

Dobrescu, Emilian. *Optimul Economiei Socialiste (The Optimum for a Socialist Economy).* Bucharest: Editur Politica, 1976.

East-West, no. 150 (March 25, 1976).

East-West Markets (April 5 and October 4, 1976).

Eurostat, no. 2-1976 (1976).

External Trade of the Socialist Republic of Romania. Bucharest: Ministry of Foreign Trade and Central Statistics Office, 1973.

Food and Agricultural Organization of the United Nations. *Yearbook of Agricultural Production.* Rome: United Nations, 1974.

Herescu, Ioan. "Development of the Power Base." *Revista Economica* (July 16 and 23, 1976).

Investitii-Constructii in Republica Socialista Romania (Investment and Construction in the Socialist Republic of Romania). Bucharest: Central Statistics Office, 1966.

Law (no. 1) on Foreign Trade of 1971. Article 3. *Official Bulletin of the Socialist Republic of Romania,* no. 33 (March 17, 1971).

Law (no. 4) on Adoption of the Unified National Plan of Economic and Social Development of the Socialist Republic of Romania for 1976–80. *Official Bulletin of the Socialist Republic of Romania,* no. 65 (July 7, 1976).

Law (no. 10) of 1971 on the Adoption of the Five-Year Plan for 1971–75 for the Economic and Social Development of the Socialist Republic of Romania. *Official Bulletin of the Socialist Republic of Romania,* year 6, no. 129 (October 21, 1971).

Law (no. 11) on the Organization and Management of State Socialist Units of 1971. *Official Bulletin of the Socialist Republic of Romania*, no. 130 (October 21, 1971).

Law (no. 11) of 1972: Law Adopting the National Economic and Social Development Plan for 1973. *Official Bulletin of the Socialist Republic of Romania*, year 8, no. 137 (November 28, 1972).

Law (no. 16) of 1971: Law Adopting the National Economic and Social Development Plan for 1972. *Official Bulletin of the Socialist Republic of Romania*, year 7, no. 153 (December 16, 1971).

Law (no. 19) on Prices and Tariffs of 1971. Preamble. *Official Bulletin of the Socialist Republic of Romania*, no. 154 (December 16, 1971).

Law (no. 57) on Remuneration According to the Quantity and Quality of Labor. *Official Bulletin of the Socialist Republic of Romania*, no. 133-134 (November 1, 1974).

Law (no. 64) of 1974: Law Adopting the National Economic and Social Development Plan for 1975. *Official Bulletin of the Socialist Republic of Romania*, year 10, no. 160 (December 23, 1974).

Law (no. 71) on Economic Contracts of 1969. *Official Bulletin of the Socialist Republic of Romania*, no. 154 (December 29, 1969).

Law (no. 72) on the Organization, Planning, and Execution of Investment Projects of 1969. *Official Bulletin of the Socialist Republic of Romania*, no. 154 (December 29, 1969).

Law (no. 105) of 1973: Law Adopting the National Economic and Social Development Plan for 1974. *Official Bulletin of the Socialist Republic of Romania*, year 9, no. 190 (December 3, 1973).

Ministry of Education. Information provided by Romanian authorities during discussions with the authors.

Ministry of Finance. Information provided by Romanian authorities during discussions with the authors.

Ministry of Foreign Trade and International Cooperation. Information provided by Romanian authorities during discussions with the authors.

Ministry of Mines, Petroleum, and Geology. Information provided by Romanian authorities during discussions with the authors.

Ministry of Tourism. *Capactiati de cazare si utilizarea lor in anul 1975 (Capacity of Accommodations and Occupancy Rates in 1975)*, June 1976.

Ministry of Tourism. Information provided by Romanian authorities during discussions with the authors.

Ministry of Transport. Information provided by Romanian authorities during discussions with the authors.

Montias, J. M. *Economic Development in Communist Romania*. Cambridge, Mass.: MIT Press, 1967.

Mooz, William E. *Energy in the Transportation Sector.* Santa Monica: Rand Corporation, 1973.

National Party Conference. Report. Bucharest, December 1967. Pages 6, 54.

Orascu, Serban. *Specializares si cooperarea in industrie (Specialization and Cooperation in Industry).* Bucharest, 1974, pp. 55–56.

Pescaru, V., and V. Mierlea. "Model De Planificare Optima A Productiei In Subramura De Prelucrare A Titeiului." ("Model for the Optimal Planning of Production in the Oil-Processing Subsector").

Population Census of Romania, 1956, 1966.

Resolution (no. 900/1970) of the Council of Ministers on the Preparation and Execution of Investment Operations. *Official Bulletin of the Socialist Republic of Romania,* no. 75-76 (July 7, 1970).

Revista de Statistica. Bucharest (November 21, 1970).

Seymer, N. *Intermodal Comparisons of Energy Intensiveness in Long Distance Transports.* London: Programme Press, 1976.

Sica, G. H. *Projection and Planning of Wholesale Prices.* Bucharest: Editura Academii, 1973.

State Planning Commission. *Modele Economico—Matematica De Prognoza De Permen Lung Pentru Optimizarea Structurii Productiei Agricole (A Mathematical Model of Long-Term Projection for the Optimization of the Structure of Agricultural Production).* Bucharest: Agerpres, 1975.

State Planning Commission. *Program De Perspectiva Privind Constructia De Centrale Hidroelectrice in RSR (Perspective Program for Construction in the Hydroelectric Central in Romania).*

United Nations Economic Commission for Europe. *Economic Survey of Europe.* Geneva, 1975.

United Nations Secretariat, Department of Economic and Social Affairs, Population Division, "Selected World Demographic Indicators, by Countries, 1950–2000." New York: United Nations, May 1975.

United Nations Statistical Office. *Monthly Bulletin of Statistics* (October 1976).

United Nations Statitiscal Office. *Statistical Papers.* "Series J, World Energy Supplies." New York: United Nations.

United Nations Statistical Office. *Statistical Yearbook.* New York: United Nations, 1975.

United Nations Statistical Office. *Yearbook of Industrial Statistics.* New York: United Nations, 1974.

World Bank. "Appraisal of the Riul Mare-Retezat Hydropower Project in Romania." Report no. 1103-RO. A restricted-circulation document. Washington, D.C., March 1976. Processed.

World Bank. "Current Economic Position and Prospects of Romania." Report no. 492a-RO. A restricted-circulation document. Washington, D.C., October 1974. Processed.

World Bank. Economic Memorandum. Report no. 818a-RO. A restricted-circulation document. Washington, D.C., December 1975. Processed.

World Bank. "Economy of Romania." Report no. 181b-RO. A restricted-circulation document. Washington, D.C., November 1973. Processed.

World Bank. "Romania: Agricultural Sector Survey." Report no. 953a-RO. A restricted-circulation document. Washington, D.C., October 1976. Processed.

World Bank. *World Bank Atlas.* Washington, D.C., published yearly.

Zymelman, Manuel. "Patterns of Educational Expenditure." World Bank Staff Working Paper, no. 246. Washington, D.C.: World Bank, November 1976.